2023年度上海高校市级重点课程
"国际税法"阶段性建设成果

高等院校经济管理类主干课程教材
上海立信会计金融学院精品教材

国际税法

主　编◎龙英锋
副主编◎陈阵香　赵　鹏

立信会计出版社
LIXIN ACCOUNTING PUBLISHING HOUSE

图书在版编目（CIP）数据

国际税法：汉英对照 / 龙英锋主编 . -- 上海：立信会计出版社，2025.4. -- ISBN 978-7-5429-7818-9
Ⅰ. D996.3
中国国家版本馆 CIP 数据核字第 2025Q6H155 号

策划编辑　方士华
责任编辑　孙　勇
美术编辑　北京任燕飞工作室

国际税法
GUOJI SHUIFA

出版发行	立信会计出版社
地　　址	上海市中山西路 2230 号　　邮政编码　200235
电　　话	（021）64411389　　传　　真　（021）64411325
网　　址	www.lixinaph.com　　电子邮箱　lixinaph2019@126.com
网上书店	http://lixin.jd.com　　http://lxkjcbs.tmall.com
经　　销	各地新华书店
印　　刷	浙江临安曙光印务有限公司
开　　本	787 毫米 × 1092 毫米　　1/16
印　　张	31
字　　数	813 千字
版　　次	2025 年 4 月第 1 版
印　　次	2025 年 4 月第 1 次
书　　号	ISBN 978-7-5429-7818-9/D
定　　价	89.00 元

如有印订差错，请与本社联系调换

国际税法是一门年轻的法学学科，其基本范畴与基本理论尚处在形成时期。学者关于国际税法的概念也有一些分歧，本教材采纳了广义的国际税法概念，并认为，国际税法是调整国家与国家之间的税收利益分配关系以及国家与其涉外纳税人之间的税收征纳关系的法律规范的总称。国际税法不仅涉及直接税，也涉及间接税；不仅包含实体法规范，也包含程序法规范。国际税法是一个独立的法的部门，国际税法的体系是由国际税收协定和其他国际条约中有关税收的规定、国际税收习惯以及各国的国内税法和涉外税法组成的。学科意义上的国际税法所包含的内容与范围应当广于部门法意义上的国际税法。

从国际税法发展的历史可以看出，国际税法最初的任务就是消除和避免国际双重征税，合理分配税收管辖权和税收利益。随着国际税法的发展，国际逃税和国际避税逐渐成了危害国家税收主权和国际税收秩序的大敌。因此，防止国际逃税和避税也逐渐成了国际税法的重要任务之一。消除和避免双重征税、防止国际逃税和国际避税是传统国际税法的两大主要任务。第二次世界大战以后，国际税务领域的合作与交流越来越频繁，也越来越重要。由于缺少国际税务领域的合作，传统国际税法的两大任务已经很难完成或很难圆满地完成，实现国际税务领域的合作也逐渐成了现代国际税法的重要任务之一。综上，国际税法的作用主要体现在消除和避免国际双重征税、防止国际逃税和国际避税以及实现国际税务合作三个方面。

上海立信会计金融学院（以下简称"我校"）是一所财经类院校，我校法学院培养通法律、懂会计、懂金融与税务的复合型、应用型、国际化财经法律人才，"国际税法"是我校法学院法学专业学生的专业必修课程，也是法学专业学生培养方案的特色之一。"国际税法"课程调整国家与国家之间的税收利益分配关系以及国家与涉外纳税人之间的涉外税收征纳关系，课程的大量内容都涉及外国因素，案例及资料很多都是英文版本。另外，国家对于培养具有国际视野，通晓国际规则，能够参与国际事务的高层次法律人才一直倍加重视。为此，"国际税法"课程采用全英文或者双语授课，《国际税法》教材采用全英文或者中英双语编写是十分必要的。我校法学院开设全英文与双语"国际税法"课程的历史比较长，在以往的授课经历中，我们发现，利用全英文教材及全英文授课的效果并不理想，反而双语教材及双语授课的效果会更佳。究其原因，其实是很简单，因为我们毕竟生活在非英语国家，学生的母语是中文，学生对于全英文教材和全英文授课的接受程度会因为语言障碍受到较大的影响，学生经常会对一些概念、术语、原则等囫囵吞枣、一知半解。而如果采用双语教学则不会出现这些问题，同时，双语教学兼具全英文教学的好处，除了课程理论学习的深度不受影响，学生的视野、英文水平与能力都能够得到极大的提高。

  为此，我们决定，组织好力量认真编写这本《国际税法》(中英文双语版)教材。除了双语特色，本教材的另一大特色是理论与实践相结合。本教材不仅注重对学科理论知识的全面梳理，而且也注重对实践案例的分析，通过案例分析甚至讲故事的方式将相关的理论知识呈现给学生，被证明为既是有效的教学途径，也是容易让学生理解和接受的教学方式。本教材各章的内容都是先安排理论知识点，随后讲解与该章理论知识点相匹配的案例分析或研究。编者尽量从现实的案例中选择教材的案例，部分章节在没有真实对应案例的情况下，由编写人员结合相关理论知识点编写模拟案例并进行分析。考虑到中英文表达的差异性及双语教材写作的惯例，本教材中的中英文内容并非完全一一对应，仅保持核心内容的一致性。

  本教材共分为13章，主要内容涉及税收管辖权，个人所得税法，企业所得税法，国际双重征税，国际税收协定，跨国营业所得征税的协调，跨国劳务所得征税协调规则，跨国投资所得征税的协调，跨国不动产所得、财产收益、财产价值征税的协调，消除国际双重征税的方法、国际逃避税及其法律规制，国际税务争议的解决等。本教材适用于普通高等教育法学专业和税务相关专业的双语课程。

  本教材由龙英锋主编，陈阵香、赵鹏为副主编，本教材编写的具体分工如下：龙英锋编写第一章，陈阵香编写第二章、第三章，廖莉编写第四章、第五章，赵鹏编写第六章、第十三章，王丽华编写第七章，崔晓静编写第八章，李娜编写第九章，熊伟编写第十章，叶莉娜编写第十一章、第十二章。以上编者都长期从事国际税法教学与研究，在国际税法领域具有深厚的学养与积累。

  在此，要特别感谢武汉大学熊伟教授和崔晓静教授、上海政法学院王丽华教授以及华东政法大学李娜副教授，他们对于本教材的编写给予了无私的帮助！学者间友谊之树常青！

  最后，特别声明一点，由于编者水平的局限性，本教材如果有不足之处，恳请读者理解与包容。编者非常感谢指出教材中遗漏和错误的专家学者！

龙英锋

2025年4月

第一章 绪论 1
CHAPTER I Introduction 1

第一节 国际税收关系和国际税法的概念 1
Section 1 Concepts of International Tax Relationship and International Tax Law 1

第二节 国际税法的历史发展 13
Section 2 Historical Development of International Tax Law 13

第三节 国际税法的宗旨和原则 23
Section 3 Purposes and Principles of International Tax Law 23

第四节 国际税法与国际税法学 31
Section 4 International Tax Law and the Discipline of International Tax Law 31

第二章 税收管辖权 38
CHAPTER II Tax Jurisdiction 38

第一节 税收管辖权概述 38
Section 1 Overview of Tax Jurisdiction 38

第二节 居民税收管辖权的行使 44
Section 2 Exercise of Resident Tax Jurisdiction 44

第三节 国籍税收管辖权的行使 52
Section 3 Exercise of Nationality Tax Jurisdiction 52

第四节 所得来源地税收管辖权的行使 56
Section 4 Exercise of Source Tax Jurisdiction 56

第五节 财产所在地税收管辖权的行使 63
Section 5 Exercise of Property Location Tax Jurisdiction 63

第三章 个人所得税法
CHAPTER III Individual Income Tax Law

第一节 个人所得税法概述
Section 1 Overview of Individual Income Tax Law ... 65

第二节 个人所得税法的具体规定
Section 2 Specific Provisions of Individual Income Tax Law ... 74

第四章 企业所得税法
CHAPTER IV Enterprise Income Tax Law ... 103

第一节 统一企业所得税法的经过和意义
Section 1 Process and Significance of the Consolidation of Enterprise Income Tax Law ... 103

第二节 国内外企业所得税法的历史沿革
Section 2 History and Development of Domestic and Foreign Enterprise Income Tax Law ... 107

第三节 统一企业所得税法的必要性和可能性
Section 3 Necessity and Possibility of the Consolidation of Enterprise Income Tax Law ... 112

第四节 建立各类企业统一适用的科学和规范的企业所得税制度
Section 4 Establishment of a Unified, Scientific and Standardized Enterprise Income Tax System Applicable to All Types of Enterprises ... 116

第五节 源泉扣除和税收征管
Section 5 Source Deduction and Administration of Tax Collection ... 124

第六节 相关案例
Section 6 Related Cases ... 127

第五章 国际双重征税
CHAPTER V International Double Taxation ... 134

第一节 国际双重征税产生的原因
Section 1 Causes for the Generation of International Double Taxation ... 134

第二节 国际双重征税的概念
Section 2 Concept of International Double Taxation ... 138

第三节 国际双重征税的危害性 142

Section 3   Harmfulness of International Double Taxation 142

第四节 相关案例 144

Section 4   Related Cases 144

第六章 国际税收协定 152

CHAPTER VI   International Tax Treaty 152

第一节 国际税收协定概述 152

Section 1   Overview of International Tax Treaty 152

第二节 国际税收协定的主要内容 157

Section 2   Main Elements of International Tax Treaty 157

第三节 国际税收协定与国内税法的关系 192

Section 3   Relationship between International Tax Agreements and Domestic Tax Laws 192

第四节 国际税收协定的解释 202

Section 4   Interpretation of International Tax Agreements 202

第五节 相关案例 211

Section 5   Related Cases 211

第七章 跨国营业所得征税的协调 216

CHAPTER VII   Tax Harmonization on Cross-border Business Profit 216

第一节 基本原则 216

Section 1   Basic Principles 216

第二节 常设机构的概念和范围 219

Section 2   Concept and Scope of Permanent Establishment 219

第三节 常设机构的利润归属 233

Section 3   Attribution of the Profits of Permanent Establishment 233

第四节 常设机构应税所得额的确定 236

Section 4   Determination of the Taxable Incomes of Permanent Establishment 236

第五节 相关案例 242

Section 5   Related Cases 242

第八章　跨国劳务所得征税协调规则 258
CHAPTER VIII　Tax Harmonization on Cross-border Income from Personal Services 258

第一节　独立个人劳务 259
Section 1　Independent Personal Services 259

第二节　受雇所得 266
Section 2　Income from Employment 266

第三节　对特定人员跨国劳务所得征税的分配规则 272
Section 3　Distributive Rules on Cross-border Service Income of Specific Persons 272

第九章　跨国投资所得征税的协调 287
CHAPTER IX　Tax Harmonization on Cross-border Investment Income 287

第一节　概述 287
Section 1　General Introduction 287

第二节　对跨国投资所得征税的协调 294
Section 2　Harmonization on Taxation on Incomes from Cross-border Investment 294

第三节　相关案例 313
Section 3　Related Cases 313

第十章　跨国不动产所得、财产收益、财产价值征税的协调 324
CHAPTER X　Tax Harmonization on Cross-border Income from Immovable Property, Capital Gains and Property Value 324

第一节　跨国不动产所得征税的协调 326
Section 1　Tax Harmonization on Cross-border Income from Immovable Property 326

第二节　跨国财产收益征税的协调 333
Section 2　Tax Harmonization on Cross-border Income from Capital Gains 333

第三节　跨国财产价值征税的协调 346
Section 3　Tax Harmonization on Cross-border Property Value 346

第四节　相关案例 350
Section 4　Related Cases 350

第十一章　消除国际双重征税的方法 360
CHAPTER XI　Ways to Eliminate International Double Taxation 360

第一节　概述 360
Section 1　Overview 360
第二节　免税法 363
Section 2　Exemption Methods 363
第三节　抵免法 365
Section 3　Credit Methods 365
第四节　直接抵免法 369
Section 4　Direct Credit Method 369
第五节　间接抵免法 370
Section 5　Indirect Credit Method 370
第六节　税收饶让制度 371
Section 6　Tax Sparing Mechanism 371

第十二章　国际逃避税及其法律规制 373
CHAPTER XII　International Tax Evasion and Avoidance as Well as Their Legal Regulations 373

第一节　国际逃税和避税概述 373
Section 1　Overview of International Tax Evasion and Tax Avoidance 373
第二节　国际逃税 376
Section 2　International Tax Evasion 376
第三节　国际避税的主要方式和各国的法律管制 377
Section 3　Main Ways to Tax Evasion and its Regulations 377
第四节　转让定价及其法律管制 388
Section 4　Transfer Pricing and Its Legal Regulations 388
第五节　防止国际逃税与避税的国际税收合作 396
Section 5　Prevention of International Tax Evasion and Avoidance by International Tax Cooperation 396
第六节　反避税案例 401
Section 6　Anti-tax Avoidance Cases 401

第十三章 国际税务争议的解决 ... 410
CHAPTER XIII Settlement of International Tax Disputes ... 410

第一节 国际税务争议概况 ... 410
Section 1 Overview of International Tax Disputes ... 410
第二节 国际税务争议解决的原则和方法 ... 419
Section 2 Principles and Methods for the Settlement of International Tax Disputes ... 419
第三节 国际税务争议解决的国内法程序 ... 424
Section 3 Domestic Law Procedures for the Settlement of International Tax Disputes ... 424
第四节 国际税务争议解决的国际法程序 ... 436
Section 4 International Legal Procedures for the Settlement of International Tax Disputes ... 436
第五节 相关案例 ... 471
Section 5 Related Cases ... 471

参考文献 ... 485
Reference ... 485

第一章 CHAPTER I

绪 论
Introduction

第一节 国际税收关系和国际税法的概念
Section 1 Concepts of International Tax Relationship and International Tax Law

国际税法(international tax law)是适应调整国际税收关系的需要,逐渐从国内税法部门中产生和发展起来的综合性税法分支,同时也属于国际经济法的范畴。它是国际经济交往发展到一定阶段的产物,是随着国际税收关系的出现和国家间税收管辖权的冲突而产生的。

Originating from domestic tax law, international tax law is a comprehensive branch of tax laws for governing international tax relationships. Being part of the international economic law, it is a product of the development of international economic interaction to a certain stage, emerging with the formation of international tax relationships and cross-border conflicts over tax jurisdiction.

一、国际税收关系的产生
The Emergence of International Tax Relationship

国际税法随国际税收关系的产生而产生,而国际经济交往的发展则是国际税收关系产生的前提。当经济活动局限在一个国家的范围之内时,纳税人就其参与的经济活动收益只对一个国家承担纳税义务,此时不会存在国家与国家之间的税收利益分配关系,不存在国家间的税收管辖权(tax jurisdiction)冲突和双重征税(double taxation)。随着跨国经济活动的发展,纳税人就其参与的跨国经济活动收益需同时向两个以上的国家承担纳税义务,此时,就会产生国家与国家之间的税收利益分配关系,会发生国家间的税收管辖权冲突和双重征税,从而产生国际税收关系。

International tax law emerged following the formation of international tax relationships, whose precondition was the development of international economic interaction. When economic activities were restricted within the territory of one country, taxpayers undertook tax burdens to that country on the economic activities in which they were engaged. There were neither situations that demanded the distribution of tax revenues nor transnational tax jurisdiction conflicts and double taxation. With the development of cross-border economic activities, taxpayers began to assume tax burdens to two or more countries on such activities, resulting in the distribution of tax revenues between different countries as well as tax jurisdiction conflicts and double taxation, hence the formation of international tax relationships.

在资本主义社会之前,社会生产力比较低下,自给自足的封闭式自然经济占主导地位,农业是社会经济结构中最主要的生产部门,手工业及比较简单的商品经济处于附属地位,这一时期的社会生产与交换基本限于一国境内进行,在这种基本封闭的生产条件下产生的税收征纳关系被严格局限在一国地域范围之内,不涉及其他国家的税收利益,不存在国际税收关系。

Self-sufficient and closed natural economy played a leading role in precapitalist societies with low social productive forces, where agriculture was the most important sector of production in the socioeconomic structure while handicraft and simple commodity economy were in a subsidiary status. During this period of time, social production and exchange were virtually limited within the boundaries of one country. The tax relationship under almost closed production conditions was in turn strictly limited within the territory of one country, without involving any tax benefit of other countries. Therefore, there was no international tax relationship.

进入资本主义社会后,社会经济进入商品经济时代,商品交易行为逐步从国内市场扩展到国际市场,国家对进出口的货物实施关税制度。关税的征收已包含了一定的涉外因素,但从严格意义上来说,关税仍然属于在一国境内发生的税收分配,国家的税收管辖权并没有跨越国境,不会产生管辖权冲突或者国家间税收利益分配矛盾。19世纪末,社会经济进入垄断资本主义时代,垄断资本主义的主要特征是资本输出,包括资本直接输出和资本间接输出。资本直接输出,是指投资人直接在资本输入国投资开办企业,在资本输入国从事生产经营活动,从而获取来源于当地的营业利润和其他所得。资本间接输出,是指投资人购买资本输入国的股票、债券或向资本输入国提供贷款、技术等,从而获取股息、红利、利息、租金或特许权使用费等。垄断资本家为了获取更大的利益,不断扩大资本的国际输出,促使商品、资金、技术和劳动力等经济要素的跨国流动日趋频繁。从事跨国投资和其他经济活动的企业和个人的收入和财产日益国际化,这为国际税收关系及国际税法的产生奠定了客观的经济基础。

The capitalist society ushered in an era of commodity economy, during which commodity transactions gradually extended from domestic markets to international ones and many countries carried out tariffs on imported and exported goods. Some foreign-related factors were already involved in the imposition of tariffs. In the strict sense, however, tariffs still belonged to the category of domestic tax revenue distribution, while national tax jurisdiction did not cross the borders and would not lead to conflicts of tax jurisdiction or of tax revenue distribution between countries. At the end of the 19th century, the world witnessed the beginning of the era of monopoly capitalism, which features the export of capital, including both direct and indirect export of capital. By direct export of capital we refer to situations whereby investors start businesses in the capital-importing countries, thus acquiring business profits and other incomes from local sources. By indirect export of capital we refer to situations whereby investors purchase stocks, bonds from capital-importing countries or provide loans, technology, etc. to these countries to obtain dividends, bonuses, interests, rents or royalties. To earn more, monopoly capitalists continuously expanded international export of capital, leading to the increasingly frequent cross-border movement of commodities, funds, technology, labor, etc. The income and assets of the enterprises or individuals who were engaged in transnational investment and other economic activities became more and more internationalized, creating the economic foundation of international tax relationship and international tax law.

与此同时,各个国家所得税制度和一般财产税制度的普遍确立,为国际税收关系和国际税法的产生创造了必要的法律条件。18世纪末,英国首创了所得税。所得税的征税对象是纳税人的生产经营所得和其他所得及收益。到20世纪初,所得税已在世界上大多数国家得到普遍推行,在一些资本主义国家代替间接税成为主要的税种。在资本跨国流动和收入国际化的背景下,各主权国家为维护本国税收利益,一般对所得税同时行使属地原则和属人原则两种税收管辖权。税收管辖权是国家主权在税收领域的体现。其中,属地原则是指征税国根据纳税人的所得来源于本国境内的事实主张征税,无论纳税人是位于征税国境内还是境外;属人原则则是指征税国依据纳税人与本国存在居民或国籍的身份隶属关系主张对其来源于征税国境内和境外的各种所得征税。一般来讲,征税国都主张同时适用属人原则和属地原则,既对本国居民的纳税人来源于本国境内外的收入征税,又对非本国居民或公民的纳税人来源于本国境内的所得征税。由此可见,对于同一纳税人的同一跨国所得,所得来源国根据属地原则征税,纳税人居住国或国籍国根据属人原则也要征税,国际税收关系因而产生,国际双重征税现象同时出现。另外,纳税人除了在居住国或国籍国拥有财产,也会在其他国家拥有财产,而对于以纳税人的一般财产作为征税对象的财产税,很多国家在征税原则上同所得税一样,也主张属人原则与属地原则同时适用,纳税人居住国或国籍国对于财产的属人管辖权与跨国财产所在地国家的属地管辖权也会产生冲突,从而导致国际双重征税现象。

In the meantime, the establishment of income tax and general property tax system in many countries created the judicial condition for the advent of international tax relationship and international tax law. At the end of the 18th century, income tax, whose taxable object was the taxpayers' operational income and other earnings, was introduced in the UK for the first time in the world. Income tax had become prevalent in most countries by the beginning of the 20th century, and replaced indirect tax to be the primary category of tax in several capitalist countries. With the cross-border movement of capital and the increasingly global nature of income, sovereign countries usually carry out, as regards income tax, two different principles of tax jurisdiction simultaneously, namely territorial jurisdiction and personal jurisdiction, to protect their own tax benefit. Tax jurisdiction was a reflection of a country's sovereignty in the area of taxation. According to the principle of territorial jurisdiction, a country would levy a tax based on the fact that the income was sourced from within its territory, no matter whether the taxpayer was located inside or outside its territory. According to the principle of personal jurisdiction, however, a country would levy a tax based on the fact that the taxpayer had the identity of residence or citizen of the country. Generally speaking, most countries adopted simultaneously personal jurisdiction and territorial jurisdiction, that is to say, for resident taxpayers applying personal jurisdiction to tax on incomes sourced globally, and for non-resident or non-citizen applying territorial jurisdiction to tax on incomes sourced from its territory. Thus, for the transnational income of a same taxpayer, the source country would tax based on the principle of territorial jurisdiction, while the resident country or citizen country would tax based on the principle of personal jurisdiction. The international tax relationship was created thereon, and international double taxation emerged at the same time. Besides, in addition to owning property in the resident country or citizen country, the taxpayer might also own property in other countries. Regarding the property tax with general property as the taxable object, many countries simultaneously carried out the principles of personal jurisdiction and territorial jurisdiction, as in the case of income tax. This might cause conflict between the personal jurisdiction on property of the resident country or citizen country and the territorial jurisdiction of the countries where the property was located, leading to international double taxation.

国际双重征税现象的普遍大量存在并不利于实现各国的经济利益与长远发展，同时也与遭受重复征税纳税人的切身利益相悖。首先，国际双重征税使跨国纳税人要依法向两个以上的国家纳税，担负了沉重的纳税义务，违背了税负公平原则。仅有国内财产和所得的纳税人与在国外拥有财产和所得的跨国纳税人相比较，就同样的所得，跨国纳税人要承担重得多的税负。其次，国际双重征税影响国际投资经营决策，违背税收中性原则。税收中性原则，又称税收中立原则，是指税收不应对纳税人的投资取向、经营决策和行为选择产生直接影响，特别是纳税人对投资区域、行业领域和经营方式的选择，应主要由价值规律和市场竞争来驱动，而国家税收政策的影响应该是中性的。但在国际双重征税的情况下，纳税人计划的投资可能因为税负加重使收益降低的因素而发生改变。最后，国际双重征税严重阻碍国际经济的发展。过重的税收负担使跨国交易成本增高，严重挫伤纳税人从事国际经济活动的积极性，从而影响了国际资金、商品流动和技术合作及文化交流。对于缺少资金和技术的发展中国家来说，国际双重征税阻碍了其有效吸引外资和引进技术；对于发达国家来说，国际双重征税也不利于其国内剩余资金向国外流动以获取利润。

The prevalence of international double taxation went against the economic interests and long-term development of all countries, and was not in the interests of taxpayers who suffered it. Firstly, the taxpayer who sufferes international double taxation should pay taxes to two or more countries on a same income, a heavy burden that violates the principle of tax equality. Compared with taxpayers with only domestic property and income, taxpayers with overseas property and income assume much heavier tax burdens on the same income. Secondly, international double taxation will impact transnational investment and business decision-making, thus violating the principle of tax neutrality. The principle of tax neutrality means that taxation should not exert any direct impact on investment orientation, operation decision and other behavioral choices of the taxpayer. In particular, the choices concerning the location of investment, industrial sector and business methods should be driven primarily by the law of value and market competition, while the impact of tax policies should be neutral. In the situation of international double taxation, however, a taxpayer's planned investment might be changed because of the lower profit caused by heavier tax burdens. Thirdly, international double taxation would severely impede the development of the world economy. Overweight tax burden would increase the cost of international transaction and demotivate the taxpayers to engage in international economic activities, with negative impact on international flow of funds and commodities as well as on technological cooperation and cultural exchanges. For developing countries lacking funds and technologies, international double taxation would hamper the effective attraction of FDI and technologies; for developed countries, it would discourage their domestic surplus funds from flowing outwards to gain profit.

如何减少、避免和消除国际双重征税,促进国际经济活动的正常发展,是各国政府和从事国际经济活动的人们的共同愿望和要求。在各国政府之间建立一种合理的税收利益分配关系,协调好各国间的税收管辖权,消除和减轻国际双重征税成为国际税法的重要内容。

It has become the common aspiration and requirement of national governments as well as individuals engaged in international economic activities to reduce, avoid and eliminate international double taxation and boost international economic activities. International tax law is mainly about the elimination or alleviation of international double taxation, by the establishment of a reasonable tax benefit distribution relationship among governments and the coordination of tax jurisdictions of different countries.

（二）国际税法的概念
The Concept of International Tax Law

国际税法是调整国际税收关系的法律规范的总称。国际税收关系既包括国家与国家之间的税收利益分配关系,也包括主权国家与纳税人之间的涉外税收征纳关系。理论界对于国际税收关系范围的界定存在一定的分歧。第一个分歧是国际税收是否包括涉外税收。狭义论认为,国际税收仅指国家与国家之间的税收利益分配关系;广义论认为,国际税收除涉及国家间的税收利益分配关系外,还包括主权国家与纳税人的涉外税收征纳关系。第二个分歧是间接税是否应包括在国际税收范围之内。狭义论认为,国际税收涉及的税种范围只包括所得税和财产税,而不包括关税、增值税等流转税税种;广义论认为,国际税收涉及的税种范围除所得税和财产税之外,还包括关税、增值税等流转税。[①]本教材采纳广义的国际税收范围,主张国际税法不仅包括调整国家间税收管辖权冲突和权益分配的国际公法性质的冲突法和实体法规范,还包括各国制定的调整国家与涉外纳税人之间利益分配的国内法规范。[②]

International tax law is defined as a general term for laws and regulations governing international tax relationship. International tax relationship includes not only tax benefit

---
① 参见刘隆亨主编:《国际税法》(第二版),法律出版社2007年版,第8—9页。
② 参见高尔森主编:《国际税法》(第二版),法律出版社1992年版,第6—7页。

distribution relationship between countries but also foreign tax-levying relationship between sovereign countries and foreign taxpayers. There are several divergences of opinion in the academic world regarding the scope of international tax relationship. The first divergence is about whether international tax includes foreign tax. The narrow-sense point of view believes that international tax refers only to the tax benefit distribution relationship between countries, whereas the broad-sense point of view regards international tax as including not only the tax benefit distribution relationship between countries but also the tax-levying relationship between sovereign countries and foreign taxpayers. The second divergence is about whether indirect taxes are within the scope of international tax. From the narrow-sense point of view, international tax includes only income taxes and property taxes, and turnover taxes such as tariff and value added taxes are excluded. From the broad-sense point of view, however, international tax includes not only income taxes and property taxes but also turnover taxes such as tariff and value added taxes. The broad-sense opinion is adopted in this book, arguing that international tax law includes not only international public law governing tax jurisdiction conflicts and tax benefit distribution between countries, but also domestic laws and regulations made by different countries governing foreign tax-levying relationship between sovereign countries and foreign taxpayers.

国际税收涉及的税种不仅有所得税、财产税等直接税,也包括关税、增值税等间接税;相应地,不仅国内所得税法、财产税法隶属于国际税法的范畴,而且国内增值税法、关税法等也同样隶属于国际税法的范畴。①

International tax includes not only direct taxes such as income taxes and property taxes, but also indirect taxes such as tariff and value added taxes. Correspondingly, domestic value added tax laws and tariff laws, in addition to domestic income tax laws and property tax laws, belong to the category of international tax law.

国际税法的渊源包括国内法渊源和国际法渊源两部分。两部分虽具有各自的功能和作用,但彼此配合,相互渗透,共同对国际税收关系进行法律调整。

The sources of international tax law include domestic law sources and international law sources. The two parts, with their respective functions and roles, are mutually supporting and closely interwoven, jointly governing international tax relationships.

国际税法的国内法渊源,包括各国单方面制定的适用于对纳税人涉外所得和财产征税的所得税法和财产税法,以及适用于对纳税人商品、资金、劳务、技术、知识产权、数据信息等的流转额征税的增值税法、关税法等。在一些普通法系国家,法院的税务案件判例也是具有约束力的国内法渊源。各国通过这些国内法渊源明确了税收管辖权的范围和内涵,对纳税人的居民和非居民身份及其相应的纳税责任作出规定,确定各个税种的税目、税率、应税所得额、减免税优惠、可予扣除的成本、费用、损失以及征收方式和程序等,也可以确定逃避税的法律责任以及应对逃避税行为的方法和措施,甚至主权国家可以单方制定国内法来消除和减轻国际双重征税。国际税法的国内法渊源,从广义上来说,除了国家立法机关制定的税收法律,还包括各国行政机关根据法律的授权发布的税收税务行政法规、行政规章和部门规

---

① 参见刘剑文主编:《国际税法学》(第二版),北京大学出版社2004年版,第30—31页。

章,以及地方立法机关、地方行政机关发布的地方性法规和地方规章。当然,宪法性文件、法律、行政法规、部门规章、地方性法规、地方规章中的税法规范的法律效力和法律地位是有所不同的,在中国,需要按照宪法及立法法的有关规定来确定各种法律渊源在法的体系中的地位和效力。

  The domestic sources of international tax law include income tax laws and property tax laws, unilaterally made by every country to be applied on foreign incomes and properties of taxpayers, as well as value added tax laws and tariff laws applied on the turnover of commodities, funds, labor services, technologies, intellectual properties, data information, etc. In some common-law countries, the judicial precedents of tax cases made by court are also deemed as among domestic sources of law with binding effect. Every country clarifies the scope and connotation of the tax jurisdiction through domestic sources of law, determines the resident/non-resident identification and the corresponding tax responsibilities, stipulates the tax items, tax rate, taxable income, tax preferential treatment, deductible costs, expenditures and losses, as well as collection methods and procedures, and defines legal responsibilities for tax avoidance and evasion as well as countermeasures against them. A sovereign country can even unilaterally make domestic laws to eliminate or mitigate international double taxation. The domestic sources of international tax law, in a broad sense, include the tax laws made by a national legislative body, as well as administrative regulations, administrative rules and department regulations made by administrative organizations authorized by law, and local statutes and regulations made by local legislative bodies or local administrative organizations. There are differences, of course, in the legal effects or legal status of constitutional documents, laws, administrative regulations, department regulations, and local regulations. In China, the legal effects and legal status of legal sources are to be determined by the Constitution and the Law on Legislation.

  国际税法的国际法渊源,主要是指各国相互间为协调对跨国征税对象的课税关系而签订的双边或多边的国际税收协定或条约和各国在国际税收实践中普遍遵行的国际税收习惯(usual practices of international tax law)。它们的主要作用在于协调各国税收管辖权之间的冲突,避免国际双重征税和确立国际税务行政协助关系。[①] 国际税收协定是各国政府为协调相互之间的国际税收利益分配关系而缔结的条约及协定,一些不以调整国际税收关系为主要目的的国际条约或协定,如双边投资协定、友好通商航海条约,也存在关于国际税收关系的约定,这些约定也属于国际税法的渊源。也有观点认为,某些国际组织制定的规范性文件中关于国际税法的内容也是国际税法的渊源。国际税法的国际法渊源的另一重要组成部分是国际税收习惯,它是指在国际税收实践中反复出现并被各国普遍采用且承认具有法律约束力的惯常行为和做法。例如,在国际税收实践中逐渐形成的国际税收习惯,如外交税收豁免、税收无差别待遇、非居民承担有限纳税责任等,这些国际税收习惯大多逐渐被各国国内立法或税收协定确定并成为成文法规则,那些仍然存在的不成文的国际税收习惯则越来越少。与国际税收习惯密切相关的是国际税收惯例(customary rule of international tax),两者之间既

[①] 参见廖益新主编、朱炎生副主编:《国际税法学》,高等教育出版社2013年版,第5—6页。

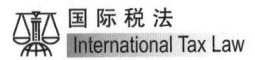

有区别又相互联系。区别在于，国际税收惯例虽然也是实践中各国普遍适用的行为方法，但在没有约定的情况下，尚不具有法律约束力；联系在于，国际税收惯例是国际税收习惯形成的基础和必经阶段，某一种国际税收行为方法必须经过国际税收惯例这个阶段才能上升为具有法律约束力的国际税收习惯。

The international sources of international tax law refer mainly to bilateral or multilateral tax treaties signed by countries to coordinate the tax-levying relationship regarding transnational tax objects and usual practices of international tax which are complied with in international taxation. They are intended to settle conflicts among different tax jurisdictions, avoid international double taxation, and establish international tax administrative assistance relationship. International tax treaties are treaties or agreements signed by governments to coordinate mutual tax benefit distribution. Some international treaties or agreements whose main purposes are not the governing of international tax relationship, such as bilateral investment agreement, treaty of commerce and navigation, also include agreement regarding international tax relationship. Such agreement is part of the sources of international tax law. Contents relevant to international tax issues in the normative documents made by international organizations are sometimes regarded to be part of the sources of international tax law as well. Another important part of the international sources of international tax law is usual practices of international tax, i.e., the usual behaviors or practices with binding effect which are repeatedly found in international taxation and widely adopted by countries, such as diplomatic tax exemption, non-discriminate treatment, non-resident taxpayer taking limited tax responsibilities. Step by step, these practices are confirmed by domestic legislation or tax treaties and become written law, with increasingly fewer practices still being unwritten ones. The Customary rule of international tax, which is closely related to usual practices of international tax, distinguishes itself from the latter by the fact that it does not have any binding effect without previous agreement though it is also widely adopted by many countries. The two are closely related because customary rule of international tax is the foundation and a necessary stage for the formation of usual practices of international tax; a method cannot become a usual practice of international tax with binding effect before it is accepted as a customary rule.

（三）国际税收法律关系的特征
The Characteristics of International Tax Legal Relationship

国际税收法律关系与国际税收关系，两者分属上层建筑和经济基础层面，是同一个事物的不同层面。国际税收关系既包括国家与国家之间的税收利益分配关系，也包括主权国家与纳税人之间的涉外税收征纳关系，当这种关系被国际税法调整时，参与各方形成国际税法下的权利义务关系就成为了国际税收法律关系。国际税收法律关系在其主体、客体和内容上都有自己的特点。

International tax legal relationship and international tax relationship, belonging to a society's superstructure and economic base respectively, are two different aspects of a same phenomenon. International taxation relationship include tax benefit distribution between countries, as well as the foreign tax-levying relationship between a sovereign country and taxpayers. When international taxation relationship is governed by international tax law, the rights and obligations of all parties involved under international tax law form an international taxation legal relationship, with uniqueness in its subjects, objects and content.

(一) 国际税收法律关系主体
The Subject of International Tax Legal Relationship

国际税收法律关系的主体是指参加国际税收法律关系，在国际税收法律关系中承担义务并享有权利的主体。作为法律关系的主体应当具有法律规定的主体资格，即应当具备权利能力和行为能力。自然人、法人、其他组织和团体、国际组织、国家都可以作为国际税收法律关系的主体。国际税收法律关系的主体分为纳税主体与征税主体两大类。

Subjects of international tax legal relationship are the participants who join the legal relationship, assuming obligations and enjoying rights. A subject of the legal relationship should have the eligibility stipulated by law, i.e., having the legal capacity and disposing capacity. Subjects of international taxation legal relationship could be natural persons, legal persons, other organizations or institutions, international organizations or nations. They can be divided into two categories: taxpayers and tax authorities.

从征税主体来看，国内税收的征税主体仅为一个国家，而国际税收的征税主体则必须同时存在两个以上的国家。国内税收关系主要是国家与纳税主体之间的税收征纳关系，国家为获得财政收入向纳税人强制无偿征收税款，作为征税主体的国家实质上只享有征税权利，并不承担义务。而在国际税收关系中，既有国家与跨国纳税主体的税收征纳关系，也有国家间的税收利益分配关系。国家与跨国纳税主体的税收征纳关系与国内税收征纳关系基本相同，但有一点不同之处是国际税法对国家间税收管辖权和税收利益分配的调整将影响国际税收征纳关系。在国家间的税收利益分配关系之中，不同国家作为平等的主体协商签订税收协定，在享有权利的同时也承担相应的义务。国家在国际税收法律关系中同时具有征税主体和税收利益分配主体的双重身份。

The tax authority of domestic taxation is only one country, whereas the tax authorities of international taxation have to be two or more countries at the same time. The domestic tax relationship includes primarily the tax-levying relationship between the country and the taxpayers, in which the country compulsorily collects taxes from taxpayers without compensation to acquire fiscal revenue. As the tax authority, the country enjoys the rights to collect taxes without assuming obligations. In international tax relationship, however, there exist not only tax-levying relationship between countries but also tax revenue distribution relationship between the country and transnational taxpayers. The tax-levying relationship between the country and the transnational taxpayers is basically the same as the domestic taxation relationship, with one difference that the international tax law will affect the international tax-levying relationship by adjusting tax jurisdiction and tax revenue distribution between countries. In the tax revenue distribution between countries, countries negotiate and sign tax agreements as equal subjects, enjoying rights and bearing corresponding obligations at the same time. In international tax legal relationship, a country has the dual identity of a tax authority and a subject of tax revenue distribution.

在国际税收关系中，多数国家在所得税和财产税上都同时主张属人原则和属地原则两种税收管辖权。国家是征税主体，一方面，作为居住国，根据属人原则要求本国居民就其来源于国内国外的所得和财产纳税；另一方面，其作为收入来源国或财产所在国，对非居民行使属地税收管辖权，要求非居民就来源于该国的所得或存在于该国的财产纳税。同一个国家往往同时具有居住国和来源国的双重征税主体地位。而该种身份的确定必须针对某个特定的纳税主体来进行，对于不同的纳税主体，征税国会以居住国或来源国的不同身份出现。

In international tax relationships, most countries assert both personal and territorial jurisdictions on income and property taxation. On the one hand, the state, or the tax authority, as the resident country, requires its residents to be taxed on their income and property derived from domestic and foreign sources based on the personal jurisdiction. On the other hand, as the country of income or property, it exercises territorial jurisdiction over non-residents and requires them to pay taxes on income or property that originates or is present in that country. The same country often has the dual taxing subject status of both the resident country and the source country. The determination of such status must be made with respect to a particular tax subject, and for different tax subjects, the taxing state will appear in a different capacity as the resident or the source country.

国际税收法律关系中的纳税主体，也被称为跨国纳税主体或涉外纳税主体，包括自然人、法人、其他非法人组织和一些国际组织。跨国纳税主体与国内纳税主体的不同之处在于，前者就同一笔课税对象需向两个以上国家承担纳税义务，后者只需向一个国家承担纳税义务。正是因为跨国纳税主体在其居住国依属人原则纳税，同时还需对跨国财产或所得向来源国承担税负，才导致了国家之间税收管辖权的冲突与税收利益的分配关系。必须特别注意的是，一个纳税主体是否构成国际税收法律关系中的跨国纳税人，关键在于纳税人是否就其同一笔征税对象对两个以上的征税国家承担纳税义务。如果一个纳税人分别就不同的征税对象对两个以上的征税国承担纳税义务，则其不是国际税法意义上的跨国纳税人。另外，纳税人的国籍也不是认定其是否为跨国纳税人的标志。一个具有外国国籍的纳税人并非当然是跨国纳税人，一个具有本国国籍的纳税人也并不一定只是国内税收关系中的纳税人。[1]

The tax subjects in international tax legal relationships, also known as transnational tax subjects or foreign tax subjects, include natural persons, legal persons, other unincorporated organizations and some international organizations. The difference between a transnational tax subject and a domestic tax subject is that the former is liable to two or more countries for the same tax object, while the latter is liable to one country only. A multinational tax subject pays tax in its country of residence according to the principle of personal jurisdiction, and at the same

---

[1] 参见廖益新主编：《国际税法学》，高等教育出版社2008年版，第7—8页。

time bears the tax liability to the source country for the multinational property or income, which leads to the conflict of tax jurisdiction and the distribution of tax benefits between countries. It is important to note that whether a tax subject is a transnational taxpayer in international tax legal relationships depends on whether the taxpayer is liable to more than two taxing countries for the same tax object. If a taxpayer is liable to more than two taxing countries for different tax objects, this taxpayer is not a transnational taxpayer in the sense of international tax law. In addition, the nationality of a taxpayer is not an indication of whether it is a multinational taxpayer. A taxpayer with foreign nationality is not necessarily a transnational taxpayer, and a taxpayer with domestic nationality is not necessarily a taxpayer of domestic tax relationship.

（二）国际税收法律关系客体
The Object of International Tax Legal Relationship

国际税收法律关系客体是指国际税收法律关系主体之间权利、义务指向的对象。由于国际税法的调整对象为国家与跨国纳税人之间的涉外税收征纳关系和国家之间的税收利益分配关系，相对应的国际税收法律关系客体也包括两方面内容，即国际税收的征税对象和在国家间分配的国际税收收入。国际税收的征税对象即国家就哪些税种与跨国纳税人发生法律关系。本教材认同广义的国际税法概念，认为国际双重征税不仅发生在所得税、财产税上，流转税领域同样存在重复征税问题以及国际逃避税现象，也需要国与国之间进行税收利益的分配，因此，所得税、财产税和流转税都应包括在国际税收的征税对象范围。而国家间进行分配的国际税收收入则包含在各征税主体依据国际税收协定划分的征税权直接征收的税款中。

The object of international tax legal relationship refers to the object to which the rights and obligations between the subjects of international tax legal relationship are directed. Since the object of international tax law is the foreign tax collection and payment relationship between the state and the transnational taxpayers and the tax benefit distribution relationship between the states, the corresponding object of international tax legal relationship includes two aspects, namely, the object of international taxation and the international tax revenue distributed between the states. The object of international taxation is the legal relationship between the state and the transnational taxpayers on which taxes are levied. In this book we agree with the concept of international tax law in a broad sense. International double taxation not only occurs in income tax and property tax, but also exists in the field of turnover tax, which also requires the allocation of tax benefits between countries. Therefore, income tax, property tax and turnover tax should be included in international taxation. The international tax revenues allocated among countries are included in the taxes directly collected by each taxing body according to the taxing rights divided by international tax agreements.

（三）国际税收法律关系内容
The Content of International Tax Legal Relationship

国际税收法律关系内容是指国际税收法律关系主体相互之间存在的权利和义务。在国家之间的税收利益分配关系中,国家所享有的权利一般包括税款征收权、税收调整权、税务管理权以及国际税收协定约定的其他权利;国家所承担的义务一般包括限额征税义务、税收减免义务、税务合作义务以及国际税收协定约定的其他义务。在国家与跨国纳税人之间的涉外税收征纳关系中,国家所享有的权利一般包括税款征收权、税收调整权、税务管理权、减免审批权以及税收处罚权等;国家所承担的义务主要包括限额征税义务、税收减免义务和税收服务义务等。跨国纳税人所承担的义务主要包括纳税义务、接受税收调整义务、接受税务管理义务以及接受税收处罚义务等,其享有的权利主要包括依法纳税和限额纳税权、税收减免权、享受税收服务权、保守秘密权、行政诉讼和行政复议等诉讼救济权。

The content of international tax legal relationship is the rights and obligations that exist between the subjects of international tax legal relationship. In the tax benefit distribution relationship between states, the rights enjoyed by the state generally include the right of tax collection, tax adjustment, tax administration and other rights agreed in the international tax agreement; the obligations undertaken by the state generally include the obligation of tax limitation, tax relief, tax cooperation and other obligations agreed in the international tax agreement. In the foreign tax-levying relationship between the state and the multinational taxpayers, the rights enjoyed by the state generally include the right of tax collection, tax adjustment, tax administration, tax relief approval and tax penalty, etc. ; the obligations undertaken by the state mainly include the obligation of tax limitation, tax relief and tax service, etc. The obligations of multinational taxpayers mainly include the obligation to pay tax, as well as to accept tax adjustment, tax administration and tax punishment, etc. The rights they enjoy mainly include the right to pay tax according to law and the limit, the right to tax relief, the right to enjoy tax services, the right to keep secrets, the right to administrative litigation and administrative reconsideration and other litigation remedies.

在国内税收法律关系中,由国家作为主导对课税利益进行分配,主体之间的权利义务总体上是不对等的,而在国际税收法律关系中,因为多了国家间的税收利益分配,国家与跨国纳税人之间的权利义务已经不完全取决于一个征税主体的单方意志。国家之间地位平等,国家之间对国际税收利益分配形成的权利义务关系,是建立在对等互利的基础上,国家间税收利益的分配通过各国对跨国纳税人的具体征税措施体现出来,因而,国家与跨国纳税人之间的权利义务在一定程度上是两个甚至两个以上征税主体之间意志协调的结果。

In domestic taxation relationship, the state is the dominant authority in the distribution of tax benefits, and the rights and obligations between subjects are generally unequal, while in international taxation relationship, because of the distribution of tax benefits between countries, the rights and obligations between the state and transnational taxpayers no longer depend entirely on the unilateral will of a taxing subject. The rights and obligations between countries are equal in status, and the relationship of rights and obligations formed by the distribution of international tax benefits between countries is based on reciprocity and mutual benefit, and the distribution of the tax benefits between countries is reflected through the specific taxation measures of each country to transnational taxpayers, thus, the rights and obligations between countries and transnational taxpayers are to a certain extent the result of the harmonization of the will between two or even more taxing subjects.

第二节　国际税法的历史发展
Section 2　Historical Development of International Tax Law

一、国际税收协定的签订是国际税法产生的标志
The Signing of International Tax Treaty as a Symbol of the Creation of International Tax Law

据记载，世界上第一个税收协定可以追溯到1843年比利时与法国签订的协定，该协定主要解决两国在税务问题上的相互合作和情报交换等问题。在遗产税方面的第一个国际税收协定是于1872年由瑞士沃州政府同英国缔结的避免双重征税的协定。在所得税方面的第一个综合性税收协定是于1899年6月21日由奥匈帝国和普鲁士王国签订的避免双重征税的协定，该协定首次提出对不动产所得、抵押贷款利息所得、常驻代表机构所得以及个人劳务所得，可以由收入的来源国征税，其他类型所得由居住国征税。

According to the relevant information, the first tax agreement in the world can be traced back to the agreement signed between Belgium and France in 1843, which mainly solved the problems of mutual cooperation and information exchange between the two countries in tax matters. The first international tax agreement in the field of inheritance taxation was concluded in 1872 between the Swiss Canton of Vaud and the United Kingdom for the avoidance of double taxation. The first comprehensive tax agreement in the field of income tax was the agreement for the avoidance of double taxation between Austria-Hungary and the Kingdom of Prussia, signed on June 21, 1899, which for the first time introduced the possibility of taxation of income from real estate, interest on mortgages, income from permanent representations and income from personal services in the country of origin and other types of income in the resident country.

纵观国际税收协定的发展历史，具有现代意义的对所得和财产避免国际双重征税的综合性的税收协定起步于20世纪20年代。第一次世界大战后，随着所得税在各国的相继开征、所得税的负担日益加重，资本输出国（如当时的英国，后来的美国）中纳税人的国际双重征税问题尖锐地表现出来。为此，国际商会（International Chamber of Commerce, ICC）曾于1921年、1922年、1923年和1924年组织成员对双重征税进行了4次专题讨论。1921年，国际联盟（League of Nations）根据1920年布鲁塞尔国际财政会议的要求，建立了一个由美国的塞利格曼、荷兰的布鲁英斯、意大利的艾因诺第和英国的斯坦普组成的四人税务专家组，着手研究国际双重征税问题。

Throughout the history of the development of international tax treaties, comprehensive tax treaties with modern significance for the avoidance of international double taxation on income and property started in the 1920s. After the First World War, with the introduction of income tax in various countries and the increasing burden of income tax, the problem of international double taxation of taxpayers in capital-exporting countries (such as the United Kingdom at that time, and the United States later) came out sharply. For this reason, the International Chamber of Commerce (ICC) organized four special discussions on double taxation among its member countries in 1921, 1922, 1923 and 1924. In 1921, the League of Nations established a four-member tax expert group consisting of Seligman from the United States, Bruins from the Netherlands, Einaudi from Italy and Sir Josiah Stamp from the United Kingdom to study the issue of international double taxation, as requested by the International Fiscal Conference in Brussels in 1920.

1923年4月3日,税务专家组发表了一份关于国际双重征税对经济影响的研究报告。报告首次从理论上阐述了双重征税对国际资本流动的影响、税收管辖权的执行依据,试图找到资本输出国与资本输入国之间财政利益分配的各种组合。报告提出了确定纳税义务的两个主要因素,即财富所有人的居住地和财富的来源地(所谓来源地,是指经济上的含义,并非单纯的地理上的含义),而课税权主体应对此作出选择。确定纳税义务的其他因素还包括国籍、临时居住地、课税主体的实际所在地、课税主体的登记注册地。专家们对不同类型所得和财产的课税原则提出了自己的观点,如对土地、采矿企业、商业企业、工业企业、农业用具,应优先由财富来源地所在国课税,而对有价证券、财产所有权和个人劳务,应由财富所有人居住地国家课税。同时,报告还提出了避免国际双重征税可供选择的四种方案:一是居民所在国对其居民在外国缴纳的税收予以减除;二是收入来源国免征非居民来源于境内收入的税收;三是居民所在国和收入来源国相互间在一定条件下对税收进行分配;四是采取分类法,即对某些专项所得可明确由居民所在国或由收入来源国独占征税权。

On April 3, 1923, the tax expert group published a report on the economic impact of international double taxation. For the first time, the report theorized the effects of double taxation on international capital flows, the basis for enforcement of tax jurisdiction, and attempts to find various combinations of the distribution of fiscal benefits between capital-exporting and capital-importing countries. The report suggested two main factors in determining the tax liability, namely the residence of the owner of the wealth and the place of origin of the wealth (the *place of origin* was defined in an economic sense, not in a purely geographical sense) for which the subject of the taxing power should make a choice. Other factors that determine the tax liability include nationality, temporary residence, physical location of the subject of taxation, and place of registration of the subject of taxation. The experts presented their views on the principles of taxation of different types of income and property, such as the priority of taxation of land, mining enterprises, commercial enterprises, industrial enterprises and agricultural appliances in the country where the wealth is sourced, and the taxation of securities, property ownership and personal services in the country where the wealth owner resides. At the same time, The report also proposed four options to avoid international double taxation: first, the resident country should deduct the tax paid by its residents in foreign countries; second, the source country should exempt non-residents from taxation on income derived from its territory; third, the resident country and the source country should allocate the tax between each other under certain conditions; fourth, the classification method should be adopted, i.e., certain special income can be explicitly taxed by the resident country or the source country. The taxing right is exclusively reserved by the source country.

尽管在当时的四个方案中没有一项方案被所有国家一致接纳,显然,这是因为各国的经济状况不尽一致,难以统一满足各国经济利益的税收分配原则,但报告在最后提出的希望是,随着落后国家工业化进程的不断发展,居住地纳税原则即第二种方案,应被认为是解决国际双重征税难题的最有效和最能为各国所接受的原则。可以认为,以塞利格曼为首的专家组提出的研究报告对以后国际税收的研究和国际税收协定范本的产生、发展有着重要的影响。与此同时,1922年,为了研究国际双重征税和防止国际偷漏税的管理等实际问题,国际联盟在财政委员会范围内成立了一个由比利时、英国、意大利、捷克斯洛伐克、法国、荷兰和瑞士七国高级税务官员组成的工作组。1925年,德国、阿根廷、波兰、日本和委内瑞拉的代表相继参加了工作组。美国代表于1927年也进入了这个工作组工作。工作组在1923—1927年起草了下列4个有关双边税收协定的文件,即《关于避免对直接税重复征税的双边协定》《关于避免对财产继承重复征税的双边协定》《关于征税的行政管理援助的双边协定》和《关于征税的司法援助的双边协定》。所有这些范本及其注释主要是提供给国际联盟的成员和非成员政府研究和参考的。1928年10月,在日内瓦召开了由27个国家代表参加的专门会议。会议草拟了包含消除国际双重征税和防止国际偷漏税的国际税收协定初稿,并首次提出了"常设机构"在国际税收中的概念内涵。1929年,国际联盟的常设机构之一——财政委员会宣告成立。委员会经过对35个国家的调查研究,起草了一份有关国家间所得分配的协定草案。这个草案首先由国际商会美国部在华盛顿和纽约组织召开的专门会议上进行讨论,之后又在1933年6月召开的财政委员会全体会议上再次讨论。在1935年6月召开的财政委员会全体会议上略加修改的这个草案,被批准为1935年协定范本。1940年,财政委员会在荷兰召开的会议总结了税收协定研究工作的成果,并对1928年和1935年的协定范本作了一系列补充。由于第二次世界大战爆发,财政委员会难以进一步开展工作,被迫中断了某些活动。然而,1940年和1943年,在墨西哥的墨西哥城还是召开了两次高级税务会议,参加会议的有美国和拉丁美洲的国家。

Although none of the four options was unanimously accepted by all countries at that time, apparently because the economic situation of each country was not identical and it was difficult to unify the tax allocation principles that could satisfy the economic interests of each country, the report concluded with the hope that later, with the continuous development of industrialization in the backward countries, the principle of residence taxation, i.e., the second option, should be considered as the most effective and the most acceptable principle for all countries. It can be considered that the study presented by the expert group headed by Seligman had an important influence on the subsequent research on international taxation and the emergence and development of the model international tax agreements. At the same time, in 1922, in order to study practical problems of international double taxation and administration of prevention of international tax evasion, the League of Nations established a working group within the Finance Committee consisting of senior tax officials from seven countries — Belgium, Great Britain, Italy, Czechoslovakia, France, the Netherlands and Switzerland. In 1925, representatives from Germany, Argentina, Poland, Japan and Venezuela joined the working group. In 1927, representatives of the United States also joined this working group. The working group drafted the following four documents on bilateral tax agreements during the period from 1923 to 1927, namely, *the Bilateral Agreement for the Avoidance of Double Taxation on Direct Taxes*, *the Bilateral Agreement for the Avoidance of Double Taxation on Inheritance of Property*, *the Bilateral Agreement for Administrative Assistance in the Collection of Taxes*, and *the Bilateral Agreement for Judicial Assistance in the Collection of Taxes*. In October 1928, a special conference was held in Geneva with the participation of representatives of 27 countries. In 1929, the Fiscal Committee, one of the permanent bodies of the League of Nations, was established. After research into 35 countries, the Committee prepared a draft agreement on the distribution of income between countries. This draft was first discussed at special meetings organized by the U. S. Department of the International Chamber of Commerce in Washington and New York, and then again at the plenary session of the Fiscal Committee in June 1933. In 1940, at a meeting held in the Netherlands, the Fiscal Committee summarized the results of its work on tax treaties and made a series of additions to the 1928 and 1935 model agreements. The outbreak of World War II made it difficult for the Committee to carry out further work and forced it to discontinue certain activities. Nevertheless, two high-level tax conferences were held in Mexico City in 1940 and 1943, with participation from the United States and Latin American countries.

此后一次会议又拟订了一些新的协定范本草案,其中包括有关避免所得双重征税的协定范本、有关避免遗产双重征税的协定范本和有关政府间就直接税的计征建立协作关系的协定范本。所有这些协定范本草案被称为《墨西哥草案》。《墨西哥草案》的特征是,采取了对资本输入国有利的课税原则,即强调了收入来源国的优先征税权,对非居民的所得几乎完全由来源国课税;对来自工业、商业和农业的所得或其他营利性活动的所得,仅在实际经营地课税,而不是在纳税人的国籍国或居住国课税。1946年3月,国际联盟财政委员会在伦敦召开了第10届全体会议,会议重新讨论了墨西哥城会议拟订的协定范本草案,并提出了《伦敦草案》。《伦敦草案》并未接受《墨西哥草案》对股息事项所得的源泉课税原则,但同意对利息按一定的百分比由源泉国课征预提税;对特许权使用费则要求在扣除成本和费用的基础上,实行有限制的源泉国课税。委员会希望,在国际联盟解散后的新历史条件下,有关国际税收问题的讨论,能够对以前的工作成果给予充分利用。

At the latter meeting, a number of new draft model agreements were prepared, including a model agreement for the avoidance of double taxation on income, a model agreement for the avoidance of double taxation on estates, and an agreement on intergovernmental collaboration on the collection of direct taxes. All of these draft model agreements are referred to as the "Mexican Draft." The "Mexican Draft" is characterized by the adoption of taxation principles favorable to the country of importation of capital, i.e., it emphasizes the priority of taxation in the country of origin of the income, and the income of non-residents is taxed almost exclusively in the country of origin; income from industry, commerce, agriculture or other profit-making activities is taxed only in the place of actual operation and not in the country of the taxpayer's nationality or residence. In March 1946, the 10th plenary session of the Fiscal Committee of the League of Nations was held in London, where the draft model agreement prepared at the Mexico City Conference was revisited and the "London Draft" was proposed. The "London Draft" did not accept the principle of source taxation on dividends, but agreed that interest should be subject to a certain percentage of source country withholding tax; royalties should be subject to limited source country taxation on the basis of deduction of costs and expenses. The Committee hoped that, after the dissolution of the League of Nations, it would be possible to impose a limited source-country tax. The Committee hopes that in the new historical conditions following the dissolution of the League of Nations, discussions on international tax issues will make full use of the results of previous work.

（二）《经济合作与发展组织关于对所得和财产课税的协定范本》为各国间签订税收协定提供了样本

The OECD Model Tax on Incomes and Property Provided an Example Text

联合国成立后，在其经济和社会理事会1946年10月1日第2（Ⅲ）号文件的决议中，肯定了前国际联盟财政委员会的工作成果继续有效；并决定建立一个财政委员会来帮助联合国经济和社会委员会研究国家财政，特别是某些法律、行政管理和技术上的问题。此后，由于国际局势中"冷战"加剧，1954年，财政委员会及其工作小组的工作曾一度中断。于是，欧洲经济合作组织（Organization for European Economic Cooperation, OEEC）便成为国际财政问题合作的中心。1961年，OEEC为经济合作和发展组织（Organization for Economic Co-operation and Development, OECD，以下简称经合发组织）所取代。1956年3月，欧洲经济合作组织财政委员会宣告成立。自1958年起，欧洲经济合作组织财政委员会着手为这个组织的成员国起草有关避免所得和财产双重征税的新的协定范本。1958—1961年，财政委员会进行了大量的工作，最后于1963年公布了有关避免所得和财产双重征税的协定范本草案（简称为《经济合作与发展组织1963年协定范本草案》）。这个协定范本草案得到很多国家的承认，并成为协调国际税收关系的重要参考文件。事实上，1977年前，国际上签订的大部分税收协定都是建立在这个文件基础之上的。除此之外，财政委员会于1966年又起草了《关于对财产和遗产避免双重征税的协定范本》。1967年，财政委员会（1971年起易名为财政事务委员会）开始修订《经济合作与发展组织1963年协定范本草案》，这是因为各国的税收制度发生了较大的变化，国际间税收关系扩大了，某些企业和公司在跨国活动中的组织形式也日趋复杂。1977年，OECD正式公布了首次修订后的新的《经济合作与发展组织关于避免对所得和财产双重征税的协定范本》（简称为《经济合作与发展组织1977年协定范本》）以及内容丰富的注释本。30多年来，《经济合作与发展组织1977年协定范本》对于合理划分缔约国的征税权、消除国际双重征税及加强国家间的税务协作起到了指导作用，得到了世界舆论的肯定。但是在实践过程中，该范本也显露了许多不完善之处。为此，OECD

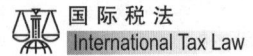

根据经济国际化发展新形势的要求，总结了各国的实践经验，并进行了大量的调查研究，于1992年提出了税收协定新范本，新范本易名为《经济合作与发展组织关于对所得和财产课税的协定范本》（简称为《经济合作与发展组织1992年协定范本》）。

After the establishment of the United Nations, in its Economic and Social Council resolution No. 2 (III) of October 1, 1946, it affirmed the continued validity of the work of the former Fiscal Committee of the League of Nations; and decided to establish a Finance Committee to assist the United Nations Economic and Social Council in studying national finances, particularly certain legal, administrative and technical issues. After that, the work of the Finance Committee and its working groups was interrupted in 1954 due to the intensification of the "Cold War" in the international situation. In March 1956, the OEEC Fiscal Committee was established. Since 1958, the OEEC Fiscal Committee has been working on a new model agreement on the avoidance of double taxation of income and property for the member countries of the organization. From 1958 to 1961, the Fiscal Committee carried out extensive work, which culminated in the publication of the Draft Model Agreement for the Avoidance of Double Taxation on Income and Property in 1963 (referred to as the "OECD 1963 Draft Model Agreement"). This draft model agreement was recognized by many countries and served as an important reference document for the harmonization of international taxation relations. In fact, most of the tax agreements concluded internationally before 1977 were based on this document. In addition, in 1966, the Committee drafted the Model Agreement for the Avoidance of Double Taxation on Property and Estates, and in 1967, the Fiscal Committee (renamed Committee on Fiscal Affairs in 1971) began to revise the OECD 1963 Draft Model Agreement, because the tax systems of various countries had changed considerably, and the international tax system had become more complex. In 1977, the OECD officially published the first revised version of the new OECD Model Convention for the Avoidance of Double Taxation on Income and Property (the OECD Model Convention). The OECD Model Convention for the Avoidance of Double Taxation with Respect to Taxes on Income and on Capital (OECD Model Convention 1977), together with a rich annotated version, has been instrumental for more than 30 years in rationalizing the division of taxing rights among contracting countries, eliminating international double taxation, and strengthening the international tax system. For more than 30 years, the OECD 1977 Model Agreement has played a guiding role in the rational division of taxing rights of contracting countries, elimination of international double taxation and strengthening of tax coordination among countries, and has been recognized by the public opinion worldwide. However, in the process of practice, the Model has also revealed many imperfections. For this reason, the OECD, in accordance with the requirements of the new situation of economic internationalization, summarized the practical experience of countries and conducted a lot of research and studies, and proposed a new model tax treaty in 1992, which was renamed "The OECD Model Tax on Income and Property."

与原范本比较，新范本更改的主要内容有14个方面，包括条文和注释两个部分。为了不断地完善协定范本，财政事务委员会认为，今后要在广泛吸收成员国和非成员国建议的基础上，对协定范本作周期性的修订。迄今，OECD范本经历了11次修改，最近一次修改发生在2017年。

Compared with the original model agreement, the main changes include 14 aspects, including both articles and notes. In order to continuously improve the model agreement, the Committee believes that the model agreement should be revised periodically in the future, based on extensive incorporation of suggestions from member and non-member countries. To date, the OECD model has undergone 11 revisions, with the most recent one in 2017.

20世纪60年代以后，大量的发展中国家加入联合国。1968年，联合国秘书长根据联合国经济和社会理事会1967年8月4日第1273号文件的决议，组织了一个专家小组来起草发达国家与发展中国家之间的税收协定范本。在专家小组的第七次全体会议上，专家们以《经济合作与发展组织协定范本》为样本，提出了《发达国家与发展中国家间关于税收协定的指南》。1977年，专家小组又进一步修订了这个指南，把它修改成一个附有注释的协定范本，即《联合国关于发达国家与发展中国家间双重征税的协定范本（草案）》（简称为联合国范本）。1979年12月，专家小组第八次全体会议重新审查并通过了这个范本草案，将其作为联合国用于协调发达国家与发展中国家税务关系的正式参考文件。该范本与《经济合作与发展组织协定范本》相比，为所得来源国有全部或部分征税优先权提供了更多的依据。

After the 1960s, a large number of developing countries joined the United Nations. In 1968, the UN Secretary General, in accordance with the UN Economic and Social Council Resolution No. 1273 of August 4, 1967, organized an expert group to draft a model international tax agreement between developed and developing countries. At the seventh plenary session of the expert group, the experts proposed a Guide on Tax Agreements between Developed and Developing Countries, using the OECD Model Agreement as a model. In 1977, the expert group further revised this guide into an annotated model agreement, The UN Draft Model Double Taxation Convention Between Developed and Developing Countries (The UN Draft Model Double Taxation Convention). The UN Draft Model Double Taxation Convention Between Developed and Developing Countries (the UN Model) was re-examined and adopted by the Eighth Plenary Meeting of the expert group in December 1979 as the official UN reference document for the harmonization of tax relations between developed and developing countries. The Model provides a greater basis for full or partial tax priority for source countries than does the OECD Model Agreement.

（三）区域税收一体化呈现加快态势
Regional Tax Integration Showed an Accelerating Trend

自20世纪80年代以来，随着国际经济合作与交往日益向集团化、区域化方向发展，特别是国际贸易的关税壁垒和非关税壁垒逐步得到消除，商品、资本、技术和劳动力的跨国流动更为密切，出现了税收一体化的新格局。在推行税收一体化的进程中，欧共体国家一直走在前列。1968年，欧共体取消了工业品内部关税，并统一了对外关税税率，翌年又取消了农产品的内部关税，而后在增值税方面也采取了一系列重大措施，如缩小成员国之间的税率差别、规定统一的征税原则、规范清算制度等。目前，欧盟已开始就与所得税协调有关的股息转让定价、企业重组等问题展开协调。继欧盟之后，区域性经济组织相继成立，如中美洲共同市场、新西兰—澳大利亚自由贸易区、北美自由贸易区、东南亚国家联盟、安第斯共同市场、非洲统一组织等。目前，世界上已形成西欧、北美和东亚三大经济区域，充分体现着不同国家间内外部的经济及税收利益矛盾与协调关系，这些经济区域里的国家经济发展状况相近、经济体制和结构类似、经济交往密切等，都为区域税收一体化创造了良好的条件。

Since the 1980s, with the increasing development of international economic cooperation and interaction in the direction of grouping and regionalization, especially the gradual elimination of tariff and non-tariff barriers to international trade, and the closer cross-border flows of commodities, capital, technology and labor among countries, a new pattern of tax integration has emerged. In 1968, the EC abolished internal tariffs on industrial goods and unified external tariff rates. In the following year, internal tariffs on agricultural products were abolished, and a series of major steps were taken in the area of VAT, such as reducing the differences in tax rates among member states, stipulating uniform taxation principles, and regulating the clearing system. Currently, the EU has started to coordinate on issues such as transfer pricing of dividends and corporate restructuring related to income tax harmonization. Following the EU, regional economic organizations have been established, such as the Central American Common Market, the New Zealand-Australia Free Trade Area, the North American Free Trade Area, the Association of Southeast Asian Nations, the Andean Common Market, and the Organization of African Unity. At present, three major economic regions, namely, Western Europe, North America and East Asia, have been formed, fully reflecting the contradictory and coordinated relations of internal and external economic and taxation interests among different countries. The similar economic development status, similar economic systems and structures, and close economic interactions among countries in these economic regions have created good conditions for regional tax integration.

（四）国际税务合作逐渐向多边发展
The International Tax Cooperation Gradually Developed to a Multilateral Direction

在国际税务合作领域，合作模式长期以来都是以双边协定为基础，直到20世纪后半期才出现了一些区域性多边协定。由于各国税制差异大以及担心税收主权受到限制等，全球性多边税收公约一直未能形成。但随着经济全球化的进一步发展，各国已普遍认识到双边或区域性多边协定已不能满足调整国际税收秩序的需要，必须在更广泛的全球范围内通过多边协定来协调立场和加强合作。正是在这个背景下，经合发组织于2010年对《多边税收征管互助公约》进行修订并向所有国家开放，使其成为一个全球性多边税务合作公约。修订后的公约采取了国际通行的税收透明度标准，取消了信息交换要求的"双重犯罪标准"，突破了国内税收利益要求和银行保密制度的阻碍。① 但不可否认，《多边税收征管互助公约》还只是一个开

---

① 参见崔晓静著：《国际税收行政合作的新发展及其法律问题研究》，中国社会科学出版社2014年版，第99—102页。

端,公约本身也规定了多项保留条款,国际税务多边合作的路注定还很漫长。

In the field of international tax cooperation, the cooperation model has long been based on bilateral agreements, and only in the second half of the 20th century did some regional multilateral agreements emerge. Due to the large differences in tax systems among countries and the fear of tax sovereignty being restricted, global multivariate tax conventions have not been formed. However, with the further development of economic globalization, countries have generally recognized that bilateral or regional multilateral agreements can no longer meet the need to adjust the international tax order, and it is necessary to coordinate positions and strengthen cooperation through multilateral agreements in a broader global context. It is against this background that the OECD revised and opened the Multilateral Convention on Mutual Assistance in Tax Matters to all countries in 2010, making it a global multilateral tax cooperation convention. The revised convention adopts the internationally accepted standard of tax transparency, eliminates the "double criminality standard" for information exchange requirements, and breaks the barriers of domestic tax interest requirements and bank secrecy. However, it is undeniable that the Multivariate Tax Administration Mutual Assistance Convention is only a beginning, and the convention itself provides for a number of reservations, which dooms the road of international tax multilateral cooperation to be a long one.

近年来,国际税收领域反避税力度加大,在税收情报交换、征管互助等领域取得了突破性进展。同时,官方及非官方的国际税收交流与讨论得到增强,它促进了各国税务机关加强合作,以共同应对各种国际税收挑战。2013年经合发组织《税基侵蚀和利润转移报告》指出,导致税基侵蚀和利润转移的根本原因在于国际税收一般原则即分享税收管辖权原则与不断发展变化的商业环境不同步。各国国内和国际的国际税法规则还植根于低水平的跨国经济融合的商业环境,而非目前以知识产权作为价值驱动、信息及通信技术不断发展为特征的全球环境。简而言之,各国税收制度融合的程度远远落后于各国经济的融合程度。鉴于国际税收领域内政策、制度等方面的协调内容日趋复杂,范围日益扩大,已有专家建议成立"世界税收组织",使其同世界贸易组织、国际货币基金组织一样发挥功能,就某些世界性税基征税,提供某些世界性公共产品,并协调各国税制。①

In recent years, anti-avoidance efforts in the field of international taxation have increased, and breakthroughs have been made in the areas of tax information exchange and mutual assistance in tax collection and administration. At the same time, both official and unofficial international tax exchanges and discussions have been enhanced to strengthen cooperation among national tax authorities and to jointly address various international tax challenges. The 2013 OECD Report on Base Erosion and Profit Shifting points out that the root cause of base erosion and profit shifting is international taxation. The root cause of base erosion and profit shifting is the lack of synchronization between the general principles of international taxation, i.e., the principle of shared tax jurisdiction, and the evolving business environment.

---

① 参见汤贡亮主编:《2012年中国税收发展报告——中国国际税收发展战略研究》,中国税务出版社2013年版,第50页。

International tax law rules, both domestic and international, are also rooted in a business environment with low levels of cross-border economic integration, rather than the current global environment characterized by intellectual property as a value driver and evolving information and communication technologies. In short, the degree of integration of national tax systems lags far behind the degree of integration of national economies. In view of the increasing complexity and scope of policy and institutional coordination in the field of international taxation, experts have suggested the establishment of a "World Tax Organization" to function like the World Trade Organization and the International Monetary Fund, to levy taxes on certain global tax bases, to provide certain global public goods, and to coordinate national tax systems.

特别值得一提的是，近年来我国税务部门积极推动建立"一带一路"税收征管合作机制，该机制是在"共商共建共享"总原则的指导下，是参与"一带一路"建设的国家（地区）积极推进、共同形成的机制，是对现有税收国际组织和多边税收机制的有益补充与完善，旨在为"一带一路"建设参与国家（地区）提供税收政策沟通和征管合作平台，共同提升税收征管能力，有效促进贸易自由化和投资便利化，实现互利共赢。

It is especially worth mentioning that in recent years, China's taxation authorities have actively promoted the establishment of the "Belt and Road" tax collection and administration cooperation mechanism, which is a mechanism actively promoted and jointly formed by the countries (regions) participating in the "Belt and Road" construction under the guidance of the general principle of "common consultation, construction and sharing". It is a useful supplement and improvement to the existing international tax organizations and multilateral tax mechanisms, aiming to provide a platform for tax policy communication and cooperation in tax administration for the countries (regions) participating in the "Belt and Road" construction, to jointly improve the tax administration capacity and effectively promote trade liberalization and investment facilitation for mutual benefits.

（五）跨国电子商务的国际税务问题日益受到关注
International Tax Issues of Transnational Electronic Commerce Were Receiving More Attentions

电子商务是指采用数字化电子方式进行商务数据交换和开展商务活动。由于其经营模式的特殊性，电子商务的使用和推广给传统秩序和规则带来了全面的冲击和挑战。就对国际税法的冲击而言，有学者归纳为以下几个方面：传统的常设机构概念受到挑战；来源地税收管辖权和居民税收管辖权的划分受到冲击，国际税收管辖权的冲突更加复杂；营业利润、劳务所得以及特许权使用费所得等之间的区别变得模糊；转让定价等引起的国际避税问题更加突出；税收征管难以获得真实的信息，给税务征管带来了困难[1]等。经合发组织为应对电子商务给国际税法规则带来的挑战，于1999年专门成立了技术咨询小组来指导营业利润

---

[1] 参见张泽平主编：《国际税法》，北京大学出版社2014年版，第21页。

征税条约规范的适用,研究现有的对营业利润征税的条约规则如何在电子商务环境下适用并提出替代性规则。2000年12月,经合发组织财政事务委员会发布了《常设机构概念在电子商务背景下的运用:对经济合作与发展组织税收协定范本第五条的注释的建议性说明》,2001年2月,发布了《电子商务环境下常设机构的利润归属》讨论草案,2011年11月提交了《电子商务引起的税收条约定性问题报告》,2003年11月,发布了《对营业利润率征税的现行税收条约规则对电子商务而言是否适当》的讨论草案,并在各方评论的基础上进行完善,于2004年6月发布了最终报告。①

E-commerce refers to the use of digital electronic means to exchange business data and conduct business activities. Due to the specificity of its business model, the use and promotion of e-commerce has brought a comprehensive impact and challenge to the traditional order and rules. As far as the impact on international tax law is concerned, some scholars have summarized it into the following aspects: the traditional concept of permanent establishment is challenged; the division of source tax jurisdiction and resident tax jurisdiction is impacted and the conflict of international tax jurisdiction becomes more complicated; the distinction between business profits, labor income and royalty income becomes blurred; the international tax avoidance problem caused by transfer pricing becomes more prominent; it is difficult to obtain real information for tax administration, bringing difficulties to tax collection and management.

第三节　国际税法的宗旨和原则
Section 3　Purposes and Principles of International Tax Law

一、国际税法的宗旨
The Purposes of International Tax Law

国际税法的宗旨是指国际税法的目的与意图,是人们创造国际税法的出发点和归宿。宗旨与作用和原则不同,宗旨带有较多的主观色彩,强调的是国家制定国际税法的主观目的与意图。作用则强调的是某一事物的用途与功能,具有较强的客观色彩。原则则是达到目的、宗旨所依据的法则和标准,正确的国际税法原则是实现国际税法宗旨的必要条件。

The purposes of international tax law refer to the aims and intentions of international tax law, it is the starting point and destination to create international tax law. Different from roles and principles,

---

① 参见张泽平主编:《国际税法》,北京大学出版社2014年版,第21页。

purposes are more subjective and emphasize the subjective aim and intention of the country to make international tax law. Roles emphasize the use and function of something and are more objective. Principles are the rules and standards to achieve the aims and purposes, and the correct principles of international tax law are the necessary conditions to achieve the purposes of international tax law.

目前,理论界对国际税法的宗旨有两种不同的观点。一种观点认为,国际税法的宗旨是实现对跨国征税利益的公平分配,建立一个公平合理的国际税收秩序,促进国际贸易投资的健康发展。实现对跨国征税对象利益的公平分配,包括对跨国纳税人征税公平和国家之间国际税收利益公平分配两个方面。征税公平意味着针对同一征税对象,非居民纳税人应与居民纳税人承担一样的税负,不应因身份的差别而产生税负上的差别。国家间要实现税收利益分配上的公平合理,不仅要重视分配形式上的对等和互利,更要充分考虑国家之间经济发展水平的差距和在国际资金、技术交流中所处的地位,以达到实质上的平等互利。另一种观点认为,国际税法的宗旨是维护国家税收主权和涉外纳税人的合法权益。本教材赞同第二种观点。第一,法是有阶级性和国家属性的,是维护一国占统治地位利益集团的工具,任何一个国家的国际税法都不可避免地负有维护本国利益、保障本国税收主权及本国跨国纳税人利益的基本义务。例如,美国一直拒绝承认"税收饶让抵免",多数成员为发达国家的经济合作与发展组织《关于对所得和财产征税的协定范本》在内容上倾向于对发达资本主义国家利益的保护。第二,世界上并不存在一个超国家的权力主体,国际税法并不是由一个高于国家的主体制定的法律体系,而是各个国家为了保护本国税收利益,参与国际税收协定或条约,创造适用于本国主权范围内的国际税收制度而实现的。

There are currently two different types of views on the purpose of international tax law. One view is that the purpose of international tax law is to realize the fair distribution of the benefits of transnational taxation, establish a fair and reasonable international taxation order and promote the healthy development of international trade and investment. Realizing the fair distribution of the benefits of transnational taxation includes two aspects: fairness in taxation of cross-border taxpayers and fair distribution of international tax benefits among countries. Fairness in taxation means that non-resident taxpayers should bear the same tax burden as resident taxpayers for the same taxable object, and there should not be any difference in tax burden due to the difference in status. Countries which try to realize fairness and reasonableness in the distribution of tax benefits among countries should not only pay attention to the reciprocity and mutual benefit in the form of distribution, but also fully consider the difference in the level of economic development between countries and the position in the international capital and technology exchange, so as to achieve equality and mutual benefit in substance. Another view is that the purpose of international tax law is to safeguard national tax sovereignty and the legitimate rights and interests of taxpayers involved in foreign countries. In this book, we agree with the second view. The international tax law of any country inevitably has the basic obligation of safeguarding the interests of the country, protecting its tax sovereignty and the interests of its multinational taxpayers. For example, the United States has always refused to recognize the "tax sparing credit", while the Organization for Economic Cooperation and Development (OECD) Model Agreement on Taxation of Income and Property, which has a majority of developed countries as members, tends to protect the interests of developed capitalist countries. Secondly, there is no supranational authority in the world, and international tax law is not a legal system made by a subject superior to the state, but is realized by each country participating in international tax agreements or treaties in order to protect its tax interests and create an international tax system applicable to its sovereignty.

各国制定国际税法的目的在于维护本国的利益,国际税法对本国利益的维护主要体现在维护国家税收主权和维护涉外纳税人的权益。国家税收主权是国家主权在税收领域的体现,是国际税收关系存在的前提。没有国家税收主权的存在也就谈不上国家间税收利益分配的协调与合作。每个国家认为的公平合理的国际税收秩序都是从维护自身税收主权出发,以是否符合本国税收利益最大化为判断标准。发达国家与发展中国家支持的国际税收秩序不同,其原因在于不同国家税收主权的要求存在差异。维护涉外纳税人的权益既包括维护本国的涉外纳税人的权益,也包括维护在本国投资的外国涉外纳税人的权益。维护本国涉外纳税人的权益等同于对本国利益的维护,是一国法律应具备的作用与功能。维护在本国投资的外国涉外纳税人的权益,则主要是出于吸引外资的目的,实质上仍是对本国利益的维护。维护涉外纳税人权益就是要求涉外纳税人与国内纳税人承担相同的纳税义务,纳税义务不因涉外因素而有所不同,对涉外纳税人可能遭受的重复征税需采取措施减轻或者免除。

The purpose of formulating international tax laws is to safeguard the interests of countries, and the safeguard of national interests by international tax laws is mainly reflected in safeguarding national tax sovereignty and safeguarding the rights and interests of foreign taxpayers. National tax sovereignty is the embodiment of national sovereignty in the field of taxation, which is the precondition for the existence of international taxation relationship. Without the existence of national tax sovereignty, there is no coordination and cooperation in the distribution of tax benefits among countries. The fair and reasonable international tax order that each country considers is based on safeguarding its own tax sovereignty and judged by whether it is in line with the maximization of its tax interests. The difference between the international tax order supported by developed countries and developing countries lies in the difference in the requirements of tax sovereignty among different countries. Safeguarding the rights and interests of foreign taxpayers includes both the rights and interests of domestic foreign taxpayers and foreign taxpayers who invest in their own countries. Protecting the rights and interests of domestic foreign-related taxpayers is the same as protecting the interests of the country, which is the role and function of the law of a country. The protection of the rights and interests of foreign taxpayers investing in the country is mainly for the purpose of attracting foreign investment, which is still in essence the protection of the interests of the country. To protect the rights and interests of foreign taxpayers is to require foreign taxpayers to bear the same tax obligations as domestic taxpayers, and the tax obligations should not be different because of foreign factors, and measures should be taken to reduce or exempt the double taxation that foreign taxpayers may suffer.

国际税法的两个宗旨是统一不可分割的。维护涉外纳税人权益是维护国家税收主权的途径,没有国家税收主权也就没有涉外纳税人基本权益可言,只有涉外纳税人权益和国家税收主权两方面同时实现,才能真正实现国际税法的宗旨。

The two purposes of international tax law are unified and inseparable. Only when the rights

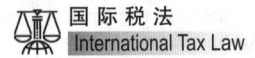

and interests of foreign taxpayers and national tax sovereignty are realized simultaneously can the purpose of international tax law be truly realized.

二、国际税法的基本原则
The Basic Principles of International Tax Law

国际税法的基本原则是指贯穿全部国际税法规则，对国际税法规则的制定和实施具有指导作用的原理和准则。本教材认为国际税法的基本原则包括以下几项：国家税收管辖权独立原则、国际税收公平原则、国际税收中性原则、国际税收效率原则。

The basic principles of international tax law refer to the principles and guidelines throughout all international tax law rules with a guiding effect on the formulation and implementation of international tax law rules. We believe that the basic principles of international tax law include the following ones: the principle of independence of national tax jurisdiction, the principle of international tax fairness, the principle of international tax neutrality, and the principle of international tax efficiency.

（一）国家税收管辖权独立原则
The Principle of Independence of National Tax Jurisdiction

国家税收管辖权独立原则是国家主权独立在国际税收领域的具体表现，是指一国政府有权决定实行何种涉外税收制度及政策，有权确定本国开设的税种，各个税种的征税对象、征税范围、征税程序以及征税方式等，不受任何其他国家或组织的干涉。

The principle of independence of national tax jurisdiction is a concrete manifestation of national sovereign independence in the field of international taxation, which means that a government has the right to decide what kind of foreign-related taxation system and policies to implement, and the right to determine the types of taxes to be introduced in the country, the objects, scope, procedures and manners of taxation for each tax item, without interference from any other countries or organizations.

国家税收管辖权独立的一个重要体现在于各国可以任意制定本国的涉外税收法律制度，其他任何国家或组织无权干涉。国际税法是国内立法的产物，并不来源于国际组织立法或各种习惯，国际协定或条约也是通过国内立法而对各国纳税人产生约束力。世界各国根据本国经济发展的实际需要确定本国的税收法律制度，从而导致各国税收法律制度之间存在重大差异，国家间也很难形成一个统一协调各国税收权益的国际组织，国际上也并不存在对各国税收法律制度具有约束力的统一法律规范或标准。但是国家税收管辖权独立不是绝对的，而是相对独立的，这表现在以下几个方面：第一，国家之间各自的税收管辖权独立，但国家间需互相尊重对方的税收管辖权。第二，国家税收管辖权必须在其边界之内行使，任何国家都不能超越其边界行使税收管辖权。第三，每个国家都要履行其在国际税收协定或条约下的义务。第四，每个国家都要遵守国际税收实践中逐渐形成的国际税收习惯。

An important manifestation of the independence of national tax jurisdictions is that each country is free to develop its own legal system for foreign taxation, and no other country or organization has the right to interfere. International tax law is a product of domestic legislation and does not derive from the legislation of international organizations or various customs, and international agreements or treaties are binding on national taxpayers through domestic legislation. Countries around the world determine their own tax legal systems according to the actual needs of their economic development, which leads to significant differences between national tax legal systems, and it is difficult to reach an international organization that unifies and coordinates the tax rights and interests of countries, and there is no uniform legal norm or standard that binds national tax legal systems internationally. However, the independence of national tax jurisdiction is not absolute, but relative, which is manifested in the following aspects: First, each country is independent in its tax jurisdiction, but the countries need to respect each other's tax jurisdiction. Second, national tax jurisdiction must be exercised within its borders, and no country can exercise tax jurisdiction beyond its borders. Third, each country has to fulfill its obligations under international tax agreements or treaties. Fourth, each country has to comply with the international tax customs that have gradually developed in the international tax practice.

（二）国际税收公平原则
The Principle of International Tax Fairness

国际税收公平原则涉及国家间税收利益分配关系的公平和涉外税收征纳关系的公平。国家间税收利益分配关系的公平是国际经济法中公平互利原则在国际税收领域的体现。国家间税收利益分配关系是国际税法调整的重要对象，各国涉外税收立法以及签订国际税收协定的一个重要目的就是确保公平的税收分配。而实现国际税收分配公平的关键在于合理划分各国的税收管辖权。税收来源地管辖权与居民管辖权的内在矛盾导致国际双重征税，跨国纳税人的一项跨国所得既要向来源国承担税负也要向居住国承担税负，为避免双重征税，就得对各国税收管辖权进行划分。强调来源地管辖权对所得来源国或资本输入国较为有利，强调居民税收管辖权则对居住国或资本输出国较为有利。当两个国家间资本输出与资本输入基本平衡时，实行何种税收管辖权都能基本保持两国间税收利益分配的公平。当两个国家间资本输出与资本输入不能保持平衡时，就要对来源地管辖权与居民税收管辖权进行合理的划分，以实现两个国家间税收利益分配的公平。

The principle of international tax fairness refers to fairness in the relationship of tax benefit distribution between countries and fairness in the relationship of foreign tax collection and acceptance. The fairness of interstate tax interest distribution relations is the embodiment of the principle of fairness and mutual benefit in international economic law in the field of international taxation. One of the important purposes of foreign tax legislation and international tax agreements is to ensure fair tax distribution. The key to realizing the fair distribution of international taxation lies in the reasonable division of tax jurisdiction of each country. Due to the inherent contradiction between source jurisdiction and resident jurisdiction, international double taxation is caused, and a transnational taxpayer's transnational income has to bear tax liability to both the source country and the resident country. In order to avoid double taxation, the tax jurisdiction of each country has to be divided. The emphasis on source jurisdiction is more

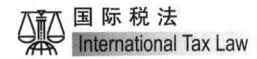

favorable to the source country or capital-importing country of income, while the emphasis on resident tax jurisdiction is more favorable to the resident country or capital-exporting country. When the capital export and capital import between two countries are basically balanced, the tax jurisdiction can basically maintain the fair distribution of tax benefits between the two countries. When the balance between capital export and capital import cannot be maintained between two countries, a reasonable division between source jurisdiction and resident tax jurisdiction is needed to achieve a fair distribution of tax benefits between the two countries.

涉外税收征纳关系中的公平原则是指涉外纳税人所承担的税负应与其负担能力相适应,包括横向公平与纵向公平。横向公平是指经济情况相同的纳税人承担相同的税负;纵向公平则是指经济情况不同的纳税人应承担与其经济情况相适应的不同的税收负担。在发生重复征税和逃避税的情况下,相同经济情况的纳税人承担的税负不相同,因而违背了国际税收公平原则。各国关于避免重复征税和防止逃避税行为的相关规范和制度都体现了涉外税收征纳关系中的公平原则。另外,国际税收公平和国内税收公平有一定的区别。国内税收公平不涉及涉外纳税人,也不存在不同国家的税收管辖权冲突导致的重复征税问题。在国际税收公平中,同一跨国纳税人要向居住国和来源国分别纳税,因此就存在两个评判跨国纳税人税负是否公平的标准,当两个标准不同时,纳税人只能保证在一个国家实现税负公平而不能同时在两个国家都实现税负公平。

The principle of fairness in foreign-related tax collection relationship refers to the fact that the tax burden borne by foreign taxpayers should be commensurate with their affordability. It includes horizontal equity and vertical equity. Horizontal equity means that taxpayers with the same economic situation should bear the same tax burden; vertical equity means that taxpayers with different economic situations should bear different tax burdens in accordance with their economic situations. In the case of double taxation and tax evasion, taxpayers with the same economic situation bear different tax burdens, thus violating the principle of international tax equity. The relevant norms and systems of each country on avoidance of double taxation and prevention of tax evasion embody the principle of fairness in foreign tax collection and payment relationship. In addition, there are certain differences between international tax equity and domestic tax equity. Domestic tax equity does not involve foreign taxpayers, and there is no problem of double taxation due to the conflict of tax jurisdictions of different countries. In international tax equity, the same multinational taxpayer has to pay taxes to the resident country and the source country respectively, so there are two criteria to judge whether the tax burden of multinational taxpayers is fair or not, and when the two criteria are different, the taxpayer can only ensure the fairness of tax burden in one country but not in both countries at the same time.

(三)国际税收中性原则
The Principle of Neutrality of International Tax

税收中性是指国家征税应避免对市场经济正常运行的干扰,特别是不能使税收超越市场机制而成为资源配置的决定因素。税收中性体现在国际税法领域是指资本、劳务、技术、货物等在国家间流动不会受国际税法影响,可在各国之间自由流动,充分发挥市场机制的作用,从而有助于实现各种资源在世界范围内被合理利用。

Tax neutrality means that state taxation should avoid interfering with the normal operation of the market economy, especially not to make taxation become a decisive factor in resource allocation beyond the market mechanism. Tax neutrality in the field of international tax law means that the flow of capital, labor, technology, goods, etc., between countries will not be affected by international tax law and can flow freely between countries, giving full play to the role of the market mechanism, thus helping to realize the rational use of various resources in the world.

国际税收中性又分为资本输出中性和资本输入中性。前者是从居住国角度提出的,一国政府对其居民纳税人境内投资所得和境外投资所得课征的税收负担应当相同,不能因为资本的输出造成差别税负;后者则是站在来源国的角度提出的,一国政府对在该国进行相同经营活动的所有纳税人,不问其资本来源如何,施加税收负担应当一视同仁。如果税收制度是中性的,则意味着其不会影响纳税人在跨国交易中的经济选择。通常来讲,发达国家更倾向于资本输出中性,这样纳税人在选择投资国内或者投资国外时不受影响,也就是追求全球效率。相反,发展中国家则更倾向于资本输入中性,以确保国内投资者和国外投资者税收负担水平相同,也就是追求国内效率。资本输出中性与资本输入中性存在一定矛盾,实现资本输入中性的措施会妨碍资本输出中性的实现,反之亦然。一个国家无法同时既强调资本输出中性又强调资本输入中性,税收中性只是一种理论上的设想,在现实中很难实现。实践中,发达国家经济实力较强,比发展中国家更倾向于资本输出中性,发展中国家为了吸引国外投资,制定的政策往往鼓励资本输入、限制资本输出,更倾向于资本输入中性。虽然资本输入中性与资本输出中性存在一定的矛盾,但是在国际税法领域坚持中性原则仍具有重要意义,避免重复征税和防止逃避税制度及规范,管辖权划分的原则的确定等都体现了国际税收中性。为了有助于资本等经济要素在全世界范围内的优化配置,国际税法仍需要坚持税收中性原则。

International tax neutrality includes capital export neutrality and capital import neutrality. The former is proposed from the perspective of the resident country, where a government should impose the same tax burden on the income of its resident taxpayers from domestic and foreign investments, and should not create different tax burdens due to the export of capital; the latter is proposed from the perspective of the source country, where a government should impose the same tax burden on all taxpayers conducting the same business activities in that country, regardless of the source of their capital. If the tax system is neutral, it means that it does not affect the economic choices of taxpayers in cross-border transactions. Generally speaking, developed countries prefer capital export neutrality so that taxpayers are not affected in their choice to invest domestically or abroad, i.e., to pursue global efficiency. On the contrary, developing countries prefer capital import neutrality to ensure the same level of tax burden for domestic and foreign investors, i.e., to pursue domestic efficiency. There is a contradiction between capital export neutrality and capital import neutrality in that measures to achieve capital import neutrality can impede the achievement of capital export neutrality, and vice versa. A country cannot emphasize both capital export neutrality and capital import neutrality at the same time, and tax neutrality is only a theoretical idea, which is difficult to realize in reality. In practice, developed countries with stronger economies tend to have more neutral tax laws than developing countries, while developing countries, in order to attract foreign investment, often formulate policies that encourage capital import and restrict capital export, preferring capital import neutrality. Although there is a certain contradiction between capital import neutrality and capital export neutrality, it is still important to adhere to the principle of neutrality in the field of international tax law. The avoidance of double taxation and prevention of tax evasion systems and norms, the determination of the principle of jurisdictional division, etc., all reflect international tax neutrality. In order to contribute to the optimal allocation of economic factors such as capital around the world, it is still necessary to adhere to the principle of tax neutrality in international tax law.

（四）国际税收效率原则
The Principle of International Tax Efficiency

国际税收效率原则是国内税法的税收效率原则向国际税法领域延伸的结果，即以最小的税收成本获取最大的国际税收收入，并利用税收的经济调控作用最大限度地促进国际贸易投资的正常发展，或最大限度地减轻国际经济交流的障碍。

The principle of international tax efficiency is the result of the extension of the principle of efficiency of domestic tax law to the field of international tax law, that is, to obtain the maximum international tax revenue with the minimum tax cost, and to use the economic regulation effect of taxation to promote the normal development of international trade and investment to the maximum extent, or to minimize the obstacles to international economic exchange.

国际税收效率原则包括税收行政效率和税收经济效率两个方面。税收行政效率是指各征税国家应进行税收的行政协调与合作，使国家的征税成本以及纳税人的纳税成本最低。即国家提高税收的行政效率，给纳税人提供税收缴纳便利，包括纳税时间、方法、手续等的简便易行，节省纳税人为纳税而承担的缴纳成本。同时，国家在征税时应尽量减少征税费用，政府的征税成本不应超出征收的收益。税收经济效率则要求尽量减小国际税收对国际经济的正常发展的影响。税收经济效率是税收效率的更高层次。在通过市场手段配置资源失灵时，政府有必要进行干预，税收则是国家干预经济的有效手段。不合理的税制会引起资源配置的扭曲，但如果税制设计合理、税收政策得当，则不仅可以降低税收的经济成本，还可以弥补市场失灵的缺陷，提高经济运行效率。国际税收效率原则体现在国际税收法律制度的各个方面。避免重复征税和防止逃避税的各种制度及规范、国家间缔结协定对税收管辖权的划分等，都是为了避免给国际经济交往造成障碍以及对各国经济和世界经济带来负面影响。

The principle of international tax efficiency includes both administrative efficiency of taxation and economic efficiency of taxation. Administrative efficiency of taxation means that each taxing country should coordinate and cooperate in taxation administration so that the cost of taxation of the country and the cost of taxation of taxpayers is minimized. In other words, the administrative efficiency of taxation should be improved, and taxpayers should be provided with the convenience of tax payment, including the simplicity of taxation time, methods and procedures, so as to save the cost of tax payment borne by taxpayers. At the same time, the state should minimize the cost of tax collection, and the government's cost of tax collection should not exceed the revenue collected. Economic efficiency of taxation refers to the requirement that international taxation should minimize the impact on the normal development of the international economy. Tax economic efficiency is a higher level of tax efficiency. When the allocation of resources through market means fails, it is necessary for the government to intervene, and taxation is an effective means for the state to intervene in the economy, and an unreasonable taxation system will cause distortion in the allocation of resources. The principle of international tax efficiency is reflected in all aspects of the international taxation legal system, including the various systems and norms to avoid double taxation and prevent tax evasion, and the division of tax jurisdiction by agreements concluded between countries, all of which are aimed at avoiding obstacles to international economic interactions and negative impacts on national economies and the world economy.

第四节 国际税法与国际税法学
Section 4　International Tax Law and the Discipline of International Tax Law

一、国际税法与国际税法学的概念
The Concept of International Tax Law and the Discipline of International Tax Law

国际税法是指调整国际税收关系的法律规范的总称。从国际税法的渊源上来看，国际税法并不是以一部完整的法典形式呈现。在各国的法律实践中，具有国际税法性质的法律规范散落于各国国内法律体系关于财产税、所得税及其他涉外税种以及税收征管程序的法律法规中，还体现在各国参加和签订的双边或多边国际税收协定或条约以及国际税收习惯中。这些分散存在的法律规范兼具调整国际税收利益分配和涉外税收征纳关系的作用，在国际税收活动中互相紧密配合，对国际税收关系发挥调控功能，共同构成了国际税法的法律体系，维护一国国家税收主权和涉外纳税人的基本权利。

International tax law refers to the general term of legal norms that regulate international tax relations. In the legal practice of each country, the legal norms with the nature of international tax law are scattered in the laws and regulations on property tax, income tax and other foreign-related taxes and tax collection and administration procedures in the domestic legal system of each country, and also reflected in the bilateral or multilateral international tax agreements or treaties that each country participates in and signs as well as usual practices of international tax. These scattered legal norms are used to adjust the distribution of international tax benefits and foreign tax collection and payment relations, and they closely cooperate with each other in international taxation activities to play a regulatory function on international tax relations, which together constitute the legal system of international tax law and safeguard the national tax sovereignty of a country and the basic rights of foreign taxpayers.

国际税法作为一门部门法和作为一个法学学科的国际税法学是不同的，国际税法属于上层建筑中的政治法律制度组成部分，而国际税法学则是一门综合性社会学科。国际税法是国际税法学赖以建立和存在的前提和基础，是国际税法学研究的主要内容，并且影响着国际税法学的形成、发展、内容和范围。国际税法学的研究范围比国际税法规范体系要广泛得多，它不仅要研究国际税法规范，还要研究与之有关的其他学科，如国际贸易、国际金融、国际投资以及国内税法等。国际税收行为和现象与各种国际贸易、国际投资、国际金融活动伴生交织在一起而发生，并且国际双重征税和逃避税行为的产生也多是由在国际贸易、投资、金融活动中利用不同国家税收政策进行税务安排而导致的。国际贸易、投资、金融活动状况会对国际税收状况产生直接影响，一国的税收政策往往随该国贸易投资金融政策的变化而变化，并为该国的贸易投资金融服务。反之，一国的国际税收政策与制度也会直接对国际贸易投资金融产生影响。

International tax law, as a department of law, is different from the discipline of international tax law as a jurisprudence discipline. International tax law belongs to the political and legal system component of the superstructure, while the discipline of international tax law is a comprehensive social discipline. International tax law is the premise and foundation on which the discipline of international tax law is established and exists, and it constitutes the main content of research in the discipline of international tax law, and influences the formation and development of the discipline of international tax law as well as its content and scope. The scope of the discipline of international tax law is much broader than the system of international tax law norms, and it not only studies international tax law norms but also other disciplines related to them, such as international trade, international finance, international investment and domestic tax law. The international taxation behaviors and phenomena occur together with various international trade, international investment and international financial activities, and the international double taxation and tax evasion behaviors are mostly caused by the taxation arrangements in international trade, investment and financial activities by using different national tax policies. The status of international trade, investment and financial activities will have a direct impact on the status of international taxation, and the taxation policy of a country often changes with the change of the country's trade, investment and financial policies and provides financial services for the country's trade and investment. Conversely, a country's international tax policy and system will also have a direct impact on international trade and investment finance.

国际税法学的地位，即国际税法学在法学学科体系中的位置。虽然法律部门的划分与部门法学的划分并不完全对应，但是国际税法学的地位与国际税法的地位紧密相连。本教材认为，根据国际税法学的研究对象和内容，国际税法学既属于国际经济法的分支学科，又属于税法的分支学科，即属于国际经济法学与税法学的交叉学科。

Let's consider the status of the discipline of international tax law, i.e., its position in the system of jurisprudence disciplines. Although the division of legal departments does not correspond exactly to the division of departmental jurisprudence, the status of the discipline of international tax law is closely connected with the status of international tax law. We believe that the discipline of international tax law belongs to both the sub-discipline of international economic law and the sub-discipline of tax law, and is a cross-discipline of international economic law and tax law, as determined by the research object and content of international tax jurisprudence.

（二）国际税法学的研究内容
The Research Contents of the Discipline of International Tax Law

国际税法学的主要研究内容包括以下几个方面。

The main research contents of the discipline of international tax law include the following aspects:

（一）国际税法的基本理论问题
The Basic Theoretical Issues of International Tax Law

国际税法的基本理论问题包括国际税法的概念、性质、构成及国际税法的渊源；国际税收法律关系的内容、特征、涉及的税种；国际税法的宗旨、任务、作用、地位和基本原则；国际税法产生、发展、变化的历史等。目前，国际税法的基本理论问题还在研究与确立的过程中，也仍然存在一定的分歧和争议。我们需要抱着发展的态度对待国际税法基本理论，使国际税法的基本理论在实践中不断得到检验与发展。

The basic theoretical issues of international tax law include the concept, nature, composition of international tax law and the sources of international tax law; the content, characteristics and tax items involved in international taxation legal relationship; the purpose, mission, role, status and basic principles of international tax law; the history of the emergence, development and changes of international tax law; and so on. At present, the basic theoretical issues of international tax law are still in the process of research and establishment, and there are still some differences and controversies. We need to treat the basic theory of international tax law with an attitude of development, so that the basic theory of international tax law can be tested and developed in practice continuously.

（二）税收管辖权的理论与实践
The Theories and Practices of Tax Jurisdiction

税收管辖权是国际税法的一个基本概念，也是国际税法学研究的根本性问题，国际税法的各种现象与问题的产生都与各国行使的税收管辖权密切相关。我们认为，国际税法学需要研究的税收管辖权问题主要包括各国政府对跨国征税对象分别主张的属人性质和属地性质的税收管辖权的理论依据和内在矛盾；各国在所得税和一般财产税及其他税种上主张的属人及属地性质税收管辖权的表现和实践问题；各国所得税和一般财产税制度及其他涉外税种的课税范围、课税程度、征税方式和程序上的异同；各国采取相同或不同的税收管辖权对国际经济交往的作用与影响；税收管辖权冲突的表现形式和协调冲突的具体规则、措施等。

Tax jurisdiction is a basic concept of international tax law and a fundamental issue of the discipline of international tax law, and various phenomena and problems of international tax law are closely related to the tax jurisdiction exercised by countries. In our opinion, the tax jurisdiction issues that need to be studied include the theoretical basis and inherent contradictions of the personal and territorial tax jurisdictions claimed by the governments of each country over the transnational tax objects; the manifestation and practice of the personal and territorial tax jurisdictions claimed by each country over income tax, general property tax and other taxes; the similarities and differences in the scope, extent, methods and procedures of taxation concerning income tax, general property tax and other foreign-related taxes; the effects and impacts of the same or different tax jurisdictions on international economic interactions; the manifestations of tax jurisdiction conflicts and the specific rules and measures to coordinate them, etc.

（三）国际双重征税问题及其解决
International Double Taxation and Its Solution

国际双重征税问题是国际税收关系中矛盾的集中体现和核心问题，避免和消除国际双重征税现象，也是国际税法的主要任务之一。国际双重征税现象的产生原因、表现形式、对有关国际经济交往活动的影响程度，以及各国目前通过国内单边立法或双边税收协定采取的解决各种国际双重征税问题的方法和效果等问题，都是国际税法应认真研究的内容。

The issue of international double taxation is the concentrated and core issue of conflicts in international taxation relationship, while the avoidance and elimination of international double taxation is one of the main tasks of international tax law. The causes of international double taxation, its manifestations, the extent of its impact on the relevant international economic activities, and the methods adopted by countries through domestic unilateral legislation or bilateral tax agreements to solve various international double taxation problems are all issues that should be carefully studied in international tax law.

（四）国际逃避税行为及其防范
International Tax Evasion and Avoidance and Their Prevention

与国际双重征税现象相反，国际逃避税行为从另一个极端阻碍了国际税收公平合理秩序的建立，跨国纳税主体利用世界各国所采用的不同税收制度以及税收环境之间客观存在的矛盾与漏洞，采取转移定价、变更纳税主体所在地、利用避税港等方式进行逃避税。尤其是近年来，各种生产要素在国际间更加快速自由流动，跨国纳税主体的逃避税行为越来越活跃，方式也越来越多样化，这引起了各国政府的更多关注，世界各国必须采取更有效的措施来对抗国际逃避税行为。国际税法学需顺应这种趋势，加强对国际逃避税行为、手段及方式的研究，提出更为有效的管制措施，防范打击国际逃避税行为，保证国际经济秩序的健康有序发展。

In contrast to the phenomenon of international double taxation, international tax evasion and avoidance hinders the establishment of a fair and reasonable international taxation order from the other extreme. Transnational tax subjects take advantage of the objective contradictions and loopholes between different taxation systems and taxation environments adopted by different countries in the world to evade tax by means of transfer pricing, changing the location of tax subjects, using tax havens and so on. Especially in recent years, various production factors have become more rapidly and freely flowing internationally, and the tax evasion behaviors of transnational tax subjects have become more and more active and diversified, attracting more attention from governments. Countries around the world must take more effective measures to combat international tax evasion behaviors. The discipline of international tax law needs to follow this trend, strengthen the research on international tax evasion behaviors, means and methods, propose more effective control measures, prevent and combat international tax evasion, and ensure the healthy and orderly development of the international economic order.

（五）国际税收协定及其与国内税法的关系
International Tax Treaties and Their Relationship with Domestic Tax Law

国家之间通过签订国际税收协定，协调各国税收管辖权冲突，减少国际双重征税与国际逃避税行为。近年来，各国签订、参加的国际税收协定或条约数量越来越多，协定内容也随着实践和发展中国家的努力而不断完善更新，国际税收协定或条约对于促进国际经济的正常发展起到越来越重要的作用。而国内税法与国际税收协定有着密不可分的联系，它们都是国际税法的主要渊源，它们之间的关系实质上是国际法和国内法关系的一个侧面，它们既相互独立，又相互配合、相互补充，共同调整着国际税收关系。

By signing international tax agreements countries can coordinate their tax jurisdiction conflicts and reduce international double taxation and international tax evasion. In recent years, countries have signed more and more international tax agreements or treaties, and the contents of the agreements have been improved and updated with the practice and efforts of developing countries, and international tax agreements or treaties play an increasingly important role in promoting the normal development of the international economy. Domestic tax laws and international tax agreements are inextricably linked, and they are both the main sources of international tax laws, and the relationship between them is essentially an aspect of the relationship between international law and domestic law, which are both independent of each other and complementary to each other, and jointly adjust international tax relations.

（六）国际税收的协调与合作
Harmonization and Cooperation in International Taxation

进入20世纪90年代以来，有关国际组织努力协调各国税收政策和税制，以消除可能存在的国际双重征税和国际逃避税，防止恶性税收竞争，加强税务情报交换和税收征管国际合作，这已成为新时期国际税法发展的主要内容。国际税法学应该充分关注国际税收协调与合作的内容和发展倾向，研究国际税收协调和国际税务合作与国家税收主权的关系，明确鼓励吸引外国投资税收优惠与恶性税收竞争的区别界限，促进国际税收协调与合作的发展，建立公平合理的国际经济法律秩序。

Since the 1990s, the efforts of international organizations to coordinate the differences in tax policies and tax systems among countries in order to eliminate possible international double taxation and international tax evasion, prevent vicious tax competition and strengthen tax information exchange and international cooperation in tax collection and administration have become the main content of the development of international tax law in the new era. The discipline of international tax law should pay full attention to the content and development tendency of international tax coordination and cooperation, examine the relationship between international tax coordination and international tax cooperation and national tax sovereignty, clarify the boundary of distinction between encouraging tax incentives to attract foreign investment and vicious tax competition, promote the development of international tax coordination and cooperation, and establish a fair and reasonable international economic legal order.

（七）国际税务争议的解决
Resolution of International Tax Disputes

国际税务争议包括国家之间的税务争议和国家与跨国纳税人之间的税务争议。在一定条件下，国家与跨国纳税人之间的税务争议会转化为国家之间的税务争议。当跨国纳税人与国家之间的税务争议被税务主管当局受理并启动国际相互协商程序时，就会上升为国家间的税务争议。国际税务争议不利于国际经济的交流合作，影响良好国际投资环境的形成以及国际投资的正常流动，对于资本输出国和输入国的经济均有不良影响，因此，在解决国际税务争议方面，世界各国具有共同的利益。国际税务争议的解决对于跨国纳税人和相关国家都具有重要意义，是公平、效率原则和国际经济合作原则的任务与要求。如何解决国际税务争议是国际税法学的重要研究内容之一。国际税法学要研究国家之间税务争议和国家与跨国纳税人之间税务争议的不同特点与不同的处理解决方式，解决争议的方式和途径，行政复议、行政诉讼及仲裁等国内法程序处理争议的适用性以及相互协商，仲裁程序的不足与完善等。

International tax disputes include tax disputes between countries and tax disputes between countries and transnational taxpayers. Under certain conditions, tax disputes between countries and transnational taxpayers will be transformed into interstate tax disputes. When tax disputes between multinational taxpayers and countries are accepted by tax authorities and international mutual consultation procedures are initiated, they will escalate into international tax disputes. International tax disputes are not conducive to international economic exchanges and cooperation, affect the formation of a good international investment environment and the normal flow of international investment, and have adverse effects on the economies of both capital exporting and importing countries. The resolution of international tax disputes is of great significance to both transnational taxpayers and relevant countries, and is the task and requirement of the principles of fairness and efficiency and the principles of international economic cooperation. The solution of international tax disputes is one of the important research contents of the discipline of international tax law, which ought to study the different characteristics and different ways of handling and resolving tax disputes between countries and between countries and transnational taxpayers, the ways and means of resolving disputes, the applicability of domestic law procedures such as administrative reconsideration, administrative litigation and arbitration to deal with disputes, as well as the shortcomings and improvements of mutual consultation and arbitration procedures.

第一章 绪 论
CHAPTER I Introduction

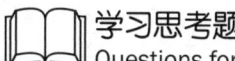
Questions for Study

1. 国际税法产生的原因是什么?
   What is the reason for the creation of international tax law?
2. 国际税收法律关系的特点是什么?它与国内税收法律关系的区别是什么?
   What are the characteristics of the international tax legal relationship? What are the differences compared with the domestic tax legal relationship?
3. 怎样正确理解国际税收公平和效率原则?
   How to understand the principles of the fairness and efficiency of the international tax?
4. 国际税法和国际税法学的关系是什么?
   What is the relationship between international tax law and the discipline of international tax law?
5. 怎样正确理解国家税收管辖权独立原则?
   How to understand the principle of independence of the tax jurisdiction?
6. 国际税法发展的趋势是什么?
   What are the tendencies of the development of international tax law?

第二章 CHAPTER II

税收管辖权
Tax Jurisdiction

第一节　税收管辖权概述
Section 1　Overview of Tax Jurisdiction

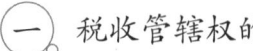

一、税收管辖权的概念
Concept of Tax Jurisdiction

税收管辖权是指一国政府享有的征税权,是一国政府自主决定对一定范围内的人或对象进行征税的权力。税收管辖权的内容包括了五个方面:(1)征税主权,即由谁征税,具体而言是由国家行使征税权,由国家的税务部门行使税收的管理权;(2)纳税主体,即对谁征税,负有纳税义务的主体范围由一国政府自行规定;(3)纳税客体,即对什么征税,一般包括收益、所得、财产和行为;(4)纳税数量,即征多少税,包括税基、税率、税种的确定;(5)征税程序,即如何征纳,涉及征税的时间、期限方式以及地点等。

Tax jurisdiction refers to the authority of a government to impose and collect taxes within a specified scope, covering individuals and entities subject to taxation. The contents of tax jurisdiction include five aspects: (1) The sovereignty of taxation means who collects the tax, specifically by the state uses the right to collect tax, and the tax administration power being exercised by the tax department of the state. (2) The scope of the subject of tax payment, i.e., who is taxed and who is obliged to pay taxes, shall be determined by the government itself. (3) The object of taxation, i.e., what is taxed, generally including income, property and behavior. (4) The amount of tax paid, i.e., how much tax is collected, including the determination of the tax base, tax rate and tax type. (5) Procedure of tax collection, which means how the tax is collected, the time of taxation, term and location, etc.

税收管辖权是国家主权在税收领域中的体现,是国家主权的重要组成部分,一国政府行使税收管辖权的依据是国家的主权。根据国际法,主权国家是国际法的基本主体,主权国家享有的国家基本权利包括独立权、平等权、自卫和管辖权。管辖权是国家权力的一种体现,管辖权一般是指在国际社会中,主权国家对其领域内的一切人(除享受豁免权者外)和事物以及一切居住在国外的本国人行使管辖的权力。税收管辖权是国家管辖权的一项重要组成部分。按照国际法的基本准则,任何一个主权国家都有权在不受任何外来干涉的情况下自由地行使管辖权，正是由于国家的税收管辖权来源于国家主权，因而它是一种完全独立自主的、不受外来干预的权力。一国政府可以在完全独立自主、不受外来干预的条件下，依据本国的政治经济状况来制定税收政策、确立税制和规定纳税人与征税对象等，这一税收管辖权独立自主的原则，已为世界各国所普遍承认和遵守。

The embodiment of state sovereignty in the field of taxation is by tax jurisdiction, which is a significant part of national sovereignty, a government's exercising of tax jurisdiction is based on national sovereignty. According to international law, the sovereign state is the basic subject, its basic rights include independence, equality, self-defence and jurisdiction. Jurisdiction is a reflection of the rights of states, which generally refer to the exercise of jurisdiction by sovereign states in the international community over all persons and things in their field (except those enjoying immunity) and all nationals residing abroad. Tax jurisdiction is an important component of national jurisdiction. In accordance with the basic norms of international law, any sovereign state has the right to exercise its jurisdiction freely without any external interference, precisely because its tax jurisdiction derives from national sovereignty and is therefore a fully independent power free from outside interference. A government can formulate tax policies according to its own political and economic conditions, establish a tax system and stipulate taxpayers and tax objects, the principle of independent tax jurisdiction has been widely accepted and observed by all countries over the world.

伴随着国际交往合作的进一步发展，纳税人的所得与财产不再局限于一个国家，出现两个或两个以上的国家对同一征税对象课税、不同国家税收管辖权发生交叉的现象，导致国际双重征税等国际税收问题，税收管辖权问题在国际上才显得日益突出和复杂。

With the deeper development of international cooperation, taxpayers' income and property are no longer confined to one country, the phenomenon of two or more countries taxing on the same tax object tax results in international tax issues such as international double taxation, and tax jurisdiction issues become more and more complicated in the international community.

从一个独立国家的角度来看，税收管辖权是一种不受任何约束和限制的权力。但是，国际社会是由众多大小不同但主权平等的国家构成的，并且各国的税收管辖权都应是平等的，这一客观事实本身就决定了税收管辖权独立自主的原则，虽是如此，但这并不意味着一国政府可以肆意地扩大其税收管辖权的范围。一国政府在行使税收管辖权时，也不可能绝对地不受任何限制和约束。

From the perspective of an independent state, tax jurisdiction is a power that is not bound by any constraints or restrictions. However, the objective fact that the international community was composed of many states, large and small, but sovereign and equal, and that each state's tax jurisdiction should be equal, in itself determined the principle of the independence of tax jurisdiction, but it did not mean that a government could arbitrarily expand the scope of its tax jurisdiction, nor can a government exercise its tax jurisdiction without any restrictions or constraints.

国家主权平等是近代国际法的基础，也是当代国际关系与国际法中最重要和最基本的原则。国家主权平等原则是指在国际交往中，国家不分强弱大小，无论其经济、政治、社会状况如何,一律平等,都是国际社会中的平等主体,均有平等权利与责任,各国都充分享有国家主权的固有权力,各国的法律人格、领土完整和政治独立必须得到充分的尊重,任何国家不能对他国提出强权要求,也不能为了满足自己的要求干涉他国内政,损害对方的利益。同时,根据国际法,各国都应当诚实履行自己的国际责任和义务。国家主权平等原则已得到《联合国宪章》、1965年《关于各国内政不容干涉及其独立与主权之保护宣言》、1970年《国际法原则宣言》等现代国际法律文件的确认,无论是联合国或是其他区域性国际组织,在它们通过的有关国家间关系的基本原则的文件中,均列有国家主权平等原则,甚至将它列为各项原则之首。税收管辖权源于国家主权,理应适用国际公法的相应原则,各国税收管辖权一律平等,一国应当尊重其他国家的税收管辖权,并不得随意进行干涉。当两国之间没有进行相应的特殊约定时,一国税务机关不得在另一国境内进行税收行政行为,否则会构成对另一国主权的侵犯。

State sovereign equality is the foundation of modern international law, it is also the most important and basic principle of contemporary international relations and law. The sovereign equality principle refers to the fact that international intercourse countries regardless of their size or strength, no matter of their economic, political and social status, are all equal subjects in the international community, all have equal rights and responsibilities, and these countries fully enjoy the inherent power of state sovereignty, national legal personality, territorial integrity and political independence, which must be fully respected. No country should make hegemonic demands on other countries, nor should it interfere in other countries' internal affairs or undermine their interests to meet its own demands. At the same time, according to international law, all countries should honestly fulfill their international responsibilities and obligations. The principle of the sovereign equality of states has been recognized by modern international legal documents such as the Charter of the United Nations, the 1965 Declaration on the Non-Interference in the Internal Affairs of States and the Protection of Their Independence and Sovereignty, and the 1970 Declaration of Principles of International Law. Tax jurisdiction originates from national sovereignty and should be applied to the corresponding principles of public international law. All countries have equal tax jurisdiction, and one country must respect the tax jurisdiction of other countries and not interfere at will. When there is no corresponding special agreement between two countries, the tax authorities of one country may not engage in tax administration in the territory of the other, otherwise it constitutes a violation of the sovereignty of the other.

税收管辖权的行使除了要尊重他国主权、遵守税收管辖权平等的原则外,还要受到外交税收豁免这一国际习惯的限制。1961年4月订立的《维也纳外交关系公约》与1963年的《维也纳领事关系公约》,对适用于外国代表机构和使领馆人员的外交税收豁免原则和范围作出了规定,上述两个公约分别于1975年12月和1979年8月在中国生效,中国在个人所得税法及有关税收法规中对外交税收豁免也作出了相应规定。而在外交实践中,为便于外国及国际组织代表更好地执行公务,表示对外交代表所代表的国家及国际组织的尊重,外交税收豁免已成为被国际上普遍接受的外交惯例,而有关国家无论是否参加了上述条约,都应当遵守这一惯例,这样各国行使税收管辖权时无疑都要受到外交税收豁免的限制，一国税收机关不得向享有税收豁免权的外交代表机构和使领馆人员及国际组织代表行使税收管辖权，如果某国强行剥夺相关机构人员的外交税收豁免权，拒绝给予外交税收豁免待遇，则在国际法上被视为一种违法行为，会受到国际社会的谴责与制裁。

In addition to respecting the sovereignty of other states and observing the principle of equality of tax jurisdiction, the exercise of tax jurisdiction is subject to the international practice of diplomatic immunity. The Vienna Convention on Diplomatic Relations, concluded in April 1961, and the Vienna Convention on Consular Relations of 1963 provide for the principle and scope of diplomatic tax exemptions applicable to foreign representative bodies and consular personnel, which entered into force in China in December 1975 and August 1979 respectively. In diplomatic practice, in order to facilitate the better performance of official duties by representatives of foreign and international organizations and to show respect for the states and international organizations represented by diplomatic representatives, diplomatic tax immunity has become an internationally accepted diplomatic practice, which should be observed regardless of whether the state concerned participates in the above-mentioned treaties, so that states will undoubtedly be subject to diplomatic tax immunity in the exercise of their tax jurisdiction. A country's tax authorities may not exercise tax jurisdiction over diplomatic missions and consulates and representatives of international organizations that enjoy tax immunity, and if a state forcibly deprives the personnel of the relevant institutions of diplomatic tax immunity and refuses to grant diplomatic tax immunity, it is considered as an illegal act under international law and will be condemned and sanctioned by the international community.

（二）税收管辖权的分类
Classification of Tax Jurisdiction

根据确定征税权力的原则不同，即遵从国际法两个基本原则——属人主义原则和属地主义原则，税收管辖权可分为属人性质的税收管辖权和属地性质的税收管辖权。

According to the different principles of tax power, and the two principles in the international tax jurisdiction, tax jurisdiction can be divided into the personal tax jurisdiction and geographical tax jurisdiction.

（一）属人性质的税收管辖权
Personal Tax Jurisdiction

属人性质的税收管辖权是指征税国根据纳税人与征税国之间存在着的某种人身隶属关系性质的法律事实，对纳税人来自征税国境内、境外的全部所得和财产价值进行征税。各国主张的属人性质税收管辖权，根据纳税人与征税国之间不同性质的人身隶属关系，具体分为居民税收管辖权与国籍税收管辖权两种表现形式，以下将分别对这两种管辖权形式进行介绍。

The personal tax jurisdiction means the taxing state taxes taxpayers according to the legal facts of some kind of personal affiliation between the taxpayer and the taxing state. The personal tax jurisdiction advocated by each country, according to the personal affiliation of different nature between the taxpayer and the taxing state, is divided into two manifestations, the resident tax jurisdiction and the nationality tax jurisdiction, which will be introduced in the following two forms.

1. 居民税收管辖权

Resident Tax Jurisdiction

居民税收管辖权,也称居民课税原则,是指征税国根据纳税人与征税国之间存在居民身份关系的法律事实主张行使征税的管辖权。居民身份关系的法律事实是指纳税人满足征税国法律规定的居民(包括自然人与非自然人)条件。凡是满足某个国家的居民条件,与该国家存在税收居所联系的纳税人,就是该国的居民纳税人,而这个国家相应地称为纳税人居住国。凡是不符合某国税法规定的居民构成条件的主体,则属于该国税法意义上的非居民,相对于非居民来说,该国则是其非居住国。需要注意的是,符合某国居民条件的居民并不一定是具备该国国籍的公民,一国居民可能包括外国国籍的人。在行使居民税收管辖权的情况下,征税国可以要求纳税人就其来源于境内和境外即世界范围内的全部所得或财产价值承担纳税义务,因此,纳税人承担的是无限纳税义务。

The resident tax jurisdiction, also called resident tax principle, means the exercise of taxation jurisdiction by the taxing state on the basis of the legal facts of the relationship between the taxpayer and the taxing state. The legal facts of resident status relationship refers to the taxpayer meeting the conditions of residents (including natural and non-natural persons) stipulated by the law of the taxing state. Taxpayers who meet the living conditions of a country and have such a tax residence in that country are the resident taxpayers of that country, which is accordingly referred to as the country of residence of the taxpayer. Subjects who do not meet the conditions for the composition of resident under a country's tax law are non-residents within the meaning of the country's tax law, and the country is its non-resident country relative to non-residents. It is important to note that a resident who meets the conditions for resident of a state is not necessarily a citizen with the nationality of that state and that a resident of a state may include a person of foreign nationality. In the exercise of resident tax jurisdiction, the taxing state may require the taxpayer to bear tax liability for all income or property value derived from within and outside the country, worldwide. Thus, the taxpayer is responsible for unlimited tax payment.

2. 国籍税收管辖权

Nationality Tax Jurisdiction

国籍税收管辖权,也称公民税收管辖权,是按属人原则确立的一种税收管辖权。国籍税收管辖权是指征税国根据纳税人与征税国之间存在的国籍关系,主张行使适于征税的管辖权。此种税收管辖权强调按纳税人的公民身份,以纳税主体与国籍国之间的国籍法律关系作为行使税收管辖权的依据,并不考虑纳税人与国家之间是否存在经济利益联系。依据国籍税收管辖权,具有该国国籍的人应就其来自国内国外的全部所得与财产向国籍国承担无限纳税义务。

Nationality tax jurisdiction, also called citizen tax jurisdiction, is a kind of tax jurisdiction established according to the principle of personality. Nationality tax jurisdiction refers to the exercise of taxable jurisdiction by the taxing state on the basis of the nationality relationship between the taxpayer and the taxing state. Such tax jurisdiction emphasizes the legal relationship of nationality between the subject and the state of nationality as the basis for the exercise of tax jurisdiction on the basis of the taxpayer's citizenship, and doesn't take into account the existence of an economic interest link between the taxpayer and the state. Under the nationality tax jurisdiction, a person with that nationality shall be responsible to the state of nationality for unlimited taxation of all his/her income and property derived from domestic or overseas.

(二)属地性质的税收管辖权
Territorial Tax Jurisdiction

属地性质的税收管辖权,也称来源地税收管辖权,它只对来自本国境内的所得或财产征税,亦称地域管辖权。按照属地主义原则,税收管辖权以国家主权所能达到的地域范围为依据,基于所得来源地或财产所在地而行使。属地性质的税收管辖权主要表现形式有所得来源地税收管辖权和财产所在地税收管辖权。

Territorial tax jurisdiction, also called tax jurisdiction of origin, only taxed on domestic income or property, also known as region jurisdiction. According to the principle of territorialism, tax jurisdiction is exercised on the basis of the origin or location of the property and on the geographical extent to which national sovereignty can be realized. The main manifestations of this tax jurisdiction are tax jurisdiction of the source of income and tax jurisdiction of property situation.

1. 所得来源地税收管辖权
Tax Jurisdiction of the Source of Income

所得来源地税收管辖权,是征税国基于纳税人所得来源于本国境内的事实而主张行使的税收管辖权。所得来源地管辖权是依据属地原则确立起来的税收管辖权,以征税对象与本国领域存在着地域上的联系作为征税依据,不考虑纳税人的国籍和居民身份归属。行使所得来源地税收管辖的国家仅限于向纳税人源于本国境内的收入征税,纳税人源于境外国家的收入则不在该国的所得来源地税收管辖范围之内,因此,纳税人承担的是有限的纳税义务。

Tax jurisdiction of the source of income is the tax jurisdiction that the taxing state claims to exercise on the basis of the fact that the taxpayer's income originated in its territory. The jurisdiction of the source of income is the tax jurisdiction established according to the principle of territoriality, which is based on the geographical connection between the object of taxation and the territory of the country, regardless of the nationality of the taxpayer and the attribution of the resident status. The state exercising the tax jurisdiction of the source of income is limited to taxing the income of the taxpayer originated in its territory, and the income of the taxpayer originated from outside is not within the tax jurisdiction of the source of income of that state. Thus, the taxpayer has a limited tax liability.

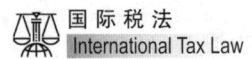

2. 财产所在地税收管辖权

Tax Jurisdiction of Property Situation

财产所在地税收管辖权，是征税国在财产税方面基于财产或财产价值存在于一国境内的事实而主张行使的征税权。在财产所在地税收管辖权下，征税国主张征税的依据在于作为征税对象的财产或财产价值位于征税国境内的事实。与所得来源地税收管辖权相似，征税国也不考虑纳税人的国籍和居民身份的归属情况。由于纳税人承担纳税义务的课税对象，仅限于存在于征税国境内的财产及财产价值，那些位于征税国境外的纳税人财产或财产价值，则不属于征税国的财产所在地税收管辖权的管辖范围，因此，纳税人承担的也是一种有限的纳税义务。相对于所得来源地的识别而言，关于各种财产或财产价值的所在地认定则相对简单明确。在各国税法上，土地、房屋等不动产所在地基本都是以其实际坐落地为准，至于各种动产，多数国家以其实际存在的地点作为其所在地，船舶、飞机、汽车等交通运输工具则多以注册登记地为其所在地，由其注册登记地国家行使财产所在地税收管辖权。

Tax jurisdiction of property situation, is the tax right claimed in respect of property tax on the basis of the fact that the property or the value of the property exists in the territory of a state. Under the tax jurisdiction of the place where the property is located, the taxing state claims that the tax is based on the fact that the property or the value of property to which it is subject are located in the territory of the taxing state. Similar to the jurisdiction of the source of income, the taxing state doesn't take into account the nationality of the taxpayer and the attribution of the resident status. Since the object of taxation of the taxpayer's tax obligation is limited to the value of property or property that exists in the taxing state, the value of the property or property of those taxpayers located outside the taxing state is not within the jurisdiction, the taxpayer bears a limited tax obligation. The determination of the location of various properties and their values of the property is relatively simple and clear in relation to the identification of the source of the proceeds. In the national tax law, land, housing and other real estate location is basically based on its actual landing, as for all kinds of movable property, most countries with its actual location as its location, ships, aircraft, automobiles and other means of transportation are mostly registered as its location, by its registered state to exercise the tax jurisdiction of property situation.

第二节 居民税收管辖权的行使
Section 2　Exercise of Resident Tax Jurisdiction

由于居民身份关系的存在是一国行使居民税收管辖权的前提，只有符合居民身份的纳税人才被视为该国的居民纳税人，其有义务向居民国承担无限纳税义务并享受该国相关的税收优惠,因此,居民身份的确认对行使居民税收管辖权的国家及相应纳税主体具有重要意义。迄今为止,国际上存在多种居民身份确认标准,并未形成统一的居民身份确认标准。在税收实践中,世界各国综合本国政治、经济和社会状况,从维护本国税收权益的角度出发,通过国内立法的形式确定本国的居民身份的确认标准。

Due to the existence of resident status relationship is the premise of a country to exercise resident tax jurisdiction, only taxpayers, who meet the resident status can be regarded as resident taxpayers, have the obligation to take on unlimited tax obligations to their resident country and take the relevant tax benefits from the country, therefore, the confirmation of resident status is of great significance to the country exercising resident tax jurisdiction and the corresponding tax subject. Now, there're a variety of resident identity comfirmation standards in the world, and no unified one has been formed. In the perspective of taxation practice, the countries around the world usually determine the identification criteria of their own residents by the form of domestic legislation, taking into account their own political, economic and social situations, to protect their own tax interests.

一、居民税收管辖权的确立
Establishment of Resident Tax Jurisdiction

(一)自然人居民身份的确认
Resident Identification for Natural Persons

关于自然人居民身份的确认,在各国的税收实践中主要采用的标准有以下几种。

With regard to resident identification for natural persons, the following standards are mainly used in tax practice in various countries.

1. 住所标准

Domicile Standard

住所标准是指以自然人在一国境内是否拥有住所这一法律事实,作为判断该自然人是否具有此国居民纳税人身份的标准。关于住所的概念在民法学界有不同主张,但在国际税法领域中一般认为住所是指一个自然人具有永久性、固定性的居住场所。住所通常与自然人的户籍所在地、住宅所在地、主要财产关系所在地以及家庭所在地相联系。住所与国籍不同,国籍是公法上的概念,反映了自然人与某一国家之间的政治联系;住所属于私法上的概念,反映了自然人与特定地域的民事联系。在某国拥有住所的人并不一定是该国的公民,随着国际人员的流动自由性增加,拥有某国国籍的人也有可能在该国没有住所,如果该国未适用国籍税收管辖权,则其不会对该国承担无限纳税义务。

Domicile standard means the legal fact that a natural person has a domicile in the territory of a state as a criterion for determining whether the natural person has the taxpayer status of a resident of that state. The concept of domicile has different ideas in civil law circles, but in the territoriality of international tax law it is generally considered that domicile refers to a natural person's permanent and fixed place of residence. The domicile is usually linked to the place of residence of a natural person, the location of the residence, the location of the principal property relationship and the place of the family. Domicile is different from nationality, which is a concept in public law, reflecting the political connection between a natural person and a state. A person who has a domicile in a state is not necessarily a citizen of that state, and as the freedom of movement of persons internationally increases, a person who has the nationality of that state may also have no domicile in that state, and if that state doesn't have the nationality tax jurisdiction, he/she will not be responsible for unlimited tax liability in that state.

鉴于住所具备永久性和固定性的特征，采用住所标准易于确定纳税人的居民身份，但由于国际经济交往的日益频繁，个人的经济活动范围不断扩大，个人住所与其从事经济活动的地点不一致的现象越来越普遍，住所作为一种法定的个人永久居住场所，已经不能完全代表个人真实的活动场所。因此，单纯以住所确定某个人的居民身份，并以此行使税收管辖权，将不可避免地造成纳税义务地与实际经济活动地不符的问题的出现。采用住所标准的各国在税收实践中通常同时采用其他的标准以弥补住所标准的不足。如在荷兰，拥有住处、家庭或者有长期居住意向的即属于荷兰居民。在英国，拥有住宅，且不在国外从事全日制工作者才属于居民纳税人。日本则规定，有永久性住所或者在日本居住满1年者属于日本居民。

According to the character of permanent and fixed nature of the domicile, it is easy to determine the resident status of the taxpayer by adopting the residence standard. However, due to the increasing frequency of international economic exchanges, the scope of personal economic activities continues to expand, and the phenomenon that personal residence is inconsistent with the location of economic activities, it is becoming more and more common that domicile, as a statutory permanent residence for individuals, can no longer fully represent the real place of personal activities. Therefore, simply determining a person's resident status by domicile and exercising tax jurisdiction will inevitably cause the problem of inconsistency between the tax liability and the actual economic activity. Therefore, in the practice of taxation, countries that adopt the domicile standard usually adopt other standards at the same time to make up for the deficiencies of the domicile standard. If you have a residence, family or long-term residence intention in the Netherlands, you are a resident of the Netherlands. In the UK, it is a resident taxpayer to be eligible to own a home in the UK and not work full-time abroad. Japan stipulates that persons who have permanent residence or have lived in Japan for one year are Japanese residents.

2. 居所标准

Residence Standard

居所标准是指以自然人在某国是否拥有居所作为判断其是否为该国居民纳税人的标准。居所是指自然人经常居住，但不具有永久居住性质的场所。与住所标准相比，居所是更能反映自然人真实活动的地域。居所不同于国籍，是否具有某国国籍与是否在该国拥有居所没有必然的联系。自然人居民可以包括拥有外国国籍的人。居所与住所的区别在于，居所并不代表永久性居住的意图，自然人可能因某种原因暂时停留于一国，而住所则体现着自然人永久性居住在某国的意图。居所标准比住所标准更能准确地反映自然人的主要活动地点。居所标准的缺点在于居所的认定标准缺乏统一的客观识别标志。在各个国家的税收实践中，对居所的认定具有较大的弹性，容易引起纳税人与税务主管机构之间的争议。因此，在实践中多数国家采用居所与居住时间结合的标准来判定自然人的居民纳税人身份。

Residence standard refers to the criterion of whether a natural person has a residence in a country for determining whether he or she is a resident taxpayer of that country. Residence refers to a place where natural persons live regularly but not permanently. Compared with the standard of domicile, residence is more reflective of the real activities of natural persons. Residence is different from nationality, there is no evitable link between a nationality of a state and whether or not to have residence in that country. Residents of natural persons may include persons of foreign nationality. The difference between residence and domicile is that residence doesn't means he or she will live in some place forever, just because a natural person stays in a country temporarily due to some reasons, while domicile reflects the intention of a natural person to reside permanently in a state. The standard of residence more accurately reflects the main place of activity of natural persons than the standard of domicile. The disadvantage of the residence standard is that the residence identification standard lacks a unified objective identification mark, and in the tax practice of each country, the determination of residence has greater flexibility, which can easily lead to disputes between taxpayers and tax authorities. Therefore, most countries define the natural persons and resident taxpayers based on the combination of domicile and residence time.

3. 居住时间标准

Standard of Residence Time

居住时间标准是指以自然人在一国境内居住或停留的时间长短来判断其是否属于该国居民纳税人的标准。居住时间标准不考虑自然人是否在该国境内拥有居所或住所，也不考虑其是否具有该国的国籍。自然人只要在某国停留的时间达到该国的法定期限，就有可能成为该国的居民纳税人。

The standard of residence time refers to the standard to judge whether a natural person belongs to the resident taxpayer of a country according to the length of his or her residence or stay in the country. The standard of residence time does not take into account whether a natural person has a place of residence or residence in the territory of the state or whether he/she has the nationality of that state. As long as an individual natural person has been stayed enough time that matches that country's legal term, then he/she may become a resident taxpayer of that country.

在税收实践中，采用居住时间标准的国家，在具体实施的标准上也大不相同。

In tax practice, countries adopttting the standard of residence time also have different specific implementation rules.

（1）对达到该标准需在本国停留的时间规定不同。如日本、韩国规定为1年，英国、法国、澳大利亚、中国规定在一个纳税年度连续或者累计居住183天；（2）对在本国停留时间的计算方式不同。有的国家规定，自然人在本国境内连续停留时间达到法定期限，才属于本国的居民纳税人；有的国家则规定，自然人在本国境内累计停留时间达到本国的法定期限，属于本国的居民纳税人，即自然人可以中途离开该国，只要累计在该国居住时间超过规定就属于该国居民；（3）对是否按纳税年度计算，各国也有所不同。有些国家规定，在任何12个月内达到成为本国居民纳税人要求逗留的期限就是本国居民；而有些国家按一个纳税年度的停留时间计算。一般而言，一个纳税年度是指从公历的1月1日到12月31日。如果一个自然人在采用纳税年度为计算标准的国家,虽然其在该国境内居住的时间已超出了该国规定的期限,但由于居住时间跨越了两个纳税年度,且在每个纳税年度内居住停留时间都没有达到法定时间标准,那么这个自然人不能被认定为这个国家的居民纳税人。《中华人民共和国个人所得税法》规定,在中国境内有住所,或者无住所而一个纳税年度内在中国境内居住累计满183天的个人为居民纳税人。

(1) Different rules for meeting this standard are made for the time period required to stay in the country. For example, 1 year for Japan and the Republic of Korea, 183 consecutive or cumulative days of residence in a tax year for the United Kingdom, France, Australia and China; (2) Some states provide that a natural person's continuous stay in the territory of the country has reached the statutory period of time, belongs to the resident taxpayer of the country, while others provide that the cumulative length of stay of a natural person in the territory of the country has reached the statutory period of time in the country, and that the resident taxpayer of the country, i.e., the natural person, may leave the country midway, as long as the cumulative length of residence in the country exceeds the prescribed period; (3) Some countries provide that the period of stay required by the taxpayer who becomes a resident within any 12-month period is the resident of the country, while others are calculated on the basis of the length of stay in a tax year. Generally speaking, a tax year is from January 1st to December 31st of the Gregorian calendar. A natural person cannot be recognized as a resident taxpayer of a country where the tax year is the criterion for calculation, although the period of residence in that country has exceeded the period specified in that country, but has spanned two tax years and the length of stay in each tax year has not met the statutory time standard. China's Personal Income Tax Law stipulates that an individual who has a domicile in China, or has no domicile, and who has lived in China for a cumulative period of 183 days in a tax year, is a resident taxpayer.

居住时间标准相对于居所标准更具有优势。居住时间标准明确固定,并且可以通过出入境登记机构具体掌握,便于操作,同时可以准确反映自然人与居住国之间的经济联系程度。因此,居住时间标准在国际上被广泛认可与采用。为了弥补不同标准的不足,更好地体现自然人实现经济活动的地域,在采用居住时间标准的同时,各国通常同时使用居所或住所标准,自然人只要符合其中一项标准即可判定为居民。例如,中国、日本都是同时采用住所标准与居住时间标准的国家。

The residence period standard is better than the domicile standard. The residence period standard is apparently fixed, and can be specifically mastered by the immigration registration agency, easy to operate, and can accurately reflect the degree of economic ties between natural persons and the country of residence. Therefore, the standard of residence time is widely recognized and adopted internationally. In order to make up for the shortcomings of different standards and better reflect the geographical realization of economic activities of natural persons, while using standard of residence time, countries usually apply the standard of residence or domicile at the same time, and natural persons can be judged as residents as long as they meet one of the criteria. For example, China and Japan are countries that adopt both the domicile standard and the residence period standard.

4. 意愿标准
Criterion of Willingness

按照意愿标准，自然人在行使居民管辖权的国家内有长期居住的主观意愿或被认定为有长期居住意愿的，即被视为该国居民。凡在一国有长期居住意愿，并依法取得入境护照、移居签证和各种居留证明的外国侨民，都属于该国居民，该国政府都有权对其来源于世界范围的全部所得进行征税，如希腊、土耳其、美国等国都有上述规定。判断某一自然人是否有在本国长期居住的主观意图，通常要综合考虑其签证时间长短、劳务合同期限、是否建立家庭或购置永久性生活设施等因素。美国在1984年税收法案实施以后，对取得在美国永久居留权的外国人，即所谓"绿卡"持有者，在税收上视为美国居民。因为持有"绿卡"这一行为本身，就表明该人在美国有长期居住的愿望。

According to the criterion of willingness, a natural person who has the subjective intention or is recognized as having the intention of long-term residence in the country exercising resident jurisdiction is regarded as a resident of that country. Foreign nationals who have long-term residence in a country and who have obtained a national passport, immigration visa and various residence certificates in accordance with the law are residents of that country, and the government has the right to tax all income derived from worldwide, as provided for in Greece, Turkey, the United States and other countries. The subjective intention of a natural person to determine whether he or she has long-term residence in the country is usually based on factors such as the length of his visa, the duration of the labour contract, the establishment of a family or the acquisition of permanent living facilities. After the implementation of the US Tax Act of 1984, foreigners who have obtained permanent residency in the United States, the so-called "green card" holders, are considered US residents for taxes. Because the act of holding a "green card" in itself indicates that the person has an intention to live in the United States for a long time.

（二）法人居民身份的确认
Resident Identification for Legal Person Residents or Enterprise

法人是依法成立的、有必要的财产与组织机构、能够独立享有民事权利、承担民事义务的社会组织。法人的经济活动范围相较于自然人而言更为广泛，因而在国际税法上，"税收居民"和"税收公民"的概念包含法人。世界各国关于法人居民身份认定的标准各有不同，主要包括以下几个标准。

A legal person is a social organization established according to law, with necessary property and organizational institutions, which can independently enjoy civil rights and assume civil obligations. Legal persons have a wider range of economic activities than natural persons, so in international tax law, the concepts of "tax residents" and "tax citizens" include legal persons. The criteria for the identification of legal persons vary from country to country, including the following.

1. 注册成立地标准
The Standard of Place of Incorporation

注册成立地标准，又称准据法标准，在该标准下，按一国法律在该国注册成立的法人即为该国的居民纳税人,应向该国承担无限纳税义务。凡是在一国注册成立的法人,不论其投资者是哪国人,不论其实际管理机构在哪国,不论其总机构在哪国,都是该国的居民纳税人。反之,不在本国注册成立的法人则为非居民纳税人。此标准的优势在于一般法人的登记注册地点比较确定,易于识别,因为法人的注册地一旦被确定,不经法人登记注册国同意并办理变更手续,法人的注册地原则上不能变更。但注册成立地标准不一定能够反映法人的真实活动地点,法人很有可能完全脱离注册地国家而在其他国家从事经营活动,并且可以通过选择注册登记地的方法,达到规避有关国家税收管辖权的目的。美国是采用注册登记地标准的典型国家,美国对法人国籍与居民身份的确认,同样仅凭注册登记地标准进行。除美国之外,瑞士、芬兰也采用此标准。

The standard of place of incorporation, also called the standard of applicable law, means that a legal person registered in that country under the law of that country is a resident taxpayer of that country and shall bear unlimited tax obligations to that country. All legal persons registered in that country, irrespective of the person whose investors are from, regardless of the country in which they are actually governed and regardless of the country in which their head office is based, are resident taxpayers of that country. Conversely, legal persons not registered in their home countries are non-resident taxpayers. The advantage of this standard is that the registration place of the general legal person is relatively certain and easy to identify, because once the place of registration of the legal person is determined, the place of registration of the legal person cannot be changed in principle without the consent of the legal person registration state and the procedure for change. However, since the standard of place of incorporation does not necessarily reflect the real place of activity of the legal person, the legal person is likely to leave the country of the place of registration and engage in business activities in other countries, and can be selected by means of the place of registration to avoid the tax jurisdiction of the state concerned. The United States is a typical country that adopts the standard of place of registration, and the recognition of the nationality and resident status of legal persons in the United States is also carried out only by the standard of place of registration. In addition, Switzerland and Finland also use this standard.

2. 实际管理与控制中心所在地标准

The Standards of the Location of the Actual Management and Control Center

实际管理与控制中心所在地标准,是以法人在一国境内是否设有管理与控制中心作为判定其是否具有该国居民身份的标准。法人的实际管理与控制中心是指法人重大经营决策和决定形成和作出的地点,主要是指法人的董事会或监事会所在地。此地点与法人的经营管理机构所在地有可能相同,也有可能不同。依据此标准,控制中心属于哪个国家,此法人就为哪国的居民纳税人,并对其承担无限纳税义务。在国际上,采用此标准的国家主要有英国、德国、希腊等。我国也采用了此标准。我国《企业所得税法》第2条规定:"居民企业,是指依法在中国境内成立,或者依照外国(地区)法律成立但实际管理机构在中国境内的企业。"以实际管理与控制中心标准认定法人的居住地具有理论上的合理性,但在实践中存在一定的弊端。由于各国对于如何认定实际管理与控制中心的标准不统一,纳税人能够通过改变决策地点实现逃避税的目的。

The standard of the location of the actual management and control center is whether the legal person has management and control in the territory of a country. The center serves as a criterion for determining its status as a resident of the country. The actual management and control center of a legal person refers to the place where the major business decisions and decisions of the legal person are formed and made, mainly referring to the seat of the board of directors or the board of supervisors of the legal person. This location may be the same or different from the location of the legal person's business administration. According to this standard, the corporation is a resident taxpayer of the country in which the control center is located, and bears unlimited tax liability to it. Internationally, the countries that adopt this standard are mainly the United Kingdom, Germany, Greece and so on. Our country has also adopted this standard. Article 2 of China's Enterprise Income Tax Law stipulates: "Resident enterprises are those established in China in accordance with the law, or established in accordance with the laws of foreign regions but with actual regulatory bodies in China." The standard of actual management and control center to determine the residence of legal persons has theoretical rationality, but in practice there are certain disadvantages. Because countries have different standards on how to identify the actual management and control center, taxpayers can avoid tax by changing the location of decision making.

3. 总机构所在地标准

The Standards of the Location of the Head Office

总机构所在地标准是指以法人的总机构所在地认定法人居民身份的标准。依据此标准，法人的总机构设在哪个国家，该法人就是哪个国家的居民纳税人，其向居住国承担无限纳税义务。法人总机构指的是负责管理和控制法人日常经营业务活动，统一核算法人盈亏的中心机构，如总公司、总部、总店、主要事务所等。总机构标准与实际管理与控制中心标准的区别在于，总机构强调的是法人经营管理机构的重要性，实际管理与控制中心强调的是法人权力决策中心的重要性。采用本标准的国家主要有中国和日本。日本所得税法意义上的本国法人，指的是在国内具有总店和主要事务所的法人。总机构标准的确定相对简单，但同样也存在法人通过改变总机构地点逃避税收的可能，因此采用此标准的国家通常在公司法中规定在本国设立的公司必须将其总机构设立在本国内，最典型的例子就是日本。

The standard of the location of the head office means the standard for determining the resident status of a legal person by the location of its general body. According to this standard, the general body of a legal person is located in which country, the legal person is the resident taxpayer of that country, which has unlimited tax obligations to the country of residence. The head office of a legal person refers to the central body responsible for managing and controlling the day-to-day business activities of a legal person and the unified accounting of the profits and losses of a legal person, such as the head office, headquarters, main office, etc. The difference between the general agency standard and the actual management and control center standard is that the head office emphasizes the importance of the legal person management organization, and the actual management and control center emphasizes the importance of the legal person decision-making center. The main countries that adopt this standard are China and Japan. A domestic legal person in the sense of Japan's income tax law refers to a legal person with a head office and a major office in Japan.

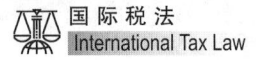

The determination of the head office standard is relatively simple, but there is also the possibility that legal persons evade taxes by changing the location of the head office, so that a state adopting this standard usually provides in the company law that companies incorporated domestically must establish their head office in the country, just like Japan.

第三节　国籍税收管辖权的行使
Section 3　Exercise of Nationality Tax Jurisdiction

国籍是指个人具有的属于某个国家公民或国民的法律身份,是一个人与某个国家固定的法律关系。同时,它也是指飞机、船舶等属于某个国家的隶属关系。国籍税收管辖权又可称为公民税收管辖权,它的行使及判定也可分为自然人与法人两方面内容。

Nationality means an individual's legal status as a citizen or national of a country, and is a fixed legal relationship between someone and a state. It also refers to the affiliation of aircraft and ships, etc., to a country. Nationality tax jurisdiction can also be called citizen tax jurisdiction, its exercise and determination can also be divided into natural and legal persons.

一　自然人国籍的确认
Confirmation of the Nationality of Natural Persons

一个国家在行使公民管辖权时,首先应确定纳税人是否具有本国公民身份。根据各国的国籍立法和实践,自然人取得一国国籍的方式主要有如下两种。

When a state exercises its civil jurisdiction, the first step is to determine whether the taxpayer has its national citizenship. According to the nationality legislation and practice of states, there are mainly two ways for natural persons acquire the nationality of a state.

(1) 因出生而取得国籍。因出生而取得国籍采用两种原则：出生地主义和血统主义。采用出生地主义的国家,不论父母双方是否拥有该国的国籍,孩子出生在该国即取得该国的国籍。采用血统主义的国家,则不论孩子出生地为何处,孩子的国籍必须随父母双方或一方的国籍。

(1) To get the nationality by birth. There are two principles for acquiring nationality by birth, i.e., place-of-birthism and descentism. In a country of place of birthism, the child acquires the nationality of the country if the child was born in that country, regardless of whether the parents have the nationality of that country or not. In countries where pedigree is adopted, the nationality of the child must be the nationality of either or both parents, regardless of the place of birth of the child.

（2）通过申请加入取得一国国籍。申请加入国籍也称入籍和继有国籍，是指外国人或无国籍的人，按照某一国家法律规定提出申请，经批准后取得该国国籍。继有国籍的取得方式很多，如因近亲属关系取得、因婚姻关系取得、因经济关系取得等。

(2) To get the nationality by applying for accession. The application for nationality is also called naturalization and successor nationality, which means an alien or stateless person who has obtained the nationality of that state upon approval in accordance with the law of a state. There are many ways to acquire nationality, such as through close relatives, marriage, economic relations, etc.

在行使国籍税收管辖权的国家，不论该自然人是否在该国境内居住，不论其是否在该国境内拥有居所，只要依据该国国籍法确认其为该国公民，自然人就是该国的纳税人，并负有无限的纳税义务。各国的国内法在自然人国籍认定上存在差异，可能会导致一个自然人拥有双重国籍或多重国籍的情况发生。当一个自然人同时拥有两国或多国国籍时，所属国籍国均可依据公民管辖权要求其履行纳税义务，则必然发生公民管辖权的冲突。因此，大多数国家普遍主张坚持"一人一籍"的国籍原则，即在一国公民合法取得别国国籍时，原国籍国应将其原有国籍取消或使之丧失，并且对于保留别国国籍的自然人不给予本国国籍。

In a state exercising the tax jurisdiction of nationality, no matter whether the natural person resides in that state or not, and no matter whether he or she has a residence in that state or not, the natural person is a taxpayer of that state, provided that he or she is recognized as a citizen of that state under the Nationality Act of that state. This may lead to a situation in which a natural person has dual or multiple nationality, owing to differences in the determination of the nationality of natural persons in the domestic laws of states. When a natural person has two or more nationalities at the same time, the states of nationality may all require him/her to perform his/her tax obligations in accordance with the jurisdiction of citizen, and there arises a conflict of civil jurisdiction. Thus, most states generally insist on the principle of "one person, one nationality", meaning when a citizen of a state legally acquires the nationality of another state, the state of origin should cancel its original nationality and not grant its nationality to natural persons who retain the nationality of another state.

公民税收管辖权单纯以自然人与国籍国之间存在国籍法律关系作为行使税收管辖权的依据，而不考虑其与国籍国之间是否存在实际的经济关系。依据公民与国家之间的国籍从属关系行使公民税收管辖权，主张对公民境内外的全部所得与财产征税，虽然在法律上有充分的依据并且认定标准也相对简单明了，但是随着经济的全球化、跨国公司的迅速发展，人员的跨国流动日益普遍和频繁，一国单纯以是否具有本国国籍为依据向公民主张承担无限纳税义务，缺乏经济上的合理性，容易与其他国家的税收管辖权发生冲突，并在实施上也存在一定困难。因此，目前世界上大部分的国家普遍适用居民管辖权，少数国家实行国籍税收管辖权，如美国、墨西哥、荷兰等。

A citizen's tax jurisdiction is based solely on the existence of a legal relationship of nationality between a natural person and a state as the basis for the exercise of tax jurisdiction, regardless of the existence of an actual economic relationship between him or her and the state of nationality.

Though it is legally justifiable to implement citizens' tax jurisdiction on the basis of nationality affiliation and claim tax liability on all income and property of citizens both within and outside the country, with relatively simple and clear criteria of determination, it is economically unreasonable for a country, with the rapid development of multinational corporations in a globalized economy and the increasingly common and frequent transnational mobility of people, to claim unlimited tax liability from its citizens solely on the basis of whether or not they have the nationality of their own country, which makes it easy to clash with the tax jurisdictions of other countries and poses certain difficulties in its implementation. Therefore, most countries currently adopt resident jurisdiction, and only a few countries have nationality tax jurisdiction, such as the United States, Mexico, the Netherlands, etc.

二、法人的国籍身份确认
Confirmation of the Nationality of a Legal Person

法人的国籍表明法人与特定国家之间的固定法律联系。关于法人国籍的认定，有以下几种学说。

The nationality of a legal person indicates a fixed legal link between a legal person and a particular state. With regard to the determination of the nationality of legal persons, there are several doctrines as below.

（1）注册登记地主义，又称准据法主义，即法人依照哪国法注册登记，其所在国国籍就是法人的国籍。

(1) Registration localism, also known as the doctrine of applicable law, that is, the nationality of a legal person is that of the state in accordance with whose law it is registered.

（2）设立地主义，即法人在一国内设立的公司为国内公司，在外国设立的公司即为外国公司。

(2) Establishmentism means that a company established by a legal person in a country is a domestic company, and a company established in a foreign country is a foreign company.

（3）国籍主义，即以法人资本控制者的国籍来确定法人的国籍。例如，公司总部所在地标准、公司主要办事机构所在地标准、公司主要营业地标准、公司实际管理地标准、章程指定住所标准等。

(3) Nationalsim means that the nationality of a legal person is determined by the nationality of the person who controls the capital of the legal person, such as the standard of the location of the company's headquarters, the standard of the location of the company's main office, the standard of the company's main place of business, the standard of the company's actual place of management, the standard of designated residence by association, etc.

（4）住所地主义，即法人的国籍由法人的住所地决定。

(4) Domicileism means that the nationality of a legal person is determined by its domicile.

（5）实际控制主义，即主张公司实际由哪国控制就为哪国国籍。

(5) Actual controlism, that is, it claims that the company is actually controlled by which

country belongs to the nationality of that country.

（6）复合标准说，即在公司国籍判断标准中兼采前述两种以上的学说，特别是兼采准据法主义和住所地主义两大标准来确定公司的国籍。

(6) The composite criterion is that the nationality of the company is determined by combining the above two or more theocrats in the criteria of the company's nationality judgement, in particular the two criteria of legalism and domicileism.

目前，多数国家在确定公司的身份时采用注册登记地主义，尤其是英美法系国家基本上采用这种标准。例如，美国法规定，根据美国任一州的法律注册成立的公司，就是美国公司，要向美国就其来源于世界范围的财产与所得纳税；非在美国注册成立的公司则为外国公司，仅就来源于美国境内的财产与所得向美国纳税。中国目前采用的是注册登记地主义确定法人国籍，凡依我国法律在我国境内登记成立的法人（无论其是否有外资成分），均为中国法人；凡依外国法律在外国登记成立的法人，均为外国法人。也有其他国家同时采用几种标准确立法人的国籍身份，如德国、日本等。

Nowadys, most countries use registration localism in determining the identity law of companies, especially in the United Kingdom and the United States. For example, US law requires companies registered under the laws of any US state to pay US taxes on property and income originating worldwide. Companies that are not registered in the United States are foreign companies that pay taxes to the United States only on property and income originating in the United States. At present, China adopts registrationism to determine the nationality of legal persons, and all legal persons registered in our territory in accordance with our laws (whether or not they have foreign capital components) are Chinese legal persons, and all legal persons registered in foreign countries under foreign laws are foreign legal persons. Other countries have also adopted several criteria to establish the nationality status of legal persons, such as Germany, Japan and so on.

关于公司等法人主体是否具有国籍，各国虽存在争议，但区分公司国籍仍有其法律和实践上的意义。法人同样存在国籍变动、双重国籍的问题，也需遵循"一人一籍"的国籍原则，并通过国际协商处理。在同时实行居民和公民税收管辖权的国家税法中，法人国籍与法人的居民身份的概念是同一的，两者适用于同样的法律原则或法律标准。比如，根据美国法律，确定法人国籍的标准也就是确定法人居民身份的标准。

Although there are some arguments among different countries as to whether legal persons have nationality or not, it is still of legal and practical significance to distinguish the nationality of companies. Legal persons also have the problem of change of nationality, dual nationality, which should be resolved through international consultations, following the promotion of "the one person, one nationality" principle. In national tax laws which exercise the tax jurisdiction of both residents and citizens, the concept of the nationality of the legal person and the resident status of the legal person is the same, and the same legal principles or legal standards are applied to both. For example, under US law, the criterion for determining the nationality of a legal person is also the criterion for determining the resident status of a legal person.

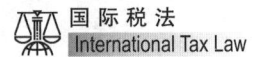

第四节 所得来源地税收管辖权的行使
Section 4 Exercise of Source Tax Jurisdiction

在国际税法领域,确认所得来源地是判断一个国家是否能够有效地行使所得来源地税收管辖权的基本前提。一个单一采用所得来源地税收管辖权的国家,在征税时不区分居民和非居民纳税人身份。而在所得来源地税收管辖权和居民税收管辖权并用的国家,居民纳税人取得的来源于境内和境外的财产与收入受到属人性质的税收管辖,国家税务机关可以行使居民或者国籍税收管辖权进行征税,而非居民纳税人则不受此限制,因此,所得来源地管辖权是针对非居民纳税人行使的征税权。即使非居民纳税人不在来源地国境内,非居民的所得和财产在非居民纳税人未向来源国履行纳税义务前是不被允许转移出境的,所以来源地国的属地税收管辖权实现是有保障的。与属人性质管辖权相比,属地性质的管辖权的实行方便了税务行政管理的划分,同时又使国际经济利益的分配合理化,所以其在国际税收上被认为是一条比较合理、合适的原则,为各个国家所接受,从而得到普遍采用。

In the field of international tax law, the recognition of the source of income is a fundamental prerequisite for determining whether a state can effectively exercise its tax jurisdiction of the source of income. A state that only uses the tax jurisdiction of the source of income does not distinguish between resident and non-resident taxpayers when taxing. In the country where the tax jurisdiction of the source of income and the tax jurisdiction of the residents are both used, the property and income obtained by the resident taxpayers from within and outside the territory are subject to tax jurisdiction of a personal nature, and the state tax authorities may exercise the tax jurisdiction of the residents or nationalities to collect taxes, while the non-resident taxpayers are not subject to such restrictions, so the jurisdiction of the source of income is the right to tax the non-resident taxpayers. Even if the non-resident taxpayer is not in the territory of the country of origin, the income and property of the non-resident taxpayer are not allowed to be transferred out of the country of origin between the non-resident taxpayers and the non-resident taxpayers who fail to perform their tax obligations to the country of origin, so the territory tax jurisdiction of the country of origin is guaranteed. Compared with the jurisdiction of human nature, the exercise of jurisdiction of the nature of the territory facilitates the division of tax administration and rationalizes the distribution of international economic benefits, so it is considered as a more reasonable and appropriate principle in international taxation, which is accepted by various countries, and thus widely adopted.

一、所得来源地的确认意义
The Confirmation of the Source of the income

行使来源地税收管辖权的重点在于如何确定纳税人是否拥有源于本国的所得与一般财产,因此,来源地的判定对于实行来源地管辖的国家具有重要意义。不仅如此,对于行使居民税收管辖权的国家而言,如何确定来源地也具有重要意义。

The exercise of tax jurisdiction at the place of origin focuses on determining whether the taxpayer has income derived from the country and general property, and the determination of the place of origin is therefore important for the state in which the jurisdiction of the source is exercised. Not only that, how to determine the source is also important for countries exercising residents' tax jurisdiction.

(1)一个国家在行使税收管辖权时,先是确定自然人或法人是否具有居民纳税人身份,然后是确定课税对象,其中的重要内容之一就是确认纳税人所得的来源地,即判定纳税人所得是来源于本国境内还是境外。因此,所得来源地的确认关系到一国能否对取得有关所得的非居民主张行使征税权。所得来源地是一国对非居民主张来源地税收管辖权的前提。

(1) In the exercise of tax jurisdiction, the first step is to determine whether a natural or legal person has the status of a resident taxpayer, followed by the determination of the object of taxation, one of the important elements of which is to confirm the source of the taxpayer's income, that is, to determine whether the taxpayer's income originated within or outside its territory. Therefore, the recognition of the source of the income relates to the power of a state to exercise the right to tax on non-residents. The source of income is a prerequisite for a state's tax jurisdiction over non-residents claiming the source.

(2)对于一国的税收居民而言,所得来源地的确认也具有重要意义。对于居民征税虽不分境内、境外所得,但由于各国税制的差异,不可避免地会产生重复征税的问题。在实践中,很多国家将纳税人的境外所得已纳税款从其全部应纳税款中扣除。所得来源地的确定有利于一国正确行使其税收管辖权,有利于不同国家间解决国际税务争端,有利于避免国际双重征税的发生。

(2) For a country's tax residents, the identification of the source of income is also important. Although the tax for residents does not regard domestic and foreign income, because of the differences in tax systems, the problem of double taxation arises inevitably. In practice, many countries take taxes paid on taxpayers' overseas earnings out of all taxes payable. The determination of the source of income is conducive to the correct exercise of a state's tax jurisdiction, the settlement of international tax disputes between different countries, and the avoidance of international double taxation.

(3)所得来源地的确定,方便一国税务机关判断所得来源是来自境内还是境外,以此在征税时赋予其不同的税收待遇,或者适用不同的课税规则。

(3) The determination of the source of income makes it convenient for a country's tax authorities to determine whether the source of income is from within or outside the country,

thereby granting it different tax treatment at the time of taxation or applying different taxation rules.

二、所得来源地的确认标准
Criteria for Confirmation of the Source of Income

从所得来源地税收管辖权的概念可知，征税国行使此种管辖权的依据在于确认纳税人的收入源于本国境内，因此，对所得来源地进行识别认定，关系到该项税收管辖权的具体实施，是研究实施所得来源地税收管辖权的重要内容。根据各国的所得税法，纳税人的所得种类一般可分为营业所得、劳务所得、投资所得和财产所得四类。以下主要介绍各国税法识别各类所得的来源地常用的标准。

The concept of tax jurisdiction from the place of origin of income is known to be based on the confirmed fact that the taxing state exercises such jurisdiction. Recognizing that the taxpayer's income originates within the territory of the country, the identification of the source of income relates to the specific implementation of the tax jurisdiction, which is an important part of the study and implementation of the tax jurisdiction of the source of income. According to the income tax law of each country, the types of income of taxpayers can generally be divided into four categories: business income, labor income, investment income and property income. The following mainly describes the common criteria used by national tax laws to identify the origin of various types of income.

（一）营业所得的来源地认定
Identification of the Source of the Proceeds of Business

营业所得，又称经营所得或营业利润，是指纳税人（自然人、法人）在某个固定场所从事各种工商经营性质的活动所取得的所得或利润，包括从事生产、采购、销售、服务等系列经营业务在内的一种综合经济活动所获得的所得。判断一笔所得是否属于纳税人的营业所得，要确定取得这项所得的经营活动是否属于纳税人的主要营业范围。例如，一家公司的主要经营活动是生产、销售产品，那么其营业所得是指生产、销售产品所获得的所得或利润，它对其他公司的投资取得的股息、利息则属于投资所得。而一家证券公司投资所得的股息、红利则属于该公司的营业所得。

Income from business, also known as operating income or operating profit, refers to the income or profit obtained by taxpayers (natural persons, legal persons) engaged in various industrial and commercial activities in a fixed place, including the income from a comprehensive economic activity, like production, procurement, sales, services and other series of business activities. To determine whether an income belongs to the taxpayer's business income, it is possible to determine whether the business activities for which the income is obtained fall within the main business scope of the taxpayer. For example, if a company's main business activity is the production and sale of products, its operating income refers to the income or profit from the production and sale of products, the dividends and interest earned on its investments in other companies are the income from investments. Dividends and bonuses from a securities company's investments belong to the company's operating income.

关于营业所得来源地的认定，各国税法通常都采用营业活动发生地原则，即以经营活动的发生地作为营业所得来源地。对于营业活动发生地，各国税法提出了不同的判定原则与标准。各国依据税收管辖权独立原则选择适用：

With regard to the determination of the place of origin of business income, national tax laws generally adopt the principle of the place of origin of business activities, i.e. the place of origin of business activities as the mark of the place of origin of business income. For the place where the business activities take place, different determination principles and standards are put forward in the tax laws of various countries. Each state chooses to apply the following rules on the basis of the principle of independence of tax jurisdiction:

（1）交易合同的签订地标准，即以交易双方缔结合同的地点作为营业活动的发生地；（2）生产所在地标准，以利润的来源地作为营业活动的发生地，该标准主要适用于制造业；（3）货物的交付地标准，以货物所有权转移的交货地点作为营业活动的发生地；（4）货款支付地标准，以货款支付的所在地作为营业活动的发生地；（5）营业机构所在地标准，以从事经营活动场所设立地作为营业活动的发生地。

(1) The standard of the place of conclusion of the transaction contract, i.e., the place where the contract is concluded is considered as the place of occurrence of business activities; (2) The standard of the place of production, i.e., the place of origin of profits is considered as the place of occurrence of business activities. This standard mainly applies to the manufacturing industry; (3) The standard of place of delivery of goods, i.e., the place of delivery and transfer of ownership of goods is considered as the place of business activities; (4) The place of payment for goods as the place of business activities; (5) The standard of the place of business, which is considered as the place of business activities.

除此之外，跨国营业所得来源地认定的标准十分复杂，这容易导致国际双重征税问题。为了防止国际双重征税，各国普遍采用常设机构原则对非居民纳税人的跨国营业所得进行征税。常设机构原则是指来源国仅对非居民纳税人通过设立在来源国境内的常设机构的活动所取得的营业所得征税。

Besides, the complexity of the criteria for determining the source of cross-border business income can easily lead to the problem of international double taxation. In order to prevent international double taxation, the principle of permanent establishment is generally used to tax on the transnational business income of non-resident taxpayers. The principle of permanent establishment means that the country of origin taxes only on the proceeds of business obtained by non-resident taxpayers through the activities of the permanent establishment in the country of origin.

（二）劳务所得来源地的认定
Determination of Source of Labour Services Income

劳务所得是指纳税人因对他人提供服务而获得的报酬。企业获得的劳务所得在国际税法上一般认定为营业所得。个人劳务所得可区分为独立劳务所得和非独立劳务所得两大类。独立劳务所得是指自由职业者以自己的名义从事某种专业性劳务或其他独立性活动所取得的报酬。其中,专业性劳务和独立性活动是指个人从事医师、律师、建筑师、会计师等专业性劳务以及个人独立从事科学、艺术、教育等活动。非独立劳务所得是指个人受雇于他人从事劳务工作而获得的工资薪金、津贴、资金等报酬。值得注意的是,个人独立从事工业或商业经营所获取的工商经营所得,在国际税法上一般不认为是劳务所得,而属于营业所得的范围。

Income from labor services is the compensation that taxpayers receive for providing services to others. The income from labor services obtained by an enterprise is generally recognized as business income in international tax law. The personal labor income is divided into two categories: independent labor income and non-independent labor income. Income from independent services refers to remuneration obtained for engaging in certain professional services or other independent activities in the name of the freelancer himself. Among them, professional labor service and independent activities refer to the individual labor as physicians, lawyers, architects, accountants and other professional services, as well as independent activities in science, art, education and other activities. Income from non-independent services refers to the salary, allowances, funds and other remuneration received by an individual who is employed by another person to perform labor work. It is worth noting that income obtained by individuals from independent industrial and commercial operations is generally not considered as income from labor services in international tax laws, but falls within the scope of business income.

由于劳务所得的类型不同,各国税法对于劳务所得来源地的确定,采用的标准不一,主要有劳务提供地标准、劳务所得支付地标准、劳务报酬支付人居住地标准以及停留时间标准。

Due to the different types of income from services, the tax laws of various countries adopt different standards for determining the source of income from services, the main criteria include the standard of the place of service supply, the standard of the place of payment of the income of labor services, the standard of residence of the payer of remuneration for labor services and the standard of the length of stay.

(1)劳务提供地标准是指纳税人在哪个国家提供劳务,由此获得的劳务报酬即为来源于哪个国家的所得,由该国先行使收入来源地管辖权征税。对于从事独立劳务的提供者,劳务提供地的判断主要根据其从事活动的固定基地设在哪个国家,而对于从事非独立劳务者而言,主要是根据其受雇提供劳务的地点,即其劳务行为发生在哪国,判定其劳务所得来源于哪国;(2)劳务所得支付地标准是指以支付劳务报酬的居民、固定机构、常设机构所在国为劳务所得的来源地国;(3)劳务报酬支付人居住地标准是指以支付劳务报酬的支付人的居住地所在国为劳务所得的来源地国;(4)停留时间标准是指以跨国劳务提供者在另一国境内因提供劳务而停留的时间连续或累计已达到一定的天数(一般为183天)为依据,来确定劳务所得的来源地。

(1) The standard of the place where the service is provided refers to the country in which the taxpayer provides the service, and the service remuneration obtained from it is the income from it, the country may first exercise the tax jurisdiction of the source of income. For the independent labor service provider, the judgment of the place where the labor service is provided mainly depends on

the country where the fixed base of his or her activities is located, while for the non-independent labor service provider, it mainly depends on the place where he or she is employed to provide the labor service, that is, the country where his or her labor service takes place, so as to determine the source of his or her labor service income. (2) The payment standard of labor income refers to the country where the residents, fixed institutions and permanent establishments paying labor remuneration is considered as the source state of labor income. (3) The standard of the place of residence of the payer of labor remuneration refers to the country where the payer of labor remuneration lives as the source country of labor income. (4) The standard of stay time is to determine the source of labor income based on the continuous or cumulative stay time of transnational labor service providers in another country (generally 183 days).

（三）投资所得的来源地认定
Determination of the Source of Investment Income

投资所得是指纳税人从事各种间接性投资活动所获得股息、红利、利息、特许权使用费和租金收益。投资所得又可称为纳税人的消极所得。投资者不直接参与企业的经营活动，而是通过提供资金、技术、权利而获得收益，投资所得都具有权利所得的性质。股息、红利是投资者因拥有股份、股权以及其他与股权相似的非债权性公司权利而取得的所得；利息是投资者凭借债权而取得的所得；特许权使用费是指因向他人提供专利权、商标权、商誉、经销权、专有技术等无形资产的使用权而取得的收益；租金是转让有形财产的使用权而产生的收益。

Investment income refers to dividends, bonuses, interest, royalties and rental income obtained by taxpayers in various indirect investment activities. The income from investment can also be called the negative income of the taxpayer. Investors are not directly involved in the business activities of the enterprise, but gain income through the financing, technology, rights. Investment income has the nature of rights. Dividends and bonuses are income obtained by investors from owning shares, equity and other non-debt company rights similar to equity, interest is earned by investors by virtue of creditor's rights, royalties are income from the provision of patent rights, trademark rights, goodwill, distribution rights, proprietary technology and other intangible assets to others, and rent is the proceeds from the transfer of the right to use tangible property.

当以上这些权利的提供者与使用者，即投资所得的取得者与支付者处在同一国家时，投资所得来源地很容易确定，但如果处在不同的国家，对所得来源地的确定就会产生很大的分歧。目前，世界各国对于确认各类投资所得来源地，主要采用的标准如下：

When the providers and users of these rights, i.e. if the recipient and payer of the proceeds of the investment, are in the same country, the source of the proceeds of the investment is easily identified. But if they are in different countries, the determination of the source of the proceeds can be highly divisive. At present, countries around the world have adopted the following criteria for identifying the sources of income from various types of investments:

（1）权利提供地标准，又称投资权利发生地原则，即将权利拥有人的居住地认定为所得的来源地。(2) 权利使用地标准，又称所得支付地标准，即以权利或资产的使用地或实际承担投资所得的义务人居住地为所得来源地。(3) 常设机构所在地标准，是指将常设机构的国内外的全部投资所得视为本国境内所得，其实质是按属人管辖权对常设机构的全部所得进行征税。

(1) The standard of the place where the right is provided, also known as the principle of the place where the right to invest occurs, identifies the place of residence of the owner of the right as the source of the income. (2) The standard of place of use of rights, also known as the criterion of place of payment of income, that is, the place of residence of the duty bearer using the right or asset, or who actually bears the investment income as the source of income. (3) The standard of the location of the permanent establishment, that is to regard all the investment income including overseas income of the permanent establishment as domestic income, the essence is to tax the permanent establishment on all incomes according to personnel tax jurisdiction.

（四）财产所得的来源地认定
Determination of the Source of Income

财产所得主要包括不动产所得和财产转让所得。不动产所得是指纳税人在不转让所有权的前提下，让渡不动产的收益权而取得的收益，即出租、使用不动产的所得。对于不动产所得，各国通常都以不动产的所在地或坐落地作为所得来源地。财产转让所得又称资本所得，是指转让动产和不动产所有权取得的所得。对不动产转让所得和不动产所得的认定标准是相同的，各国一般都以不动产的所在地或坐落地作为所得来源地。对于不动产以外其他财产的转让所得，各国主要以转让者的居住国或财产的实际销售地或成交地为来源国。

Income from property mainly includes income from immovable property and income from the transfer of property. Real estate income refers to the income obtained by the taxpayer by lying to the real estate on the condition that it does not transfer ownership, that is, the income from leasing and using it. In the area of immovable property income, states usually use the location or land of immovable property as the source of income. The income from the transfer of property, also known as the income from capital, refers to the income obtained from the transfer of ownership of movable and immovable property. The criteria for determining the proceeds of the transfer of immovable property and the income from immovable property are the same, and states generally use the location or land of immovable property as the source of the proceeds. Proceeds from the transfer of property other than immovable property are mainly derived from the transferor's country of residence or the actual place of sale or settlement of the property.

此外，根据财产的不同种类，还存在以下不同的处理方式。
Besides, depending on different types of property, there are different ways of dealing with it.

（1）转让或出售在非居住国的常设机构的营业所得，或从事个人独立劳务的固定基地的财产所得，通常以常设机构或固定基地的所在国作为财产所得来源国。(2) 关于转让股票、债券等所取得的收益，各国的做法各异，目前国际上普遍通行的有两个标准，一是认定转让者居民国为来源国；二是认定被转让股份、债券公司的所在国作为来源国。(3) 对于出售从事国际运输的船舶、飞机及附属于上述船舶、飞机的动产所取得的收入,按照国际惯例,一般应以这些所得所属企业的实际管理机构所在国为来源国。

(1) Proceeds from the transfer or sale of the proceeds of the operations of a permanent establishment in a non-resident state, or from the property of a fixed base engaged in independent labour for individuals, usually by the state in which the permanent establishment or fixed base is located, as the source of the proceeds of the property. (2) For transfer of stocks, bonds and other gains between different countries do it differently. The current two widely-accepted international standards are to identify the transferor's nationality as the country of origin and to identify the country of the company in which the shares or bonds are transferred as the country of origin. (3) In accordance with international practice, the country of origin shall be identified as the country where the actual administrative organization of the enterprise whose income derived from sale of ships and aircrafts engaged in international transport and movable property attached to such ships and aircrafts to which they belong.

第五节　财产所在地税收管辖权的行使
Section 5　Exercise of Property Location Tax Jurisdiction

财产所在地税收管辖权,是财产税方面一国基于财产或财产价值存在于一国境内的事实而主张行使的征税权。在财产所在地税收管辖权下,征税国主张征税的依据在于作为征税对象的财产或财产价值位于征税国境内的事实。征税国并不考虑纳税人的国籍和居民身份的归属情况。征税国仅就纳税人位于征税国境内的财产及财产价值进行征税,因此,纳税人承担的是一种有限的纳税义务。相对于所得来源地的判定,对各种财产或财产价值的所在地认定相对简单。在各国税法上,土地、房屋等不动产所在地基本都是以其实际坐落地为准,而对于各种动产,多数国家则以其实际存在的地点作为其所在地,船舶、飞机、汽车等交通运输工具则多以注册登记地为其所在地,由其注册登记地国家行使财产所在地税收管辖权。

The tax jurisdiction of the place where the property is located is that the property tax is based on the property or the value of the property that exists in the territory of a state. Under this jurisdiction, the taxing state claims the basis of tax on the fact that the property or the value of property exists in the territory of this state. The taxing state does not take into account the nationality of the taxpayer and the attribution of the resident status. The taxing state collects taxes only on the value of the property or property of the taxpayer located in the territory of the taxing state, and therefore the taxpayer has a limited tax liability. Compared with the determination of the source of the income, it is relatively simple to determine the location of the various properties and the value of the property. In national tax laws, the location of land, housing and other real estate is basically based on its actual location; As to movable properties, the location of which is determined in most countries by its actual location; the location of ships, aircrafts, automobiles and other means of transportation are mostly in accordance with their registered location, and its registered state is to exercise the tax jurisdiction.

学习思考题
Questions for Study

1. 什么是国家的税收管辖权？
   What is national tax jurisdiction?
2. 何谓居民税收管辖权？各国税法确定居民纳税人的主要标准具体有哪些？
   What is resident tax jurisdiction? What are the main standards for determining resident taxpayers in national tax laws?
3. 不同所得来源地认定的标准分别是什么？
   What are the standards for determining different sources of income?

第三章 CHAPTER III

个人所得税法
Individual Income Tax Law

第一节 个人所得税法概述
Section 1　Overview of Individual Income Tax Law

一、个人所得税法的概念与制度模式
Concept and Institutional Model of Individual Income Tax Law

（一）个人所得税法的概念
Concept of Individual Income Tax Law

个人所得税是指对个人（即自然人）在一定期间取得的各项应税所得所征收的一种税。

Individual (personal) income tax is a tax levied on the taxable income obtained by an individual (a natural person) during a certain period of time.

个人所得税法在概念上有广义和狭义之分。广义的个人所得税法是指调整征税机关与自然人（居民个人、非居民个人）之间在个人所得税的征纳与管理过程中所发生的社会关系的法律规范的总称，其中包括个人所得税法、个人所得税法实施条例，以及与个人所得税有关的法律规范。例如，税收征收管理法中涉及个人所得税的法律规范等。狭义的个人所得税法即指全国人大制定的单个税种的法律——《中华人民共和国个人所得税法》。

Individual income tax law can be defined broadly and narrowly. Broadly, personal income tax law refers to the general term of the legal norms that adjust the social relations between the tax collection authorities and natural persons (individual residents, non-residents) in the process of collecting and managing personal income tax, including the Personal Income Tax Law, the regulations on the implementation of the personal income tax law, and the legal norms related to personal income tax such as the related legal norms in the tax collection and administration law. Narrowly, personal income tax law refers to the personal tax law formulated by the National People's Congress, that is Individual Income Tax Law of the People's Republic of China, this book also calls it the Personal Income Tax Law.

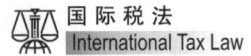

（二）个人所得税法的制度模式
Institutional Model of Individual Income Tax Law

个人所得税法的制度模式在国际上通常分为综合所得税制（一般所得税制）、分类所得税制（个别所得税制）、分类综合所得税制（混合所得税制）三种主要模式。

Internationally, there are mainly three types of institutional model for individual income tax law: comprehensive income tax system (general income tax system), classified income tax system (individual income tax system) and classified comprehensive income tax system (mixed income tax system).

1. 综合所得税制
Comprehensive Income Tax System

综合所得税制（一般所得税制），是将纳税人在一定期间内（通常是一个纳税年度）各种不同来源的所得综合起来，依法进行宽免或扣除后，对其余额依法计征的一种所得税制度。在此种税制下，纳税人一定时期的各类所得不分类别，由纳税人统一进行汇总申报，一般采用超额累进税率计算征税。其优点在于：（1）税基宽，能够综合反映纳税人实际的纳税能力，符合量能课税原则；（2）税基广泛，在一定程度上能够有效地保证国家获取足够的税收收入；（3）对纳税人的净所得采用累进税率，发挥税收的调节功能，调节纳税人之间所得的税负，促进税收公平的实现。其缺点在于：计税依据的确定较为复杂和困难，征税成本较高，不便实行源泉扣缴，税收逃避现象较为严重。综合所得税制通常在较为发达的国家实行。

The comprehensive income tax system (general income tax system) is an income tax system that combines the income of different sources of taxpayers over a certain period of time (usually a tax year) and, after relief or deduction according to law, the balance is calculated according to law. Under such a tax system, all kinds of income of taxpayers for a certain period of time, without being categorized, are declared in a unified summary, and the tax is generally calculated using the excess progressive tax rate. Its advantages include: (1) With a wide tax base, it can comprehensively reflect the actual tax ability of taxpayers, in line with the principle of taxability; (2) With a broad tax base, it can effectively ensure that the state obtains sufficient tax revenue to a certain extent; (3) By adopting a progressive tax rate for the net income of taxpayers, it plays the role of tax adjustment, adjusts the tax burden between taxpayers, and promotes the realization of tax fairness. The disadvantages are that the determination of tax basis is complex and difficult, with higher cost of taxation, inconvenience for source deduction, and more serious problem of tax evasion. Therefore, the comprehensive income tax system is usually adopted by developed countries.

2. 分类所得税制
Classified Income Tax System

分类所得税制（个别所得税制），是指依据所得来源的不同，依法将所得分为不同的类别，对不同种类的所得分别计征的所得税制度，对于税法中没有明确的所得类别不予课征。对不同性质的所得项目应适用不同的税率，纳税人分别承担轻重不同的税负。此种税制的优点在于：（1）对于特定的所得来源，比较容易掌握，有利于源泉课征，并且可减少汇算清缴的繁琐，节省税收成本；（2）按不同性质的所得，分别采用不同的税率，实行差别待遇。例如，对于工资薪金，这类需要付出辛勤劳动的所得，课税较轻。对于营业利润、股息、利息、租金等凭借财产投资而获得的所得，课税相对较重。分类所得税制的缺点在于：（1）征税范围有限，主要针对单项所得进行征税，不能持续取得较多的财政收入；（2）不能全面、综合地判断纳税人实际的纳税能力，不符合量能课税原则；（3）无法充分发挥累进税率调节社会财富的功能。因而分类所得税制通常在不发达国家和发展中国家实行。在2018年10月1日之前，我国个人所得税实行的是分类所得税制。

The classified income tax system (individual income tax system) refers to an income tax system in which income is divided into different categories according to different sources of income and different types of income are taxed separately according to law. Categories of income that are not specified in the tax law are not taxable. Different tax rates should be applied to income items of different nature, and taxpayers should bear different tax burdens respectively. The advantages of such a tax system include: (1) Easier to obtain the information of a specific source of income, it is conducive to the source deduction, reduces the red tape of final settlement, and therefore saves cost of taxation; (2) Different tax rates are applied according to the different nature of income, implementing the differential treatment. The taxes are lighter for incomes such as wages and salaries which require hard labor. The taxes are heavier for business profits, dividends, interest, rent, etc., which are obtained by virtue of property investment. The disadvantages of the classified income tax system are: (1) With limited scope of taxation, mainly for individual incomes, it cannot secure fiscal revenue on a sustainable basis; (2) It fails to fully and comprehensively judge the taxpayers' actual ability to pay taxes, which is not in line with the ability-to-pay principle of taxation; (3) It is unable to give full play to the function of progressive tax rates in adjusting social wealth. Thus, the classification of income tax system is usually implemented in underdeveloped countries and developing countries. It was adopted in China's personal tax system prior to October 1, 2018.

3.分类综合所得税制
Classified Comprehensive Income Tax System
分类综合所得税制（混合所得税制），是将分类所得税制和综合所得税制相结合的所得税制度。此种税制依法对纳税人不同类别的所得先按照各类所得的规则从所得来源扣缴，然后将纳税人在一个纳税年度中的各种所得综合进行年度汇算清缴。其优点在于：（1）此种税制既符合按支付能力课税的原则，对纳税人不同来源的收入实行综合计算征收，又符合差别对待的原则，对不同性质的收入实行区别对待，对所列举的特定收入项目按特定办法和税率课征；（2）由于稽征便利，有利于防止偷漏税。

The classified comprehensive income tax system (mixed income tax system) is a combination of the classified income tax system and the comprehensive income tax system. Under this system, the different types of income of taxpayers shall be withheld in accordance with the rules of various types of income from the source of income, and then an annual final settlement and payment will be carried out for the various income of the taxpayer in a tax year. Its advantages include: (1) It is in line with the ability-to-pay principle of taxation, that is to say, the income from different sources will be calculated and collected by a comprehensive method, while it is also in line with the principle of differential treatment, that is to say, different treatment is used for income of different nature and specific income items are taxed according to specific methods and rates; (2) The facilitated process of inspection and collection helps prevent tax evasion.

目前世界上几乎没有一个国家实行纯粹的综合所得税制或是分类所得税制。一般均为综合与分类的混合制。唯一的区别是有的国家以综合税制为主，有的国家以分类税制为主，两者所占的比重有所不同。我国现行《中华人民共和国个人所得税法》实行分类综合所得税制。

Currently almost no country in the world adopts a purely comprehensive or classified tax system. A mixture of the two systems is usually used. The only difference is that the comprehensive tax system plays a leading role in some countries while the classified system is dominant in other countries, with different proportion of the two. China's current Individual Income Tax Law implements a classified comprehensive income tax system.

（二）我国个人所得税法的历史沿革与最新发展
History and Latest Development of China's Personal Individual Tax Law

（一）我国个人所得税法的历史沿革
Historical Reform of China's Individual IncomeTax Law

1980年9月10日，第五届全国人大第三次会议通过并公布了我国第一部《中华人民共和国个人所得税法》。该法的适用对象主要是境外人员，包括华侨和港、澳、台同胞。至此，我国个人所得税法方始建立。

On September 10, 1980, the Third Session of the Fifth National People's Congress passed and promulgated China's first Individual Income Tax Law. The Law was mainly applicable to foreigners, including overseas Chinese and compatriots in Hong Kong, Macao and Taiwan. This was the beginning of the establishment of China's individual income tax law.

1993年10月31日，第八届全国人大常委会第四次会议审议通过《关于修改〈中华人民共和国个人所得税法〉的决定》。此次对《中华人民共和国个人所得税法》的修改是我国个人所得税法发展历史上的一次具有标志性的重大改革，象征着《中华人民共和国个人所得税法》立法进一步规范化、科学化和国际化。具体修改如下：

On October 31, 1993, the Fourth Session of the Standing Committee of the Eighth National People's Congress adopted the Decision on Revising the Individual Income Tax Law of the People's Republic of China. This revision of the Personal Income Tax Law is an iconic and important reform in the history of the development of China's individual income tax law, demonstrating the more standardized, scientific and international nature of China's personal income tax legislation . Specifically speaking, the revision includes the following aspects:

（1）"居民"概念的引入，扩大了纳税主体的范围。旧的《中华人民共和国个人所得税法》对纳税意义上的"居民"和"非居民"缺乏较为明确的界定，此次修改的《中华人民共和国个人所得税法》则按照国际惯例，采用了住所和居住时间两种标准，将纳税人分为居民和非居民。因此居住国和来源地国都能够更好地行使居民管辖权和所得来源地管辖权。

(1) The introduction of the concept of "resident" expanded the scope of taxpayers. The old Individual Income Tax Law lacked a clear definition of "residents" and "non-residents" in the sense of tax payment, while the revised Personal Income Tax Law adopted two criteria, domicile and residence time, whereby all taxpayers were divided into residents and non-residents. Both the country of residence and the country of origin were therefore enabled to better exercise the jurisdiction of the residents and the jurisdiction of the source of the proceeds.

（2）应税所得范围的拓宽。此次修改的《中华人民共和国个人所得税法》将旧的《中华人民共和国个人所得税法》的6个应税项目增列为11项。

(2) Widening of the scope of taxable income. In the revised Personal Income Tax Law, the previous six taxable items in the old Personal Income Tax Law were expanded to 11 ones.

（3）适用税率和减除费用的调整。在税率方面，对不同所得分别采用不同的比例税率和累进税率。在原有的5%~45%超额累进税率的中间增设了15%、25%和35%三级税率。对各项所得的费用扣除作了原则或具体规定。

(3) Adjustments to applicable tax rates and deductions. In terms of tax rates, different proportional rates and progressive rates were applied for different incomes. Three tax rates of 15%, 25% and 35% were added to the original 5%~45% excess progressive tax rates. The deductions for expenses earned were stipulated in principle or specifically.

（4）个人所得税计征方法的统一。旧的《中华人民共和国个人所得税法》实行分项征收，个人收入调节税是单项与综合征收相结合的模式。此次修改的《中华人民共和国个人所得税法》对计征方法实行分项扣除、分项定率和分项征收。

(4) The uniform method of personal income tax collection. The old Individual Income Tax Law adopted itemized collection, and the personal income adjustment tax was combination of individual and comprehensive collection. The revised Individual Income Tax Law introduced itemized deductions, itemized rates and itemized levies for the method of calculation.

（5）根据我国具体国情，适当增加了免税的相关内容。

(5) Stipulations about tax exemption were added in accordance with China's specific national conditions.

1999年8月30日，第九届全国人大常委会第十一次会议对《中华人民共和国个人所得税法》进行了第二次修改。其针对当时投资不足、消费疲软的经济特点取消了储蓄存款利息的免税待遇，并授权国务院确定对储蓄存款利息所得征收个人所得税的开征时间和征收办法。1999年9月30日，国务院颁布《对储蓄存款利息所得征收个人所得税的实施办法》，决定自1999年11月1日起恢复征收储蓄存款利息个人所得税，并对其适用20%的比例税率。

On August 30, 1999, the 11th Session of the Standing Committee of the Ninth National People's Congress made a second revision of the Personal Income Tax Law. In view of the economic backgrounds of insufficient investment and weak consumption at that time, the revision eliminated the tax exemption of interest on savings deposits, and authorized the State Council to determine the time and method regarding the income tax on interest earned on savings deposits. On September 30, 1999, the State Council promulgated the Implementation Measures for the Collection of Personal Income Tax on Interest Income from Savings Deposits, and decided to resume the collection of personal income tax on interest on savings deposits from November 1, 1999, with a proportional tax rate of 20%.

2005年10月27日，第十届全国人大常委会第十八次会议对《中华人民共和国个人所得税法》进行了第三次修改。具体修改如下：

On October 27, 2005, the 18th session of the Standing Committee of the 10th National People's Congress revised the Personal Income Tax Law for the third time. The specific changes are as follows:

（1）调整了"工资、薪金所得"的费用扣除标准，由每月800元提至每月1 600元。承包经营、出租经营所得的费用扣除标准，个体工商户业主、个人独资企业和合伙企业投资者的费用扣除标准，提至每月1 600元或每年19 200元。

(1) The expense deduction standard of "wage and salary income" was adjusted from 800 yuan per month to 1,600 yuan per month. The fee deduction standard for the income obtained from contracting or leasing operations, as well as the expense deduction standard for individual industrial and commercial owners, sole proprietorship and investors of partnerships was raised to 1,600 yuan per month or 19,200 yuan per year.

（2）扩大了纳税人自行申报的范围，个人所得超过国务院规定数额的和具有国务院规定的其他情形的纳税人需自行申报。

(2) The scope of self-declaration by taxpayers was expanded, and taxpayers with personal income exceeding the amount prescribed by the State Council and in other circumstances prescribed by the State Council were required to declare by themselves.

（3）增加了扣缴义务人实行全员全额扣缴申报的内容。

(3) Full withholding declaration of the withholding agents were required.

2007年6月29日，第十届全国人大常委会第二十八次会议对《中华人民共和国个人所得税法》进行了第四次修改。具体修改如下：

On June 29, 2007, the 28th Session of the Standing Committee of the 10th National People's Congress made the fourth revision to the Personal Income Tax Law. The specific changes are as follows:

将旧法第12条"对储蓄存款利息所得征收个人所得税的开征时间和征收办法由国务院规定"修改为"对储蓄存款利息所得开征、减征、停征个人所得税及其具体办法，由国务院规定"。由此扩大了国务院对个人所得税的征收范围的决定权力。随后，国务院决定自2007年8月15日起，将储蓄存款利息所得个人所得税的适用税率由20%调减为5%。之后，面对我国经济社会发展的新情况，为了增加个人的储蓄存款，国务院决定自2008年10月9日起，对储蓄存款利息所得暂免征收个人所得税。

Article 12 of the old Law, "The time and method for the collection of personal income tax on interest earned on savings deposits shall be amended by the State Council" was revised to: "The introduction, reduction and suspension of personal income tax on interest earned on savings deposits and their specific measures shall be prescribed by the State Council." This expanded the State Council's power to collect personal income tax. Subsequently, the State Council decided to reduce the applicable personal income tax rate on interest earned on savings deposits from 20% to 5% from August 15, 2007. Later, in order to increase the individual's savings deposits with the new situation of China's economic and social development, the State Council decided that from October 9, 2008, the interest income from savings deposits would be exempted from personal income tax.

2007年12月29日，第十届全国人大常委会第三十一次会议对《中华人民共和国个人所得税法》进行了第五次修改，并于2008年3月1日起开始实施。此次修订主要调整了"工资、薪金所得"项目费用扣除标准，从每月1 600元提至每月2 000元。承包经营、出租经营所得的费用扣除标准从每月1 600元提至每月2 000元。

On December 29, 2007, the 31st Session of the Standing Committee of the 10th National People's Congress made the fifth revision of the Personal Income Tax Law, which came into effect on March 1, 2008. The revision mainly adjusted the fee deduction standard of "wages and salaries income" from 1,600 yuan per month to 2,000 yuan per month. The standard deduction for expenses from contract operation and rental operation was raised from 1,600 yuan per month to 2,000 yuan per month.

2011年6月30日，第十一届全国人大常委会第二十一次会议对《中华人民共和国个人所得税法》进行了第六次修改，并于2011年9月1日起开始实施。具体修改如下：

On June 30, 2011, at the 21st session of the Standing Committee of the 11th National People's Congress, the Personal Income Tax Law was revised for the sixth time and came into effect on September 1, 2011. The specific changes are as follows:

（1）调整了"工资、薪金所得"项目费用扣除标准，从每月2 000元提至每月3 500元。承包经营、出租经营所得的费用扣除标准从每月2 000元提至每月3 500元。

(1) The expenses deduction standard of "wages and salaries income" was raised from 2,000 yuan per month to 3,500 yuan per month. The standard deduction for expenses from contract operation and rental operation is raised from 2,000 yuan per month to 3,500 yuan per month.

（2）将"工资、薪金所得"项目适用的税率，由旧法中的9级超额累进税率改为7级超额累进税率，并修改了"个体工商户生产、经营所得和对企事业单位的承包、承租经营所得"项目的累进级距。

(2) The applicable tax rates for "wages and salaries income" was changed from the 9-level excess progressive tax rates in the old law to the 7-level excess progressive tax rates, and the progressive level distances of the "income from individual industrial and commercial households' production and operation, and income from the contracting and leasing operations of enterprises and institutions" were revised.

（3）将部分税款缴入国库的期限从7日延长至15日。

(3) The period for the payment of part of the tax to the Treasury has been extended from 7 to 15 days.

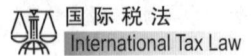

（二）我国个人所得税法的最新发展
Latest Development of China's Individual Income Tax Law

2018年8月31日，十三届全国人大常委会第五次会议对《中华人民共和国个人所得税法》进行了第七次修改，并于2019年1月1日起开始实施。具体修改如下：

On August 31, 2018, the Fifth Session of the Standing Committee of the 13th National People's Congress made the seventh amendment to the Personal Income Tax Law, which will come into effect on January 1, 2019. The specific changes are as follows:

（1）明确了居民个人和非居民个人的概念，修改了居民纳税人判定的标准，增加了纳税年度的条款，与国际惯例保持一致。如将居民纳税人判定的时间标准，由"在中国境内居住累计满一年"，改为"一个纳税年度内在中国境内居住累计满一百八十三天"；将非居民个人确定为在中国境内无住所又不居住，或者无住所而一个纳税年度内在中国境内居住累计不满183天的个人，并规定了纳税年度是自公历1月1日起至12月31日止。

(1) The concepts of individual residents and non-residents have been clarified, the criteria for the determination of resident taxpayers have been revised, the provisions of the tax year have been added, and consistency with international practice has been achieved. For example, the time standard determined by the resident taxpayer is changed from "accumulated residence in China for one year" to "cumulative residence in China for 183 days in a tax year". Non-resident individuals are defined as individuals who have no domicile in China and no residence, or who have no domicile and have a cumulative residence in China for less than 183 days in a tax year, and provide that the tax year is from January 1 to December 31 in the solar calendar.

（2）简并所得项目，由旧法的11个所得项目变为9项；确定了综合所得范围，删除了旧法第2条的最后一款，进一步落实了税收法定原则。最新的个人所得税法依据个税改革的要求，结合目前我国的税收征管能力与实际的配套措施，修改了第2条，将工资薪金、劳务报酬、稿酬和特许权使用费4项劳动性所得（以下称为"综合所得"）纳入综合征税范围，适用统一的超额累进税率，居民个人按年合并计算个人所得税，非居民个人按月或者按次分项计算个人所得税；将"个体工商户的生产、经营所得"调整为"经营所得"，不再保留"对企事业单位的承包经营、承租经营所得"，该项所得根据具体情况，分别并入综合所得或者经营所得。对经营所得，利息、股息、红利所得，财产租赁所得，财产转让所得，偶然所得以及其他所得，仍采用分类征税方式，按照规定分别计算个人所得税。

(2) The items obtained were changed from 11 items of income under the old law to 9 items, the scope of comprehensive income was established, the last paragraph of article 2 of the old law was deleted, and the statutory principles of taxation were further implemented. In accordance with the requirements of personal tax reform and combined with the current tax collection and management capacity and actual supporting measures in China, Article 2 of the Individual Income Tax Law was revised to include four labor income (hereafter referred to as "comprehensive income") of wages and salaries, remuneration for services and royalties into the comprehensive tax scope, applying a unified excess progressive tax rate. Individual residents calculate personal income tax on an annual basis, and individual non-residents calculate

personal income tax on a monthly or sub-item basis. "Income from individual industrial and commercial households' production and operation" was adjusted to "operating income" and "income from the contracting and leasing operations of enterprises and institutions" was integrated into the comprehensive income or the operating income respectively according to the specific circumstances. Income from operations, interest, dividends, bonuses, property lease income, property transfer income, incidental income and other income were still to be taxed by classification, and personal income tax was calculated separately in accordance with the provisions.

（3）优化调整税率结构，扩大了较低档税率级距。综合所得适用税率：拉长3%、10%、20%税率级距，相应缩小25%税率级距，维持30%、35%、45%税率级距不变。经营所得适用税率：维持5%~35%税率不变，大幅拉长各级税率级距。

(3) Optimize and adjust the tax rate structure and expand the lower tax rate range. As for the applicable tax rates for comprehensive income, the tax rate ranges at 3%, 10% and 20% have been lengthened, correspondingly reducing the tax rate range to 25%, while the tax rate ranges at 30%, 35%, 45% remained unchanged. As for the applicable tax rate for operating income, the tax rates of 5%~35% have not changed and the tax rate ranges at all levels have been significantly lengthened.

（4）完善扣除模式，提高综合所得基本减除费用标准，新增专项附加扣除。

(4) Improve the deduction model, improve the standard of basic deduction of expenses for comprehensive income, and add special additional deductions.

新的《中华人民共和国个人所得税法》综合所得基本减除费用标准调整至6万元/年（5 000元/月）。此项标准对于在中国境内无住所而在中国境内取得工资、薪金所得的纳税人和在中国境内有住所而在中国境外取得工资、薪金所得的纳税人统一适用，不再保留原来专门的附加减除费用（1 300元/月）。对专项扣除未作修订，继续执行，如个人基本养老保险、基本医疗保险、失业保险、住房公积金等专项扣除项目以及依法确定的其他扣除项目。新增了专项附加扣除相关条款，包括子女教育支出、继续教育支出、大病医疗支出、住房贷款利息和住房租金、赡养老人、3岁以下婴幼儿照护专项附加扣除。

The new Personal Income Tax Law adjusts the basic deduction fee standard to 60,000 yuan/year (5,000 yuan/month). This standard applies uniformly to taxpayers who have no domicile in China and who have obtained wages and salaries in China, and to taxpayers who have domicile in China and who have obtained wages and salaries outside China, and no longer retain the original special additional deduction fee (1,300 yuan/month). The special deductions have not been revised and shall continue to be implemented, including special deduction items such as personal basic old-age insurance, basic medical insurance, unemployment insurance, housing provident fund and other deduction items as determined in accordance with the law. Special additional deductions have been added, including special additional deductions for children's education expenses, continuing education expenses, medical expenses for major diseases, interest on housing loans and housing rent, supporting the Elderly, care of infants and children under 3 years of age.

（5）增加反避税条款，维护国家税收权益。此次新《中华人民共和国个人所得税法》还增加了反避税条款，目的是堵塞税收漏洞，防止个人运用各种手段逃避个税。为了堵塞税收漏洞，维护国家税收权益，参照企业所得税法有关反避税规定，针对个人不按独立交易原则转让财产、在境外避税地避税、实施不合理商业安排获取不当税收利益等避税行为，赋予税务机关按合理方法进行纳税调整的权力。规定税务机关作出纳税调整，需要补征税款的，应当补征税款，并依法加收利息。

(5) To add anti-avoidance provisions to safeguard the state's tax rights and interests. The new Personal Income Tax Law also adds anti-avoidance provisions aiming at closing tax loopholes and preventing individuals from using various means to avoid tax. In order to close tax loopholes and safeguard the state's tax rights and interests, the tax authorities are given the power to adjust their taxes in accordance with reasonable methods for tax avoidance, such as the transfer of property by individuals in accordance with the principle of independent transactions, tax avoidance in offshore tax havens, and the implementation of unreasonable business arrangements to obtain improper tax benefits. If the tax authorities make tax adjustments that require the imposition of additional taxes, the additional taxes shall be imposed and interest shall be added in accordance with the law.

（6）改革税收征管制度。为保障个人所得税改革的顺利实施，新个人所得税法还进一步健全了与个人所得税改革相适应的税收征管制度，如引入纳税人识别码制度、明确纳税人信息共享机制等。

(6) Reform the tax collection and management system. In order to ensure the smooth implementation of the personal income tax reform, the new Individual Income Tax Law has further improved the corresponding tax collection and management code, such as introducing the taxpayer identification number system and clarifying the taxpayer information sharing mechanism.

第二节　个人所得税法的具体规定
Section 2　Specific Provisions of Individual Income Tax Law

一、纳税人
Taxpayers

自20世纪60年代以来，国家征收个人所得税是按照居民税收管辖权和来源地税收管辖权行使权力的。我国个人所得税的纳税人是在中国境内有住所取得所得的人，以及在中国境内无住所而从中国境内取得所得的个人。根据国际惯例，我国《个人所得税法》采用了住所和居住时间两个标准,明确了"居民"的概念,并将个人所得税的纳税人分为居民个人和非居民个人。

Since the 1960s, the state has exercised its right to collect personal income tax in accordance with the jurisdiction of residents' tax and the jurisdiction of source tax. The taxpayers of personal income tax in China are those who have obtained income from their residence in China. According to international practice, China's Personal Income Tax Law adopts the two criteria of domicile and residence time, defines the concept of "resident" and divides the taxpayers of personal income tax into individual residents and non-residents.

(一)居民个人
Resident Individual

在中国境内有住所,或者无住所而一个纳税年度内在中国境内居住累计满183天的个人,为居民个人。居民个人从中国境内和境外取得的所得,依法缴纳个人所得税。居民个人承担无限纳税义务。

An individual who has a domicile in China, or who has no domicile and has lived in China for a cumulative period of 183 days in a tax year, is a resident. Income obtained by individual residents from within and outside China shall be subject to personal income tax in accordance with the law. Individual residents are liable for unlimited tax payments.

居民个人的认定标准包括:(1)住所标准:在我国境内有住所的人,即因户籍、家庭、经济利益关系在我国境内习惯性居住(判定纳税人是居民或是非居民个人的法律意义上的标准,不是指实际居住或在某一特定时期内的居住);(2)时间标准:在我国境内居住累计满183天。

The criteria for the identification of individual residents include: (1) the standard of domicile: the time standard for persons with domiciles in China, i.e., those who habitually reside in China because of household registration, family and economic interests (the criteria for determining whether the taxpayer is a resident or a non-resident in the legal sense, not the actual residence or residence within a certain period of time); (2) the standard of time: the cumulative total of 183 days of residence in our country.

我国《个人所得税法实施条例》规定的例外情形,即在我国境内无住所的个人,在我国境内居住累计满183天的年度连续不满6年的,经向主管税务机关备案,其来源于我国境外且由境外单位或者个人支付的所得,免予缴纳个人所得税;在我国境内居住累计满183天的任一年度中有一次离境超过30天的,其在中国境内居住累计满183天的年度的连续年限重新起算。

The exceptions stipulated in the Regulations on the Implementation of China's Personal Income Tax Law, that is, individuals without domiciles in China who have lived in China for a cumulative period of 183 days for less than six consecutive years shall be exempted from paying personal income tax upon filing with the competent tax authorities for income derived from outside China and paid by foreign units or individuals. Where the taxpayer has left China for 30 days or more in a single trip in any of the years in which he or she has stayed for a total of 183

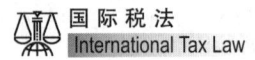

days or more in China, the starting time of the specified consecutive years in which he or she has stayed for a total of 183 days or more in China shall be recounted.

(二)非居民个人
Non-resident Individual

在中国境内无住所又不居住,或者无住所而一个纳税年度内在中国境内居住累计不满183天的个人,为非居民个人。非居民个人仅就其从中国境内取得的所得,依法缴纳个人所得税。非居民个人承担有限纳税义务。

An individual who has no domicile or residence in China, or who has no domicile but has lived in China for a cumulative period of less than 183 days in a tax year, is a non-resident individual. Non-resident individuals pay personal income tax in accordance with the law only on the income they obtain from within China. Non-resident individuals are liable for limited tax payments.

《中华人民共和国个人所得税法》依据所得来源地税收管辖权,确定以下自然人为非居民纳税人:(1)在我国境内无住所又不居住在我国的自然人;(2)在我国境内无住所而居住在我国境内不满183天的自然人。

China's Personal Income Tax Law, on the basis of the tax jurisdiction of the source of income, stipulates that the following natural persons are non-resident taxpayers: (1) Natural persons who have no domicile and do not reside in China; (2) natural person who has no domicile in China but has lived in China for less than 183 days.

另外,在中国境内无住所的个人,在一个纳税年度内在中国境内居住累计不超过90天的,其来源于中国境内的所得,由境外雇主支付并且不由该雇主在中国境内的机构、场所负担的部分,免予缴纳个人所得税。

In addition, an individual without a domicile in China who has resided in China for a cumulative period of not more than 90 days in a tax year shall be exempted from personal income tax if he or she has income derived from the territory of China and is paid by an overseas employer and is not borne by the employer's institutions or places in China.

二、征税对象
Object of Taxation

我国《个人所得税法》将个人所得税分为境内所得和境外所得。所称从中国境内和境外取得的所得,分别是指来源于中国境内的所得和来源于中国境外的所得。

China's Personal Income Tax Law divides personal income tax into domestic income and overseas income. The "income obtained from within and outside China" refers to income derived from China and income derived from outside China, respectively.

《个人所得税法实施条例》规定,除国务院财政、税务主管部门另有规定外,下列所得,不论支付地点是否在中国境内,均为来源于中国境内的所得:(1)因任职、受雇、履约等在中国境内提供劳务取得的所得;(2)将财产出租给承租人在中国境内使用而取得的所得;(3)许可各种特许权在中国境内使用而取得的所得;(4)转让中国境内的不动产等财产或者在中国境内转让其他财产取得的所得;(5)从中国境内企业、事业单位、其他组织以及居民个人取得的利息、股息、红利所得。

The Regulations on the Implementation of the Individual Income Tax Law stipulate that, unless otherwise provided by the competent department of finance and taxation under the State Council, the following income, whether or not the place of payment is within the territory of China, shall be considered as income from the territory of China: (1) income derived from the provision of services within the territory of China, such as employment, engagement and performance; (2) income from the rental of property to the lessee for use in China; (3) income from permitting the use of various concessions in China; (4) proceeds from the transfer of real estate and other property in China or transfer of other property within China; and (5) income from interest, dividends and bonuses obtained from enterprises, institutions, other organizations and individual residents in China.

《中华人民共和国个人所得税法》明确规定了9项个人所得的范围。

China's Personal Income Tax Law clearly defines the scope of nine items of personal income.

(1)工资、薪金所得,是指个人因任职或者受雇取得的工资、薪金、奖金、年终加薪、劳动分红、津贴、补贴以及与任职或者受雇有关的其他所得。

(1) Income from wages and salaries refers to wages, salaries, bonuses, year-end salary increases, labor dividends, allowances, subsidies and other income related to employment of an individual as a result of his or her employment.

(2)劳务报酬所得,是指个人从事劳务取得的所得,包括从事设计、装潢、安装、制图、化验、测试、医疗、法律、会计、咨询、讲学、翻译、审稿、书画、雕刻、影视、录音、录像、演出、表演、广告、展览、技术服务、介绍服务、经纪服务、代办服务以及其他劳务取得的所得。

(2) Income from remuneration for labor services refers to income obtained by individuals engaged in labor services, including from design, decoration, installation, drawing, testing, medical treatment, law, accounting, consulting, lectures, translation, review, painting, sculpture, film and television, audio recording, video, performance, advertising, exhibition, technical services, referral services, brokerage services, agency services and other services.

(3)稿酬所得,是指个人因其作品以图书、报刊等形式出版、发表而取得的所得。

(3) The income from manuscript remuneration refers to the income obtained by an individual as a result of the publication of his works in the form of books, newspapers and periodicals, etc.

(4)特许权使用费所得,是指个人提供专利权、商标权、著作权、非专利技术以及其他特许权的使用权取得的所得;提供著作权的使用权取得的所得,不包括稿酬所得。

(4) The income from royalties refers to the income obtained by an individual from the provision of patent rights, trademark rights, copyrights, non-patented technologies and other royalties.

(5)经营所得,是指:① 个体工商户从事生产、经营活动取得的所得,个人独资企业投资人、合伙企业的个人合伙人来源于境内注册的个人独资企业、合伙企业生产、经营的所得;

② 个人依法从事办学、医疗、咨询以及其他有偿服务活动取得的所得；③ 个人对企业、事业单位承包经营、承租经营以及转包、转租取得的所得；④ 个人从事其他生产、经营活动取得的所得。

(5) Income from business means: (i) income obtained by individual industrial and commercial households engaged in production and business activities, income derived from the production and operation of a sole proprietorship enterprise or partnership enterprise registered in China; (ii) income obtained by an individual engaged in running a school, medical treatment, consulting and other paid service activities in accordance with the law; (iii) Income derived from contracting, leasing, subcontracting and subletting by individuals to enterprises and institutions; (iv) income derived from other business activities.

其中，居民个人取得的(1)—(4)项所得称为综合所得，按纳税年度合并计算个人所得税；非居民个人取得(1)—(4)项所得，按月或者按次分项计算个人所得税。纳税人取得其他5项所得，依照法律规定分别计算个人所得税。

Among them, (1)—(4) income obtained by individual residents is referred to as comprehensive income, and personal income tax is calculated on a consolidated basis according to the tax year, while (1)—(4) income obtained by non-resident individuals is calculated on a monthly or sub-item basis. Taxpayers who obtain the other 5 items of income shall be calculated separately in accordance with the law.

个人所得的形式，包括现金、实物、有价证券和其他形式的经济利益；所得为实物的，应当按照取得的凭证上注明的价格计算应纳税所得额，无凭证的实物或者凭证上所注明的价格明显偏低的，参照市场价格核定应纳税所得额；所得为有价证券的，根据票面价格和市场价格核定应纳税所得额；所得为其他形式的经济利益的，参照市场价格核定应纳税所得额。

The form of individual income includes cash, physical, marketable securities and other forms of economic benefits. If the income is in kind, the taxable income shall be calculated according to the price indicated on the obtained documents, and if the price indicated on the unsealed physical or voucher is significantly lower, the taxable income shall be approved by reference to the market price. If the proceeds are in the form of marketable securities, the taxable income is authorized on the basis of the face price and market price. If the proceeds are in other forms of economic benefits, the taxable income is authorized with reference to the market price.

三、税率

Tax Rate

个人所得税税率是个人所得税应纳税额与应纳税所得额之间的比例。个人所得税根据综合所得和其他不同的征税项目，分别规定了不同的税率（表3-1）。

The personal income tax rate is the ratio between the taxable amount of individual income tax and the taxable income. Individual income tax rates are based on consolidated income and other different tax items (table 3-1).

表3-1 个人所得税税率表(总览)
Table 3-1 Individual Income Tax Rates(Overview)

税 率 rates	适 用 情 况 application Situation
3%~45% 七级超额累进税率 rates ranging from 3% to 45%	综合所得(工资、薪金所得;劳务报酬所得;稿酬所得;特许使用费所得) comprehensive income
5%~35% 五级累进税率 rates ranging from 5% to 35%	经营所得 business income
20% 比例税率 flat rate of 20%	财产租赁所得、财产转让所得、利息股息红利所得、偶然所得 income from author's remuneration

(1)综合所得,适用7级超额累进税率,最低为3%,最高至45%(表3-2)。

(1) Comprehensive income is subject to a progressive tax rate of 7 levels of excess, with a minimum of 3% and a maximum of 45% (table 3-2).

表3-2 个人所得税税率(综合所得适用)
Table 3-2 Personal Income Tax Rate(Comprehensive Income)

级 数 grade	全年应纳税所得额 whole year taxable income	税率 tax rate
1	不超过36 000元的 income of 36,000 yuan or less	3%
2	超过36 000元至144 000元的部分 that part of income in excess of 36,000 to 144,000 yuan	10%
3	超过144 000元至300 000元的部分 that part of income in excess of 144,000 to 300,000 yuan	20%
4	超过300 000元至420 000元的部分 that part of income in excess of 300,000 to 420,000 yuan	25%
5	超过420 000元至660 000元的部分 that part of income in excess of 420,000 to 660,000 yuan	30%
6	超过660 000元至960 000元的部分 that part of income in excess of 660,000 to 960,000 yuan	35%
7	超过960 000元的部分 that part of income in excess of 960,000 yuan	45%

注:非居民个人取得工资、薪金所得,劳务报酬所得,稿酬所得和特许权使用费所得,依照本表按月换算后计算应纳税额。
Tips: Income from wages, salaries, remuneration for services, remuneration for manuscripts and royalties earned by individual non-residents shall be calculated in accordance with the monthly conversion of the taxable amount in accordance with this table.

(2)经营所得,适用5级超额累进税率,最低为5%,最高至35%(表3-3)。

(2) Operating income is subject to a progressive tax rate of 5 levels of excess, with a

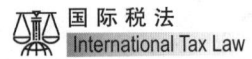

minimum of 5% and a maximum of 35% (table 3-3).

表3-3 个人所得税税率（经营所得适用）
Table 3-3　Individual Income Tax Rate
(Applicable to Income from Production or Business Operation)

级　数 grade	全年应纳税所得额 annual taxable income amount	税率 tax rate
1	不超过30 000元的 income of 30,000 yuan or less	5%
2	超过30 000元至90 000元的部分 that part of income in excess of 30,000 to 90,000 yuan	10%
3	超过90 000元至300 000元的部分 that part of income in excess of 90,000 to 300,000 yuan	20%
4	超过300 000元至500 000元的部分 that part of income in excess of 300,000 to 500,000 yuan	30%
5	超过500 000元的部分 that part of income in excess of 500,000 yuan	35%

（3）利息、股息、红利所得，财产租赁所得，财产转让所得和偶然所得，适用比例税率，税率为20%。

(3) A proportional tax rate of 20% applies to interest, dividend and bonus income, property rental income, property transfer income and incidental income.

（四）应纳税所得额的计算
Calculation of Taxable Income

个人所得税的计税依据是应纳税所得额，需要强调的是应纳税所得额并不等同于收入总额。

Personal income tax is based on taxable income, and it should be emphasized that taxable income is not equivalent to total income.

（一）居民个人取得综合所得的应纳税所得额
The Taxable Income Earned by Individual Residents on Comprehensive Income

居民个人的综合所得，以一个纳税年度的收入总额减除费用60 000元以及专项扣除、专项附加扣除和依法确定的其他扣除后的余额，为应纳税所得额。计算公式为：

The comprehensive income of individual residents shall be the amount of taxable income with the total income of one tax year minus the expenses of 60,000 yuan and the balance after special deductions, special additional deductions and other deductions determined in accordance with the law. The formula is:

居民个人的综合所得的应纳税所得额＝一个纳税年度的收入总额-60 000元-专项扣除-专项附加扣除-依法确定的其他扣除

the amount of taxable income from the comprehensive income of individual residents = the total income of a tax year － 60,000 yuan － special deduction － special additional deduction － other deductions determined according to law

居民个人取得的劳务报酬所得、稿酬所得、特许权使用费所得以收入减去20%的费用后的余额为收入额。稿酬所得的收入额减按70%计算。劳务报酬所得、稿酬所得、特许权使用费所得，属于一次性收入的，以取得该项收入为一次；属于同一项目连续性收入的，以一个月内取得的收入为一次。计算公式为：

For income from remuneration for services obtained by individual residents, income from remuneration for manuscripts, and income from royalties shall be the amount of income after income minus 20% of the expenses. Income from remuneration is calculated by 70%. Income from remuneration for services, remuneration for manuscripts and royalties shall be a one-time income, with the income obtained once, and income obtained once within one month for continuous income for the same project. The formula is:

居民个人的劳务报酬所得的收入额＝每次收入×（1－20%）

income from the remuneration of individual residents for their services = per income × (1－20%)

居民个人的稿酬所得的收入额＝每次收入×（1－20%）×70%

income from the remuneration of individual residents × (1－20%) × 70%

居民个人的特许权使用费所得的收入额＝每次收入×（1－20%）

income from royalties earned by individual residents = per income × (1－20%)

专项扣除，包括居民个人按照国家规定的范围和标准缴纳的基本养老保险、基本医疗保险、失业保险等社会保险费和住房公积金等。

Special deductions, including basic old-age insurance, basic medical insurance, unemployment insurance and other social insurance premiums and housing provident funds paid by individual residents in accordance with the scope and standards stipulated by the state.

专项附加扣除，包括子女教育、继续教育、大病医疗、住房贷款利息或者住房租金、赡养老人、3岁以下婴幼儿照护支出，扣除的具体范围、标准和实施步骤由国务院在2018年颁布的《个人所得税专项附加扣除暂行办法》中进一步规定。

Special additional deductions, including expenses such as children's education, continuing education, medical care for major illnesses, interest on housing loans or housing rent and support for the elderly, care of infants and children under 3 years of age. shall be further stipulated in the Interim Measures for Special Additional Deductions for Personal Income Tax promulgated by the State Council in 2018.

依法确定的其他扣除，包括个人缴付符合国家规定的企业年金、职业年金，个人购买符合国家规定的商业健康保险、税收递延型商业养老保险的支出，以及国务院规定可以扣除的其他项目。

Other deductions determined in accordance with the law include the payment by an individual of enterprise annuity or occupational annuity in accordance with the provisions of the state, the purchase by an individual of expenditure in accordance with the provisions of the state for commercial health insurance, tax deferred commercial old-age insurance, and other items that may be deducted as prescribed by the State Council.

上述专项扣除、专项附加扣除和依法确定的其他扣除,以居民个人一个纳税年度的应纳税所得额为限额;一个纳税年度扣除不完的,不结转以后年度扣除。

The above-mentioned special deductions, special additional deductions and other deductions determined in accordance with the law shall be limited to the amount of taxable income of an individual resident in a tax year. If the deduction is not completed in one tax year, the deduction shall not be carried forward to future years.

(二)非居民个人的工资、薪金所得、劳务报酬所得、稿酬所得、特许权使用费所得的应纳税所得额

Taxable Income from Wages, Salary Income, Remuneration for Services, Remuneration for Manuscripts and Royalties for Non-residents

非居民个人的工资、薪金所得,以每月收入额减除费用5 000元后的余额为应纳税所得额;劳务报酬所得、稿酬所得、特许权使用费所得,以每次收入额为应纳税所得额。

Income from wages and salaries of non-residents shall be taxable income with the balance of the monthly income deducting expenses of 5,000 yuan, and the income from remuneration for services, remuneration for manuscripts and royalties shall be taxable income for each income amount.

与居民个人相同,非居民个人取得的劳务报酬所得、稿酬所得、特许权使用费所得以收入减除20%的费用后的余额为收入额。稿酬所得的收入额减按70%计算。劳务报酬所得、稿酬所得、特许权使用费所得,属于一次性收入的,以取得该项收入为一次;属于同一项目连续性收入的,以一个月内取得的收入为一次。计算公式为:

Same as for individual residents, the income from remuneration for services, remuneration from manuscripts and royalties obtained by individual non-residents shall be the amount of income after income minus 20% of the expenses. Income from remuneration is reduced by 70%. Income from remuneration for services, remuneration for manuscripts and royalties shall be a one-time income, with the income obtained once, and income obtained once within one month for continuous income for the same project. The formula is as follows:

非居民个人的工资、薪金所得的应纳税所得额=每月收入额−5 000元

taxable income from wages and salaries of non-resident individuals = monthly income − 5,000 yuan

非居民个人的劳务报酬所得的应纳税所得额=每次收入额×(1−20%)

taxable income from labour remuneration of non-resident individuals = amount of income per time × (1−20%)

非居民个人的稿酬所得的应纳税所得额=每次收入额×（1−20%）×70%

taxable income from the remuneration of non-resident individuals = amount of income per time × (1−20%) × 70%

非居民个人的特许权使用费所得的应纳税所得额=每次收入额×（1−20%）

taxable income from royalties earned by non-resident individuals = amount of income per time × (1−20%)

（三）经营所得的应纳税所得额
Taxable Income from Operating Income

经营所得，以每一纳税年度的收入总额减除成本、费用以及损失后的余额，为应纳税所得额。取得经营所得的个人，没有综合所得的，计算其每一纳税年度的应纳税所得额时，应当减除费用60 000元、专项扣除、专项附加扣除以及依法确定的其他扣除。专项附加扣除在办理汇算清缴时减除。计算公式为：

Income from operations shall be taxable income in terms of the total amount of income in each tax year less costs, expenses and the balance after loss. Where an individual who has obtained income from business operations does not have comprehensive income, he shall, when calculating the amount of his taxable income for each tax year, deduct the expenses of 60,000 yuan, special deductions, special additional deductions and other deductions determined in accordance with the law. Special additional deductions shall be made in the final settlement and payment. The formula is as follows:

经营所得的应纳税所得额=每一纳税年度的收入总额−成本−费用−损失

taxable income from operating income = total income − cost − expense − loss for each tax year

（四）财产租赁所得的应纳税所得额
The Taxable Income from the Lease of Property

财产租赁所得，每次收入不超过4 000元的，减除费用800元；4 000元以上的，减除20%的费用，其余额为应纳税所得额。财产租赁所得，以一个月内取得的收入为一次。计算公式为：

Income from property lease shall be reduced by 800 yuan per income not exceeding 4,000 yuan, and if the cost of 4,000 yuan or more is reduced by 20%, the balance shall be taxable income. Income from the lease of property shall be earned once within one month. The formula is as follows:

不超过4 000元的财产租赁所得的应纳税所得额=每次收入−800元

taxable income from property leases not exceeding 4,000 yuan ＝ per income − 800 yuan

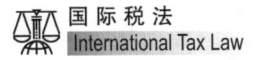

超过4 000元的财产租赁所得的应纳税所得额＝每次收入×（1−20%）

taxable income from property leases of more than 4,000 yuan = per income × (1−20%)

（五）财产转让所得的应纳税所得额
The Taxable Income from the Transfer of Property

财产转让所得，以转让财产的收入额减除财产原值和合理费用后的余额，为应纳税所得额。具体公式为：

Income from the transfer of property shall be taxable income by subtracting the balance of the original value and reasonable expenses of the property from the amount of income from the transfer of property. The formula is as follows:

财产转让所得的应纳税所得额＝收入额−财产原值−合理费用

Taxable income from the transfer of property−amount of income−original value of property−reasonable expenses.

（六）利息、股息、红利所得和偶然所得的应纳税所得额
The Taxable Income from Interest, Dividends, Bonuses and Incidental Income

利息、股息、红利所得和偶然所得，以每次收入额为应纳税所得额。利息、股息、红利所得，以支付利息、股息、红利时取得的收入为一次。偶然所得，以每次取得该项收入为一次。

For income from interest, dividend, bonus and contingent income, the taxable income shall be the amount of each income. The income from interest, dividend and bonus shall be the income obtained when the interest, dividend and bonus are paid. In case of accidental income, it shall be regarded as one time.

除上述扣除以外，个人将其所得对教育、扶贫、济困等公益慈善事业进行捐赠，捐赠额未超过纳税人申报的应纳税所得额30%的部分，可以从其应纳税所得额中扣除；同时，国务院如规定对公益慈善事业捐赠实行全额税前扣除的，从其规定。

In addition to the above deductions, individuals who donate their income to public welfare charities such as education, poverty alleviation and relief shall be deducted from their taxable income if the amount of the donation does not exceed 30% of the taxable income declared by the taxpayer. Meanwhile, follow the requirements by the State Council if it demands the full-amount pre-tax deduction for donations to the public welfare and charitable purposes.

五、应纳税额的计算
Calculation of the Taxable Amount

根据我国的实际情况，本着有利于防止税款流失和便于征管的原则，个人所得税除对工资、薪金所得、劳务报酬所得、稿酬所得、特许权使用费所得综合征收以外，采取对其他所得分项扣除、分项定率、分项征收的计征办法。居民个人从中国境内和境外取得的综合所得、经营所得，应当分别合并计算应纳税额；从中国境内和境外取得的其他所得，应当分别单独

计算应纳税额。

According to the actual circumstances in our country, in line with the principle of preventing the loss of tax and facilitating the collection and administration, personal income tax shall be levied on the deduction, sub-rate and item-by-item collection of wages, salary income, labor remuneration income, manuscript remuneration income and royalties income. The comprehensive income and operating income obtained by individual residents from within and outside China shall be calculated separately and the taxable amount shall be calculated separately, and other income obtained from China and abroad shall be calculated separately.

(一) 居民个人综合所得的应纳税额
The Taxable Amount of the Resident's Personal Comprehensive Income

居民个人综合所得的全年应纳税额=(全年收入额-60 000元-专项扣除-专项附加扣除-其他扣除)×适用税率-速算扣除数

the annual taxable amount of the resident's personal comprehensive income = (the annual income amount − 60,000 yuan − special deduction − special additional deduction − other deduction) × the applicable tax rate − the quick calculation deduction

(二) 非居民个人取得工资、薪金所得,劳务报酬所得,稿酬所得和特许权使用费所得的应纳税额
The Taxable Amount of Income from Wages, Salaries, Remuneration for Services, Remuneration for Manuscripts and Royalties Earned by Individuals Who are Not Residents

非居民个人取得工资、薪金所得,劳务报酬所得,稿酬所得和特许权使用费所得按月或者按次分项计算个人所得税,具体如下:

Income from wages, salaries, remuneration for services, remuneration for manuscripts and royalties obtained by individual non-residents shall be calculated on a monthly or sub-item basis, as follows:

工资、薪金所得的应纳税额=(每月收入额-5 000元)×适用税率-速算扣除数

the taxable amount of salary and salary income = (monthly income amount −5,000 yuan) × applicable tax rate − quick calculation deduction

劳务报酬所得的应纳税额=收入额×(1-20%)×适用税率-速算扣除数

taxable amount of income from remuneration for services = amount of income × (1−20%) × applicable tax rate − quick calculation deduction

特许权使用费所得的应纳税额=收入额×(1-20%)×适用税率-速算扣除数

taxable amount of royalties income = income × (1−20%) × applicable tax rate − quick calculation deduction

稿酬所得的应纳税额=收入额×(1−20%)×70%×适用税率−速算扣除数

the taxable amount of the remuneration income = the amount of income × (1−20%) × 70% × the applicable tax rate − the quick calculation deduction

(三) 经营所得的应纳税额
The Taxable Amount of the Operating Income

经营所得的应纳税额=全年应纳税所得额×适用税率−速算扣除数
　　　　　　　　=(全年收入总额−成本、费用及损失)×适用税率−速算扣除数

the taxable amount of the operating income = the amount of taxable income for the whole year × the applicable tax rate − the quick calculation deduction
= (total annual revenue − costs, expenses and losses) × applicable tax rate − quick calculation deduction

(四) 财产租赁所得的应纳税额
The Taxable Amount of the Income from the Lease of Property

财产租赁所得(每次收入不超过4 000元)的应纳税额=(每次所得收入−800元)×20%

taxable amount of property lease income (not more than 4,000 yuan per income) − (income per income − 800 yuan per income) × 20%

财产租赁所得(每次收入超过4 000元)的应纳税额=每次所得收入×(1−20%)×20%

taxable amount of property lease income (more than 4,000 yuan per income) = income per income × (1−20%) × 20%

(五) 财产转让所得的应纳税额
The Taxable Amount of Income from the Transfer of Property

财产转让所得的应纳税额=(收入额−财产原值−合理费用)×20%

taxable amount of income from property transfer = (income − original value of property − reasonable expenses) × 20%

(六) 利息、股息、红利所得的应纳税额
The Taxable Amount of Interest, Dividends and Bonuses

利息、股息、红利所得的应纳税额=每次收入额×20%

taxable amount of interest, dividends, bonuses = amount of income per time × 20%

(七) 偶然所得的应纳税额
The Taxable Amount of the Incidental Income

偶然所得的应纳税额=每次收入额×20%

taxable amount of incidental income = amount of income per time × 20%

六 税收优惠
Tax Benefits

（一）个人所得税的减免
Individual Income Tax Relief

对个人所得税的减免有直接减免和间接减免两种方式。我国个人所得税采取前一种方式，具体内容如下。

There are direct and indirect ways to reduce personal income tax. China's personal income tax relief takes the former approach, and the specific content is as follows.

1. 个人所得税的免征

Exemption from Personal Income Tax

《中华人民共和国个人所得税法》第4条规定下列各项个人所得，免征个人所得税：

Article 4 of China's Personal Income Tax Law stipulates that the following personal income shall be exempted from personal income tax:

（1）省级人民政府、国务院部委和中国人民解放军军以上单位，以及外国组织、国际组织颁发的科学、教育、技术、文化、卫生、体育、环境保护等方面的奖金；

(1) prizes awarded by provincial people's governments, ministries under the State Council and units above the level of major military command of the Chinese People's Liberation Army, as well as by foreign organizations and international organizations, for science, education, technology, culture, health, sports and environmental protection;

（2）国债和国家发行的金融债券利息；

(2) interest on government bonds and financial bonds issued by the state;

（3）按照国家统一规定发给的补贴、津贴；

(3) subsidies and allowances issued in accordance with the unified provisions of the state;

（4）福利费、抚恤金、救济金；

(4) welfare expenses, pensions and benefits;

（5）保险赔款；

(5) insurance compensation;

（6）军人的转业费、复员费、退役金；

(6) military severance pay, demobilization pay and retirement fee of the military personnel;

（7）按照国家统一规定发给干部、职工的安家费、退职费、基本养老金或者退休费、离休费、离休生活补助费；

(7) the payment of home, retirement, basic pension or retirement expenses, leave expenses and living allowances to cadres and workers in accordance with the unified provisions of the state;

（8）依照有关法律规定应予免税的各国驻华使馆、领事馆的外交代表、领事官员和其他人员的所得；

(8) the income of diplomatic representatives, consular officials and other personnel of

embassies and consulates in China who are exempt from tax in accordance with the relevant laws;

（9）中国政府参加的国际公约、签订的协议中规定免税的所得；

(9) income exempt from tax exemption stipulated in international conventions and agreements to which the Chinese Government is a party;

（10）国务院规定的其他免税所得。

(10) other tax-exempt income as prescribed by the State Council.

前款第十项免税规定，由国务院报全国人民代表大会常务委员会备案。

The 10th tax exemption provision of the previous paragraph shall be reported by the State Council to the Standing Committee of the National People's Congress for the record.

2. 个人所得税的减征

A Reduction in Personal Income Tax

《中华人民共和国个人所得税法》明确规定有下列情形之一的，可以减征个人所得税，具体幅度和期限，由省、自治区、直辖市人民政府规定，并报同级人民代表大会常务委员会备案：

China's personal Income Tax Law clearly stipulates that individual income tax may be reduced if there are any of the following circumstances, the specific range and duration of which shall be prescribed by the people's governments of the provinces, autonomous regions and municipalities directly under the Central Government and reported to the Standing Committee of the People's Congress at the same level for the record:

（1）残疾、孤老人员和烈属的所得；

(1) the income of the disabled, the elderly and the martyr's dependents;

（2）因自然灾害遭受重大损失的。

(2) suffered heavy losses as a result of natural disasters.

国务院可以规定其他减税情形，报全国人民代表大会常务委员会备案。

The State Council may prescribe other tax reductions and report them to the Standing Committee of the National People's Congress for the record.

（二）个人所得税的抵免

Personal Income Tax Credit

个人所得税的抵免是避免重复征税的重要措施之一。

Personal income tax credit is one of the important measures to avoid double taxation.

《中华人民共和国个人所得税法》规定，居民个人从中国境外取得的所得，可以从其应纳税额中抵免已在境外缴纳的个人所得税税额，但抵免额不得超过该纳税人境外所得依照本法规定计算的应纳税额。

China's Personal Income Tax Law stipulates that income obtained by an individual resident from outside China may be credited from his or her taxable amount to the amount of personal income tax paid abroad, provided that the amount of credit does not exceed the taxable amount calculated by the taxpayer's overseas income in accordance with the provisions of this Law.

《个人所得税法实施条例》规定,除国务院财政、税务主管部门另有规定外,来源于中国境外一个国家(地区)的综合所得抵免限额、经营所得抵免限额以及其他所得抵免限额之和,为来源于该国家(地区)所得的抵免限额。

The Regulations on the Implementation of the Personal Income Tax Law stipulate that, unless otherwise provided by the competent department of finance and taxation under the State Council, the total income credit limit, the operating income credit limit and other income credit limits from a country outside China shall be the credit limits derived from that country.

居民个人在中国境外一个国家(地区)实际已经缴纳的个人所得税税额,低于依照前款规定计算出的来源于该国家(地区)所得的抵免限额的,应当在中国缴纳差额部分的税款;超过来源于该国家(地区)所得的抵免限额的,其超过部分不得在本纳税年度的应纳税额中抵免,但是可以在以后纳税年度来源于该国家(地区)所得的抵免限额的余额中补扣。补扣期限最长不得超过五年。

If the amount of individual income tax actually paid by a resident individual in a country (region) outside China is less than the credit limit for income derived from that country (region) calculated in accordance with the preceding paragraph, the resident individual shall pay the difference in China; if the amount exceeds the credit limit for income derived from that country (region), the exceeding amount shall not be credited against the tax payable for the current tax year, but can be deducted from the balance of the credit limit for income derived from that country (region) for the subsequent tax years. However, the excess shall not be deducted from the taxable amount of the current tax year, but can be deducted from the balance of the credit limit of the country (region) in the subsequent tax year. The maximum period for making up the credit shall not exceed five years.

居民个人申请抵免已在境外缴纳的个人所得税税额,应当提供境外税务机关出具的税款所属年度的有关纳税凭证。

When an individual resident requests a credit for the amount of personal income tax paid abroad, he or she shall provide the relevant tax certificate for the year to which the tax is issued by the overseas tax authority.

七、特别纳税调整

Special Tax Adjustment

《中华人民共和国个人所得税法》第8条规定,有下列情形之一的,税务机关有权按照合理方法进行纳税调整:

Article 8 of the Personal Income Tax Law stipulates that the tax authorities shall have the power to make tax adjustments in accordance with reasonable methods in one of the following cases:

(1) 个人与其关联方之间的业务往来不符合独立交易原则而减少本人或者其关联方应纳税额,且无正当理由;

(1) The business dealings between an individual and his or her related parties do not conform to the principle of independent transactions and reduce the taxable amount of himself or

herself or his or her related parties without justification;

（2）居民个人控制的，或者居民个人和居民企业共同控制的设立在实际税负明显偏低的国家（地区）的企业，无合理经营需要，对应当归属于居民个人的利润不作分配或者减少分配；

(2) An enterprise established in a country (region) under the control of individual residents, or jointly controlled by individual residents and resident enterprises, shall not allocate or reduce the distribution of profits that should be attributed to individual residents without reasonable business needs.

（3）个人实施其他不具有合理商业目的的安排而获取不当税收利益。

(3) An individual obtains improper tax benefits by implementing other arrangements that do not have a reasonable business purpose.

税务机关依照前款规定作出纳税调整，需要补征税款的，应当补征税款，并依法加收利息。

Where a tax authority makes tax adjustments in accordance with the provisions of the previous paragraph and needs to make up the tax payment, it shall make up the tax payment and add interest in accordance with the law.

八、征收管理
Administration of Tax Collection

（一）自行纳税申报
Self-tax Return

自行申报纳税是指纳税人自行在税法规定的期限向税务机关申报取得的应税所得项目和数额，如实填写个人所得税的纳税申报表，并按照税法规定计算应纳税额，据此缴纳个人所得税。纳税人可以采用远程办税端、邮寄等方式申报，也可以直接到主管税务机关申报。《中华人民共和国个人所得税法》第9条规定，个人所得税以所得人为纳税人。

Self-reporting of tax means that taxpayers themselves report to the tax authorities within the time limit stipulated in the tax law the items and amounts of taxable income obtained, fill out the tax return of personal income tax truthfully, and calculate the taxable amount in accordance with the provisions of the tax law, according to which personal income tax is paid. Taxpayers may file by remote tax office, mail, etc., or directly to the competent tax authorities. Article 9 of China's Personal Income Tax Law stipulates that the income tax shall be paid by the earner.

《中华人民共和国个人所得税法》第10条规定，有下列情形之一的，纳税人应当依法办理纳税申报：

Article 10 of the Personal Income Tax Law stipulates that taxpayers shall file tax returns in accordance with the law if one of the following circumstances occurs:

（1）取得综合所得需要办理汇算清缴；

(1) to obtain the comprehensive income, it is necessary to handle settlement and payment;

（2）取得应税所得没有扣缴义务人；

(2) no withholding duty payer for obtaining taxable income;

（3）取得应税所得，扣缴义务人未扣缴税款；

(3) to obtain taxable income, the withholding obligation has not withheld the tax;

（4）取得境外所得；

(4) obtaining overseas income;

（5）因移居境外注销中国户籍；

(5) canceling Chinese household registration due to emigration;

（6）非居民个人在中国境内从两处以上取得工资、薪金所得；

(6) income from wages and salaries obtained by non-resident individuals from more than two places within the territory of China;

（7）国务院规定的其他情形。

(7) other circumstances as prescribed by the State Council.

扣缴义务人应当按照国家规定办理全员全额扣缴申报，并向纳税人提供其个人所得和已扣缴税款等信息。

The withholding agent shall, in accordance with the provisions of the state, handle the full withholding declaration and provide the taxpayer with information such as his or her personal income and withheld tax.

据此，国家税务总局于2018年12月13日发布了《关于个人所得税自行纳税申报有关问题的公告》，对个人所得税自行纳税申报的内容、方法、期限、地点等作了更加细致的规定。

Accordingly, on December 13, 2018, the State Administration of Taxation issued the Notice on Issues Related to Personal Income Tax Self-Tax Return, which made more detailed provisions on the content, method, duration and location of individual income tax self-tax return.

1. 取得综合所得需要办理汇算清缴的纳税申报

Tax Returns for which Final Settlement and Payment are Required for Obtaining Comprehensive Income

要获得综合收益，需要提交结汇纳税申报表。

To obtain comprehensive income, it is necessary to file a tax return for the settlement and payment.

取得综合所得需要办理汇算清缴的情形包括：（1）从两处以上取得综合所得，且综合所得年收入额减除专项扣除的余额超过6万元；（2）取得劳务报酬所得、稿酬所得、特许权使用费所得中一项或者多项所得，且综合所得年收入额减除专项扣除的余额超过6万元；（3）纳税年度内预缴税额低于应纳税额；（4）纳税人申请退税。

The circumstances in which the comprehensive income needs to be processed for settlement include: (1) the comprehensive income is obtained from more than two places, and the balance of the annual income of the comprehensive income minus the special deduction exceeds 60,000 yuan; (2) Obtaining one or more of the income from remuneration for labor, remuneration for manuscripts, or royalties, and the balance of the annual income from comprehensive income minus special deductions exceeds 60,000 yuan; (3) the amount of prepaid tax is lower than the amount of tax payable for the taxable year; and (4) the taxpayer applies for a tax refund.

需要办理汇算清缴的纳税人,应当在取得所得的次年3月1日至6月30日内,向任职、受雇单位所在地主管税务机关办理纳税申报,并报送《个人所得税年度自行纳税申报表》。纳税人有两处以上任职、受雇单位的,选择向其中一处任职、受雇单位所在地主管税务机关办理纳税申报;纳税人没有任职、受雇单位的,向户籍所在地或经常居住地主管税务机关办理纳税申报。

Taxpayers who need to handle the final settlement and payment shall, within the period from March 1 to June 30 of the following year, file their tax returns with the competent tax authorities in the places where they are employed, and file their own tax returns for the individual income tax year. If a taxpayer has more than two employment units, he or she shall choose to file a tax return with the competent tax authority at the place where one of the units is located. If the taxpayer is not employed, he or she shall file a tax return with the competent tax authority at the place where he or she is domicile or resided.

纳税人办理综合所得汇算清缴,应当准备与收入、专项扣除、专项附加扣除、依法确定的其他扣除、捐赠、享受税收优惠等相关的资料,并按规定留存备查或报送。

Taxpayers shall prepare information related to income, special deductions, special additional deductions, other deductions determined in accordance with the law, donations, enjoying tax benefits, etc. for the settlement of the consolidated income, and shall keep them for inspection or reporting in accordance with the provisions.

2. 取得经营所得的纳税申报

Obtain a Tax Return on Operating Income

税法对经营所得没有规定扣缴义务人。纳税人取得经营所得,按年计算个人所得税,由纳税人在月度或季度终了后15日内,向经营管理所在地主管税务机关办理预缴纳税申报。在取得所得的次年3月31日前,向经营管理所在地主管税务机关办理汇算清缴;从两处以上取得经营所得的,选择向其中一处经营管理所在地主管税务机关办理年度汇总申报。

The tax law does not provide for withholding of income from business. Taxpayers who obtain business income shall calculate personal income tax on an annual basis, and the taxpayer shall, within 15 days after the end of the monthly or quarterly period, file a pre-payment tax return with the competent tax authority at the place where the operation and management is located. Before March 31 of the year in which the income is obtained, the final settlement and payment shall be made to the competent tax authority at the place where the operation and management is located, and if the income from the operation is obtained from more than two places, the competent tax authority at the place where the operation and management is located shall be selected to make an annual summary declaration.

3. 取得应税所得,扣缴义务人未扣缴税款的纳税申报

To Obtain Taxable Income, Withhold the Tax Return of the Non-withholding of Tax by the Withholding Obligation

纳税人取得应税所得,扣缴义务人未扣缴税款的,应当区别以下情形办理纳税申报:

(1) 居民个人取得综合所得的,按照综合所得汇算清缴的规定办理;(2) 非居民个人取得工资、薪金所得,劳务报酬所得,稿酬所得,特许权使用费所得的,应当在取得所得的次年6月30日前,向扣缴义务人所在地主管税务机关办理纳税申报。有两个以上扣缴义务人均未扣缴税款的,选择向其中一处扣缴义务人所在地主管税务机关办理纳税申报。非居民个人在次年6月30日前离境(临时离境除外)的,应当在离境前办理纳税申报。(3) 纳税人取得利息、股息、红利所得,财产租赁所得,财产转让所得和偶然所得的,应当在取得所得的次年6月30日前,按相关规定向主管税务机关办理纳税申报。税务机关通知限期缴纳的,纳税人应当按照期限缴纳税款。

Where a taxpayer obtains taxable income and the withholding of tax by the withholding obligation is not withheld, the tax declaration shall be handled in a different way: (1) if an individual resident obtains comprehensive income, it shall be handled in accordance with the provisions of the settlement of the comprehensive income; (2) Individual non-resident who earn wages, salaries income, remuneration for services, remuneration for manuscripts, royalties shall file tax returns with the competent tax authority in the place where the withholding agents are located before June 30 of the year following the year in which the income is earned, if each of the two or more withholding obligations has not withheld tax, he or she shall choose to file a tax return with the competent tax authority in the place where one of the withholding obligations is located. If an individual non-resident leaves the country before June 30 of the following year (except for temporary departure), he or she shall file a tax return before leaving the country. (3) If a taxpayer obtains interest, dividends or dividends, income from leasing property, income from the transfer of property and incidental income, he shall file a tax return with the competent tax authority in accordance with the relevant provisions before June 30 of the following year. If the tax authority notifies the tax authorities of the payment within the time limit, the taxpayer shall pay the tax in accordance with the time limit.

4. 取得境外所得的纳税申报

Obtain a Tax Return for Overseas Income

居民个人从中国境外取得所得的,应当在取得所得的次年3月1日至6月30日内,向中国境内任职、受雇单位所在地主管税务机关办理纳税申报;在中国境内没有任职、受雇单位的,向户籍所在地或中国境内经常居住地主管税务机关办理纳税申报;户籍所在地与中国境内经常居住地不一致的,选择其中一地主管税务机关办理纳税申报;在中国境内没有户籍的,向中国境内经常居住地主管税务机关办理纳税申报。

If an individual resident obtains income from outside China, he or she shall, within the next year from March 1 to June 30 of the year in which he obtained the income, file a tax return with the competent tax authority in the territory of China where he or she is employed. If not employed in China, he or she shall apply for tax declaration to the tax authority in charge of the place where he or she has the household registration or the place where he or she habitually resides. If the place of household registration and the place where he or she habitually resides are not the same, one of them shall be chosen to apply for tax declaration. Without household registration in China, one shall apply for tax declaration to the tax authority in charge of the place where he or she habitually resides in China.

5. 因移居境外注销中国户籍的纳税申报

Tax Returns for the Cancellation of Chinese Household Registration Due to Emigration

纳税人因移居境外注销中国户籍的,应当在申请注销中国户籍前,向户籍所在地主管税务机关办理纳税申报,进行税款清算。(1)纳税人在注销户籍年度取得综合所得的,应当在注销户籍前,办理当年综合所得的汇算清缴。尚未办理上一年度综合所得汇算清缴的,应当在办理注销户籍纳税申报时一并办理。(2)纳税人在注销户籍年度取得经营所得的,应当在注销户籍前,办理当年经营所得的汇算清缴。尚未办理上一年度经营所得汇算清缴的,应当在办理注销户籍纳税申报时一并办理。(3)纳税人在注销户籍当年取得利息、股息、红利所得,财产租赁所得,财产转让所得和偶然所得的,应当在注销户籍前,申报当年上述所得的完税情况。(4)纳税人有未缴或者少缴税款的,应当在注销户籍前,结清欠缴或未缴的税款。纳税人存在分期缴税且未缴纳完毕的,应当在注销户籍前,结清尚未缴纳的税款。(5)纳税人办理注销户籍纳税申报时,需要办理专项附加扣除、依法确定的其他扣除的,应当向税务机关报送《个人所得税专项附加扣除信息表》《商业健康保险税前扣除情况明细表》《个人税收递延型商业养老保险税前扣除情况明细表》等。

If a taxpayer cancels a Chinese household registration because he has emigrated abroad, he shall file a tax return with the competent tax authority at the place where the household registration is located and carry out tax liquidation before applying to cancel his or her Chinese household registration. (1) If a taxpayer obtains comprehensive income in the year of cancellation of household registration, he shall handle the settlement of and payment of the comprehensive income in the current year before writing off household registration. If the settlement of the previous year's comprehensive income has not been processed, it shall be handled together with the cancellation of the household registration tax return. (2) If a taxpayer obtains the operating income in the year of cancellation of the household registration, he shall handle the settlement and payment for income from the current year's operation before the cancellation of the household registration. If the settlement and payment of the operating income of the previous year has not been processed, it shall be handled in the same way as the tax declaration for the cancellation of household registration. (3) Taxpayers who obtain interest, dividends and bonuses, income from property leases, income from property transfer and incidental income in the year of household registration cancellation shall declare the tax payment of the above-mentioned income in the current year before deregistration. (4) If a taxpayer has unpaid or under-paid taxes, the outstanding or unpaid taxes shall be paid before the household registration is cancelled. If a taxpayer pays taxes in installments and has not paid them, he shall clear the outstanding taxes before writing off his household registration.(5) If a taxpayer needs to handle special additional deductions and other deductions determined in accordance with the law when handling the cancellation of household registration tax returns, he shall report to the tax authorities the Personal Income Tax Special Additional Deduction Information Form, the Details of Commercial Health Insurance Pre-tax Deductions, the Details of Personal Tax Deferred Commercial Pension Insurance Deductions, etc.

6. 非居民个人在中国境内从两处以上取得工资、薪金所得的纳税申报

Tax Returns on Wages and Salary Income Obtained by Non-resident Individuals from more than Two Places within the Territory of China

非居民个人在中国境内从两处以上取得工资、薪金所得的,应当在取得所得的次月15日内,向其中一处任职、受雇单位所在地主管税务机关办理纳税申报。

Where a non-resident individual obtains wages or salaries from more than two places within the territory of China, he shall file a tax return with the competent tax authority at the place where one of the units is located within 15 days of obtaining the income.

(二) 源泉扣缴

Source Withholding

《中华人民共和国个人所得税法》第9条规定,个人所得税以所得人为纳税人,以支付所得的单位或者个人为扣缴义务人。此条款中的支付单位,包括支付储蓄存款利息的银行、支付股息的股份公司、支付工资薪金的单位、支付专利使用费的被许可人等。

Article 9 of China's Personal Income Tax Law stipulates that personal income tax shall be paid by the income person as the taxpayer and the unit or individual who pays the income shall be the withholding agent. The units of payment in this clause include banks that pay interest on savings deposits, stock companies that pay dividends, units that pay wages, licensees who pay royalties, and so on.

《中华人民共和国个人所得税法》第10条规定,扣缴义务人应当按照国家规定办理全员全额扣缴申报,并向纳税人提供其个人所得和已扣缴税款等信息。全员全额扣缴申报,是指扣缴义务人在代扣税款的次月15日内,向主管税务机关报送其支付所得的所有个人的有关信息、支付所得数额、扣除事项和数额、扣缴税款的具体数额和总额以及其他相关涉税信息资料。扣缴义务人每月或者每次预扣、代扣的税款,应当在次月15日内缴入国库,并向税务机关报送《个人所得税扣缴申报表》。

Article 10 of China's Personal Income Tax Law stipulates that the withholding agent shall handle the full withholding declaration in accordance with the provisions of the state and provide the taxpayer with information such as his or her personal income and withheld tax. Full withholding declaration means that the withholding agent shall report to the competent tax authority the relevant information, the amount of the payment income, the deductions and amounts, the specific amount and total amount of the withholding tax and other relevant tax-related information within 15 days of the following month. The withholding agent shall, on a monthly or every withholding or withholding tax, be paid into the state treasury within 15 days of the following month and shall submit the Personal Income Tax Withholding Declaration Form to the tax authorities.

国家税务总局据此于2018年12月21日发布了《个人所得税扣缴申报管理办法(试行)》,对个人所得税的扣缴申报作了规定。

On the basis of this, the State Administration of Taxation issued the Measures for the Administration of Personal Income Tax Withholding Declaration (Trial) on December 21, 2018, which provides for the withholding declaration of personal income tax.

1. *居民个人的工资、薪金所得*

Income from the Wages and Salaries of Individual Residents

扣缴义务人向居民个人支付工资、薪金所得时,应当按照累计预扣法计算预扣税款,并按月办理扣缴申报。累计预扣法,是指扣缴义务人在一个纳税年度内预扣预缴税款时,以纳税人在本单位截至当前月份工资、薪金所得累计收入减除累计免税收入、累计减除费用、累计专项扣除、累计专项附加扣除和累计依法确定的其他扣除后的余额为累计预扣预缴应纳税所得额(表3-4),用累计预扣预缴应纳税所得额计算累计应预扣预缴税额,再减除累计减免税额和累计已预扣预缴税额,其余额为本期应预扣预缴税额。余额为负值时,暂不退税。纳税年度终了后余额仍为负值时,由纳税人通过办理综合所得年度汇算清缴,税款多退少补。计算公式如下:

When the withholding obligation pays wages and salaries to individual residents, the withholding tax shall be calculated in accordance with the cumulative withholding method and the withholding declaration shall be processed on a monthly basis. The cumulative withholding method refers to the cumulative withholding of taxable income determined by the withholding payer in a tax year, and the cumulative withholding tax amount of the taxpayer's accumulated income from wages and salaries income as of the current month, the cumulative deduction of expenses, the cumulative special deduction, the cumulative special extra deduction and other deductions determined by the law shall be the cumulative withholding tax amount, and the cumulative withholding tax shall be calculated (table 3-4). The balance is withholding tax for the current period. When the balance is negative, no tax refund is available. When the balance is still negative after the end of the tax year, the taxpayer shall pay the consolidated income by processing the annual remittance of the comprehensive income, and the balances will be paid to either side as the case may be. The formula is as follows:

本期应预扣预缴税额=(累计预扣预缴应纳税所得额×预扣率-速算扣除数)-累计减免税额-累计已预扣预缴税额

withholding tax payable for the current period = (cumulative withholding taxable income × withholding rate - quick deduction) - cumulative tax relief - cumulative withholding tax amount

累计预扣预缴应纳税所得额=累计收入-累计免税收入-累计减除费用-累计专项扣除-累计专项附加扣除-累计依法确定的其他扣除

accumulated withholding taxable income amount = cumulative income - cumulative tax-exempt income - cumulative deduction of expenses - cumulative special deductions - cumulative special additional deductions - cumulative other deductions determined in accordance with the law

其中累计减除费用,按照5 000元/月乘以纳税人当年截至本月在本单位的任职受雇月份数计算。

The cumulative deduction of expenses shall be calculated by multiplying 5,000 yuan/month by the number of months of employment of the taxpayer in the unit as of this month.

表3-4 个人所得税预扣率表
（居民个人工资、薪金所得预扣预缴适用）
Table 3-4 Personal Income Tax Withholding Rate Table
(The Withholding of Personal Wages and Salaries of Residents Shall Apply)

级数 grade	累计预扣预缴应纳税所得额 accumulated withholding of taxable income	预扣率 withholding rate	速算扣除数 quick calculation deductions
1	不超过36 000元 income of 36,000 yuan or less	3%	0
2	超过36 000元至144 000元的部分 that part of income in excess of 36,000 to 144,000 yuan	10%	2 520
3	超过144 000元至300 000元的部分 that part of income in excess of 144,000 to 300,000 yuan	20%	16 920
4	超过300 000元至420 000元的部分 that part of income in excess of 300,000 to 420,000 yuan	25%	31 920
5	超过420 000元至660 000元的部分 that part of income in excess of 420,000 to 660,000 yuan	30%	52 920
6	超过660 000元至960 000元的部分 that part of income in excess of 660,000 to 960,000 yuan	35%	85 920
7	超过960 000元的部分 that part of income in excess of 960,000 yuan	45%	181 920

居民个人向扣缴义务人提供有关信息并依法要求办理专项附加扣除的，扣缴义务人应当按照规定在工资、薪金所得按月预扣预缴税款时予以扣除，不得拒绝。

If an individual resident provides relevant information to the withholding agent and requests special additional deductions in accordance with the law, the withholding agent shall, in accordance with the provisions, deduct the withholding tax on the monthly withholding of the income from wages and salaries, and shall not refuse to do so.

2. 居民个人的劳务报酬所得、稿酬所得、特许权使用费所得

Income from the Remuneration of Individual Residents for Their Services, Remuneration for Manuscripts and Royalties

扣缴义务人向居民个人支付劳务报酬所得、稿酬所得、特许权使用费所得时，应当按照以下方法按次或者按月预扣预缴税款：劳务报酬所得、稿酬所得、特许权使用费所得以收入减除费用后的余额为收入额；其中，稿酬所得的收入额减按70%计算。预扣预缴税款时，劳务报酬所得、稿酬所得、特许权使用费所得每次收入不超过4 000元的，减除费用按800元计算；每次收入4 000元以上的，减除费用按收入的20%计算。劳务报酬所得、稿酬所得、特许权使用费所得，以每次收入额为预扣预缴应纳税所得额，计算应预扣预缴税额。劳务报酬所得适用表3-5，稿酬所得、特许权使用费所得适用20%的比例预扣率。居民个人办理年度综合所得汇算清缴时，应当依法计算劳务报酬所得、稿酬所得、特许权使用费所得的收入额，并

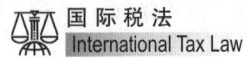

入年度综合所得计算应纳税款,税款多退少补。

When the withholding agent pays to the individual residents the income from remuneration for services, remuneration for manuscripts, and royalties, the withholding tax shall be withheld on a sub-monthly basis or in accordance with the following methods: income from remuneration for services, income from remuneration for manuscripts, income from royalties and income after expenses have been deducted from expenses; Of which, the amount manuscript remuneration income is reduced to 70%. When withholding tax, the income from labor remuneration, remuneration from manuscripts and royalties shall not exceed 4,000 yuan per income, the deduction fee shall be calculated at 800 yuan; Income from remuneration for services, income from remuneration for manuscripts, and income from royalties shall be calculated as withholding taxable income with withholding of each income amount. Table 3-5 applies to income from remuneration for services, with a 20% withholding rate for income from remuneration and royalties. When individual residents handle the settlement of the annual comprehensive income, they shall calculate the income from the remuneration of labor services, the income from the remuneration of manuscripts and the income from royalties in accordance with the law, and combine the income from the annual comprehensive income to calculate the tax payable, with more or less tax to be paid back.

表3-5 个人所得税预扣率表
(居民个人劳务报酬所得预扣预缴适用)
Table 3-5 Personal Income Tax Withholding Rate Form
(The Withholding of Income from the Remuneration of Individual Services of Residents Shall Apply)

级 数 grade	预扣预缴应纳税所得额 withholding of taxable income	预扣率 withholding rate	速算扣除数 quick calculation deductions
1	不超过20 000元 income of 20,000 yuan or less	20%	0
2	超过20 000元至50 000元的部分 that part of income in excess of 20,000 to 50,000 yuan	30%	2 000
3	超过50 000元的部分 that part of income in excess of 50,000 yuan	40%	7 000

3. 非居民个人的工资、薪金所得,劳务报酬所得,稿酬所得和特许权使用费所得

Income from Wages, Salaries, Remuneration for Services, Remuneration for Manuscripts and Royalties for Non-residents

扣缴义务人向非居民个人支付工资、薪金所得,劳务报酬所得,稿酬所得和特许权使用费所得时,应当按照以下方法按月或者按次代扣代缴税款:非居民个人的工资、薪金所得,以每月收入额减除费用5 000元后的余额为应纳税所得额;劳务报酬所得、稿酬所得、特许权使用费所得,以每次收入额为应纳税所得额,适用表3-6计算应纳税额。劳务报酬所得、

稿酬所得、特许权使用费所得以收入减除20%的费用后的余额为收入额；其中，稿酬所得的收入额减按70%计算。非居民个人在一个纳税年度内税款扣缴方法保持不变，达到居民个人条件时，应当告知扣缴义务人基础信息变化情况，年度终了后按照居民个人有关规定办理汇算清缴。

When the withholding agent pays wages, salary income, labor remuneration income, manuscript remuneration income and royalties income to non-resident individuals, it shall withhold tax monthly or sub-deduction according to the following methods: Wages and salary income of non-resident individuals shall be taxable income with the balance of 5,000 yuan of monthly income minus expenses; Income from remuneration for services, income from remuneration for manuscripts and income from royalties is the balance of income after 20% of the cost is reduced; Of which, the amount manuscript remuneration income is reduced to 70%. When a non-resident individual's method of tax withholding remains unchanged in a tax year and the resident's personal conditions are met, he shall inform the withholding agent of the change in the basic information and handle the final settlement in accordance with the relevant provisions of the individual resident after the end of the year.

表3–6　个人所得税税率表
（非居民个人工资、薪金所得，劳务报酬所得，稿酬所得，特许权使用费所得适用）
Table 3-6　Personal Income Tax Rate Table
(Income from Wages and Salaries of Non-residents, Income from Remuneration for Services, Income from Remuneration for Manuscripts, and Income from Royalties Shall Apply)

级数 grade	应纳税所得额 taxable income	税率 tax rate	速算扣除数 quick calculation deductions
1	不超过3 000元 income of 3,000 yuan or less	3%	0
2	超过3 000元至12 000元的部分 that part of income in excess of 3,000 to 12,000 yuan	10%	210
3	超过12 000元至25 000元的部分 that part of income in excess of 12,000 to 25,000 yuan	20%	1 410
4	超过25 000元至35 000元的部分 that part of income in excess of 25,000 to 35,000 yuan	25%	2 660
5	超过35 000元至55 000元的部分 that part of income in excess of 35,000 to 55,000 yuan	30%	4 410
6	超过55 000元至80 000元的部分 that part of income in excess of 55,000 to 80,000 yuan	35%	7 160
7	超过80 000元的部分 that part of income in excess of 80,000 yuan	45%	15 160

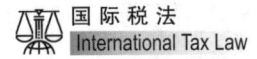

4. 利息、股息、红利所得,财产租赁所得,财产转让所得或者偶然所得

Income from Interest, Dividends and Bonuses, Income from Lease of Property, Income from the Transfer of Property or Incidental Income

扣缴义务人支付利息、股息、红利所得,财产租赁所得,财产转让所得或者偶然所得时,应当依法按次或者按月代扣代缴税款。纳税人需要享受税收协定待遇的,应当在取得应税所得时主动向扣缴义务人提出,并提交相关信息、资料,扣缴义务人代扣代缴税款时按照享受税收协定待遇有关办法办理。

When the withholding agent pays interest, dividends, bonuses, income from property lease, income from the transfer of property or incidental income, it shall withhold tax payments on a monthly rate in accordance with the law. Where a taxpayer requires to enjoy the treatment of the tax treaty, he shall, when obtaining the taxable income, voluntarily submit to the withholding agent, and submit relevant information and documents, and the withholding of the tax by the withholding agent shall be handled in accordance with the relevant measures for enjoying the tax treaty treatment.

支付工资、薪金所得的扣缴义务人应当于年度终了后两个月内,向纳税人提供其个人所得和已扣缴税款等信息。纳税人年度中间需要提供上述信息的,扣缴义务人应当提供。纳税人取得除工资、薪金所得以外的其他所得,扣缴义务人应当在扣缴税款后,及时向纳税人提供其个人所得和已扣缴税款等信息。

The withholding agent for the payment of wages and salaries shall, within two months after the end of the year, provide the taxpayer with information on his personal income and withholding tax. If the taxpayer is required to provide such information in the middle of the year, the withholding agent shall provide it. If a taxpayer obtains any income other than wages or salaries, the withholding agent shall, after withholding tax, provide the taxpayer with timely information on his personal income and withholding tax.

扣缴义务人应当按照纳税人提供的信息计算税款、办理扣缴申报,不得擅自更改纳税人提供的信息。扣缴义务人发现纳税人提供的信息与实际情况不符的,可以要求纳税人修改。纳税人拒绝修改的,扣缴义务人应当报告税务机关,税务机关应当及时处理。纳税人发现扣缴义务人提供或者扣缴申报的个人信息、支付所得、扣缴税款等信息与实际情况不符的,有权要求扣缴义务人修改。扣缴义务人拒绝修改的,纳税人应当报告税务机关,税务机关应当及时处理。

The withholding agent shall calculate the tax according to the information provided by the taxpayer and handle the withholding declaration, and shall not change the information provided by the taxpayer without authorization. If the withholding agent finds that the information provided by the taxpayer does not conform to the actual situation, it may request the taxpayer to amend it. If the taxpayer refuses to amend the matter, the withholding agent shall report it to the tax authority, which shall deal with it in a timely manner. If the taxpayer discovers that the personal information provided or withheld by the withholding agent, the income from payment, the withholding tax and other information does not conform to the actual situation, he shall have the right to request the withholding agent to amend it. If the withholding agent refuses to amend it, the taxpayer shall report it to the tax authority, which shall deal with it in a timely manner.

扣缴义务人应当依法对纳税人报送的专项附加扣除等相关涉税信息和资料保密。扣缴义务人依法履行代扣代缴义务，纳税人不得拒绝。纳税人拒绝的，扣缴义务人应当及时报告税务机关。

The withholding agent shall, in accordance with law, keep confidential the relevant tax-related information and materials, such as special additional deductions kept by the taxpayer. The withholding agent shall fulfill the withholding obligation in accordance with the law, and the taxpayer may not refuse it. If the taxpayer refuses, the withholding agent shall promptly report it to the tax authorities.

（三）纳税人识别号
Taxpayer Identity Number

自然人纳税人识别号是自然人纳税人办理各项涉税事项的唯一代码标识。《中华人民共和国个人所得税法》第9条规定，纳税人有中国公民身份证号码的，以中国公民身份证号码为纳税人识别号；纳税人没有中国公民身份证号码的，由税务机关赋予其纳税人识别号。扣缴义务人扣缴税款时，纳税人应当向扣缴义务人提供纳税人识别号。

The natural person taxpayer identification number is the unique code identification for the natural person taxpayer to handle various tax-related matters. Article 9 of China's Personal Income Tax Law stipulates that if a taxpayer has a Chinese citizenship number, the Chinese citizenship number shall be the taxpayer identification number, and if the taxpayer does not have a Chinese citizenship number, the tax authorities shall give him or her the taxpayer identification number. When withholding tax from the withholding agent, the taxpayer shall provide the withholding dutyholder with the taxpayer identification number.

（四）信息共享
Information Sharing

《中华人民共和国个人所得税法》第15条规定，公安、人民银行、金融监督管理等相关部门应当协助税务机关确认纳税人的身份、金融账户信息。教育、卫生、医疗保障、民政、人力资源和社会保障、住房和城乡建设、公安、人民银行、金融监督管理等相关部门应当向税务机关提供纳税人子女教育、继续教育、大病医疗、住房贷款利息、住房租金、赡养老人等专项附加扣除信息。个人转让不动产的，税务机关应当根据不动产登记等相关信息核验应缴的个人所得税，登记机构办理转移登记时，应当查验与该不动产转让相关的个人所得税的完税凭证。个人转让股权办理变更登记的，市场主体登记机关应当查验与该股权交易相关的个人所得税的完税凭证。有关部门依法将纳税人、扣缴义务人遵守本法的情况纳入信用信息系统，并实施联合激励或者惩戒。

Article 15 of China's Personal Income Tax Law stipulates that relevant departments such as public security, people's banking and financial supervision and management shall assist tax authorities in confirming the identity of taxpayers and financial account information. Relevant departments such as education, health, medical security, civil affairs, human resources and social security, housing and urban and rural construction, public security, People's Bank of China, financial supervision and management shall provide the tax authorities with special additional deduction information on the education of the children of taxpayers, continuing education, medical treatment for major diseases, interest on housing loans, housing rent, support for the elderly, etc. If an individual transfers real estate, the tax authority shall verify the personal income tax payable on the basis of relevant information such as real estate registration, and when the registration institution handles the transfer registration, it shall examine the tax payment certificates of the personal income tax related to the transfer of the real estate. If an individual transfers an equity to handle the registration of changes, the registration authority of the market subject shall examine the tax payment certificates of the personal income tax related to the equity transaction. Relevant departments shall, in accordance with law, incorporate the compliance of taxpayers and withholding obligations with this law into the credit information system and implement joint incentives or disciplinary measures.

学习思考题
Questions for Study

1. 请谈谈《中华人民共和国个人所得税法》修订的意义。
   Please talk about the significance of the amendment of the Personal Income Tax Law.
2. 判断居民纳税人与非居民纳税人的标准具体是什么？
   What are the specific standard for judging resident taxpayers and non-resident taxpayers?
3. 请谈谈新的《中华人民共和国个人所得税法》对于国际税法的影响。
   Please talk about the influence of the new personal income tax law on international tax law.

第四章 CHAPTER IV

企业所得税法
Enterprise Income Tax Law

第一节 统一企业所得税法的经过和意义
Section 1　Process and Significance of the Consolidation of Enterprise Income Tax Law

统一内外资企业所得税的工作,最早于1994年内资企业所得税合并完成之后就着手开始,但由于政治、经济等诸多方面因素的影响,统一企业所得税法之路充满坎坷,一度未能提到全国人大的立法议程中,直到21世纪特别是中国加入WTO以后,统一企业所得税法的步伐才开始加快。

The consolidation of domestic enterprise income tax and foreign enterprise income tax began as early as 1994 after the completion of the merger of domestic enterprise income taxes. However, due to the influence of political and economic factors, the road to consolidation of enterprise income tax law was full of ups and downs, and the draft was never submitted to the National People's Congress. Until the 21st century, especially after China's accession to the WTO, the pace of unifying the enterprise income tax law began to accelerate.

2001年,财政部、国家税务总局起草了《企业所得税法(草案)》上报国务院。

In 2001, the Ministry of Finance and the State Administration of Taxation drafted the enterprise income tax law and submitted it to the State Council.

2004年,国家税务总局和国务院法制办共同起草了《中华人民共和国企业所得税法(征求意见稿)》,书面征求了全国人大财经委,全国人大常委会法工委、预工委,各省、自治区、直辖市和计划单列市人民政府以及国务院有关部门的意见。

In 2004, the State Administration of Taxation and the Legislative Affairs Office of the State Council jointly drafted the Enterprise Income Tax Law of the People's Republic of China (Draft for Comment), which was consulted in writing by the Finance and Economics Committee of the National People's Congress, the Legislative Work Committee and the Preliminary Work Committee of the Standing Committee of the National People's Congress, various provinces, autonomous regions, and Opinions of the people's governments of municipalities directly under the Central Government and cities specifically designated in the state plan and relevant departments of the State Council.

2006年年初，全国人大常委会将企业所得税立法工作确定为2007年一类立法计划。2006年8月，国务院常务会议通过了《企业所得税法（草案）》，并于2006年9月28日提请全国人大常委会审议。第十届全国人大常委会第二十五次会议通过了该草案。

At the beginning of 2006, the Standing Committee of the National People's Congress determined the enterprise income tax legislative work as a priority in the legislative plan for 2007. In August 2006, the State Council executive meeting passed the Enterprise Income Tax Law (draft), which was submitted to the Standing Committee of the National People's Congress for deliberation on September 28, 2006. The draft was passed at the 25th meeting of the Standing Committee of the Tenth National People's Congress.

2007年3月16日，《中华人民共和国企业所得税法》于第十届全国人民代表大会第五次会议通过，并以主席令第63号发布，自2008年1月1日起施行。这标志着内外资企业所得税的最终统一。

On March 16, 2007, the Enterprise Income Tax Law of the People's Republic of China was passed at the fifth meeting of the Tenth National People's Congress and promulgated as Chairman's Order No. 63. It came into force on January 1, 2008, marking the final consolidation of domestic enterprise income tax and foreign enterprise income tax.

2007年11月28日，《中华人民共和国企业所得税法实施条例》于国务院第197次常务会议通过，以国务院第512号令公布，自2008年1月1日起施行。

On November 28, 2007, the Regulations for the Implementation of the Enterprise Income Tax Law of the People's Republic of China were passed at the 197th executive meeting of the State Council and promulgated by Order No. 512 of the State Council, and came into effect on January 1, 2008.

统一企业所得法是中国经济制度走向成熟、规范的标志性进程之一，也是社会各界的普遍共识和呼声，具有重要的现实意义和深远的历史意义。

The consolidation of enterprise income tax law is one of the landmark processes of China's more mature and standardized economic system, and it is also the common consensus and voice of all sectors of society. It is of important practical and far-reaching historical significance.

（1）统一企业所得税法，有利于创造公平竞争环境和完善市场经济体制。

(1) The consolidation of enterprise income tax law is conducive to creating a level playing field and improving the market economy system.

内外有别的企业所得税制导致税收政策差异巨大，企业税负苦乐不均。通过统一企业所得税法可以在税收制度方面（五个统一）为各类企业创造一个公平竞争的市场环境，从而促进我国社会主义市场经济体制的进一步完善。

Different internal and external corporate income tax systems have led to huge differences in tax policies and uneven corporate tax burdens. The unified corporate income tax law can create a fair and competitive market environment for all types of enterprises in the tax system (five unifications), thereby promoting China's socialist market economic system.

（2）统一企业所得税法，有利于促进经济增长方式转变和产业结构升级。

(2) The consolidation of enterprise income tax law is conducive to promoting the transformation of economic growth mode and upgrading the industrial structure.

原税制下企业优惠政策设计过于宽泛,重点不突出。统一企业所得税法,明确实行鼓励节约资源能源、保护环境以及发展高新技术等以产业优惠为主的税收优惠政策,有利于进一步发挥税收的调控作用,有利于引导我国经济增长方式向集约型转变,推动我国产业结构的优化升级。

Under the previous tax system, the design of preferential policies for enterprises was too broad and the focus was not prominent. With the consolidation of the enterprise income tax law, preferential tax policies have been implemented based on industrial preferences, such as policies encouraging resource conservation, environmental protection, and development of high-tech. It is conducive to further exerting the regulatory role of taxation, and guiding China's economic growth mode to an intensive transformation, boosting the optimization and upgrading of China's industrial structure.

(3) 统一企业所得税法,有利于促进区域经济的协调发展与和谐社会的建立。

(3) The consolidation of enterprise income tax law is conducive to the coordinated development of regional economies and the establishment of a harmonious society.

统一企业所得税法,将优惠重点由以区域优惠为主转向以产业优惠为主、区域优惠为辅,其中第57条对西部地区需要重点扶持的产业继续实行所得税优惠政策,有利于推动西部地区加快发展,逐步缩小东、中、西部地区差距。

The consolidation of enterprise income tax law shift the priority of preferential treatment from regional preferential treatment to industrial preferential treatment, supplemented by regional preferential treatment. Article 57 of the Enterprise Income Tax Law will continue to be implemented to provide income tax preferential policies for industries that need key support in the western region, which will help the western region speed up development and gradually narrow the gap between the eastern, central and western regions.

（4）统一企业所得税法,有利于提高我国利用外资的质量和水平。

(4) The consolidation of enterprise income tax law is conducive to improving the quality and level of China's utilization of foreign capital.

在国内资金比较充足、外贸出口稳步增长的情况下,统一企业所得税法,调整优惠政策,可以积极引导外资投资方向,在更高层次上促进国民经济结构调整和经济增长方式转变,提高我国利用外资的质量和水平。

With sufficient domestic funds and steady growth in foreign trade exports, consolidating the enterprise income tax law and adjusting preferential policies can actively guide the direction of foreign investment, promote the adjustment of the national economic structure and the transformation of economic growth patterns at a higher level, and improve the quality and level of China's utilization of foreign capital.

（5）统一企业所得税法,有利于推动我国税制的现代化建设。

(5) The consolidation of enterprise income tax law is conducive to promoting the modernization of China's tax system.

20世纪80年代以来,世界各国纷纷推出了新减税计划,从而形成了以"降低税率、扩大税基、税收中性、严格征管"为主要特征的世界性税制改革。在此背景下,我国统一企业所得税法,降低法定税率,调整税收优惠政策,不仅符合"宽税基,低税率"的国际税制改革源流,而且使我国企业所得税制更与国际接轨,这对于促进我国税制的总体现代化具有重要的作用。

Since the 1980s, countries all over the world have launched new tax reduction plans, thus forming a worldwide tax system reform featuring "reducing tax rates, expanding tax bases, tax neutrality, and strict collection and management". In this context, China's unification of the enterprise income tax law, reduction of statutory tax rates, and adjustment of preferential tax policies not only conform to the international tax system reform of "wide tax base and low tax rate", but also make China's enterprise income tax system more in line with international standards. It plays an important role in the overall modernization of China's tax system.

(6)统一企业所得税法,有利于加强税收征管和堵塞税收漏洞。

(6) The consolidation of enterprise income tax law is conducive to strengthening tax collection and management and plugging tax loopholes.

"两法并存"导致一些通过"假合资""返程投资"等方式骗取税收优惠的问题发生,造成国家财政收入的流失。统一企业所得税法施行后,由于实现了统一内资、外资企业所得税,统一了所得税税率,统一和规范税前扣除办法和标准,统一税收优惠政策,因而改变了这类"假外资"生存的土壤。同时由于统一企业所得税法加入了有关反避税条款,也能令外资企业重新检讨转移定价等关联交易带来的风险。

The "coexistence of the two laws" has led to the occurrence of some problems of fraudulently obtaining tax incentives through "fake joint ventures" "return investment", resulting in the loss of national fiscal revenue. After the implementation of the new Enterprise Income Tax Law, the consolidation of domestic and foreign-funded enterprise income tax, income tax rates, and standardized pre-tax deduction methods and standards, and tax preferential policies leads to the changing of the living soil of this type of "fake foreign capital". At the same time, the new tax law has added relevant anti-avoidance provisions, which will also cause foreign-funded enterprises to re-examine the risks brought by related-party transactions such as transfer pricing.

总之,统一内外资企业所得税法,有利于促进我国经济结构优化和产业升级,有利于为各类企业创造一个公平竞争的税收法治环境,是适应我国社会主义市场经济发展新阶段的一项制度。

In short, the consolidation of enterprise income tax law is conducive to promoting the optimization of China's economic structure and industrial upgrading, and creating a fair and competitive taxation legal environment for all types of enterprises. It is a system that adapts to the new stage of China's socialist market economy.

第四章 企业所得税法
CHAPTER IV Enterprise Income Tax Law

第二节 国内外企业所得税法的历史沿革
Section 2 History and Development of Domestic and Foreign Enterprise Income Tax Law

一、国内企业所得税的历史沿革
History and Development of Domestic Enterprise Income Tax

（一）改革开放前的企业所得税制度（1949—1978年）
Enterprise Income Tax System before the Reform and Opening Up Policy (from 1949 to 1978)

1949年，第一届全国税务会议通过了统一全国税收政策的基本方案，其中包括对企业所得和个人所得征税的办法。

In 1949, the First National Tax Conference adopted the basic plan for unifying the national taxation policy, including the taxation of enterprise income and personal income.

1950年，政务院发布了《全国税政实施要则》，开设工商业税（所得税部分）、存款利息所得税和薪给报酬所得税等3种税收。

In 1950, the State Council promulgated the "National Tax Policy Implementation Principles", establishing three types of taxes, including industrial and commercial tax (income tax), deposit interest income tax, and salary income tax.

工商业税（所得税部分）自1950年开征以后，主要征税对象是私营企业、集体企业和个体工商户的应税所得。国营企业因政府有关部门直接参与经营和管理，其财务核算制度也与一般企业差异较大，所以国营企业实行利润上缴制度，不缴纳所得税。在这种制度下，国营企业上缴的利润仍是国家财政收入主要来源之一。在税收收入中，国内销售环节征收的货物税和劳务税是主体收入，占税收总额的比例在70%以上，工商企业上缴的所得税收入占税收总额的比重较小。这种制度的设计适应了当时中国高度集中的计划经济管理体制的需要。

After the industrial and commercial tax (income tax) was levied in 1950, the main tax objects were the taxable income of private enterprises, collective enterprises and individual industrial and commercial households. State-owned enterprises are directly involved in the operation and management of relevant government departments, and their financial accounting system is quite different from that of ordinary enterprises. Therefore, state-owned enterprises implement a profit transfer system without paying income tax. Under this system, the profits turned in by state-owned enterprises are still one of the main sources of national fiscal revenue. In the tax revenue, the goods tax and labor tax collected in the domestic sales link are the main income, accounting for more than 70% of the total tax revenue. The income tax revenue paid by industrial and commercial enterprises accounts for a small proportion of the total tax revenue. The design of this system adapted to the needs of China's highly centralized planned economy management system at that time.

(二) 改革开放初期的企业所得税制度 (1978—1990年)
Enterprise Income Tax System at the Beginning of Reform and Opening Up (from 1978 to 1990)

从1978年起,中国开始实行改革开放政策,税制建设进入了一个新的发展时期,税收收入逐步成为政府财政收入主要的来源,同时税收成为国家宏观经济调控的重要手段。

Since 1978, China began to implement the Reform and Opening Up policy, and the construction of the tax system has entered a new period of development. Tax revenue has gradually become the main source of government revenue, and taxation has become an important means of national macroeconomic regulation.

1. 1978年至1982年的企业所得税制度

Enterprise Income Tax System from 1978 to 1982

改革开放以后,出于引进国外资金、技术和人才,开展对外经济技术合作的需要,根据党中央统一部署,税制改革工作在"七五"计划期间逐步推开。

After the Reform and Opening Up, in order to meet the needs of introducing foreign capital, technology and talents, and to carry out foreign economic and technological cooperation, according to the unified deployment of the Party Central Committee, the tax system reform was gradually carried out during the Seventh Five-Year Plan period.

1980年9月,第五届全国人民代表大会第三次会议通过了《中华人民共和国中外合资经营企业所得税法》并公布施行。该法将企业所得税税率确定为30%,另按应纳所得税额附征10%的地方所得税。

In September 1980, the Third Session of the Fifth National People's Congress passed the Income Tax Law of the People's Republic of China on Sino-foreign Joint Ventures and announced its implementation. The enterprise income tax rate was determined to be 30%, and a local income tax of 10% was levied on the amount of income tax payable.

1981年12月,第五届全国人民代表大会第四次会议通过了《中华人民共和国外国企业所得税法》,实行20%至40%的五级超额累进税率,另按应纳税的所得额附征10%的地方所得税。

In December 1981, the Fourth Session of the Fifth National People's Congress passed the Foreign Enterprise Income Tax Law of the People's Republic of China, which implemented a five-tier excess progressive tax rate of 20% to 40%, plus taxable income 10% local income tax.

上述改革标志着与中国社会主义有计划的市场经济体制相适应的所得税制度改革开始起步。

The above-mentioned reforms marked the beginning of the reform of the income tax system compatible with China's socialist planned market economic system.

2. 1983年至1990年的企业所得税制度

Enterprise Income Tax System from 1983 to 1990

1983年,国务院试行国营企业"利改税",即将国营企业向国家上缴利润的制度改为缴纳企业所得税的制度。

In 1983, the State Council piloted the "profit-to-tax conversion" of state-owned enterprises, that is, the system for state-owned enterprises to pay profits to the state was changed to a system for paying corporate income tax.

1984年9月,国务院发布了《中华人民共和国国营企业所得税条例(草案)》和《国营企业调节税征收办法》,国营企业所得税的纳税人为实行独立经济核算的国营企业,国营大中型企业实行55%的比例税率,国营小型企业按10%至55%的八级超额累进税率,并对国营大中型企业征收国营企业调节税,税率由财税部门商企业主管部门核定。税后利润原则上归企业支配。

In September 1984, the State Council promulgated the Regulations of the People's Republic of China on State-owned Enterprise Income Tax (Draft) and the Measures for the Collection of State-owned Enterprise Adjustment Tax. The taxpayers of the income tax of state-owned enterprises are state enterprises practicing independent economic accounting, and a proportional tax rate of 55% is applied to large and medium-sized state enterprises. State-owned small enterprises are subject to an eight-level progressive tax rate ranging from 10% to 55%, and state-owned enterprise adjustment tax is levied on large and medium-sized state-owned enterprises. The tax rate is determined by the financial and taxation department and the competent department of the enterprise. In principle, after-tax profits belong to the enterprise.

1985年4月,国务院发布了《中华人民共和国集体企业所得税暂行条例》,实行10%至55%的八级超额累进税率,同时停止执行原来对集体企业征收的工商税(所得税部分)。

In April 1985, the State Council promulgated the Interim Regulations of the People's Republic of China on Collective Enterprise Income Tax, which implemented an eight-level excess progressive tax rate of 10% to 55%. The original industrial and commercial tax (income tax) imposed on collective enterprises was suspended at the same time.

1988年6月,国务院发布了《中华人民共和国私营企业所得税暂行条例》;1988年11月,财政部颁发了《私营企业所得税暂行条例施行细则》,这两部法将私营企业所得税的税率定为35%的比例税率。

In June 1988, the State Council issued the Interim Regulations of the People's Republic of China on Income Tax for Private Enterprises, and in November 1988, the Ministry of Finance issued the Detailed Rules for the Implementation of the Interim Regulations on Income Tax for Private Enterprises. The private enterprise income tax rate is a proportional rate of 35%.

(三)内外资有别的企业所得税制度(1991—2007年)

Different Enterprise Income Tax Systems for Domestic and Foreign Investment (1991–2007)

为适应中国建立社会主义市场经济体制的新形势,进一步扩大改革开放,努力把国有企业推向市场,按照统一税法、简化税制、公平税负、促进竞争的原则,国家先后完成了外资企业所得税的统一和内资企业所得税的统一。

In order to adapt to the new situation of China's establishment of a socialist market economic system, further expand reform and opening up, and strive to promote state-owned enterprises to the market, in accordance with the principles of unified tax law, simplified tax system, fair tax burden, and promotion of competition, the state has completed the unification of the income tax for foreign-funded enterprises and the income tax for the domestic-funded enterprises.

1991年4月,第七届全国人民代表大会通过了《中华人民共和国外商投资企业和外国企业所得税法》(对《中华人民共和国中外合资经营企业所得税法》与《中华人民共和国外国企业所得税法》进行了合并),于同年7月1日起施行,实行30%的比例税率,另按应纳税所得额征收3%的地方所得税,综合税率33%。

In April 1991, the Seventh National People's Congress passed the Income Tax Law of the People's Republic of China on Foreign-invested Enterprises and Foreign Enterprises (consolidated the Income Tax Law of the People's Republic of China Concerning Chinese-Foreign Joint Ventures with the Income Tax Law of People's Republic of China Concerning Foreign Enterprises), which came into effect on July 1 of the same year, with a 30% proportional tax rate and a 3% local income tax based on taxable income, with a comprehensive tax rate of 33%.

1993年12月,国务院制定了《中华人民共和国企业所得税暂行条例》[对《中华人民共和国国营企业所得税条例(草案)》《国营企业调节税征收办法》《中华人民共和国集体企业所得税暂行条例》和《中华人民共和国私营企业所得税暂行条例》的整合],于1994年1月1日起施行,法定税率33%。

In December 1993, the State Council formulated the Interim Regulations of the People's Republic of China on Enterprise Income Tax [the integration of the Regulations of the People's Republic of China on State-owned Enterprise Income Tax (Draft), Measures for the Collection of Regulation Tax on State-owned Enterprises, and Interim Regulations of the People's Republic of China on Collective-owned Enterprise Income Tax and the Interim Regulations of the People's Republic of China on Private Enterprise Income Tax], which came into effect on January 1, 1994, and the statutory tax rate is 33%.

(四)内外资统一的企业所得税(2008年至今)

Consolidation of Domestic Enterprise Income Tax and Foreign Enterprise Income Tax (2008—)

如前所述,内外资有别的企业所得税一定程度上导致税负不公,进而出现假外资获取税收优惠等问题。

As mentioned earlier, the difference in enterprise income tax between domestic and foreign capital has led to unfair tax burdens to a certain extent, and problems arose such as false foreign investment in order to obtain tax incentives.

2007年3月16日,第十届全国人大第五次会议通过《企业所得税法》,同年11月28

日国务院第197次常务会议通过《中华人民共和国企业所得税法实施条例》,两法均于2008年1月1日起施行。企业所得税基本税率为25%;非居民企业适用税率为20%;符合条件的小型微利企业适用税率为20%;国家需要重点扶持的高新技术企业适用税率为15%。

On March 16, 2007, the Fifth Session of the Tenth National People's Congress passed the Enterprise Income Tax Law. On November 28 of the same year, the 197th Executive Meeting of the State Council passed the Regulations for the Implementation of the Enterprise Income Tax Law of the People's Republic of China. Both laws came into effect on January 1, 2008. The basic corporate income tax rate is 25% and the applicable tax rate for non-resident enterprises is 20%; the applicable tax rate for qualified small and low-profit enterprises is 20%; and the applicable tax rate for high-tech enterprises that need support from the state is 15%.

《企业所得税法》的施行,平衡了内、外资企业的所得税负担,完善了所得税税法和税率统一了税前扣除的办法和标准,统一了优惠等政策,规范了征收管理。这标志着我国税制现代化建设迈出重大步伐,具有划时代的意义。

The implementation of the Enterprise Income Tax Law balances the income tax burdens of domestic and foreign-funded enterprises, improves the income tax law and tax rate, unifies the methods and standards for pre-tax deductions, unifies preferential policies, and standardizes collection management. It marks a major step forward in the modernization of China's tax system and is of epoch-making significance.

（二）国外企业所得税历史沿革
History and Development of Domestic Enterprise Income Tax

现代税收制度和税收法律制度,形成于第一次世界大战以后暂时的经济衰退时期到第二次世界大战以前。一战对世界各国的财政经济产生极其深刻的影响,包括税收制度。第一次世界大战以后,各国长期以来实行的以关税壁垒、消费税为中心的落后税收制度,以第一次世界大战为转机,变革为现代税收制度,从而进入以商品税(包括产品税、营业税乃至消费税)为中心的现代税收制度。第二次世界大战以后,世界各国建立以所得税为中心、以增值税适应普遍调节的现代税收制度。

The modern taxation system and taxation legal system were formed during the temporary economic recession after the First World War and before the Second World War. The First World War had an extremely profound impact on the fiscal economy of countries around the world, including taxation systems. After the First World War, the backward taxation systems that had been implemented by various countries for a long time, centered on tariff barriers and consumption taxes, took the First World War as an opportunity to transform into a modern tax system, thus entering into a commodity tax (including product tax, business tax and even consumption tax) as the center of the modern tax system. After the Second World War, countries around the world established a modern tax system which took income tax as the center and adopted value-added tax to adapt to general adjustment.

其一，以美国为代表的国家，致力于增加所得税，并且建立以所得税为中心的税收制度。同样，也是以一战为转机，以英国为代表的国家将其以消费税为中心的税收制度转向以所得税为中心的税收制度。德国在1920年把所得税和法人所得税统一纳入国税。法国也在1914年引入所得税。

First, countries represented by the United States were committed to increasing income taxes and establishing a tax system centered on income taxes. Similarly, with the First World War as a turning point, countries represented by the United Kingdom turned their taxation system centered on consumption tax to a tax system centered on income tax. In 1920, Germany unified income tax and corporate income tax into the national tax. France also introduced income tax in 1914.

其二，一战期间，各国在调整、增加征收所得税的同时，相继创设了营业税来作为增加税收的强大武器。德国、法国、意大利、加拿大、比利时都相继创设了营业税。营业税的迅速发展，在一战期间的一些国家中几乎处于中心地位。

Second, during the First World War, while adjusting and increasing income taxes, various countries successively created business taxes as a powerful weapon to increase tax revenue. Germany, France, Italy, Canada, and Belgium have all created business tax. The rapid development of business tax was almost at the center of some countries during the First World War.

第三节　统一企业所得税法的必要性和可能性
Section 3　Necessity and Possibility of the Consolidation of Enterprise Income Tax Law

 统一企业所得税法的必要性

The Necessity of the Consolidation of Enterprise Income Tax Law

改革开放以来，中国进行了一系列与社会主义市场经济体制相适应的所得税制度改革，但是，随着我国改革开放的深入及市场经济体制的建立和完善，特别是我国加入WTO后，内、外资企业两套所得税制度并存的税制模式，已无法适应市场经济发展的要求，矛盾日趋突出，统一企业所得税势在必行。

Since the Reform and Opening-up, China has carried out a series of income tax system reforms that are compatible with the socialist market economic system. However, as China's reform and opening up and the establishment and improvement of the market, the coexistence of the two sets of corporate income tax systems has been unable to meet the requirements of the development of the market economy, and the contradictions have become increasingly prominent. It is imperative to unify corporate income tax.

一是内、外资企业所得税制度的差异，使得在税率、税收优惠、税前扣除、税收征管等方面，存在外资企业偏松、内资企业偏紧的问题，另外企业通过"假投资""返程投资"等手段骗取税收优惠政策，不仅造成企业之间税负不公平，更造成国家税款的流失，为此企业要求统一税收待遇、公平竞争的呼声较高。

The first contradiction lies in the difference in the income tax system between domestic and foreign-funded enterprises, which has caused problems such as the looseness of foreign-funded enterprises and the tightness of domestic-funded enterprises in terms of tax rates, tax incentives, pre-tax deductions, and tax collection. In addition, enterprises have adopted "fake investment" "return trips". Defrauding preferential tax policies by means such as "investment" has not only caused unfair tax burdens among enterprises, but also caused the loss of national taxes. For this reason, enterprises have a higher voice for unified tax treatment and fair competition.

二是经过40多年的改革开放，我国的政治经济形势发生了巨大变化，国有经济、民营经济和外资经济三足鼎立、共同发展，特别是随着国有企业改制改组和投融资体制改革的深入，企业资本融合速度加快，不同性质企业之间相互参股、控股情况十分普遍，企业经济呈现多元化和混合化发展的趋势，致使原按内、外资企业分设的两套税法制度已不适应当前经济发展的客观要求。

The second contradiction is that China's political and economic situation has undergone tremendous changes after more than 40 years of Reform and Opening-up. The state-owned economy, private economy, and foreign-funded economy have developed together. Especially with the deepening of state-owned enterprise restructuring and investment and financing system reforms, the speed of corporate capital integration accelerated. As a result, the mutual participation and holding of shares between companies of different natures has become very common, and the corporate economy is showing a trend of diversification and mixed development. Therefore, the two sets of tax law systems that were originally separated by domestic and foreign companies are no longer suitable for the objective of current economic development.

三是内、外资企业所得税的立法级次不同，外资企业所得税法为全国人大制定的法律，而内资企业所得税法是国务院制定的条例，从而在实际执行中的法律效力也有所差别；内资企业所得税暂行条例只有20条，外资企业所得税法只有30条，税法内容过于简单，大量税收政策以部门规范性文件的形式发布。过于简单的税法和大量法律效力低的部门规定，削弱了企业所得税法的严肃性和刚性，且存在较多释义不清的问题，给税收征管工作带来困难，加大了征管成本。

The third contradiction is that the legislative levels of income tax for domestic and foreign-funded enterprises are different. Because the income tax law for foreign-funded enterprises is a law formulated by the National People's Congress and the domestic-funded enterprise income tax law is a regulation formulated by the State Council, the legal effect in actual implementation is also different. There are only 20 provisions in the Interim Regulations on Corporate Income Tax and 30 provisions in the Foreign-invested Enterprise Income Tax Law. The content of the tax law is too simple, and a large number of tax policies are issued in the form of departmental regulatory documents. Too-simple tax laws and a large number of departmental regulations with low legal effects weaken the seriousness and rigidity of the corporate income tax law, and there are many problems with unclear interpretations, which bring difficulties to tax collection and management, and increase the cost of collection and management.

四是受国际税制改革的影响,为适应我国社会经济情况与国际的接轨,许多新的税收政策内容也亟须补充到税法当中去。

The fourth contradiction is that due to the impact of the reform of the international tax system and in order to adapt to the country's social and economic situation and the international standards, many new tax policies must be added to the tax law.

二、统一企业所得税法的可能性
Possibility of the Consolidation of Enterprise Income Tax Law

中国政治形势稳定,经济持续平稳、快速增长,国家财政充裕,企业投资和发展环境日益成熟,根据完善社会主义市场经济体制的重要任务,借鉴国际经验,按照"简税制、宽税基、低税率、严征管"的要求,建立统一适用、规范的所得税制度的时机也已经成熟。

China's political situation is stable, the economy continues to grow steadily and rapidly, and the environment for corporate investment and development is becoming increasingly mature. In accordance with the important task of improving the socialist market economic system and drawing on international experience, China will follow the simplified tax system featured with wide tax base, low tax rate, and strict collection. It is time to establish a uniformly applicable and standardized income tax system.

(1) 改革开放深入,经济持续快速发展为统一企业所得税法奠定了良好的宏观经济基础。

(1) With the deepening of reform and opening up, the sustained and rapid economic development has laid a good macroeconomic foundation for the consolidation of enterprise income tax law.

宏观经济数据显示,我国经济在2002年基本走出低谷的基础上,2003年至2006年继续保持了较快增长的势头,2006年我国GDP达到20.94万亿元,比上年增长10.7%。2007年前三季度,我国GDP同比增长11.5%,继续保持平稳快速增长势头。另有数据显示,改革开放以来,我国的对外开放程度已大大提高,在当代国际分工体系中扮演了一个越来越重要的角色:2006年对外贸易总额达到17 606.9亿元,居世界第三位,成为名副其实的贸易大国。外贸依存度从1978年的10%提高到2006年的65%,这表明我国经济对外开放取得了显著成就。

Macroeconomic data shows that on the basis that China's economy basically bottomed out in 2002, it continued to maintain a relatively rapid growth momentum from 2003 to 2006. In 2006, China's GDP reached 20.94 trillion yuan, an increase of 10.7% over the previous year. In the first three quarters of 2007, China's GDP increased by 11.5% year-on-year, continuing to maintain a steady and rapid growth momentum. Other data show that since the reform and opening up, China's opening to the outside world has greatly improved, and it has played an increasingly important role in the contemporary international division of labor: in 2006, the total foreign trade reached 1,760.69 billion yuan, ranking third in the world and becoming a veritable trading nation. The degree of dependence on foreign trade increased from 10% in 1978 to 65% in 2006, which shows that China's economy has made remarkable achievements in opening up to outside the territory.

（2）税收连续几年超额增长，为统一企业所得税法提供了充裕的财力支持和充分的操作空间。

(2) Tax revenue has increased excessively for several consecutive years, providing ample financial support and sufficient operating space for the consolidation of enterprise tax law.

2006年，全国税收收入（不包括关税、耕地占用税和契税，未扣减出口退税）完成37 636亿元，比上年增长21.9%，增收6 770亿元。2007年前三季度，全国税收收入累计完成37 161亿元，比上年同期增收8 741亿元，增长30.8%，已接近2006年全年水平。

In 2006, the national tax revenue (excluding tariffs, farmland occupation tax and deed tax, without deduction of export tax rebates) completed 3,763.6 billion yuan, an increase of 21.9% over the previous year and an increase of 677 billion yuan. In the first three quarters of 2007, the national tax revenue totaled 3,716.1 billion yuan, an increase of 874.1 billion yuan over the same period last year, an increase of 30.8%, which is close to the level of 2006.

如果统一企业所得税法，与现行税法的口径相比，财政当年减收约930亿元，仅占2006年税收收入增长额的13.7%，也比2006年内外资企业所得税的增收额1 570亿元低640亿元。应该说，这时进行"两法合并"改革，财政是完全可以承受的。

If the consolidation of enterprise income tax law is achieved, compared with the current tax law, fiscal revenue will be reduced by about 93 billion yuan that year, accounting for only 13.7% of the increase in tax revenue in 2006, which is 64 billion yuan lower than the 157 billion yuan increase in domestic and foreign-funded enterprise income tax in 2006. It should be said that the reform of the "merger of the two laws" at this time is completely affordable.

（3）各国企业所得税改革的趋势，为我国税改创造了一个可参照的国际大背景。

(3) The trend of enterprise income tax reform in various countries has created an international background as a reference for China's tax reform.

世界趋势集中表现为公司所得税综合税率的持续下降。从2000年到2006年，OECD 30个成员国的公司所得税的平均税率经历了一个逐年下降的变化趋势，各年平均税率分别为：33.6%、32.5%、31.2%、30.7%、29.8%、28.6%和28.4%。此外，英国、德国等许多国家也陆续宣布未来几年公司所得税率的下调计划。

The global trend is concentrated in the continuous decline in the comprehensive corporate income tax rate. From 2000 to 2006, the average corporate income tax rates of the 30 member countries of the OECD experienced a downward trend year by year. The average annual tax rates were 33.6%, 32.5%, 31.2%, 30.7%, 29.8%, 28.6% and 28.4%. In addition, many countries such as the United Kingdom and Germany have successively announced plans to reduce corporate income tax rates in the next few years.

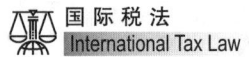

第四节 建立各类企业统一适用的科学和规范的企业所得税制度
Section 4 Establishment of a Unified, Scientific and Standardized Enterprise Income Tax System Applicable to All Types of Enterprises

 统一内外资企业所得税法的原则

Principles of the Consolidation of Enterprise Income Tax Law for Domestic and Foreign Companies

改革开放以来，企业所得税按企业性质分别立法，对维护国家权益、吸引外资、促进企业制度改革和经济发展，起到了积极的作用。但是，随着我国社会主义市场经济体制的建立和完善，特别是我国加入世界贸易组织后，建立各类企业统一适用的科学和规范的企业所得税制度的呼声日益高涨。

Since the reform and opening up, separate legislation on corporate income tax according to the nature of the enterprise has played a positive role in safeguarding national rights and interests, attracting foreign investment, and promoting corporate system reform and economic development. However, with the establishment and improvement of China's socialist market economic system, especially after China's accession to the World Trade Organization, the call is increasing for the establishment of a scientific and standardized corporate income tax system applicable to all types of enterprises.

（一）遵循WTO公平竞争原则，创造公平竞争的税收政策环境，促进国民经济更好更快发展

Follow the Principle of Fair Competition of WTO, Create a Tax Policy Environment of Fair Competition, and Promote Better and Faster Development of the National Economy

根据全国企业所得税税源调查资料测算，2007年全国内资企业的平均税负为25%，比外资企业的平均15%的税负高出10个百分点。税负上的差距使内资企业处于不公平地位，竞争力也相应大大削弱。在世界经济一体化迅速加快的情况下，我们鼓励内资企业"走出去"开拓海外市场，提高知名度，这是国家提高民族经济竞争力和保障国家经济安全的重要战略。因此，应按照WTO公平竞争原则，积极为各类企业创造公平竞争的税收政策环境，以促进国民经济更好更快地发展。

According to the survey data of national enterprise income tax sources, the average tax burden of domestic enterprises nationwide in 2007 was about 25%, which was 10% higher than the average tax burden of foreign-funded enterprises of 15%. The gap in tax burden puts domestic enterprises in an unfair position, and the corresponding competitiveness is also greatly weakened. With the rapid acceleration of world economic integration, domestic-funded enterprises are encouraged to "go global" to open up overseas markets and increase visibility. This is an important strategy for the country to improve national economic competitiveness and ensure national economic security. Therefore, in accordance with the WTO fair competition principle, we should actively create a fair competition tax policy environment for all types of enterprises to promote better and faster development of the national economy.

(二) 提高利用外资水平，建立规范的企业所得税制度，促进国民经济健康有序地发展
Improve the Level of Foreign Capital Utilization, Establish a Standardized Enterprise Income Tax System, and Promote the Healthy and Orderly Development of the National Economy

根据统计，2006年我国非金融类的外国直接投资达161亿美元，位居全球首位。按照党的十六届三中全会关于"抓住新一轮全球生产要素优化重组和产业转移的重大机遇，提高利用外资水平"的精神，新企业所得税应通过建立规范公平的企业所得税制度和产业税收优惠体系，取消低层次税收优惠，将税收优惠重点放在鼓励高科技产业发展、提高产品技术含量等高层次引资上来，更好地发挥外资作用，更多地引进先进技术和管理经验，促进国民经济有序健康发展。

According to statistics, China's non-financial foreign direct investment (FDI) reached 16.1 billion US dollars in 2006, ranking first in the world. In accordance with the spirit of the Third Plenary Session of the 16th Central Committee of the Communist Party of China on "seizing the new round of major opportunities in the optimization and reorganization of global production factors and industrial transfer, and improving the level of foreign capital utilization", the new enterprise income tax should focus on tax incentives to encourage the development of high-tech industries, improve product technology content and other high-level investment, through the establishment of a standardized and fair enterprise income tax system and industrial tax preferences system, abolish low-level tax incentives, to better play the role of foreign capital, introduce more advanced technology and management experience, and promote the orderly and healthy development of the national economy.

(三) 统筹区域发展，合理调整税收优惠政策，促进社会全面进步
Coordinate Regional Development, Rationally Adjust Tax Preferential Policies, and Promote Overall Social Progress

我国吸收的外商直接投资中，东部沿海11省市占了绝大部分，中部8省市次之，西部地区12省市最少。因此，新企业所得税法应从建立全国统一市场出发，削减东部地区优惠，增加中西部地区的优惠，与党的十六届三中全会制定的"统筹区域发展、形成促进区域经济协调发展的机制"的政策目标和任务相一致。同时，应充分利用税收政策杠杆，适当加大支持

社会公益事业和环保事业发展的政策力度,促进社会经济可持续发展和全面进步。

Among China's foreign direct investment, 11 provinces and cities on the east coast accounted for the majority, followed by 8 provinces and cities in the central region, and 12 provinces and cities in the western region the least. Therefore, the new enterprise income tax law should start from the establishment of a unified national market, reduce the preferential treatment in the eastern region, and increase the preferential treatment in the central and western regions, and the goals and tasks be consistent with the policy of "coordinating regional development and forming a mechanism to promote coordinated regional economic development" formulated by the Third Plenary Session of the 16th Central Committee. At the same time, it is necessary to make full use of tax policy levers, appropriately increase policy support for the development of social welfare undertakings and environmental protection undertakings, and promote sustainable social and economic development and overall progress.

二、税率、收入、扣除和资产税务处理的规定
Tax Treatment Regulations on Tax Rates, Income, Deductions and Assets

(一) 税率
Tax Rates

税率是对征税对象的征收比例或征收额度,是衡量纳税人税负轻重的基本要素。根据不同的角度,税率可以划分为中央税率和地方税率;正税率和负税率;比例税率、累进税率和固定税率。我国《企业所得税法》采用了中央税率、正税率和比例税率。

The tax rate is the percentage or amount of tax levied on the subject, and it is the basic element to measure the tax burden of taxpayers. According to different perspectives, tax rates can be divided into central tax rates and local tax rates; positive tax rates and negative tax rates; proportional tax rates, progressive tax rates and fixed tax rates. China's Enterprise Income Tax Law adopts the central tax rate, positive tax rate and proportional tax rate.

《企业所得税法》第4条第一款规定了企业所得税的税率为25%,同时对符合条件的小型微利企业规定了20%的优惠税率、国家需要重点扶持的高新技术企业规定了15%的优惠税率。另外,对于非居民企业,我国《企业所得税法》规定,非居民企业在中国境内未设立机构、场所,或者虽设立机构、场所但取得的所得与其所设机构、场所有实际联系的所得,缴纳20%的企业所得税。为扶持西部地区的产业发展,我国财政部发布的财政部公告2011年第58号文还规定,自2011年1月1日至2020年12月31日,对设在西部地区的鼓励类企业产业征收15%的企业所得税。

The first paragraph of Article 4 of the Enterprise Income Tax Law stipulates that the corporate income tax rate is 25%. At the same time, it provides a preferential tax rate of 20% for qualified small and low-profit enterprises, and a 15% tax rate for high-tech enterprises that need key support from the state. In addition, for non-resident enterprises, our country's Enterprise Income Tax Law stipulates that non-resident enterprises that have not established institutions or premises in China, or have established institutions or premises but obtained income from actual contact with the institutions and premises established by them shall pay 20% corporate income tax. In order to support the industrial development of the western region, the Ministry of Finance Announcement No. 58 of 2011 issued by the Ministry of Finance stipulated that from January 1, 2011 to December 31, 2020, the Ministry of Finance would levy a 15% enterprise income tax on encouraged corporate industries located in the western region.

（二）企业的收入
Corporate Income

企业收入是政府对企业征税的前提，也是企业纳税的基础。为防止纳税人将应征税的经济利益排除在应税收入之外，《企业所得税法》第6条将企业收入定义为"企业以货币形式和非货币形式从各种来源取得的收入"，包括：(1) 销售货物收入；(2) 提供劳务收入；(3) 转让财产收入；(4) 股息、红利等权益性投资收益；(5) 利息收入；(6) 租金收入；(7) 特许权使用费收入；(8) 接受捐赠收入；(9) 其他收入。

Corporate income is the prerequisite for the government to levy taxes on enterprises, and it is also the basis for corporations to pay taxes. In order to prevent taxpayers from excluding taxable economic benefits from taxable income, Article 6 of the Corporate Income Tax Law defines corporate income as "income obtained by an enterprise from various sources in monetary and non-monetary forms", including: (1) income from the sale of goods; (2) income from the provision of labor services; (3) income from the transfer of property; (4) income from equity investment such as dividends and bonuses; (5) interest income; (6) rental income; (7) royalties income; (8) income from donations received; (9) other income.

同时，《企业所得税法》第7条还规定了不征税收入，即财政拨款；依法收取并纳入财政管理的行政事业性收费、政府性基金；国务院规定的其他不征税收入。由于这些属于财政性资金的收入，《企业所得税法》将其排除在应征税收的范围之外。此外，《企业所得税法》第26条就企业的免税收入进行规定，包括国债利息收入；符合条件的居民企业之间的股息、红利等权益性投资收益；在中国境内设立机构、场所的非居民企业从居民企业取得与该机构、场所有实际联系的股息、红利等权益性投资收益；符合条件的非营利组织的收入。

At the same time, Article 7 of the Enterprise Income Tax Law also stipulates non-taxable income, that is, fiscal appropriation; administrative fees and government funds collected in accordance with the law and included in financial management; and other non-taxable incomes stipulated by the State Council. Because these are revenues of fiscal funds, the Corporate Income Tax Law excludes them from the scope of taxation. In addition, Article 26 of the Enterprise Income Tax Law stipulates the tax-free income of enterprises, including interest income from government bonds, dividends and bonuses and other equity investment income between qualified resident enterprises, non-resident enterprises obtain dividends, bonuses and other equity investment income from resident enterprises that are actually connected to the institution or the venue, income from qualified non-profit organizations.

(三) 扣除
Deduction

《企业所得税法》对扣除原则和框架作了规定,要求扣除应当符合相关性和合理性原则。《企业所得税法》第8条规定,企业实际发生的与取得收入有关的、合理的支出,包括成本、费用、税金、损失和其他支出,准予在计算应纳税所得额时扣除。相关性和合理性是企业所得税税前扣除的基本要求和重要条件。《企业所得税法实施条例》第8条对于相关性和合理性作了解释,相关性是指"与取得收入直接相关的支出",合理性是指"符合生产经营活动常规,应当计入当期损益或者有关资产成本的必要和正常的支出"。

The Enterprise Income Tax Law stipulates the deduction principle and framework, and the requirement that deductions should comply with the principle of relevance and reasonableness. Article 8 of the Enterprise Income Tax Law stipulates that reasonable expenses related to income obtained by an enterprise, including costs, expenses, taxes, losses and other expenses, are allowed to be deducted when calculating taxable income. Relevance and rationality are the basic requirements and important conditions for the deduction of corporate income tax. Article 8 of the Implementation Regulations of the Enterprise Income Tax Law explains relevance and rationality. Relevance refers to "expenses directly related to the income obtained", and rationality refers to "compliance with the routine of production and operation activities and should be included in the current profits and losses, or necessary and normal expenditures related to asset costs".

同时,《企业所得税法》第10条规定了禁止扣除项目,包括:(1)向投资者支付的股息、红利等权益性投资收益款项;(2)企业所得税税款;(3)税收滞纳金;(4)罚金、罚款和被没收财物的损失;(5)本法第9条规定以外的捐赠支出;(6)赞助支出;(7)未经核定的准备金支出;(8)与取得收入无关的其他支出。

At the same time, Article 10 of the Enterprise Income Tax Law stipulates prohibited deduction items, including: (1) dividends, bonuses and other equity investment income paid to investors; (2) enterprise income tax; (3) tax late fee; (4) penalty, fines and loss of confiscated property; (5) donation expenditures other than those specified in Article 9 of this law; (6) sponsorship expenditures; (7) unapproved reserve expenditures; (8) other expenditures that are not related to income.

《企业所得税法》明确对企业实际发生的与取得收入有关的、合理的支出允许税前扣除的一般规则,同时明确不得税前扣除项目的禁止扣除规则,又规定了允许扣除的特殊项目。这些一般扣除规则、禁止扣除规则和特殊扣除规则,构成了我国企业所得税制度税前扣除的一般框架。①

The Enterprise Income Tax Law clarifies the general rules for allowable pre-tax deductions for reasonable expenditures related to income obtained by enterprises, and at the same time clarifies the prohibition deduction rules for items that cannot be pre-tax deductions, and also

---

① 国家税务总局关于印发《新企业所得税法精神宣传提纲》的通知,国税函〔2008〕159号文第11条。

stipulates the special items allowed for deductions. These general deduction rules, prohibition deduction rules, and special deduction rules constitute the general framework of pre-tax deductions in China's corporate income tax system.

(四)资产税务处理
Asset Tax Treatment

资产税务处理,一般是指企业所得税对各项资产如何在税前折旧、摊销和扣除。资产的税务处理主要包括资产的分类、确认计价、扣除方法和处置等内容。《企业所得税法》对企业的各项资产作了规定,具体包括:

Asset tax treatment generally refers to how various assets are depreciated, amortized, and deducted before taxing. The tax treatment of assets mainly includes the classification of assets, confirmation of valuation, deduction methods, and disposal. The Enterprise Income Tax Law stipulates various assets of enterprises, including:

(1)固定资产。固定资产是指企业为生产产品、提供劳务、出租或经营管理而持有的、使用寿命超过12个月、单位价值在规定标准以上的有形资产;

(1) Fixed assets refer to tangible assets held by an enterprise for the purpose of producing products, providing labor services, leasing or operating management, with a service life of more than 12 months and a unit value above the prescribed standard;

(2)无形资产。无形资产是指企业拥有或控制的无实物形态可供辨认的非货币性资产;

(2) Intangible assets refer to non-monetary assets owned or controlled by an enterprise that have no recognizable physical form;

(3)长期待摊费用。长期待摊费用是指企业已经支出,但摊销期限在1年以上(不含1年)的各项费用,包括固定资产大修理支出、租入固定资产的改良支出、已足额提取折旧的固定资产的改建支出、企业的开办费等;

(3) Long-term prepaid expenses refer to the expenses that the enterprise has already paid, but the amortization period is more than one year (excluding one year), including the expenses for major repairs of fixed assets, the improvement expenses of rented fixed assets, and the expenditures for reconstruction of fixed assets, start-up expenses of enterprises, that have been fully depreciated, etc;

(4)投资资产。投资资产是指企业对外进行权益性投资、债权性投资和混合性投资所形成的资产;

(4) Investment assets refer to the assets formed by enterprises' external equity investments, debt investments and mixed investments;

(5)存货等。存货是指企业在日常活动中持有以备出售的成品或商品、处在生产过程中的在产品、在生产过程或提供劳务过程中耗用的材料和物料等。

(5) Inventory refers to the finished products or commodities that an enterprise holds for sale in daily activities, the products in the production process, the materials and supplies consumed in the production process or the process of providing labor services, etc.

三、应纳税所得额和应纳税额的计算和规定
Calculation and Regulation of Taxable Income and Taxable Amount

(一) 应纳税所得额的概念及其计算
Concept and Calculation of Taxable Income

应纳税所得额是指企业各项应税收入的毛收入。《企业所得税法》第5条规定：应纳税所得额=企业每一纳税年度的收入总额-不征税收入-免税收入-各项扣除-允许弥补的以前年度亏损。

Taxable income refers to the gross income of various incomes of the enterprise. Article 5 of the Enterprise Income Tax Law stipulates: taxable income = total income of the enterprise for each tax year − non-taxable income − tax exempt income − various deductions − allowable compensation for previous years' losses.

企业应纳税所得额的计算，以权责发生制为原则。权责发生制要求，属于当期的收入和费用，不论款项是否收付，均作为当期的收入和费用；不属于当期的收入和费用，即使款项已经在当期收付，均不作为当期的收入和费用。权责发生制以企业经济权利和经济义务是否发生作为计算应纳税所得额的依据，注重强调企业收入与费用的时间配比，要求企业收入费用的确认时间不得提前或滞后。企业在不同纳税期间享受不同的税收优惠政策时，坚持按权责发生制原则计算应纳税所得额，可以有效防止企业利用收入和支出确认时间的不同规避税收。

The calculation of taxable income of an enterprise is based on the principle of accrual. The accrual system requires that the income and expenses that belong to the current period, regardless of whether the money is received or paid, are regarded as the income and expenses of the current period; the income and expenses that do not belong to the current period, even if the money has been received and paid in the current period, are not regarded as the current income and expenses. The accrual system takes the occurrence of economic rights and obligations of the enterprise as the basis for calculating taxable income, emphasizes the time ratio of enterprise income and expenses, and requires that the recognition time of enterprise income and expenses shall not be advanced or delayed. When enterprises enjoy different preferential tax policies during different tax periods, they adhere to the principle of accrual calculation of taxable income, which can effectively prevent enterprises from taking advantage of the difference in the confirmation time of income and expenditure to avoid taxation.

另外，企业会计准则规定，企业要以权责发生制为原则确认当期收入或费用，计算企业生产经营结果。《企业所得税法》与会计采用同一原则确认当期收入或费用，有利于减少两者的差异，减轻纳税人税收遵从成本。

In addition, the Accounting Standards for Business Enterprises stipulate that companies should use the accrual basis as the principle to confirm current income or expenses and calculate the results of their production and operations. The Enterprise Income Tax Law and accounting adopt the same principle to confirm the current income or expenses, which is conducive to reducing the difference between the two and reducing the tax compliance cost of taxpayers.

此外,《企业所得税法》第17条规定,企业在汇总计算缴纳企业所得税时,其境外营业机构的亏损不得抵减境内营业机构的盈利。

In addition, Article 17 of the Enterprise Income Tax Law stipulates that when enterprises collectively calculate and pay corporate income tax, the losses of their overseas business institutions shall not be offset against the profits of domestic business institutions.

《企业所得税法》第18条规定,企业纳税年度发生的亏损,准予向以后年度结转,用以后年度的所得弥补,但结转年限最长不得超过5年。

Article 18 of the Enterprise Income Tax Law stipulates that the losses incurred in the tax year of an enterprise may be carried forward to subsequent years and be made up with the income of the subsequent years, but the carry-forward period shall not exceed five years.

(二)应纳税额的概念及其计算
Concept and Calculation of Tax Payable

应纳税额是指纳税人应缴纳的税款,是应纳税所得额乘以税率所得出的实质上应缴纳的税款,即税收负担。《企业所得税法》第22条规定:应纳税额=应纳税所得额×适用税率-减免税额-允许抵免的税额。

Tax payable refers to the tax payable by the taxpayer, which is the actual tax payable obtained by multiplying the taxable income by the tax rate, that is, the tax burden. According to Article 22 of the Enterprise Income Tax Law: tax payable = taxable income × applicable tax rate − tax deduction − allowable tax credit.

(三)企业所得税的抵免及其计算
Enterprise Income Tax Credit and Its Calculation

抵免是避免重复征税的手段之一。企业在境外开展投资活动,通过抵免使企业在境外已缴纳的所得税回到境内缴纳所得税时可以得到扣除;但这种扣除是有限额的,不准超过按照本国税率所计算出来的应纳税额;超过部分不得抵免。

Credit is one of the means of avoiding double taxation. Enterprises that carry out investment activities abroad can deduct the income tax that the enterprise has paid abroad when they return to the country to pay income tax through credits; however, such deductions are subject to a limit and cannot exceed the tax payable calculated according to the domestic tax rate. The excess part cannot be credited.

《企业所得税法》第23条规定,企业取得的下列所得已在境外缴纳的所得税税额,可以从其当期应纳税额中抵免,抵免限额为该项所得依照本法规定计算的应纳税额;超过抵免限额的部分,可以在以后五个年度内,用每年度抵免限额抵免当年应抵税额后的余额进行抵补:(1)居民企业来源于中国境外的应税所得;(2)非居民企业在中国境内设立机构、场所,取得发生在中国境外但与该机构、场所有实际联系的应税所得。

Article 23 of the Enterprise Income Tax Law stipulates that the following income tax paid abroad by an enterprise can be deducted from its current tax payable. The credit limit is the amount of income calculated in accordance with the provisions of this law. The part that exceeds the credit limit can be used to offset the taxable amount of the current year with the annual credit limit for the following five years: (1) the taxable income of a resident enterprise derived from outside China; (2) a non-resident enterprise establishes an institution or place in China, and obtains taxable income that occurs outside China but actually contacts the institution or place.

《企业所得税法》第24条规定,居民企业从其直接或者间接控制的外国企业分得的来源于中国境外的股息、红利等权益性投资收益,外国企业在境外实际缴纳的所得税税额中属于该项所得负担的部分,可以作为该居民企业的可抵免境外所得税税额,在本法第23条规定的抵免限额内抵免。

Article 24 of the Enterprise Income Tax Law stipulates that the dividends, bonuses and other equity investment income that a resident enterprise receives from a foreign enterprise directly or indirectly controlled by it is derived from equity investment income outside China, and the foreign enterprise actually pays overseas income tax. The part of the income burden can be used as the deductible foreign income tax amount of the resident enterprise, and it can be deducted within the credit limit stipulated in Article 23 of this law.

《企业所得税法》第21条规定,在计算应纳税所得额时,企业财务、会计处理办法与税收法律、行政法规的规定不一致的,应当依照税收法律、行政法规的规定计算。

Article 21 of the Enterprise Income Tax Law stipulates that when calculating taxable income, if the enterprise's financial and accounting treatment methods are inconsistent with the tax laws and administrative regulations, the calculation shall be carried out in accordance with the tax laws and administrative regulations.

第五节　源泉扣除和税收征管
Section 5　Source Deduction and Administration of Tax Collection

改革开放和市场经济的发展让企业的机构和组织形式趋向多样化,也让企业收入来源的渠道和形式更加多元,因此增加了企业所得税征收管理的复杂性。在此过程中,一方面应当做到为纳税人提供方便,降低纳税成本,更好地服务纳税人,另一方面也要有利于税务机关实施高效的税收管理。因此,这是统一企业所得税法立法过程中的一个重要问题,除了应当依法执行我国税收征管法的相关规定,对于企业所得税征收管理中出现的一些特殊问题,有的应当进行反复强调,有的应该作出补充规定。例如,新税法就纳税地点、分支机构汇总纳税等作了补充规定。

Reform and opening up and the development of the market economy have diversified the institutions and organizational forms of enterprises, and have also made the channels and forms of corporate income sources more diversified, thus increasing the complexity of corporate income tax collection and management. In this process, on the one hand, it should provide convenience for taxpayers, reduce tax costs, and better serve taxpayers. On the other hand, it should also help tax authorities implement efficient tax management. Therefore, this is an important issue in the legislative process of unifying the corporate income tax law. In addition to the implementation of the relevant provisions of China's tax collection and management law, some special issues arising in the management of corporate income tax collection should be repeatedly emphasized, and some supplementary provisions should be made. For example, the new tax law makes supplementary provisions on taxation locations and branch taxation.

 源泉扣除

Source Deduction

源泉扣除,指的是以所得支付者为扣缴义务人,在每次向纳税人支付有关所得款项时,化为扣缴税款的做法。这种扣除实际上是对税收征管的发生地与支付单位所得收入进行控制,并且予以源泉扣除,而非税前列支的扣除。

Source deduction refers to the practice of withholding tax on behalf of the taxpayer when the income payer is the withholding agent. This kind of deduction actually controls the place of tax collection and management and the income of the payment unit, and is deducted from the source, rather than the deduction of pre-tax expenses.

《企业所得税法》第3条规定,非居民企业在中国境内设立机构、场所的,应当就其所设机构、场所取得的来源于中国境内的所得,以及发生在中国境外但与其所设机构、场所有实际联系的所得,缴纳企业所得税。非居民企业在中国境内未设立机构、场所的,或者虽设立机构、场所但取得的所得与其所设机构、场所没有实际联系的,应当就其来源于中国境内的所得缴纳企业所得税。第37条规定,对非居民企业取得的所得应缴纳的所得税,实行源泉扣缴,以支付人为扣缴义务人。税款由扣缴义务人在每次支付或者到期应支付时,从支付或者到期应支付的款项中扣缴。

Article 3 of the Enterprise Income Tax Law stipulates that "For a non-resident enterprise having offices or establishments inside China, it shall pay enterprise income tax on its incomes derived from China as well as on incomes that it earns outside China but which has real connection with the said offices or establishments. For a non-resident enterprise having no office or establishment inside China, or for a non-resident enterprise whose incomes have no actual connection to its institution or establishment inside China, it shall pay enterprise income tax on the incomes derived from China". Article 37 of the Enterprise Income Tax Law stipulates that the income tax payable on the income obtained by non-resident enterprises shall be withheld from the source, and the payer shall be the withholding agent. The tax shall be withheld by the withholding agent from the amount paid or due each time it is paid or due.

《企业所得税法》第38条规定,对非居民企业在中国境内取得工程作业和劳务所得应缴纳的所得税,税务机关可以指定工程价款或者劳务费的支付人为扣缴义务人。

Article 38 of the Enterprise Income Tax Law stipulates that for non-resident companies that obtain income from construction operations and labor services within China, the tax authority may designate the payer of the project price or labor service fee as the withholding agent.

《企业所得税法》第39条规定,实行税源扣缴的所得税,扣缴义务人未依法扣缴或者无法履行扣缴义务的,由纳税人在所得发生地缴纳。纳税人未依法缴纳的,税务机关可以从该纳税人在中国境内其他收入项目的支付人应付的款项中,追缴该纳税人的应纳税款。

Article 39 of the Enterprise Income Tax Law stipulates that income tax withheld from tax sources is implemented. If the withholding agent fails to withhold the tax according to law or fails to perform the withholding obligation, the taxpayer shall pay it at the place where the income is generated. If a tax payer fails to pay taxes according to the law, the tax authorities may recover the tax payable by the taxpayer from the amount payable by the payer of other income items within the territory of China.

二、纳税方式
Approach of Tax Payment

《企业所得税法》第49条规定,企业所得税的征收管理除《企业所得税法》的规定外,依照《中华人民共和国税收征收管理法》的规定执行。第50条规定,除税收法律、行政法规另有规定外,居民企业以企业登记注册地为纳税地点;但登记注册地在境外的,以实际管理机构所在地为纳税地点。

Article 49 of the Enterprise Income Tax Law stipulates that, in addition to the provisions of the Enterprise Income Tax Law, the collection and management of enterprise income tax shall be implemented in accordance with the Tax Collection Management Law of the People's Republic of China. Article 50 stipulates that, unless otherwise provided by tax laws and administrative regulations, resident enterprises shall take the place of registration of the enterprise as the place of tax payment; but if the place of registration is overseas, the place of actual management institution shall be the place of tax payment.

《企业所得税法》第52条规定,除国务院另有规定外,企业之间不得合并缴纳企业所得税。

Article 52 of the Enterprise Income Tax Law stipulates that, unless otherwise stipulated by the State Council, no enterprise income tax shall be paid jointly among enterprises.

《企业所得税法》第53条规定,企业在一个纳税年度中间开业,或者终止经营活动,使该纳税年度的实际经营期不足12个月的,应当以其实际经营期为一个纳税年度。企业依法清算时,应当以清算期间作为一个纳税年度。

Article 53 of the Enterprise Income Tax Law stipulates that if an enterprise opens in the middle of a tax year or terminates its business activities, so that the actual operating period of the tax year is less than twelve months, its actual operating period shall be a tax year. When an enterprise is liquidated according to law, the liquidation period shall be regarded as a tax year.

以上这些规定,一方面对企业所得税的征收管理有所加强,另一方面又方便了纳税人,服务了纳税人。

On the one hand, the above regulations have strengthened the collection and management of corporate income tax, and on the other hand, they have provided convenience for taxpayers.

第六节 相 关 案 例
Section 6　Related Cases

此节中所选案例为意大利意迩瓦萨隆诺控股股份公司诉山东省烟台市芝罘国家税务局税收争议案。

Italian Illva Saronno Holding SpA v. Zhifu State Taxation Bureau of Yantai City, Shandong Province.

一、案情介绍
Introduction of the Case

原告:意大利意迩瓦萨隆诺控股股份公司

Plaintiff: Italian Illva Saronno Holding SpA

被告:山东省烟台市芝罘国家税务局

Defendant: Zhifu State Taxation Bureau

原告意大利意迩瓦萨隆诺控股股份公司系意大利意迩瓦萨隆诺投资有限公司(以下简称"意迩瓦投资公司")的母公司,意迩瓦投资公司系原告的全资子公司,两公司均为意大利的法人公司。2005年9月29日,意迩瓦投资公司经山东省对外贸易经济合作厅批准,以人民币481 424 260元的对价取得烟台张裕集团有限公司33%股权。2012年7月17日,原告意迩瓦控股公司与意迩瓦投资公司分别通过股东大会决议,决定由原告对意迩瓦投资公司实施吸收合并,接受该投资公司的全部资产与负债,其中包括烟台张裕集团有限公司的33%股权。在合并吸收之后,意迩瓦投资公司已于2012年11月21日依法注销了公司登记,由原告意迩瓦控股公司直接持有烟台张裕集团有限公司的33%股权。2012年7月17日,原告意迩瓦控股公司将两公司的合并吸收情况,致函告知了烟台张裕集团有限公司。

The plaintiff Illva Saronno Holding SpA (hereinafter referred to as "Illva Holding") is the parent company of Italian Illva Investment Co., Ltd. (hereinafter referred to as "Illva Investment"). Illva Investment is a wholly-owned subsidiary of the plaintiff. Both companies are corporate companies in Italy. On 29 September 2005, approved by Shandong Foreign Trade and Economic Cooperation Department, the plaintiff acquired 33% equity of Yantai Changyu

Group Co., Ltd. at a consideration of RMB 481,424,260. On 17 July 2012, after the resolution of the general meeting of shareholders, Illva Holding and Illva Investment decided that the plaintiff implemented the merger of Illva Investment Company and accepted all the assets and liabilities of the investment company, including 33% equity of Yantai Changyu Group Co., Ltd. After the merger, Illva Investment cancelled its company registration in accordance with the law on November 21, 2012, and Illva Holding directly held 33% equity of Yantai Changyu Group Co., Ltd.. On 17 July 2012, Illva Holding informed Yantai Changyu Group Co., Ltd. of the merger and absorption of the two companies.

被告山东省烟台市芝罘国家税务局于2013年9月9日作出了一项税务事项通知书,认定原告意迩瓦控股公司于2012年7月17日通过股东大会决议吸收合并了意迩瓦投资公司,致使烟台张裕集团有限公司的股东由意迩瓦投资公司变更为原告意迩瓦控股公司。依据国税函〔2009〕698号文件(以下简称"国税函698号文件")第7条"非居民企业向其关联方转让中国居民企业股权,其转让价格不符合独立交易原则而减少应纳税所得额的,税务机关有权按照合理方法进行调整"之规定,应对该合并事宜进行纳税调整,以烟台张裕集团有限公司2012年6月30日账面净资产数额2 863 169 524.88元为基准,原告意迩瓦控股公司应缴纳企业所得税46 342 168.32元,被告通知原告于2013年9月25日前到被告处进行纳税申报。原告意迩瓦控股公司不服被告作出的税务事项通知书,于2013年11月20日向山东省烟台市国家税务局提起了行政复议,要求撤销被告的税务事项通知书。山东省烟台市国家税务局则认为,根据财税59号文,外方关联公司之间转让境内公司股权,除了要符合该规章第5条的规定,还要同时适用第7条第1款的规定,而原告对意迩瓦诺投资公司的吸收合并行为,并不符合该规定,仍应适用国税函698号文件的规定,据此维持了被告作出的税务事项通知书。原告对山东省烟台市国家税务局的行政复议决定仍然不服,便向山东省烟台市芝罘区人民法院提起了行政诉讼,请求法院撤销被告作出的税务事项通知书,并退还原告已缴纳的所得税46 342 168.32元。

The defendant Zhifu State Taxation Bureau issued a tax notice on September 9, 2013, determining that Illva Holding absorbed and merged Illva Investment through a resolution of the shareholders' general meeting on July 17, 2012, as a result, the shareholders of Yantai Changyu Group Co., Ltd. changed from Illva Investment to Illva Holding. In accordance with Article 7 of document No. 698 of the State tax letter (2009) (hereinafter referred to as document No. 698 of the State tax letter) which stipulates that "If a non-resident enterprise transfers the equity of a Chinese resident enterprise to its related party, and the transfer price does not comply with the principle of arm's length transactions and reduces the taxable income, the tax authority has the right to make adjustments in accordance with reasonable methods", tax adjustments should be made to the merger based on the book value of 2,863,169,524.88 yuan on June 30, 2012, and Illva Holding should pay enterprise income tax 46,342,168.32 yuan. The defendant informed the plaintiff to make a tax declaration to the defendant by September 25, 2013. The plaintiff was dissatisfied with the notice of tax matters made by the defendant, and filed an administrative reconsideration with the State Taxation Bureau of Yantai City, Shandong Province on 20 November 2013, requesting for rescission of the defendant's notice of tax matters. The State Taxation Bureau of Yantai City, Shandong Province decides that in accordance with article 59, the transfer of equity of a domestic company between foreign affiliates shall not only comply with the provisions of Article 5 of the Regulations, but also comply with the provisions of Article 7 Paragraph 1 at the same time. As the plaintiff's absorption and merger of Illva Investment did not comply with this requirement, document No. 698 of the State tax letter shall still be applied. Accordingly, the defendant's notice of tax matters was maintained. The plaintiff was still dissatisfied with the administrative reconsideration decision of the State Taxation Bureau of Yantai City, Shandong Province, filed an administrative lawsuit with the Zhifu District People's Court of Yantai City, Shandong Province, requesting the court to revoke the notice of tax matters made by the defendant and return 46,342,168.32 yuan.

原告诉称,意迩瓦投资公司系原告的全资子公司,为优化集团内部结构,简化控股及管理机制,原告与该公司于2012年7月17日分别通过股东大会决定实施吸收合并。原告的本次交易符合财政部、国家税务总局《关于企业重组业务企业所得税处理若干问题的通知》[财税〔2009〕59号文](以下简称"财税59号文")的相关规定,税务待遇应按该通知的有关合并的特殊重组一般条件享受免税待遇,而被告却将该合并认定为股权转让,并依据国税函698号文件第7条的规定对我公司征税46 342 168.32元。被告的征税行为违反了税收法定原则、中意两国关于税收无差别待遇原则、中意两国关于避免双重征税的原则、中意两国政府保护投资协定的相关原则,片面选择性地引用对其有利的独立交易原则对此次交易征税,而对原告有利的税收法定原则、财税59号文、中意两国相关协定及企业重组等符合国际惯例的相关法规,却拒绝予以适用,有违税收公平正义原则。

The plaintiff stated that Illva Investment was a wholly-owned subsidiary of the plaintiff, and in order to optimize the group's internal structure and simplify the holding and management mechanisms, the plaintiff and Illva Investment decided to implement the merger through the shareholders' general meeting on July 17, 2012. The plaintiff's transaction complied with the relevant regulations of the Ministry of Finance and the State Administration of Taxation on the handling of certain issues of enterprise income tax in the business of enterprise reorganization [Fiscal and Tax (2009) 59] (hereinafter referred to as "Fiscal and tax 59"), thus shall enjoy the tax treatment in accordance with the general conditions of the notice relating to the merger. However, the defendant identified the merger as an equity transfer, and levied 46,342,168.32 yuan on the plaintiff. The defendant's taxation violates the statutory principle of taxation, the principle of non-discrimination in taxation between China and Italy, the principle of avoiding double taxation between China and Italy, and the relevant principles of investment protection agreements between China and Italy; The defendant one-sidedly and selectively cited the principle of independent transactions in its favour, and refused to apply the legal principle of taxation in favour of the plaintiff, Fiscal and Tax 59, the relevant agreements between China and Italy and the relevant regulations of enterprise reorganization, thus violating the principle of fairness and justice in tax collection.

被告辩称,原告意迩瓦控股公司与意迩瓦投资公司的上述吸收合并,实质是意迩瓦投资公司将其持有的烟台张裕集团有限公司33%股权转让给了其母公司即原告意迩瓦控股公司,应认定是直接股权转让,且转让价格不符合独立交易原则。依据国税函698号文件第7条"非居民企业向其关联方转让中国居民企业股权,其转让价格不符合独立交易原则而减少应纳税所得额的,税务机关有权按照合理方法进行调整"之规定,采用成本法对股权转让价格进行纳税调整。根据张裕集团2012年6月份资产负债表,归属于张裕集团的净资产为2 863 169 524.88元,原告意大利意迩瓦萨隆诺控股股份公司投资比例为33%,股权成本为481 424 260.00元,应缴纳企业所得税46 342 168.32元。

The defendant argued that the above absorption and merger was essentially the transfer of 33% of Illva Investment's shares in Yantai Changyu Group Co., Ltd. to Illva Holding, which should be considered as a direct equity transfer, also, the transfer price did not conform to the principle of independent trading. According to Article 7 of Document No. 698 of the State Tax Letter "if a non-resident enterprise transfers the shares of a Chinese resident enterprise to its related party and its transfer price does not conform to the principle of independent transaction and reduces the amount of taxable income, the tax authorities shall have the right to adjust it in accordance with reasonable methods", the cost method was used to adjust the price of equity transfer. According to the balance sheet of Changyu Group in June 2012, the net assets attributable to Changyu Group were 2,863,169,524.88 yuan, the investment ratio of the plaintiff Italy Illva Holding is 33%, the cost of equity was 481,424,260.00 yuan, and the enterprise income tax should be 46,342,168.32 yuan.

原告还提出,根据中意税收协定第24条,原告应与中国居民企业享受同样的财税59号文规定的特殊税收待遇;根据中意税收协定第23条第1款,被告对本次交易征税决定也明显违背中国和意大利不应当双重征税的规定;根据中意投资协定的第3条第1款,中意两国政府给予对方国民或公司不能低于任何第三国的投资待遇,而同时根据中芬投资协定第3条第2款,中国、芬兰两国政府已给予了对方国民或公司国民待遇,故被告对原告也应给予同样的国民待遇,即原告应与中国居民企业享受财税59号文规定的同样特殊税收待遇。被告在答辩状中则认为,原告不能根据中意双方协定的某一原则性条款就来反对中国税务机关根据具体明确的税法所作出的行政行为;假如按照中华人民共和国的税法将导致对原告双重征税,那么这涉及两国之间哪一方作出调整的问题,应按照中意税收协定议定书的规定,启动政府间协商机制,由两国政府通过协商程序解决。

The plaintiff also submitted that, according to Article 24 of the Sino-Italian tax agreement, the plaintiff should enjoy the same special tax treatment as the Chinese resident enterprise, as stipulated in Fiscal and Tax 59; according to Article 23, Paragraph 1 of the Sino-Italian tax agreement, the defendant's tax decision on this transaction was also clearly contrary to the stipulation that China and Italy should not double tax; in accordance with Article 3, Paragraph 1 of the Sino-Italian Investment Agreement, the Governments of the two countries shall treat each other's nationals or companies no less than that of any third country, while, in accordance with Article 3, Paragraph 2 of the Sino-Finen Investment Agreement, the Governments of China and Finland have already treated each other's nationals or companies, so the defendant shall treat the plaintiff with the same national treatment, that is, the plaintiff shall enjoy the same special tax treatment as that stipulated in Fiscal and Tax 59. In its reply, the defendant held that the plaintiff could not oppose the administrative act of the Chinese tax authorities under the specific and clear tax laws on the basis of a certain principle clause of the agreement between China and Italy; If the tax laws of the People's Republic of China would lead to double taxation of the plaintiff, then the question of which party to make adjustments between the two countries should be set up in accordance with the provisions of the protocol to the Sino-Italian Tax Agreement, and the intergovernmental consultation mechanism should be initiated by the two governments through consultation procedures.

法院经过审理,决定驳回原告的诉讼请求。

After hearing, the court decided to reject the plaintiff's claim.

(二) 案件分析
Case Analysis

本案的主要争议焦点在于:第一,原告和意迩瓦投资公司此次重组交易的性质是合并还是股权转让;第二,原告此次对意迩瓦投资公司的重组交易是否符合财税59号文的享受免税待遇的规定;第三,原告是否应当根据中意税收协定、中意投资协定、中芬投资协定的最惠国待遇规定而在本次交易中享受免税待遇。

The main focus of the dispute in this case is: first, whether the nature of the reorganization transaction between the plaintiff and Illva Investment is a merger or an equity transfer; second, whether the plaintiff's reorganization transaction with Illva Investment conforms to the tax exemption provisions of Fiscal and Tax 59; third, whether the plaintiff should enjoy tax exemption in this transaction in accordance with the most-favoured-nation treatment provisions of the Sino-Italy Tax Agreement, the Sino-Italy Investment Agreement and the Sino-Finen Investment Agreement.

第一,原告和意迩瓦投资公司此次重组交易的性质是合并还是股权转让。原告的子公司意迩瓦投资公司仅持有烟台张裕集团有限公司一家的股份,意迩瓦投资公司的主要资产就是对张裕集团的股权投资,此次吸收合并直接导致了张裕集团的股东由意迩瓦投资公司变更为原告,实现了原告对烟台张裕集团公司的直接控制。同时,在2013年12月12日国家税务总局72号文所载明的境外企业合并导致中国居民企业股权被转让属于非居民企业股权转让的规定,也进一步可以证明此次重组交易的性质应当被认定为股权转让。

First, the nature of the reorganization transaction between the plaintiff and Illva Investment is merger or equity transfer. The plaintiff's subsidiary, Illva Investment only holds a stake in Yantai Changyu Group Co., Ltd., whose main asset is equity investment in Changyu Group. The merger directly led to the change of shareholders from Illva Investment Company to plaintiff, realizing the plaintiff's direct control of Yantai Changyu Group Company. At the same time, the stipulation that "The transfer of equity of Chinese resident enterprises caused by the merger of overseas enterprises is a non-resident enterprise equity transfer" stated in the State Administration of Taxation No. 72 of December 12, 2013 can also be further proved that the nature of the reorganization transaction should be recognized as equity transfer.

第二,原告此次对意迩瓦投资公司的重组交易是否符合财税59号文的享受免税待遇的规定。原告的此次境外股权交易虽然符合财税59号文第5条的适用特殊性税务处理规定,但财税59号文第7条还规定企业发生涉及中国境内与境外之间的股权和资产收购交易,除应符合本通知第5条规定的条件外,还应同时符合下列条件才可选择适用特殊性税务处理规定,即非居民企业向其100%直接控股的另一非居民企业转让其拥有的居民企业股权的,也就是"母转子公司"的情形,而原告的此次交易是"子转母公司"的情形,因此原告不应当享受财税59号文规定的免税待遇,被告根据国税函698号文制作的纳税通知符合法律规定。

Second, whether the plaintiff's restructuring of Illva Investment is in line with the tax exemption provisions of Fiscal and Tax 59. Although the plaintiff's overseas equity transaction conforms to the applicable special tax treatment provisions of Article 5 of Fiscal and Tax 59, Article 7 of Fiscal and Tax 59 also stipulates that in addition to meeting the conditions stipulated in Article 5 of this Circular, a non-resident enterprise may choose to apply the special tax treatment provisions, that is, if a non-resident enterprise transfers its special tax treatment provisions, that is, where a non-resident enterprise transfers its own shares in a resident enterprise to another non-resident enterprise with 100% direct control, that is, the case of a "parent-to-subsidiary company", and the plaintiff's transaction is a "sub-to-mother company" situation. Therefore, the plaintiff should not enjoy the tax-free treatment stipulated in Fiscal and Tax 59, and the tax notice made by the defendant according to the tax letter No. 698 conforms to the law.

第三,原告是否应当根据中意税收协定、中意投资协定、中芬投资协定的最惠国待遇规定而在本次交易中享受免税待遇。根据《中华人民共和国企业所得税法》《中华人民共和国企业所得税法实施细则》以及国税函698号文的规定,对于股权转让行为的征税,境内居民企业和境外非居民企业的适用,以及境外各国非居民企业之间的适用都是一致的,并不存在任何歧视。在中国企业所得税法的制度体系中,对境外非居民企业按照其独有特点制定专门的征收管理规定,不能认为这就是对作为非居民企业的原告的歧视,这也是目前的国际惯例。尤其根据中意税收协定第25条以及中意税收协定议定书第7条的规定,原告对中国税务机关的征税决定有疑义,在进行国内诉讼程序后,可以启动中意两国的税收协商程序,仍有可能的救济途径。

Third, whether the plaintiff should enjoy tax exemption in this transaction according to the most-favoured-nation treatment provisions of the Sino-Italian tax agreement, Sino-Finnish investment agreement. In accordance with the provisions of the Enterprise Income Tax Law of the People's Republic of China, the Detailed Rules for the Implementation of the Enterprise Income Tax Law of the People's Republic of China and the State Tax Letter No. 698, the taxation of the transfer of shares, the application of domestic resident enterprises and foreign non-resident enterprises, and the application of non-resident enterprises in foreign countries are consistent without any discrimination. In the system of Chinese enterprise income tax law, foreign non-resident enterprises make special regulations on collection and management according to their unique characteristics, which can not be considered as discrimination against the plaintiff as a non-resident enterprise, which is also the current world practice. In particular, according to Article 25 of the Sino-Italian Tax Agreement and Article 7 of the Protocol to the Sino-Italian Tax Agreement, the plaintiff has doubts about the tax decision of the Chinese tax authorities. After domestic proceedings, the tax negotiation procedure between China and Italy can be initiated. There are still possible remedies.

学习思考题
Questions for Study

1. 我国企业所得税法对居民企业和非居民企业是怎样认定的?
   How to identify resident enterprises and non-resident enterprises in China's Law of Enterprise Income Tax?
2. 我国企业所得税的税率是多少?
   What is the tax rate of China's enterprise income tax?
3. 居民企业和非居民企业的应纳税所得额分别是怎样计算的?
   How to calculate the taxable income of resident enterprises and non-resident enterprises?
4. 企业所得税法规定的非税所得和免税所得分别有哪些?
   What are the non-tax income and tax-free income stipulated in the Law of Enterprise Income Tax?
5. 企业所得税法对于固定资产、无形资产以及长期待摊费用是如何处理的?
   How to deal with fixed assets, intangible assets and long-term deferred expenses in the Law of Enterprise Income Tax?
6. 企业境外取得所得如何确定应纳税所得额?
   How to determine the taxable income for enterprises' overseas income?
7. 企业所得税法规定了哪些情形需要特别纳税调整? 什么是转移定价和预约定价安排?
   What circumstances need special tax adjustment in the Law of Enterprise Income Tax? What is transfer pricing and advance pricing arrangement?

第五章 CHAPTER V

国际双重征税
International Double Taxation

第一节 国际双重征税产生的原因
Section 1 Causes for the Generation of International Double Taxation

在国际层面，由于各国税收管辖权并存，存在着从事跨国经济活动的同一纳税主体的同一笔所得被多次征税的可能。国际双重征税，指的就是两个以上的国家或地区，对属于不同纳税人的来源于同一税源的课税对象同时行使税收管辖权。

Internationally, due to the coexistence of tax jurisdictions in various countries, there is a possibility that the same income of the same taxpayer engaged in transnational economic activities may be double taxed. International double taxation refers to the situation that two or more countries or regions simultaneously exercise tax jurisdiction over taxation objects from the same tax source that come from different taxpayers.

在税收征管实践中，导致国际双重征税的原因是多方面的，但究其根本，是由于国家税收管辖权之间的冲突。国家税收管辖权之间的冲突，主要体现为居民税收管辖权与来源地税收管辖权之间的冲突、两个国家的居民税收管辖权之间的冲突、两个国家的来源地税收管辖权之间的冲突三个方面。

In the practice of tax administration, there are many causes for the generation of international double taxation, but the fundamental one is the conflicts over tax jurisdiction between countries. The conflicts over tax jurisdiction between countries are mainly reflected in the conflicts over resident tax jurisdiction and source tax jurisdiction, the conflicts over resident tax jurisdiction between countries, and the conflicts over source tax jurisdiction.

一、居民税收管辖权与来源地税收管辖权之间的冲突
Conflicts over Resident Tax Jurisdiction and Source Tax Jurisdiction

居民税收管辖权与来源地税收管辖权之间的冲突形成的背后原因是各国可以采用不同的原则行使税收管辖权，因此对于一国居民纳税人在境外从事经济活动的所得与财产，既可以由实行居民管辖权的国家依据属人主义原则对本国纳税人的境外所得进行征税，也可

以由实行地域管辖权的国家依据属地主义原则对外国纳税人从本国境内取得的财产进行征税,从而出现同一跨国纳税人的同一笔所得被两个国家双重征税的问题。例如,作为A国居民纳税人的甲在乙国从事经济活动并取得所得,对于该笔所得,A国依据属人主义原则行使居民管辖权征税,B国依据属地主义原则行使来源地管辖权征税,这样A国人甲在B国的所得便被A、B两国同时征税。

The cause for the generation of conflicts over resident tax jurisdiction and source-based tax jurisdiction is that countries can adopt different principles to exercise tax jurisdiction. Therefore, the income and property of a resident taxpayer from overseas economic activities can be taxed by countries that exercise resident jurisdiction based on the principle of humanism, while the property acquired by foreign taxpayers from the host countries can also be taxed by that country based on the principle of territorialism, which can lead to the situation that the same income of the same transnational taxpayer is double taxed by two countries. For example, assuming a resident taxpayer of country A engages in economic activities in country B and obtains income, and for this income, if country A exercises its resident jurisdiction to levy taxes based on the principle of humanism, and country B exercises its jurisdiction of source based on the principle of territorialism, the result is that such income will be double taxed by both A and B at the same time.

在该种类型的国际双重征税下,跨国经济活动者的税收负担大大加重,不仅可能影响跨国经济活动者的相关投资、经营决策,也可能会扭曲正常的国际经济交往活动,从而对各国国家利益产生负面影响。要消除或者减轻该种类型的国际双重征税带来的不良影响,核心要素是解决居民税收管辖权与来源地税收管辖权之间的冲突,要求相关国家通过单边、双边或多边的方法限制各自的税收管辖权的行使范围,以达到国际税收的利益协调与平衡。然而由于税收涉及国家主权问题,同时也与一国的财政收入密切相关,因此很难实现这种协调与平衡状态。

Under this type of international double taxation, the tax burden of people engaged in transnational economic activities is greatly increased, which may not only affect the relevant investment and business decisions, but may also distort normal international economic exchange activities, thereby imposing negative impact on countries. To eliminate or mitigate the adverse effects of this type of international double taxation, the core solution is to resolve the conflicts over resident tax jurisdiction and source tax jurisdiction, which can be achieved by restricting the scope of countries' respective tax jurisdiction through unilateral, bilateral or multilateral methods to achieve the coordination and balance of international taxation interests. However, as taxation involves national sovereignty issues and is also closely related to a country's fiscal revenue, it is difficult to achieve this kind of coordination and balance.

 两个国家的居民税收管辖权之间的冲突

Conflicts over Resident Tax Jurisdiction between Countries

两个国家的居民税收管辖权之间的冲突,本质上是税收领域的属人管辖权之间的重叠。这种重叠表现为：居民税收管辖权与居民税收管辖权的冲突；居民税收管辖权与公民税收管辖权的冲突；居民税收管辖权与公民税收管辖权的冲突。不过，由于采用公民税收管辖权的国家很少，属人管辖权之间的重叠主要表现为两个国家的居民税收管辖权之间的冲突。

The conflicts over resident tax jurisdiction between two countries is essentially an overlap between the personal jurisdictions in the tax field. This overlap is manifested in the following conflicts: the conflicts over resident tax jurisdiction and resident tax jurisdiction; the conflicts over resident tax jurisdiction and citizen tax jurisdiction; and the conflicts over resident tax jurisdiction and citizen tax jurisdiction. However, since few countries adopt citizen tax jurisdiction, the overlap between personal jurisdiction is mainly manifested in the conflicts over two countries' resident tax jurisdiction.

由于不同国家在行使居民税收管辖权时对居民标准的认定存在不同，一个自然人或者法人可能同时被两个国家认定为其各自国家的居民（公民）纳税人，因此对于该纳税人，两个国家都认为其应该履行纳税义务，在这种情况下的纳税人将在两个国家承担无限纳税义务。根据国际税法实践，跨国自然人的居民身份的判断标准有：住所标准、时间标准和意愿标准等。跨国法人的居民身份的判断标准有：注册成立地标准、总机构所在地标准、实际管理控制中心标准、主要经济活动地标准等。这些标准的差异无疑会使双重征税的问题更加复杂。例如，甲乙两国都采用居民管辖权，甲国税法规定，凡在甲国拥有住所且离开甲国不满1年者为甲国纳税居民。乙国规定，凡在乙国居住时间超过半年的为乙国居民。现在甲国公民A在甲国拥有住所并离开甲国到乙国从事生产经营活动，在乙国居住了240天并取得收入，对于该笔收入，甲国根据本国税法认定A为纳税居民并对其征税，乙国也因A在本国居住时间超过半年而认定A为纳税居民并对其征税。在这种情况下，甲乙两国均根据本国税法对A行使居民管辖权，从而产生了国际双重征税的问题。同样，跨国法人也会因为两个国家在行使居民税收管辖权时对于居民身份的判断标准不同而产生纳税冲突。

Since different countries have different identification of resident standards when exercising resident tax jurisdiction, a natural person or legal person may be recognized by two countries as resident (citizen) taxpayers of their respective countries. Therefore, for this taxpayer, both countries believed that he or she should fulfill his or her tax obligations, in this case the taxpayer will have unlimited tax obligations in both countries. According to the practice of international tax law, the criteria for the identification of the resident status of a transnational natural person are domicile standards, time standards and willingness standards. The criteria for judging the resident status of a transnational legal person are standards for the place of incorporation, standards for the location of the head office, standards for the actual management control center, standards for major economic activities, etc. The differences in these standards will undoubtedly make the problem of double taxation more complicated. For example, both country A and country B adopt resident jurisdcition. The tax law of country A stipulates that anyone who has a residence in country A and has been away from country A for less than one year is a tax resident of country A, and the tax law of country B stipulates that anyone who has lived in country B for more than half a year is regarded as a resident of country B. Now a citizen of country A has a domicile in country A and left country A to engage in production and business activities in country B. He or she has lived in country B for 240 days and obtained income. Country A recognizes this person as a tax resident according to its own tax law. Country B also recognizes this person as a tax resident and levies taxes on it because he or she has lived in the country for more than half a year. In this case, both Country A and Country B exercise resident jurisdiction over him or her in accordance with their domestic tax laws, resulting in the problem of international double taxation. Similarly, transnational legal persons may also have this problem due to different criteria for judging resident status when the two countries exercise resident tax jurisdiction.

三、两个国家的来源地税收管辖权之间的冲突
Conflicts over Source Tax Jurisdiction between Countries

来源地税收管辖权之间的冲突,主要是由不同国家对所得的来源地的判断标准不同所引起。具体来说,在判断财产所得来源地时,各国税法对于动产及不动产的确定标准是不同的。在认定不动产转让所得的来源地时,各国税法一般以不动产所在地为所得来源地;在转让不动产以外的其他财产所得的来源地认定上,各国主张的标准不一。例如,对于跨国特许权使用费所得,有些国家认为可以将特许权使用费受益人的居住地认定为所得来源地,有些国家认为可以将支付特许权使用费的发生地认定为所得来源地,还有国家以支付特许权使用费的公司所在地为所得来源地。①这样,对于同一笔跨国特许权使用费,受益人的居住地国、支付特许权使用费的发生地国及支付特许权使用费的公司所在地国都可能行使税收管辖权,从而产生了国际双重征税问题。

The conflicts over source tax jurisdiction between countries are mainly caused by the different criteria of the source of income in different countries. Specifically, when determining the source of property or income, the tax laws of various countries have different standards for determining movable and immovable properties. When determining the source of income from the transfer of real estate, the tax laws of various countries generally substitute real estate as the source of income; in determining the source of income from the transfer of other properties, the recognized standards vary from country to country. Some countries believe that the place of residence of the beneficiary of royalties can be identified as the source of income, some countries believe that the place where royalties are paid can be identified as the source of income, and some countries use the location of the company paying the royalties as the source of income. In this way, for the same ancillary royalties, the country of residence of the beneficiary, the country where the royalties are paid, and the place where the company that pays the royalties may all be embezzled, resulting in international double taxation issues.

---

① 参见刘剑文主编:《国际税法学》,北京大学出版社2004年版,第127—128页。

第二节　国际双重征税的概念
Section 2　Concept of International Double Taxation

从国际税收的实践来看,国际双重征税既可能是法律上的,也可能是经济上的。前者被称为"法律性国际双重征税"或"法律意义的国际双重征税",后者被称为"经济性国际双重征税"或"经济意义的国际双重征税"。

From the practice of international taxation, international double taxation may be legal or economic. The former is called "International Juridical Double Taxation", and the latter is called "International Economic Double Taxation".

一、法律性国际双重征税
International Juridical Double Taxation

OECD将法律性国际重复征税定义为:两个以上的国家,对同一纳税人就同一征税对象,在同一征税期内征收相同或类似的税收。法律性国际双重征税是国家间因税收制度不同而发生冲突的产物。国家有权依据国家主权原则制定本国的税收管理制度,对于相互关联的经济行为,当两个以上国家同时认定其享有对该行为的税收管辖权时,就会导致税收管辖冲突,进而产生国际双重征税问题。

The OECD defines international legal double taxation as: two or more countries impose the same or similar taxes on the same taxpayer for the same taxation object during the same taxation period. International legal double taxation is the product of conflicts of different taxation systems between countries. The country has the right to formulate its own tax management system based on the principle of national sovereignty. For interconnected economic activities, when two or more countries simultaneously determine that they have tax jurisdiction over the activity, it will lead to tax jurisdiction conflicts, which will further lead to conflicts over tax jurisdiction and cause international double taxation.

根据OECD的定义,法律性国际双重征税包括五项构成要件。

According to the definition of the OECD, legal international double taxation includes five components.

第一,存在着两个以上的征税主体,涉及两国或多国的税收管辖权。征税主体一般是国家的中央税务机关,但也存在一方是中央政府税务机关,另一方是地方政府税务机关,抑或双方的层级都是地方政府税务机关的情况。但无论两个征税主体的层级如何,两者必须分属两个国家的税务机关,否则不构成法律性国际双重征税,这也是法律性国际双重征税成立的必要条件。

First, there are two or more taxation subjects, involving the tax jurisdiction of two or more countries. The subject of taxation is generally the central tax agency of the country, but there are also cases where one party is the central government tax agency and the other is the local government tax agency, or both levels are local government tax agencies. However, regardless of the level of the two taxation subjects, the two must belong to the tax authorities of the two countries, otherwise they will not constitute legal international double taxation, which is also a necessary condition for the establishment of legal international double taxation.

第二,存在着同一个纳税主体,即同一纳税人对两个以上的国家都负有纳税义务。从纳税主体的性质上看,包括自然人和属于同一个法人的总机构和分支机构。法人在从事跨国经济活动时,经常会在另一国设立常设机构或运营机构。对于该法人的常设机构或运营机构在东道国获得的经营所得,东道国可能依据属地主义原则行使来源地管辖权征税,而法人的母国可能依据属人主义原则行使居民管辖权征税,这就导致该法人的常设机构或运营机构同时被两个国家认定为纳税主体并负有双重纳税义务。

Second, there is the same taxpayer, that is, the same taxpayer is liable to pay taxes to two or more countries. In terms of the nature of taxpayers, it includes natural persons and head offices and branches that belong to the same legal person. When a legal person is engaged in transnational economic activities, it often establishes a permanent establishment or an operating organization in another country. For the business income of the permanent establishment or operating institution of the legal person in the host country, the host country may levy taxes based on the territorial principle of the source jurisdiction, and the home country of the legal person may levy taxes based on the humanist principle of the resident jurisdiction. The permanent establishment or operating institution of the legal person is recognized as a taxpayer by two countries at the same time and is liable for double taxation.

第三,存在同一征税对象,即同一笔所得或财产被重复征税。只有同一纳税主体的同一笔所得或财产同时落入两个以上国家的税收管辖权范围,并在实际上被重复征税,才构成法律性国际双重征税;相反,如果两个以上国家对同一纳税主体的不同来源的所得或财产同时征税,则不成立法律性国际双重征税。例如,A国的a公司在B国设立了子公司并从事生产经营活动,在B国生产并销售相关产品。如果A国对a公司在B国的子公司就该生产经营所得征收经营所得税,B国对子公司在销售产品的过程中实现的增值额征收增值税,尽管两个征税主体对同一个纳税主体均进行了征税,但由于征税对象不同,此种情况并不构成法律性国际双重征税。

Third, there is the same taxation object, that is, the same income or property is taxed repeatedly. Only when the same income or property of the same taxpayer falls into the tax jurisdiction of two or more countries at the same time, and is actually taxed repeatedly, can it constitute legal international double taxation; on the contrary, if two or more countries impose taxes on the same taxpayer's income or property from different sources at the same time, there is no legal international double taxation. For example, company a in country A has established a subsidiary in country B and engaged in production and business activities, and produced and sold related products in country B. If country A imposes an operating income tax on a company

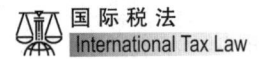

a's subsidiary in country B on the income from production and operation, country B imposes a value-added tax on the value-added value realized by the subsidiary in the process of selling products, even though two taxing entities pay the same tax entities have levied taxes, but due to different taxation objects, this situation does not constitute legal international double taxation.

第四,征收相同或类似的税收。这是指两个以上的征税主体在对同一征税对象就同一笔所得或财产征税时,适用的是相同或相似的税种。例如,A国的a公司就本公司的一项专利与B国的乙公司在B国签订专利使用许可合同,并收取专利使用费用,对于甲公司获得的该笔所得,如果A国将特许权使用费受益人的居住地认定为所得来源地对甲公司征收税款,B国将支付特许权使用费的发生地认定为所得来源地对甲公司征收税款,此种情况下才构成法律性国际双重征税。

Fourth, levy the same or similar taxes. This means that two or more taxation entities apply the same or similar taxes when taxing the same income or property on the same taxation object. For example, company a in country A signs a patent license contract with company b in country B for one of its patents. The residence of the beneficiary of the royalties is deemed to be the source of income to impose taxes on company a, and country B shall impose taxes on company a by identifying the place where royalties are paid as the source of income. In this case, it constitutes legal international double taxation.

第五,在同一征税期内。这是指两个征税主体对同一纳税人在同一个纳税期间的所得或财产征税,而不是指两国征税的具体日期是相同的。这里的"纳税期间"指的是纳税的计算期间,尽管纳税人在对两个国家履行税款缴纳义务的时间存在先后,但是只要是在相同的纳税计算期间就同一笔所得或财产被两个国家征税,就成立在同一征税期缴纳税款这一要件。

Fifth, within the same taxation period. This means that two taxation entities levy taxes on the income or property of the same taxpayer during the same taxation period, rather than that the specific dates for taxation in the two countries are the same. The "tax period" here refers to the tax calculation period. Although the taxpayer has a priority in the time when the taxpayer pays taxes to the two countries, as long as it is during the same tax calculation period, the same income or property is covered by two national taxation is the requirement of paying taxes in the same taxation period.

(二) 经济性国际双重征税

International Economic Double Taxation

经济性国际双重征税是对有内在经济联系的不同纳税人的同一经济渊源进行重复征税,即对两个或两个以上的不同纳税主体就同一项所得或财产进行分别征税。经济性国际双重征税主要有以下几种形式。

International economic double taxation is the repeated taxation of the same economic origin of different taxpayers who have inherent economic connections, that is, two or more different taxpayers are taxed separately on the same income or property. Economic international double taxation mainly takes the following forms.

一是对跨国公司利润和跨国股东分红的双重征税。广泛实行所得税法的国家,其税收制度规定对公司、企业的营业利润所得征收公司所得税或企业所得税,并且同时规定对于股东所取得的股息红利征收个人所得税。此种税收制度因涉及企业与股东同一经济渊源而导致经济性国际双重征税问题的发生。

The first is the double taxation of profits of multinational companies and dividends of multinational shareholders. In countries with extensive income tax laws, the taxation system stipulates the levy of corporate income tax or corporate income tax on the operating profits of companies and enterprises, and also stipulates the levy of personal income tax on dividends received by shareholders. This kind of taxation system involves the same economic source of the enterprise and the shareholders, which leads to the occurrence of international economic double taxation.

二是对跨国财产转移双方的双重征税。当财产转移在两个或多个国家之间发生,如跨国财产的赠与、跨国财产的继承、跨国抚养费的支付及跨国信托的分红,纳税义务将在跨国财产的转移双方之间因同一经济渊源的财产产生,从而引发经济性国际双重征税。

The second is the double taxation on both parties of the transnational property transfer. When property transfer occurs between two or more countries, such as the gift of transnational property, the inheritance of transnational property, the payment of transnational support and the dividend of transnational trust, the tax liability will be the same between the two parties in the transfer of transnational property. The property of economic origin is produced, which leads to international economic double taxation.

三是所得税计税办法引起的双重征税。不同国家对与所得税相关的扣除项目规定存在区别,以及不同国家对国际关联企业内部转让定价进行调整的价格标准规定的矛盾,也会导致经济性国际双重征税问题的发生。[1]

The third is the double taxation caused by the income tax calculation method. Different countries have different regulations on income tax-related deduction items, as well as contradictions in the price standard regulations of different countries to adjust the internal transfer pricing of international affiliates, which will also lead to the occurrence of international economic double taxation.

通过将法律性国际双重征税与经济性国际双重征税相比较,可以看到经济性国际双重征税除了不具备同一纳税主体这一特征外,同样具备法律性国际双重征税的其他四项构成要件。即法律性国际双重征税是对同一纳税人就同一所得或财产双重征税,经济性国际双重征税是对不同纳税主体就同一项所得或财产重复征税。

By comparing international legal double taxation with international economic double taxation, we can see that economic international double taxation does not have the characteristic of the same taxpayer, but has the other four elements of legal international double taxation. That is, legal international double taxation is the repeated taxation of the same taxpayer on the same

---

[1] 参加付志宇主编:《国际税法》,清华大学出版社2015年版,第45页。

income or property, and economic international double taxation is the repeated taxation of the same income or property on different taxpayers.

第三节　国际双重征税的危害性
Section 3　Harmfulness of International Double Taxation

无论是法律性国际双重征税抑或经济性国际双重征税,其在经济上和法律上产生的负面影响基本相同,都会在一定范围内损害相关国家税收利益和纳税人经济权益的实现,在不同程度上阻碍国际经济贸易发展。

Either international juridical double taxation and international economic double taxation can lead to legal and economic negative impacts, which will damage the relevant national tax interests and the realization of taxpayers' economic rights to a certain extent, and even hinder the development of international economy and trade to varying degrees.

一、违背税收公平原则
Violate the Principle of Tax Equity

税收公平原则是税收的一项基本原则,要求纳税人承担的税负与其纳税能力相适应,并使纳税人之间的负担水平保持平衡。如果从事跨国经济活动的纳税人因被双重征税而导致其需要缴纳的税款远远超过其经济能力,其承担的税负大大超过没有从事跨国经济活动的纳税人,这不仅加大了跨国纳税人的负担,还会造成两类纳税人之间税负的不公平,并干扰纳税人之间在经济活动中的公平竞争,扭曲税收对经济的中性作用。

The principle of tax equity is a basic principle of taxation, which requires taxpayers to bear the tax burden in line with their taxpaying ability and to maintain a balance between the taxpayers' burden level. If a taxpayer engaged in transnational economic activities is subject to double taxation, the tax he or she needs to pay far exceeds his or her economic capacity, and his or her tax burden will greatly exceed that of taxpayers who are not engaged in transnational economic activities. The burden of taxpayers will also cause unfair tax burdens between the two types of taxpayers, interfere with fair competition between taxpayers in economic activities, and distort the neutral effect of taxation on the economy.

二、违背税收中性原则
Violate the Principle of Tax Neutrality

税收中性原则,是指一国的税收制度应该是中性的,不应扭曲市场经济的正常运行。税收中性原则的理论基础是确信市场能充分实现资源配置，避免税收对市场机制的干扰。一国的税收必然会对纳税人的经济行为产生影响，而国际双重征税的存在加重了跨国经济行为人的税负，降低其经济利益，并对其对外投资计划、经营决策产生直接影响，可能使其放弃对预定的领域或行业的投资计划，转向国内投资。因此，国际双重征税违背了税收中性原则。

The principle of tax neutrality means that a country's taxation system should be neutral and should not distort the normal operation of the market economy. The theoretical basis of the principle of tax neutrality is to believe that the market can fully realize the allocation of resources and avoid the interference of taxation on the market mechanism. A country's taxation will inevitably have an impact on the taxpayer's economic behavior, and the existence of international double taxation increases the tax burden of transnational economic actors, reduces their economic benefits, and has a direct impact on their foreign investment plans and business decisions. It may make it abandon investment plans in predetermined fields or industries and switch to domestic investment. Therefore, international double taxation violates the principle of tax neutrality.

（三）影响国家间财权利益关系
Affect the Fiscal Relationship and Interests between Countries

一般情况下，当跨国交易发生在双方当事人之间并使当事人从中受益时，双方当事人的政府可以通过行使税收管辖权就该收益征税，进而增加本国的税收利益。但国际双重征税的存在使得跨国纳税人承担比国内经济活动纳税人更重的税负，可能放弃对外投资计划，这样一来，资本输入国便无法吸引到外国投资者的投资，不利于本国经济的发展，资本输出国无法通过对外投资消化本国的过剩资本，实际上也无法增加本国税收。

In general, when a cross-border transaction occurs between two parties and benefits the parties, the governments of both parties can tax the proceeds by exercising tax jurisdiction, thereby increasing the tax benefits of the country. However, the existence of international double taxation makes multinational taxpayers bear heavier tax burdens than taxpayers of domestic economic activities, and may abandon foreign investment plans. In this way, capital importing countries cannot attract foreign investors, which is not good for their own countries. With economic development, capital-exporting countries cannot absorb their own excess capital through foreign investment, and in fact cannot increase their own taxes.

（四）阻碍国际经济发展
Hinder the Development of International Economic

经济全球化的深入发展使得资本、技术、人员和商品各要素在世界范围内得到更为合理的配置。但是，国际双重征税因加重跨国纳税人税负而挫伤其开展跨国经济活动的积极性，阻碍了资本、技术、人员和商品各流动要素在国家间的流动和利用，既严重影响了纳税人的跨国经济活动和各国的经济发展，更在很大程度上阻碍了国际经济贸易的发展。

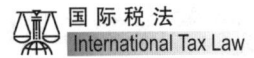

The in-depth development of economic globalization has resulted in a more reasonable allocation of capital, technology, personnel, and commodities worldwide. However, international double taxation has increased the tax burden of multinational taxpayers, which has dampened their enthusiasm for transnational economic activities, hindered the flow and utilization of capital, technology, personnel, and commodities among countries, and seriously affected taxpayers' transnational economic activities and the economic development of various countries, hindered the development of international economic trade to a large extent.

第四节 相 关 案 例
Section 4　Related Cases

本案是中国双重雇佣个人所得税第一案。
This case is the No.1 case of double employment individual income tax in China.

一、案情介绍
Introduction to the Case

原告（上诉人）：英国公民 Andrew Ronald MacDonald-Hardie
Plaintiff (appellant): Andrew Ronald MacDonald-Hardie of British citizens
被告（被上诉人）：广州市地方税务局第一稽查局（广州市地方税务局涉外稽查局）
Defendant (Appellee): First Inspection Bureau of Guangzhou Local Taxation Bureau (Foreign Inspection Bureau of Guangzhou Local Taxation Bureau)
第三人：阿奎特（广州）水处理有限公司
Third Person: Aquit (Guangzhou) Water Treatment Co., Ltd.

原告在2005年至2007年期间是阿奎特（广州）水处理有限公司（以下简称阿奎特广州公司）的法定代表人、董事长。原告在2005年至2007年每年在中国境内居住的时间分别是259.5天、289天和286天。2005年至2007年，原告在阿奎特广州公司工作的同时也任职于阿奎特国际公司，在此期间，阿奎特国际公司每年向原告支付的薪金（含工资、小费、奖金和其他报酬）分别是107 124美元、176 566美元和120 081美元，每年为原告支付的商业保险是7 764美元。

The plaintiff served as the legal representative and Chairman of Aquit (Guangzhou) Water Treatment Co., Ltd. (hereinafter referred to as Aquit Guangzhou Company) from 2005 to 2007. From 2005 to 2007, the plaintiff lived in China for 259.5 days, 289 days and 286 days respectively. From 2005 to 2007, the plaintiff worked simultaneously for Aquit Guangzhou and for Aquit International. In the meantime, the annual salary (including wages, tips, bonuses and other remuneration) paid by Aquit International to the plaintiff was $107,124, $176,566 and $120,081. The annual commercial insurance payment for the plaintiff was $7,764.

2009年9月29日,被告作出一项税务处理决定,认定阿奎特广州公司在2005年1月至2007年12月未按税法规定为原告足额代扣代缴个人所得税,根据《中华人民共和国个人所得税法》第一条、第二条、第三条、第八条及《中华人民共和国个人所得税法实施条例》第八条规定,责成阿奎特广州公司补缴个人所得税658 556.01元。原告得知该税务处理决定后不服,于2013年8月14日向广州市地方税务局申请行政复议,广州市地方税务局于2013年10月12日作出维持被告行政税务处理决定的行政复议决定。原告仍不服,以被告认定事实不清,违反中美税收协定及法律规定,且未向其送达税务处理决定、程序违法等为由,诉至一审法院,要求撤销被告作出的税务处理决定。

On 29 September 2009, The defendant made a tax decision, determining that Aquit Guangzhou Company failed to withhold personal income tax in full for the plaintiff from January 2005 to December 2007, In accordance with Articles 1, 2, 3 and 8 of the Personal Income Tax Law of the People's Republic of China and Article 8 of the Regulations on the Implementation of the Personal Income Tax Law of the People's Republic of China, Aquit Guangzhou Company to pay personal income tax 658,556.01 yuan. The plaintiff did not accept the decision, applying for administrative reconsideration to the Guangzhou Local Taxation Bureau on 14 August 2013, The Guangzhou Local Taxation Bureau made an administrative reconsideration decision on October 12, 2013 to maintain the defendant's administrative tax treatment decision. The plaintiff still disagrees, the defendant found the facts unclear, in violation of Sino-US tax agreements and laws, and did not serve the tax processing decision, the procedure illegal and so on, to the court of first instance, requesting for rescission of the tax decision made by the defendant.

一审中,原告表示其在2005年至2007年同时任职于中国境内、境外两家独立的公司,工作时间、工作地点均相互独立,其在中国境内是履行阿奎特广州公司的工作内容,在中国境外是履行阿奎特国际公司的工作内容。由于阿奎特国际公司向其支付的薪金是其离境后处理境外事务的收入所得,被告不应当就阿奎特国际公司支付给上诉人的薪金进行征税。被告则表示其对原告征收的税收是按原告实际在境内的天数占全年天数比例计征,符合税法规定。第三人则表示对被告作出的税务处理决定无异议。

In the first instance, the plaintiff stated that between 2005 and 2007, he worked for two independent companies in China and abroad, working hours and working places independently of each other, performing the work of Aquit Guangzhou Company in China and performing the work of Aquit International Company outside China. Since the salary paid to it by Aquit International was the proceeds of its overseas affairs after departure, the defendant should not tax the salary paid by Aquit International to the appellant. The defendant said that the tax levied on the plaintiff was calculated according to the proportion of the actual number of days in the territory of the plaintiff to the number of days in the whole year, in accordance with the provisions of the tax law. The third party indicated that there was no objection to the tax treatment decision made by the defendant.

一审法院认为,根据我国的相关税收法律法规和《中华人民共和国政府和美利坚合众国政府关于对所得避免双重征税和防止偷漏税的协定》(以下简称"中美税收协定")的相关规定,原告因在阿奎特国际公司受雇取得的报酬,属于来源于中国境内的所得,且不符合《中美税收协定》规定的仅在美国征税的情形,因此应当依照我国法律、法规及相关规定依法缴纳个人所得税。

The court of first instance held that, in accordance with the relevant tax laws and regulations of our country and the relevant provisions of the agreement between the government of the People's Republic of China and the government of the United States of America on the avoidance of double taxation of income and the prevention of tax evasion (hereinafter referred to as the Sino-US Tax Agreement), the remuneration obtained by the plaintiff for his employment with Aquit International derived from the territory of China and was not in conformity with the provisions of the Sino-US Tax Agreement and was taxed only in the United States, so personal income tax should be paid in accordance with the laws, regulations and relevant provisions of our country.

原告不服一审法院判决,向二审法院提起上诉称:一、阿奎特国际公司支付给原告的工资薪金为原告的境外所得,被告无权就原告的境外所得向原告征收个人所得税。二、原告对其中国境外所得已经向美国税务机关申报纳税,并缴纳了全部税款。被告的征税行为已经构成双重征税,违反了《中美税收协定》。

The plaintiff appealed to the court of second instance against the judgment of the court of first instance, claiming that the salary paid by Aquit International to the plaintiff was the plaintiff's overseas income, and that the defendant had no right to levy personal income tax on the plaintiff's overseas income. In addition, the plaintiff has declared and paid all taxes to the United States tax authorities on his income outside China. The defendant's taxation has constituted double taxation, in violation of the Sino-US Tax Agreement.

被告答辩称:一、原告在中国境内工作期间取得的由中国境外企业阿奎特国际公司支付的工资薪金,依法属于来源于中国境内的所得,应当按照中国有关税收法律规定征缴个人所得税。二、被告作出的税务处理决定符合《中美税收协定》。原告在2005年至2007年担任阿奎特广州公司总裁一职,在中国境内受雇,并且在中国境内停留连续或累计超过183天。根据《中美税收协定》第十四条第一款、第二款规定,被告对原告在中国境内受雇取得来源于中国境内的所得征税符合《中美税收协定》。对于在中国缴纳的个人所得税,原告可根据《中美税收协定》有关规定向美国政府申请税收抵免,消除双重征税;确因超期无法抵免的,被告可依法循其他法律途径解决。

The defendant replied: First, the wages and salaries paid by the Chinese foreign enterprise Aquit International Company during the plaintiff's work in China belong to the income derived from the territory of China according to law, and the individual income tax shall be collected and paid in accordance with the relevant tax laws of China. Second, the defendant's decision on tax treatment is in accordance with the Sino-US Tax Agreement. The plaintiff held the position of President of Aquit Guangzhou Company from 2005 to 2007, was employed in China and stayed in China for a continuous or cumulative period of more than

183 days. According to Article 14, Paragraphs 1 and 2, of the Sino-US Tax Agreement, the defendant's tax on the plaintiff's employment in China to obtain income derived from China is in accordance with the Sino-US Tax Agreement. For personal income tax paid in China, the plaintiff may apply to the United States Government for a tax credit in accordance with the relevant provisions of the Sino-US Tax Agreement to eliminate double taxation; if it is true that the period of time can not be deducted, the defendant may settle the matter by other legal means according to law.

二审法院经审理认为，一审法院认定事实清楚，适用法律正确，决定驳回上诉，维持原判。

The court of second instance held that the court of first instance found the facts clearly and applied the law correctly, and upholds the original judgment.

二、案件分析
Case Analysis

从一审和二审来看，本案的主要争议焦点之一是：原告是否应当就其在2005年至2007年取得的由中国境外企业阿奎特国际公司支付的工资薪金按照中国有关税收法律规定缴纳个人所得税。这个问题的关键在于三点：第一，原告在2005年至2007年从阿奎特国际公司获得的报酬是否属于来源于中国境内的所得；第二，原告是否应当就来源于中国境内的所得缴纳个人所得税；第三，原告的情形是否符合《中美税收协定》第十四条规定的仅在美国征税的情形。

From the first and second instances, we can see that one of the main points of dispute in this case is whether the plaintiff should pay personal income tax in accordance with the relevant tax laws of China on the wages and salaries paid by the Chinese foreign enterprise Aquit International Company from 2005 to 2007. The key to this question lies in three points: first, whether the remuneration received by the plaintiff from Aquit International from 2005 to 2007 was derived from the territory of China; second, whether the plaintiff should pay personal income tax on income derived from the territory of China; and third, whether the plaintiff's circumstances were in conformity with the United States-only provided for in Article 14 of the Sino-US Tax Agreement.

第一，原告在2005年至2007年从阿奎特国际公司获得的报酬是否属于来源于中国境内的所得。国税发〔1994〕148号《国家税务总局关于在中国境内无住所的个人取得工资薪金所得纳税义务问题的通知》（以下简称"第148号文件"）第三条第一款、第二款规定："三、关于在中国境内无住所而在一个纳税年度中在中国境内连续或累计居住超过90日或在税收协定规定的期间中在中国境内连续或累计居住超过183日但不满一年的个人纳税义务的确定。根据税法第一条第二款以及税收协定的有关规定，在中国境内无住所而在一个纳税年度中在中国境内连续或累计工作超过90日或在税收协定规定的期间中在中国境内连续或累计居住超过183日但不满1年的个人，其实际在中国境内工作期间取得的由中国境内企业或个人雇主支付和由境外企业或个人雇主支付的工资薪金所得，均应申报缴纳个人所得税;其在中国境外工作期间取得的工资薪金所得,除属于本通知第五条规定的情况外,不予征收个人所得税。"第五条规定:"五、中国境内企业董事、高层管理人员纳税义务的确定。担任中国境内企业董事或高层管理职务的个人,其取得的由该中国境内企业支付的董事费或工资薪金,不适用本通知第二条、第三条的规定,而应自其担任该中国境内企业董事或高层管理职务起,至其解除上述职务止的期间,不论其是否在中国境外履行职务,均应申报缴纳个人所得税;其取得的由中国境外企业支付的工资薪金,应依照本通知第二条、第三条、第四条的规定确定纳税义务。"根据第148号文件的上述规定,尽管原告是在境外履行阿奎特国际公司的工作内容而取得由阿奎特国际公司支付的报酬,但是由于原告在中国境内担任阿奎特广州公司的董事长,因此原告自阿奎特国际公司取得的报酬应当被视为来源于中国境内的所得。

First, whether the plaintiff's remuneration from Aquit International from 2005 to 2007 was derived from Chinese territory. The Circular of the State Administration of Taxation (No. 1994) 148 on the Tax Obligations of Individuals without Residence in China to Obtain Wage and Salary Income (hereinafter referred to as "Document No. 148") stipulates in Article 3, Paragraphs 1 and 2: "3. Determination of the Tax Obligations of Individuals without Residence in China who have resided continuously or accumulatively in China for more than 90 days in a tax year or who have resided continuously or accumulatively in China for more than 183 days but less than one year during the period stipulated in the Tax Agreement. In accordance with Article 1, Paragraph 2, of the Tax Code and the relevant provisions of the Tax Agreement, individuals who have no domicile in China and have worked continuously or accumulatively in China for more than 90 days in a tax year or have resided continuously or accumulatively in China for more than 183 days but less than one year during the period specified in the tax agreement, wages and salaries paid by an enterprise or individual employer in China and paid by an enterprise or individual employer abroad, should declare and pay individual income tax; income from wages and salaries earned while working outside China, subject to the provisions of Article 5 of this notice, individual income tax shall not be levied." Article 5: "5. Determination of the tax obligations of directors and senior managers of enterprises within China. Article 2 and Article 3 of this Circular shall not apply to the directors or salaries paid by the enterprises in China, but shall declare and pay personal income tax for the period from the time they hold the position of directors or senior management of the enterprises in China to the end of their discharge, whether or not they perform their duties outside China. The wages and salaries paid by the enterprises outside China shall be determined in accordance with the provisions of Article 2, Article 3 and Article 4 of this Circular." According to the above provisions of document No. 148, although the plaintiff was paid by Aquit International for the performance of the work of Aquit International abroad, the plaintiff's remuneration from Aquit Guangzhou Company should be regarded as derived from the territory of China because the plaintiff was the chairman of the company in China.

第二,原告是否应当就来源于中国境内的所得缴纳个人所得税。《中华人民共和国个人所得税法》(2007年修正)(以下简称《个人所得税法》)第1条规定:"在中国境内有住所,或者无住所而在境内居住满一年的个人,从中国境内和境外取得的所得,依照本法规定缴纳个人所得税。在中国境内无住所又不居住或者无住所而在境内居住不满一年的个人,从中国境内取得的所得,依照本法规定缴纳个人所得税。"第二条规定:"下列各项个人所得,应当缴纳个人所得税:(一)工资、薪金所得;(二)个体工商户的生产、经营所得;(三)对企事业单位的承包经营、承租经营所得;(四)劳务报酬所得;(五)稿酬所得;(六)特许权使用费所得;(七)利息、股息、红利所得;(八)财产租赁所得;(九)财产转让所得;(十)偶然所得;(十一)经国务院财政部门确定征税的其他所得。"第8条规定:"个人所得税,以所得人为纳税义务人,以支付所得的单位或者个人为扣缴义务人。个人所得超过国务院规定数额的,在两处以上取得工资、薪金所得或者没有扣缴义务人的,以及具有国务院规定的其他情形的,纳税义务人应当按照国家规定办理纳税申报。扣缴义务人应当按照国家规定办理全员全额扣缴申报。"《中华人民共和国个人所得税法实施条例》(以下简称《个税法实施条例》)第四条规定:"税法第一条第一款、第二款所说的从中国境内取得的所得,是指来源于中国境内的所得;所说的从中国境外取得的所得,是指来源于中国境外的所得。"根据《中华人民共和国个人所得税法》和《中华人民共和国个人所得税法实施条例》的相关规定,由于原告自阿奎特国际公司取得的报酬是从中国境内取得的所得,因此应当依法在我国缴纳个人所得税。

Second, whether the plaintiff should pay personal income tax on income derived from China. Article 1 of the Personal Income Tax Law of the People's Republic of China (Revised 2007) (hereinafter referred to as the "Personal Income Tax Law") stipulates: "Individual income tax shall be paid in accordance with the provisions of this law for individuals who have domicile in China or who have resided in China for one year without domicile. Individual income tax shall be paid in accordance with the provisions of this law for the income obtained from the territory of China by an individual who has no domicile, no residence or no residence and has resided within the territory of China for less than one year." Article 2 stipulates: "The following individual income shall be subject to income tax of one person: (1) income from wages and salaries; (2) income from the production and operation of individual industrial and commercial households; (3) income from the contracted operation of enterprises and institutions and from the lease operation; (4) income from remuneration for labour services; (5) income from remuneration for manuscripts; (6) income from royalties; (7) income from interest, dividends and bonuses; (8) income from lease of property; (9) income from transfer of property; (10) income by chance; (11) other income subject to taxation determined by the financial department of the State Council." Article 8 stipulates: "Personal income tax shall be paid by the income payer and by the unit or individual paying the income as the withholding agent. Where an individual's income exceeds the amount prescribed by the State Council, the taxpayer shall, in accordance with the provisions of the State Council, file a tax return in two or more places where the income from wages or salaries is obtained or there is no withholding agent, and in other cases as prescribed by the State Council. The withholding agent shall, in accordance with the provisions of the state, handle the full amount of the withholding declaration." Article 4 of the Regulations of the People's Republic of China on the Implementation of the Personal Income Tax Law (hereinafter referred to as the "Regulations on the Implementation of the Personal Income Tax Law") stipulates: "The income derived from the territory of China referred to in Paragraphs 1 and 2 of Article 1 of the Tax Law is the income obtained from the territory of China, and the income obtained from the territory out of China refers to the income obtained from the territory out of China. According to the relevant provisions of the Personal Income Tax Law and the Regulations on the Implementation of the Personal Income Tax Law, since the remuneration obtained by the plaintiff from Aquit International Company is derived from the territory of China, personal income tax shall be paid in accordance with the law in our country."

第三,原告的情形是否符合《中美税收协定》第14条规定的仅在美国征税的情形。《中美税收协定》第1条规定:"本协定适用于缔约国一方或者双方居民的人。"第2条规定:"一、本协定适用于下列税种:(一)在中华人民共和国:1.个人所得税;2.中外合资经营企业所得税;3.外国企业所得税;4.地方所得税;(以下简称"中国税收")(二)在美利坚合众国:根据国内收入法征收的联邦所得税。(以下简称"美国税收")二、本协定也适用于本协定签订之日后增加或者代替第一款所列税种的相同或者实质相似的税收,缔约国双方主管当局将各自有关税法所作的实质变动适当时间内通知对方。"此外,《中美税收协定》第十四条第二款就免于双重征税的条件作了规定:"虽有第一款的规定,缔约国一方居民因在缔约国另一方受雇取得的报酬,同时具有以下三个条件的,应仅在该缔约国一方征税:(一)收款人在有关历年中在该缔约国另一方停留连续或累计不超过183天;(二)该项报酬由并非该缔约国另一方居民的雇主支付或代表雇主支付;(三)该项报酬不是由雇主设在该缔约国另一方的常设机构或固定基地所负担。"本案中原告在2005年至2007年担任阿奎特广州公司的法定代表人,职务为董事长,是中国境内企业的高层管理人员,每年在中国境内居住的时间分别是259.5天、289天和286天,均超过183天,因此原告在阿奎特广州公司受雇取得的报酬,不属于《中美税收协定》第14条第二款规定的应就其在阿奎特国际公司受雇取得的报酬仅在美国征税的情形,因此仍然应当按照我国的相关法律规定依法缴纳个人所得税。

Third, whether the plaintiff's case is in accordance with Article 14 of the Sino-US Tax Agreement only in the United States. Article 1 of the Sino-US Tax Agreement states: "This Agreement shall apply to any person who is resident of one or both parties." Article 2 stipulates: "1. This agreement applies to the following taxes: (1) In the People's Republic of China: ① individual income tax; ② income tax on joint ventures; ③ foreign enterprise income tax; ④ local income tax; (2) In the United States of America: federal income tax under the domestic income law (hereinafter referred to as "United States Taxes"). 2. This agreement shall also apply to the competent authorities of the contracting parties which, after the date of the signing of this agreement, increase or replace the same or substantially similar taxes listed in Paragraph 1, notify the other party within an appropriate time of the material changes made in their respective tax laws." In addition, Article 14, Paragraph 2, of the Sino-US Tax Agreement sets out the conditions for exemption from double taxation: "Notwithstanding Paragraph 1, remuneration of a resident of a contracting state for employment in another contracting state, having the following three conditions, (i) The payee shall remain in the other party for a continuous or cumulative period of not more than 183 days in the relevant calendar year; (ii) The remuneration shall be paid by or on behalf of an employer who is not a resident of the other party; (iii) The remuneration is not borne by the employer's permanent establishment or fixed base located on the other party of the state party." From this case, the plaintiff was the legal representative of Aquit Guangzhou Company from 2005 to 2007, the chairman of the board of directors, the senior management of enterprises in China, and lived in China for 259.5 days, 289 days and 286 days each year, all exceeding 183 days. Therefore, the remuneration obtained by the plaintiff for his employment in Aquit Guangzhou Company does not belong to the case that the remuneration for his employment in Aquit International Company shall be taxed only in the United States, as stipulated in Article 14, Paragraph 2, of the Sino-US Tax Agreement, and therefore the personal income tax shall still be paid in accordance with the relevant laws of China.

学习思考题 / Questions for Study

1. 国际双重征税的定义是什么？产生国际双重征税的原因是什么？
   What is the definition of international double taxation? What are the causes of international double taxation?
2. 法律性国际双重征税和经济性国际双重征税的区别是什么？
   What is the difference between legal international double taxation and economic international double taxation?
3. 国际双重征税有什么危害？
   What is the harm of international double taxation?
4. 消除和减轻国际双重征税有什么途径？
   How to eliminate and reduce international double taxation?

第六章 CHAPTER VI

国际税收协定
International Tax Treaty

第一节　国际税收协定概述
Section 1　Overview of International Tax Treaty

国际税收协定是有关国家之间签订的旨在协调彼此间税收权益分配关系和实现国际税务行政协助的书面协议,对缔约国而言,税收协定构成规范约束它们各自征税行为的特别国际法。根据签订和参加协定的国家数量的多寡,国际税收协定可分为双边税收协定(bilateral tax treaty)和多边税收协定(multilateral tax treaty);按协定适用的税种的不同,则可分为关税协定、增值税协定、所得税协定和财产税协定;根据协定涉及的内容范围不同,又可分为综合性税收协定和专门性税收协定。专门性税收协定通常是缔约国双方为协调处理某一特定项目的税收分配关系或税务事项所签订的协定,如关于税务情报交换的协定等。综合性税收协定则是指缔约各方签订的广泛协调各种所得税和财产税的权益分配关系和有关税务合作事项的协定,如各国间普遍签订的双边性的关于避免对所得和财产的双重征税协定(以下简称"双重征税协定"),即属于典型的综合性国际税收协定。本章所要重点阐述的即是这类双重征税协定及其与缔约国各自单方面制定的国内所得税法和一般财产税法之间的关系问题。

An international tax agreement (tax treaty) is a written agreement between the states concerned for the purpose of coordinating the distribution of tax rights and interests and achieving international assistance in tax administration. For the constracting state, tax agreements constitute special international law that governs their respective taxation. Based on the number of countries that have signed and participated, international tax agreements can be divided into bilateral tax agreements (bilateral tax treaty) and multilateral tax agreements (multilateral tax treaty). According to different taxes applicable to the treaties, they can be divided into tariff agreement, value-added tax agreement, income tax agreement and property tax agreement. Depending on the scope of the agreement, they can also be divided into comprehensive tax agreements (comprehensive tax treaty) and special tax agreements (specific tax treaty). A special tax agreement is usually an agreement between the parties to coordinate tax distribution or tax matters for a particular project, such as agreements on the exchange of tax information. A comprehensive tax agreement refers to an agreement signed by the contracting parties to widely coordinate the distribution of interests in various income and property taxes and related tax cooperation matters, such as bilateral agreements on the avoidance of double taxation of income and property (hereinafter referred to as "double taxation agreements"), which are generally concluded between states, that is, a typical comprehensive international tax agreement. This chapter focuses on such double taxation agreements and their relationship to the domestic income tax law and the general property tax law unilaterally enacted by the state parties.

缔约国政府制定的可适用于对纳税人的跨国所得和跨国财产价值征税的国内所得税法和一般财产税法,是缔约国单方面的主权意志的体现,它们与缔约国对外签订的双边或多边的避免双重征税协定之间的关系,从根本性质上说,属于国内法与国际条约之间的关系。但是,由于此类国际税收协定调整的国际税收关系的特殊性和复杂性,决定了它们具有区别于一般的双边国际经贸协定的法律特点,以及它们与缔约国国内有关税法关系的特殊问题。正确地认识此类国际税收协定与缔约国国内有关税法之间的关系,对于我们准确地适用此类协定条款规定,妥善处理好国际税收实践中的各种复杂的法律问题,具有重要的实际意义。

The domestic income tax law and the general property tax law enacted by the government of a contracting state, which are applicable to the taxation of the value of transnational income and property of taxpayers, are a manifestation of the unilateral sovereign will of the contracting states and the relationship between them and bilateral or multilateral agreements on the avoidance of double taxation concluded by the contracting states, which, by their very nature, is the one that between domestic law and international treaties. However, because of the particularity and complexity of the international tax relations adjusted by such international tax agreements, they have legal characteristics different from the general bilateral international economic and trade agreements, as well as their special problems with the domestic tax law relations of the contracting states. A correct understanding of the relationship between such international tax agreements and the relevant domestic tax laws of states parties is of great practical significance for us to accurately apply the provisions of such agreements and properly handle various complex legal problems in international tax practice.

国家之间通过缔结双重征税协定来协调彼此间的税收权益分配和解决国际双重征税问题的历史,最早可以追溯到1872年8月瑞士与英国之间签订的关于避免对遗产的双重征税协定。而国际上第一个综合性的避免对所得的双重征税协定是1899年6月奥匈帝国和普鲁士所缔结的税收条约。一百多年来,双重征税协定的发展经历了一个内容由简单到综合、条款由各具特色到规范统一的演进过程。在这个过程中,有关国际组织在推动此类协定的规范化发展方面,发挥了积极的作用。

The history of states coordinating the distribution of tax interests among themselves and resolving the problem of international double taxation through the conclusion of double taxation agreements dates back to the double taxation agreement between Switzerland and the United Kingdom on the avoidance of inheritance signed in August 1872. The first comprehensive double taxation agreement to avoid repeated taxation on income was the tax treaty concluded between Austria-Hungarian and Prussia in June 1899. Over the past 100 years, the development of double taxation agreements has experienced a process of evolution from simple to comprehensive content and from different characteristics to normative unity. In this process, relevant international organizations have played an active role in promoting the normative development of such agreements.

早在20世纪初,当时的国际联盟下设的国际税务委员会就开始致力于推动这类协定的规范化,先后研究拟定了一系列有关双重征税的双边协定范本。这些协定范本虽然没有得到当时各国的普遍接受和采用,但为后来双重征税协定条款的规范统一奠定了基础。不过,对此类双边协定内容和形式的规范化影响最大的,应是分别由经合发组织(OECD)以及联合国经济和社会理事会(以下简称"经社理事会")制定公布的双重税收协定范本。

As early as the beginning of the 20th century, the International Taxation Committee of the League of Nations began to work to standardize such agreements, and successively studied and developed a series of model bilateral agreements on double taxation. Although these model agreements were not generally accepted and adopted by states at that time, they laid the foundation for the normative harmonization of the provisions of subsequent double taxation agreements. However, the most significant impact on the standardization of the content and form of such bilateral agreements should be the model double taxation agreements published by the OECD (OECD) and the United Nations Economic and Social Council (hereinafter referred to as the Economic and Social Council), respectively.

经合发组织下设的税务委员会于1963年公布了由税收专家小组起草的《关于对所得和财产避免双重征税的协定范本草案》(以下简称"经合发组织范本"),这是经合发组织范本的第一个文本,并得到当时经合发组织成员国的普遍认同和采用。1967年经合发组织对草案进行了修订,并于1977年正式通过了修改后的范本及其注释。由于经合发组织范本强调居住国课税原则,注重保护居住国的税收利益,代表和反映了发达国家在处理国际税收分配问题上的利益和观点,因此不利于在国际税收分配关系中多处于来源地国地位的发展中国家的利益。为指导发展中国家与发达国家签订双重征税协定,1967年,经社理事会专门成立了由发达国家和发展中国家的代表组成的税收专家小组,经过近10年的努力,于1977年拟定了《发达国家与发展中国家关于双重征税的协定范本(草案)》及其注释,于1980年正式颁布,此即所谓联合国范本。在协定形式结构上,该范本与经合发组织范本相同,但有关条款强调来源地国税收管辖权原则,更多地照顾到资本输入国的权益,较多地考虑了发展中国家的要求,因此,它出台以来得到广大发展中国家的广泛采用。

A draft Model Agreement on the Avoidance of Double Taxation of Income and Property (hereinafter referred to as the OECD Model), prepared by the Group of Tax Experts, was published by the Committee on Fiscal Affairs (CFA) in 1963 as the first version of the OECD Model and was generally accepted and adopted by the then OECD member countries. The draft was revised by OECD in 1967 and the revised model and its annotations were formally adopted in 1977. Since the OECD Model emphasizes the principle of taxation in the country of residence and focuses on the protection of the tax interests of the country of residence, it represents and reflects the interests and views of developed countries in dealing with the issue of international tax distribution, and therefore is not conducive to the interests of developing countries that are mostly source countries in international tax distribution relations. In order to guide the conclusion of double taxation agreements between developing and developed countries, in 1967, the Economic and Social Council established a panel of tax experts composed of representatives of developed and developing countries. After nearly 10 years of efforts, the Model Agreement between Developed and Developing Countries on Double Taxation (draft) and its annotations were prepared in 1977 and officially promulgated in 1980, the so-called United Nations Model. In terms of the formal structure of the agreement, the model is the same as the OECD model, but the relevant provisions emphasize the principle of tax jurisdiction in the source state, take more account of the interests of the capital importing country, and take more account of the requirements of the developing countries.

经合发组织范本和联合国范本，是对长期以来各国双重税收协定实践经验的总结。它们的诞生，标志着双重征税协定的发展，开始进入成熟阶段。各国在谈判签署税收协定时，基本上都参照甚至套用两个范本所建议的条文和规则。两个范本的注释，也成为各国解释和适用双重征税协定条款时的重要参考文件。截至目前，世界上已有187个国家签署了4 000多个税收协定。中国从1981年年初就开始同有关国家签订双重征税协定，截至2020年4月底，我国已对外正式签署107个避免双重征税协定，其中101个协定已生效。①税收协定数量位居全球第三，已形成了比较完善的税收协定网络。全球的区域分布具体情况请见下文。由于中国是一个发展中国家，在国际税收分配关系中多处于收入来源地国的地位，中国在对外谈判缔结税收协定时，更多地参考采用联合国范本的建议条款，坚持所得来源地税收管辖权优先的原则，以尽可能维护本国应有的税收权益。

The OECD model and the United Nations model are a summary of the long-standing practical experience of national double tax agreements. Their birth marked the development of double taxation agreements and began to mature. When countries negotiate tax agreements, they basically refer to or even apply the two models in negotiating tax agreements, states have basically referred to or even applied the provisions and rules recommended in the two model texts. The notes of the two models also serve as an important reference document for states in interpreting and applying the provisions of double taxation agreements. So far, 187 countries in the world have signed more than 4,000 tax agreements. Since the beginning of 1981, China has signed double taxation agreements with countries concerned. By the end of April 2020, China had officially signed 107 double taxation avoidance agreements, of which 101 have entered into force. The number of tax agreements ranked third in the world, and had formed a relatively perfect network of tax agreements. As to the global regional distribution, see below for details. Since China is a developing country and is mostly a source of income country in the international tax distribution relationship, when negotiating and concluding tax agreements with foreign countries, China should refer more to the suggested provisions of the United Nations model and adhere to the principle of priority of jurisdiction over income in order to safeguard its due tax rights and interests as far as possible.

---

① 详见国家税务总局官网，www.chinatax.gov.cn/chinatax/n810341/n810770/index.html. 登录时间2020年10月。

双重税收协定的主要功能目的,是避免和消除缔约国相互之间所得和财产价值的国际双重征税。此类协定中的大多数实体性条款,都是围绕实现这一作用目的而设。各国相互缔结此类国际税收协定,尤其是第二次世界大战后签订此类税收协定的另一个作用目的,是防止国际逃税。不过,尽管防止国际逃税也是此类协定的明确目的之一,但按照前述两个范本模式签订的大多数此类税收协定中,直接服务于这一功能目的的协定条款为数却不多,甚至协定关于逃税概念用语本身的含义范围,也没有一个明确的解释。除上述两个主要的功能目的外,此类税收协定还有其他一些附属性的功能目的,如消除对外国人和非居民纳税人的税收歧视待遇,建立税收情报交换和税款征收协助方面的国际税务合作关系,以及处理国际税收争议解决程序等。

The main functional purpose of a double taxation agreement is to avoid and eliminate international double taxation of the value of income and property of the states parties. Most of the substantive provisions of such agreements are designed to serve the purpose of this role by setting up states to conclude such international tax agreements with one another, in particular after the Second World War, with a view to preventing international tax evasion. However, while the prevention of international tax evasion is also one of the explicit purposes of such agreements, the majority of such border tax agreements concluded under the aforementioned two-way formula do not have a large number of provisions that directly serve this functional purpose, and even there is no clear definition of the meaning of the terms themselves of the agreement on the concept of tax evasion. In addition to the above two main functional purposes, such tax agreements have other subsidiary functional purposes, such as the elimination of tax discrimination against foreign and non-resident taxpayers, the establishment of international tax cooperation in tax information exchange and tax collection assistance, and the handling of international tax dispute resolution procedures.

国家间缔结税收协定的目的是避免双重征税和双重不征税。然而,国家间签订了税收协定并不意味着就能自动实现这一目标。国际税收协定的内容主要是征税权的冲突规则。国际税收协定的规则主要是征税权(税收管辖权)划分规则。[①]国际税收协定不能为缔约国双方的公民或居民创设权利,除非税收协定的规定按国内立法方式被制定为法律,个人因缺乏国际法地位不得直接依协定主张权利但根据税收协定中的相互协商程序,纳税人享有争议解决的程序权利。缔约主体是国家,权利义务主体也是国家,但税收协定最直接的受益者是跨国纳税人,不是缔约国双方的税务部门,因此,税收协定主要适用于跨国纳税人,作用于缔约国税务机关和纳税人。

The purpose of tax agreements between states is to avoid double taxation and double non-

---

① 如,Art.7(1) 2010 OECD Model, (Profits of an enterprise of a contracting state shall be taxable only in that state unless the enterprise carries on business in the other contracting state through a permanent establishment situated therein.);《中华人民共和国政府和大不列颠及北爱尔兰联合王国政府关于对所得和财产收益相互避免双重征税和防止偷漏税的协定》第10条关于股息的规定:"1. 缔约国另一方居民从缔约国一方居民公司取得的股息,可以在该另一国征税。2. 然而,这些股息也可以在支付股息的公司是其居民的缔约国,按照该国的法律征税。但是,如果该项股息的受益所有人是缔约国另一方居民,则所征税款不应超过该股息总额的百分之十。"

taxation. However, the conclusion of tax agreements between countries does not mean that this goal can be achieved automatically. The content of international tax agreements are mainly the conflict rule of tax right. The rules of international tax agreements are mainly the rules of tax right (tax jurisdiction) division. International tax agreements can not create rights for citizens or residents of both parties, unless the provisions of the tax agreements are enacted into law in the form of domestic legislation, and individuals can not claim rights directly under the agreement because of their lack of international law status, but taxpayers have procedural rights to dispute under the mutual consultation procedure in the tax agreement. The subject of contracting is the state, the subject of rights and obligations is also the state, but the most direct beneficiary of the tax agreement is the transnational taxpayer, not the tax department of both parties. Therefore, the tax agreement mainly applies to transnational taxpayers and acts on the tax authorities and taxpayers of the parties.

经合发组织税收协定范本及其注释是诸多税收协定谈判和缔结的基础,对国际税收协定的谈判、解释和适用具有重要意义,也是国际税收争议解决方式的主要法律渊源。

The OECD Model Tax Agreement (the OECD Model Convention) and its Notes (the Commentaries on the OECD Model) are the basis for the negotiation and conclusion of many tax agreements, which are of great significance to the negotiation, interpretation and application of international tax agreements, and are also the main legal sources of international tax dispute resolution.

第二节　国际税收协定的主要内容
Section 2　Main Elements of International Tax Treaty

现代各国间参照上述两个范本签订的双重税收协定,主要包括以下四方面内容。

The double tax agreement signed between modern countries with reference to the above two models mainly includes the following four aspects.

 双重征税协定的适用范围
Scope of Application of Double Taxation Agreements

1. 双重征税协定空间和时间上的效力范围
Scope of Effectiveness in Space and Time of Double Taxation Agreements

双重征税协定在空间上的效力范围,是指此类协定适用的地域范围。协定在地域上的适用范围一般与缔约国各方税法有效适用的地域范围一致。缔约国税法有效适用的地域范围,包括缔约国领土、领海,以及领海以外缔约国根据国际法拥有勘探开发海底和底土资源以及海底以上水域资源权利区域。双重征税协定时间上的效力范围，则是指此类协定条款有效适用约束缔约国征税行为的期间。它与协定本身作为一种国际法律文件的生效是不同的概念。双重征税协定经缔约国双方授权代表谈判签署后，在缔约国各方往往还需履行各自国内法上有关条约通过或批准程序，并由双方互换批准通知书后才能生效。双重征税协定通常规定在生效后的下一个纳税年度起适用，此双边协定一般长期有效，但缔约双方往往也规定自协定生效起若干年后（一般为5年）可以单方面通知对方终止协定。

The scope of space validity of double taxation agreements refers to the geographical scope of application of such agreements. The territorial scope of application of the agreement is generally consistent with the territorial scope of the effective application of the tax laws of the parties to the agreement. The territorial scope of the effective application of the state tax law of a contracting state includes the territory, territorial sea of a contracting state and the area of the right of a contracting state other than the territorial sea to explore for and exploit the resources of the seabed and subsoil and the resources of the territorial waters above the seabed in accordance with international law. The scope of validity of a double taxation agreement in time refers to the period during which the provisions of such an agreement are effectively applied to the taxation acts of the contracting states. It is a different concept from the entry into force of the agreement itself as an international legal document. After a double taxation agreement has been negotiated and signed on behalf of the authorized representatives of the parties, the parties often have to perform the procedures for the adoption or ratification of the relevant treaty in their domestic law, and the parties exchange notifications of ratification before it can enter into force. Double taxation agreements usually provide for their application in the following tax year after their entry into force, and bilateral agreements generally remain in force for a long time, but contracting parties often also provide for the possibility of unilaterally notifying the other party to terminate the agreement after a number of years (generally 5 years) from the entry into force of the agreement.

2. 双重征税协定适用的税种范围

Scope of Taxes Applicable to the Agreements

双重征税协定一般只适用于以所得或财产价值为征税对象的税种，即缔约国双方各自开征的各种属于所得税或一般财产税性质的税收。协定通常要具体列出缔约国双方各自适用于协定的现行税种，同时考虑到双方各自税制在协定签订后可能发生的变化，一般还明确规定协定也适用于签订后缔约国任何一方增加的或代替与现行税种相同或实质相似的税收。

Double taxation agreements generally apply only to taxes that take the value of income or property as the object of taxation, that is, various taxes of the nature of income tax or general property tax imposed by both parties. The agreement would normally specify the existing taxes applicable to the agreement by each of the contracting parties, taking into account the possible changes in the respective tax systems of the parties following the signing of the agreement, and would generally specify that the agreement would also apply to taxes added by either of the contracting parties after the signing or in lieu of taxes identical or substantially similar to the existing taxes.

3. 双重征税协定对人的适用范围

Scope of Persons Applicable to the Agreements

现代各国之间签订的双重征税协定，除个别条款外，一般都明确规定仅适用于具有缔约国一方或双方居民身份从而对缔约国负有居民纳税义务的纳税人。只有那些被认定为是缔约国一方居民的纳税人，才能享受协定条款提供的优惠待遇。因此，为了明确限定协定对纳税人的适用范围，此类税收协定通常都参照两个范本的模式，对"缔约国一方居民"这一关键用语作出定义解释。按照两个范本第4条的定义解释，"缔约国一方居民"是指根据该国法律，因住所、居所、公司注册地、管理地或者其他类似性质的标准应当在该国纳税的人，也包括该国及其任何政治分支机构或者地方当局。这一定义首先表明，判断一个人是否为缔约国一方居民，应该根据该缔约国国内税法有关居民纳税人身份确认标准的规定进行识别认定。其次，它明确限定了居民身份原则上应依据住所、居所、管理场所或其他类似居住状态性质的标准来确定。这就意味着在判定一个人是否为税收协定意义上的缔约国一方居民时，虽然原则上应依照该缔约国国内税法的有关居民身份规定来认定，但也不能完全以该缔约国的国内法规定为准。税收协定同时对缔约国各方税法规定的居民身份确认标准要作适当的范围限制，即应限于目前绝大多数国家普遍采用的属于居住状态性质的标准，不包括少数国家税法上采用的国籍、注册成立地等法律性质的标准，以防止税收协定待遇被滥用。最后，按照这种定义，能够适用协定的人，还必须是在该缔约一方由于居民身份而负有无限纳税义务的人。不在该缔约国负有无限纳税义务的人，不能享受协定的待遇，尽管他（她）具有缔约国一方居民的身份。

Double taxation agreements concluded between modern states generally expressly apply, with the exception of individual provisions, only to taxpayers who have the status of resident of one or both of the contracting states and thus have the obligation to pay taxes to the residents of the contracting states. The preferential treatment provided for in the terms of the agreement is granted only to taxpayers who are recognized as residents of one of the contracting states. Therefore, in order to clearly define the scope of application of the agreement to taxpayers, such tax agreements usually interpret the key term "resident of one of the contracting states" by reference to the two Models. According to the definition in Paragraph 4 of the two Model Provisions, the term "resident of a contracting state" means any person who, under the laws of that state, is liable to tax therein by reason of his or her domicile, residence, place of incorporation, place of management or any other criterion of a similar nature, and also includes that state and any political subdivision or local authority thereof. This definition first indicates that the determination of whether a person is a resident of one of the contracting states should be made in accordance with the provisions of the domestic tax law of that state relating to the criteria for the identification of resident taxpayers. Secondly, it clearly defines that the identity of the resident shall in principle be determined on the basis of the criteria of the nature of the domicile, residence, place of administration or other similar state of residence. This means that, in determining whether a person is a resident of a contracting state within the meaning of a tax agreement, while in principle it should be determined in accordance with the relevant resident status provisions of the domestic tax law of that contracting state, it can not be entirely governed by the domestic law of that contracting state. The tax agreement, at the same time, imposes an appropriate scope limit on the criteria for the identification of residents under the tax laws of the contracting states, i.e. the criteria of a resident status which are generally used in the vast majority of states at present, excluding those of the legal nature of nationality, place of incorporation, etc., adopted in the tax laws of a few states, in order to prevent the abuse of the treatment of tax agreements. Finally, according to this definition, the person who can apply the agreement must also be the person who has an unlimited tax obligation on that contracting party because of its resident status. A person who does not have an unlimited duty to pay taxes in that contracting state is not entitled to the treatment agreed upon, even though he or she is a resident of one of the states parties.

适用上述缔约国一方居民的概念定义，如果一个纳税人按照缔约国甲方的国内税法规定认定属于其居民，但同时依照缔约国乙方国内税法规定的标准，也可以认定为是乙方的居民，在发生这种"双重居民身份冲突"的情形下，缔约国双方为了协定适用，必须确定这个纳税人的居民身份究竟应归属于何方，否则该税收协定无法对这个纳税人适用。根据两个范本建议的系列冲突规则，自然人的双重居民身份冲突应按照以下规则顺序确定其居民身份的归属：首先应认定这个自然人是其拥有永久性住所在国一方的居民；如果这个自然人在缔约国双方同时有永久性住所，应认为仅是与其个人和经济关系更密切（重要利益中心）所在国的居民。如果这个自然人的重要利益中心所在国无法确定，或者他（她）在其中任何一方都没有永久性住所，应认为仅是其有习惯性居处所在国的居民。如果他（她）在缔约国双方都有，或者都没有习惯性居处，应认为仅是其国籍所属国一方的居民。如果这个自然人同时是缔约国双方的国民，或者是其中任何一方的国民，应由缔约国双方主管当局通过协商确定其居民身份的归属。在公司和法人组织发生双重居民身份冲突的情形下，按照两个范本建议的规则，应认定该法人团体仅是其实际管理机构所在地国一方的居民。应该指出的是，在出现双重居民身份冲突的情形下，缔约国双方适用上述系列冲突规则确定某个纳税人的居民身份归属缔约国一方，完全仅是为了就该特定纳税人适用彼此间签订的税收协定的需要，并不妨碍缔约国另一方在对该纳税人课税时继续适用国内税法上有关居民纳税人的课税规定。在双重征税协定适用意义上，某个特定的纳税人一旦确定为缔约国一方居民纳税人，该缔约国一方就是他（她）的居住国，而这个特定的纳税人相对于缔约国另一方而言，就是其非居民纳税人。

If a taxpayer is recognized as a resident of Party A in accordance with the provisions of Party A's domestic tax law, but at the same time according to the standards stipulated in Party B's domestic tax law, it may also be recognized as a resident of Party B. In the event of such "double resident status conflict", the contracting state must determine where the taxpayer's resident status belongs, otherwise the tax agreement can not apply to the taxpayer. According to the series of conflict rules proposed by the two models, the dual-resident status conflict of a natural person should determine the attribution of his or her resident status in the order of the following rules: First, the natural person should be considered as a resident of the country in which he or she has permanent residence on the constracting state's side; if the natural person has permanent residence on both sides of the constracting state, he or she should be considered as a resident of the country in which he or she has a closer personal and economic relationship (centre of significant interest). Second, if the state in which the natural person's centre of important interests is located can not be determined, or if he or she does not have permanent residence in either of them, he or she should be considered as only a resident of the state in which he or she habitually resides. Third, if he or she has or is not habitually resident in both states parties, he or she shall be considered as a resident of one of the states to which he or she belongs. Fourth, if the natural person is also a national of both parties, or a national of either party, the attribution of his or her resident status shall be determined by consultation between the competent authorities of both parties. In the case of dual resident status conflict between the company and the legal person organization, according to the rules suggested by the two models, it should be determined that the legal person organization is only a resident of one party of the country where its actual administrative organization is located. It should be noted that, in the event of a dual-resident status conflict, the application by the parties of the above-mentioned conflict rules to establish the resident status of a taxpayer to one of the parties is solely for the purpose of applying the tax agreement concluded between the two parties to that particular taxpayer, without prejudice to the continued application by the other party of the tax provisions of the domestic tax law relating to the resident taxpayer in respect of that particular taxpayer. In the sense of application of a double taxation agreement, once a particular taxpayer is identified as a resident taxpayer of one of the contracting states, one of the contracting states is his or her country of residence, and that particular taxpayer is its non-resident taxpayer relative to the other of the contracting states.

值得注意的是，虽然双重征税协定原则上仅适用于具有缔约国一方居民身份的纳税人，但由于跨国纳税人滥用此类税收协定进行国际避税的现象日益普遍，近些年来，为防止第三国居民通过在缔约国一方境内设置所谓"导管公司"套取协定的优惠待遇，许多国家在此类协定中增设了反滥用协定条款。根据这类反滥用协定条款，如果某个具有缔约国一方居民身份的公司被证实属于第三国居民设置的旨在套取某个协定优惠待遇的"导管公司"，则该协定中有关减免税和其他优惠待遇的条款不适用于这种居民。

It is worth noting that, while double taxation agreements in principle apply only to taxpayers with the resident status of one of the contracting parties, they have been prevented in recent years by the increasing prevalence of international tax avoidance by transnational taxpayers abusing such tax agreements. Many countries have added anti-abuse agreement provisions to the so-called "conduit companies" arbitrage agreements by residents of the three countries through the establishment of preferential treatment in the territory of one party. Under the terms of such an anti-abuse agreement, the provisions of the agreement relating to tax relief and other preferences do not apply to a company with a resident status of one of the contracting states that is proved to be a "conduit company" established by a resident of a third country to obtain preferential treatment under an agreement.

4. 确定缔约国一方对各类跨国所得行使来源地税收管辖权的条件和范围

Determination of the Conditions and Scope for a Contracting Party to Exercise its Jurisdiction over the Source of Taxes on Various Types of Transnational Proceeds

如前指出，跨国所得和财产价值的国际双重征税，在大多数情况下是由一国对其居民纳税人来源于居住国境外的所得主张行使居民税收管辖权，与有关所得的来源地国主张的来源地税收管辖权发生冲突的结果造成的。要解决国际双重征税问题，双重征税协定首先要区分各种不同性质的跨国所得，如不动产所得，营业所得，国际运输企业利润、股息、利息和特许权使用费等投资所得，劳务所得和财产收益等，再分别规定作为来源地国的缔约国一方，对缔约国另一方居民来源于其境内的上述各项跨国所得，在何种条件下或范围内可以行使来源地课税权征税，而不能完全依照其国内税法的规定课税。这样才能在一定程度和范围内避免和减缓双方税收管辖权的冲突。下面结合我国税收协定的规定，分别介绍这些核心条款。

As noted earlier, international double taxation of the value of transnational income and property is, in most cases, the result of a conflict between a state's exercise of resident tax jurisdiction over a claim by its resident taxpayer for income derived from outside the country of residence and the tax jurisdiction of the place of origin claimed by the country of origin of the income concerned. To solve the problem of international double taxation, a double taxation agreement must first distinguish between transnational income of various natures, such as income from real estate, income from business, income from investments such as profits from international transport enterprises, dividends, interest and royalties, income from services and income from property, and provide, respectively, that one of the contracting states that is the country of origin may, under what conditions or to what extent, exercise the right to taxation of the place of origin against the above-mentioned transnational income derived from the territory of the other resident of the contracting state, and not exclusively in accordance with its domestic tax laws. This is the only way to avoid and mitigate the conflict of tax jurisdiction between the two sides to a certain extent. The following are the main provisions of China's tax agreement.

（1）常设机构

Permanent Establishment

常设机构条款是税收协定的重要条款，它主要与营业利润条款结合，组成对缔约一方所取得营业利润的征税规则，以限制所得来源国的征税权，避免双重征税。

The permanent establishment clause is an important one in the tax agreement. It is mainly combined with the operating profit clause to form a tax rule on the operating profit obtained by the contracting party in order to limit the tax right of the source country and avoid double taxation.

常设机构条款主要用来确定企业是否在某国具有纳税义务，从而使该国能对归属于常设机构的所得进行征税。常设机构条款不仅是征税的前提条件，还是辨别应税所得征收方式的基础。一般来说，对归属于常设机构的所得要按照常设机构营业利润征税，对不归属于常设机构的所得则按照其他条款征税。

The permanent establishment is primarily used to determine whether an enterprise has a tax obligation in a country, thereby enabling that country to tax income attributable to the permanent establishment. The rules of permanent establishment are not only the precondition of taxation, but also the basis of distinguishing the way of collection of taxable income. In general, income attributable to the permanent establishment is taxed on the basis of the operating profit of the permanent establishment and income not attributable to the permanent establishment is taxed on other terms.

【适用主体】

Subject of Application

从缔约对方国家(地区)取得营业利润所得的居民。(税收协定中的居民是税法上的一个概念,指的是税收居民,是以缔约国国内法上的居民定义为基础的。要成为税收协定上的居民,首先必须符合缔约国国内税法上的居民定义。)

Residents who obtain operating profits from the country (region) of the contracting party. (Residents in tax agreements are a concept in the tax law, referring to tax residents, based on the definition of residents in the domestic law of the constracting state. To become a resident in a tax agreement, it must first comply with the definition of resident in the domestic tax law of the constracting state.)

【协定规定】

Provisions of the Agreement

我国对外签订的税收协定,对常设机构的一般性条款主要表述为:协定中,"常设机构"一语是指企业进行全部或部分营业的固定营业场所。"常设机构"一语特别包括:管理场所、分支机构、办事处、工厂、车间(作业场所)、矿场、油井或气井、采石场或者其他开采自然资源的场所。除上述列举外,我国与部分国家还增列了部分项目。

In the tax agreement signed by China, the general clause of the permanent establishment is mainly expressed as: the term "permanent establishment" in the agreement refers to the fixed business place where the enterprise carries out all or part of its business. The term "permanent establishment" includes, inter alia: management sites, branches, offices, factories, workshops (workplaces), mines, wells or gas wells, quarries or other sites for the exploitation of natural resources. In addition to the above list, some items have been added to our country and some countries.

在常设机构一般性条款之外,通常还对承包工程、提供劳务构成常设机构以及代理型常设机构的标准进行专门规定。

In addition to the general provisions of the permanent establishment, the criteria for contracting works, providing services to constitute the permanent establishment and acting permanent establishment are usually specified.

此外,我国同部分国家签订的税收协定还增加了有关保险业务构成常设机构的特殊规定。

In addition, tax agreements between China and some countries have added special provisions on the formation of permanent establishments in the insurance business.

【适用条件】

Conditions of Application

一般常设机构。一般常设机构是指具有固定性、持续性和经营性的营业场所,但不包括从事协定所列举的专门从事准备性、辅助性活动的机构。

General permanent establishment. The general permanent establishment has a fixed, continuous and operational place of business, but does not include institutions specialized in preparatory, auxiliary activities as enumerated in the agreement.

工程型常设机构。"常设机构"一语包括建筑工地,建筑、装配或安装工程,或者与其有关的监督管理活动,但仅以该工地、工程或活动连续达到规定时间(通常为6个月)以上的为限,未达到该规定时间的则不构成常设机构。我国与不同国家签订的协定,通常以一般表述为基准,但在项目的持续时间上,会存在几种不同的形式。此外,少数协定没有纳入有关的监督管理活动。不同协定中有关承包工程构成常设机构的表述存在差异。

Engineering permanent establishment. The term "permanent establishment" includes construction site, construction, assembly or installation works, or supervision and management activities relating thereto, but only if the site, works or activities have continuously reached the prescribed time (usually 6 months), and if they have not reached the prescribed time, it does not constitute a permanent establishment. Agreements with different countries are usually based on general statements, but there are several different forms in the duration of the project. In addition, a few agreements do not include related monitoring and management activities. In different agreements, there are differences in the description of the construction of a permanent establishment.

劳务型常设机构。提供劳务构成常设机构的一般表述为:缔约国一方企业通过雇员或者其他人员,在缔约国另一方为同一个项目或相关联的项目提供劳务,包括咨询劳务,仅以在任何一个月中连续或累计超过____天/月为限,未达到该规定时间的则不构成常设机构。不同协定对时间长度的计算方法有所不同,通常为任何12个月中连续或累计超过6个月或183天。

Labor type permanent establishment. The general expression of the provision of services as constituting a permanent establishment is that an enterprise of one contracting state, through its employees or other personnel, provides services, including advisory services, in the other contracting state for the same or associated project, only for a continuous or cumulative period of more than ____ days/months in any month, and does not constitute a permanent establishment if the prescribed time is not reached. The calculation of the length of time varies from agreement to agreement, usually for more than 6 months or 183 days in any 12 months.

代理型常设机构。当一个人(除适用第6款的独立代理人外)在缔约国一方代表缔约国另一方的企业进行活动时,有权以该企业的名义签订合同并经常行使这种权利,这个人为该企业进行任何活动,均应认为该企业在该缔约国一方设有常设机构。

Acting permanent establishment. When a person (other than an independent agent to which Paragraph 6 applies) carries out activities on behalf of an enterprise of the other contracting state, he or she has the right to enter into a contract on behalf of that enterprise and to exercise such right on a regular basis, any activity carried out by that enterprise for that enterprise shall be deemed to have a permanent establishment in one of the contracting states.

保险业务常设机构。我国同突尼斯、墨西哥、芬兰、文莱、斯里兰卡、摩洛哥、印度尼西亚、尼泊尔、埃及、越南、巴基斯坦、泰国增加有关保险行业构成常设机构的内容。

A Permanent establishment of insurance business. With Tunisia, Mexico, Finland, Brunei, Sri Lanka, Morocco, Indonesia, Nepal, Egypt, Viet Nam, Pakistan and Thailand, China has increased the content of the insurance industry as a permanent establishment.

（2）营业利润

Operating Profit

税收协定规定,只有在构成常设机构的情况下,来源国才有权对营业利润征税。因此营业利润条款是与常设机构密切相关的条款。常设机构条款主要起界定作用,明确哪些活动在何种情况下构成常设机构,从而确定来源国拥有对该常设机构的征税权。而"营业利润"条款是指一旦构成常设机构,企业从事跨国经营产生的利润如何在国家间划分征税权。

Tax agreements provide that source countries are entitled to tax operating profits only if they constitute a permanent establishment. Therefore, the operating profit clause is closely related to the permanent establishment. The provisions of the permanent establishment primarily define what activities constitute the permanent establishment in which case the source country has the right to tax the permanent establishment. The "operating profit" clause refers to how the tax rights over the profits generated by the multinational operation of a permanent establishment enterprise are divided between countries.

要注意常设机构优先原则,除营业利润外,当其他所得与常设机构有实际联系时,应将有关的部分所得归属于常设机构征税,余下所得再按照其他条款处理。

Attention should be paid to the principle of permanent establishment priority. In addition to operating profits, when other income is actually related to the permanent establishment, the relevant part of the income shall be taxed by the permanent establishment, and the remaining income shall be treated in accordance with other provisions.

【适用主体】

Subject of Application

通过设在缔约对方国家（地区）的常设机构取得营业利润所得的居民企业。

A resident enterprise that obtains the proceeds of operating profits through a permanent establishment in the state (region) of the contracting party.

【协定规定】

Provisions of the Agreement

缔约国一方企业的利润应仅在该国征税,但该企业通过设在缔约国另一方的常设机构进行营业的除外。如果该企业通过在缔约国另一方的常设机构进行营业,其利润可以在另一国征税,但应仅以归属于该常设机构的利润为限。

The profits of an enterprise of one contracting state shall be taxed in that state only, except where the enterprise operates through a permanent establishment located in the other contracting state. If the enterprise operates through a permanent establishment in the other contracting state, its profits may be taxed in the other state, but only to the extent of the profits attributable to that permanent establishment.

【适用条件】

Conditions of Application

我国居民企业在缔约对方国家（地区）设立常设机构进行营业,归属于该常设机构的利润,在缔约对方国家（地区）按照营业利润纳税。

For our resident enterprises in the other contracting country (region) to establish a permanent establishment for business, profits attributable to the permanent establishment shall be taxed on the basis of business profits in the other contracting party's country cregion.

国际运输企业利润的特殊处理

Special treatment of profits of international transportation companies

我国对外签订的税收协定中,除与美国的协定外,都有海运和空运等涉及国际运输的条款。海运和空运一般为税收协定的第8条,共两款,分别规定了对国际运输所得的征税和国际合作形式下国际运输所得的税收处理。

In China's foreign tax agreements, except the agreement with the United States, there are maritime and air transport and other provisions related to international transport. Maritime and air transport are generally Article 8 of the tax agreement, which consists of two paragraphs, respectively provide for the tax treatment of the proceeds of international transport and the tax treatment of the proceeds of international transport in the form of international cooperation.

我国签订的大多数税收协定对国际运输所得采用居民国独占征税权的原则和总机构或实际管理机构所在国独占征税权的原则,少部分采用来源国拥有部分征税权的原则。

Most of the tax agreements signed by China adopt the principle of exclusive tax right of the resident state and the principle of exclusive tax right of the host country of the general institution or the actual administrative institution, and a few adopt the principle of partial tax right of the source country.

【适用主体】

Subject of Application

以船舶或飞机从事国际运输业务取得收入的居民企业。

A resident enterprise engaged in international transport business by ship or aircraft.

【协定规定】

Provisions of the Agreement

我国对外签订的税收协定一般表述为:缔约国一方企业以船舶或飞机经营国际运输业务取得的利润,应仅在该缔约国征税。部分税收协定采用总机构所在国独占征税权原则,部分税收协定采用实际管理机构所在国独占征税权原则,部分则采用总机构或实际管理机构所在国独占征税权原则。

 The tax agreements signed by China are generally expressed as follows: the profits obtained by an enterprise of a contracting state in the operation of international transport by ship or aircraft shall be taxed only in that contracting state. Some tax agreements adopt the principle of exclusive tax right in the country where the general agency is located, some tax agreements adopt the principle of exclusive tax right in the country where the actual administrative agency is located, and some adopt the principle of exclusive tax right in the country where the general agency or the actual administrative agency is located.

采用总机构所在国独占征税权原则的税收协定,该条第一款一般表述为:以船舶或飞机经营国际运输业务所取得的利润,应仅在企业总机构所在缔约国征税。并且通常增加第二款"母港确定规则":船运企业的总机构设在船舶上的,应以船舶母港所在缔约国为所在国；没有母港的，以船舶经营者为其居民的缔约国为所在国。需要说明的是，我国与比利时的协定虽然对国际运输所得也采用总机构所在国独占征税权原则，并且使用上述一般表述，但却没有母港确定规则。

The first paragraph of this article, which adopts the principle of exclusive taxation of the state in which the general body is located, expresses as follows: profits from the operation of international transport operations on board a ship or aircraft shall be taxed only in the contracting state in which the general body of the enterprise is located. And the second paragraph of the rules for determining the home port shall be added: if the general body of the shipping enterprise is located on board a ship, the contracting state in which the ship's home port is located shall be the contracting state in which the ship's home port is located; if there is no home port, the state party in which the ship operator is its resident shall be the contracting state in which the ship operator is located. It should be noted that although the agreement between China and Belgium also adopts the principle of exclusive taxation right of the country where the head office is located for international transport income, and uses the above general expression, there is no home port determination rule.

采用实际管理机构所在国独占征税权原则的协定，该条第一款一般表述为：以船舶或飞机经营国际运输的利润，应仅在企业实际管理机构所在缔约国征税。并且通常增加第二款"母港确定规则"，一般表述为：船运企业的实际管理机构设在船舶上的，应以船舶母港所在缔约国为所在国；没有母港的，以船舶经营者为其居民的缔约国为所在国。

Agreement adopting the principle of exclusive taxation of the state in which the actual regulatory agency is located, the first paragraph of this article is generally stated as follows: the profits from the operation of international transport by ships or aircraft shall be taxed only in the contracting state in which the actual regulatory agency of the enterprise is located, and the second paragraph shall normally be added to the rules for the determination of the home port. If the actual administrative body is located on board a ship, the state party in which the ship's home port is located shall be the contracting state in which the ship's home port is located; if there is no home port, the state party in which the ship's operator is resident shall be the contracting state in which the ship's operator is located.

采用总机构或实际管理机构所在国独占征税权原则的协定，该条第一款一般表述为：以船舶或飞机经营国际运输业务所取得的利润，应仅在企业总机构或实际管理机构所在缔约国征税。并且通常增加第二款"母港确定规则"：船运企业的总机构或实际管理机构设在船舶上的，应以船舶母港所在缔约国为所在国；没有母港的，以船舶经营者为其居民的缔约国为所在国。

An agreement adopting the principle of exclusive taxation in the state in which the general body or the actual administrative body is located, the first paragraph of this article is generally stated as follows: the profits derived from the operation of international transport operations on board a ship or aircraft shall be taxed only in the state party in which the enterprise's general or actual administrative body is located, and the second paragraph is usually added: if the general or actual administrative body of the shipping enterprise is located on the ship, the state party in

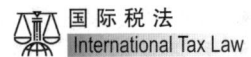

which the ship's home port is located shall be the state in which the ship is located; if there is no home port, the constracting state in which the ship operator is its resident shall be the state in which the ship is located.

需要注意的是，虽然我国签订的大部分税收协定都规定国际运输所得适用的税种是所得税，但我国与部分国家的税收协定及议定书，或者其他协议、换函中也涉及间接税。

It should be noted that although most of the tax agreements signed by China stipulate that the tax applicable to the income from international transportation is income tax, the tax agreements and protocols between our country and some countries, or other agreements, exchange letters also involve indirect taxes.

【适用条件】

Conditions of Application

以船舶或飞机经营，取得属于税收协定或其他协议、换函规定的国际运输收入的居民企业。

A resident enterprise operating on a ship or aircraft and obtaining income from international transport as provided for in a tax agreement or other agreements or exchange of letters.

（3）股息

Dividend

我国签订的税收协定中明确了我国和来源国对股息都有征税权，来源国即指分配股息的公司所在国。一般而言，来源国基于税收协定对股息收入实行限制性税率（具体税率与持股比例相关，一般低于来源国国内税法规定的税率）。

The tax agreement signed by China makes it clear that both our country and the source country have the right to tax dividends, and the source country refers to the country where the company distributes the dividend. In general, the source country imposes a restrictive tax rate on dividend income based on tax agreements (the specific tax rate is related to the shareholding ratio and is generally lower than the tax rate stipulated in the domestic tax law of the source country).

取得股息的人在具有该所得受益所有人身份的情况下，才能在来源国享受协定规定的优惠税率，否则将按来源国的国内法进行征税。受益所有人是指对所得和所得据以产生的权利或财产具有所有权和支配权的人，一般从事实质性的经营活动，可以是个人、公司或其他任何团体。在判定受益所有人身份时，应按照实质重于形式的原则，结合具体的实际情况，在综合考虑各种相关因素的基础上，进行分析判断。

A person who has obtained a dividend shall be entitled to the preferential tax rate provided for in the agreement in the country of origin only if he or she has the status of beneficial owner of the income, otherwise the tax will be levied in accordance with the domestic law of the country of origin. The beneficial owner is a person who has the right of ownership and control over the right or property derived from the proceeds, generally engaged in substantive business activities, and may be an individual, a company or any other group. In determining the identity of the beneficial owner, we should analyze and judge according to the principle that substance is more important than form, combined with the concrete actual situation, and on the basis of comprehensive consideration of various relevant factors.

需要注意的是，对所支付的股息同常设机构有实际联系的不适用股息条款，而应按营业利润处理。

It should be noted that the dividend clause does not apply to dividends paid that are actually linked to the permanent establishment and it should be treated as operating profit.

【适用主体】

Subject of Application

从缔约对方国家（地区）取得股息所得的我国居民。

A resident of the country (region) that obtains dividends from the other party.

【协定规定】

Provisions of the Agreement

股息条款一般表述为：如果该项股息的受益所有人是缔约国另一方居民，则所征税款不应超过股息总额的____%。我国与其他国家或地区所签订税收协定的股息限制税率存在差异，协定税率分别为5%到20%之间。

The dividend clause is generally expressed as follows: if the beneficial owner of the dividend is a resident of the other party of the contracting state, the tax levied shall not exceed ____% of the total dividend amount. There are differences in dividend restriction rates for tax agreements between China and other countries or regions, ranging between 5% and 20% respectively.

【适用条件】

Conditions of Application

从缔约对方国家（地区）取得股息所得符合税收协定股息条款有关持股比例等特定要求。

Dividend income obtained from the country (region) of the contracting party shall comply with the specific requirements of the dividend provisions of the tax treaty such as the shareholding ratio.

股息免税的情形

Dividend Exemption

我国签订的税收协定中，对于个别国家，来源国放弃股息收入征税权，即我国居民取得的股息收入享受协定免税待遇。

In the tax agreement signed by China, for individual countries, the source country waives the right to tax dividend income, that is, the dividend income obtained by our residents enjoys the agreement tax-free treatment.

在适用股息条款时，存在受益所有人的问题。当股息收入的居民符合协定关于受益所有人的规定，并满足一定条件时，来源国才会放弃对该股息所得的征税权。

In the application of dividend terms, there is a problem of beneficial owners. Only when the residents of the dividend income meet the requirements of the agreement for the beneficial owner and meet certain conditions will the source country waive the right to tax the dividend income.

【适用主体】

Subject of Application

从特定缔约对方国家（地区）取得股息所得的居民。

A resident who obtains dividends from the country (region) of a particular contracting party.

【协定规定】
Provisions of the Agreement

我国与科威特、阿联酋签订的税收协定规定：虽有第一款和第二款的规定，由缔约国一方居民公司支付给缔约国另一方居民的股息，应仅在该缔约国另一方征税，条件是该项股息的受益所有人是：① 缔约国另一方政府、其政府机构、或为该缔约国另一方政府直接或间接全部拥有的其他实体；或 ② 由该缔约国另一方政府直接或间接拥有至少20%股份的该缔约国另一方居民公司。

China's tax agreements with Kuwait and the United Arab Emirates provide that, notwithstanding Paragraphs 1 and 2, dividends paid by a resident company of one contracting state to a resident of the other contracting state shall be taxed only in the other contracting state if the beneficial owner of the dividend is: (i) the government of the other contracting state, its governmental agencies, or other entity owned directly or indirectly by the government of the other contracting state; or (ii) a resident company of the other contracting state owns at least 20 per cent of the shares directly or indirectly by the government of the other contracting state.

我国与沙特阿拉伯签订的税收协定规定：虽有第一款和第二款的规定，如果股息的受益所有人是缔约国另一方政府、其所属机构或其直接或间接完全拥有的其他实体，缔约国一方的居民公司支付给缔约国另一方居民的股息仅应在该缔约国另一方征税。

China's tax agreement with Saudi Arabia provides that, notwithstanding Paragraphs 1 and 2, dividends paid by a resident company of one contracting state to a resident of the other contracting state shall be taxed only in the other contracting state if the beneficial owner of the dividend is the government of the other contracting state, its institutions or other entities wholly owned, directly or indirectly, by that state.

我国与英国签订的税收协定规定：虽有第一款和第二款的规定，由缔约国一方居民公司支付给缔约国另一方居民的股息，如果受益所有人是缔约国另一方政府及其机构，或者是缔约国另一方政府直接或间接全资所有的其他实体，应仅在该缔约国另一方征税。

China's tax agreement with the United Kingdom provides that, notwithstanding Paragraphs 1 and 2, dividends paid by a resident company of one contracting state to another resident of the contracting state shall be taxed only in the other contracting state if the beneficial owner is the government of the other contracting state and its institutions, or other entities wholly owned, directly or indirectly, by the government of the other contracting state.

我国与格鲁吉亚签订的税收协定规定：如果该受益所有人直接或间接拥有支付股息公司至少50%股份，并在该公司投资超过200万欧元，为股息总额的百分之零。

China's tax agreement with Georgia stipulates that if the beneficial owner directly or indirectly owns at least 50% of the dividend paying company and invests more than 2 million euros in the company, it is 0% of the total dividend.

【适用条件】
Conditions of Application

从科威特、阿联酋、沙特阿拉伯、英国或格鲁吉亚取得股息所得并符合我国与上述五国签订的税收协定股息条款相关规定。

Dividends received from Kuwait, the United Arab Emirates, Saudi Arabia, the United Kingdom or Georgia are in accordance with the dividend terms of our tax agreements with the above five countries.

(4) 利息

Interest

我国已签税收协定或安排中的利息条款通常表述为:"利息"一语是指从各种债权取得的所得,不论其有无抵押担保或者是否有权分享债务人的利润;特别是从公债、债券或者信用债券取得的所得,包括其溢价和奖金。由于延期支付的罚款,不应视为本条所规定的利息。

Interest clauses in tax agreements or arrangements that have been signed in China are usually expressed as follows: "interest" refers to income obtained from various claims, whether secured or not, or entitled to share the profits of the debtor; in particular, income obtained from bonds, bonds or credit bonds, including premiums and bonuses. The penalty due to deferred payment shall not be regarded as interest under this Article.

一般而言,来源国基于税收协定对利息收入实行限制性税率。

In general, source countries impose restrictive tax rates on interest income based on tax agreements.

需要注意的是,对所支付的利息同常设机构有实际联系的不适用利息条款,而应按营业利润处理。

It is important to note that interest payments that are actually linked to the permanent establishment do not apply to interest clauses and should be treated as operating profits.

在适用利息条款时,同样存在受益所有人的问题。来源国没有义务仅因利息所得是由与其缔约的另一方国家的某个居民所直接接受而放弃对该利息所得的征税权。

In the application of interest clauses, there is also the problem of beneficial owners. The source state is not obliged to waive its right to tax the proceeds of interest solely on the grounds that the proceeds of interest are directly accepted by a resident of the state to which it is a party.

【适用主体】

Subject of Application

从缔约对方国家(地区)取得利息所得的居民。

Residents who earn interest from the other country (region) of the contracting party.

【协定规定】

Provisions of the Agreement

利息条款一般表述为:如果收款人是该利息受益所有人,则所征税款不应超过利息总额的____%。

The interest clause is generally expressed as follows: if the payee is the beneficial owner of the interest, the tax levied shall not exceed ____% of the total interest amount.

关于利息税收协定还存在特殊规定,如部分国家(地区)体现为对税基进行限制,如奥地利支付给我国银行或金融机构的利息,应仅按该利息总额的70%征税。

There are also special provisions on interest tax agreements, such as some countries (regions) reflect restrictions on the tax base, such as interest paid by Austria to our banks or financial institutions, which should be taxed at only 70% of the total interest.

我国与部分国家签订的税收协定中对利息来源国的限制税率存在差异，在0%到10%之间。

There are differences in the restrictive tax rates of interest source countries in the tax agreements signed between China and some countries. The tax rates of some agreements are from 0% to 10%.

【适用条件】

Conditions of Application

从缔约对方国家（地区）取得利息所得符合税收协定利息限制税率规定的具体要求。

Income from interest earned from the state (territory) of the contracting party is in accordance with the specific requirements of the tax agreement interest limit tax rate.

利息免税的情形

interest tax exemption

部分情况下，来源国放弃利息收入征税权，即我国居民取得的利息收入享受协定免税待遇。

In some cases, the source country waives the right to tax interest income, that is, the interest income obtained by China's residents enjoys the agreement tax exemption.

【适用主体】

Subject of Application

从缔约对方国家（地区）取得利息所得的居民。

Residents who earn interest from the other country (region) of the contracting party.

【协定规定】

Provisions of the Agreement

我国与大部分国家签署的税收协定中的利息条款存在免税规定，即发生在缔约国对方而为我国政府、地方政府及中央银行或者完全为我国政府所有的金融机构取得的利息；或者为我国居民所取得的利息，其债权是由我国政府、地方政府及中央银行或者完全为我国政府所有的金融机构间接提供资金的，应在该缔约国对方免税。通常，这些金融机构在具体协定中采取列名方式。

Tax exemptions exist in the interest clauses in tax agreements signed by China with most countries, i.e. interest earned on behalf of our government, local governments and central banks, or solely for China's government-owned financial institutions, occurring in the other party of the state parties; or interest earned on behalf of our residents, whose claims are indirectly financed by our government, local governments and central banks or by financial institutions wholly owned by China's government, shall be exempt from tax in that party. Typically, these financial institutions adopt listing modalities in specific agreements.

我国与新加坡、马耳他、葡萄牙、墨西哥、土库曼斯坦、特立尼达和多巴哥、摩洛哥、巴巴多斯、冰岛、泰国、委内瑞拉等国家签署的协定中对政府全部或主要拥有的任何机构或其他类似机构贷款利息均免予征税。

China's agreements with Singapore, Malta, Portugal, Mexico, Turkmenistan, Trinidad and Tobago, Morocco, Barbados, Iceland, Thailand, Venezuela and other countries exempt from taxation interest on loans made by any institution or other similar institution wholly or mainly owned by the government.

【适用条件】

Conditions of Application

从缔约对方国家(地区)取得利息所得符合税收协定利息免税规定的具体要求。

Income earned from the state (territory) of the contracting party meets the specific requirements of the tax exemption for interest under the tax agreement.

(5) 特许权使用费

Royalties

我国签订的税收协定明确了我国和所得来源国对特许权使用费都有征税权,来源国是指实际支付特许权使用费的企业所在国。

The tax agreement signed by China's country clarifies that both China and the source country of income have the right to tax royalties, and the source country refers to the country where the enterprise actually pays the royalties.

我国与大多数国家签订的税收协定对特许权使用费通常表述为:"特许权使用费"一语是指使用或有权使用文学、艺术或科学著作,包括电影影片、无线电或电视广播使用的胶片、磁带的版权,专利、商标、设计、模型、图纸、秘密配方或秘密程序所支付的作为报酬的各种款项,也包括使用或有权使用工业、商业、科学设备或有关工业、商业、科学经验的情报所支付的作为报酬的各种款项。

Royalties are usually expressed in China's tax agreements with most countries as follows: "royalties" refers to the use or right to use literary, artistic or scientific works, including the copyright of films, tapes, patents, trademarks, designs, models, drawings, secret formulations or secret proceedings, as well as the various payments paid as compensation for the use or right to use industrial, commercial, scientific equipment or information relating to industrial, commercial and scientific experience.

一般而言,来源国基于税收协定对特许权使用费收入实行限制性税率。

In general, source countries impose restrictive tax rates on royalty income based on tax agreements.

需要注意的是,对所支付的特许权使用费同常设机构有实际联系的不适用特许权使用费条款,而应按营业利润处理。

It should be noted that the royalty clause does not apply to royalty payments that are actually linked to the permanent establishment and should be treated as operating profit.

在适用特许权使用费条款时,同样存在受益所有人的问题。来源国没有义务仅因特许权使用费所得是由与其缔约的另一方国家的某个居民所直接接受而放弃对该项所得的征税权。

In the application of the royalty clause, there is also the problem of beneficial owners. The source state is not obliged to waive the right to tax the proceeds of the royalties solely because they are directly accepted by a resident of the state to which it is a party.

【适用主体】

Subject of Application

从缔约对方国家(地区)取得特许权使用费所得的居民。

Residents who obtain royalties from the country (region) of the contracting party.

【协定规定】

Provisions of the Agreement

特许权使用费条款一般表述为：如果特许权使用费受益所有人是缔约国另一方居民，则所征税款不应超过特许权使用费总额的＿＿＿％。我国与其他国家或地区所签订税收协定特许权使用费限制税率存在差异，在5%~10%。

The royalty clause is generally expressed as follows: if the beneficial owner of the royalty is a resident of the other party of the contracting state, the tax levied shall not exceed ＿＿＿ % of the total royalty amount. There are differences in the royalty limit tax rates between China and other countries or regions, and some of the agreement tax rates are from 5% to 10%.

【适用条件】

Conditions of Application

从缔约对方国家（地区）取得特许权使用费所得符合税收协定关于特许权使用费规定的具体要求。

The acquisition of royalties from the state (territory) of the contracting party is in accordance with the specific requirements of the tax agreement regarding royalties.

（6）技术服务费

Technical Services

我国与印度和巴基斯坦签订的税收协定中单独对技术服务费作了规定。

Technical services are provided separately in China's tax agreements with India and Pakistan.

【适用主体】

Subject of Application

从缔约对方国家（地区）取得技术服务费所得的居民。

Residents who obtain technical services from the other country (region) of the contracting party.

【协定规定】

Provisions of the Agreement

我国与印度、巴基斯坦签订的双边税收协定中包括技术服务费条款。

China's bilateral tax agreements with India and Pakistan include provisions on technical services.

中印（印度）协定第12条为特许权使用费和技术服务费条款。特许权使用费的表述与一般表述相同。对技术服务费的表述为，"技术服务费"一语是指缔约国一方居民在缔约国另一方提供管理、技术或咨询服务而收取的任何报酬，但不包括本协定第5条第二款第（11）项和第15条所提及的活动的报酬。

Article 12 of the Sino-Indian (India) Agreement is the terms of royalties and technical service fees, which are expressed in the same manner as the general expression. The term "technical service fee" refers to any remuneration received by a resident of one of the contracting parties for the provision of administrative, technical or advisory services to the other of the contracting parties, excluding remuneration for activities referred to in Article 5, Paragraph 2(e) and Article 15 of this Agreement.

中巴（巴基斯坦）协定除特许权使用费条款外，还单独设置第13条技术服务费条款，表述为："技术服务费"一语是指缔约国一方居民在缔约国另一方提供管理、技术或咨询服务（包括该居民通过其他人员提供的技术服务）而收取的任何报酬（包括一次总付的报酬），但不包括本协定第5条第3款和第15条所提及的活动的报酬。

In addition to the royalty clause, the China-Pakistan (Pakistan) Agreement has a separate Article 13 technical service fee clause, which states that the term "technical service fee" means any remuneration (including lump-sum remuneration) received by a resident of a contracting party for the provision of administrative, technical or advisory services (including technical services provided by that resident through other personnel) by the other contracting party, but does not include remuneration for activities referred to in Articles 5(3) and 15 of this Agreement.

【适用条件】
Conditions of Application

从印度或巴基斯坦取得技术服务费所得符合税收协定关于技术服务费规定的具体要求。

Technical service fees obtained from India or Pakistan are in accordance with the specific requirements of the tax agreement for technical service fees.

（7）转让财产
Transfer of Properties

① 转让不动产
Transfer of Immovable Property

转让不动产属于税收协定财产收益条款的重要内容。财产收益条款主要涉及转让各类财产所有权取得收益的征税权的划分，包括不动产、常设机构财产、运输工具、股份以及其他财产。

The transfer of immovable property is an important part of the property income clause of the tax agreement. The property income clause mainly relates to the division of the tax right to transfer the ownership of all kinds of properties, including real estate, permanent establishment property, means of transport, shares and other properties.

税收协定对财产转让收益在居民国的征税权通常没有限制，但在赋予来源国对财产转让收益的征税权时，设有限制条款。换言之，我国"走出去"企业在境外转让财产取得收益一般在我国征税，但在某些情况下，与我国签订税收协定的缔约对方国家也拥有征税权。协定规定缔约对方国家对财产收益拥有征税权的，按其国内法规定进行征税。

Tax agreements usually do not limit the right to tax the proceeds of the transfer of property in the country of residence, but there are restrictions when granting the source country the right to tax the proceeds of the transfer of property. In other words, China's "going out" enterprises in the transfer of property abroad to obtain income are generally taxed in our country, but in some cases, the other party to the tax agreement with our country also has the right to tax. Where the agreement provides that the state of the contracting party has the right to tax the proceeds of property, it shall be taxed in accordance with its domestic law.

【适用主体】
Subject of Application

转让位于缔约对方国家（地区）的不动产并取得收益的居民。

Residents who transfer immovable property located in the state (territory) of the contracting party and obtain income.

【协定规定】

Provisions of the Agreement

我国签订的税收协定中规定,对我国居民转让位于缔约对方国家(地区)的不动产取得的收益,可以由缔约对方国家(地区)征税。

The tax agreement signed by China stipulates that the income from the transfer of immovable property located in the country (region) of the contracting party may be taxed in the country (region) of the contracting party.

【适用条件】

Conditions of Application

转让位于缔约对方国家(地区)的不动产取得收益并符合税收协定财产收益相关条款的具体要求。

The transfer of immovable property located in the state (territory) of the contracting party acquires proceeds and meets the specific requirements of the relevant provisions of the tax agreement on property proceeds.

② 转让常设机构营业财产

Transfer of Business Property of a Permanent Establishment

【适用主体】

Subject of Application

转让位于在缔约对方国家(地区)常设机构的营业财产并取得收益的居民。

The residents who transfer business property located in a permanent establishment in the state (territory) of the contracting party and obtain income.

【政策规定】

Policy Provisions

按照我国目前签订的税收协定规定,转让我国居民在缔约对方国家(地区)的常设机构营业财产部分的动产,包括转让该常设机构(单独或者随同整个企业)取得的收益,可以由缔约对方国家(地区)征税。

In accordance with the provisions of the tax agreement currently signed by China, the transfer of movable property of the residents of China in the part of the business property of the permanent establishment of the other party's country (region), including the transfer of permanent establishment (alone or with the whole enterprise), may be taxed in the other party's country (region).

【适用条件】

Conditions of Application

转让设立在缔约对方国家(地区)的常设机构的营业财产取得收益并符合税收协定财产收益相关条款的具体要求。

The transfer of the business property of a permanent establishment established in the state (territory) of the contracting party proceeds and meets the specific requirements of the provisions relating to property proceeds of tax agreements.

③ 转让船舶、飞机等运输工具

Transfer of Means of Transport, Such as Ships and Aircrafts

【适用主体】

Subject of Application

转让在缔约对方国家(地区)经营的船舶、飞机等运输工具并取得收益的居民。

The residents who transfer means of transport such as ships and aircrafts operating in the state (territory) of the contracting party and obtain income.

【协定规定】

Provisions of the Agreement

按照我国目前签订的税收协定规定,缔约国一方居民转让从事国际运输的船舶或飞机,或者转让属于经营上述船舶、飞机的动产取得的收益,应仅在经营上述船舶或飞机的企业为其居民的国家征税。其中与土库曼斯坦、吉尔吉斯斯坦、哈萨克斯坦、乌兹别克斯坦、土耳其的协定中转让从事国际运输的陆运车辆适用此规定;与塔吉克斯坦的协定中转让从事国际运输的公路或铁路车辆适用此规定;与俄罗斯的协定中转让从事国际运输的火车以及机动交通工具适用此规定;与中国香港的安排中转让从事陆运的车辆适用此规定。

In accordance with the provisions of the tax agreement currently signed by China, the transfer of ships or aircraft engaged in international transport by a resident of a contracting state or the transfer of proceeds from movable property belonging to the said ships or aircrafts shall be taxed only in the state where the enterprise operating the said ships or aircraft is the resident of that state. This provision applies to the transfer of land transport vehicles engaged in international transport in agreements with Turkmenistan, Kyrgyzstan, Kazakhstan, Uzbekistan and Turkey; to the transfer of road or rail vehicles engaged in international transport in agreements with Tajikistan; to the transfer of trains and motor vehicles engaged in international transport in agreements with Russia; and to the transfer of vehicles engaged in land transport in arrangements with Hong Kong of China.

根据中国与希腊的协定规定,转让从事国际运输的船舶或飞机,或者转让属于经营上述船舶或飞机的动产取得的收益,应仅在按第8条的规定对该船舶或飞机取得的利润征税的缔约国征税。

According to the agreement between China and Greece, the transfer of a ship or aircraft engaged in international transport, or the transfer of proceeds from movable property belonging to the said ship or aircraft, shall be taxed only in the contracting state where profits from that ship or aircraft are taxed in accordance with the provisions of Article 8.

我国签订的部分协定还有规定由企业实际管理机构所在的国家征税以及由该企业总机构所在的国家征税等情形。

Some of the agreements signed by China also provide for taxation in the country where the actual management organization of the enterprise is located and in the country where the general organization of the enterprise is located.

【适用条件】

Conditions of Application

转让在缔约对方国家(地区)经营的船舶、飞机等运输工具并取得收益的居民企业。

The residential enterprises who transfer means of transport such as ships and aircrafts operating in the state (territory) of the contracting party and obtain income.

④ 转让主要由不动产组成的公司股权

Transfer of Equity in a Company Consisting Mainly of Immovable Property

【适用主体】

Subject of Application

转让位于缔约对方国家（地区）主要由不动产组成的公司股权并取得收益的居民。

The residents who transfer equity in a company consisting mainly of immovable property located in the state (territory) of the contracting party and obtain income.

【协定规定】

Policy Provisions

目前我国签订的部分税收协定中规定，转让一个公司财产股份的股票取得的收益，该公司的财产又主要直接或间接由位于一方的不动产所组成，可以由不动产所在国征税。其中我国与马来西亚的协定中转让一个合伙企业或信托机构的股权适用此规定；我国与阿尔巴尼亚的协定中转让在合伙企业或信托中的利益也适用此规定。

At present, some tax agreements signed by China stipulate that the proceeds obtained from the transfer of shares in the property of a company, the property of which is mainly directly or indirectly composed of immovable property located on one side, may be taxed in the country where the immovable property is located. This provision applies to the transfer of equity in partnership or trust in the agreement between China and Malaysia. This provision is also applicable to the transfer of interests in partnership or trust in the agreement between China and Albania.

我国与澳大利亚的税收协定规定："缔约国一方居民转让一个公司的股票或类似权益取得的所得或收益，该公司的财产又全部或主要由第六条'不动产所得'所述的位于缔约国另一方的不动产所组成，可以在该缔约国另一方征税。"我国与部分国家的协定对不动产占比作了明确规定，部分协定没有单列对转让主要财产为不动产的公司的股份取得收益的税收处理规定。

China's tax agreement with Australia provides that: "Income or proceeds derived by a resident of a contracting state from the transfer of shares or similar interests in a company whose property consists wholly or primarily of immovable property located in the other contracting state, as referred to in Article VI 'real property proceeds', may be taxed in the other contracting state." The proportion of real estate has been clearly stipulated in the agreement between China and some countries. Some agreements do not list the tax treatment provisions for the transfer of shares of companies whose main property is immovable property.

【适用条件】

Conditions of Application

转让位于缔约对方国家（地区）主要由不动产组成的公司股权并取得收益的居民企业。

The residential enterprises who transfer shares in a company mainly composed of immovable property in the country (region) of the contracting party and obtain income.

⑤ 转让公司股权(主要由不动产构成的股权除外)
Transfer of Equity in the Company (Other than Equity Consisting Mainly of Immovable Property)

【适用主体】
Subject of Application

从缔约对方国家(地区)取得转让不动产组成的公司股权以外的股权所得的居民。
Residents who acquire from the other party's country (region) equity other than the transfer of immovable property.

【协定规定】
Policy Provisions

对于该项所得,我国与不同国家(地区)的协定规定有所不同,部分表述为:转让不动产组成的公司股份以外的其他股票取得的收益,该项股票又相当于参与缔约国一方居民公司的股权的25%的,可以在该缔约国征税;部分协定还要求,该收益的收款人在转让行为前的12个月内,曾经直接或间接拥有该公司至少25%的股份;我国与一部分国家的税收协定则没有单列对转让其他公司股份取得收益的税务处理规定。具体征税要求见表6-1。

The provisions of China's agreements with different countries (regions) differ in respect of this income, in part as follows: the proceeds from the transfer of shares other than the shares of a corporation consisting of immovable property, which in turn amounts to 25 per cent of the shares of a resident corporation of a participating constracting state, may be taxed in that constracting state; in part, the agreement also requires the payee of the proceeds to have owned at least 25 per cent of the shares of the corporation directly or indirectly within 12 months prior to the transfer; and in part, the tax agreement with some states does not contain separate provisions on the tax treatment of proceeds from the transfer of shares of other companies. The specific tax requirements are shown in table 6-1 below.

表6-1 转让不动产组成的公司股份以外,相当于公司 25% 股权的征税权的划分一览表
Table 6-1 A List of Tax Rights Equivalent to 25 Shares of a Company Other than the Shares of a Company that Are Part of the Transfer of Immovable Property

转让相当于缔约国一方公司25%股权	转让前直接或间接拥有公司25%股份	未单列"转让相当于缔约国一方公司25%股权"规定
美国、挪威、瑞典、意大利、斯洛伐克、保加利亚、巴基斯坦、塞浦路斯、西班牙、罗马尼亚、蒙古国、卢森堡、巴布亚新几内亚、克罗地亚、越南、乌克兰、牙买加、冰岛、乌兹别克斯坦、苏丹、马其顿、埃及、老挝、塞舌尔、南非、摩尔多瓦、卡塔尔、尼泊尔、阿曼、巴林、吉尔吉斯斯坦、斯里兰卡、沙特	丹麦、毛里求斯、巴巴多斯、新加坡、芬兰、马耳他、中国香港、中国澳门、比利时、法国、英国、德国、荷兰、瑞士	日本、马来西亚、加拿大、新西兰、泰国、波兰、澳大利亚、波黑、科威特、巴西、匈牙利、阿联酋、韩国、印度、白俄罗斯、斯洛文尼亚、以色列、土耳其、亚美尼亚、立陶宛、拉脱维亚、孟加拉国、塞尔维亚和黑山、葡萄牙、爱沙尼亚、菲律宾、爱尔兰、古巴、委内瑞拉、哈萨克斯坦、印尼、尼日利亚、突尼斯、伊朗、希腊、摩洛哥、特立尼达和多巴哥、阿尔巴尼亚、文莱、阿塞拜疆、格鲁吉亚、阿尔及利亚、塔吉克斯坦、埃塞俄比亚、土库曼斯坦、赞比亚、叙利亚、俄罗斯

注:信息仅供参考,详细情况以税收协定文本规定为准。
Note: The information is for reference only. The details are subject to the provisions of the tax agreement.

我国与捷克、奥地利的税收协定规定，不论控股比例大小，均在被转让股份的公司所在国征税。

China's tax agreements with the Czech Republic and Austria provide for taxation in the country where the transferred shares are located, regardless of the holding ratio.

我国与墨西哥的税收协定规定：转让第二款所述以外的代表缔约国一方居民公司参股的股票取得的收益，可以在该缔约国一方征税。

The tax agreement between China and Mexico provides that the proceeds from the transfer of shares in a company other than those referred to in Paragraph 2 representing a resident of a contracting state may be taxed on that contracting state.

【适用条件】

Conditions of Application

从缔约对方国家（地区）取得转让不动产组成的公司股权以外的股权所得的居民企业。

The residential enterprises that acquire from the other party's country (region) equity other than the transfer of immovable property.

⑥ 转让其他财产

Transfer of other Property

【适用主体】

Subject of Application

从缔约对方国家（地区）取得转让其他财产所得的居民。

Residents who acquire income from the transfer of other property from the state (territory) of the contracting party.

【协定规定】

Policy Provisions

对于该项所得，我国与不同国家（地区）的协定规定有所不同，对征税权的划分差异较大。

For this income, since China and different countries' (regions') agreement provisions are different, the division of tax rights is quite different.

【适用条件】

Conditions of Application

从缔约对方国家（地区）取得转让其他财产所得的居民企业。

The residential enterprises that obtain income from the transfer of other property from the state (region) of the contracting party.

（8）受雇所得

Income from Employment

我国以前签署的税收协定中此条款表述为非独立个人劳务，近年来签署的税收协定将此条款表述为受雇所得，上述两种表述并无实质差别，主要明确了对受雇所得划分征税权的一般原则即来源国拥有优先征税权，但对于同时满足三个条件（详见下文所述）的受雇所得来源国应给予免税，居民国独占征税权，并且明确了与国际运输活动有关的受雇所得的特殊处理。

There is no substantive difference between the provisions of the tax agreements previously signed by China, which are described as non-independent personal services, and the tax agreements signed in recent years, which define the general principle of the right to tax the income of employment, that is, the country of origin has a preferential right to tax the income of employment, provided that the source of the income of employment that meets the three conditions (see below for more details) shall be exempt from taxation, the country of residence has exclusive right to tax, and the special treatment of the income of employment related to international transport activities is clarified.

【适用主体】

Subject of Application

在境外以受雇身份(雇员)从事劳务活动取得所得的居民个人。

An individual resident who, as an employed person (employee), engages in labour activities abroad.

【协定规定】

Provisions of the Agreement

一般性表述为,缔约国一方居民因受雇取得的薪金、工资和其他类似报酬,除在缔约国另一方从事受雇的活动以外,应仅在该缔约国一方征税。在缔约国另一方从事受雇的活动取得的报酬,可在该缔约国另一方征税。

The general expression is that salaries, wages and other similar remuneration earned by a resident of a contracting state for employment shall be taxed only on that contracting state except in respect of activities engaged in by another contracting state. The remuneration obtained for activities employed in another state party may be taxed in that other state party.

【适用条件】

Conditions of Application

我国目前对外签订的税收协定受雇所得条款一般在第一款明确受雇所得的一般征税原则,即应在缔约国一方居民个人从事受雇活动的所在国征税。

The provisions on the income from employment in the tax agreements currently concluded by China are generally defined in Paragraph 1 as the general principle of taxation of the income from employment. That is to say, the tax shall be levied in the country where one of the residents of a contracting state is engaged in the activities of employment.

第2款明确规定受雇所得要在来源国(即劳务发生国)获得免税待遇必须同时具备三个条件,反之,只要有一个条件未符合,就构成在来源国的纳税义务。这三个条件是:① 居民个人在有关历年中或会计(财政、纳税)年度中或任何12个月(任何365天)中在该缔约国另一方停留连续或累计不超过183天;② 该项报酬由并非该缔约国另一方居民的雇主支付或代表雇主支付;③ 该项报酬不是由雇主设在该缔约国另一方的常设机构或固定基地所负担。

Paragraph 2 makes it clear that the income from employment must have three simultaneous conditions for obtaining tax exemption in the country of origin (i.e. the country of employment), whereas, if one condition is not met, it constitutes a tax obligation in the country of origin.

These three conditions are: (i) that the individual resident shall remain in the other constracting state for a continuous or cumulative period of not more than 183 days in the calendar year in question or in the accounting (financial, tax) year or in any 12 months (any 365 days); (ii) that the remuneration shall be paid by or on behalf of the employer who is not a resident of the other constracting state; and (iii) that the remuneration shall not be borne by the employer's permanent establishment or fixed base in the other constracting state.

第三款对与国际运输活动有关的受雇所得划分征税权作出了特殊处理规定。

Paragraph 3 provides for special treatment of the right to tax on employment income related to international transport activities.

(9) 董事费

Directors' Fees

我国居民个人作为缔约国对方居民公司的董事会成员取得的董事费适用董事费条款规定，由缔约国对方征税。但是，假如董事会成员因在公司任职、受雇取得的那部分报酬则应适用受雇所得条款中的一般原则。

The director's fee obtained by the individual resident of China as a member of the board of directors of the opposite party's resident company shall be subject to the provisions of the director's fee and shall be taxed by the other party. However, the general principle contained in the terms of employment shall apply to members of the board of directors in respect of the part of remuneration obtained for their employment in the company.

【适用主体】

Subject of Application

在境外担任董事会成员及相应税收协定规定人员的居民个人。

Individual resident who is a member of the board of directors and the personnel stipulated in the corresponding tax agreement abroad.

【协定规定】

Provisions of the Agreement

一般性表述为，缔约国一方居民作为缔约国另一方居民公司的董事会成员取得的董事费和其他类似款项，可以在该缔约国另一方征税。

A general statement indicates that directors' fees and other similar payments made by a resident of a contracting state as a member of the board of directors of a resident company of the other contracting state may be taxed in the other contracting state.

【适用条件】

Conditions of Application

我国对外签订的税收协定中，都坚持了由支付董事费的公司所在地的国家征税，但人员范围有所不同，有的适用于董事会成员，有的同样适用于监事会或其他类似机构的成员，有的同样适用于高级管理人员。

In the tax agreements signed by China, we insist on the taxation of the country where the company pays the director's fee, but the scope of personnel is different. Some apply to the members of the board of directors, some also apply to the members of the board of supervisors or other similar institutions. Some also apply to senior managers.

所谓的"其他类似款项",包括个人以公司董事会成员身份取得的实物福利,如股票期权、居所或交通工具、健康或人寿保险及俱乐部成员资格等。

The so-called "other similar funds" include physical benefits obtained by individuals as members of the company's board of directors, such as stock options, residence or transportation, health or life insurance, club membership, and so on.

（10）艺术家和运动员

Artists and Athletes

对于艺术家或运动员的报酬,原则上由来源国即其提供活动所在国征税,由来源国政府优先行使收入来源地管辖权。但是,如果该活动是由双方政府的文化交流计划安排的,来源国对其报酬应予免税。

The remuneration of artists or athletes is, in principle, taxed by the country of origin, i.e. the country in which the activity is provided, and the source government exercises priority jurisdiction over the source of income. However, if the event is organized by a cultural exchange programme between the two governments, the country of origin shall grant tax exemptions for its remuneration.

【适用主体】

Subject of Application

作为艺术家和运动员的居民个人。

Individual residents as artists and athletes.

【协定规定】

Provisions of the Agreement

一般表述为:①缔约国一方居民,作为表演家,如戏剧、电影、广播或电视艺术家、音乐家或作为运动员,在缔约国另一方从事其个人活动取得的所得,可以在该缔约国另一方征税。② 表演家或运动员从事其个人活动取得的所得,并非归属于表演家或运动员本人,而是归属于其他人,该所得可以在该表演家或运动员从事其活动的缔约国征税。

It is generally expressed as follows: (i) Income derived by a resident of a contracting state, as a performer, such as a theatre, film, radio or television artist, musician or athlete, may be taxed in the other contracting state. (ii) The proceeds obtained by the performer or athlete in the performance of his or her personal activities are not attributable to the performer or the athlete himself or herself, but to other persons, may be taxed in the constracting state in which the performer or athlete engages in his or her activities.

【适用条件】

Conditions of Application

我国对外签订的税收协定中,"艺术家和运动员"条款主要包括三项内容:第一项是艺术家和运动员从事个人活动所取得的所得,由活动所在国征税;第二项是艺术家或运动员由于雇佣关系取得的归属于其他人（包括公司）的所得,也由活动所在国征税;第三项是艺术家或运动员从事政府间的文化交流或者是由政府或其地方当局公共基金资助进行的表演活动取得的所得,应予以免税。

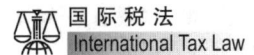

The "artists and athletes" clause in the tax agreement signed by China mainly includes three items: the first is the income obtained by artists and athletes in their personal activities, which is taxed by the country in which the activity is carried out; the second is the income earned by artists or athletes as a result of, belonging to others (including companies), which is also taxed by the country in which the activity is carried out; and the third is the income obtained by artists or athletes engaged in intergovernmental cultural exchanges or performing activities financed by the government or the public funds of their local authorities, is exempt from tax.

（11）退休金

Pensions

退休金是受雇所得（非独立个人劳务）的特殊情况，优先于受雇所得（非独立个人劳务）条款执行。一般情况下，居民国对退休金独占征税权，但政府或地方当局按照社会保险制度（公共福利计划）支付退休金和其他款项，（此时）支付国独占征税权。

Pension is a special case of employment income (non-independent personal services), which takes precedence over employment income (non-independent personal services) provisions. In general, the state of residence has exclusive rights to tax pensions. As to pensions and other payments paid by the government or local authorities according to the public welfare scheme, the exclusive tax rights belong to the payer.

【适用主体】

Subject of Application

取得退休金和其他类似报酬所得的居民个人。

Individual residents who receive pension and other similar remuneration.

【协定规定】

Provisions of the Agreement

一般表述为，除适用"政府服务"第二款的规定以外，因以前的雇佣关系支付给缔约国一方居民的退休金和其他类似报酬，应仅在该缔约国一方征税。

The general expression is that, in addition to the application of Paragraph 2 of "government services", pensions and other similar remuneration paid to a resident of a contracting state due to previous employment relations shall be taxed only on that contracting state.

【适用条件】

Conditions of Application

我国对外签订的税收协定对退休金征税权一般规定：居民国享有退休金征税权。除"政府服务"条款第二款规定的情形外，居民国享有退休金的征税权；居民国对退休金独占征税权。不论取得退休金的人以前的工作地点如何，取得退休金时该个人为其居民的国家对该项退休金独占征税权。

The tax agreement signed by China generally stipulates that the resident country has the right to tax the pension. Except as provided for in Paragraph 2 of the "Government Services" clause, the resident state shall have the right to tax the pension; the resident state shall have the exclusive right to tax the pension. Regardless of the former place of work of the person obtaining the pension, the state in which the individual was a resident at the time of obtaining the pension has exclusive rights to tax the pension.

（12）教师和研究人员

Teachers and Researchers

我国签署的部分税收协定中列有专门的教师和研究人员条款,对符合一定条件的教师和研究人员给予免税待遇。截至目前,除与加拿大、乌兹别克斯坦、阿塞拜疆、阿尔及利亚、赞比亚、捷克、芬兰、新加坡、中国香港等国家和地区的税收协定(安排)中没有该条款外,其他协定都有专门规定。

Some tax agreements signed by China include special provisions for teachers and researchers, and tax-free treatment for teachers and researchers who meet certain conditions. So far, except for tax agreements (arrangements) with Canada, Uzbekistan, Azerbaijan, Algeria, Zambia, the Czech Republic, Finland, Singapore, Hong Kong of China and other countries and regions, there are special provisions.

【适用主体】

Subject of Application

从事教学或科研机构工作的居民个人。

An individual resident engaged in teaching or scientific research.

【协定规定】

Provisions of the Agreement

一般表述为,任何个人是,或者在直接前往缔约国一方之前曾是缔约国另一方居民,主要由于在该缔约国一方的大学、学院、学校或其他公认的教育机构从事教学、讲学或研究的目的暂时停留在该缔约国一方,从其第一次到达之日起停留时间不超过三年的,该缔约国一方应对其由于教学、讲学或研究取得的报酬,免于征税。

It is generally stated that any individual who is, or has been, a resident of the other contracting state prior to direct travel to one of the contracting states shall be exempt from taxation from remuneration for teaching, teaching or research, primarily for the purpose of temporarily staying in the contracting state for a period not exceeding three years from the date of his or her first arrival, for the purpose of teaching, or research at a university, college, school or other recognized educational institution of the contracting state.

【适用条件】

Conditions of Application

对缔约国一方居民个人到缔约国另一方的大学、学院或其他公认的教育机构或科研机构从事教学、讲学或研究取得的报酬,该缔约国另一方应给予定期的免税待遇。有的协定规定免税期,即对在符合免税条件的机构从事活动的教师、研究人员给予三年(或两年)免税,三年(或两年)后征税。

The other constracting state shall grant a periodic exemption from tax for the remuneration of a resident of a state party for teaching, or research at a university, college or other recognized educational or scientific institution of the other constracting state. There are agreements that provide for a tax exemption period, i.e. three years (or two years) for teachers and researchers performing activities in institutions that meet the conditions of the exemption, and three years (or two years) after the tax.

（13）学生和实习人员

Students and Interns

税收协定中的学生通常包括实习生和企业学徒，是指接受教育或培训的人。作为一类特殊人群，税收协定对其以维持生活、接受教育或培训为目的而取得的款项给予了一定的免税待遇。

Students in tax agreements usually include interns and business apprentices, referring to people who receive education or training. As a special group of people, the money they obtain for the purpose of maintaining their lives, receiving education or training is granted tax exemption in tax agreements.

【适用主体】

Subject of Application

作为学生、企业学徒或实习生的居民个人。

Individual resident as a student, business apprentice or intern.

【协定规定】

Provisions of the Agreement

一般表述为，学生或企业学徒是，或在直接前往缔约国一方访问前曾是缔约国另一方居民，仅由于接受教育或培训的目的停留在首先提及的国家，其为维持生活、接受教育或培训收到来源于该国以外的款项，该国免于征税。

It is generally stated that a student or business apprentice who is, or was, a resident of the other party of the constracting state prior to a direct visit to one of the states parties, is exempt from taxation for the sole purpose of receiving education or training in the first-mentioned country, for which funds are received from outside that country for subsistence, education or training.

【适用条件】

Conditions of Application

我国已签订的税收协定中，部分协定只有原则性规定对学生、企业学徒或实习生为了维持生活、接受教育或培训的目的收到的款项，在其学习、接受教育或培训的所在国免于征税；部分协定（安排）根据学生收到的所得的不同来源、性质，分别明确不同的税收待遇；部分协定还对免税时间进行了规定。

In the tax agreements that China has signed, some agreements only provide in principle for exemption from taxation of payments received by students, business apprentices or interns for the purpose of living, receiving education or training in the countries where they study, receive education or training; some agreements (arrangements) specify different tax treatment according to the different sources and nature of the income received by students; and some agreements also provide for tax exemption periods.

（二）消除国际双重征税的方法

Methods for Eliminating International Double Taxation

除了少数几种跨国所得外，双重征税协定在大多数跨国所得项目上，只是限定了作为来源地国的缔约国一方可以优先行使来源地税收管辖权的条件和范围,并没有排除作为纳税人的居住国的缔约国另一方对这些跨国所得可以继续主张居民税收管辖权课税的权力。因此,对于已经被来源地国一方优先课税了的有关跨国所得,双重征税协定规定作为居住国的缔约国另一方在继续主张其居民税收管辖权课税时,必须采取相应的消除国际双重征税的方法和措施,如采用免税方法或税收抵免方法,才能基本解决国际双重征税问题。因此,相对于前述协定第一部分的内容而言,协定有关消除国际双重征税方法的规定,可以理解为是对缔约国一方作为居住国的义务设定的。

With the exception of a few types of transnational income, double taxation agreements, in most cross-border income items, merely limit the conditions and scope under which one of the contracting states which is the source state may exercise its jurisdiction of taxation of the place of origin as a matter of priority, and do not exclude the power of the other contracting state that is the resident states of the taxpayer to continue to claim taxation of such cross-border income. Thus, for relevant transnational income that has already been preferentially taxed by one of the source countries, the double taxation agreement provides that the other party of the state of residence, in continuing to assert its resident tax jurisdiction, must adopt appropriate methods and measures to eliminate international double taxation, such as tax exemption or tax credit, in order to basically solve the problem of international double taxation. Thus, in relation to the content of part (i) of the aforementioned agreement, the provisions of the agreement relating to the elimination of international double taxation can be understood as creating obligations for one of the contracting states as the State of residence.

三、禁止税收歧视
Prohibition of Tax Discrimination

禁止税收歧视,也称税收无差别待遇,指的是缔约国一方国民在缔约国另一方境内负担的税收或有关纳税条件,不应与缔约国另一方国民在相同情况下负担,或可能负担的税收或有关纳税条件不同,或比其更重。这实际上是国民待遇原则在税收领域内的体现。在税收协定中,约定非歧视待遇的目的在于协调国与国之间的税收权利和财政利益以及避免税收歧视,它一般包括国籍非歧视、常设机构非歧视、费用扣除非歧视、资本非歧视四个方面的定义解释和保留条款。

The prohibition of tax discrimination, also known as non-discrimination in taxation, refers to taxes or related tax conditions borne by a national of a contracting state in the territory of the other contracting state and should not be borne in the same circumstances or may be borne by a national of the other contracting state or by a tax or related tax condition or heavier than that. This is actually the embodiment of the principle of national treatment in the field of taxation. In tax agreements, the purpose of non-discriminatory treatment is to coordinate tax rights and financial interests between states and to avoid tax discrimination. It generally includes four aspects: non-discrimination of nationality, non-discrimination of permanent establishment, deduction of non-discrimination, non-discrimination of capital, etc.

（1）国籍非歧视是非歧视待遇条款的重要内容，即纳税人不因国籍不同而在纳税上受到歧视待遇。

Non-discrimination on the basis of nationality is an important part of the non-discrimination clause, that is, taxpayers are not discriminated against on the basis of nationality.

【适用主体】

Subject of Application

居民企业及个人。

Resident enterprises and individuals.

【协定规定】

Provisions of the Agreement

一般表述为：缔约国一方的国民在缔约国另一方负担的税收或者有关条件，在相同情况下，特别是在居民身份相同的情况下，不应与该缔约国另一方的国民负担或可能负担的税收或者有关条件不同或比其更重。虽有第一条（本协定适用于缔约国一方或者同时为双方居民的人）的规定，本款规定也应适用于不是缔约国一方或者双方居民的人。

The general expression is that a national of one of the contracting states shall bear a tax or related condition on the other of the contracting states, and in the same circumstances, in particular in the same situation as a national of the other contracting state, or may bear a tax or related condition, which shall not be different or heavier than that of the national of the other contracting state. Notwithstanding the provisions of Article 1(this agreement applies to one of the contracting states or to persons who are both residents), the provisions of this paragraph shall also apply to persons who are not residents of one or both of the contracting states.

【适用条件】

Conditions of Application

符合税收协定规定条件的居民企业或个人。

Resident enterprises or individuals that meet the conditions stipulated in the tax agreement.

（2）常设机构非歧视，即缔约国一方企业设在缔约国另一方的常设机构的税收负担，不应高于进行同样活动的缔约国另一方企业。

A permanent establishment is non-discriminatory, i.e. The tax burden of a permanent establishment in which one of the contracting states' enterprises is located on the other of the contracting states shall not be higher than that of the other contracting state's enterprises conducting the same activity.

【适用主体】

Subject of Application

在缔约国另一方设立常设机构的居民企业。

The establishment of a resident enterprise with a permanent establishment on the other side of the constracting state.

【协定规定】

Provisions of the Agreement

一般表述为：缔约国一方企业在缔约国另一方常设机构的税收负担，不应高于缔约国另一方对从事同样活动的本国企业征收的税收。本规定不应理解为缔约国一方由于民事地位、家庭责任给予缔约国一方居民的个人补贴、优惠和减免也必须给予缔约国另一方居民。

The general expression is that the tax burden on an enterprise of one contracting state in a permanent establishment of the other contracting state shall not be higher than the tax levied by the other contracting state on a domestic enterprise engaged in the same activity. This provision should not be understood to mean that individual subsidies, preferences and exemptions granted by one of the contracting parties to a resident of one of the contracting states on the basis of civil status, family responsibilities must also be granted to a resident of the other contracting state.

【适用条件】

Conditions of Application

符合税收协定规定条件的居民企业。

Resident enterprises that meet the conditions stipulated in the tax agreement.

（3）费用扣除非歧视，指在企业之间没有特殊关系的正常交易情况下，缔约国一方企业支付给缔约国另一方居民的利息、特许权使用费和其他费用款项，在确定该企业应税所得额时，应与在相同情况下支付给缔约国一方居民一样给予扣除。

Expense deduction non-discriminatory refers to interest, royalties and other expenses paid by an enterprise of a contracting state to a resident of the other contracting state in the case of a normal transaction in which there is no special relationship between the enterprises, which shall be deducted in the same way as the amount of taxable income paid to a resident of a contracting state under the same circumstances.

【适用主体】

Subject of Application

居民企业。

Resident Enterprises.

【协定规定】

Provisions of the Agreement

一般表述为：除适用第9条（关联企业）、第11条（利息）第7款或第12条（特许权使用费）第6款规定外，缔约国一方企业支付给缔约国另一方居民的利息、特许权使用费和其他款项，在确定该企业应纳税利润时，应与在同样情况下支付给该缔约国一方居民同样予以扣除。

The general expression is that, in addition to the application of Article 9(affiliated enterprises), Article 11(interest), Paragraph 7, or Article 12(royalties), Paragraph 6, interest, royalties and other payments made by an enterprise of a contracting state to a resident of the other contracting state shall be deducted in the determination of the taxable profits of that enterprise in the same manner as those paid to a resident of that contracting state under the same circumstances.

【适用条件】

Conditions of Application

符合税收协定规定条件的居民企业。

Resident enterprises that meet the conditions stipulated in the tax agreement.

（4）资本非歧视，即缔约国一方企业的资本，不论是全部或部分直接或间接为缔约国另一方居民所拥有或控制，该企业负担的税收或纳税条件，不应与该缔约国一方其他企业不同或比其更重。

Non-discrimination of capital means that the tax or related conditions on the enterprise of one contracting state, whether the capital of that enterprise is wholly or partly owned or controlled, directly or indirectly, by a resident of the other contracting state, shall not be different from or heavier than that of the other enterprise of that contracting state.

【适用主体】
Subject of Application
居民企业。
Resident Enterprises.

【协定规定】
Provisions of the Agreement
一般规定表述为：缔约国一方企业的资本全部或部分，直接或间接为缔约国另一方一个或更多居民拥有或控制，该企业在该缔约国一方负担的税收或者有关条件，不应与该缔约国一方其他同类企业的负担或可能负担的税收或者有关条件不同或比其更重。

The general provision is expressed as follows: if the capital of an enterprise of one contracting state is owned or controlled, directly or indirectly, by one or more residents of the other contracting state, the tax or related conditions on which the enterprise is liable in that contracting state shall not be different from or heavier than the tax or related conditions on which the enterprise is liable or may be liable for other similar enterprises of that contracting state.

【适用条件】
Conditions of Application
符合税收协定规定条件的居民企业。
Resident enterprises that meet the conditions stipulated in the tax agreement.

资本非歧视待遇禁止缔约国一方对资本全部或部分、直接或间接由缔约国另一方一个或多个居民拥有或控制的企业，在税收上给予比较不利的待遇。该项规定及其要防止的差别待遇，仅与企业税收有关，而与拥有或控制其资本的人无关。因此，规定的目的是对居住于同一国家的纳税人保证平等待遇，而不是对合伙人或股东持有的外国资本给予用于国内资本的同样待遇。资本非歧视待遇并不妨碍借款人所在国应用国内关于对居民企业支付给非居民企业关联企业的利息不允许扣除的资本弱化的有关规定。

Non-discriminatory treatment of capital prohibits a contracting party from treating a business owned or controlled, in whole or in part, directly or indirectly, by one or more residents of the other contracting party less favourably in tax matters. This provision and the differential treatment to be prevented relate only to corporate taxation and not to those who own or control their capital. Therefore, the purpose of the provision is to guarantee equal treatment to taxpayers residing in the same country, rather than to give the same treatment to foreign capital held by partners or shareholders for domestic capital. The non-discriminatory treatment of capital does not prevent the borrower from applying the relevant domestic regulations on the weakening of capital that is not allowed to be deducted from the interest paid by the resident enterprise to the affiliated enterprise of the non-resident enterprise.

(四) 相互协商程序与情报交换制度
Mutual Consultation Procedures and Information Exchange System

相互协商程序是双重征税协定规定的一种独特的解决协定在适用过程中发生争议问题和解释分歧的程序。它无须通过正式的外交途径进行，可以由缔约国双方的税务主管当局相互直接联系接洽处理，具有形式不拘、灵活便利的优点。相互协商程序主要有以下三方面作用：(1) 对纳税人提出的有关违反协定的征税的申诉，如果其居住国一方税务主管当局认为申诉有理，又不能单方面采取措施解决问题时，可以通过这种程序同缔约国另一方税务主管机关进行协商解决。(2) 缔约国双方对协定未明确定义的条款用语的解释，彼此存在意见分歧和疑义，可由双方税务主管当局通过这种程序解决。(3) 对协定中没有规定的双重征税问题，双方税务主管当局可通过此种程序相互协商解决。在缔约国税务主管机关之间建立税务情报交换制度，是正确适用协定，防范国际偷税和避税的必要措施。因此，现代各国间签订的双重征税协定中一般都规定，缔约各方税务机关有义务向对方提供协定所涉及的有关税种的国内法律规定，包括其修改变化的情况资料，尤其是应相互提供防止偷漏税所需要的情报。协定中规定的情报交换制度，主要包括双方交换情报的种类和范围、情报交换的方法、交换情报的使用和保密义务规定等方面内容。鉴于近年来经济全球化的迅猛发展进一步刺激了纳税人国际逃税和避税现象的泛滥，加强有关国家税务主管当局之间的税务行政协助日益显得必要，2010年修订后的经合发组织范本增设了缔约国之间进行有关税款征收协助的条款。

A mutual consultation procedure is a unique procedure for resolving disputes and interpreting differences in the application of a double taxation agreement. It does not need to be carried out through formal diplomatic channels, and can be dealt with by direct contact between the tax authorities of both parties, with the advantages of informal form and flexibility. The mutual consultation procedure has the following three main functions: (1) A complaint against a taxpayer concerning a tax violation of an agreement may be settled through consultation with the tax authority of the other party of the states parties if the tax authority of one of the states in which the complaint is found to be justified and can not unilaterally take measures to resolve the problem. (2) Differences of opinion and doubts between the parties regarding the interpretation of the terms of the provisions not clearly defined in the agreement may be resolved by the competent tax authorities of both parties through such a procedure. (3) The issue of double taxation, which is not provided for in the agreement, may be settled by mutual consultation between the tax authorities of the two parties through such a procedure. The establishment of a system of exchange of tax information between the tax authorities of states parties is a necessary measure to correctly apply agreements and prevent international tax evasion and tax avoidance. Thus, double

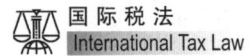

taxation agreements concluded between modern countries generally provide that the tax authorities of the contracting parties are obliged to provide the other party with information on the domestic legal provisions relating to taxes covered by the agreement, including changes in their information. In particular, mutual information is needed to prevent tax evasion. The information exchange system stipulated in the agreement mainly includes the types and scope of information exchange between the two parties, the method of information exchange, the use of information exchange and the provisions of confidentiality obligations. In view of the fact that the rapid development of economic globalization in recent years has further stimulated the proliferation of international tax evasion and avoidance by taxpayers and the growing need to strengthen tax administrative assistance among the competent tax authorities of the countries concerned, the 2010 revised OECD model adds provisions on tax collection assistance among the states parties.

第三节 国际税收协定与国内税法的关系
Section 3　Relationship between International Tax Agreements and Domestic Tax Laws

缔约国相互间缔结的双重征税协定与缔约国制定的国内所得税法和一般财产税法之间的关系，是一个非常重要的法律问题。在双重征税协定与国内税法冲突时，我国税法规定协定条款原则上应有优先适用的效力。双重征税协定性质上属于约束缔约国双方的特别国际法。在国际法与国内法的效力关系上，有些国家实行前者优先于后者的原则，在协定与国内税法规定发生抵触和冲突时，主张协定有优先适用的效力。但在一些认定国际法与国内法具有同等效力地位的国家，对协定与国内税法的冲突则采取孰后优先的处理原则。我国宪法上虽然没有规定国际法优越于国内法的一般原则，但基于"条约应当信守"这一国际法基本原则，我国在一些具体的国内立法中，一般都确认条约规定具有优先于国内立法规定的地位。根据《企业所得税法》第58条规定，中国对外签订的双重税收协定的有关规定与国内税法的规定不一致时，应优先适用协定的规定。确认协定原则上具有优先于国内税法适用的效力地位，是实现这类协定宗旨和作用的需要，也是"条约应当信守"这一国际法准则的基本要求。

The relationship between the double taxation agreement concluded by the states parties and the domestic income tax law and the general property tax law unilaterally formulated by the states parties is a very important legal issue. In the event of a conflict between a double taxation agreement and the domestic tax law, China's tax laws stipulate that the provisions of the agreement shall, in principle, have the effect of precedence. Double taxation agreements are by nature special international law binding both parties. In the effective relationship between international law and domestic law, some countries apply the principle that the former takes precedence over the latter, and in the event of conflict and conflict between the agreement and the provisions of domestic tax law, they advocate the prior application of the agreement. However, in some countries where international law is found to have the same effect as domestic law, the conflict between agreements and domestic tax law is treated with the principle of precedence. Although our Constitution does not stipulate the general principle that international law is superior to domestic law, based on the basic principle of international law, "treaties should be adhered to", China generally recognizes in some specific domestic legislation that treaty provisions have precedence over domestic legislative provisions. According to the provisions of Article 58 of the Enterprise Income Tax Law, the provisions of the agreement shall be applied first when the relevant provisions of the double taxation agreement signed by China with foreign countries are inconsistent with the provisions of the domestic tax law. The recognition of agreements as having precedence in principle over the application of domestic tax law is a need to fulfil the purpose and role of such agreements and a fundamental requirement of the international law norm that treaties should be respected.

但是,鉴于跨国纳税人越来越频繁地利用双重征税协定进行国际避税的现实,协定优先于缔约国国内税法的地位不宜绝对化。双重征税协定条款优先于缔约国国内税法规定适用的地位,要受到税收协定消极作用原则的约束。以下几方面将有助于正确理解两者的关系:

However, given the increasingly frequent use of double taxation agreements by transnational taxpayers for international tax avoidance, the primacy of agreements over the domestic tax laws of states parties should not be absolute. It should also be noted that the provisions of double taxation agreements take precedence over the application of the provisions of the domestic tax law of the contracting states are bound by the principle of the negative effects of the agreements. Hereinafter may help to have a correct understanding of the relationships:

第一,双重征税协定与缔约国国内税法是统一的国际税法规范体系中功能各有侧重的两个组成部分,两者在调整国际税收分配关系时发挥的作用有所不同。

First, the double taxation agreement and the domestic tax law of the contracting parties are two parts of the unified international tax law standard system, which play different roles in adjusting the international tax distribution relationship.

国际税收分配关系本质上是两个或两个以上的主权国家与纳税人相互间在跨国征税对象(跨国所得和跨国财产价值)上产生的经济权益分配关系,它涉及三方面主体的利益分配问题,即从事经济交往活动获得跨国所得或拥有跨国财产价值的纳税人(也称跨国纳税人)、跨国纳税人的居住国政府和跨国所得的来源地国(或跨国财产价值的所在地国)。要实现上述三方主体在跨国征税对象上经济权益分配的公平合理,需要同时兼顾三方的利益,才能维护和促进国际经济交往的正常发展。避免对跨国所得和财产价值的国际双重征税,以及防范跨国纳税人的国际逃税与避税,都是为了实现这一国际税法的根本宗旨和目的。

In essence, the international tax distribution relationship is the distribution of economic rights and interests between two or more sovereign countries and taxpayers on the object of transnational taxation (transnational income and the value of transnational property). It involves the distribution of interests of three subjects, namely, taxpayers engaged in economic activities to obtain transnational income or have the value of transnational property (also known as transnational taxpayers), the governments of countries where transnational taxpayers live and the countries of origin of transnational income (or the countries where transnational property values are located). In order to realize the fairness and reasonableness of the distribution of economic rights and interests on the transnational tax object, it is necessary to take into account the interests of the three parties at the same time in order to maintain and promote the normal development of international economic exchanges. The avoidance of international double taxation of the value of transnational income and property, as well as the prevention of international tax evasion and avoidance by transnational taxpayers, are all aimed at realizing the fundamental purpose and purpose of this international tax law.

在调整和规范国际税收关系的国际税法体系中,缔约国单方依据其主权意志制定的国内所得税法和一般财产税法,属于统一的国际税法体系中的国内法渊源部分。它们在调整规范在跨国征税对象上产生的国际税收分配关系过程中的主要功能和作用是规定对谁征税、征多少税以及如何征税。也就是说,对跨国征税对象的征税权的创设、课税对象范围(包括纳税主体和征税客体)和课税程度(税基与税率)以及征税的程序方式的确定,首先或主要是由各国通过其国内有关税法确定的。例如,关于纳税人的居民身份的认定,应税的所得种类、性质和应税的财产范围的确定,有关所得项目的来源地或财产价值的所在地的识别,以及适用的税率和课税方式等一系列重要事项,首先或主要是取决于缔约国各自的国内有关税法的规定,只要缔约国双方各自的国内有关税法规定的适用不发生冲突,双重征税协定原则上并不干预和协调缔约国各自国内税法规定的适用。

In the international tax law system of adjusting and standardizing international tax relations, the domestic income tax law and the general property tax law formulated unilaterally by the constracting state according to its sovereign will belong to the source of domestic law in the unified international tax law system. Their main function in the process of regulating the international tax distribution relationship generated by transnational taxation is to specify the issues of how and to whom to levy tax. That is to say, the creation of the right to tax the object of transnational taxation, the scope of the object of taxation (including the subject and object of taxation) and the degree of taxation (tax base and tax rate) and the determination of the procedure of taxation are primarily determined by each country through its domestic relevant tax laws. For example, the determination of the resident status of the taxpayer, the determination of the type, nature and scope of taxable income, the identification of the place of origin or the value of the property in question, and the applicable tax rates and methods of taxation depend, first or primarily, on the provisions of the respective domestic tax laws of the contracting states, provided that the application of the provisions of the respective domestic tax laws of the contracting states does not conflict, the double taxation agreement does not in principle interfere with and coordinate the application of the provisions of the respective domestic tax laws of the contracting states.

如前指出,缔约国相互间缔结双重征税协定的主要目的之一,是避免和消除对本国居民纳税人来源于缔约国对方境内的跨国所得或存在于缔约国对方境内的财产价值的国际双重课税,在维护本国的税收权益的同时,保证和促进彼此间的经济、技术和人员交往的正常发展。因此,作为国际税法体系中的国际法渊源部分的主要构成内容,此类双重征税协定在调整规范国际税收分配关系过程中发挥的主要功能和作用,在于协调缔约国各方国内有关税法上主张的居民税收管辖权和来源地税收管辖权之间的矛盾和冲突,在各类跨国所得和财产价值上划分和分配作为纳税人的居住国和作为征税对象的所得来源地国或财产所在地国的税收权益份额,明确缔约国应该采取的避免重复征税的措施方法,消除对缔约国对方国民的税收歧视待遇,以及建立彼此提供税务行政协助的合作机制和相互协商解决国际税收争议的程序方式。

As noted earlier, one of the main purposes of the conclusion of double taxation agreements between states parties is to avoid and eliminate international double taxation of the value of property derived from transnational proceeds or existing in the territory of the other constracting state by its resident taxpayers, and to safeguard and promote the normal development of economic, technical and human interaction with one another while safeguarding its tax interests. Therefore, as a major component of the source of international law in the international tax system, the main function and role of such double taxation agreements in regulating the relationship between international tax distribution is to settle the contradictions and conflicts between the resident tax jurisdiction and the source tax jurisdiction advocated in the relevant tax laws of the parties, to divide and distribute the tax rights and interests of the country of residence as a taxpayer and the country of origin (or property) as the object of taxation in terms of the value of various types of transnational income and property, to clarify the measures to be taken by the parties to avoid double taxation, to eliminate discriminatory tax treatment of nationals of the other state party, and to establish a cooperative mechanism for mutual assistance in tax administration and the procedural modalities for the settlement of international tax disputes through mutual consultation.

第二,双重征税协定对缔约国国内税法确立的征税权只能维持或加以限制,不能为缔约国创设或扩大征税权。

Second, double taxation agreements can only maintain or restrict the right to tax established by the domestic tax law of a constracting state, and can not create or expand the right to tax for a constracting state.

由于双重征税协定在调整规范国际税收分配关系过程中的主要功能作用之一,在于协调缔约国双方国内有关税法上主张的居民税收管辖权和来源地税收管辖权之间的冲突,适当分配居住国和所得来源地国在各类跨国所得和财产价值上的税收权益,以避免和消除国际双重征税,这就决定了此类税收协定对缔约国双方各自国内有关税法上规定的征税权和课税范围和程度,只能或应该是遵循所谓的消极作用原则进行调整和约束。这种消极作用原则意味着双重征税协定只能维持或者是限制缔约国国内税法确立的征税权,不能为缔约国创设或扩大征税权。这是我们在理解双重征税协定与缔约国国内有关税法关系上应该明确的重要一点。

Since one of the main functions of double taxation agreements in the process of regulating the international tax distribution relationship is to coordinate the conflict between the resident tax jurisdiction and the source tax jurisdiction advocated in the relevant tax laws of the parties, and to properly distribute the tax interest of the country of residence and the country of origin in the value of various types of transnational income and property in order to avoid and eliminate international double taxation, this determines that such tax agreements can only or should be adjusted and bound by the so-called principle of negative role in the tax rights and scope and extent of taxation stipulated in the relevant tax laws of the parties. This principle of negative effects means that double taxation agreements can only maintain or restrict the right to tax established by the domestic tax law of the constracting state and can not create or expand the right to tax for the constracting state. This is an important point that we should make clear in our understanding of the relationship between double taxation agreements and the relevant tax laws in the states parties.

跨国所得的国际双重征税现象之所以产生,是因为纳税人的居住国国内所得税法上主张的居民税收管辖权,与来源地国国内税法上主张的来源地税收管辖权在跨国所得上发生冲突。因此,要避免和消除国际双重征税,双重征税协定首先要尽可能地协调缔约国双方在各类跨国所得上彼此主张的居民税收管辖权和所得来源地税收管辖权之间的冲突。这种协调就是贯彻上述消极作用原则,在确认作为居住国的缔约国一方原则上有权对其居民纳税人获得的来源于作为所得来源地国的缔约国对方境内的各种跨国所得行使居民税收管辖权课税的基础上,一方面对缔约国对方国内税法上对各种跨国所得主张的来源地征税权的行使施加条件和范围的限制,另一方面规定居住国一方对本国居民纳税人来源于缔约国对方境内的所得,如果已经由来源地国依照双重征税协定规定征了税,在继续行使居民税收管辖权课税时应采取相应的消除双重征税的措施。

The main reason for the phenomenon of international double taxation of transnational income is the resident tax jurisdiction advocated in the domestic income tax law of the country where the taxpayer acquires transnational income. The result of conflict between the source tax jurisdiction and the transnational income as the object of taxation. Therefore, in order to avoid and eliminate international double taxation, the double taxation agreement must, as far as possible, coordinate the conflict between the resident tax jurisdiction and the tax jurisdiction of the source of the income between the two parties on various types of transnational income. Such coordination is the implementation of the above-mentioned principle of negative effects, by imposing conditions and limits on the exercise of the right to tax on the place of origin of various claims of transnational income in the domestic tax law of the contracting state, on the one hand, on the basis of the recognition that one of the contracting states which is the state of residence is, in principle, entitled to exercise its jurisdiction to tax on the various transnational income derived from the territory of the contracting state which is the source of the income, and on the other hand, on the income derived from the territory of the other state, if the source state has already been taxed by the state in the continued exercise of tax jurisdiction of residents appropriate measures should be taken to eliminate double taxation.

1. 双重征税协定对所得来源地国一方国内税法规定适用的限制

Limitation on the Application of Double Taxation Agreements to the Provisions of the Domestic Tax Law of One of the Countries of Origin of Income

概括而言,针对不同种类和性质的跨国所得项目,双重征税协定对所得来源地国一方国内税法规定的征税权的限制,大体分为以下三种方式。

In summary, for cross-border income items of different types and natures, the restrictions imposed by the double taxation agreement on the right to tax under the domestic tax law of one of the source countries of income are broadly divided into the following three ways.

(1) 对跨国营业利润、个人独立和非独立劳务所得以及不动产所得等大多数跨国所得项目,双重征税协定在确认来源地国一方有优先课税权的同时,对来源地国国内有关所得税法规定的征税条件和征税范围加以限制,从而使来源地国一方对缔约国对方居民纳税人来源于境内的有关所得能够行使征税权课税的条件和范围更为严格有限。这里所谓的优先课税权,是指在符合双重征税协定规定的课税条件和范围内,来源地国可以完全依照其国内税法规定的税率和征税程序方式对有关的跨国所得计征所得税。虽然对这些可以由来源地国优先课税的跨国所得项目,双重征税协定并没有排除居住国一方仍然可以行使居民税收管辖权征税,但是要求居住国一方承担采取消除双重征税措施的条约义务,如给予其居民纳税人外国税收抵免。因此,居住国在实行外国税收抵免后,是否能够继续征收到一部分税额,则取决于其国内所得税税率的高低。

(1) For most cross-border income items, such as transnational operating profits, income from individual independent and non-independent services and income from immovable property, double taxation agreements, while recognizing the preferential right of taxation of one party in the source country, restrict the conditions and scope of taxation under the relevant income tax laws in the source country, thus making the conditions and scope for one party in the source country to be able to exercise the right of taxation on income derived from the territory of the other party's residents more strictly limited. The so-called preferential right of taxation here refers to the income tax of the source country on the relevant transnational income in full accordance with the tax rate and tax procedure stipulated in its domestic tax law within the conditions and scope of taxation stipulated in the double taxation agreement. While for these cross-border income items, which may be subject to preferential taxation by the source country, the double taxation agreement does not exclude that one of the resident countries may still exercise resident tax jurisdiction, the resident country is required to assume a treaty obligation to take measures to eliminate double taxation, such as granting foreign tax credits to its resident taxpayers. Therefore, whether the country of residence can continue to collect part of the tax after the introduction of foreign tax credit depends on its domestic income tax rate.

(2) 对跨国投资所得,即股息(红利)、利息和特许权使用费所得项目,双重征税协定是采用税收分享原则,在确认缔约国双方对这些跨国投资所得项目均有权课税的同时,明确在协定中规定来源地国一方对缔约国对方居民取得的这些投资所得项目源泉扣缴预提所得税的上限税率,这种协定限制税率通常要低于来源地国国内所得税法上规定的对非居民适用的预提税税率。这属于对来源地国国内税法规定的征税程度的限制,目的是尽可能保

197

证居住国在这些跨国投资所得项目上能够分享到一定的税收利益。例如,依照中国个人所得税法规定,非居民个人取得的来源于中国境内的特许权使用费,应适用源泉扣缴方式征收20%的个人所得税。而在中国对外签订的双边税收协定中,通常协定规定的预提税率不得高于10%。

(2) For cross-border investment income items, i.e. dividends (bonuses), interest and royalty income items, a double taxation agreement is based on the principle of tax sharing, while recognizing the right of both parties to tax these cross-border investment income items, specifying in the agreement that the source country party withholds the upper limit tax rate on the source of these investment income items acquired by the other party's residents, which is usually lower than the withholding tax rate applicable to non-residents under the domestic income tax law of the source country. This is a limitation on the extent of taxation under the domestic tax law of the source country, with the aim of ensuring, to the extent possible, that the country of residence can share certain tax benefits in these cross-border investment income items. For example, according to the provisions of the China's Personal Income Tax Law, 20% of the personal income tax shall be levied by the source withholding method on the royalties obtained by non-resident individuals from the territory of China. In bilateral tax agreements signed by China, the withholding tax rate usually stipulated in the agreement shall not exceed 10%.

(3)对少数种类的跨国所得,如国际运输企业利润、一般退休金所得和协定未有具体规定的其他跨国所得等,双重征税协定则是按照独占征税原则,将征税权排他性地完全划归纳税人的居住国一方行使,来源地国不得主张其国内税法上规定的属地征税权。

(3) For a small number of types of transnational income, such as profits from international transport enterprises, general pension income and other transnational income not specifically provided for in the agreement, double taxation agreements exercise the right of taxation exclusively under the principle of exclusive taxation on the part of the state of residence of the taxpayer, and the state of origin may not claim the right of territorial taxation under its domestic tax law.

2. 双重征税协定对居住国国内税法规定适用的限制

Restrictions on the Application of the Provisions of the Domestic Tax Law of the Country of Residence under the Double Taxation Agreement

虽然双重征税协定中大多数条款内容是针对来源地国国内税法上对非居民来源于境内的各种所得所主张行使的征税权加以限制的规定,但对居住国国内所得税法规定的适用,也不是毫无节制。这方面的限制主要体现在以下诸点。

Although most of the provisions of the double taxation agreement are provisions that restrict the right to tax on income derived from the territory of a non-resident in the domestic tax law of the country of origin, the application of the provisions of the domestic income tax law of the country of residence is not unrestrained. The limitations in this regard are mainly reflected in the following points.

双重征税协定通常都明确规定了居住国一方应该采用的消除双重征税的具体方法(如免税法或外国税收限额抵免方法),如果居住国国内所得税法上有规定不同的解决国际双重征税问题的措施(如扣除法或减税法等),这种措施不能适用于本国居民纳税人来源于缔约国对方境内的所得的课税。

Double taxation agreements usually specify the specific methods of eliminating double taxation (e.g. tax exemption or foreign tax limit credit) to be applied by one party to the country of residence, which can not be applied to the taxation of income derived from the territory of the other party of the state of residence if there are different measures (e.g. deductions or tax deductions) in the domestic income tax law of the country of residence.

在居住国国内税法规定的有关所得来源地认定标准与双重征税协定中或来源地国国内税法上规定的该项所得的来源地识别规则不一致的情形下,为消除国际双重征税的需要,居住国不能坚持适用其国内税法规定的认定标准,而应适用双重征税协定中的统一规定或接受来源地国一方国内税法上规定的所得来源地识别标准。例如,关于利息所得的来源地认定,如果作为缔约国一方的居住国国内税法上实行以利息的支付人所在地为其来源地识别标准,而双重征税协定或缔约国对方国内税法中规定,在利息的支付人所在地与实际负担利息费用的机构、场所不一致的情形下,应以实际负担利息的机构或场所所在地为其所得来源地,则居住国一方国内税法上有关利息来源地的认定标准,不能适用于对由位于缔约国对方境内的常设机构或固定基地实际负担的跨国利息所得的来源地判定。

In cases where the criteria for the identification of the origin of the proceeds under the domestic tax law of the state of residence are inconsistent with the rules for the identification of the origin of the proceeds under the double taxation agreement or under the domestic tax law of the state of origin, in order to eliminate the need for international double taxation, the state of residence cannot adhere to the criteria for identification under its domestic tax law, but should apply the uniform provisions in the double taxation agreement or the criteria for the identification of the origin of the proceeds under the domestic tax law of the state of origin. For example, with regard to the determination of the place of origin of interest income, if the domestic tax law of the state of residence of one of the contracting states applies a criterion for the identification of the place of origin of the payer of interest as the place of origin of the payer of interest, and the double taxation agreement or the domestic tax law of the other contracting state provides that, in the event of inconsistency between the place where the payer of interest is located and the institution or place where the interest is actually charged, the place of origin of the income shall be the place of origin of the institution or place where the interest is actually charged. It can not be applied to the determination of the origin of transnational interest earned by a permanent establishment or fixed base located in the territory of the other constracting state.

居住国由于其国内税法规定的原因而对双重征税协定中的有关征税权冲突协调规则的理解和适用,可能与来源地国对双重征税协定中的有关征税权冲突协调规则的解释和适用不一致。由此可能导致对有关所得重复征税,为避免这种情形,居住国应接受来源地国对税收协定有关条款的解释和适用结果。例如,如果来源地国国内税法上规定,合伙企业本身不是独立的纳税人,合伙人应就其在合伙企业中的所得份额纳税,而按照居住国国内税法,合伙企业与公司法人一样,本身具有独立的纳税主体资格。当一个居住国的居民合伙人转让其在来源地国境内设立的合伙企业中的股份财产取得转让财产收益,并且两国间签订的双重征税协定在跨国财产转让所得的征税协调问题上完全采用了经合发组织范本第13条规定，这种情形下，对于作为缔约国对方居民的合伙人取得的上述转让财产所得，来源地国一方认为是协定第13条第2款规定意义上的对方居民转让位于来源地国境内的常设机构营业财产所得，可以在来源地国课税；而居住国则可能认为上述转让财产所得属于转让公司法人中的股份财产所得，应适用协定第13条第4款规定，只能由转让人的居住国征税，作为公司所在地国的来源地国不得课税。在发生这种两国各自国内税法对合伙企业的纳税主体资格规定不同而导致的适用协定条款分歧的情形下，为避免由此而引起的国际双重征税，居住国一方应接受来源地国一方对税收协定条款的解释和适用结果，在对其居民合伙人取得的上述转让合伙企业中的股份财产所得征税时，对来源地国已征所得税额应给予税收抵免待遇。

The understanding and application by the state of residence, for reasons provided for in its domestic tax law, of the rules for the coordination of conflicts of taxation rights in double taxation agreements may be inconsistent with the interpretation and application by the state of origin of the rules for the coordination of conflicts of taxation rights in double taxation agreements. It may lead to a double taxation of the income concerned, in which case, in order to avoid double taxation, the state of residence shall accept the interpretation and application of the relevant provisions of the tax agreement by the state of origin. For example, if the domestic tax law of the country of origin provides that the partnership itself is not an independent taxpayer, the partner shall pay taxes on his share of income in the partnership, and according to the domestic tax law of the country of residence, the partnership is the same as the corporate legal person. Where a resident partner of a state of residence acquires proceeds from the transfer of equity property in a partnership established in the territory of the state of origin, and where a double taxation agreement between the two states fully applies the provisions of article 13 of the OECD Model with respect to the harmonization of taxation of proceeds from the transfer of transnational property, the proceeds from the transfer of such property acquired by the partner of the other resident of the constracting state may be taxed in the state of origin, in the opinion of one of the source countries, in the sense of article 13, paragraph 2, of the agreement, from the transfer by the resident of the other party of the business property of a permanent establishment located in the territory of the state of origin. However, the state of residence may consider the above-mentioned proceeds of the transfer of property to be proceeds of shares in the legal person of the transfer company, subject to the provisions of article 13, paragraph 4, of the Agreement, which may be taxed only by the state of residence of the assignor and may not be taxed as the state of origin in which the company is located. In the event of such differences in the terms of the applicable agreement resulting from the differences in the provisions of the respective domestic tax laws on the tax subject of the partnership, in order to avoid the resulting international double taxation, the state of residence shall accept the interpretation and application of the terms of the tax agreement by the source country and, in the case of taxation of the income derived from the share property in the above-mentioned transfer partnership obtained by its resident partner, shall be treated with tax credit for the income tax levied by the source country.

第三,双重征税协定和缔约国国内税法既有各自独立的法律概念体系,又存在着彼此配合、相互补充和共同作用的关系。

Third, double taxation agreements and the domestic tax laws of states parties have separate systems of legal concepts. There is also a relationship of cooperation, complementarity and interaction.

双重征税协定是缔约国双方经协商谈判达成的国际法律文件,有其相对独立的法律概念体系。这首先表现在协定中使用的某些法律概念用语是协定本身所独有的,在缔约国国内有关税法中并不存在或没有单独列出。例如,协定中使用"常设机构""固定基地"等概念,我国现行税法上并没有使用或单独列出。其次,尽管协定在规定所得种类方面所使用的概念用语,如"特许权使用费""股息"和"利息"等用语,在相当大程度上等同或类似于国内税法上的概念术语,但彼此在内涵或外延上,可能仍有一定程度或范围的差异。因此,从准确适用协定的角度出发,应该从两种不同的概念体系来理解协定中的概念和缔约国国内税法上的概念。由于协定有自己相对独立的概念体系和特定的功能作用,在涉及对缔约国对方居民的课税事项时,首先应依照协定的概念规定来审查协定对缔约国的课税权是否作出了限制以及有何种程度的限制。

The Double taxation agreement is an international legal document negotiated by both parties and has its relatively independent legal concept system. This is first manifested in the fact that certain legal conceptual terms used in the agreement are unique to the agreement itself and do not exist or are not separately listed in the relevant tax laws of the constracting state. For example, the concept of "permanent establishment" and "fixed base" is used in the agreement, which is not used or listed separately in the current tax law of our country. Secondly, although the conceptual terms used in the agreement in terms of the type of income, such as "royalties", " dividends" and "interest", are to a considerable extent equivalent or similar to the conceptual terms in domestic tax law, there may still be some degree or scope differences in connotation or extension. Therefore, from the point of view of the accurate application of the agreement, the concept in the agreement and the concept in the domestic tax law of the contracting party should be understood from two different conceptual systems. Since the agreement has its own relatively independent conceptual system and specific functional role, when it comes to taxation of residents of the other party, it is first up to the conceptual provisions of the agreement to examine whether and to what extent the agreement limits the right of states parties to tax.

另外,双重征税协定又是一种以缔约国双方的国内有关税法为基础的法律文件,有人形象地将其喻为联结缔约国双方国内税法的桥梁和纽带。它与缔约国国内有关税法存在着彼此配合、相互补充、共同作用于调整国际税收关系的密切联系。首先,协定中的冲突规范和实体规范的功能作用,需要缔约国国内税法上的有关实体规范和程序规范的配合补充,才能得以施行和实现。例如,协定仅适用于缔约国的居民,但居民身份的确定则有赖于缔约国国内税法的规定。协定运用冲突规范将某种跨国所得的征税权分配给缔约国一方行使,如果没有缔约国相应的国内税法上实体规范和程序规则的配合实施,则不可能实现协定的宗旨。其次,协定与缔约国的国内税法虽然各有相对独立的法律概念体系,但协定同时也明确规定了某些用语的含义以缔约国国内法律规定的含义为准。对于协定本身未明确定义的用语,按照协定的解释规则,允许依照缔约国国内有关税法概念进行解释。因此,只有通过协定和

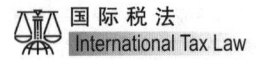

缔约国双方国内有关税法的互相配合、彼此补充和共同作用,才能实现对国际税收关系的完整的法律调整。

In addition, the double taxation agreement is a kind of legal document based on the relevant domestic tax laws of both parties, which is vividly described as the bridge and link between the domestic tax laws of both parties. It has a close relationship with the relevant domestic tax laws of the state parties, which complement each other and act together to adjust the international tax relations. First of all, the conflict norms in the agreement and the functional role of entity norms need to be supplemented by the relevant entity norms and procedural norms in the domestic tax law of the parties in order to be implemented and realized. For example, the agreement applies only to residents of a contracting state, but the determination of resident status depends on the provisions of the domestic tax law of the contracting state. The purpose of the agreement cannot be achieved without the cooperation of the substantive norms and procedural rules of the respective domestic tax laws of the contracting states in the application of conflict norms to the exercise of the right to tax on certain transnational proceeds by one party. Secondly, although the Agreement and the domestic tax laws of the contracting states have a relatively independent system of legal concepts, the Agreement also clearly stipulates that the meaning of certain terms is subject to the meaning prescribed by the domestic laws of the contracting states. For terms that are not clearly defined in the agreement itself, interpretation is permitted in accordance with the relevant concepts of the tax law in the state party, in accordance with the rules of interpretation of the agreement. Therefore, a complete legal adjustment to international tax relations can be achieved only through the mutual cooperation, complementarity and interaction between the agreement and the relevant domestic tax laws of the parties.

第四节　国际税收协定的解释
Section 4　Interpretation of International Tax Agreements

一、条约的解释
Interpretation of Treaties

尼采说,"没有事实,只有解释"。根据尼采的"透视主义"概念,协议很容易产生争端,而且很难解决,因为所有的决定、事实和主张都是主观的,即它们代表了协议各方对这些事实的不同解释。①条约的解释是一门艺术,而不是一门精确的科学,是一项非常具有挑战性

---

① Harm J. Oortwijin, *Dispute Resolution in Cross-Border Tax Matters* (European Taxation, 2016), 163.

的事业。近来,世界各地的条约解释者受到这些问题的挑战,例如滥用条约、滥用法律、冒犯性解释和其他类似的解释,这些解释创造了一种新的条约语言的表达方式,已被引入国际税务条约法,从最近的解决一般反避税条款的法定规则以及最近法院案件的判决中得到体现。产生解释需要的主要疑问是条约中词语是否明确表达了条约缔约方在其法律范围内的意图。这是条约解释中需要解决的关键问题。《维也纳条约法公约》(以下简称《条约法公约》)第31条被视为规定了条约解释的一般规则。

Nietzsche said, "there are no facts, only interpretations". According to Nietzsche's concept of "perspectiveism", agreements can easily produce disputes and are difficult to resolve because all decisions, facts and claims are subjective, that is, they represent different interpretations of these facts by the parties to the agreement. The interpretation of treaties is an art, not a precise science, and a very challenging undertaking. Recently, treaty interpreters around the world have been challenged by these issues, such as the abuse of treaties, the abuse of laws, offensive interpretations and other similar interpretations, which have created a new expression of treaty language and have been introduced into international tax treaty law, as reflected in recent statutory rules for the resolution of general anti-tax avoidance provisions and in recent court decisions. The main question that gave rise to the need for interpretation was whether the words in the treaty clearly expressed the intention of the parties to the treaty within their legal framework. This is a key issue to be addressed in treaty interpretation. Article 31 of the Vienna Convention on the Law of Treaties (hereinafter referred to as the Convention on the Law of Treaties) is considered to provide for the general rules governing the interpretation of treaties.

第31条内容如下:

1. 条约应依其上下文及目的和宗旨,依其用语之一般含义,作出善意解释。

2. 条约解释的上下文除约文外,还应包括其序言和附件:

(a) 所有缔约方就缔结条约而达成的与条约有关的任何协定;

(b) 一个或多个缔约方在缔结条约时提出并被其他缔约方接受为与条约有关的任何文书。

3. 应结合上下文考虑:

(a) 缔约方就条约的解释或其条款的适用达成的任何嗣后协定;

(b) 条约适用方面的任何嗣后惯例,以确立缔约方对条约解释的协议;

(c) 适用于双方关系的任何相关国际法规则;

(d) 如果确定当事人有此意图,则应赋予一个术语一个特殊的含义。

Article 31 reads as follows:

1. A treaty shall be interpreted in good faith in accordance with the ordinary meaning to be given to the terms of the treaty in their context and in the light of its object and purpose.

2. The context for the purpose of the interpretation of a treaty shall comprise, in addition to the text, its preamble and annexes:

(a) Any agreement relating to the treaty which was made between all the parties in connection with the conclusion of the treaty;

(b) Any instrument which was made by one or more parties in connection with the conclusion of the treaty and accepted by the other parties as an instrument related to the treaty.

3. There shall be taken into account, together with the context:

(a) Any subsequent agreement between the parties regarding the interpretation of the treaty or the application of its provisions;

(b) Any subsequent practice in the application of the treaty which establishes the agreement of the parties regarding its interpretation;

(c) Any relevant rules of international law applicable in the relations between the parties;

(d) A special meaning shall be given to a term if it is established that the parties so intended.

按照国际法委员会的释义,第31条所依据的观点是,必须假定约文是当事人意图的真实表达,因此,解释的出发点是阐明约文的含义,而不是从头调查当事方的意图。[①]此外,国际法院的判例已经确定,对条约解释的文本方法被视为既定法律。1966年条款草案第27条评注第12段声明如下:第31条第1款包含三项不同的原则。第一个原则是善意解释条约,直接来自条约必须遵守的规则。第二个原则是文本方法的精髓:当事人应当被推定具有其所用术语的通常含义所表示的意思。第三个原则是一项融合了常识和善意的原则:词语的通常含义不应抽象地确定,而是根据条约的上下文并参考其目的和宗旨来确定。第31条第2款明确界定了为条约解释目的对"上下文"一词的理解。问题是与条约有关的其他文件在多大程度上应被视为构成解释目的上下文的一部分。第27条评注第14段声明如下:有时可能会出现一个事实问题,即在谈判期间就某一条款的含义达成的谅解是否意在构成对该条款解释的商定基础。但是,如果关于一项条款的解释的协议被确定为在缔结条约之前或当时达成的,则应被视为构成条约的一部分。……同样,在缔结条约之后达成的关于一项条款的解释的协议代表了条约缔约方的真实解释,为了解释条约,必须将其读入条约。《条约法公约》第31条第3款b项规定"条约适用方面的任何嗣后惯例,以确定缔约方对条约解释的协议",是一个需要考虑的因素。第27条评注第15段解释说:这种嗣后惯例,作为解释的一个要素在条约适用中的重要性是显而易见的;因为它是缔约方理解条约含义的客观证据。嗣后惯例的价值各不相同,因为它表明各方对术语的含义有共同的理解。国际法委员会认为,确立缔约方对条约解释的理解的嗣后惯例应列入第3款,作为解释性协定之外的真实解释资料。《条约法公约》第31条第3款c项增加了另一项需要考虑的因素,即适用于当事人之间关系的任何有关国际法规则。第27条评注第16段解释说:这一要素对第2款所界定的约文和上下文来说,都是外在的因素。无论如何,使用这一解释要素需要根据缔约方在签署条约时的意图作出善意解释。在涉及税务条约解释的情况下,可能没有必要使用有关国际法规则,因为赋予一个术语的特殊含义必须列入先前或之后的谈判。在这种情况下,这一谈判将构成条约文本、其上下文或可以和上下文一起考虑的一份文件。

According to the International Law Commission, Article 31 is based on the view that, it must be assumed that the text is a true expression of the intention of the parties, therefore, the

---

[①] 1966 Draft Articles, supra n. 301, at 220, para. 11.

point of interpretation is to clarify the meaning of the text, rather than investigating the intention of the parties from scratch. In addition, the jurisprudence of the International Court of Justice has established, the textual approach to treaty interpretation is considered to be established law. Paragraph 12 of the commentary to draft Article 27 of 1966 stated that Article 31, Paragraph 1, contained three different principles. The first principle is benevolent interpretation which comes directly from the rules that the treaty must abide by. The second principle is the essence of the text method: the parties should be presumed to have the meaning expressed in the usual meaning of the terms used. The third principle is a principle that combines common sense and goodwill. The usual meaning of words should not be determined abstractly. It is determined by the context of the treaty and by reference to its object and purpose. Paragraph 2 of Article 31 clearly defines the understanding of the term "context" for the purposes of treaty interpretation. The question was to what extent other treaty-related documents should be considered as part of the context for the purpose of interpretation. Paragraph 14 of the commentary to Article 27 states that there may sometimes be a question of fact, that is, whether the understanding reached during the negotiations on the meaning of a provision is intended to constitute an agreed basis for its interpretation. But, uh, if an agreement on the interpretation of a provision is determined to have been reached before or at the time of the conclusion of the treaty, it should be considered as part of the treaty... the same, the agreement reached after the conclusion of the treaty on the interpretation of a provision represents the true interpretation by the parties to the treaty, to interpret treaties, it must be read into the treaty. Convention on the Law of Treaties Article 31, Paragraph 3(b), any subsequent practice in the application of the treaty which establishes the agreement of the parties regarding its interpretation, is a factor to consider. Paragraph 15 of the commentary to Article 27 explains that the importance of such subsequent practice as an element of interpretation in the application of the treaty is obvious, because it is objective evidence that the parties understand the meaning of the treaty. The value of subsequent practice varies, because it shows that the parties have a common understanding of the meaning of the term. According to the International Law Commission, subsequent practice establishing the understanding of the parties of the interpretation of the treaty should be included in Paragraph 3, as a true explanatory material other than an interpretative agreement. Article 31, Paragraph 3(c), of the Convention on the Law of Treaties adds another factor to be considered, that is, any relevant rules of international law applicable to the relationship between the parties. Paragraph 16 of the commentary to Article 27 explains that this element is relevant to the text and context as defined in Paragraph 2, are external factors. Anyway, the use of this element of interpretation would need to be interpreted in good faith in the light of the intention of the parties at the time of signing the treaty. In the case of tax treaty interpretation, it may not be necessary to use the relevant rules of international law, because the special meaning given to a term must be included in previous or subsequent negotiations. In this case, this negotiation would constitute the text of the treaty, its context or a document that could be considered together with the context.

二、税收协定的解释
Interpretation of Tax Agreements

经合发组织在2000年4月的《否决条约效力》的报告[①]中就依据《条约法公约》规定的条约解释的规则来解释税收协定,表明了两个主要立场:首先,条约解释的规则仅适用于个案的基础上;其次,这些规则适用于各国及其政府税务当局。税收协定,就其根据《条约法公约》规定的规则所作的解释而言,可以说是由两个缔约国以书面形式订立的国际公法文件,根据该文件,这些缔约国确定或商定对一个或两个缔约国居民所得的收入或利润项目按照其国内法合法适用的征税归属。此外,税收协定的其中一个目的和宗旨涉及两个缔约国保证采取适当措施防止一个或两个缔约国居民跨境逃税的方式和方法。税收协定不能防止第三国居民逃税。我们可以简单地将《条约法公约》第31条规定的解释原则理解为,缔约国的征税归属或防止逃税的措施必须善意地解释,根据缔约国在条约文本及其上下文中表达的意图,根据条约中用于在签署条约时表达这一意图的用语的一般含义,并以条约缔约国签署时的情况为依据。

In its April 2000 Report on Denial of the Validity of Treaties, the OECD expressed two main positions on the interpretation of tax agreements based on the rules of treaty interpretation under the Convention on the Law of Treaties, namely, first that the rules of treaty interpretation apply only on a case-by-case basis, and secondly that they apply to states and their governmental tax authorities. Tax agreements, as far as their interpretation under the rules provided for in the Convention on the Law of Treaties is concerned, can be said to be public international law documents concluded in writing by two states parties, according to which they determine or agree on the tax attribution of income or profit items earned by residents of one or two states parties that are lawfully applicable under their domestic law. In addition, one object and purpose of the tax agreement relates to ways and means by which two states parties undertake to take appropriate measures to prevent cross-border tax evasion by residents of one or two states parties. Tax agreements can not prevent tax evasion by residents of the third country. We can simply interpret the principle of interpretation provided for in Article 31 of the Convention on the Law of Treaties as that the attribution of taxes to states parties or measures to prevent tax evasion must be interpreted in good faith, based on the intention expressed by states parties in the text of the treaty and in its context, and the general meaning of the terms used in the treaty to express this intention at the time of signature of the treaty and in accordance with the circumstances at the time of signature by the parties to the treaty.

对税收协定的善意解释必须是事实性的,而不仅仅是概念性的。应被视为事实性的税收协定善意解释的指标包括:

(1)解释必须确保税收协定的目的和宗旨实现了。也就是说,解释必须确保缔约国的意图在协定和缔约国授予或同意的征税归属的范围内得到充分确立。

(2)如果对协定有两种解释,一种有助于实现协定的目的和宗旨,另一种显然没有,则

[①] OECD, Tax Treaty Override (Apr.2000), paras. 19-20.

必须采用前者。

（3）当纳税人是从其居住地国或另一缔约国的著名国际税务条约顾问处获得建议时，必须推定纳税人善意解释税务条约。

（4）善意的解释总是遵循基于协定上下文的约文术语的普通含义。必须立即无视导致违背协定目的和宗旨的结果的字面解释。

（5）主管机关在协商解决解释问题时，必须推定其对税收协定的解释是善意的，无论主管机关是否根据相互协商程序或咨询程序达成协议。

（6）当主管当局根据相互协商程序开始谈判以解决纳税人可能的双重征税问题时，主管当局必须达成一项协议，全面免除双重征税。例如，在转让定价调整引起的分配案件中，一个主管机关可以采取完全免除双重征税的立场，而另一个主管机关只能采取部分免除的立场，则诚实信用原则要求采用前一种立场。

（7）缔约国国内法随后发生的变化，不得以任何方式改变或影响在缔结税收协定时达成的最初谅解。如果确实发生这种变化，则必须根据缔约国的宪法程序缔结一项附加议定书或一项新条约，以便使该条约成为该国具有约束力的法律。

（8）法院必须只执行法律，法律要求税收协定必须善意解释。[①]

The interpretation of tax treaties in good faith must be factual and not merely conceptual. Indicators of what should be regarded as a factual good faith tax treaty interpretation includes:

(1) The interpretation must ensure that the object and purpose of the treaty are achieved. That is, the interpretation must be certain that the intentions of the treaty parties are well established within the context of the treaty and the taxing attributions conferred or consented by the contracting states.

(2) If two interpretations of the treaty arise, one facilitating the achievement of the object and purpose of the treaty and the other clearly not, the former must be adopted.

(3) A taxpayer must be presumed to interpret a tax treaty in good faith when the taxpayer obtains advice from a reputable international tax treaty advisor in either the taxpayer's country of residence or the other contracting state.

(4) An interpretation in good faith always follows the ordinary meaning of the treaty terms based on the treaty context. A literal interpretation that leads to a result contrary to the treaty's object and purpose must be disregarded at once.

(5) The competent authorities must be presumed to interpret a tax treaty in good faith when they confer with each other to resolve an interpretation issue, whether or not a competent authority agreement is reached under the mutual agreement procedure or a consultation process.

(6) When the competent authorities commence negotiations under the mutual agreement procedure to resolve a taxpayer's problem of potential double taxation, the competent authorities must reach an agreement that provides full relief from double taxation. If for example in an allocation case

---

① Juan Angel Becerra, Interpretation and Application of Tax Treaties in North America, Second Revised Edition. (IBFD 2013). p. 118.

arising from a transfer pricing adjustment, one competent authority may take a position that provides full relief from double taxation while the other competent authority takes a position that provides only partial relief, the principle of good faith demands that the former position be adopted.

(7) A subsequent change in the domestic law of a contracting state must not change or affect in any way the original understandings reached at the conclusion of a tax treaty. If such changes do occur, an additional protocol or a new treaty must be concluded in accordance with the constitutional procedures of the contracting states in order to make the treaty the binding law of the land.

(8) The courts must only give effect to the law, which demands that a tax treaty be interpreted in good faith.

经合发组织税收协定范本及其注释是诸多税收协定谈判和缔结的基础，也是国际税收协定解释和适用的主要法律渊源。使用经合发组织协定范本注释来解释特定税收协定也可以从不同的层面来看待：在缔约国的国际公法层面，仅限于条约谈判者将协定范本和注释作为条约谈判过程和结论的出发点，当税务机关在相互协商程序下对税收协定条款达成共识时，这一点很可能适用；在纳税人层面，仅在有允许使用范本注释的法定规则的情况下，或在税收协定条款明确源自协定范本的情况下，但仅在用尽适用于特定案件的所有法律背景后，才可以使用范本注释作为解释的补充手段；在法院层面，（限于）法院有足够的空间将范本注释用作适用某一国内法定规则所产生的法律背景，法院的惯例确立了诉诸范本注释的足够权威时，并且/或当条约本身给予范本注释足够的法律地位以解释注释。可以看出，经合发组织协定范本注释的使用必须根据具体国家的法律制度或习惯，对逐个国家进行研究。然而，在所有情况下，考虑协定范本注释在世界范围都是有意义的，因为如上所述，经合发组织税收协定范本和注释代表了对过去120年来国际税收协定语言和实践的编纂。

The OECD Model Tax Agreement and its Notes are the basis for the negotiation and conclusion of many tax agreements and the main legal source for the interpretation and application of international tax agreements. The use of the OECD Model Agreement Notes to interpret specific tax agreements can also be seen at different levels: at the public international law level of states parties, the treaty negotiators are limited to using the Model Agreement and Notes as the starting point for the treaty negotiation process and conclusions, which is likely to apply when tax authorities reach consensus on the provisions of tax agreements under mutual consultation procedures; at the taxpayer level, the model annotation may be used as a supplementary means of interpretation only if there are statutory rules allowing the use of the model annotation, or if the provisions of the tax agreement clearly derived from the model agreement, but only after exhausting all the legal contexts applicable to a particular case; at the court level, if the court has sufficient space to use the model annotation as the legal context arising from the application of a domestic legal rule, when the practice of the court establishes sufficient authority to resort to the model annotation and/or when the treaty itself gives the model annotation sufficient legal status to explain the annotation. As can be seen, the use of the OECD Model Agreement Notes must be country-by-country based on country-specific legal systems or customs. In all cases, however, consideration of the Model Agreement Notes is relevant worldwide, as noted above, the OECD Model Tax Agreements and Notes represent a codification of the language and practice of international tax agreements over the past 120 years.

联合国范本和经合发组织范本第3条第2款规定:"缔约国一方实施本协定时,对未经本协定明确定义的用语,除上下文联系另有要求外,应当具有该缔约国关于适用本协定税种的法律所规定的涵义。"在解释国际税收协定的过程中,在某些情况下,允许缔约国一方依据其国内有关税法规定的涵义来解释协定中的用语涵义。[①]因此,第3条第2款也被视为国际税收协定解释的特别规定。有学者指出,这一条款来自1945年美国和英国双边税收协定的第二条第3款。[②]所以也称其是一个"盎格鲁—撒克逊发明"。[③]经合发组织范本第3条第2款借用了1945年美英税收协定的表述而且范本注释混淆了税收协定的适用和解释。联合国范本注释没有犯同样的错误。第3条第2款可以采用灵活方式提及国内法,只要它不扭曲税收协定缔约国(作为解释主体)的真实和最初的意图。第3条第2款所界定的术语包括薪金、雇主、营业利润、其他收入和收益。当对征税归属(当事人的意图或上下文)没有问题时,第3条第2款仅用于适用目的。

In accordance with Article 3, Paragraph 2, of the United Nations Model and the OECD Model: "In the implementation of this Agreement by one of the contracting parties, for terms not expressly defined in this Agreement, unless the context requires otherwise, it shall have the meaning provided for in the law of the contracting state on the application of taxes under this Agreement." In interpreting international tax agreements, in some cases, a contracting party is permitted to interpret the meaning of the terms of the Agreement in the light of the meaning provided for in the relevant domestic tax law. Therefore, Article 3, Paragraph 2, is also considered a special provision for the interpretation of international tax agreements. Some scholars have pointed out that, this provision derives from Article 2, Paragraph 3, of the 1945 bilateral tax agreement between the United States and the United Kingdom. So it is also called an "Anglo-Saxon invention". Article 3, Paragraph 2, of the OECD Model borrows the expression of the 1945 US-British Tax Agreement and the Model Note confuses the application and interpretation of tax agreements. The UN Model Notes did not make the same mistake. Article 3, Paragraph 2, may refer to domestic law in a flexible manner, as long as it does not distort the true and original intent of the parties to the tax agreement as the subject of interpretation. The terms defined in Article 3, Paragraph 2, include salary, employer, operating profit, other income and earnings.

---

① 廖益新主编,《国际税法学》,高等教育出版社2008年版,第78页。

② Article II (3) of the 1945 tax treaty between the United States and the United Kingdom read as follows. In the application of the provisions of the present Convention by one of the contracting parties any term not otherwise defined shall, unless the context otherwise requires, have the meaning which it has under the laws of that contracting party relating to the taxes which are the subject of the present Convention.
Article 3(2) of the 1963 Draft Model states as follows. As regards the application of the Convention by a contracting state, any term not defined therein shall, unless the context otherwise requires, have the meaning which it has under the law of that state concerning the taxes to which the Convention applies.

③ Juan Angel Becerra, Interpretation and Application of Tax Treaties in North America, Second Revised Edition. (IBFD 2013). p. 138.

When there is no problem with the attribution of taxation (the intent or context of the parties), Article 3, Paragraph 2, is used only for applicable purposes.

综合上述解释规则，正如学者所述，"缔结税收协定的目的是避免双重征税和双重不征税。然而国家间签订了税收协定并不意味着就能自动实现这一目标。在许多案件中，税收协定往往成为国家法律博弈中的另类。在税收协定解释方面，并没有国际性的法院作出指导原则，目前对税收协定的解释由国内法院来管辖。国内法院运用各自的国内方法解释税收协定。因此，不同国家的法院解释规则不同，裁判的结果也不同。例如，英国法院在解释协定时重点放在协定本身的文字和结构上，即采用文义解释的方法，而德国和荷兰则更倾向于采用目的解释。结果是同样的协定条文产生不同的解释，导致双重征税或双重不征税。尽管有现有的这些争议解决措施，如相互协商程序、OECD税收协定范本的注释、联合国税收协定范本的注释，以及仲裁解决分歧解释，但形成一套统一的税收协定解释规则是极为重要的。近十年来，在国际上出现了各种解决此问题的建议，例如使用统一的国际税收语言、赋予普遍解释原则效力、通知缔约方相关判例法，但是还没有一种建议获得一致认可。"①

Synthesizing the above rules of interpretation, as scholars have said, "The purpose of concluding tax agreements is to avoid double taxation and double non-taxation. However, the conclusion of tax agreements between countries does not mean that this goal can be achieved automatically. In many cases, tax agreements often become an alternative to national legal games. There are no international courts to guide the interpretation of tax agreements, and the current interpretation of tax agreements is governed by domestic courts. Domestic courts use their own domestic methods to interpret tax agreements. Therefore, the rules of interpretation of courts in different countries are different, and the results of decisions are different. For example, British courts have focused on the letter and structure of the agreement itself in interpreting the agreement, i.e. using the method of literal interpretation, while Germany and the Netherlands prefer the purpose interpretation. As a result, the same articles of agreement produced different interpretations, leading to double taxation or double non-taxation. Although these existing dispute resolution measures, such as the mutual consultation procedure, the annotation of the OECD Model Tax Agreement, the annotation of the United Nations Model Tax Agreement, and the interpretation of arbitration settlement differences, it is extremely important to form a unified set of rules for the interpretation of tax agreements. Over the past decade, various proposals have emerged at the international level to address this issue, such as the use of a uniform international tax language, giving effect to the principle of universal interpretation, and informing parties of relevant case law, but none has been unanimously endorsed."

---

① Wim Wiinen, *Some Thoughts on Convergence and Tax Treaty Interpretation*, Bulletin for International Taxation, 2013 (Volume 67), No. 11.

第五节 相 关 案 例
Section 5　Related Cases

本节选取施乐案。

This Section is about the Xerox case.

一、案件经过
Course of the Case

施乐一案初审由联邦索赔法院于1988年作出裁决,在1994年由美国联邦巡回上诉法院作出终裁。

The first trial in the Xerox case was decided by the Federal Claims Court in 1988 and finalised by the United States Federal Circuit Court of Appeal in 1994.

本案涉及美国税收程序(IRS Rev. Pro. 80-18. this revenue procedure)的使用和法律地位,该程序基于美国-英国税收协定下的税务主管当局协议。这一税收程序是以美英两国税务主管机关依据美英两国税收协定相互协商程序达成的协议为基础的,该协议通过换文完成但没有通过外交渠道,而且未经美国参议院批准。

The case relates to the use and legal status of the United States tax procedure (IRS Rev. Pro.80-18. this revenue procedure), which is based on a tax authority agreement under the United States-UK tax agreement. The tax process is based on an agreement between the U.S. and British tax authorities based on a mutual consultation process between the U.S. and British tax agreements, completed by exchange of letters but not through diplomatic channels, and without the approval of the United States Senate.

美国索赔法院非常重视税收程序,指出税务主管当局协议是美英两国税收协定缔约方意图的表达,因为协定第25条第三款特别授权主管税务当局可以解决在解释或适用协定方面出现的任何困难或疑问。

The United States Claims Court attached great importance to the tax procedure, noting that the agreement of the competent tax authority was an expression of the intention of the parties to the United States-UK tax agreement, since Article 25(3) of the agreement specifically authorized the competent tax authority to resolve any difficulties or questions arising in the interpretation or application of the agreement.

---

① US: CC, 1988, Xerox Corp. v. United States, 14 CI. Ct. 455(1988), US: AC, 1994, Xerox Corp. V. United States, 41 F. 3d 647 (Fed. Cir. 1994).

美国索赔法院还表示,它没有发现"异常有力的相反证据",表明主管税务当局协议曲解了税收协定的语言或美英两缔约国的意图。

The United States Claims Court also stated that it had not found "unusually strong evidence to the contrary" indicating that the agreement of the competent tax authorities misinterpreted the language of the tax agreement or the intention of the United States and British States parties.

本案首先判决被告美国国税局胜诉。法院的判决是基于这样一个事实,即按照法院的规定,施乐无法证明其有权获得超出税收协定条款规定和主管税务当局协议的外国税收抵免。

The case was first decided in favour of the defendant, the IRS. The court's decision was based on the fact that, under the court's terms, Xerox could not prove that it was entitled to a foreign tax credit that exceeded the provisions of the tax agreement and the agreement of the competent tax authority.

施乐向联邦巡回上诉法院上诉,并于1994年12月6日获得了有利的裁决。这项有利的上诉裁决指出,税务主管当局协议不符合税收协定的宗旨。此外,上诉法院指出,尽管税收程序不具有根据《国内税收法典》颁布的规章的效力,但税收裁决仍有权作为对税务专员的规章解释的反映而具有一定的分量。法院还指出,税收程序可能有助于解释规章,但对法院没有约束力。法院强调,尽管税收程序需要公平考虑,以反映财政部的立场,但它们并没有与调查隔离开来。更具体地说,"税收程序不能改变协定的条款和宗旨"。

Xerox appealed to the Federal Circuit Court of Appeal and obtained a favourable ruling on 6 December 1994. This favourable appeal decision states that the agreement of the tax authorities is incompatible with the purpose of the tax agreement. In addition, the Court of Appeal noted that, although the tax procedure does not have the effect of a regulation issued under the Domestic Tax Code, the tax award is still entitled to a certain weight as a reflection of the tax commissioner's interpretation of the regulation. The court also noted that the tax procedure may help to interpret the regulations but is not binding on the court. The court stressed that although tax procedures required fair consideration to reflect the position of the Treasury Department, they were not isolated from the investigation. More specifically, "the tax procedure can not alter the terms and purposes of the agreement".

美国财政部(作为上诉的有效被告)辩称,主管税务当局协议第5段很重要,因为它指出美国法律决定外国税收抵免的时间,税收程序80–18阐述了美国法律,因此在本案中具有控制作用。在驳回这一论点时,上诉法院重申,税收程序既不是法律也不是规章,对法院没有约束力。

The US Treasury Department (as a valid defendant on appeal) argued that Paragraph 5 of the agreement between the competent tax authorities was important because it stated that United States law determined the timing of foreign tax credits and that the tax procedure 80–18 set out United States law and therefore had a controlling role in the case. In rejecting this argument, the Court of Appeal reiterated that the tax procedure was neither legal nor regulatory and was not binding on the Court.

上诉法院判决施乐公司胜诉,这样纳税人就可以抵免英国预付公司税(ACT)。法院认为,美英两国税收协定关于这一问题的含义是明确无误的,不应将其解释为与该协定避免双重征税的明确目的相违背。

A court of appeal ruled in favour of Xerox so that taxpayers could credit the UK prepaid company tax (ACT). The Court held that the meaning of the United States-UK tax agreement on this issue was clear and should not be interpreted as contrary to the express purpose of the agreement to avoid double taxation.

上诉法院援引美国最高法院判决的若干案件作为其决议的依据。[①] 上诉法院从这些案件中得出结论：在解释一项条约时，该条约的术语在该条约的上下文中具有一般含义，并根据该含义以最符合条约宗旨的方式加以解释。……法官的义务是在解释条约条款时满足签署双方的意图。

The Court of Appeal relied on several cases decided by the United States Supreme Court as the basis for its resolution. The Court of Appeal concluded from these cases that when interpreting a treaty, the terms of the treaty have a general meaning in the context of the treaty and are interpreted in the manner most consistent with its purpose. ... The Judge's obligation is to satisfy the intention of the signatories when interpreting the provisions of the treaty.

尽管这里可以引述本案更多的引文，但有一条不能省略的引文清楚地确定了关于条约解释的相互协议的性质是外在材料。如果它是外在的，就不能是条约文本或上下文，因此，如上所述，它至多只是一种条约解释的补充手段，只有在条约文本不明确或模棱两可时才有用。

While more citations in this case can be cited here, one that can not be omitted clearly determines that the nature of mutual agreement on treaty interpretation is external material. If it is external, it can not be a treaty text or context, and therefore, as mentioned above, it is at best a supplementary means of treaty interpretation and is useful only if the treaty text is unclear or ambiguous.

引文如下：除非条约条款表面上不清楚，或适用于所出现的情况不清楚，否则很少有必要依靠外部证据来解释条约，因为几乎不可能重新考虑导致签署国签署最终文件的所有考虑因素和妥协。然而，外部材料往往有助于理解条约及其宗旨，从而为审查条约条款提供一个开明的框架。

The quotation is as follows: unless the provisions of the treaty are ostensibly unclear or the situation to which they are applicable are not clear, it is rarely necessary to rely on external evidence to interpret the treaty, as it is almost impossible to reconsider all considerations and compromises that led the signatory states to sign the final document. However, external material often helps to understand the treaty and its purpose, thus provides an enlightened framework for reviewing its provisions.

显然，本案中的主管税务当局协议被驳回。因此，很明显，它不能等同于对纳税人或法院具有约束力的法律。

---

① United States V. Stuart, supra n. 251, at 365-366 (1989): Kolovrat v. Oregon, 366 US 187, 193-194 (1961); Sumitomo Shoji America, Inc. v. Avagliano, supran. 274, at 185; Valentine v. United States, 299 US 5, 11 (1936); Air France V. Saks, supra n. 400, at 400; United States V. Lee Yen Tai, supra n. 247, at 220-222; Maximov v. United States, supra n. 274, at 54.

Clearly, the agreement of the competent tax authorities in this case was rejected. Therefore, it is clear that it can not be equated with a law binding on taxpayers or courts.

二、案件分析
Case Analysis

相互协商程序这一术语在国际税收协定用语中是由经合发组织的前身欧洲经济合作组织（Organisation for European Economic Co-operation, OEEC）于1956年首次使用的。援引欧洲经济合作组织财政委员会的表述：本报告附件E第25条的目的是在缔约国之间提供一种磋商和协议的程序以及根据该程序的条件和适用来解决相关案件。

The term mutual consultation procedure was first used in the terms of international tax agreements by the European Economic Cooperation Organization (Organisation for European Economic Co-operation, OEEC), the predecessor of the OECD, in 1956. As stated by the Finance Committee of the European Economic Cooperation Organization, Article 25 of Annex E to the present report is intended to provide a procedure for consultation and agreement between states parties and to resolve the relevant cases in accordance with the terms and application of the procedure.

通常有两种相互协商程序，一种适用于特定纳税人税收协定事项的解决程序，如转移定价的情形或纳税人双重居所冲突的解决；另一种是税务主管机关就税收协定的解释或适用产生的事项程序。特定纳税人相互协商程序的数量要远远大于通常协定解释程序的数量。根据这两种相互协商程序，由税务主管机关分别达成两种相互协议。

There are usually two procedures for mutual consultation, one for the settlement of tax agreement matters applicable to specific taxpayers, such as the case of transfer pricing or the settlement of conflicts of dual residence of taxpayers; and the other for matters arising from the interpretation or application of tax agreements by tax authorities. The number of procedures for consultation between specific taxpayers is much greater than the number of procedures for the interpretation of agreements. According to these two mutual consultation procedures, the tax authorities reach two mutual agreements.

第一种是普通相互协议。普通相互协议是由授权税务主管机关就税收协定具体条款的解释或适用通过协商或谈判达成一致的一份协议。这种协议对于完善或澄清原来税收协定中缺漏或模糊的规定是非常必要的。另外也会出现，当一个缔约国国内税法发生变化时，在不损害税收协定的情况下如何就协定中的特定条款的解释或适用由主管机关达成一致协议。这种协议的法律地位在大多数案件中是由缔约国国内宪法或税法界定的。通说认为，它对法院没有约束力，在协定有效时它们可以被终止。在"Xerox Corp. v. United States"一案中，美国联邦上诉法院裁定：由美英两国主管机关依据美英两国税收协定相互协商程序达成的税收程序（revenue procedure）既不属于法律也不属于法规，对法院没有法律效力。而且它不能改变税收协定的内容和目的。① 在1992年的另一个案件"Snap-On Tools, Inc. v.

---

① US: CC, 1988, Xerox Corp. v. United States, 14 Cl.Ct.455 (1988).

United States"中,法院也认为根据美英两国税收协定相互协商程序达成的一项主管机关协议,有助于法院解释相关法律,但并不能约束法院。①

The first is common mutual agreement. Ordinary mutual agreement is an agreement by which the competent tax authority is authorized to reach consensus through consultation or negotiation on the interpretation or application of specific provisions of a tax agreement. This agreement is necessary to perfect or clarify the missing or vague provisions of the original tax agreement. It may also occur that when the domestic tax law of a contracting state changes, it is up to the competent authorities to agree on the interpretation or application of specific provisions of the agreement without prejudice to the tax agreement. The legal status of these agreements is defined in most cases by the domestic constitution or tax laws of the constracting state. The general view was that they were not binding on the court and could be terminated when the agreement was in force. The United States Federal Court of Appeal ruled in the "Xerox Corp. v. United States" that the tax procedure (Revenue Procedure) reached by the competent authorities of the United States and Britain under the mutual consultation procedure between the United States and Britain under the tax agreement between the two countries is neither a law nor a statute and has no legal effect on the court. And it can not change the content and purpose of tax agreements. In another case, "Snap-On Tools, Inc. v. United States", in 1992, the court also found that an agreement of the competent authorities reached under the mutual consultation procedure between the United States and Britain in the tax agreement helped the court to interpret the relevant law, but could not bind the court.

学习思考题
Questions for Study

1. 签订国际税收协定的目的是什么?
   What is the purpose of international taxation agreements?
2. 为什么国际税收协定通常是双边的而不是多边的?
   Why are international taxation agreements usually bilateral rather than multilateral?
3. 国际税收协定的主要内容有哪些?
   What are the main contents of international taxation agreements?
4. 怎样正确理解税收协定与国内税法的关系?
   How to correctly understand the relationship between taxation agreements and internal tax laws?
5. 对国际税收协定进行解释的规则是什么?
   What are the rules for interpreting international taxation agreements?

---

① US: CC/AC, 1992/1994, Snap-On Tools, Inc. v. United States, 26 Cl.Ct.1045 (1992), aff'd, 26 F.3d 137 (Fed.Cir. 1994), Tax Treaty Case Law IBFD.

第七章
CHAPTER VII

跨国营业所得征税的协调
Tax Harmonization on Cross-border Business Profit

第一节　基本原则
Section 1　Basic Principles

国际税法上的跨国营业所得,也称为跨国营业利润,是指作为一国居民的纳税人取得的来源于居住国境外(即某个非居住国境内)的营业所得或收益。如果纳税人的居住国和来源地国之间没有签订避免双重征税协定,则居住国政府可以依据居民税收管辖权、来源地国政府可以依据来源地税收管辖权对纳税人的跨国经营所得课税。这就会产生居住国和来源地国税收管辖权的冲突,从而导致对跨国经营所得的双重征税。为解决跨国经营所得管辖权的冲突,避免双重征税,经合发组织范本和联合国范本均在第7条建议采用常设机构原则来划分居住国和来源地国的征税权,即"缔约国一方企业的利润应仅在该国征税,但该企业通过设在缔约国另一方的常设机构进行营业的除外。如果该企业通过在缔约国另一方的常设机构进行营业,其利润可以在另一国征税,但其利润应仅以属于该常设机构的为限"。这类双边税收协定往往在定义解释中把"缔约国一方企业"解释为"缔约国一方居民经营的企业"。根据上述常设机构原则,居住国一方居民经营的企业取得的营业利润,应仅由该缔约国征税,但如果该企业通过在另一缔约国设立的常设机构进行营业,则另一缔约国可对该企业从本国取得并可归属于该常设机构的经营利润行使来源地税收管辖权优先征税。对不属于该常设机构的营业利润,即使按照另一缔约国的税法认定来源于其境内,另一缔约国也不得行使来源地税收管辖权征税。

In international tax law, transnational business income, also known as transnational business profit, refers to the business income or profit that is obtained by taxpayers of a country and that comes from outside the country where they reside (i.e. within a non-residence country).If there is no double taxation avoidance agreement between the taxpayer's residence country and the source country, the government of the residence country can tax the taxpayer's transnational business income according to domiciliary jurisdiction. So can the source country according to

---

① 廖益新主编:《国际税法学》,北京大学出版社2001年版,第170页。

the tax jurisdiction of income source. This will result in the conflict of tax jurisdiction between the residence country and the source country, which further leads to double taxation on income in transnational trade. In order to solve the conflict of jurisdiction over the income in transnational trade and avoid double taxation, Article 7 both in the OECD Model and in the United Nations Model proposes that the principle of permanent establishment should be adopted to divide the taxation rights of the two countries. In other words, profits of an enterprise of a contracting state shall be taxed only in that state, unless the enterprise carries on business through a permanent establishment situated in the other contracting state. In the case of the latter circumstance, its profits may be taxed in the other state, but shall be limited to that permanent establishment. Such bilateral tax treaties often interpret "an enterprise of a contracting state" as "an enterprise carried on by a resident of a contracting state". According to the above-mentioned principle of permanent establishment, the business profits of an enterprise run by those in the residence country shall be taxed only by that contracting state. However, if the enterprise carries on business through a permanent establishment in another contracting state, the contracting state in question, by exercising its jurisdiction of source tax priority, can tax the business profits that are obtained within its territory and attributable to the permanent establishment. As for the business profits that are not attributable to the permanent establishment, the other contracting state shall not tax them on the ground of exercising the source jurisdiction even if they are identified to be derived within its territory in accordance with the tax of the country in question.

常设机构原则是协调跨国经营所得征税冲突的原则，该原则将跨国营业所得来源地国的征税权限制在设有常设机构的条件下且只能对可归属于常设机构的利润征税，避免了来源地国和居住国税收管辖权的冲突。当来源地国对该部分跨国经营所得征税后，居住国往往根据税收协定中对来源地国承担的义务的规定，对该项所得给予免税或外国税收抵免待遇。①

The principle of permanent establishment is to coordinate tax conflict in transnational business income. The principle confines the taxing rights of the source country to the condition that there is a permanent establishment and the profits which can be attributed to the permanent establishment, thus avoids the conflict of tax jurisdiction between the source country and residence country. When the source country taxes this part of transnational business income, the residence country often gives tax-free or foreign tax credit treatment to the income according to its obligations to the source country stipulated in the tax treaty.

常设机构原则是解决跨国经营所得征税权冲突的原则，因此，只有当跨国纳税人的所得被界定为经营所得时才适用该原则。如果纳税人的所得被界定为非营业所得性质的其他所得，如劳务所得、投资所得、财产所得等，则不适用常设机构原则来调整居住国和来源地国的税收管辖权冲突，除非这些特定种类的跨国所得与纳税人的常设机构有实际联系从而应归属于常设机构的利润范围。

---

① 参见经合发组织范本和联合国范本第23条。

The principle of permanent establishment is to solve the conflict of the power to tax transnational business income. Therefore, it is only applied when the income of transnational taxpayers is defined as business income. If the taxpayer's income is defined as other types of income of a non-business nature, such as labor income, investment income, property income, etc., the principle of permanent establishment is not applicable to coordinate the conflict of tax jurisdiction between the residence country and the source country, unless these specific types of transnational income have actual connection with the taxpayer's permanent establishment and therefore are supposed to belong to the profit scope of the permanent establishment.

经营利润,也被称为交易收入,广义上包括制造业、服务业或销售货物、商品的收入。[①] 但如何界定经营利润的范围,经合发组织范本和联合国范本本身没有明确规定,各国间参照这两个范本签订的税收协定对"利润"这一基本概念术语往往没有专门的定义进行解释。[②] 根据避免双重征税协定的解释规则,缔约国一方实施此类税收协定时,对未经协定本身明确定义的用语,除上下文另有规定外,应当具有缔约国关于适用本协定税种的法律所规定的含义。因此,如果在适用税收协定时出现对纳税人跨国经营所得是否属于经营利润的争议,原则上应由适用协定的缔约国一方依据其国内税法上的相应概念来识别认定,但该识别认定的结果不应与税收协定的上下文有矛盾。

Business profit, also known as trading income, is broadly defined to include income from manufacturing, service or sale of goods or commodities. However, how to define the scope of operating profit is not clearly defined in the OECD Model and the UN model itself, and there is often no special definition for the basic concept of "profit" in the tax treaties signed with reference to these two models. According to the rules of interpretation for double taxation treaties, when a contracting state implements such tax treaties, the terms that are not explicitly defined in the treaties shall, unless the context requires otherwise, specify the meanings prescribed by the laws of the contracting state governing the taxes applicable to these treaties. Therefore, if there is a dispute over whether the taxpayers' income from transnational trade belongs to business profits in the application of tax treaties, it should in principle be identified by the contracting state applicable to the treaty according to the meaning of corresponding concepts in its domestic tax law, but the result of the identification should not be inconsistent with the context of the tax treaties.

---

① 2017年经合发组织范本第1条注释第104段。
② 廖益新主编:《国际税法学》,北京大学出版社2001年版,第172页。

第二节 常设机构的概念和范围
Section 2　Concept and Scope of Permanent Establishment

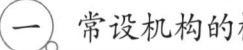

一、常设机构的概念
Concepts of Permanent Establishment

常设机构存在与否直接关系到作为跨国营业利润来源地的缔约国一方能否对缔约国另一方企业来源于其境内的营业利润行使来源地税收管辖权。如果纳税人的营业活动构成在缔约国一方设有常设机构，则该缔约国有权依据其本国税法的规定，对来源于本国的可归属于常设机构的利润优先课税；如果纳税人的营业活动未构成在缔约国一方设有常设机构，则通过该营业活动取得的营业所得应仅由作为纳税人居住国的缔约国另一方征税，缔约国一方无权主张行使来源地税收管辖权。因此，税收协定中常设机构的概念和范围直接关系到缔约双方对跨国经营所得的课税权益分配。它历来是缔约双方谈判中争执的焦点。经合发组织范本和联合国范本对常设机构范围的规定存在明显差异，各国签订的双边协定也对常设机构范围的规定存在很大不同，税收实践中跨国纳税人和税收当局就常设机构存在与否所引发的争议也屡见不鲜。

The existence of a permanent establishment is directly related to whether a contracting state, as the source of transnational business profits, can exercise the jurisdiction of source tax collection over the business profits derived from its territory by an enterprise of other contracting states. If a taxpayer's business operations constitute the existence of a permanent establishment in a contracting state, the contracting state shall, in accordance with the provisions of its domestic tax law, have priority in taxation on profits that are derived from its own territory and attributable to the permanent establishment. If a taxpayer's business operations do not constitute the existence of a permanent establishment in a contracting state, the business income derived from such business operations shall be taxed only by the other contracting state of the taxpayer's residence country, and that contracting state shall not have the right to claim the source jurisdiction. Therefore, the concept and scope of permanent establishment in tax treaties are directly related to the distribution of taxation rights and interests of the contracting parties on the income from transnational trade, which has always been the focus of disputes in the negotiation between the contracting parties. There are obvious differences between the OECD Model and the UN Model regarding the scope of permanent establishment, and the same is true of the bilateral agreements signed by various countries. In practice, there are many disputes between transnational taxpayers and tax authorities over the existence of permanent establishments.

根据经合组织范本和联合国范本的规定,常设机构可能基于某种物的因素——固定的营业场所或设施构成,也可能由于某种人的因素——特定的营业代理人的活动而存在。前者属于场所型常设机构,后者属于代理型常设机构。

According to the OECD Model and the United Nations Model, a permanent establishment may exist on the basis of a material factor such as the existence of a fixed place of business or facilities, or a person's factor such as the activities of a specific business agent. The former belongs to the place type permanent establishment; the latter belongs to the agency type permanent establishment.

(一)场所型常设机构
Place Permanent Establishment

经合发组织范本和联合国范本对场所型常设机构作出了一般性定义。根据上述两个范本的规定,所谓场所型常设机构是指一个企业进行全部或部分营业的固定场所。一个固定场所是否构成常设机构需要具备如下三个要件。

The OECD Model and the UN Model give a general definition of the place permanent establishment. According to the two models, the so-called place type permanent establishment refers to the fixed place where an enterprise conducts all or part of its business. Whether a fixed place constitutes a permanent establishment requires the following three elements.

1. 必须有一个受企业支配的营业场所
There must be a Business Place under the Control of the Enterprise

经合组织范本和联合国范本没有对何谓"营业场所"作出解释。按照《OECD税收协定范本注释》的解释,"营业场所"一语包括企业用于从事营业的厂房、设施或装置,而不论它们是否也用于其他目的。①营业场所不需要具有完整性,例如,商场中的一个摊位、酒店的一个房间、厂房中的一个设施或设备都有可能构成营业场所。企业必须对营业场所具有支配能力,这种支配能力与企业取得营业场所的方式以及是否具有合法权利无关。也就是说,企业既可以通过自有取得,也可以通过租用取得,甚至可以非法占有取得某营业场所。判断某企业对于某固定场所是否具有支配能力应注重实质,例如某公司雇员长期在另一公司的办公室办公,以确保两家公司的合同能够顺利履行,这种情况下,该雇员从事的业务与公司的业务相关,只要雇员对该办公室的支配时间足够长,就可以构成上述营业场所。但是如果某公路运输公司每天使用客户的一个码头进行交货,并且该公路运输公司每天对码头的使用时间有限,因此不能认为该码头位于公路运输公司的支配之下,不能认为该码头属于该公司的营业场所。

The OECD Model and the UN Model do not give an explanation of a "business place". According to the OECD Model Tax Convention on Income and on Capital, the term "business place" includes the plants, facilities or equipment used by an enterprise to carry on business, whether or not they are also used for other purposes. A business place does not need to be a united whole. For instance, a stall in the shopping mall, a room in the hotel, a facility or

---

① 《OECD税收协定范本注释》第5条第4款。

equipment in the workshop may all constitute a business place. An enterprise must have the ability to control the business place, which has nothing to do with the way the enterprise obtains it and whether it enjoys legal rights. That is to say, the enterprise can obtain a business place by owning or renting or even illegally occupying one. Whether an enterprise has the ability to control a fixed place needs to be judged on the basis of the crux of the matter. For instance, an employee of a company has been working in the office of another company for a long time to ensure the smooth performance of the contract between the two companies. In this case, the business that the employee is engaged in is related to the business of the company. As long as the employee controls the office long enough, the above-mentioned business place can therefore be formed. However, if a road-haulage company uses one of the customer's wharfs for delivery every day, and due to the limited hours of using the wharf, it cannot be considered that the wharf is under the control of the road-haulage company. Therefore the wharf cannot be considered as the business place of the company.

2. 该营业场所具有固定性

The Business Place Needs to be Fixed

营业场所型常设机构要求具有固定性,既包括空间上的固定性,也包括时间上的长久性。空间上的固定性强调构成常设机构的营业场所或设施具有地域上的固定性,和某确定地理位置产生物理联系,如果某场所没有固定在某特定地点之上,那么即使它的存续时间再长,也不符合固定性的要求。营业场所的固定性并不要求其固定于土地之上,位于某一确定场所的设备也可能符合营业场所固定性的要求。《OECD 税收协定范本注释》在解释固定性一词时,强调设备能不能构成营业场所,设备能否移动不重要,重要的是它是不是实际移动了,只要该设备固定于某一特定的地点即满足固定性对于空间的要求。[①] 时间上的长久性是指构成常设机构的营业场所不是出于临时经营活动的需要设置的,而是具有长期经营目的。时间上的长久性并不要求通过这种场所或设施进行的营业活动持续达到一定期限,如果企业设置营业场所或设施的目的是长期经营,即便企业在经营过程中发生特殊情况(如投资失败破产等)而提前结束经营,也不妨碍对常设机构存在的认定。鉴于实践中依靠主观标准判断营业场所时间上的长久性容易产生争执,因此各国在签订的双边税收协定中会对某些特定的营业活动的营业场所规定明确的时间期限。

The permanent establishment in the form of a business place needs to be fixed in space and long in time. The spatial fixity emphasizes that the business place or facilities that constitute the permanent establishment are geographically fixed and physically connected with a certain geographical location. If a place is not fixed on a specific place, it will not meet the requirements of spatial fixity despite its long duration. The spatial fixity of a business place does not require that it be fixed on the land, and the equipment located in a certain place may also meet the requirement. When interpreting the term "fixity", the OECD Model Tax Convention on Income and on Capital emphasizes that what matters is its … instead of its spatial movability regarding whether the equipment can constitute a business place. As long as the equipment is fixed in a

---

[①] 《OECD 税收协定范本注释》第5条第1款。

specific place, it can meet the standard of being spatially fixed. The long duration of time means that the business place which constitutes the permanent establishment is not set up for the need of temporary business operations, but for the purpose of long-term operation. The long duration does not require that the business operations be carried out through such places or facilities should reach a certain time limit. If the purpose of setting up business places or facilities is for long-term business dealings, and even if the enterprise ends its business ahead of time due to special circumstances (such as investment failure and bankruptcy), it will not hinder the identification of the existence of its permanent establishment. In view of the fact that disputes arise easily when the time limit for business places is judged based on subjective criteria in practice, a clear time limit for certain business places will be stipulated in bilateral tax treaties signed by various countries.

如经合发组织范本对于建筑工地或者建筑的时间要求为12个月,联合国范本对此的要求为6个月;对于企业通过雇员或雇佣的其他人员为上述目的提供的劳务,联合国范本对于时间的要求为在任何12个月中连续或累计为期6个月以上,我国与新加坡的税收协定对此的要求为任何12个月内雇员为从事劳务活动在对方停留连续或累计超过183天。[1]我国国家税务总局发布的《税收协定条款解读之三——常设机构》强调在理解固定性时要综合把握常设机构是否有固定的中心、固定的边界,以及是否有商业或地理上的一致性。在理解时要注意以下两点:一是所谓固定的场所不必真的固定于某一点不动,但必须有固定的活动中心场所;二是如果场所不固定,即使营业活动持续时间够长,也不存在构成常设机构的问题,因此地理上的固定性是构成营业场所的前提。对于时间上的要求,判断营业场所的持续性时,既要考虑设立营业场所的目的,也要考虑其实际存续的时间。如果一个营业场所的设立是以长期使用为目的的,即使由于企业活动的特殊性质或其他原因而提前清算,其实际存在的时间很短,仍应视为常设机构;如果一个营业场所的设立是为了短期目的,事实上也如此,那么就不构成常设机构。但如果其实际存在超过了临时性质的期限,则可构成固定场所并可追溯性地构成常设机构。[2]

---

[1] 《中华人民共和国政府和新加坡共和国政府关于对所得避免双重征税和防止偷漏税的协定》及议定书条文解释。在执行中新协定条文解释规定时,应注意:我国对外所签协定有关条款规定与中新协定条款规定内容一致的,中新协定条文解释规定同样适用于其他协定相同条款的解释及执行;中新协定条文解释与此前下发的有关税收协定解释与执行文件不同的,以中新协定条文解释为准。
The Agreement between the government of the people's Republic of China and the government of the Republic of Singapore concerning the avoidance of double taxation and the prevention of tax evasion and the interpretation of the provisions of the protocol. When interpreting the provisions of the Sino-Singapore Agreement, it should be noted that if the relevant provisions of the agreements signed by China with foreign countries are consistent with the provisions of the Sino-Singapore Agreement, the interpretation of the provisions of the Sino-Singapore Agreement are also applicable to the interpretation and implementation of the same provisions in other agreements. If the interpretation of the provisions of the Sino-Singapore Agreement is different from the interpretation of tax agreements and the implementation documents previously issued, the interpretation of the provisions of the Sino-Singapore Agreement shall prevail.

[2] 国家税务总局:《税收协定条款解读之三——常设机构》。

第七章 跨国营业所得征税的协调
CHAPTER VII　Tax Harmonization on Cross-border Business Profit

For example, the OECD Model requires that a construction site or building site last for 12 months, while the UN Model requires 6 months for this. For the services provided by the enterprises' employees or other personnel employed for the above purposes, the UN Model requires a continuous or cumulative period of more than 6 months in any 12 months. The tax treaties between China and Singapore require that employees stay in the other party continuously or cumulatively for more than 183 days in any 12 months. The interpretation of the provisions of tax treaties No. 3: permanent establishment issued by the State Administration of Taxation emphasizes that we should have a comprehensive grasp of whether the permanent establishment has a fixed center, a fixed boundary, and whether it has commercial or geographical consistency. The following two points are worth our attention. Firstly, the so-called fixed place does not really need to be fixed at a certain point, but there must be a fixed activity center; secondly, if the place is not fixed, and even if the business operations last long enough, there is no way of constituting a permanent establishment. Therefore, geographical fixity is the premise of a business place. When it comes to judgment of the duration of a business place, we should consider not only the purpose of setting up the business place, but also the actual duration of its existence. If a business place is established for long-term use, it shall be regarded as a permanent establishment even if it is liquidated in advance due to the special nature of the enterprise activities or other reasons, resulting in short actual existence time. If a business place is established for a short-term purpose, and rightly so, it does not constitute a permanent establishment. However, if its actual existence lasts longer than a temporary period, it can constitute a fixed place and can retroactively constitute a permanent establishment.

3. 企业的营业活动全部或部分通过该营业场所进行

All or Parts of the Business Activities Are Carried out through such Business Place

经合发组织范本和联合国范本规定，营业性的场所才可能构成常设机构，因此这一要件成为场所型常设机构最重要的要件。这一要件要求企业通过固定营业场所或设施实施的活动，应是属于企业经营活动范围内的活动。这种活动并不要求必须是生产性或营利性的行为，只要为该企业服务并构成企业经营活动的组成部分的行为，就符合本要件的要求。但如果企业通过固定营业场所或设施实施的活动，属于某种准备性或辅助性的非营业活动，在企业实现利润中所起作用甚微，则该经营场所一般不被认定构成常设机构。如经合发组织范本第5条4款就规定"常设机构"一语不包括如下几种场所或库存：（1）专为储存、陈列或交付本企业货物或商品的目的而使用的设施；（2）专为储存、陈列或交付目的而保存本企业货物或商品的库存；（3）专为通过另一企业加工目的而保存本企业货物或商品的库存；（4）专为本企业采购货物或商品，或者收集情报的目的而设有的固定营业场所；（5）专为本企业进行任何其他准备性或辅助性活动目的而设有的固定营业场所；（6）专为本款第（1）项至第（5）项活动的结合而设有的固定营业场所，如果这种结合使该固定营业场所的全部活动属于准备性质或辅助性质。

According to the OECD Model and the UN Model, only a business place can constitute a permanent establishment. Therefore, this element has become the most important element of the place type permanent establishment. This element requires that the activities be carried

223

out by the enterprise through fixed business places or facilities be within the scope of business of the enterprise. This kind of activity does not have to be productive or profitable. As long as they serve the enterprise and constitute an integral part of its business operations, they meet the criterion of this element. However, if the activities carried out by an enterprise through a fixed business place or facilities are some kind of reparatory or auxiliary non-business operation and play a very small role in the enterprise's profit realization, such business place is generally not recognized as a permanent establishment. For example, the fourth paragraph of Article 5 of the OECD Model stipulates that the term "permanent establishment" excludes the following types of place or warehouse: (1) the facility designed for the storage, display or delivery of goods or merchandise of the enterprise; (2) the warehouse for keeping the goods or merchandise of the enterprise for storage, display or delivery; (3) the warehouse for keeping the goods and merchandise of the enterprise for processing by another enterprise; (4) the fixed business place specially set up for purchasing goods or commodities or collecting information for the enterprise; (5) the fixed business place specially set up for any other preparatory or auxiliary activities of the enterprise; (6) the fixed business place specially established for the combination of activities mentioned from (1) to (5) of this paragraph, if such combination makes all the activities of such fixed business place of a preparatory or auxiliary nature.

  随着全球化的推进以及信息技术、新兴商业模式的发展，上述排除豁免规则受到了挑战。传统商务背景下"专为储存、陈列或交付本企业货物或商品的目的而使用的设施"不构成常设机构，但在电子商务环境下跨境电商为方便进行交易活动所设置的仓储机构在整个经营活动中的重要性日益凸显，如果把这种仓储机构也列入上述规定中的设施而无法被认定为常设机构，则会导致跨境电子商务中的常设机构认定范围大大缩小。为应对电子商务对常设机构概念的冲击，经合发组织尝试了多种修订策略。根据2017年修订的经合发组织范本注释，[①]涉及储存、陈列或交付货物或商品的目的而使用的设施，是否具有辅助性或准备性将根据企业整体活动在内的因素确定。如果一个企业在缔约国另一方从事在线货物销售，拥有一个非常大的仓库，仓库大量雇员工作的主要目的是储存和交付在线销售企业拥有的货物，则该仓库不适用第4款的规定，因为仓库所进行的储存和交付活动意味着企业投入了重要的资产和大量人员，这构成了企业销售和分销活动的重要部分，因此应排除其准备性质或辅助性质。

  With the advancement of globalization and the development of information technology and emerging business models, the above exclusion rules have been challenged. In the context of traditional business, "facilities used exclusively for the purpose of storing, displaying or delivering the goods or commodities of the enterprise" do not constitute a permanent establishment. However, in the environment of e-commerce, a warehouse set up for the convenience of the trade is becoming increasingly important in the whole business activities. If such a warehouse is included in the above-mentioned facilities but cannot be recognized as a permanent establishment, the scope of the identification of permanent establishment in

---

① 2017年经合发组织范本第5条注释的第62段。

cross-border e-commerce will be greatly reduced. In response to the impact of e-commerce on the concept of permanent establishment, OECD has tried a variety of revisions. According to the OECD Model note revised in 2017, whether the facilities used for storing, displaying or delivering the goods or commodities are of a preparatory or auxiliary character will be determined based on the overall activities of the enterprise. If an enterprise is engaged in the online sale of goods in the other contracting state and has a very large warehouse with a large number of employees whose main purpose is to store and deliver the goods for online sales, the provisions of the above-mentioned fourth paragraph shall not apply to such warehouse, because the storage and delivery activities carried out by the warehouse mean that the enterprise has invested important assets and a large number of personnel, which constitutes an important part of sales and distribution, hence excluding its preparatory or auxiliary character.

越来越多的跨国公司通过拆分常设机构进行逃税、避税从而侵蚀来源国税基,如单一企业通过将经济紧密相联的经营活动在别国进行拆分,或者关联企业间将商业活动进行重组以对常设机构进行划分,最终减少在别国存在的常设机构。为了应对常设机构遭受人为拆分从而逃、避税的情况,经合发组织范本和联合国范本都规定了反拆分条款,不认可紧密关联方之间的拆分以及将一项活动从常设机构中拆分出来的行为属于准备性质或辅助性质。

An increasing number of cross-border companies have split up their permanent establishments for tax evasion and avoidance, leading to base erosion of source countries. For instance, the business activities that are closely related to the economy can be split up by a single enterprise in other countries, or commercial activities can be reorganized among the affiliated enterprises, either of which is to divide the permanent establishment and reduce the existence of permanent establishments in other countries. In order to deal with the tax evasion and avoidance caused by artificial splitting of a permanent establishment, both the OECD Model and the United Nations Model have made anti-split provisions, which do not recognize the separation between closely related parties and the separation of an activity from the permanent establishment as preparatory or auxiliary.

我国国家税务总局对"准备性或辅助性"的判断方法作出了明确规定:一是看固定基地或场所的业务性质是否与总机构一致;二是看固定基地或场所是否仅为总机构服务,还是与他人有业务往来;三是看固定基地或场所的业务是否构成总机构业务的重要组成部分。如果固定基地或场所不仅为总机构服务,而且与其他机构有业务往来,或固定场所的业务性质与总机构的业务性质一致,且其业务为总机构业务的重要组成部分,则不能认为该固定场所的活动是准备性或辅助性的。①

The State Administration of Taxation of China has made clear provisions on the judgment of the "preparatory or auxiliary" character. Firstly, is the business nature of the fixed place or site consistent with that of the head office? Secondly, does the fixed base or site serve the head office only, or does it have business with others? Thirdly, is the business of the fixed place or site an

---

① 《国家税务总局关于税收协定常设机构认定等有关问题的通知》(国税发[2006]35号)。

important part of the head office's business? If not only does the fixed place or site serve the head office, but also has business contacts with other organizations, or its business nature is consistent with that of the head office, and its business is an important part of the head office's business, the activities of the fixed place cannot be considered as preparatory or auxiliary.

固定营业场所或设施必须同时具备上述三个要件，才能构成协定意义上的常设机构。经合发组织范本和联合国范本对可能构成常设机构的营业场所和设施情形作了具体列举：(1) 管理场所；(2) 分支机构；(3) 办事处；(4) 工厂；(5) 车间；(6) 矿场、油井或气井、采石场或者任何其他开采自然资源的场所。但范本的上述列举并没有穷尽所有可能构成常设机构的营业场所或设施，未列举的其他营业场所或设施也可能构成常设机构。

A fixed business place or facility must meet all of the above three elements to constitute a permanent establishment stipulated in an agreement. The OECD Model and the United Nations Model list the business places and facilities that may constitute permanent establishments as follows: (1) management area; (2) branches; (3) offices; (4) plants; (5) workshops; (6) mines, oil or gas wells, quarries or any other places where natural resources are mined. However, it should be noted that the above list does not cover all the places or facilities that may constitute permanent establishments, and those not listed may also constitute qualified permanent establishments.

（二）代理型常设机构
Agency Permanent Establishment

一个企业即使不存在通过固定营业场所或设施进行营业的情形，如果通过特定的营业代理人从事经营活动，也可能基于人的因素而被认定为设有常设机构。按照营业代理人是否独立于被代理企业，代理人可分为独立地位代理人和非独立地位代理人两种，代理型常设机构所指的代理人主要是非独立地位代理人。

Even if an enterprise does not engage in business activities through fixed places or facilities but through a specific business agent, it may also be recognized as having a permanent establishment based on the human factor. On the basis on whether or not the business agent is independent of the represented enterprise, the agent can be divided into independent one and non-independent one. As the agency permanent establishment, the agent is mainly non-independent.

1. 非独立地位代理人常设机构

Non-independent Agent as a Permanent Establishment

所谓非独立地位代理人常设机构，是指一个非独立代理人代表缔约国另一方的企业在缔约国一方活动，有权并经常行使这种权利以企业的名义签订合同，对于这个人为企业进行的任何活动，应认为该企业在该国设有常设机构。[①]但企业可以通过境外授权、修改合同条款但不改变合同实质成立的方式，避免在法律形式上"签署合同"，从而规避代理型常设机构的构成。为此，经合发组织范本和联合国范本都对其原有规定作了修订，扩大了非独立地位代理人常设机构的范围。根据经合发组织范本第5条第5款的规定，非独立地位代理人构

---

① 《OECD税收协定范本》第5条第5款，《UN税收协定范本》第5条第5款。

第七章　跨国营业所得征税的协调
CHAPTER VII　Tax Harmonization on Cross-border Business Profit

成常设机构要具备如下两个条件：(1)在缔约国另一方代表企业从事具有营业性质的活动，而不是范本第5条第4款范围内的准备性质或辅助性质活动；(2)有权以企业的名义，或者涉及该企业拥有或有权使用的财产的所有权的转让或使用权的授予，抑或涉及该企业所提供的服务，经常性签订合同或经常性在合同签订中起到主要作用(企业不会对订立的合同进行实质性修改)。联合国范本第5条第5款较经合发组织范本进一步扩大了非独立地位代理人构成常设机构的范围，把没有签订合同的权利，但经常在缔约国另一方保存货物或商品的库存，并且代表企业经常从该库存中交付货物或商品的情形也认定为常设机构。此外，联合国范本还把缔约国一方的保险企业除再保险外，在缔约国另一方领土内收取保险费或者接受保险业务，也视为在该缔约国另一方设有常设机构。

The so-called permanent establishment through a non-independent agent refers to that a non-independent agent acts in one contracting state on behalf of an enterprise of the other contracting state. He or she has and often exercises the right to conclude contracts in the name of the enterprise. Considering the activities carried out by this person for the enterprise, it is acknowledged that the enterprise has a permanent establishment in that country. However, the enterprise can avoid "signing the contract" in the legal form by authorizing overseas and modifying certain contract terms without changing the actual formation of the contract with the purpose of evading the constitution of an agency permanent establishment. Therefore both the OECD Model and the UN Model have revised their original provisions and expanded the scope of non-independent agency-type permanent establishment. According to Article 5(5) of the OECD Model, the following two conditions should be met for the establishment of a permanent establishment through a non-independent agent: (1) he or she is engaged in business activities on behalf of the enterprise in the other contracting state, rather than those preparatory or auxiliary activities listed in Article 5(4) of the model; (2) he or she habitually concludes contracts, or habitually plays the principal role leading to the conclusion of contracts in the name of the enterprise, or for the transfer of the ownership of, or the granting of the right to use, property owned by that enterprise or that the enterprise has the right to use, or for the provision of services by that enterprise. (The concluded contracts are without material modification by the enterprise.) Compared with the OECD Model, Article 5(5) of the UN Model further expands the scope of non-independent agents as permanent establishments. A permanent establishment can be identified through a person, though not habitually concludes contracts, habitually maintains in the other contracting state a stock of goods or merchandise from which that person regularly delivers goods or merchandise on behalf of the enterprise. Besides, in the UN Model an insurance enterprise of a contracting state shall, except in regard to re-insurance, be deemed to have a permanent establishment in the other contracting state if it collects premiums in the territory of that other state or insures risks situated therein through a person.

非独立代理人可以是个人、公司、办事处或其他任何形式，代理活动不必经委托人正式授权，非独立代理人的确定也不受常设机构营业场所这一条件的影响。对于"经常"一词要结合具体情况判断，具体考虑合同性质、交易性质以及代理人代理活动的频率等。"签订"不仅包括签署合同行为,也包括代理人为委托人的委托活动进行的合同谈判、协商、商定合同条文等情形。"合同"是指与委托人经营活动相关的业务合同。代理人如果与委托人签订的企业内部合同,例如以企业名义签订的劳务合同等,则不能仅凭此认定代理人构成企业的常设机构。

The non-independent agent can be an individual, a company, an office or any other form. The agency activities do not need to be formally authorized by the entruster, and the determination of the non-independent agent is not affected by the business place of the permanent establishment. The judgment of the word "habitually" should be based on specific situations, considering the nature of the contract and of the transaction and the frequency of agency activities. The word "conclude" includes not only the signing of the contract, but also the entrusted activities conducted by the agent such as negotiation of the contract and discussion of contract provisions. "Contract" refers to the business contract related to the business activities of the entruster. Yet the agent may conclude an internal contract with the entruster such as the labor contract signed in the name of the enterprise, only on the basis of which the agent cannot be regarded as the permanent establishment of the enterprise.

2. 独立地位代理人常设机构

Independent Agent as a Permanent Establishment

独立地位代理人常设机构是指在法律上和经济上都独立于其所代理企业的代理人,包括经纪人、一般佣金代理人。按照经合发组织范本和联合国范本的规定,缔约国一方企业仅通过经纪人、一般佣金代理人或其他独立地位代理人在缔约国另一方营业,而这类独立地位代理人是按照常规进行业务经营的,不应认为在另一方设有常设机构。因此,独立地位代理人构成常设机构的条件是在代理委托企业进行活动时,未按照营业常规进行活动。

The permanent establishment through an independent agent refers to an agent who is legally and economically independent of the entrusted enterprise, like a broker and a general commission agent. According to the OECD Model and the United Nations Model, an enterprise of a contracting state only operates in the other contracting state through brokers, general commission agents or other independent agents. They conduct business in accordance with the usual practice and the enterprise shall not be deemed to have a permanent establishment in the other country. Therefore an independent agent can constitute a permanent establishment only when he or she does not carry out business activities in accordance with the usual practice on behalf of the entrusted enterprise.

3. 独立地位代理人与非独立代理人的不同

The Difference between Independent and Non-independent Agents

由于独立地位代理人和非独立代理人构成常设机构的条件不同,区分该代理人是独立地位代理人还是非独立地位代理人,就成为判断代理型常设机构是否存在的前提。独立地位代理人和非独立代理人是国际税法上对营业代理人的分类,其概念和范围并不完全对应民商法意义上的直接代理人和间接代理人。按照经合发组织范本和联合国范本的注释,两者的区别在于代理人和委托人在经济上和法律上的密切联系程度,如果代理人在经济上和

第七章 跨国营业所得征税的协调
CHAPTER VII　Tax Harmonization on Cross-border Business Profit

法律上均独立于被代理企业,则构成独立地位代理人,反之,如果代理人在经济上和法律上依附于被代理企业,则构成非独立地位代理人。

Because of the different conditions for independent and non-independent agents to constitute a permanent establishment, distinguishing them becomes the premise to judge whether the enterprise is deemed to have a permanent establishment. Independent and non-independent agents are the classification of business agents in international tax law. The concept and scope of them are not completely corresponding to the direct and indirect agents in the civil and commercial laws. According to the notes of the OECD Model and the UN Model, the difference between the two lies in the close economic and legal ties between the agent and the entruster. If the agent is economically and legally independent of the entrusted enterprise, he or she is deemed as an independent agent; on the contrary, if the agent is attached to the entrusted enterprise economically and legally, he or she is a non-independent agent.

根据两个范本的注释,在判定代理人是否具有独立地位时一般考虑如下因素:

According to the notes of the two models, the following factors are generally considered in determining whether the agent is independent or not:

首先是代理人代理行为的自由度,如果代理人的代理行为几乎或全面受制于委托人的控制,无法或很难自由决定业务进行方式,那么代理人一般不具有独立代理地位。例如,代理人的销售方式、销售价格等由委托人决定。

The first factor is the agent's freedom he or she exercises in the agency behavior. If the agent's agency behavior is almost or completely controlled by the entruster, and he or she is unable to freely determine the way of business, then the agent is generally not independent. For example, the sales method and the price of goods are decided by the entruster.

其次,如若代理人进行代理活动的风险由委托人承担,那么代理人一般不具有独立代理地位。例如,代理人和第三方客户签订的合同,约定违约责任由委托人承担,那么代理人一般不具有独立代理地位。

The second factor is that if the risk of the agent's agency activities is borne by the entruster, then the agent is generally not deemed to be independent. For example, if the contract signed between the agent and the third-party customer stipulates that the liability for breach of contract shall be borne by the entruster, then the agent is generally not deemed to be independent.

再次,代理人的代理业务若几乎或全部是由委托人委托,那么代理人可能没有独立代理地位。例如,某缔约国企业通过固定营业场所销售另一缔约国企业的商品,除此之外,没有其他代理业务,一般而言,该代理企业构成另一缔约国企业的常设机构。

The third factor is that if the agent's business is almost or completely entrusted by the entruster, then the agent may not be independent. For example, an enterprise of a contracting state sells goods of an enterprise of the other contracting state through a fixed place of business, and besides this there is no other agency business. In general, the agency constitutes a permanent establishment of the enterprise in the other contracting state.

最后,代理人依靠委托人的专业知识进行代理活动,则代理人一般构成非独立代理人。例如,代理人的设备安装、调试、售后工作是由委托人派遣的员工完成的,这种情况下代理人一般构成非独立代理人。①

The last factor is that if an agent relies on the entruster's professional knowledge to carry out agency activities, the agent is generally deemed to be non-independent. For example, the staff dispatched by the entruster completes the equipment installation, commissioning test and after-sales work of the agent. In this case, the agent is generally deemed to be non-independent.

（二）常设机构的范围
Scope of Permanent Establishment

除了上述一般类型的常设机构以外，税收协定还规定了几种特殊的常设机构形式，分别是工程型常设机构、劳务型常设机构等。

In addition to the above-mentioned general types of permanent establishment, tax treaties also provide for several special forms of permanent establishment, namely, engineering type permanent establishment, service permanent establishment, etc.

1. 工程型常设机构

Engineering Type Permanent Establishment

根据经合发组织范本和联合国范本的规定，缔约国一方企业在缔约国另一方境内从事承包建筑、安装和装配工程活动，可以构成常设机构。至于建筑、安装和装配工程活动延续多长时间才能构成常设机构，两个范本规定不同。经合发组织范本主张，这类工程活动须延续12个月以上才构成，联合国范本则规定延续6个月以上即构成。各国在签订的双边税收协定中对此时间规定也不尽相同，短的3个月，长的长达24个月。中国与大多数国家所签订的双边税收协定中采用6个月以上的时间标准。关于如何计算上述时间，根据经合发组织范本的有关注释，建筑、安装和装配工程活动存在的起止时间，应从承包商在工程所在国一方开始工作（包括任何准备工作）之日起计算，直至工程作业完工或被永久性放弃之日为止。工程活动涉及两个以上纳税年度的，可以跨年度计算。关于建筑、安装和装配工程活动是否包括与工程有关的监督管理活动，经合发组织范本倾向于主张将单纯的监管管理活动排除，而联合国范本则明确认为应包括在建筑、安装和装配工程活动范围内，如果这种监督管理活动持续6个月以上则构成常设机构。中国对外签订的双边税收协定一般都明确建筑、安装和装配工程活动包括与工程有关的监督管理活动。

According to the provisions of the OECD Model and the UN Model, enterprises of one contracting state may form a permanent establishment if they engage in contract construction, installation and assembly projects in the territory of the other contracting state. As for the duration of these engineering activities to form a permanent establishment, the provisions of the two models are different. According to the OECD Model, such engineering activities should last for more than 12 months, while the UN Model requires that such activities should continue for more than 6 months. In the bilateral tax treaties signed by various countries, there are different

---

① 若要构成劳务型常设机构，还要满足协定对劳务型常设机构时间的要求。

provisions on such duration. The short period is 3 months, and the long period is 24 months. The bilateral tax treaties signed between China and most other countries adopt a minimum of 6-month duration. With regard to the calculation of the above-mentioned duration, the relevant notes of the OECD Model stipulate that the starting and ending time of the construction, installation and assembly shall be calculated from the date when the contractor starts work (including any preparatory work) in the country, and ends on the date when the work is completed or permanently abandoned. If an engineering project involves more than two tax years, it may be calculated across the years. With regard to whether construction, installation and assembly include project related supervision and management, the OECD Model tends to advocate the exclusion of simple regulatory activities, while the United Nations Model clearly confirms that it should be included in the scope of such engineering activities. If such supervision and management last for more than six months, they will constitute a permanent establishment. The bilateral tax treaties signed by China generally specify construction, installation and assembly include the project related supervision and management.

2. 劳务型常设机构

Service Permanent Establishment

关于提供劳务或咨询服务是否构成常设机构,联合国范本主张缔约国一方企业在另一方从事此类劳务服务活动,在任何12个月中连续或累计超过6个月的,可视为在另一方构成常设机构。经合发组织范本对此未作明确规定。中国对外签订的双边税收协定在这个问题上采用了联合国范本的主张,规定缔约国一方企业通过雇员或雇佣的其他人员,在缔约国另一方为同一项目或相关联的项目提供劳务,包括咨询服务,在任何12个月中连续累计超过6个月的,应认为在缔约国另一方设有常设机构。

As to whether the provision of labor or consulting services constitutes a permanent establishment, the United Nations Model advocates that an enterprise of one contracting state engaged in such labor service activities in the other contracting state for more than six consecutive months in any 12 months can be regarded as constituting a permanent establishment in that state. The OECD Model does not specify this. The bilateral tax treaties signed by China have adopted the United Nations Model on this issue. It is stipulated that enterprises of one contracting state provide labor services, including consulting services, for the same project or related projects in the other contracting state through their own employees or other personnel employed by them. If the accumulative total in any 12 months exceeds 6 months, it shall be deemed that there is a permanent establishment in the other contracting state structure. A permanent establishment in the other contracting state shall be deemed to exist if the services have accumulated for more than six consecutive months in any 12-month period.

3. 有形资产租赁和无形资产许可使用型常设机构

Use-type Permanent Establishment: Leasing of Tangible Assets and Licensing of Intangible Assets

缔约国一方企业通过其设在缔约国另一方企业的某种固定营业场所,将其工业、商业或科学设备、建筑物等有形资产，以及专利、商标和专有技术等无形资产出租或许可给第三方使用，这种出租或许可交易方式一般都会使该固定营业场所构成税收协定意义上的常设机构，从而使交易产生的租金或许可交易费收入都被认定为属于该常设机构的营业所得范围，适用税收协定中有关营业所得的条款，常设机构所在地的缔约国可据此征税。但如果缔约国一方企业并未为此租赁许可交易在缔约国另一方设立固定营业场所并通过该场所进行交易，则这种情形下出租或转让使用的有形资产和无形资产本身并不构成出租人或许可方在缔约国另一方境内的常设机构。

An enterprise of one contracting state leases or licenses its industrial, commercial or scientific equipment, buildings and other tangible assets as well as intangible assets such as patents, trademarks and technical know-how to a third party through a certain fixed place of business set up in the enterprise of the other contracting state. Such leasing or licensing transaction generally makes the fixed business place a permanent establishment in the tax treaties, so that the rental fee or license transaction fee is identified as belonging to the scope of the business income of the permanent establishment. The provisions concerning business income in the tax treaty shall be applied, and the contracting state where the permanent establishment is located may tax accordingly. However, if an enterprise of a contracting state does not have a fixed place of business in the other contracting state for such a leasing license and conduct business transactions through such place, the tangible and intangible assets leased or transferred for use in such a case do not constitute a permanent establishment of the lessor or the licensor in the territory of the other contracting state.

4. 近海自然资源勘探开发型常设机构

Permanent Establishment by Exploring and Developing Offshore Natural Resources

关于缔约国一方企业在缔约国另一方的领海或领海以外但拥有勘探开发自然资源主权权利的一定海域从事海上自然资源的勘探开发活动是否构成常设机构，多数国家在税收协定中专门规定，缔约国一方企业在缔约国另一方为勘探开发自然资源目的使用的设施、装置、钻井机或其他设备，如果使用期超过一定的时限，则构成该企业在缔约国另一方的常设机构。但也有少数国家间签订的税收协定不要求期限，只要缔约国一方企业在缔约国另一方设有上述设备即构成常设机构。

Most countries have specifically stipulated in their tax treaties concerning whether the exploration and development of marine natural resources, by an enterprise of one contracting state in the territorial waters and beyond where the enterprise has the sovereign right to explore and develop natural resources, constitutes a permanent establishment. Facilities, devices, drilling machines or other equipment used by an enterprise of one contracting state for exploring and developing natural resources in the other contracting state shall constitute a permanent establishment of the enterprise in the other contracting state if the duration of using them exceeds a certain period of time. However, there are also a few tax treaties signed between countries that do not require such a time limit. As long as an enterprise of one contracting state has the above-mentioned equipment in the other contracting state, it constitutes a permanent establishment.

第三节　常设机构的利润归属
Section 3　Attribution of the Profits of Permanent Establishment

 常设机构利润归属原则

Attribution of the Profits of Permanent Establishment

在确定了缔约国一方企业的经营活动在缔约国另一方设有常设机构的情况下，确认该企业来源于缔约国另一方境内的各种所得中哪些可归属于常设机构利润范围，这个问题直接关系到缔约双方的税收权益。

On the condition that an enterprise of one contracting state has a permanent establishment in the other contracting state through its business activities, it is directly related to the tax rights and interests of both contracting parties to determine which of the various income of the enterprise deriving from the territory of the other contracting state can be attributed to the profit scope of the permanent establishment.

对于常设机构利润范围问题，主要有实际联系原则和引力原则两种观点。采用实际联系原则观点的国家认为，缔约国一方企业来源于缔约国另一方境内的各种收入中，只有那些通过常设机构的活动产生的营业所得和与常设机构有实际联系的其他各项所得（如股息、利息、特许权使用费和财产收益），才能归属于常设机构的利润范围并由常设机构所在地国的缔约另一方优先征税。未通过常设机构的经营活动实现的收益和与常设机构没有实际联系的各种所得，应排除在常设机构的利润范围之外，适用税收协定相应的其他所得课税条款处理。如缔约国一方居民来源于缔约国另一方的某项股息所得，如果被认定为与该居民在缔约国另一方境内的某个常设机构有实际联系，则股息所得应纳入该常设机构的利润范围，如果被认定无实际联系，则缔约国另一方对这笔股息所得只能按照税收协定中规定的限制税率征收预提税。经合发组织范本建议采用实际联系原则。中国和绝大多数国家在双边税收协定中采用了该原则。我国认为，"归属于该常设机构的利润"不仅包括该常设机构取得的来源于其所在国家的利润，还包括其在该国境外取得的与其有实际联系的各类所得，包括股息、利息和特许权使用费等。

As for the profit scope of the permanent establishment, there are mainly two types: the effective connection principle and the force attraction principle. Countries adopting the effective connection principle hold that of all kinds of income deriving from the territory of the other contracting state, only the business income generated through the activities of the permanent establishment and other income (such as dividends, interest, royalties and property income) which are effectively connected with the permanent establishment can be attributed to the profit scope of the permanent establishment, and by the other contracting state where the permanent establishment is located shall have the priority in collecting tax. The income not deriving from the business activities of the permanent establishment and those kinds of income without effective connection with the permanent establishment shall be excluded from the profit scope of the permanent establishment, and shall be dealt with in accordance with other income tax provisions stipulated in the tax treaty. If the income of a resident in a contracting state deriving from a dividend in the other contracting state is deemed to have an effective connection with a permanent establishment of that resident in the other contracting state, the dividend income shall be included in the profits of that permanent establishment. If it is found that there is no effective connection, the other contracting state can only impose withholding tax on the dividend income at a restricted tax rate specified in the tax treaty. The OECD Model suggests that the Principle of Effective Connection should be adopted. China and most countries have adopted this principle in bilateral tax treaties. It is generally acknowledged in China that "profits attributable to the permanent establishment" includes not only the profits deriving from the country where the permanent establishment is located, but also all kinds of income effectively connected to the permanent establishment obtained outside the country, including dividends, interest and royalties.

引力原则分为一般引力原则和有限引力原则。按照一般引力原则，只要缔约国一方企业在缔约国另一方境内构成常设机构存在，则该企业来源于缔约国另一方的全部营业所得，不论是通过该常设机构所取得，还是通过其他活动实现的，都应并入常设机构利润范围，由缔约国另一方征税。有限引力原则限制常设机构所在国可征税的利润范围，只把缔约国一方企业在缔约国另一方销售与通过常设机构销售的货物或商品相同或类似的货物或商品的利润，以及在缔约国另一方进行与通过与常设机构进行的业务相同或类似的营业活动所取得的收入纳入可归属于常设机构的利润范围。一般引力原则注重维护来源地国的税收权益，应用该原则会增加跨国纳税人的申报成本、税收机关的征管难度，不适当地干预纳税人选择商业组织和交易形式自由，因此现代国家的双边税收协定实践中很少采用一般引力原则。联合国范本考虑到维护来源地国一方的税收权益，采用了有限引力原则。由于具有一定合理性，目前一些国家的双边税收协定中采用了该原则。

The force of attraction principle is divided into the general force attraction principle and the restricted force attraction principle. According to the general force attraction principle, as long as an enterprise of one contracting state is deemed to have a permanent establishment in the territory of the other contracting state, all business income deriving from the other contracting state, be it obtained through the permanent establishment or realized through other activities, shall be incorporated into the profit scope of the permanent establishment and be taxed by the other contracting state. The restricted force attraction principle limits the scope of profits that can be taxed by the state where the permanent establishment is located. Such principle specifies the scope of profits of the permanent establishment shall only include the profits from the sales of goods or commodities of an enterprise in a contracting state that are identical or similar to those sold through a permanent establishment in the other contracting state, and the income obtained from the business activities identical or similar to those carried out through a permanent establishment in the other contracting state. The general force attraction principle focuses on safeguarding the tax rights and interests of the source country. The application of such principle will increase the declaration cost of multinational taxpayers and the difficulty of tax collection and management of tax authorities, and will improperly interfere with the freedom of taxpayers to choose commercial organizations and transaction forms. Therefore, the general force attraction principle is rarely used in the practice of bilateral tax treaties among modern countries. The UN Model takes into account the protection of the tax rights and interests of the source country and adopts the restricted force attraction principle. Due to its rationality, some countries have adopted such principle in their bilateral tax treaties.

二、实际联系原则的认定
Identification of Effective Connection Principle

如果税收协定采用了实际联系原则,则如何识别缔约国一方企业来源于缔约国另一方境内的某项具体所得或收益,与该企业在另一方境内的某个常设机构是否存在实际联系就很重要。

If the effective connection principle is adopted in tax treaties, it is of vital importance to identify whether a specific income of an enterprise in a contracting state that derives from the other contracting state has an effective connection with the permanent establishment of the enterprise set up in the territory of the other contracting state.

由于经合发组织范本和联合国范本有关条款本身没有对"实际联系"一语作出具体解释规定,两个范本的注释对该问题也缺乏具体的说明,因此根据何种标准认定"实际联系"实际上取决于缔约国国内税法的规定或缔约国法院和税务机关的解释。① 我国企业所得税法在确定非居民企业在中国境内设立"机构、场所"的所得范围时采用实际联系原则。根据《企业所得税法》第3条的规定,非居民企业在中国境内设立机构、场所的,应当就其所设机构、场所取得的来源于中国境内的所得,以及发生在中国境外但与其所设机构、场所有实际联系的所得,缴纳企业所得税。非居民企业在中国境内未设立机构、场所的,或者虽设立机构、场所但取得的所得与其所设机构、场所没有实际联系的,应当就其来源于中国境内的所得缴纳企业所得税。但如何认定"实际联系",有待国家税务部门的解释。

Since the relevant provisions of the OECD Model and the United Nations Model do not provide a specific interpretation of the term "effective connection", and the notes of the two models also lack specific explanations on this issue, the criteria for determining the term depend on the provisions of the domestic tax law of the contracting states or the interpretation of the courts and tax authorities of the contracting states. China's law of enterprise income tax adopts the principle of effective connection when determining the income scope of the "institutions and business places" set up by non-resident enterprises in China. According to the provisions

---

① 廖益新主编:《国际税法学》,北京大学出版社2001年版,第203页。

of Article 3 of the law of enterprise income tax, if a non-resident enterprise establishes an organization or a business place within the territory of China, it shall pay enterprise income tax on the income that derives from the institution or business place within the territory of China as well as on the income that derives outside China but is effectively connected with its establishment. If a non-resident enterprise does not set up an institution or a business place within the territory of China, or if it establishes one but the income it obtains has no effective connection with the institution or business place it has established, it shall pay enterprise income tax on its income originating in China. However, how to identify the "effective connection" remains to be explained by the state tax department.

第四节 常设机构应税所得额的确定
Section 4 Determination of the Taxable Incomes of Permanent Establishment

明确了常设机构的利润范围后,就需要计算归属于常设机构的利润或收益的应税所得额。这个问题原则上依照缔约国国内所得税法的相关规定计算核定,但由于该问题涉及缔约国双方的税收权益分配,税收协定往往会就该问题作出原则性规定。

After defining the profit scope of the permanent establishment, it is necessary to calculate the taxable amount of incomes or profits that are attributable to the permanent establishment. In principle, the taxable amount of incomes shall be calculated and approved in accordance with the relevant provisions of the domestic income tax law of the contracting states. However, since the issue involves the distinction of tax rights and interests between the contracting states, some principled stipulation regarding this issue will be made in tax treaties.

一、独立企业原则
The Principle of Independent Enterprise

独立企业原则,也称为公平交易原则或独立竞争原则,①该原则要求在确定常设机构的应税所得额时,应将常设机构视作一个独立于其总机构的纳税实体,按照独立企业进行盈亏计算。

The principle of independent enterprise is also known as the fair trade principle or the independent competition principle. The principle requires that in determining the taxable amount of incomes of a permanent establishment, the permanent establishment should be regarded as

---

① 廖益新主编:《国际税法学》,北京大学出版社2001年版,第205页。

a tax entity independent of its head office, and the profit and loss should be calculated as an independent enterprise.

由于常设机构不是独立的法人,所以其经营活动和利润分配都由总机构控制和决定。但为了落实常设机构原则,便利收入来源地国行使税收管辖权,必然要求将常设机构视为独立的纳税实体。由此,常设机构像一个独立的纳税实体一样要将经营活动所取得的一切利润进行归并,所发生的费用进行扣除。常设机构的经营活动不仅包括常设机构与独立企业的营业往来,也包括与总机构的营业往来,与所属企业的其他常设机构、关联公司及其所属的常设机构的营业往来。

Since the permanent establishment is not an independent legal person, its business activities and profit distribution are controlled and decided by the head office. However, in order to implement the principle of permanent establishment and facilitate the tax jurisdiction of the source country, it is necessary to regard the permanent establishment as an independent tax entity. As a result, a permanent establishment, like an independent taxable entity, should merge all profits from its business activities and deduct the expenses incurred. The business activities of a permanent establishment include not only the business contacts between the permanent establishment and independent enterprises, but also with the head office, other permanent establishments of the enterprise, affiliated companies and their permanent establishments.

(二) 费用扣除和合理分摊原则
Principle of Expense Deduction and the Reasonable Apportionment

"费用扣除和合理分摊原则"是经合发组织范本和联合国范本共同采用的在计算利润时扣除成本的原则。尽管将常设机构视为独立纳税实体,但客观上常设机构是企业的一个部分,因此在处理常设机构费用扣除时,不仅要考虑一般损益原则,还需要特别考虑与总机构相关联的有关费用。对于常设机构的费用扣除和成本分摊,两个范本的规定不尽相同。联合国范本第7条第3款规定,在确定常设机构利润时应允许扣除与常设机构经营活动相关的各种费用,包括行政和一般管理费用,不论这些费用是发生在常设机构所在国还是其他地方。根据该规定,常设机构所在国的税务机关在确定常设机构的应税所得额时,首先应当允许常设机构从其收入总额中扣除其在经营活动过程中所发生的各项成本、费用和损失,以其净利润额作为课税基数。具体允许列支扣除的成本、费用和损失项目范围,原则上按照缔约国国内税法的规定执行。其次,常设机构所在国的税务机关应当允许常设机构合理分担其总机构的部分管理费用,如根据常设机构的营业额(或毛利润)与整个企业的营业额(或毛利润)的比率来考虑管理费用分摊。但这些费用必须是与常设机构的生产、经营活动有关并实际发生的费用。①最后,明确禁止某些费用的扣除,如常设机构向企业总机构因使用其专利或其他权利而支付的特许权使用费,常设机构为其总机构提供辅助性服务而发生的费用,常设机构因使用企业总机构(银行企业除外)提供的贷款而

---

① 联合国范本第7条注释第18段。

支付的利息。

The principle of expense deduction and reasonable apportionment is the principle of deducting costs in calculating profits adopted by the OECD Model and UN Model. Although a permanent establishment is regarded as an independent taxable entity, it is objectively a part of an enterprise. Therefore, when dealing with the deduction of expenses of a permanent establishment, we should not only consider the general profit and loss principle, but also pay special attention to the relevant expenses associated with the head office. There are different provisions in the two models for the deduction of expenses and the allocation of costs of a permanent establishment. Article 7, Paragraph 3, of the United Nations Model provides that in determining the profits of a permanent establishment, deductions shall be allowed for all expenses related to the operation of the permanent establishment, including administrative and general management expenses, either incurred in the country in which the permanent establishment is located or elsewhere. According to this provision, when determining the taxable amount of incomes of a permanent establishment, the tax authorities of the country where the permanent establishment is located shall, first of all, allow the permanent establishment to deduct all costs, expenses and losses incurred in the course of business activities from its total income, and take its net profit as the tax base. The specific scope of costs, expenses and losses allowed to be deducted shall be implemented in principle in accordance with the provisions of the domestic tax law of the contracting state. Secondly, the tax authorities of the country where the permanent establishment is located shall allow the permanent establishment to reasonably share part of the administrative expenses of its head office. For example, the apportionment of administrative expenses shall be considered according to the ratio of the turnover (or gross profit) of the permanent establishment to that of the whole enterprise. However, these expenses must be related to and effectively connected with the production and business activities of the permanent establishment. Finally, the deduction of certain expenses is explicitly prohibited, such as the royalties paid by the permanent establishment to the head office of the enterprise for the use of its patent or other rights, the expenses arising from the auxiliary services provided by the permanent establishment for its head office, and the interest paid by the permanent establishment for the use of the loans provided by the head office of the enterprise (except banking enterprises).

经合发组织范本在2010年修订时删除了费用扣除的规定，但这不影响常设机构的费用扣除。根据经合发组织范本注释的规定，允许常设机构从其收入总额中扣除所发生的一切有关费用，不论发生在何处。如何扣除，将视交易发生的具体情况而定，或扣除全部或部分费用，或在常设机构与企业另一部分进行交易时扣除公平交易费用。

When the OECD Model was revised in 2010, the provision of expense deduction was deleted, but this does not affect the expense deduction of permanent establishment. According to the OECD Model notes, a permanent establishment is allowed to deduct from its total income all relevant expenses regardless of where they incur. How to deduct the expenses is based on the specific circumstances of the transaction. All or part of the expenses will be deducted, or the fair trading expenses will be deducted when the permanent establishment conducts transactions with another part of the enterprise.

三、常设机构应税所得额的确定方法
Approaches of Determining the Taxable Amount of Incomes of Permanent Establishment

在确定了常设机构利润归属中的独立企业原则和费用扣除和合理分摊原则后,采用何种具体方法计算常设机构的利润就很重要。从经合发组织范本和联合国范本来看,计算方法主要有如下几种。

After determining the principle of independent enterprise and the principle of expense deduction and reasonable apportionment, it is very important to adopt specific approaches to calculate the profits of a permanent establishment. On the basis of the OECD Model and the UN Model, there are mainly the following calculation approaches.

(一)独立企业核算方法
Independent Enterprise Accounting Approach

所谓独立企业核算方法,是指根据公平交易原则把常设机构看作一个独立纳税实体时,用反映在常设机构会计账簿上的收入来计算其应税所得的一种方法。为了了解分支机构的盈利情况,注重经营管理的企业通常都要求分支机构建账。如果常设机构建立账簿,税务机关往往以账簿为基础来确认常设机构的利润,如有调整,也应该符合公平交易原则。由于常设机构隶属于企业的总机构,其财务几乎完全在总机构的控制之下,再加上它们之间的协议不具有法律效力,据此建立的账簿的可信度因而大打折扣。但是,只要具备下列两个条件,常设机构的营业账簿就可以作为税务当局征税的基础:一是总机构和常设机构的营业账簿在内部协议基础上对称建立;二是内部协议反映了企业不同部门的职能。在早期确定常设机构的利润归属时,一些国家就开始使用独立企业核算方法。目前,绝大多数国家国内企业所得税法和双边税收协定中普遍采用这种方法。联合国范本建议缔约国优先使用该方法,2010年前的经合发组织范本也建议会员国采用这种方法。

The so-called independent enterprise accounting approach refers to a method of calculating the taxable income of a permanent establishment on the basis of the income reflected in its account books, according to the principle of fair trade that the permanent establishment is regarded as an independent taxable entity. The enterprises focusing on operation and management usually require their branches to set up accounts in order to have a clear view of their profits. If a permanent establishment has an account book, tax authorities usually determine the profits of the permanent establishment on the basis of its account book. If there is any adjustment of profit amount, it should also conform to the principle of fair trade. As the permanent establishment is subordinate to the head office of the enterprise, its finance is almost completely under the control of the latter, and the agreement between them has no legal effect, so the credibility of the account books on such basis is greatly reduced. However, as long as the following two conditions are met, the business books of the permanent establishment can serve as the basis for tax collection by the tax authorities. Firstly, the business books of the head office and the permanent establishment are set up symmetrically on the basis of the internal agreement. Secondly, the internal agreement reflects the functions of different departments of the enterprise. In the early stage of determining the profit attribution of permanent establishment, some countries began to use the independent enterprise accounting approach. At present, this approach is widely used in income tax laws for domestic enterprise and bilateral tax treaties in most countries. The UN Model recommends that contracting states give priority to this approach, and the OECD Model before 2010 also recommends that its member states adopt it.

（二）公平交易法
Fair Trade Approach

为了解决公平交易原则下常设机构利润归属方法不统一产生的双重征税和不征税问题，经合发组织范本在其第7条第2款采用了公平交易方法。根据该规定，在进行常设机构利润归属时要使用两步分析法，首先需要运用职能和事实分析法将常设机构假定为一个在经济上和法律上独立于其所属企业的总机构和其他部分的独立分设企业，并据此确定常设机构履行的职能、使用的资产、负担的风险。其次，运用可比性分析方法，类推适用于目前确定法律上彼此独立的关联企业之间的转移定价的方法，分析与常设机构所从事业务的性质、市场环境、商业战略类似的可比交易，来计算可归属于常设机构的营业利润。在这种方法下，常设机构所涵盖的利润范围包括了常设机构从事的所有经营活动，既包括常设机构与其他独立企业进行的交易，也包括常设机构与联属企业、企业的其他机构进行的交易，[1]因此，这种方法不仅承认了常设机构与企业其他机构的内部交易，也要求这些交易必须按照公平交易原则定价。美国对这种方法持保留态度。[2]

In order to solve the problem of double taxation and non taxation caused by the different approaches to profit attribution of permanent establishments under the principle of fair trade, the OECD Model adopts the method of fair trade in Article 7(2). According to the regulation, the two-step analysis should be used in the profit attribution of permanent establishments. First of all, it is necessary to employ the function and fact analysis approach to assume the permanent establishment as an independent and separate enterprise which is independent of the head office and other parts of the affiliated enterprise both economically and legally, and then determine the functions, assets and risks of the permanent establishment. Secondly, the comparability analysis approach is adopted, which applies by analogy the current approach of determining the transfer pricing between legally independent associated enterprises. The business profits attributable to the permanent establishment are calculated on the basis of the analysis of the comparable transactions similar to the nature, market environment and business strategy of the business engagement of the permanent establishment. Under this method, the profit scope covered by the permanent establishment includes all the business activities carried out by the permanent establishment, including the transactions between the permanent establishment and other

---

[1] 经合发组织范本第7条注释20段。
[2] 经合发组织范本第7条注释89段。

independent enterprises, as well as the transactions between the permanent establishment and the affiliated enterprise and other institutions of the enterprise. Therefore, this approach not only recognizes the internal transactions between the permanent establishment and other institutions of the enterprise, but also requires that these transactions must be priced according to the principle of fair trade. The United States has reservations about this approach.

（三）公式分配法
Formula Apportionment Approach

公式分配法是将一定时期（通常是1年）企业的收入汇总，然后根据公式，按照一定的要素比例分摊至各个国家的分支机构，从而计算出某个分支机构应税利润额的方法。采用公式分配法时，税务机构可以按照分支机构的营业资产占企业全部营业资产的相应比例，或分支机构流动资金、营业额或员工工资额占企业全部流动资金、营业额或员工工资额的比例，将企业的利润分配给各个分支机构。

The Formula apportionment approach is to collect the income of an enterprise in a certain period (usually a year), and then apportion it to the branches set up in each country according to a certain factor proportion in the formula, so as to calculate the taxable profit of a certain branch. When the formula apportionment approach is adopted, the tax authorities may apportion the profits of the enterprise to each branch according to the corresponding proportion of the business assets of the branch in the total business assets of the enterprise, or the corresponding proportion of the fluid capital, turnover or employee salary of the branch to the total fluid capital, turnover or employee salary of the enterprise.

公式分配方法的优点是纳税人不再承担提交账簿的负担，税务机关不必逐笔审核每项交易，简化了税务征管工作，提高了税务机关的效率。发展中国家可以根据公式中的要素比例比较公平地分配税收份额。其缺点是公式不容易达成，获得公式要素所需要的信息比较困难。此外，跨国公司可能会通过操纵要素所在地来减轻税负，实现利润转移。因此，经合发组织范本和联合国范本原则上不主张采用这类方法，但如果缔约国之间习惯采用这种方法，可以继续采用该方法。① 这种方法在一国国内跨行政区域的税收分配中使用较多，如美国、加拿大对跨州、省经营的公司就使用公式来分配经营所涉各州、省的应税所得。② 近年来，欧盟提出了共同合并公司税基制度（Common Consolidated Corporate Tax Base，简称CCCTB）提案，对在多个成员国境内经营的跨国公司，采用根据三个同比重的要素（即资产、劳动和销售额）的统一公式计算出课税税基，③再将税基归集到集团公司成员中，并规定分配需符合"全部责任"标准（假设100%相关税基均是应税的），进而通过"引力原则"将税基分配到集团在欧盟的各常设机构中去。④

The advantages of the formula apportionment approach are that taxpayers no longer bear

---

① 2017年联合国范本第7条注释第19段，《2017年经合发组织范本》第7条注释第52段。
② 王丽华：《常设机构利润归属问题研究》，东华大学出版社2011年版，第63页。
③ 叶莉娜：《常设机构利润归属：独立交易法VS公式分摊法》，《税收经济研究》2012年第3期，第71页。
④ 刘奇超、郑莹、曹明星：《CCCTB机制阐发：公式分配法欧美比较与中国引申》，《国际税收》2016年第7期，第38页。

the burden of submitting account books, and the tax authorities do not have to examine each transaction one by one, which simplifies the tax collection and management and improves the efficiency of tax authorities. Developing countries can apportion tax share fairly according to the factor proportion in the formula. The disadvantage is that the formula is not easy to achieve, and it is difficult to obtain the information of the factors required by the formula. In addition, multinational companies may reduce tax burden and realize profit transfer by manipulating the location where factors are identified. Therefore, the OECD Model and the United Nations Model do not advocate the use of such an approach in principle, but it can continue to be used if it is customary among contracting states. This approach is often used in the tax apportionment of cross administrative regions within a country. For example, the United States and Canada use such formula to apportion the taxable income of the states and provinces involved in the business operation of cross state or cross provincial enterprises. In recent years, the European Union has put forward the proposal of Common Consolidated Corporate Tax Base (CCCTB). For multinational enterprises operating in several member states, the tax base is calculated by using a unified formula based on three factors of the same proportion (i.e. assets, labor and sales). Then the tax base is apportioned among the members of the group, and the apportionment is required to meet the "full responsibility" standard (assuming that 100% of the relevant tax base is taxable). Afterwards the tax base is apportioned to the permanent establishments of the group in the EU through the force of attraction principle.

第五节 相 关 案 例
Section 5 Related Cases

一、非居民企业派遣雇员在境内提供劳务构成常设机构案[①]
Case of Non-resident Enterprises Sending Employees into the Territory to Provide Services as a Permanent Establishment

（一）案件背景及相关事实
Background of the Case and Relevant Facts

A公司注册在德国，B公司是一家中外合资公司，A公司是B公司的母公司。A公司主要从事汽车及其零部件的设计、研制、制造、销售以及售后业务。近年来，A公司与B公司签订了若干项劳务合同，由A公司派遣员工为B公司的多个项目提供技术指导和售后服务。

---

① 国家税务总局国际税务司著：《税收协定执行案例集》，中国税务出版社2019年版。

Company A is registered in Germany, company B is a Sino-foreign joint venture, company A is the parent company of company B. Company A is mainly engaged in the design, development, manufacture, sale and after-sale work of automobiles and its parts. Company A has signed a number of labor contracts with company B in recent years, and company A sends employees to provide technical guidance and after-sales service for many projects of company B.

在2009年至2015年这6年间，A、B两公司签订了10份项目合同，派遣了10批次1 000余人赴中国为B公司提供服务。每份合同的履行时间均不超过183天。案件争议的焦点在于A公司在华是否构成常设机构，因此确定派员是否需要缴纳个人所得税。A公司认为所派遣员工的工资由境外发放且任意12个月中连续或累计在华时间未超183天，因此不构成常设机构，无须缴纳个人所得税。我国税务机关认为不同批次派遣人员的活动存在商业相关性，因此需将从事关联项目人员的在华时间进行加总。由于加总的结果超过了183天，从而判定这两家公司在中国境内构成了常设机构。尽管常设机构中人员的工资存在由中国境外发放的情况，但该收入也视为来源于中国，并应在中国缴纳个人所得税。

In the six years from 2009 to 2015, the two companies A and B signed 10 project contracts, dispatching 10 batches of more than 1,000 people to China to provide services to company B. The performance time of each contract shall not exceed 183 days. The focus of the case is whether company A is a permanent establishment in China, therefore, determine whether the staff need to pay personal income tax. Company A believes that the wages of the dispatched employees are paid overseas and have not exceeded 183 days in China for any 12 months, it therefore does not constitute a permanent establishment, there is no need to pay personal income tax. Our tax authorities believe that the activities of different batches of dispatched personnel have commercial relevance, therefore, it is necessary to sum up the time spent by personnel engaged in related projects in China. Since the total result was over 183 days, it is thus determined that the two companies constitute a permanent establishment in China. Despite the fact that the salaries of persons in the permanent establishment are paid outside China, the income is also seen as coming from China, and they should pay personal income tax in China.

（二）案件处理过程
Case Handling Process

针对案件的争议焦点，税务机关就A公司向B公司派员提供劳务事项展开调查。

With regard to the focus of the case, the tax authorities have investigated the provision of services by company A to company B.

1. 确定提供劳务的时间
Determine the Time of Service Provision

税务机关仔细查阅了A、B之间的劳务合同，调查了雇员出入境情况，并与B公司一一核实，发现雇员12个月内在华时间确实未超过183天。但是，税务机关发现从第一名雇员开始在华服务到最后一名雇员离开中国累计超过600天。其中，2009年至2010年，某雇员为履行两份合同在华时间分别为96天和165天。如果这两份合同之间存在关联，则该雇员在华时间实际为261天，满足在任何12个月内连续或累计超过183天的条件，应构成常设机构。为此,税务机关就A公司与B公司之间的合同是否存在关联展开进一步调查。

And the tax authorities scrutinized A, B labor contracts, investigated the entry and exit of employees, and verified with company B, it was found that the employee did not spend more than 183 days in China for 12 months. But the tax authorities found that from the first employee to the last employee left China for more than 600 days. Among them, between 2009 and 2010, an employee spent 96 days and 165 days in China in order to perform two contracts. If there's a connection between the two contracts, the employee spent 261 days in China, having met the conditions for a continuous or cumulative period exceeding 183 days in any 12 months, shall constitute a permanent establishment. To that end, the tax authorities conduct further investigations into whether the contracts between companies A and B are related.

2. 分析A、B公司之间的合同是否存在关联

Analysis of Whether Contracts between Companies A and B are Related

《〈中华人民共和国政府和新加坡共和国政府关于对所得避免双重征税和防止偷漏税的协定〉及议定书条文解释》(国税发〔2010〕75号印发)规定同一企业从事的有商业相关性或连贯性的若干个项目应视为"同一项目或相关联的项目"。税务机关重点围绕下列因素对是否具有关联性开展调查：(1)这些项目是否被包含在同一个总合同里；(2)如果这些项目分属于不同的合同,这些合同是否与同一人或相关联的人所签订,前一项目的实施是否是后一项目实施的必要条件；(3)这些项目的性质是否相同；(4)这些项目是否由相同的雇员实施。

The Agreement between the Government of the People's Republic of China and the Government of the Republic of Singapore on the Avoidance of Double Taxation of Income and the Prevention of Tax Evasion and the Interpretation of the Provisions of the Protocol (issued〔2010〕75) stipulates that a number of projects of commercial relevance or coherence undertaken by the same enterprise shall be considered "the same project or associated project". The tax authorities focus on the following factors to investigate the relevance: (1) whether the projects are included in the same general contract; (2) if the projects are divided into different contracts, whether the contracts are signed with the same person or associated person, whether the implementation of the previous project is a necessary condition for the implementation of the latter project; (3) whether the projects are of the same nature; (4) whether the projects are implemented by the same employees.

这10个合同项目的内容主要是为汽车发动机缸体、缸盖、曲轴等分别提供技术支持,看似是各自独立的合同。税务机关通过约谈境内B公司、实地走访和分析劳工单位了解到：一是这些服务项目实质上都是为同一条发动机生产线提供技术支持和指导,合同的履行顺序与发动机生产工序一致,流程上密不可分,合同实施地点主要在发动机生产车间。二是这些合同虽没有包含在同一合同内,但是均与同一人签订,因果联系强,性质相同。三是由于A公司专业化分工比较细致,这10个项目虽然不是完全由同一批雇员完成,但是这些人员均同属于A公司的技术部门,各个合同执行时存在人员交叉派遣的情况。综合以上情况,税务机关认为A公司与B公司签订的10个合同项目,符合中新协定对"同一项目或相关联的项目"的判定规定。在具体计算劳务活动在任何12个月中是否连续或累计超过183天时,应按所有雇员为同一个项目提供劳务活动不同时期在中国境内连续或累计停留的时间来掌握。在整个项

目中，A公司在其中一个"12个月"期间在中国境内提供劳务超过183天，则应认为该企业在中国构成常设机构。经与A公司合同项目负责人核实沟通，A公司认同将10个合同项目认定为"同一项目或相关联的项目"的判定结果，其派员为B公司提供服务在我国构成常设机构。

The contents of these 10 contract items are mainly to provide technical support for automobile engine cylinder block, cylinder head, crankshaft and so on, which seem to be their own independent contracts. After interviews with domestic company B, field visits and analysis of labor units, the tax authorities understand the following facts. First, these service items are essentially to provide technical support and guidance for the same engine production line, the order of performance of the contract is consistent with the engine production process, the process is inseparable, the contract implementation site is mainly in the engine production workshop. Second, although these contracts are not included in the same contract, they are signed with the same person. Third, because the professional division of labor in company A is more meticulous, although these 10 projects are not completely completed by the same group of employees, these personnel belong to the technical department of the company A, and there is a situation of cross dispatch of personnel in the execution of each contract. To sum up the above situation, the tax authorities believe that the 10 contract items signed by company A and company B are in accordance with the judgment of the "same project or related project" in the new agreement. In calculating whether the labor service activities are continuous or accumulated for more than 183 days in any 12 months, it should be grasped according to the time of continuous or cumulative stay in China for different periods of labor service activities provided by all employees for the same project. For the whole project, A company provides services in China for more than 183 days during one of the "12 months" period, the enterprise shall be deemed to constitute a permanent establishment in China. Through verification and communication with the person in charge of the contract project of company A, company A agrees to identify 10 contract projects as "the same project or related project", and its personnel provide services to company B in our country to form a permanent organization.

（三）案例评析
Case Analysis

在上述案例中，国家税务总局在判断外国企业在中国派遣员工是否构成常设机构时，没有单纯以该派遣在中国境内停留的时间是否超过183天为标准，而是采取了实质重于形式的原则，以跨国企业的实质商业安排作为税务机关审查的重点内容可以在很大程度上减少缔约国利用我国国内法的规定进行避税的可能。当然，因特殊原因，例如因疫情滞留在我国境内的外国企业派员，税务机关也要考虑这种特殊情况。只要外国企业作出相关安排的实质意图不是为了让其员工超过常设机构时间门槛在中国开展业务活动，税务机关就应考虑实际情况作出判断。

In the above-mentioned cases, the State Administration of Taxation, in judging whether the dispatch of employees by a foreign enterprise in China constitutes a permanent establishment, has not simply taken the criterion of whether the dispatch of employees in China exceeds 183 days, but has adopted the principle of substance over form. Taking the substantive business arrangements of multinational enterprises as the focus of the examination by the tax authorities can greatly reduce the possibility of states parties using the provisions of our domestic law for tax avoidance. Of course, for special reasons, such as sending personnel from foreign enterprises stranded in China because of the epidemic situation, the tax authorities should also consider this special situation. As long as the substantive intention of the arrangement is not to allow its employees to carry out business activities in China beyond the time threshold of the permanent establishment, the tax authorities should consider the actual situation.

二、中外合作办学构成常设机构案[①]
Case Concerning the Constitution of a Permanent Establishment for Sino-foreign Cooperatively-run Schools

（一）案件背景及相关事实
Background of the Case and Relevant Facts

境内L学院创建于1984年，是国内一所知名综合学府。2015年9月，境内L学院与德国M大学签订《合作办学协议》，采用"3+1.5"双学位的跨文化人才培养模式，第一教学阶段为前3年，学生在L学院学习语言、基础课程和部分专业课程，第二教学阶段为后1.5年，学生在德国M大学完成若干专业课程学习、毕业实习和毕业论文。第一教学阶段，L学院按每位学生5 700欧元向德国M大学支付学费、注册费、管理费等。第二教学阶段，L学院按每位学生4 300欧元向德国M大学支付学费、注册费。

L Institute is founded in 1984. It is a well-known comprehensive school in China. In September 2015, the L Institute of China and the M University of Germany signed a Cooperation Agreement, adopting the "3+1.5" year Dual-degree intercultural talent training model. The first stage of teaching is the first three years at the L Institute. Students study languages, basic courses and some major courses here. The second stage is 1.5 years later, at the M University of Germany. Students complete several major courses, graduate internships and graduation thesis here. For the first stage of teaching, the L Institute pays tuition fees, registration fees, management fees and so on to the German M University at 5,700 euros per student. For the second stage of teaching, the L Institute pays tuition fees and registration fees to the German M University at 4,300 euros per student.

2017年7月，德国M大学就此合同委托L学院向税务机关提出享受税收协定待遇。中德税收协定第5条规定："缔约国一方企业通过雇员或者其他人员，在缔约国另一方为同一个项目或相关联的项目提供的劳务，包括咨询劳务，仅以在任何12个月中连续或累计超过6个月的为限。"

On July 2017, the German M University commissioned the L Institute to apply to the tax

---

[①] 国家税务总局国际税务司著：《税收协定执行案例集》，中国税务出版社2019年版，第41—44页。

authorities for tax agreement treatment under Article 5 of the Sino-German Tax Agreement, according to which: "Services, including consulting services, provided by an enterprise of one contracting state for the same project or associated project in the other contracting state through employees or other persons, shall be limited to six consecutive or cumulative months in any twelve months."

M大学认为在整个办学期间,其外籍教师在境内教学时间未达到构成常设机构标准,因此可以适用协定免税待遇。

M University considers that its foreign teachers did not meet the criteria for the establishment of permanent establishment throughout the school period, and therefore can apply the agreement tax exemption.

(二) 案件分析及处理过程
Case Analysis and Processing

主管税务机关对纳税人提交的材料进行了审核,与M大学进行了多次沟通,厘清了以下内容。

A review of the taxpayer's submissions was conducted by the competent tax authorities and a number of communications were made with M University to clarify the following.

1. 关于是否构成常设机构问题
On the Question of Whether to Constitute a Permanent Establishment

M大学称,中德税收协定第5条规定,企业提供劳务,仅以在任何12个月中连续或累计超过6个月才构成常设机构,因外籍教师入境教学的时间不长,任何12个月内入境教学都不满6个月,因此并不构成常设机构。

According to the M University, Article 5 of the Sino-German Tax Agreement stipulates that enterprises provide services only for a continuous or cumulative period of more than six months in any 12 months to form a permanent establishment. Because foreign teachers enter the country for a short period of time and no longer than six months in any 12 months, so it does not constitute a permanent establishment.

税务机关指出,根据中德税收协定第5条及《〈中华人民共和国政府和新加坡共和国政府关于对所得避免双重征税和防止偷漏税的协定〉及议定书条文解释》(国税发〔2010〕75号印发)规定,常设机构判定不仅局限于建筑工程型、劳务型常设机构,企业进行全部或部分营业的固定营业场所构成固定场所型常设机构。就中外合作办学项目而言,其完全符合固定场所型常设机构,表现在以下三个方面。

The tax authorities noted that, in accordance with Article 5 of the Sino-German Tax Agreement and the Agreement between the Governments of the People's Republic of China and the Government of the Republic of Singapore on the Avoidance of Double Taxation on Income and the Interpretation of the Provisions of the Protocol (issued〔2010〕75), the permanent establishment was not limited to construction engineering type and labor type, and that the fixed place of business where the enterprise operated in whole or in part constituted the fixed-site permanent establishment. As far as the Sino-foreign cooperatively-run school project is concerned, it fully accords with the fixed-site permanent establishment, which is manifested in the following three aspects.

（1）固定性。德国M大学和L学院的合作办学项目，通过L学院的教学场所进行，虽然所采用的授课教室在不同年度会有所调整，但都是在L学院内部，因此L学院构成了M大学在境内的营业场所，该营业场所是实质存在的，具有固定性。同时，外籍教师对营业场所具有支配权。

(1) Fixity. The cooperative project of the German M University and the L Institute is carried out through the teaching premises of the L Institute. Although the teaching classrooms will be adjusted in different years, they are all within the L Institute. Therefore, L Institute constitutes the business premises of the M University in China, which is substantial and fixed. At the same time, foreign teachers have the right to control the business premises.

（2）持久性。M大学与L学院的合作办学项目是长期事项，而非短期行为，合作双方签有协议书，协议持续时间与国内学制挂钩，总时长为4年半。在办学期间，德国M大学派遣来华的外籍教师虽会有轮换，也会有短暂的放假安排，但这些暂时性的间断并不影响办学项目时间上的持久性；此外，根据合作协议，双方建立项目管理委员会，委员会成员由双方学校管理人员任职，且各出1人担任联合项目管理主任，长期任职于国内学校。综上，可以判断德国M大学在L学院内的营业场所具有持久性。

(2) Persistence. The cooperative project between M University and L Institute is a long-term matter, not a short-term act. The two parties sign an agreement, and the duration of the agreement is linked to the domestic school system, with a total duration of 4 and a half years. During the period of running a school, foreign teachers sent by the German M University to China will have a rotation and a short holiday arrangement, but these temporary breaks do not affect the duration of the project. In addition, according to the cooperation agreement, the two sides set up a project management committee. To sum up, we can judge the persistence of German M University in L Institute.

（3）经营性。德国M大学通过教学活动取得收入，且不属于我国税法规定的非营利组织免税收入，具有经营性和盈利性特征。

(3) Operating. German M University obtains income through teaching activities, and does not belong to the tax-free income of non-profit organizations stipulated in the tax law of our country. It has the characteristics of management and profitability.

2. 关于常设机构利润归属问题

Issues Relating to the Attribution of Profits to the Permanent Establishment

M大学声称整个教学分为两个阶段，在第一教学阶段外籍教师未入境提供教学服务，这一阶段取得的收入不应予以征税。

M University claims that the entire teaching is divided into two stages, and that the income earned during the first stage of teaching, when foreign teachers do not enter our country to provide teaching services, should not be taxed.

税务机关提出，该合作办学项目已经构成常设机构，应就归属于该常设机构的利润在中国缴税。合作办学不仅限于所谓外籍教师入境提供教学服务，所有为该合作办学项目从事的活动如招生管理、教学计划制定和实施、学生培养和考核等都属于常设机构从事的活动，在计算归属该常设机构的利润时均应予考虑。虽然该合作办学形式上分为第一阶段和第二阶段,但从整体看,是属于同一教学项目下的两个阶段,应作为一个合同项下的整体事项来处理。此外,《合作办学协议》中明确规定,德国M大学的职责包含组织外籍教师承担第一教学阶段在L学院进行的部分基础课程和专业课程的教学及考试工作,L学院需要就此阶段的教学及管理向境外的M大学支付相关费用。对境外教师在第一阶段来华教学这一事实,M大学不应作虚假说明。

The tax authorities proposed that the cooperative school-running project already constituted a permanent establishment and should pay taxes in China on profits attributable to the permanent establishment. Cooperation in running schools is not limited to the so-called entry of foreign teachers to provide teaching services. All activities carried out for the cooperative project, such as enrollment management, teaching plan formulation and implementation, student training and assessment, belong to the activities of the permanent establishment and should be taken into account in calculating the profits attributable to the permanent establishment. Although the form of the cooperative school is divided into the first stage and the second stage, it belongs to the two stages under the same teaching project as a whole and should be dealt with as a whole under a contract. Moreover, the Agreement on Cooperative Schools clearly stipulates that the duties of the German M University include organizing foreign teachers to undertake the teaching and examination of some basic and professional courses conducted at the L Institute during the first stage of teaching, L Institute is required to pay the relevant fees to M University abroad for the teaching and management of this stage. For the fact that foreign teachers come to China in the first stage, M University should not make false statements.

综上,德国M大学在境内的为该合作办学项目提供教育教学活动的场所构成在境内的固定场所型常设机构,对归属于该常设机构的利润应在中国缴税。M大学最终表示了认同,并补缴了60余万元税款。

In summary, the place of providing education and teaching activities for the cooperative school running project in Germany M University constitutes a fixed place permanent establishment in the territory, and the profits attributable to the permanent establishment shall be paid tax in China. M University finally agreed and paid a supplementary tax of more than 600,000 yuan.

(三)案例评析
Case Review

我国对外签订的税收协定中,对"常设机构"的一般定义,是"企业进行全部或部分营业的固定营业场所",为便于理解,协定文本列举了在通常情况下构成常设机构的场所类型和活动类型,比如办事处、分支机构、建筑安装工程和劳务服务等。但在工作实践中,有些基层税务人员和纳税人仍存在认识误区,对常设机构的认识局限于建筑型、劳务型常设机构,而对固定场所型常设机构的判定不足。本案从固定场所型常设机构判定的三个要素出发,对外方在华构成常设机构作出判定,是准确运用常设机构条款的一个实践。《国家税务总局关于税收协定执行若干问题的公告》(国家税务总局公告2018年第11号)明确了中外合作办学项目中开展教育教学活动的场所构成常设机构,进一步增强了协定执行的确定性。

The general definition of "permanent establishment" in the tax agreement signed by our country is "fixed business place where the enterprise carries out all or part of its business". For ease of understanding, the text of the agreement lists the types of places and activities that normally constitute a permanent establishment, such as offices, branches, construction and installation works and labor services. But in the work practice, some basic level tax personnel and the taxpayer still have the misunderstanding, the understanding of the permanent establishment is limited to the construction type, the labor type permanent establishment, but the judgment of the fixed place type permanent establishment is insufficient. In this case, from the three elements of the fixed place permanent establishment, it is a practice to accurately apply the provisions of the permanent establishment. The Proclamation of the State Administration of Taxation on Certain Issues in the Implementation of Tax Agreements (No. 11 of the State Administration of Taxation Proclamation of 2018) made clear that the places for carrying out educational and teaching activities in Sino-foreign cooperatively-run school projects constitute permanent establishment, further enhancing the certainty of the implementation of the agreements.

三、防止合同拆分和不当适用例外条款规避常设机构案[①]
Case About Prevention of Disclusion of Contract and Effectiveness of Except Provisions Against the Standards

（一）案例概要
Summary of the Case

非居民企业通过拆分设备采购及安装合同规避构成常设机构的时间计算，同时不当适用中日税收协定议定书关于常设机构判定的例外条款，主张其在中国境内不构成常设机构。税务机关深入调查，认真分析，将其分拆合同视为一个合同来计算在华活动的时间，并否定该活动属于适用例外条款的咨询劳务范畴，最终判定该非居民企业在华提供工程安装及监管活动构成常设机构。

Non-resident enterprises avoid the time calculation of the permanent establishment by splitting the equipment purchase and installation contract, and at the same time improperly apply the exception clause of the Sino-Japanese Tax Agreement Protocol on the permanent establishment judgment, and claim that it does not constitute a permanent establishment in China. The tax authorities have thoroughly investigated and carefully analyzed the split contract as a contract to calculate the time of activities in China, denied that the activity belongs to the category of consulting services applicable to exceptional clauses and finally judged that the non-resident enterprise in China to provide engineering installation and supervision activities constitute a permanent establishment.

---

① 国家税务总局国际税务司著：《税收协定执行案例集》，中国税务出版社2019年版，第36—40页。

第七章 跨国营业所得征税的协调
CHAPTER VII Tax Harmonization on Cross-border Business Profit

（二）相关事实
Relevant Facts

中国境内S公司从日本X株式会社进口设备，双方签署两份合同，合同仅约定设备总价款约1.62亿元，未约定外方是否需要派员提供安装调试工作。税务机关根据经验判断，认为大型设备采购通常伴有安装劳务。经询问，境内S公司向税务机关提供了与日本X株式会社签署的合同附件，附件中包含外方派遣人员从事安装、设计和指导等内容，设备于2014年6月全部运抵厂区，到2017年2月安装调试完毕。

Company S in China imports equipment from Japan X Co., Ltd., and the two parties sign two contracts. The contract only stipulates that the total price of the equipment is about 162 million yuan, and does not agree whether the foreign party needs to send personnel to provide installation and commissioning work. According to experience, tax authorities believe that large-scale equipment procurement is usually accompanied by installation services. Upon enquiry, the domestic company S provided the tax authorities with the contract attachment signed with Japan X Co., Ltd., which contains the contents of installation, design and guidance sent by foreign parties. All the equipment arrived at the plant in June 2014 and was installed and debugged by February 2017.

日本X株式会社认为其在中国不构成常设机构，可以享受协定待遇，理由如下：一是此次进口的7台设备，分属两个合同，且均为单独运转的涂布装置，应分别按每个合同来计算是否达到常设机构时间标准，不应视为同一合同整体计算。根据中日税收协定第5条第3款规定，咨询劳务"在任何十二个月中连续或累计超过六个月的"，应认为在缔约国设有常设机构，而X株式会社为完成每个合同提供劳务的时间都不到6个月，因此在中国不构成常设机构；二是其提供的是有关机器设备方面的咨询劳务，可以适用中日税收协定议定书的例外规定。根据议定书第1条规定，"虽有协定第5条第5款的规定，缔约国一方企业通过雇员或其他人员在缔约国另一方提供与销售或者出租机器设备有关的咨询劳务，应不视为在该缔约国另一方设有常设机构"，按此规定X株式会社同样在中国没有常设机构，不需要缴纳企业所得税等相关税款。

Japan X Co., Ltd. believes that it does not constitute a permanent establishment in China and can enjoy the agreed treatment for the following reasons. First, the import of seven equipment, divided into two contracts, and are separately operated coating devices, shall be calculated according to each contract to meet the permanent establishment time standard, should not be regarded as the same contract as a whole. According to Article 5, Paragraph 3, of the Sino-Japanese Tax Agreement, consulting services "for a continuous or cumulative period of more than six months in any twelve-month period" shall be deemed to have a permanent establishment in the constructing state, while X Co., Ltd. provides services for the completion of each contract for less than six months, so it does not constitute a permanent establishment in China. Second, it provides consulting services on machinery and equipment, and may apply the exception to the Sino-Japanese Tax Agreement Protocol. According to Article 1 of the Protocol, "notwithstanding the provisions of Article 5, Paragraph 5, of the Agreement, an enterprise of a contracting state, through its employees

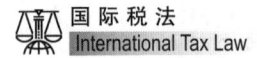

or other persons, of advisory services in connection with the sale or rental of machinery and equipment in the other contracting state shall not be deemed to have a permanent establishment in the other contracting state", according to which X Corporation also has no permanent establishment in China and does not have to pay taxes related to enterprise income tax.

（三）处理过程
Case Handling Process

依据日本X株式会社的观点,税务机关从以下三个方面进行了查证。

According to Japan's X Co., Ltd., the tax authorities start investigation from the following three aspects.

1. 确定日方派员来华提供劳务的天数
To Determine the Number of Days the Japanese Sent Personnel to China to Provide Services

税务机关从境内S公司获取外方派员信息以及在华劳务时间,同时向出入境管理部门发函,请求获取相关人员出入境记录。通过对外籍人员在华劳务时间和出入境管理部门的回函信息进行比对,税务机关确认日本X株式会社前后派15人来华。两份合同的劳务履行时间分别是165天和167天,均不满6个月。但是为完成两份合同,从第一名派员到完成全部服务最后一名人员离开,X株式会社派员共计在华停留239天。

The tax authority obtains the information of the foreign personnel from S company in China and the working time in China, and sends a letter to the Exit and Entry Administration department to request the entry and exit records of the relevant personnel. By comparing the labor time of foreign personnel in China with the information in the return letter of the entry and exit administration department, it is confirmed that 15 people from Japan's X Co., Ltd. were sent to China before and after. The labor performance time of the two contracts is 165 days and 167 days, respectively, less than 6 months. However, in order to complete the two contracts, from the first person to the last person to complete the full service, X Co., Ltd. sent staff to stay in China for a total of 239 days.

2. 分析两个合同是否具有相关性
To Analyze the Relevance of the Two Contracts

税务机关紧紧围绕相关性判定的五个方面收集和查找相关证据：一是不同的合同是否由同一个人或相关联的多方签订；二是与一个人签订的后续合同和之前与该人或相关联多方签订的合同之间是否存在因果关系；三是如果不进行税收筹划,是否会有单一合同涵盖所有活动；四是不同合同下的工作内容性质是否相同或相似；五是是否通过相同的雇员进行不同合同中的活动。

The tax authorities collect and find relevant evidence closely around five aspects of relevance determination: first, whether different contracts are signed by the same person or associated parties; second, whether there is a causal relationship between a subsequent contract with a person and a contract previously signed with that person or associated parties; third, whether there will be a single contract covering all activities without tax planning; fourth, whether the nature of the work under different contracts is the same or similar; and fifth, whether activities in different contracts are carried out through the same employees.

税务机关经过对境内S公司的实地走访、翻阅合同和设备使用说明书、约谈车间管理人员了解到：S公司通过两个合同先后从日本进口7台设备，安装在同一车间，设备使用在工艺流程上存在联动性，设备之间相互配合完成产品生产。车间管理人员同时表示，7台设备的安装工作都由同一批外方人员协助完成，按设备运抵的先后顺序进行施工，施工内容主要都是安装指导。

结合以上有力证据，税务机关判定两个合同满足以上五项因素，具有相关性，即属于同一方签订、存在因果关系、可以由单一合同涵盖、性质相同以及由相同的人员实施。故应将分拆的两个合同还原为一个合同，根据日方派员的连续或累计停留时间来判定是否构成常设机构。

Through field visits to domestic company S, the tax authorities read contracts and instructions for the use of equipment, and interviewed workshop managers, they learned that company S successively imported 7 sets of equipment from Japan through two contracts and installed them in the same workshop. The workshop manager also said that the installation of 7 sets of equipment was completed by the same batch of foreign personnel, according to the order in which the equipment arrived, the construction content was mainly installation guidance.

Combined with the above strong evidence, the tax authorities determine that the two contracts meet the above five factors, which are relevant, that is, belonging to the same party, there exists a causal relationship, can be covered by a single contract, with the same nature and executed by the same personnel. Therefore, the split two contracts should be reduced to one contract, and determine whether to form a permanent establishment according to the continuous or cumulative stay time of the Japanese party.

3. 是否符合中日税收协定议定书的例外条款

Whether comply with the Exceptions to the Protocol to the Sino-Japanese Tax Agreement

《中日税收协定议定书》第1条规定："缔约国一方企业通过雇员或其他人员在缔约国另一方提供与销售或出租机器设备有关的咨询劳务，应不视为在该缔约国另一方设有常设机构。"据此，日本X株式会社认为其提供的劳务是与销售相关的咨询劳务，符合议定书第1条的例外条款规定，即使时间上超过6个月，也不应视为常设机构。税务机关指出，根据《国家税务总局关于中日税收协定及其议定书有关条文解释的通知》(国税函〔1997〕429号)对议定书第1条作出的解释，"与销售相关的咨询劳务"仅指对销售设备在缔约国另一方的安装工程不负有指挥权和全面的技术责任的咨询性劳务。如果是成套设备销售且对设备安装提供土建设计、安装调试、试车等全面指导，以保证验收合格正常使用的劳务，则应作为监督管理劳务，适用《中日税收协定》第5条第3款规定，而不适用《中日税收协定议定书》第1条规定。根据合同附件列示，劳务内容栏明确注明是安装指导，且施工范围中设备所需管道的流程图都是由日方负责设计、施工指导，含有大量的技术参数，如果让不通晓技术参数的S公司拿着日方设计的流程图去指挥工人安装，则（施工）根本无法实现。而境内企业的管理人员也证实在安装过程中，确实是日方技术人员负责施工指导和相关调试测试。据此，税务机关否定了日本X株式会社关于适用例外条款的主张。

Article 1 of the Protocol to the Sino-Japanese Tax Agreement provides that: "An enterprise of one contracting state provides consulting services in the other contracting state, through employees or other persons, in connection with the sale or rental of machinery and equipment, shall not be deemed to have a permanent establishment in the other party". Accordingly, X Co., Ltd. believes that the services it provides are sales-related consulting services, in accordance with the exception of Article 1 of the Protocol, even if it takes more than six months, nor should it be considered permanent. The tax authorities note that, in accordance with the State Administration of Taxation Circular on the Interpretation of the Relevant Provisions of the Sino-Japanese Tax Agreement and its Protocol (Tax Letter〔1997〕429), which interprets Article 1 of the Protocol, "sales-related consultancy services" refers only to advisory services which are not subject to command and full technical responsibility for the installation of sales equipment on the other side of the contracting state. If it is a complete set of equipment sales and equipment installation to provide civil design, installation, commissioning and other comprehensive guidance, to ensure the acceptance of qualified normal use of services, should be used as supervision and management of services, applying Article 5, Paragraph 3, of the Sino-Japanese Tax Agreement, but does not apply the Sino-Japanese Tax Agreement Protocol Article 1 stipulation. According to the annex to the contract, the labor content column clearly indicates that it is the installation instruction, and the Japanese are responsible for the designation and construction guidance of the flow chart of the pipeline required by the equipment in the scope of construction, the Japanese are responsible for the designation and construction guidance of with a lot of technical parameters. If company S which does not know the technical parameters does takes the flow chart designed by Japan to direct the workers during the installation, it will be unable to proceed with construction. And the management of domestic enterprises also confirmed that in the installation process, it is true that Japanese technicians are responsible for construction guidance and related commissioning and testing. Accordingly, the tax authorities denied Japan's X Co., Ltd. on the application of exceptions.

基于以上事实和判定，日本X株式会社认可其在华提供安装和监督管理劳务构成常设机构，并按照劳务发生成本和核定利润率20%的标准，计算补缴了非居民企业所得税和滞纳金70余万元，非居民个人所得税及滞纳金200余万元。

Based on the above facts and judgments, the Japanese X Co., Ltd. approved that it provided installation, supervision and administration services in China to form a permanent establishment, and according to the standard of labor cost and approved profit margin of 20%, calculated the non-resident enterprise income tax and late payment of more than 700,000 yuan, non-resident personal income tax and late payment of more than 2 million yuan.

（四）案例点评
Case Reviews

进口大型设备往往伴随着非居民企业的安装及监督管理活动。根据我国对外签订的税收协定，非居民企业在我国提供上述活动一旦达到规定时长，通常会构成常设机构，在我国负有相应的纳税义务。税务机关在实践中应重点关注三个方面：一是与设备相关的设计、安装、调试和指导等活动是否由非居民企业承担、控制或负责。二是上述活动时间是否达到税收协定规定的时间门槛。如果存在多个合同，要特别关注这些合同是否具有"商业相关性或连贯性"。同一企业从事的具有商业性或连贯性的若干项目应视为同一个合同项目来判定常设机构。三是对非居民企业援引税收协定及其议定书中关于常设机构判定例外条款的,税务机关应根据实际情况深入调查,判定其是否符合例外条款的规定。

Importing large-scale equipment is often accompanied by the installation and supervision and management activities of non-resident enterprises. According to the tax agreement signed by our country, once the non-resident enterprises provide the above activities in our country for a specified period of time, they usually constitute a permanent establishment, and have the corresponding tax obligation in our country. In practice, tax authorities should focus on three aspects: first, whether the design, installation, commissioning and guidance activities related to equipment are undertaken, controlled or responsible by non-resident enterprises. Second, whether the above-mentioned activity time meets the time threshold stipulated in the tax agreement. If there are multiple contracts, special attention should be paid to whether they are "commercially relevant or coherent". A number of commercial or consistent projects undertaken by the same enterprise shall be regarded as the same contract project to determine the permanent establishment. Third, if a non-resident enterprise invokes the exception clause in the tax agreement and its protocol, the tax authority shall investigate deeply according to the actual situation and determine whether it conforms to the provisions of the exception clause.

(四) 谷歌爱尔兰在英国设有常设机构案①
Google Ireland's Presence in the UK

(一) 本案概要
Summary of the Case

谷歌公司设立了一家位于爱尔兰都柏林的控股公司,该控股公司旗下又设立了一家位于爱尔兰的经营公司(Google 爱尔兰),负责处理英国及其他市场的广告业务。谷歌公司位于英国的客户刊登广告均需要与"Google 爱尔兰"联系。英国税务机关(HMRC)认为,"Google 爱尔兰"的工作并非准备性质或辅助性质的工作,谷歌公司在英国的员工直接参与了"Google 爱尔兰"在英国境内的经营活动,并为其创造了重大的经济利益。最终英国税务机关判定"Google 爱尔兰"在英国构成了常设机构。

Google has set up a holding company in Dublin, Ireland, and an Irish operating company (Google Ireland) to handle advertising in the UK and other markets. Google's UK-based customers need to contact Google Ireland for advertising. The British tax authorities (HMRC) believe that Google Ireland's work is not preparatory or auxiliary, Google's employees in the UK are directly involved in Google Ireland's operations in the UK and create significant economic benefits for it. Finally, the British tax authorities decided Google Ireland constituted a permanent establishment in the UK.

---

① 延峰、冯炜、崔煜晨:《数字经济对国际税收的影响及典型案例分析》,《国际税收》2015年第3期,第16—17页。

国际税法
International Tax Law

（二）相关事实
Relevant Facts

谷歌公司（Google Inc.）是一家美国上市公司，于1998年9月7日创立，是全球最大的搜索引擎公司，在全球各地都设有销售和工程办事处，业务包括互联网搜索、云计算、广告技术等，主要利润来自赞助商链接等广告服务。谷歌公司将其搜索及广告相关无形资产注册在位于爱尔兰都柏林的一家控股公司，随后在这家控股公司旗下设立一家同样位于爱尔兰的经营公司（Google 爱尔兰），负责处理英国及其他市场的广告业务。在这种安排下，谷歌位于英国的客户如果需要刊登广告均需要与"Google 爱尔兰"联系。"Google 爱尔兰"直接向其位于英国的客户收取广告费等收入，同时约99%的英国客户仅需通过网络就可以自助完成所有交易。相比之下，仅有约1%的英国客户需要和Google在英国的员工进行接触，而相关接触也不属于真正意义上的销售活动，因此"Google 爱尔兰"认为自身在英国并不构成常设机构。但是，英国税务机关（HMRC）则给出了相反的认定。首先，虽然仅有约1%的英国客户会同Google的员工进行接触，但这些（大）客户却给"Google 爱尔兰"带来了60%至70%的收入。其次，谷歌公司在英国的员工也进行了相关的销售活动，因为尽管"Google 爱尔兰"声称其在英国的员工并不直接负责业务推广及销售，但是根据英国税务机关的调查，其在员工招聘时明确提出了对于销售背景的要求，因此可以证明其工作远远超出其所定义的准备性质或辅助性质的工作。基于以上事实，英国税务机关认定谷歌在英国的员工直接参与了"Google 爱尔兰"在英国境内的经营活动，并为其创造了重大的经济利益，因而使其在英国构成了常设机构。

Google Inc. is an American listed company, founded on 7 September 1998. It is the world's largest search engine company, with sales and engineering offices around the world, the business of which includes Internet search, cloud computing, advertising technology and so on, and its main profit comes from advertising services such as sponsor links. Google registered its search and advertising-related intangible assets with a holding company in Dublin, Ireland, and then set up an Irish-owned company under the holding company (Google Ireland), responsible for advertising in the UK and other markets. Under this arrangement, Google's UK-based customers need to contact Google Ireland if they need to advertise. Google Ireland collects advertising and other revenue directly from its clients in the UK. At the same time, about 99% of British customers can complete all transactions on their own through the Internet. By contrast, about 1% of British clients need to contact Google UK staff, and related contacts are not real sales activities. Consequently Google Ireland does not consider itself to constitute a permanent establishment in the United Kingdom. But, British tax authorities (HMRC) give the opposite determination. First, although only about 1% of British clients are in contact with Google employees, but these (big) customers generate 60% to 70% of Google revenue in Ireland. Secondly, Google's employees in the UK also carry out related sales activities, because although Google Ireland claims that its employees in the UK are not directly responsible for business promotion and sales, according to a survey by the British tax authorities, it clearly sets out the requirements for the sales background when recruiting employees, so it can prove that its work is far beyond the preparatory or auxiliary nature of its definition. Based on the above facts, the British tax authorities found that Google's employees in the United Kingdom were directly involved in Google Ireland's operations in the United Kingdom and created significant economic benefits, thus making it a permanent establishment in the United Kingdom.

(三)案例评析
Case Review

这一案例充分反映了数字经济下常设机构判定标准受到的冲击和变化。在数字经济背景下,传统的商业模式发生了变化,非居民企业可以不在来源地国设立任何有形场所,而利用数字信息技术实现远程在线交易。同时,也可以通过数字信息技术将某实质性经营活动细化成若干个辅助性的非核心活动,并由分布在不同国家的实体来完成。本案中,尽管"Google爱尔兰"没有在英国设立有形经营场所进行营业,也认为在英国的员工从事的是辅助性或准备性活动,但该销售活动是创造了重大利益的经营活动,因而不属于辅助性或准备性活动。

This case fully reflects the impact and changes in the criteria for determining permanent establishment in the digital economy. In the context of the digital economy, the traditional business model has changed, and non-resident enterprises can use digital information technology to realize remote online transactions without establishing any tangible place in the source country. At the same time, a substantive business activity can also be refined into a number of auxiliary non-core activities through digital information technology, which can be completed by entities distributed in different countries. In the present case, although Google Ireland does not have a physical place of business in the UK and considers that employees in the UK are engaged in auxiliary or preparatory activities, the sales activity is a business activity that creates a significant interest and is therefore not an auxiliary or preparatory activity.

学习思考题
Questions for Study

1. 国际税法对营业利润是怎样认定所得来源地的?
   How to identify the source of income for operating profit in International Tax Law?
2. 怎样认定场所型常设机构?
   How to identify the place-type permanent establishment?
3. 怎样认定代理型常设机构?
   How to identify the agency-type permanent establishment?
4. 常设机构利润归属有哪些原则?我国企业所得税法采纳了哪些原则?
   What are the principles of profit attribution in permanent establishment? What principles are adopted in China's Law of Enterprise Income Tax?

第八章 CHAPTER VIII

跨国劳务所得征税协调规则
Tax Harmonization on Cross-border Income from Personal Services

　　随着经济全球化的深入发展以及国际通信和交通的日益便捷化,人员的国际流动性不断加强,跨国劳务成为一种普遍现象,越来越多的劳务提供者因从事跨国劳务取得劳务报酬。因此,税收协定在避免对跨国劳务所得双重征税或双重不征税方面的作用愈加重要。为协调居民国和来源国之间的税收管辖权冲突,各国间签订的税收协定通常先把跨国劳务所得划分为独立个人劳务所得、受雇所得和特定人员劳务所得(如董事费、退休金、演艺人员和运动员所得等),然后依据这些劳务所得的特性作出如下征税权分配规则:一是由来源国与居民国对劳务所得分享征税权或者由一方独占征税权;二是在赋予来源国征税权时以劳务履行地或支付者所在地作为判断劳务所得与来源国是否存在密切经济联系的标准。为全面、准确地理解上述跨国劳务所得的税收协调规则,考虑到经合发组织范本(OECD范本)、联合国范本(UN范本)和美国范本(US范本)在税收协定谈判和签订方面的重要性,本部分以分析OECD范本、UN范本和US范本为主探讨跨国劳务所得的税收协调规则。

　　Nowadays, the development of economic globalization is deepening, and international communication and transportation are becoming more and more convenient. As a result, the international mobility of individuals remarkably increased, and cross-border personal services have become a common phenomenon and more and more service providers receive remuneration from their performance of cross-border services. Therefore, the role of tax treaties in avoiding double taxation or double non-taxation on cross-border labor income is becoming increasingly important. In order to coordinate the conflict of tax jurisdiction between the resident state and the source state, the tax treaties signed by different countries usually classify the cross-border income from personal services into income from independent personal services, employment income and service income of specific persons (such as director's fees, pension, incomes of entertainers and sportspersons, etc.), and then according to the characteristics of these service income the following tax distributive rules are laid out: a. shared taxing rights between the resident state and the source state or exclusive taxing rights by a contracting state; b. the place of activity or the place of payers as standard to identify the close economic relationship between income from personal services and the source state when granting taxing rights to the source state. In order to fully and accurately understand the above-mentioned tax coordination rules of cross-border income from personal services, this part mainly discusses the tax coordination rules of cross-border income from personal services with the analysis of the OECD Model, UN Model and US Model, which are very important in the negotiation of tax treaties.

第八章 跨国劳务所得征税协调规则
CHAPTER VIII　Tax Harmonization on Cross-border Income from Personal Services

第一节　独立个人劳务
Section 1　Independent Personal Services

一、独立个人劳务所得的概念
Concept of Independent Personal Services Income

独立个人劳务所得是指以独立的个人身份从事专业性劳务或者其他独立性活动取得的所得。对于劳务提供者作为独立合同方取得的跨国劳务所得，来源国有权依据来源地税收管辖权征税。同时，劳务提供者的居民国也有权基于居民税收管辖权对其来源于境外的劳务所得征税。这会导致对跨国独立个人劳务所得进行双重征税。为了避免对独立个人劳务所得进行双重征税，有关国家在参照OECD范本、UN范本或US范本的独立个人劳务条款的基础上在税收协定中纳入独立个人劳务条款协调税收管辖权冲突问题。在适用独立个人劳务条款对独立个人劳务所得征税时，需要正确地理解独立个人劳务所得的概念。

Income from independent personal services means the income derived by a person in respect of professional services or other activities of an independent character. The source state has the right to tax the cross-border income derived by service provider as an independent contractor based on source jurisdiction. At the same time, the state of the service provider's residence also has the right to tax the cross-border income based on the residence jurisdiction. This will lead to double taxation for cross-border income from independent personal services. In order to avoid double taxation, referring to the Independent Personal Services article of the OECD Model, UN Model or the US Model, relevant countries introduced similar article into tax treaties to coordinate the conflict of tax jurisdiction. It is necessary to correctly understand the concept of independent personal service income when applying the Independent Personal Services article to tax the cross-border income.

1. 专业性劳务和其他独立性活动

Professional Services or other Activities of an Independent Character

独立个人劳务条款要求所得必须产生于独立个人劳务或其他独立性活动。但是，OECD范本、UN范本和US范本第14条对"专业性劳务"和"其他独立性活动"的构成要件并未予以明确，只是通过非穷尽性列举的方式来对专业性劳务的特征加以解释。例如，OECD范本第14条第2款（1997版）规定，专业性劳务特别包括独立的科学、文学、艺术、教育或教学活动，以及医师、律师、工程师、建筑师、牙医师和会计师的独立活动。[①]通过上述举例可以总结出独立个人劳务具有两个特征：一是一项活动只有符合自由职业的特性才能被

---

① OECD Income and Capital Model Convention (1997): Article 14(2).

定性为独立个人劳务；二是独立个人劳务所得主要涉及劳务,资本投入数量并不能产生决定性作用。[①] 除OECD范本列举的具有代表性的独立个人劳务之外的其他活动是否属于独立个人劳务,尚需要缔约国双方通过相互协商程序来加以解释。

Independent Personal Services article only applies to income from professional services or other activities of an independent character. However, what constitutes an independent personal service or other activities of an independent character is not defined in the Article 14 of the OECD Model, UN Model and US Model, but provides examples to explain the term "professional services" in non-exhaustive way. For example, Article 14(2) of the OECD Model provides that the term "professional services" includes especially independent scientific, literary, artistic, educational or teaching activities as well as the independent activities of physicians, lawyers, engineers, architects, dentists and accountants. Through the above examples, it can be inferred that independent personal services have two characteristics: one is that an activity can only be identified as independent personal services only if it conforms to the characteristics of free occupation; the other is that the income from independent personal services mainly involves services, and the amount of capital investment does not play a decisive role. In addition to the typical independent personal services listed in the OECD Model, whether other activities constitute independent personal services still needs to be interpreted by contracting states through mutual agreement procedure.

2. 独立个人劳务所得与营业利润

Income from Independent Personal Service and Business Profit

OECD范本第14条第2款的注释明确指出,独立个人劳务属于劳务性质的活动,因此,从事具有工业性质和商业性质的活动取得的所得被排除在独立个人劳务所得之外。[②] 对此,OECD财政事务委员会认为,由于独立个人劳务活动与商业活动存在高度的相似性,在税收实践中区分纳税人从事活动取得的所得是属于独立个人劳务所得还是营业利润是非常困难的,容易诱发税收争议。

Commentary on the Article 14(2) of the OECD Model notes that independent personal services are service activities, so income derived from industrial and commercial activities is excluded from the income from independent personal services. In this regard, considering the high similarity between independent personal services and commercial activities, OECD Fiscal Committee concerns that it is difficult to distinguish whether the income derived by taxpayers is independent personal service income or business profits in tax practice, which will lead to tax disputes.

3. 独立个人劳务提供者的范围

Scope of the Providers for Independent Personal Services

在税收实践中,税收协定的独立个人劳务条款使用的是"居民"一词,导致其主体范围存在争议。一种观点认为,由于"居民"包含个人、公司和其他团体,独立个人劳务条款不仅适用于个人、其他团体,还适用于公司。另一种观点认为,独立个人劳务条款仅

---

① 迈克尔·朗著:《避免双重征税协定法导论》(第二版),朱炎生译,法律出版社2017年版,第110页。
② Commentary on Article 14(2) of the OECD Model (1997).

适用于个人、其他团体。① 对此，OECD范本和UN范本对第14条的适用范围倾向采取扩大解释，不局限于个人；而US范本第14条的注释对"居民"一词采取限缩解释，不包括法人。

In tax practice, the scope of the persons is controversial because of the term "resident" used in the Independent Personal Services article of tax treaties. One opinion holds that since "resident" includes individuals, companies and any other body of persons, the Independent Personal Services article is not only applicable to individuals and other groups, but also to companies. The other opinion is that the Independent Personal Services article is applicable to individuals and other groups. In this regard, the OECD Model and UN Model tend to expand the scope of application of Article 14, which is not limited to individuals, while the technical explanation on Article 14 of the US Model adopts a restrictive interpretation for the term "resident", excluding legal persons.

在独立个人劳务条款适用于个人的情形下，还要区分劳务提供者是从事独立个人劳务还是非独立个人劳务。独立个人劳务与非独立个人劳务之间最大的区别在于劳务提供者是否拥有固定的雇主，是否存在雇佣关系。非独立个人劳务提供者受雇于雇主，而独立个人劳务提供者具有独立性，能够自由提供劳务，自行承担风险。我国在对缔约国对方来华从事劳务的人员适用税收协定的独立个人劳务条款时，判定其是否以独立身份开展活动，一般通过审查其执业证件、劳务合同的内容进行综合判断。例如：

In the case that Independent Personal Services article is applicable to individuals, it is necessary to distinguish whether the service providers perform independent personal services or dependent personal services. The biggest difference between independent and dependent personal services lies in whether the service provider has a fixed employer and whether there is an employment relationship. The service provider of dependent personal service is controlled by employer, while the service provider of independent personal service is independent and can provide services freely and bear the risk. When China applies the Independent Personal Services article of the tax treaty to the resident of the other contracting party to provide services in China, it is generally judged by examining their professional certificates and the contents of the labor contract to determine whether they perform independent personal services. The test standard is illustrated by the following case.

新加坡居民A与我国某公司签订了一份咨询顾问合同。合同约定：A担任公司的技术顾问，在合同的有效期间内不得直接或间接接受其他聘任，从事其他工作。若A违反约定，需要承担违约责任。另外，公司按月向A发放劳务报酬，为履行职务所产生的费用由该公司承担。依据《中新协定条文解释》对独立个人劳务条款的解释，由于A在合同期间内提供多方面劳务的自由受到了实质性限制，而且其为提供合同规定的劳务所相应发生的各项费用是由公司承担，而非其个人承担，因此，新加坡居民A提供的咨询服务不属于独立个人劳务，而是非独立个人劳务，应适用非独立个人劳务所得条款征税。

---

① W. Choi, Chapter 12: Active Income of Individuals in Roy Rohatgi on International Taxation: Volume 1 Principles (O. Ostaszewska & B.R. Obuoforibo eds., IBFD 2018), Books IBFD (accessed 17 June 2021).

A, a resident of Singapore, signed a consulting contract with a Chinese company. The contract stipulates that A as the technical consultant of the company shall not directly or indirectly perform other services for other persons during the validity of the contract. If A violates the agreement, he needs to bear the responsibility for breach of contract. In addition, the company shall pay monthly remuneration to A, and the expenses incurred in performing the services shall be borne by this company. According to the interpretation of the China-Singapore Tax Treaty on the independent personal services, the freedom of A to provide various services during the contract period has been substantially restricted, and the corresponding expenses incurred for providing the services stipulated in the contract are borne by the company, not by A. Therefore, the consulting service provided by A is not independent personal service, but a dependent personal service, which should be taxed in accordance with the Dependent Personal Services article.

（二）独立个人劳务所得征税权的划分
Distributive Rules of Tax Income from Independent Personal Services

1. 固定基地原则
Principle of a Fixed Base

为协调来源国与居民国对跨国独立个人劳务所得的征税权，各国间签订的税收协定通常采用1977年OECD范本和1980年UN范本第14条第1款所共同提议的固定基地原则。OECD范本第14(1)条(1997版)规定，缔约国一方的居民由于专业性劳务或者其他独立性活动取得的所得，原则上由该居民的所在国独占征税权。但是，若缔约国一方的居民为在缔约国另一方从事其专业性劳务或者其他独立性活动而设有供其经常使用的固定基地，则缔约国另一方有权对归属于该固定基地的所得征税。依据固定基地原则，固定基地是来源国对跨国独立个人劳务所得享有征税权的前提条件，因为来源国只对缔约国对方居民归属于固定基地的独立个人劳务所得享有优先征税权。因此，准确认定固定基地将决定来源国能否对跨国独立个人劳务所得行使税收管辖权。一般认为，固定基地类似于医生的诊所、建筑师或律师的办公室等这样用于个人从事专业性劳务的固定场所。对于固定基地的具体测试标准，OECD范本、UN范本未加以规定。依据1996年UN范本第14条的法律解释，固定基地不要求劳务提供者持续地使用，只需要受劳务提供者的支配。例如，缔约国一方居民因提供独立个人劳务的需要在缔约国另一方拥有固定的办公室，无论其是否实际使用，该办公室都会被视为固定基地。若缔约国一方居民在缔约国另一方没有办公室，而将酒店作为临时办公场所，该酒店不能视为缔约国一方居民为提供独立个人劳务在缔约国另一方设立的固定基地。[①]

In order to coordinate the taxing rights of the source state and resident state on cross-border income from independent service income, the principle of a fixed base is usually adopted in tax treaties, which is proposed by Article 14(1) of the OECD Model (1977) and the UN Model

---

① Technical Explanation to Article 14 of the United States Model Income Tax Convention on Income (1996).

第八章 跨国劳务所得征税协调规则
CHAPTER VIII Tax Harmonization on Cross-border Income from Personal Services

(1980). Article 14(1) of the OECD Model provides that the recipient's residence state has the exclusive right to tax income from independent personal services and other activities of an independent character. But, if this recipient has a fixed base regularly available to him or her in the other contracting state for the purpose of performing his or her activities, the income may be taxed in the other state but only so much of it as is attributable to that fixed base. According to this principle, fixed base is the prerequisite for the source state to tax the cross-border income from independent personal service, because the source state may tax the income, but only to the extent that the income is attributable to the fixed base that is situated in the source state and is regularly available to the recipient. Accordingly, identification of fixed base will determine whether the source state can tax the income from independent personal services. It is generally believed that fixed base is similar to a physician's consulting room or the office of an architect or lawyer, which is used for providing independent personal services. For the specific test standard of fixed base, the term "fixed base" is not defined in the OECD Model and UN Model. According to the explanation to Article 14 of the 1996 UN Model, the fixed base is not required to be continually used. But, the place is at the disposal of the service provider. For example, if an individual of a contracting state has an office in the other state for performing independent personal services, that fixed base will be considered to be regularly available to him or her, regardless of whether it is actually used. An individual who had no office in the other state and occasionally rented a hotel room to serve as a temporary office would not be considered to have a fixed base regularly available to him or her.

OECD范本第14条注释指出,虽然固定基地与常设机构在理论上存在差异,但是两者都是用来判断某一经济活动与活动地国是否具有一定紧密经济联系的标准,在税收实践中是一样的。例如,在对跨国独立个人劳务所得征税中,固定基地原则的作用类似于对跨国营业所得征税中的常设机构原则,即来源国对跨国独立个人劳务所得的征税限定在可归属于该固定基地的所得。同时,在确立固定基地的应税所得时,同样遵循独立企业原则予以核定,对于固定基地发生的与该固定基地的业务活动有关的成本费用予以扣除。①因此,OECD认为可以将常设机构的判定标准适用于固定基地。对此,以Vogel为代表的一些学者认为固定基地不同于常设机构。这些学者认为,企业必须通过常设机构开展业务活动,而固定基地仅要求经常使用,所以,固定基地对"持续性"的要求程度要低于常设机构。另外,在所得归属方面,固定基地原则将独立个人劳务所得局限于劳务提供者通过该固定基地提供劳务取得的所得,而常设机构原则允许适用引力原则,可以将在常设机构以外开展商业活动取得的所得归属于常设机构所得。②

The Commentary on Article 14 of the OECD Model states that there are differences between fixed base and permanent establishment in theory. However, both of them are used to judge whether there is a close economic relationship between an economic activity and the

---

① Commentary on Article 14 of the OECD Model (1997).
② Edwin van der Bruggen, Developing Countries and the Removal of Article 14 from the OECD Model, Bulletin Taxation, Vol. 55(12), 2001, p. 602.

state of activity, and they are the same in tax practice. For example, in the taxation of income from transnational independent personal services, the fixed base principle is similar to the permanent establishment principle in the taxation of transnational business income, that is, the taxation of income from transnational independent personal services in the country of origin is limited to the income attributable to the fixed base. At the same time, in establishing the taxable income of the fixed base, it also follows the principle of independent enterprise to ratify, and the costs related to the business activities of the fixed base shall be deducted. Thus, OECD permits that permanent establishment is used as guidance for interpreting and applying fixed base. In this regard, some scholars represented by Vogel think that the fixed base is different from the permanent establishment. These scholars suggest that the degree of permanence of a fixed base should be lower than that of a permanent establishment on that fact that a business must be carried on through a permanent establishment, while a fixed base should only be regular available. In addition, in terms of income attribution, the principle of a fixed base limits the income from independent personal services to the income received by the service provider through the fixed base, while the principle of permanent establishment allows the application of the principle of the force of attraction, the income obtained from commercial activities carried outside the permanent establishment can be attributed to the income of the permanent establishment.

随着税收协定独立个人劳务条款的普遍适用，OECD考虑到该条款在界定独立个人劳务概念、区分常设机构和固定基地方面存在的问题，于2000年将OECD范本第14条删除，并且对第3条第1款的"营业"予以修改，使其包括"从事专业性劳务或者其他独立性活动"。这就使OECD范本的独立个人劳务条款被营业利润条款吸收，来源国适用营业利润条款的常设机构规则对跨国独立个人劳务所得征税。2006年US范本也删除了独立个人劳务条款。然而，UN范本仍保留了独立个人劳务条款。

With the widespread application of the Independent Personal Services article in tax treaties, considering the difficulties in defining independent personal services and difference between permanent establishment and fixed base, OECD deleted the Article 14 from the OECD Model (2000), and amended the "business" in Article 3(1) to include "engaging in professional services or other independent activities". Consequently, source taxation of income from independent personal services has been assimilated with source taxation of business profits. Source state applies permanent establishment to tax income from independent personal services. Article 14 of the US Model was also removed from the US Model (2006). The UN Model, on the other hand, continues to include Article 14, which provides rules for independent personal services.

2. 183天规则和负担规则

183-Day Rule and Burden Rule

然而，一些发展中国家认为，固定基地作为来源国享有征税权的前提条件，仅依据固定基地原则对来源国与居民国对独立个人劳务所得的征税权予以协调，将会过多地限制来源国的征税权，从而影响来源国的税收利益。为了反映广大发展中国家的利益诉求，维护发展中国家的税收利益,1980年UN范本第14条第1款在采用OECD范本的固定基地原则的同时,也规定了其他的征税权划分方式,即停留时间规则和负担规则。

However, some developing countries believe that if the fixed base is used as a prerequisite for the source state to tax and only the principle of a fixed base is applied to allocate tax rights between the source state and the resident state, the taxing rights of the source country will be limited and the interests of the source state will be impaired. In order to reflect the interests of the developing countries and safeguard the tax interests of developing countries, Article 14(1) of the UN Model (1980) takes a hybrid approach. Under Article 14 of the UN Model, taxation in the source state may arise not only from the existence of a fixed base, but also based on the "length-of-stay" rule and burden rule.

依据UN范本第14条第1款第2项的规定,缔约国对方居民为从事专业性劳务或其他独立性活动在有关会计年度内在来源国境内停留的时间累计等于或超过183天,无论是否设立固定基地,来源国对该非居民纳税人获得的独立劳务所得享有征税权。除此之外,1980年UN范本第14条第1款第3项规定,缔约国对方居民在缔约国另一方从事专业性劳务或其他独立性活动取得的报酬超过确定的金额,并且该报酬是由该缔约国另一方居民支付或者是由设在该缔约国的常设机构或固定基地负担的,此时,缔约国另一方享有征税权。依据负担规则,只要非居民纳税人取得的独立劳务所得的数额以及支付者满足上述要求,来源国就有权对来源于本国的报酬征税,而无须考虑固定基地原则和停留时间规则。但是,基于该规则在税收实践中并未得到广泛的采纳,2001年UN范本的独立个人劳务条款只保留了固定基地和停留时间规则,负担规则被删除。

Article 14(1)(b) of the UN Model allows the source state to tax the income when the services are provided by a person whose stay in the source state equals or exceeds 183 days in the fiscal year concerned, whether or not a fixed base is established, the source state may tax the income to the extent derived from the person's activities performed in the source state. Article 14(1)(c) of the UN Model(1980) provided that the remuneration for the service is paid by a resident of source country or is borne by a permanent establishment or fixed base in the source country and exceeds a certain amount, the source country has rights to tax. Under that criterion, remuneration for independent personal services could be taxed by the source country if it exceeded specified amount, regardless of the existence of a fixed base or the length of stay in that country. But, due to the fact that this rule has not been widely adopted in tax practice, it was deleted from the Article 14(1) of the UN Model (2001) that only retains the rules of fixed base and the length of stay.

与OECD范本相比,UN范本第14条更大程度上扩大了来源国对跨国独立劳务所得可予征税的范围,维护了发展中国家的税收利益。因而,许多发展中国家在具体双边税收协定谈判中采纳UN范本的固定基地原则和停留时间规则。

Article 14 of the UN Model takes a hybrid approach, under which more situations can lead to taxation in the source state than under the OECD Model and protects the tax interests of developing countries. Therefore, many developing countries adopt the fixed base and the length of stay criteria proposed by UN Model in tax treaties.

三、中外税收协定对独立个人劳务所得征税的协调规则
Tax Coordination Rules on the Income from Independent Personal Services in Tax Treaties Signed by China

我国对外签订的税收协定较多地参考了UN范本独立个人劳务条款建议的固定基地原则和停留时间规则。在采用停留时间规则方面,我国的税收协定对183天的计算适用不同的标准。例如,我国与美国、日本等国签订的税收协定中,停留时间达183天仅限于一个历年,不能跨年度计算。而在其他的一些税收协定中规定可以任何12个月计算,允许跨年度计算。另外,在我国同泰国、马来西亚等国签订的少数税收协定中,除适用固定基地原则和停留时间规则外,还采用了负担规则。

In the tax treaties signed by China, more reference is made to the fixed base and the length of stay criteria proposed by UN Model. In terms of the 183-day rule, different standards are applied to the calculation of 183 days. For example, in the tax treaties signed by China with the United States, Japan and other countries, the calculation of 183 days is limited to one calendar year and cannot be calculated across the years. However, in some other tax treaties, it can be calculated in any 12-month period and cross-year calculation is allowed. In addition, in a few tax treaties signed by China with Thailand, Malaysia and other countries, in addition to the application of the fixed base and the length of stay criteria, the burden rule is also adopted.

第二节 受雇所得
Section 2　Income from Employment

受雇所得,也称为非独立个人劳务所得,是指因受雇于他人从事劳务活动而取得的工资、薪金以及其他类似报酬。为调整跨国受雇所得征税问题,税收协定的受雇所得条款采纳了OECD范本和UN范本所建议的征税规则。考虑到UN范本、US范本的受雇所得条款与OECD范本第15条的规定基本一致,下面主要介绍OECD范本关于受雇所得征税协调的规则。

Income from employment, also known as dependent personal service income, refers to the wages, salaries and other similar remuneration derived by individuals from employment. In order to regulate the taxation of cross-border employment income, the income from employment article adopts the distributive rules proposed by OECD Model and UN Model. Considering the fact that income from employment article of the UN Model and the US Model is similar with Article 15 of the OECD Model, this chapter will discuss the distributive rules of the OECD Model on income from employment.

OECD范本第15条所确定的受雇所得征税规则是由三项规则构成的。这三项规则具体

规定了征税权的分配、适用条件以及例外情形。

Article 15 of OECD Model includes three distributive rules to regulate taxation of income from employment. These distributive rules specify the allocation rules, application conditions and exceptions of tax rights.

一、征税权分配规则一：居民国独占征税权
First Distributive Rule: Resident State's Exclusive Taxing Rights

OECD范本第15(1)条规定,缔约国一方居民因受雇取得的薪金、工资和其他类似报酬,应仅在该缔约国一方征税。该规则表明,针对纳税人在居民国从事非独立个人劳务取得的薪金、工资及其他类似报酬,居民国享有排他性征税权。因此,适用该规则需要重点把握"雇佣""所得"的含义。

Article 15(1) of the DECD Model provides that salaries, wages and other similar remuneration derived by a resident of a contracting state in respect of an employment shall be taxable only in that state. This distributive rule means that the state of the taxpayer's residence has exclusive right to tax the salaries, wages and other similar remuneration derived by this taxpayer when he or she exercises his or her employment in his or her resident state. So, the application of this rule needs to focus on the term "employment" and "income".

1. 雇佣

Employment

纳税人取得的报酬是否来源于受雇,将决定受雇所得条款的适用。但是,OECD范本第15条以及其他条款并未对"雇佣"加以定义。结合各国的税收实践,确定雇佣关系是否存在主要考虑如下因素:第一,企业风险的缺失。由于非独立个人劳务是与独立个人劳务相对应的一种劳务提供方式,若劳务提供者在提供劳务时具有以自己的名义提供劳务、自主承担经济和企业风险的特征,则属于独立个人劳务。此时,劳务提供者与劳务接受者之间不存在雇佣关系。第二,从属关系的存在。从"雇佣"的表现形式看,其最大的特征在于雇员从属于雇主。雇主能够对劳务提供的过程和结果施加控制和指导。

The application of Income from Employment article will be determined by whether the remuneration derived by the taxpayer from the employment. However, neither Article 15 nor any other article of the OECD Model defines this term "employment". According to the tax practice of various countries, the following factors should be considered to determine whether the employment relationship exists. The first factor is the lack of entrepreneurial risk. Considering the fact that dependent personal service is a kind of service opposite to the independent personal services, so, if the service provider has the characteristics of providing services in his or her own name, bearing economic and enterprise risks independently, it is an independent personal service. Thus, there is no relationship between the service provider and recipient. The second factor is the existence of relationship of subordination. From the form of "employment", the biggest feature of "employment" is that employees are subordinate to employers. Employers can control and guide the process and results of performance of the personal services.

2. 薪金、工资及其他类似报酬

Salaries, Wages and Other Similar Remuneration

纳税人因受雇取得的薪金、工资和其他类似报酬涵盖任何形式的对价,不仅包括现金支付,还包括股票期权、使用住宅或汽车、获得健康或人寿保险以及俱乐部会员资格。① 另外,纳税人取得的报酬必须来源于受雇,即报酬与受雇活动之间存在因果关系。

Salaries, wages and other similar remuneration derived by taxpayers generally cover any form of compensation, including not only cash payments, but also benefits in kind, such as stock options, the use of a residence or automobile, health or life insurance coverage and club memberships. In addition, the remuneration derived by taxpayers must come from employment, that is, there is a causal relationship between remuneration and employment.

(二) 征税权分配规则二:来源国享有征税权及其例外

Second Distributive Rule: Taxing Rights of Source State and Exceptions

OECD范本第15条第1款在规定居民国对受雇所得享有独占征税权的基础上进一步规定,缔约国一方的居民因在缔约国另一方从事受雇活动取得的报酬,可以由该缔约国另一方征税。该规定作为居民国独占征税权的例外规定,赋予居民国与劳务履行地国对跨国受雇所得共享征税权,并由劳务履行地国优先行使税收管辖权。但是,劳务履行地国对受雇所得享有的优先征税权是有条件的、有限制的。即只有受雇所得与劳务履行地国存在密切的经济关联时,劳务履行地国才有权征税。OECD范本第15条第2款对劳务履行地国享有征税权作了例外规定。该款规定,若缔约国一方居民在缔约国另一方从事受雇活动时同时满足以下三个条件,则缔约国另一方不享有征税权,仅由居民国独占征税权:第一,收款人在有关财政年度开始或结束的任何12个月中在该缔约国另一方停留连续或累计不超过183天;第二,该项报酬并非由缔约国另一方居民雇主支付或代表该雇主支付的;第三,该项报酬并非由雇主设在缔约国另一方的常设机构或固定基地所负担。这也就意味着,在满足上述三个条件时,受雇所得由居民国独占征税。在准确适用该项分配规则时,需要注意以下方面。

Article 15(1) of the OECD Model provides that the resident state has the exclusive right to tax the income from employment, and further provides that the remuneration derived by a resident of a contracting state for his or her employment in the other state, that other state may tax. As an exception to the exclusive taxing rights of the resident state, this distributive rule grants shared, non-exclusive taxing rights for the cross-border income from employment between the state of residence and the state of activity. And the state of activity has primary taxing rights. However, the primary taxing rights of the state of activity for the income from employment is conditional and limited. That is to say, only if there is a close economic relationship between the income from employment and the state of activity, the state of activity has taxing rights to tax. Article 15(2) of the OECD Model contains an exception to the taxing tights of the state of

---

① Commentary on Article 15 of the OECD Model (2017).

activity. Article 15(2) of the OECD Model provides that remuneration derived by a resident of a contracting state in respect of an employment exercised in the other contracting state shall be taxable only in the resident state if: (a) the recipient is present in the other state for a period or periods not exceeding in the aggregate 183 days in any twelve month period commencing or ending in the fiscal year concerned, and (b) the remuneration is paid by, or on behalf of, an employer who is not a resident of the other state, and (c) the remuneration is not borne by a permanent establishment which the employer has in the other state. This means that the state of residence has the exclusive right to tax income derived from employment exercised in the other state, if all of the three conditions specified in Article 15(2) are satisfied. In the application of the second distributive rule, attention should be paid to the following aspects.

1. 183 天

183 days

1977年OECD范本第15条第2款a项以受雇者"在有关财政年度内"停留时间作为计算期间,以此确定外国雇员在某个公历1月1日起至12月31日这段时间内在劳务履行地国累计或连续停留时间是否超过183天。这种判断方式虽然计算简便,但是容易造成人为安排停留时间进行避税。1992年OECD将第15条第2款a项的"在有关财政年度内"修改为"在有关财政年度开始或结束的任何12个月内"。这种计算方法由于能够跨年度计算停留时间,有助于防止受雇者利用停留时间规避纳税,保障劳务履行地国的税收利益。例如,假设美国税收居民因提供受雇活动于2019年在我国停留时间为4个月,2020年在我国停留时间为3个月。依据1977年OECD范本第15条第2款a项的措辞,该美国税收居民在2019年和2020年财政年度停留的时间均未达到183天。但是,依据修改后的措辞,该美国税收居民从2019年开始在我国停留的时间已超过183天。

Article 15(2)(a) of the OECD Model(1977) adopted "the fiscal year concerned" as the calculation period of the physical stay of employees, so as to determine whether the accumulated or continuous stay of the foreign employees in the state of activity exceeds 183 days during the period from January 1 to December 31 of a calendar. Although this calculation is simple, it is easy to avoid taxation by arranging the stay time. The OECD (1992) replaced the former wording "in the fiscal year concerned" of Article 15(2)(a) of the OECD Model(1977) with the wording "in any twelve month period commencing or ending in the fiscal year concerned". Because this method can calculate the stay time in different fiscal years, it helps to prevent employees from avoiding taxation by stay time and protect the tax interests of the state of activity. For example, assume that a US resident stay in our country for 4 months in 2019 and 3 months in 2020 for employment activities. According to the former wording of Article 15(2)(a) of the OECD Model (1977), this employee did not stay for 183 days in fiscal years 2019 and 2020. However, under the revised wording, this employee was present in our country for more than 183 days since 2019.

我国签订的税收协定中受雇所得条款在规定183天期限时,大多数表述为"在有关历年中,收款人在缔约国一方连续或累计停留的时间不超过183天。"依据该措辞,外国雇员在我国停留期间的计算仅限于一个财政年度内,不能跨年度计算。然而,在我国签订的一些其他税收协定中,有关183天的计算期限规定为"任何12个月"或"任何365天",即可以跨年度计算外国雇员在我国的停留时间。

In the tax treaties signed by China, for the article of income from employment, most of them adopted the wording "in the other State for a period or periods not exceeding in the aggregate 183 days in the fiscal year concerned". According to this wording, the calculation period of foreign employee's stay in China is limited to one calendar year and cannot be calculated across the years. However, in some other tax treaties signed by China, the calculation period of 183 days adopted the wording "any 12 months" or "any 365 days", which means cross-year calculation is allowed for the calculation period of foreign employee's stay in China.

2. 雇主

Employer

OECD范本及其注释未对"雇主"一词加以定义。依据各国国内法及税收实践来看,通常依据雇佣合同确定雇主。但是,在国际劳务租用的情况下,劳务履行地国的企业通过外国雇员所在国的中介机构间接雇用外国雇员。这些雇员与中介机构订立劳动合同,工资、薪金由该中介机构支付。因此,仅依据形式上的合同关系在国际劳务租用的情形下很难认定劳务履行地国的企业为雇主。为了避免非居民纳税人滥用国际劳务租用规避其在劳务履行地国的纳税义务,1992年修改后的OECD范本注释对国际劳务租用下的雇主身份认定作了专门的规定。OECD范本第15条的注释第8段指出,雇主是指对雇员的工作施加控制并承担责任和风险的人。在国际劳务租用的情形下,劳务履行地国的企业是真正的雇主,其对外国雇员的工作拥有控制权,并对这些雇员的工作结果承担责任和风险。在国际劳务租用下雇主认定方面,我国坚持实质重于形式原则,同样采用了1992年OECD范本注释主张的观点和标准。

OECD Model and its commentary do not provide a definition of the term "employer". "Employer" is usually determined according to the employment contract in the domestic law and tax practice of various countries. However, in the context of "international hiring-out of labor", an enterprise of the state of activity recruit foreign-resident employees through an intermediary that is established in a different state. These foreign employees concluded employment contracts with intermediaries, and their wages and salaries are paid by intermediaries. So under the "international hiring-out of labor", it is difficult to identify the enterprise of the state of activity as the employer based on the employment contracts. In order to prevent non-resident taxpayers from abusing international hiring-out of labor to avoid their tax obligations in the state of activity, OECD (1992) made special provisions in the commentary on Article 15(2)(b) for the identification of employers under international hiring-out of labor. Paragraph 8 of the Commentary on Article 15 of the OECD Model states that an employer has right to control over the work of an employee and bears responsibility and risk. In the case of international hiring-out of labor, the enterprise of the state of activity is the real employer, who has control over the work of foreign employees, and bears responsibility and risk for the work results. In this respect, our country adopts the substance over form principle and also accepts the viewpoint and standard advocated in the Commentary on OECD Model (1992).

3. 并非常设机构或固定基地负担
Not Borne by Permanent Establishment or Fixed Base

OECD范本并没有对受雇所得由设在劳务履行地国的常设机构或固定基地负担的认定问题作出明确规定。在税收实践中,通常的认定方法是设在劳务履行地国的常设机构或固定基地是否直接向非居民雇员支付工资、薪金及其他类似报酬,并且该常设机构或固定基地将其所支付的劳务报酬作为一项费用支出从营业所得中予以扣除。在判断受雇所得是否由设在我国的常设机构或固定基地负担的问题上,我国采取了一种简单的认定标准,即缔约国对方居民被派驻到设在中国的常设机构工作,不论这些人员在中国工作时间长短,也不论其工资、薪金在何处支付,都应认为其在中国常设机构工作期间的取得是由常设机构负担的。①

For the test standard that the remuneration is borne by a permanent establishment or fixed base in the state of activity, the OECD Model does not define. In tax practice, the general method is to determine whether the permanent establishment or fixed base in the state of activity directly pays wages, salaries and other similar remuneration to foreign employees, and the remuneration paid by the permanent establishment or fixed base is deducted from the business income as an expense. In identifying whether the income from employment is borne by the permanent establishment or fixed base in China, China adopts a simple standard, that is, a resident of the other contracting state who is sent to work in a permanent establishment in China shall be deemed the income derived by this foreign employees from this permanent establishment regardless of his or her stay time and where their wages and salaries are paid.

4. 第15条与第16、第18、第19条的关系
Relationship between Articles 15 and 16, 18 and 19

对于外国雇员因受雇取得的董事费、退休金以及政府服务所得,不属于第15条的调整范围,这些所得应优先适用税收协定的其他相关条款。但是,受雇所得条款实质上是对受雇所得征税的兜底条款,即除了第16、第18、第19条规定的特殊形式所得以外,其他任何形式的受雇所得将自动适用该条款。

Director's fees, pension and income from government services derived by foreign employees for their employment, which are not regulated by Article 15, other relevant special articles will take precedence over the rules set out in Article 15. However, Article 15 is essentially a closed article for the income from employment, which means that in addition to the specific types of employment income stipulated in Articles 16 (directors' fees), 18 (pensions) and 19 (government service), other kinds of employment income will be regulated by Article 15.

(三) 征税权分配规则三:国际运输征税例外规则
Third Distributive Rule: Exception for International Traffic

OECD范本第15条第3款对与国际运输有关的受雇所得征税作出了例外规定。2014年OECD范本第15条第3款规定,在缔约国一方企业经营国际运输的船舶或飞机上,或在从事内河

---

① 《中国和新加坡关于对所得避免双重征税和防止偷漏税的协定》及议定书条文解释第15条。

运输的船只上从事受雇活动取得的报酬,该企业实际管理机构所在的缔约国可以征税。2017年OECD范本第15条第3款将企业实际管理机构所在国享有征税权,修改为由居民国独占征税权。

Article 15(3) of the OECD Model also includes an exception for the income from employment exercised aboard a ship or aircraft operating in international traffic. Article 15(3) of the OECD Model (2014) provides that remuneration derived in respect of an employment exercised aboard a ship or aircraft operated in international traffic, or aboard a boat engaged in inland waterways transport, may be taxed in the contracting state in which the place of effective management of the enterprise is situated. Article 15(3) of the OECD Model (2017) changed the wording "place of effective management of the enterprise" and allocates exclusive taxing rights to the state of the employee's residence.

第三节　对特定人员跨国劳务所得征税的分配规则
Section 3　Distributive Rules on Cross-border Service Income of Specific Persons

考虑到跨国劳务活动的多样性,各国通常会在税收协定中制定专门条款来调整从事特定跨国业务活动的人取得的劳务报酬。这些特别规则作为独立个人劳务条款和受雇所得条款的特别规定,具有优先适用的地位。

Considering the diversity of cross-border service activities, countries generally formulate special articles in tax treaties to regulate the remuneration of persons engaged in specific cross-border service activities. These special articles will take precedence over the rules set out in independent personal services article and income from employment article.

一、董事费
Directors' fees

董事费是公司支付给董事会成员的劳务所得。由于董事参与公司经营决策的方式以及工作地点具有较强的灵活性和自由性,依据传统的劳务履行的原则很难确定董事所取得的董事费是因在哪个国家提供劳务产生的。因此,OECD范本第16条基于支付者所在地原则,规定:"缔约国一方居民作为缔约国另一方居民公司的董事会成员取得的董事费和其他类似所得,可以在该缔约国另一方征税。"依据该规定,来源国对董事费享有优先征税权需要满足以下条件:(1)董事因其董事身份所获得的任何利益(如股票期权、健康保险、俱乐部成员资格等)都可以被视为董事费以及类似报酬。但是,董事会成员以其他身份(如公司雇员、

---

① OECD Model: Commentary on Article 16 (2017).

顾问等）所获取的报酬不属于董事费，应适用税收协定其他相关条款征税。（2）董事与支付董事费的公司不是同一缔约国的居民，而且支付董事费的公司不能是第三国的居民。

The director's fee is received by a person as a member of the board of directors of a company. Due to the fact that directors participate in the business decision-making of the company and the place of work is more flexible and freedom, it is difficult to determine the country from which the director's fees are derived by the traditional principle of service performance place. Therefore, Article 16 of the OECD Model adopted the principle of payer's residence, which provides that "directors' fees and other similar payments derived by a resident of a contracting state in his or her capacity as a member of the board of directors of a company which is a resident of the other contracting state may be taxed in that other state". According to this article, the source state has primary taxing rights to tax directors' fees, which needs to meet the following conditions. First, directors' fees and other similar payment received by director as a member of the board of directors include benefits in kind (such as stock options, health insurance coverage and club memberships, etc). But Article 16 does not cover fees received in other capacity (such as an ordinary employee, consultant, etc), and these fees will be taxed based on other relevant articles of tax treaty. Second, Article 16 is not applicable if the company and the recipient of director's fees are residents of the same state or if the company is a resident of a third country.

UN范本第16条第1款对董事费规定的税收待遇与OECD范本一致。但是，第16条第2款赋予公司的居民国对担任公司高级管理职务的缔约国对方居民取得的薪金、工资和其他报酬享有优先征税权。依据UN范本第16条的注释，"高级管理职务"是指除董事会以外，对公司事务的管理和规划负有主要职责的职务。

Tax treatment of Article 16(1) of the UN Model reflects the OECD Model. However, the Article 16(2) of the UN Model grants primary taxing rights to the state of the company's residence with regard to salaries, wages and other similar remuneration derived by a resident of a contracting state in his or her capacity as an official in a top-level managerial position of the company. According to the Commentary on Article 16 of the UN Model, "top-level managerial position" refers to positions that involve primary responsibility for the management and general direction of the affairs of the company apart from the activities of the directors.

US范本第15条同样赋予公司居民国对缔约国对方居民作为该公司的董事会成员取得的董事费和其他报酬享有优先征税权。与OECD范本第16条不同，US范本第15条限制了公司居民国的征税权，仅董事在公司居民国提供劳务的情形下，公司居民国作为来源国，才享有优先征税权。

Article 15 of the US Model also grants primary taxing right to the state of the company's residence to tax the directors' fees and other compensation for services derived by a resident of a contracting state as a member of the board of directors. Unlike Article 16 of the OECD Model, Article 15 of the US Model limits the taxing rights of the state of the company's residence, only when directors provide services in the state of the company's residence, the state of the company's residence as the source state has the primary taxing rights.

(二) 演艺人员和运动员
Entertainers and Sportspersons

演艺人员和运动员是少数群体,其具有流动性强、停留时间短以及报酬高的特点,一直是国际税收领域重点关注的对象。各国为了防止这类高净值群体逃避税,解决税收征管困难,一般在税收协定中制定专门条款,明确规定演艺人员和运动员条款作为独立个人劳务条款和受雇所得条款的特别规定,具有优先适用的地位,从而保障来源国的税收利益。当前各国税收协定的演艺人员和运动员条款存在两种不同的立法模式:一种是以 OECD 范本、UN 范本第17条为基础;另一种是以1996年US范本第17条为基础,设定最低限额。

Entertainers and sportspersons are minority groups with highly mobility, short stay time and high remuneration, they have always been the focus of international tax. In order to prevent such high-net worth groups from avoiding taxes and solve the difficulties in tax administration, countries generally lay out special article in tax treaties, which clearly stipulate that entertainers and sportspersons article as a special rule will takes priority over articles independent personal services and income from employment, so as to protect the tax interests of source states. At present, there are two different legislative models about article entertainers and sportspersons in the tax treaties of various countries: one is based on the Article 17 of the UN Model or OECD Model; the other is to set a minimum threshold based on Article 17 of the US Model (1996).

1. OECD范本和UN范本第17条
Article 17 of the OECD Model and UN Model

OECD范本之所以制定第17条,主要是出于两个方面的原因:一是跨国演艺人员和运动员具有流动性强、停留时间短的特点,通常不符合独立个人劳务条款和受雇所得条款的构成要件;二是演艺人员和运动员一般不会向其母国报告其在国外的税收信息,从而使其来自境外的所得双重不征税。因此,OECD范本第17条偏离一般税收分配规则,能够有效防止跨国艺术家和运动员逃避税,保障来源国的税收利益。

There are two reasons for the formulation of Article 17 of the OECD Model. First, international entertainers and sportspersons have the characteristics of high mobility and short stay time, which usually do not meet the requirements of independent personal services article and income from employment article. Second, entertainers and sportspersons generally do not report their tax information abroad to their resident state, so that income from abroad will suffer to double non-taxation. Thus, Article 17 of the OECD Model deviates from the general tax distributive rules, which can effectively prevent international entertainers and sportspersons from tux avoidance and evasion and ensure the tax interests of the source state.

OECD范本第17条第1款规定:"虽有第7条和第15条的规定,缔约国一方的居民作为表演家,如戏剧、电影、广播或电视艺术家、音乐家或运动员,在缔约国另一方从事个人活动取得的所得,缔约国另一方可以征税。"依据OECD范本第17条第1款的注释,第17条作为第7条(营业利润)和第15条(受雇所得)的特别法,能够优先适用。这意味着来源国可以直接适用第17条第1款对外国艺术家和运动员在本国取得的所得征税,无论所得是营业所得还是受雇所得,也无须考虑是否存在常设机构以及停留时间。因此,第17条第1款实质上赋予了来源国无条件的优先征税权，使其能够在任何情形下都可以对外国艺术家和运动员征税。

Article 17(1) of the OECD Model provides that "notwithstanding the provisions of Articles 7 (business profits) and 15(income from employment), income derived by a resident of a contracting state as an entertainer, such as a theatre, motion picture, radio or television artist, or a musician, or as a sportsperson, from that resident's personal activities as such exercised in the other contracting state, may be taxed in that other state". According to Commentary on Article 17(1) of the OECD Model, Article 17 as a special law takes priority over Articles 7 (business profits) and 15 (income from employment). It means that Article 17 applies regardless of whether the income derived by the foreign entertainer or the sportsperson is business profit or employment income, and even if there is no permanent establishment and irrespective of the length of stay. Therefore, Article 17(1) essentially grants the source state an unconditional primary taxing rights to tax foreign entertainers or the sportspersons in any case.

为了防止演艺人员和运动员利用"星公司"规避其在演出活动地国的纳税义务，OECD范本第17条第2款纳入了"透视法"。第17条第2款规定："表演家或运动员从事其个人活动取得的所得，并非归属于表演家或运动员本人，而是归属于其他人，虽有第7条和第15条的规定，该所得可以在该表演家或运动员从事其活动的缔约国征税。"这意味着，针对缔约国一方的演艺人员或运动员以受雇于某个公司或其他人的身份在缔约国另一方从事表演活动，将其取得的表演所得归属于某个公司或其他人的情形，演出活动地国可以直接适用第17条第2款穿透公司或其他人，将其取得的所得归属于实际从事表演活动的演艺人员或运动员。然后，来源国适用第17条第1款征税。相反，如果没有规定"透视法"，来源国对表演所得归属于公司或其他人的情形需要适用第7条。若该公司不符合常设机构原则，则来源国不能对表演所得征税。

In order to prevent entertainers and sportspersons from using the "star company" to evade their tax obligations in the state of activity, Article 17(2) of the OECD Model introduces the "look-through method". Article 17(2) provides that "where income in respect of personal activities exercised by an entertainer or a sportsperson acting as such accrues not to the entertainer or sportsperson but to another person, that income may, notwithstanding the provisions of Articles 7 and 15, be taxed in the contracting state in which the activities of the entertainer or sportsperson are exercised". This means that in the case of an entertainer or a sportsperson of a contracting state performs services in the other contracting state in the capacity of employee of a company or another person, and the income derived by an entertainer or a sportsperson accrues to a company or another person, the state of activity can directly apply Article 17(2) to look through the company or another person and treat the income to the entertainer or sportsperson. Then the source state applies Article 17(1) to tax. On the other hand, if there is no look-through rule under tax treaty, Article 7 of the OECD Model would normally apply. The state of activity would have no right to tax the income if the company had no permanent establishment in that state.

UN范本第17条遵循了OECD范本第17条的规定，最大程度保障来源国的税收利益。

Article 17 of the UN Model reproduces Article 17 of the OECD Model and guarantees the tax benefits of the source state to the greatest extent.

2. 1996年US范本第17条

Article 17 of the US Model (1996)

US范本也对演艺人员和运动员从事个人活动取得的所得作出了具体规定。以1996年US范本为例，US范本第17条与OECD范本第17条相比主要存在以下不同之处。

The US Model provides specific provisions for the income in respect of personal activities exercised by entertainers and sportspersons. Taking the US Model (1996) as an example, compared with Article 17 of the OECD Model, Article 17 of the US Model mainly has the following differences.

US范本为了区分两种不同类型的演艺人员和运动员，即收入高且在活动地国停留时间短的演艺人员和运动员和所得适中的演艺人员和运动员，在第17条第1款中纳入了最低限额规则。① 第17条第1款规定："虽有第14条（独立个人劳务）和第15条（非独立个人劳务）的规定，缔约国一方的居民作为表演家或运动员，在缔约国另一方从事个人活动取得的所得，可以由缔约国另一方征税，除在有关纳税年度，在缔约国另一方取得的毛所得不超过20 000美元或同等价值的货币外。" 依据《1996年美国税收协定范本法律解释》对第17条第1款的解释，如果演艺人员和运动员的所得没有达到最低限额，来源国仍可以适用第14条或第15条征税。但是，对低于最低限额的所得如何征税，在理论上存在分歧。一种观点认为，演艺人员和运动员条款是对独立劳务所得和非独立劳务所得条款中限制来源国征税权规定的例外，并不是限制来源国的征税权。而且独立劳务所得和非独立劳务所得条款作为"保护伞"条款，可以适用相关条款对低于最低限额的所得征税。② 另一种观点认为，艺术家和运动员条款是适用于艺术家和运动员的唯一规则，对低于最低限额的所得来源国无权征税，不能适用其他条款。③

In order to distinguish between two groups of entertainers and athletes, i.e. those who are paid relatively large sums of money for very short periods of service and those who earn relatively modest amounts and are thus not easily distinguishable from those who earn other types of personal service income, Article 17(1) of the US Model contains the minimum threshold. Article 17(1) of the US Model provides that notwithstanding Articles 14 (independent personal services) and 15 (dependent personal services), income derived by an individual resident of a contracting state from activities as an entertainer or sportsperson exercised in the other contracting state may be taxed in that other state if the amount of the gross receipts derived by the performer exceeds $20, 000 or its equivalent in the currency of the other contracting state) for the taxable year. According to the technical explanation on the Article 17(1) of the US Model, an entertainer or sportsperson who does not meet the minimum threshold may still be subject to tax

---

① 《1996年美国税收协定范本法律解释》第17条第1.2段。
② Jennifer Roeleveld, KarolinaTetłak, Article17: Entertainers and Sportspersons—Global Tax Treaty Commentaries [EB/OL]. (2018-10-01) [2020-08-26]. https://research.ibfd.org/#/doc?url=/document/gttcarticle17s6.
③ Friedhelm Jacob, Martin Schiessl, Article 17: Artists and Athletes in Commentary on US-German Income Tax Convention [EB/OL]. (2010-08-09) [2020-08-26]. https://research.ibfd.org/#/doc?url=/document/gus_c17.

in the state of activity under Article 7 or Article 14. There are different opinions about whether the source state has right to tax the income below the minimum threshold. One opinion is that the entertainers and sportspersons article is an exception to the provisions restricting the taxing right of the source country by independent personal services article and income from employment article, instead of restricting the taxing rights of the source country. Moreover, the independent personal services article and income from employment article as "umbrella" articles, can be applied to the income below the minimum threshold. Another opinion is that the entertainers and sportspersons article is the only rule applicable to entertainers and sportspersons. The source state has no right to tax the income below the minimum threshold by applying other provisions.

US范本第17条第2款也规定了"透视法",允许活动地国对归属于公司或其他人的表演所得征税。但是,第17条第2款对活动地国征税作出了限制性规定。当演艺人员或运动员与"星公司"存在真实雇佣关系时,公司收取表演所得存在正当理由,因此,活动地国不得适用第17条第2款穿透"星公司"对其征税。

Article 17(2) of the US Model also contains "look-through approach" and permits the state of activity to tax the income that is derived from the activities of an entertainer or sportsperson but accrues to company or another person. However, a restriction on the taxation imposed by the state of activity is incorporated into Article 17(2) of the US Model. When an entertainer or a sportsperson has a real employment relationship with the star company, there is a legitimate reason to receive the performance income for the star company. Therefore, the state of activity shall not apply Article 17(2) to look through the star company to tax.

我国对外签订的税收协定中的演艺人员和运动员条款采纳了OECD范本第17条规定的征税权分配规则,没有引入最低限额规则。我国税收协定的演艺人员和运动员条款虽然赋予了来源国优先、无条件的征税权,但在一定程度上也加重了外国演艺人员和运动员的税收负担,不利于国家间的文化交流与合作。

Tax treaties signed by China adopted the distributive rules proposed by Article 17 of the OECD Model and do not introduce the minimum threshold. Although entertainers and sportspersons article of China's tax treaties grants primary and unconditional taxing rights to the source country, these provisions also increase the tax burden of foreign entertainers and sportspersons to a certain extent, which is not conducive to cultural exchange and cooperation between countries.

三 退休金
Pensions

退休金是个人根据有关国家的社会保险或公共福利制度,因过去的雇佣关系而在退休后继续取得的一种劳动报偿所得。① 当前,随着经济全球化的深入发展,一国的税收居民因跨国劳务取得退休金的现象愈加普遍。如果一国的居民因雇佣关系在另一国工作并从该国

---

① 廖益新主编:《国际税法学》,高等教育出版社2008年版,第149页。

取得退休金,就会产生对该笔跨国退休金是由来源国还是居民国予以征税的问题。对此,不同的国家持有不同的立场。一些国家认为,退休金作为延期支付的劳动报酬,受益人基于先前的雇佣关系取得的退休金应在劳务履行地国征税。而另一些国家基于跨国退休金的受益人退休后已不在原先受雇国境内居住的事实,则从便于税收征管的角度,主张由受益人的居民国独享征税权。由此可知,若跨国退休金的来源国基于来源地税收管辖权对本国支付的退休金征税,同时,受益人的居民国基于居民税收管辖权对该受益人取得来源于境外的退休金课税,就会导致这笔跨国退休金被双重征税,从而产生法律性双重征税的问题。为了解决跨国退休金双重征税的问题,OECD范本、UN范本以及US范本对跨国退休金征税权的划分作出了相关的规定,以此协调来源国和居民国的征税权。

Pension is a kind of compensation income of personal services that an individual continues to receive after retirement due to the past employment relationship based on the social insurance or public welfare system of the relevant country. At present, with the further development of economic globalization, it is more and more common for residents of a country to receive pension due to cross-border personal services. If a resident of a country works in another country due to employment and receives pensions from that country, the issue of whether the cross-border pensions is taxed by the source country or the resident country will arise. In this regard, different countries hold different positions. Some countries believe that as deferred payment of personal services remuneration, the pension received by the beneficiary based on the previous employment relationship should be taxed in the country where the service is performed. However, other countries, based on the fact that the beneficiary of the cross-border pension no longer lives in the original country of employment after retirement, advocates that the beneficiary's resident state should have the exclusive taxing rights in the view of tax administration. So if the source country levies the pension based on the source jurisdiction, and the beneficiary's resident country taxes the pension from abroad by resident tax jurisdiction, then the pension will suffer from double taxation, resulting in juridical double taxation. In order to solve the problem of double taxation of cross-border pension, OECD Model, UN Model and US Model have made relevant provisions on the distributive rules for cross-border pension, so as to coordinate the taxing rights of source country and resident country.

OECD范本第18条(退休金)规定:"除适用第19条第2款的规定以外,因过去的雇佣关系支付给缔约国一方居民的退休金和其他类似报酬,应仅在该缔约国一方征税。"[1]由此可知,OECD范本对跨国退休金征税的立场是由受益人的居民国独占征税权。OECD范本规定居民国独占征税权,虽然便于考虑受益人的全球范围的所得和总体纳税能力,确保量能课税和有效地避免来源国税收征管难的问题,但是,各国对退休金实施不同的税收制度在国际税收领域会产生税收错配的问题,会导致双重征税和双重不征税的问题。

Article18 (pensions) of the OECD Model provides that "Subject to the provisions of Paragraph 2 of Article 19, pensions and other similar remuneration paid to a resident of a contracting state in consideration of past employment shall be taxable only in that state." So,

---

[1] Model Tax Convention on Income and on Capital 2017 (Condensed Version): Article 18 (Pensions).

the OECD Model's position on cross-border pension is that the beneficiary's resident state has the exclusive taxing rights. Although provisions of Article 18 considers the global income and overall tax capacity of the beneficiary to ensure tax fair and effectively avoid the difficulty of tax administration of source country, due to the different tax systems implemented by different countries for pensions, there will result in tax mismatch and double taxation or double non-taxation.

各国的退休金税收制度依据是否对退休金缴费、退休金营运增值收益、退休金分配收益这三个环节征税,可以分为三种模式:一是EET(Exempt-Exempt-Tax)模式,即对退休金缴费以及营运期间产生收益免税,只对退休金分配收益征税;二是TEE(Tax-Exempt-Exempt)模式,是指对退休金缴费征税,但是对营运产生的收益以及退休金分配收益免税;三是ETE(Exempt-Tax-Exempt)模式,仅对营运收益征税。①在OECD范本居民国独占征税权的原则下,采用EET模式的来源国不享有征税权,若受益人的居民国对退休金实行TEE模式的税收制度,居民国不会对跨国退休金所得征税,从而产生双重不征税;反之,若来源国采用TEE模式的退休金税收制度,而居民国实行EET模式,依据OECD范本第18条,退休金会被双重征税。对此,OECD范本第18条的注释纳入了替代条款,如允许来源国对退休金所得享有独占征税权;来源国对退休金非独占征税权;来源国对一定比例的退休金享有有限征税权以及来源国在居民国对退休金不征税的前提下征税。②

Considering in these stages of pension payment, value-added income and distribution income whether are taxed, pension tax system of various countries can be divided into three models. One is EET (exempt-exempt-tax), that is, the pension payment and income generated during operation are tax-free, and only the pension distribution income is taxed. The other is TEE (tax-exempt-exempt). It means that only pension payment is taxed. The final model is ETE (exempt-tax-exempt), which only taxes operating income. Under the principle of exclusive taxing rights of resident state, the source country adopting EET model does not tax. And if the beneficiary's resident country adopts TEE model for pension, then the resident country will not tax, which will result in double non taxation. On the contrary, if the source country adopts the TEE model, and the resident country exercises EET system, the cross-border pension will be subject to double taxation based on Article 18. In this regard, the Commentary on Article 18 of the OECD Model includes alternative provisions, such as exclusive taxing rights by source country, shared taxing rights, the source country's limited taxing rights on a certain proportion of pension and taxation by the source country under exemption tax treatment given by resident state.

UN范本第18条(退休金和社会保险)为缔约国提供了两种可供选择的方案。第18条方案A③在OECD范本第18条的基础上增加了第2款,即缔约国一方因雇佣关系支付给缔约国另一方居民的退休金或其他类似报酬来源于依据本国的公共福利计划建立的社会保险基

---

① 雷霆:《国际税收实务与协定适用指南:原理、实务与疑难问题》,法律出版社2018年版,第493页。
② Commentary on Article 18: Concerning the Taxation of Pensions, Paragraph 15.
③ Article 18 (Pensions and Social Security Payments) of the UN Model (2017).

金,那么该笔跨国退休金应仅在该缔约国一方征税,即支付者所在国享有独占征税权。而第18条方案B[①]则规定,受益人居民国对该受益人取得的来源于缔约国另一方的退休金或类似报酬享有征税权。若该笔退休金和其他类似报酬是由缔约国另一方居民或者设在该国的常设机构支付的,也可以由该缔约国另一方征税,即受益人居民国和支付者所在国均享有征税权。但是,若上述退休金或类似报酬是由缔约国另一方依据公共福利计划建立的社会保险基金支付的,则仅由支付者所在国享有征税权。与OECD范本第18条相比,UN范本对跨国退休金征税权的协调更加倾向于保护来源国的税收利益。

Article 18 (pensions and social security payments) of UN Model provides two options for contracting states. Alternative A of Article 18 adds paragraph 2 on the basis of Article 18 of the OECD Model, that is, the pension and other similar remuneration paid by one contracting state to a resident of the other contracting state for employment is derived from the social security system, then pensions shall be taxed only in that contracting state, that is, payer's state enjoys exclusive taxation right. Alternative B of Article 18 provides that the resident state of the beneficiary has the right to tax pensions or similar remuneration derived from the other contracting state. If the pension and other similar remuneration are paid by a resident of the other contracting state or by a permanent establishment situated therein, it may also be taxed by the other contracting state, which means the resident state and the source country share the tax jurisdiction. But, if such pension or similar remuneration is paid by a social security fund of the other contracting state, this pension shall be taxable only in the state of the payer. Compared with Article 18 of the OECD Model, the UN Model is more inclined to protect the tax interests of the source country.

我国与新加坡、日本等国家签订的税收协定采用了OECD范本建议的规则,规定受益人的居民国对退休金及其他类似报酬享有独占征税权。我国同美国等国的协定中借鉴了UN范本第18条方案A,即原则上受益人居民国独占征税权,但是若来源国按照社会保险制度支付的退休金和其他类似报酬,则由支付国独占征税权。与泰国、巴西签订的协定规定,在退休金是由来源国企业或者位于该国的常设机构支付的情形下,来源国与受益人居民国均享有征税权。另外,我国同加拿大签订的税收协定未就退休金作出特别的规定,则按照税收协定中的有关受雇所得的一般规则征税。

In the tax treaties signed with Singapore, Japan and other countries, China adopts the provisions proposed in the OECD Model, stipulating that the resident state of the beneficiary has the exclusive taxing rights. In the tax treaties between China and the United States and other countries, Alternative A of Article 18 of the UN Model is adopted, that is, in principle, the resident state has the exclusive right to tax, but if the source country pays pension and other similar payments derived from the social security system, the payer's country has exclusive tax jurisdiction. Tax treaties with Thailand and Brazil provide that the source state and resident state share taxing rights when the pension is paid by a resident enterprise of the source country or a permanent establishment situated in the country. In addition, the tax treaty signed between China

---

① Article 18 (Pensions and Social Security Payments) of the UN Model (2017).

and Canada does not make any special provisions on pensions, which will be taxed according to the general rules on income from employment.

（四）政府服务
Government Services

OECD范本第19条第1款规定，缔约国一方或者其行政区或地方当局对向其提供服务的个人支付的工资、薪金和其他类似报酬，应仅由该缔约国一方享有征税权，即支付国享有排他性的征税权。但是，在某些条件下，对上述工资、薪金和其他类似报酬的排他性征税权将由该雇员的居民国享有。OECD范本第19条第1款第2项规定，如果受雇者的个人劳务是在缔约国另一方提供的，且该受雇者也是该国的公民；或者并非仅由于提供政府服务而成为该国的居民的，那么，该受雇者取得的由缔约国一方支付的工资、薪金和其他类似报酬，应该仅在该缔约国另一方征税。对于政府雇员的退休金所得，OECD范本第19条第2款规定，缔约国一方或所属行政区支付给个人的基于先前的政府服务而获得的退休金，由该缔约国一方独占征税权。但是，如果该项退休金的领取者既是缔约国另一方的居民又是该缔约国另一方的国民的，则退休金只能在该缔约国另一方征税。另外，OECD范本第19条第3款明确规定，前两款的征税规则不适用于向缔约国一方或其行政区或地方当局从事的营业活动提供服务而取得的工资、薪金、退休金和其他类似报酬。这些所得应当根据税收协定的其他条款征税。

Article 19(1) of the OECD Model provides that salaries, wages and other similar remuneration paid by a contracting state or a political subdivision or a local authority thereof to an individual in respect of services rendered to that state or subdivision or authority shall be taxable only in that state. This means the paying state shall have exclusive taxation jurisdiction. But, under certain conditions, such wages, salaries and other similar remuneration shall be taxable only in the resident country of the government service employee. Article 19(1)(b) of the OECD Model also stipulates that such salaries, wages and other similar remuneration shall be taxable only in the other contracting state if the services are rendered in that state and the individual is a resident of that state who is a national of that state or did not become a resident of that state solely for the purpose of rendering the services. With regard to pensions received by government employees, Article 19(2) of the OECD Model provides that pensions paid by a contracting state or a political subdivision to an individual in respect of services rendered to that state or subdivision or authority shall be taxable only in that state. In addition, Article 19(3) specifies that the provisions of Paragraph 1 and Paragraph 2 shall not apply to wages, salaries, pensions and other similar remuneration in respect of services rendered in connection with the business carried out by a contracting state or a political subdivision or a local authority. Such income shall be taxed in accordance with other provisions of the taxtreaty.

OECD范本关于政府雇员的工资薪金和退休金的课税规则得到了UN范本、US范本的遵循，以支付国对政府雇员的跨国工资、薪金、退休金所得享有排他性征税权为原则。我国在对外签订的税收协定中也采纳了上述规则。

Distributive rules of the OECD Model on the wages, salaries and pensions of government employees are followed by the UN Model and the US Model. The principle is that the paying state has the exclusive taxing right to tax the income of cross-border wages, salaries and pensions of government employees. China has also adopted the above distributive rules in the tax treaties signed with other contracting states.

(五) 学生和企业学徒
Students and Business Apprentices

缔约国为了促进国家间文化、技术的交流与合作，一般会在税收协定中专门制定"学生和企业学徒"条款（下文简称"学生条款"），对学生和企业学徒在缔约国对方居留期间为接受教育或培训所获得的款项给予免税待遇，从而保障跨国求学和接受培训的学生和企业学徒的生活。为鼓励东道国对来访的学生和企业学徒收到的款项给予免税待遇，OECD范本、UN范本以及US范本的学生条款明确了对学生和企业学徒的征税规则。

In order to encourage cross-border culture and training exchanges, contracting parties generally introduce the students and business apprentice article (hereinafter referred to as students article) into the tax treaty, which provides for an exemption for the payments received by students and business apprentice for the purpose of education and training in the country. The policy behind this article is to ensure the students and business apprentice to pursue their education and training in the country. As a result, OECD Model, UN Model and US Model set forth specific rules for taxing students and business apprentice for the purpose of encouraging host counties to grant exemption treatment.

OECD范本第20条规定："学生或者企业学徒是，或者在直接前往缔约国一方之前曾是缔约国另一方的居民，仅为接受教育或者培训的目的而在该缔约国一方停留，并在停留期间取得来源于该缔约国一方境外的为维持其生活、教育或培训而支付的款项，该缔约国一方不应征税。"[①]该条款表明，作为缔约国另一方税收居民的学生和企业学徒，为了接受教育或者培训的需要而前往并暂时居住在缔约国一方期间取得来源于该缔约国境外的用以维持生活、接受教育和培训的款项，应当在缔约国一方享受免税待遇。对于该规则的适用，在具体的税收实践中应当注意以下问题。

Article 20 of the OECD Model provides that payments which a student or business apprentice who is or was immediately before visiting a contracting state a resident of the other contracting state and who is present in the first-mentioned state solely for the purpose of his or her education or training receives for the purpose of his or her maintenance, education or training shall not be taxed in that state, provided that such payments arise from sources outside that state. This article implied that students and business apprentice as a resident of the other contracting state received payment from source outside the country for the purpose of maintenance, receiving education or training, the country shall not tax. For the application of the rule, attention should be

---

① Model Tax Convention on Income and on Capital 2017(Condensed Version), Article 20: students.

paid to the following issues in specific tax practices.

首先,学生和企业学徒的范围。由于OECD范本第20条及其注释未对"学生"和"企业学徒"给出明确的定义,在界定上述主体的范围时应当符合OECD范本第20条的宗旨,即促进国家间文化、技术的交流与合作。因此,学生和企业学徒应当包括前往缔约国一方接受教育和培训的各种人员。除此之外,考虑到税收协定所提供的税收优惠只能由缔约国居民享有,因此,跨国学生或者企业学徒在缔约国一方享受免税待遇的前提条件是在前往缔约国一方接受教育或者培训之前必须是缔约国另一方的税收居民。

Firstly, the definition of "student" and "business apprentice" is not specific. The terms "student" and "business apprentice" are not defined in the OECD Model and its Commentary on Article 20 of the OECD Model. Considering the purpose of Article 20 of the OECD Model, the terms should be interpreted in line with the policy objectives of Article 20 of the OECD Model, that is, encouraging cultural and technological exchange and cooperation between countries. Accordingly, the terms "student" and "business apprentice" should be regarded as encompassing all persons that are currently undergoing any kind of education or training. In addition, because residents of the contracting state have entitlement to acquire the tax benefits, student or business apprentice must be a resident of the other contracting state before visiting the other contracting state.

其次,学生和企业学徒收到的款项是为了维持生活、教育或培训。这一限制条件有两层含义:其一,上述人员在东道国的主要或者唯一目的是接受教育或者培训;其二,受到免税待遇的款项仅仅是为了维持生活、教育或培训的目的而收到的款项,而不包括第15条(受雇所得)或者第7条(营业利润)所涵盖的对上述人员提供劳务或者服务所支付的报酬或者属于该部分的给付。因此,对于上述人员的培训工作涉及工作经历的情形下,有必要对提供劳务所获得的报酬与维持生活、教育和培训所需要的款项予以区分。如果支付报酬的数目与提供类似服务但并非学生或实习生的人所获得的报酬金额类似,可以认为该报酬是为提供服务而支付的。①

Secondly, the purpose of the payments received by a student or business apprentice is to pay aintenance, receive education and training. This includes two requirements. On the one hand, the student or business apprentice who is present in the other state solely for the purpose of education or training for the duration of the education or training. On the other hand, the article covers only payments received for the purpose of the recipient's maintenance, education or training. It does not, therefore, apply to a payment, or any part thereof, that is remuneration for services rendered by the recipient and which is covered by Article 15 (or by Article 7 in the case of independent services). Where the recipient's training involves work experience, however, it is necessary to distinguish between a payment for services and a payment for the recipient's maintenance, education or training. The fact that the amount paid is similar to that paid to persons who provide similar services and are not students or business apprentices would generally indicate that the payment is remuneration for services.

---

① Commentary on Article 20 of the OECD Model (2017).

最后,学生和企业学徒收到的款项必须来自缔约国一方境外。缔约国一方境外包括学生和企业学徒的原籍国以及第三国。但是,由该缔约国一方居民或者代表该居民支付的款项,或者由某个人在该缔约国一方的常设机构负担的款项,不能认定为来自缔约国一方境外。[①]另外,当学生和企业学徒收到的用于维持生活、接受教育或培训的款项来源于该缔约国一方境内时,此时这些人员所享受的税收待遇需要依据其税收居民身份来确定。若上述人员在求学或培训期间仍是原籍国的税收居民,则适用税收协定的"其他所得"条款;相反,如果上述人员取得了停留国的税收居民的身份,则依据国内税收规则来征税。

Finally, the article only applies to payments arising from sources outside the study state. The source of the payments must be either the origin state of the student or business apprentice, or a third state. But the payments that are made by or on behalf of a resident of a contracting state or that are borne by a permanent establishment which a person has in that state are not considered to arise from sources outside that state. In other words, if payments arise from sources within the study state, its tax treatment will depend on the resident identity. If he or she remain the resident of origin state, applying the article of "other income"; otherwise, applying the domestic rule to tax.

最新版本的UN范本的学生条款及其注释遵循了OECD范本的规定。但是,与OECD范本第20条相比,US范本的学生条款的适用条件存在较大差异。一是该条的适用主体包括学生和企业实习生。2006年US范本用"实习生"代替"企业学徒",而且对实习生的范围作出了明确的规定。2006年US范本第20条(学生和实习生)第3款规定:"企业实习生包括如下个体:该个体为保证其获得胜任一个职业或职业专长所需的技能而在缔约国一方暂时停留接受培训;或者该个体作为缔约国另一方居民的雇员,在缔约国一方暂时停留的主要目的是为了从该缔约国另一方居民之外的人处获得技能、职业或者商业经验。"[②]二是对上述人员来访的目的作进一步限制。US范本的学生条款不仅要求学生和实习生在东道国停留的主要目的是为接受教育或培训,而且还要出于接受全日制教育或全日制培训的目的。三是规定了实习生的免税期间以及个人劳务所得的免税限额。就企业实习生而言,免税待遇仅适用于其为培训的目的第一次到达东道国之日起不超过12个月的期间内。而且,对上述人员在东道国暂时停留期间取得的劳务报酬给予有限豁免。

The student article of the latest version of the UN Model and its Commentary follow the OECD Model. However, compared with Article 20 of the OECD Model, the applicable conditions of student article in the US Model are quite different. Firstly, this article applies to the students and trainees. In contrast, in the US Model (2006), the term "business apprentice" was omitted and a definition of the term "business trainee" was included. Based on the Article 20(3) of the US Model, a business trainee is an individual present on a temporary basis in the host state to undertake the training required to qualify for practicing a profession or progressing in a certain professional capacity. The individual must also be employed by a resident of the origin state and must receive the training from a person that is not related to the employer.

---

① Commentary on Article 20 of the OECD Model (2017).
② United States Model Income Tax Convention (2006), Article 20: Students and Trainees.

Secondly, this article further restricts the purpose of the above-mentioned personnel's visit. Article 20 of the US Model requires students to stay in the host country not only for the purpose of receiving education or training, but also for the purpose of receiving full-time education or training. Thirdly, this article stipulates that tax exemption should meet the time and income threshold requirement. The exemption shall apply to a business trainee only for a period of time not exceeding twelve months from the date the business trainee first arrives in the first-mentioned contracting state for the purpose of training. And limited exemption shall be granted to the above-mentioned personnel for their remuneration during their temporary stay in the host country.

在我国对外签订的税收协定中,学生条款一般规定学生和实习人员在缔约国对方学习、培训期间为了维持生活、接受教育或者培训的目的取得的款项,缔约国对方应当不予征税。但是,该条款的适用条件在我国对外谈签的税收协定中存在着明显的差异。其主要表现为以下方面。

In the tax treaties concluded by China with other countries, students article generally stipulates that the other contracting state shall not impose tax on payments received by students and business apprentices during their study or training in that other contracting state for the purpose of maintenance, education and training. However, there are obvious differences in the tax treaties negotiated and signed by China. It is mainly manifested in the following aspects.

第一,税收协定的学生条款对其适用主体作出了不同的规定。例如,在我国与日本、美国等国家签订的税收协定中,该条款的适用主体是"学生""企业学徒""实习生";而与泰国、马来西亚签订的税收协定的该条款的措辞分别是"任何个人""一个人"。

First, the student article of the tax treaty makes different provisions on its subject of application. For example, the applicable subjects of the clause are "students", "business apprentices" and "trainees" (tax treaties between China and Japan, the United States and other countries). However, the wording of the tax treaty with Thailand and Malaysia is "any individual" and "one person" respectively.

第二,我国与日本、加拿大等国家签订的税收协定对学生和实习人员的所得来源不作区分,只是作原则性的免税规定。如中日税收协定规定,学生、企业学徒或者实习生,为了维持生活、接受教育或者培训的目的收到的款项或所得,接受教育和培训所在国应给予免税待遇。①

Second, the tax treaties signed between China and some countries, such as Japan and Canada, make no distinction between the sources of income, but only provide tax exemption in principle. For example, the Sino-Japanese Tax Treaty stipulates that the income received by a student, business apprentice or trainee for the purpose of maintaining, receiving education or training, the host state shall grant exemption treatment.

第三,在与美国、英国等国家签订的税收协定中区别不同的所得来源,给予不同的税收待遇。其主要包括三种情况:一是为了维持生活、接受教育和培训,从所在国以外收到的款

---

① 《中华人民共和国政府和日本国政府关于对所得避免双重征税和防止偷漏税的协定》第21条(学生和实习人员条款)。

项，该缔约国应当免于征税；二是对来源于学习、接受教育或者培训所在国政府、科学、教育或者其他免税组织的赠款或奖金，在该国免于征税；三是对来源于学习、培训所在国境内的劳务报酬在一定的年限内给予定额免税待遇。

Third, different sources of income with different tax treatment are distinguished in tax treaties signed with countries such as the United States and the United Kingdom. There are three main situations. First, payments received from outside the study state for the purpose of maintenance, education and training shall be exempt by that state. Second, grants or bonuses derived from the governments, scientific, educational or other tax-free organizations of the countries where they study, receive education or training shall be exempt by that country. Third, fixed tax-free treatment shall be provided for labor remuneration originating from the country where learning and training are conducted for a certain period of time.

第四，我国与挪威、澳大利亚等国的税收协定中，学生或者学徒在接受教育或者培训所在国境内从事个人劳务获得的所得，享有与该国税收居民同样的税收待遇。

Fourth, in the tax treaties between China and Norway, Australia and other countries, students or apprentices who engage in personal services in the study state where they are receiving education or training enjoy the same tax treatment as residents in that country.

学习思考题
Questions for Study

1. 国际税法独立个人劳务所得征税协调规则是什么？
   What are the cooperation rules for the taxation of income from independent personal services in International Tax Law?
2. 国际税法关于非独立个人劳务征税协调规则是什么？
   What are the cooperation rules for the taxation of income from non-independent personal services in International Tax Laws?
3. 非独立个人劳务所得征税雇主的认定规则是什么？雇主的认定有何重要意义？
   What are the confirmation rules for the employers of the taxation of income from non-independent personal services? What is the significance of the confirmation of employers?
4. 对于跨国个人劳务所得征税的特殊情形有哪些？
   What are the special circumstances of the taxation of income from transnational personal services?

第九章 CHAPTER IX

跨国投资所得征税的协调
Tax Harmonization on Cross-border Investment Income

第一节 概 述
Section 1　General Introduction

一、投资所得的概念及特点
The Definition and Features of Investment Income

国际税法意义上的投资所得，指的是纳税人将其资产或者技术提供给他人使用而取得的各种所得，主要包括股息、利息和特许权使用费。所谓股息所得，是指纳税人通过对被投资企业出资入股或者购买股票等方式而享有股权、股份或者其他非债权关系分享利润的权利而取得的所得或者收益。利息所得是指纳税人因提供贷款或者拥有其他形式的债权而获得的收入。特许权使用费是指权利人因提供专利、商标、专有技术、著作权等专有权的使用权而获得的报酬。区分投资所得与劳动所得以及营业利润的关键标准在于纳税人是否直接参与被投资企业的经营管理。因此，相较于劳动所得与营业利润而言，投资所得具有消极性、被动性等特征。

In the sense of international tax law, the investment income refers to all kinds of income derived by taxpayers through providing their assets or technologies to others for use, mainly including dividends, interest and royalties. Dividends refer to the income obtained by taxpayers by means of investing or buying shares of invested enterprises and thus enjoying profits from equities or other non-credit rights. Interest refers to the income obtained by taxpayers from providing loan or right of credit in other forms. Royalty refers to the remuneration obtained by the right-holders for providing the right to use the patents, trademarks, proprietary technologies, copyrights and other exclusive rights. Whether the taxpayer engaged in the operation and management of the invested company directly is the key issue to tell the difference between investment income, labor income and business profit.

---

① 张泽平主编：《国际税法》，北京大学出版社2016年版，第131页。

Thus, compared with labor income and business profit, investment incomes are characterized by their passiveness.

二、跨国投资所得征税协调的基本原则
Basic Principle of Tax Harmonization on Cross-border Investment Income

(一) 税收分享原则
Tax Sharing Principle

针对跨国投资所得中股息所得、利息所得的征税协调问题，OECD范本与UN范本均采用了税收分享原则，即可以在受益人的居住国征税，也可以在所得来源地国一方征税。但是对于跨国特许权使用费的征税协调问题，这两个范本作出了不同规定，OECD范本规定由居住国一方独占征税权，而UN范本则采用了与股息、利息征税规则相同的税收分享原则。税收分享原则旨在通过双方在税收协定的签订过程中协商预提税率的方式，来限定来源地国的扣缴比例，以确保居住国一方能够分享到一定的税收利益；同时也要避免对跨国投资者重复征税。之所以采用税收分享原则，而不采用独占征税原则，主要是由跨国投资的特点和公平合理原则所决定的。跨国投资是一个多方参与的活动，从投资所得的来源国角度而言，跨国投资的资金、财产和技术是在来源国境内投入生产、在实际运用中创造出更多财富，跨国投资所得的实现与来源国经济活动有着不可分割的联系，因此来源国应有权对投资所得征税。从纳税人居住国一方而言，虽然投资所得的产生不是在本国境内实现，但是有关资金的筹集、财产的购置和技术的研究与开发，往往是在居住国境内进行的，而且这些投资的成本费用一般已经在纳税人的居住国摊销扣除，因此也应确保居住国就其居民来自境外的投资所得分享到适当的税收利益，这样才能确保跨国投资所得的税收分配关系更加公平合理。OECD范本第12条第1款所主张的跨国特许使用费仅由受益人居住国一方享有独占征税权，该条款在适用中受到较多限制。通常情况下，该独占征税权是建立在两个假设前提之上的，一是在采用特许权使用费独占征税权的缔约国之间，跨国投资技术流动大致相等；二是双方均同意在类似的税收实践中让渡税收管辖权。因此，独占征税权一般仅在少数彼此间技术交流规模大致相当的发达国家之间采用，因为双方的资金和技术交流规模相近，即便由受益人居住国一方独占征税权，双方之间最终的税收分配结果也会是大体相当的。但是在经济技术发展水平差距较大的两个国家之间，由于双方的资金、技术交流规模等差距较大，如果由受益人居住国一方行使独占征税权，就会形成极不合理的税收分配关系，投资所得的来源地国可能将面临极不合理的税收权益分配结果。[①]因此，OECD范本第10条、第11条以及UN范本第12条都规定，对相关跨国投资所得应采用限定来源国一方可以课征预提税的最高税率，来确保受益人居住国一方将获取税收利益，从而实现税收分享的协作原则。[②]而且该税收分享原则已经被大多数国家在其双边税收协定中采用。

[①] 廖益新主编：《国际税法学》，高等教育出版社2008年版，第166页。
[②] 参见OECD范本第10条和第11条，以及UN范本第12条。

As for the issue of allocating taxing power for dividends and interest, both OCED Model Tax Convention and UN Model Tax Convention lay down the principle of tax sharing, that is, dividends and interest may be taxed in the state of residence of beneficiary owner and the state of source of income. However, OCED Model Tax Convention and UN Model Tax Convention stipulate different principles to the issue of allocating taxing power on royalties. The former grants the exclusive taxation rights on royalties to the state of beneficial owner's residence and the latter adopts the tax sharing principle. The tax sharing principle aims to limit the withholding tax rate imposed by the state of source through bilateral negotiation to ensure that the state of source does not impose an excessive tax on investment income and the tax revenue is to be shared between the state of source and the state of residence. The principle of tax sharing is widely applicable because of its reflection of fairness and reasonability. Many parties are participating in cross-border investment activities. From the perspective of state of source, the relevant capital, property and technology in cross-border investment are put into the process of production and create more wealth in practical application in its territory, hence realization of cross-border investment income is inextricably linked with the economic activities of the state of source. Thus, the state of source should have the right to tax on such investment income. From the point of state of residence, although the investment income is not realized in its territory, the raising of assets, purchase of property and the research and development of relevant technology are conducted in its territory. And generally, the cost of these investments would have been amortized and deducted by the taxpayer in its territory as well. Therefore, the residence state should be ensured to share appropriate tax benefits on the investment income of its residents from abroad, so as to make the tax allocation fairer and more reasonable for incomes from investment. The idea that royalties arising in a contracting state and beneficial owned by a resident of the other contracting state shall be only taxed in that other state was put forward in Paragraph 1 of Article 12 of OECD Model Tax Convention. However such a provision has been applied with a number of limitations. Under normal conditions, the exclusive taxation right is premised on two assumptions. Firstly, the flow of investment funds between the contracting states should be approximately equal. Secondly, the contracting states should have both agreed to grant the exclusive taxing right to the residence state. Therefore, this method is only used in a few bilateral agreements between developed countries with similar technical exchange scale, because only when having equal scale of technology and capital exchange can lead to equal allocation result if granting the residence state with the exclusive taxation right on royalties. When the gap of technical and economic development were too wide between the contracting states, granting the exclusive taxation rights to the residence state would result in an unreasonable distribution relationship for the state of source. Therefore, Articles 10 and 11 of the OECD Model Convention and Article 12 of the UN Model Convention all slipulate that the highest tax rate that can be imposed on the relevant transnational investment income derived from the source country should be limited to ensure that the beneficiary's country of residence will obtain tax benefits, so as to realize the tax sharing principle.

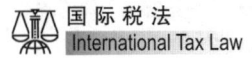

（二）税收分享原则的适用前提
The Preconditions for Application of the Tax Sharing Principle

在适用税收分享原则时，受益所有人必须为缔约国一方居民。该适用前提包含两层意思：首先，适用税收分享原则的纳税人范围应仅限于具有缔约国一方居民身份的跨国投资者，而不包括第三国居民纳税人。其次，具有缔约国一方居民身份的纳税人，应当是"受益所有人"，而非代理人、指定人或者"导管"公司。之所以将纳税人范围限定为缔约国一方居民身份的跨国投资人，是因为双边税收协定中有关投资所得项目的限制税率是由缔约国双方在对等互惠的基础上谈判确定，目的在于通过限制预提税征税税率，在缔约国之间形成合理的税收利益分配关系，避免对纳税人重复征税。如果第三国居民纳税人享受此种税收优惠待遇，则会损害投资所得来源国的正当税收利益。此外，仅仅具有缔约国一方居民身份是不够的，为了避免协定的优惠待遇不被第三国居民利用，还要求缔约国一方居民是受益所有人，即如果跨国投资所得的受益所有人不是缔约国另一方的居民纳税人，而是第三国居民，尽管跨国投资的收款人具有缔约国一方居民身份，来源国一方没有义务因为投资所得是被缔约国一方居民直接获取而放弃对该项所得征税权。来源国一方可以适用国内所得税法的规定进行源泉课税，而不受税收协定中限制税率的约束。

The precondition of the application of the principle of tax sharing is that the beneficial owner must be a resident of contracting state. This contains two-fold meanings. First, the scope of taxpayers applying the principle of tax sharing shall be limited to cross-border investors who are residents of a contracting state and shall not include resident taxpayers of a third state. Second, taxpayers who are the resident of a contracting state shall be the beneficial owner, instead of agent, nominee or "conduit" company. The reason why the provision limits the range of taxpayer within the category of residence investor is that the ceiling tax rate of relevant income in tax convention is negotiated on the basis of reciprocity in order to form reasonable distribution relationship between contracting states and avoid double taxation. Granting tax benefits to a person in third state will do harm to the benefits of source state. In case of abuse of provisions, it is not enough for the taxpayers merely have the identification of resident of contracting state, also, the residence taxpayers of contracting state ought to be beneficial owner of the investment income. If the beneficial owners of income were residence in third state rather than taxpayers of contracting state, the state of source is not obliged to give up taxing rights over the relevant income merely because that income was paid directly to a resident of a state with which the state of source had concluded convention. The state of source is not constrained by the limitation of withholding rate in convention, but tax on the relevant income according to its domestic personal income tax law.

OECD范本在注释中指出，"受益所有人"概念不同于其他文件中该词语具有的含义，对此应当加以区分。"受益所有人"概念是为了解决第10条第1款用语引发的问题，因此不能在一种狭隘的技术层面上运用，而应结合具体语境以及协定的目的和宗旨去理解，包括避免双重征税和防止逃避税。[①]OECD范本还明确了代理人、指定人以及"导管"公司不应构成

---

① 参见OECD范本第10条注释第12段。

受益所有人。在某项所得是由作为代理人或者指定人的缔约国一方居民所接收的情况下，如果来源国仅因该接收人具有缔约国一方居民身份而予以减税或者免除，这将违背协定的目的和宗旨，因为在这种情形下，直接接收人虽然具有缔约国居民身份，但是其并不会直接产生双重征税问题，因为该接收人不应构成该所得的受益所有人。与此同时，如果缔约国一方的某个居民不是通过代理人或者指定人关系，而是为另一个实际取得股息的人作为接收相关所得的"导管"，此时要求来源国减免征税的做法，也与税收协定的目的和宗旨不符。因此，经合发组织财政事务委员会在《双重征税协定与"导管"公司的运用》报告中得出结论：尽管导管公司是形式上的特定资产的所有人，但因其对资产的权力非常有限，使得其实际上是一个利害关系人的利益行事的受托人或者执行人，因此，"导管"公司一般不被认为构成受益所有人。①

The notes to the "OECD Model" point out that the concept of "beneficial owner" is different from the meaning of the term in other documents and should be distinguished. The concept of "beneficial owner" is to solve the problems caused by the terminology of Article 10, Paragraph 1, and therefore cannot be applied on a narrow technical level. It should be understood in light of the specific context and the purpose of the agreement, including avoidance double taxation and prevention of tax evasion. Also, agent, nominee and conduit company are not beneficial owner. When an item of income is paid to a resident of contracting state acting in the capacity of agent or nominee it would be inconsistent with the object and purpose of the convention for the state of source to grant relief or exemption merely on account of the status of the direct recipient of the income as a resident of the other contracting state. Because in this situation, direct recipient qualifies as a resident but no potential double taxation arises as a consequence of that status since the recipient is not treated as the owner of the income for tax purpose in the state of residence. It would be equally inconsistent with the object and purpose of the convention for the state of source to grant relief or exemption where a resident of contracting state, otherwise than through an agency or nominee relationship, simply acts as a conduit for another person who in fact receives the benefit of the income concerned. For these reasons, the report from Committee on Fiscal Affairs entitled "Double Taxation Conventions and the Use of Conduit Companies" concludes that a conduit company cannot normally be regarded as the beneficial owner if, through the former owner, it has, as a matter of fact, very narrow powers which render it, in relation to the income concerned, a merely fiduciary or administrator acting on account of the interest parties.

关于"受益所有人"的概念与认定标准，目前还存在分歧，归纳起来主要有以下问题：（1）税收协定中受益所有人用语是否具有独立的协定法意义，还是适用缔约国的国内法来认定？（2）税收协定意义上的受益所有人的判定应该依据的是一种法律性质的认定标准还是一种事实或者经济实质性的检验标准？（3）受益所有人的认定仅仅考察的是收款人对所得的控制支配权，还是应扩大考虑其对所得的基础财产或权利的控制支配权？（4）在受益所有人问题上是否应考虑缔约国国内特别反避税规则或者实质优先于形式等一般反避税规

---

① 参见OECD范本（2017）第10条注释第12.2段，第12.3段，第12.4段。

则的适用？参考OECD分别于2011年4月29日和2012年12月25日公布的《经合发组织税收协定范本中"受益所有人"含义的说明》的讨论稿，一些学者提出受益所有人概念发展将呈现如下趋势：（1）税收协定中的受益所有人概念应具有相对独立的协定法意义；（2）虽然确认受益所有人原则上应依据一种法律性质的标准进行判定，但不排除运用事实性检测标准来认定是否存在法律义务；（3）受益所有人的认定应考察其对有关款项的支配控制权，不包括对产生所得的基础财产或者权利的控制权；（4）认定受益所有人概念不适用缔约国国内法上的特别或者一般反避税规则，但具有受益所有人身份并不自动获得税收协定的优惠待遇。①

There has been much controversy over the definition and identification criteria of "beneficial owner", which could be summed up in the following cases. First, whether the term "beneficial owner" used here has independent conventional meaning or the domestic law of contracting state should be applied to determine the term? Second, whether the term "beneficial owner" in the sense of tax convention should be identified on the basis of legal criterion or on the basis of factual or economic substantial criterion? Third, whether the determination of "beneficial owner" merely examines the recipient's power of domination and control over the income or put the power of domination and control over the basic property or right from which the income derives into consideration? Fourth, whether the application of special anti-tax avoidance rules or general anti-tax avoidance rules such as substance over form in domestic law of contracting state should be taken into consideration on the issue of beneficial owner? Based on the discussion draft "Clarification of the Meaning of 'Beneficial Owner' in the OECD Model Tax Convention" released by OECD on 29 April 2011 and 25 December 2012, scholars put forward that the concept of beneficial owner will develop in the following trends. First, the concept of beneficial owner in tax convention should have relatively independent legal significance. Second, although it is recognized that the beneficial owner is determined on the basis of a standard of legal nature, it does not preclude the use of factual testing standards to determine the existence of legal obligations. Third, the determination of the beneficial owner shall take the power of dominance and control over the relevant funds into consideration, excluding the power over the underlying property or rights that generate the income. Fourth, the determination of the concept of beneficial owner shall not apply to the special or general anti-avoidance rules of the domestic law of the contracting state, and even though the recipient of income is considered to be the beneficial owner, it does not mean that limitation of tax provided in convention must automatically be granted.

（三）税收分享原则的适用例外
The Exception of Tax Sharing Principle

即使跨国纳税人同时具备缔约国一方居民与受益所有人身份，税收分享原则在适用过程中仍然存在一些例外情况。OECD范本第10条、第11条，第12条中分别对例外情况作出

---

① 张泽平主编：《国际税法》，北京大学出版社2016年版，第133、第134页。

第九章 跨国投资所得征税的协调
CHAPTER IX Tax Harmonization on Cross-border Investment Income

规定。概括地说,作为缔约国一方居民的受益所有人,如果在所得来源国一方境内设有常设机构进行营业或者设有固定基地从事个人独立劳务,并且据以支付股息、利息以及特许权使用费的股权、债权和权利财产与常设机构或者固定基地有实际联系,这种情况下的跨国投资所得不适用税收协定中关于跨国投资预提税限制规定,而应适用协定中有关营业所得课税条款,将其作为常设机构的营业利润课税,或者将其作为固定基地的个人所得,适用协定中关于独立劳务所得的征税规则。OECD范本第10条第4款仅仅规定如果支付的所得是缔约国另一方居民设立的常设机构资产的一部分或者与该常设机构有其他形式的实际联系,该项所得可以作为常设机构的营业利润征税,并没有规定向缔约国一方居民支付的来自缔约国另一方境内常设机构的收入一定与该常设机构具有联系。该种例外情况要求固定机构与跨国投资所得分配具有实际联系,即产生投资所得的股权、债权、知识产权和设备财产等属于常设机构或者固定基地直接拥有的财产,或者常设机构、固定基地与产生投资所得的财产有实际经营管理关系。OECD范本指出,所谓实际联系,不仅限于要求在常设机构会计账簿上有记载,如果股权、债权和权利财产的"经济"所有权按照《常设机构利润归属报告》中为适用第7条第2款而提出的原则分配给常设机构,则这种与支付有关的股份持有将构成常设机构的部分营业资产。股份、债权和权利财产的"经济所有权"相当于一个独立企业在所得税意义上拥有的所有权,包括随之产生的收益和负担。①

Still, there is exception stipulated in Article 10, Article 11 and Article 12 of OECD Model respectively in the application of principle of tax sharing, even though the beneficiary owner of income is the resident of contracting state. Generally speaking, the beneficial owner, which is the resident of contracting state, has permanent establishment to carry on business or fixed base to perform independent labor service in state of source, and the equity, creditor's rights and chose in action that produce dividends, interest and royalties are effectively connected with the permanent establishment. In this situation, the investment income shall be regarded as business profit of permanent or personal income of fixed base and apply taxation rules of business profit or taxation rules of independent labor income in tax convention rather than the regulation of withholding tax rate. Paragraph 4 of Article 10 of OECD Model merely provides that in the state of source the dividends are taxable as part of the profits of the permanent establishment there owned by the beneficiary which is a resident of the other state, if they are paid in respect of holding forming part of the assets of the permanent establishment or otherwise effectively connected with that establishment. It does not stipulate that income flowing to a resident of a contracting state from a source situated in the other state must be related to a permanent establishment which that resident may have in the latter state. This kind of exception requires that the fixed base or permanent establishment be effectively connected with the distribution of income, that is the equity, creditor's right, intellectual property and equipment property that generate income belong to permanent establishment or fixed base, or there exists management operation relationship between permanent establishment, fixed base and the property that generates investment income. As is pointed out in OECD Model Tax Convention that the requirement that a shareholding be

---

① 参见OECD范本第10条第4款注释第31—32.1段。

"effectively connected" to such a location requires more than merely recording the shareholding in the books of the permanent establishment for accounting purposes, if the "economic" ownership of the holding is allocated to that permanent establishment under the principles developed in the Committee's report entitled Attribution of Profits to Permanent Establishments for the purposes of the application of Paragraph 2 of Article 7. In the context of that paragraph, the "economic" ownership of a holding means the equivalent of ownership for income tax purposes by a separate enterprise, with the attendant benefits and burdens.

第二节 对跨国投资所得征税的协调
Section 2　Harmonization on Taxation on Incomes from Cross-border Investment

一、股息
Dividends

(一)股息征税规则
Taxation Rules of Dividends

OECD范本第10条确立了税收分享原则：一、对于缔约国一方居民公司支付给缔约国另一方居民的股息，可以在该缔约国一方征税。二、然而这些股息也可以在支付股息的公司是其居民的缔约国，按照该缔约国的法律征税。但是如果股息受益所有人是缔约国另外一方居民，则所征的税款：(1)如果受益所有人持续365天(包括支付股息的日期，为了计算持有时间，无须考虑持有股权的公司或者支付股息的公司可能由于合并或者分立重组而直接引起的所有权变化)直接持有支付股息公司至少25%资本的公司，不应超过股息总额的5%；(2)其他情况下，不应超过股息总额的15%。缔约国双方主管当局应通过共同协商，确定限制税率的实施方式。本款不影响针对公司的利润征税。

Article 10 of OECD Model Tax Convention lays down the principle of tax sharing as follows. Dividends paid by a company which is a resident of a contracting state to a resident of the other contracting state may be taxed in that other state. However, dividends paid by a company which is a resident of a contracting state may be also taxed in that state according to the laws of that state, but if the beneficial owner of the dividends is a resident of the other contracting state, the tax so charged shall not exceed: a. 5 per cent of the gross amount of the dividends if the beneficial owner is a company which holds directly at least 25 per cent of the capital of the company paying the dividends throughout a 365 day period that includes the day of the payment of the dividend (for the purpose of computing that period, no account shall be taken of changes of ownership that would directly result from a corporate reorganization, such as merger or divisive reorganization, of the company that holds the shares or that pays the dividend; b. 15 per cent of the gross amount of the dividends in all other cases. The competent authorities of the contracting states shall settle the mode of application of the limitations by mutual agreement. This paragraph shall not affect the taxation of the company in respect of the profits out of which the dividends are paid.

值得注意的是,相较于之前的版本而言,[①]2017年新修订的OECD范本对第10条第2款第1项中关于股息征税规则作出了两点改动:第一,将之前版本中要求受益所有人是直接持有支付股息公司至少25%资本的公司,而不包括合伙企业之规定删除;将合伙企业排除在外的规定删除,是因为认识到如果合伙企业在其所成立的缔约国税法上被当作公司对待,缔约国另一方对其适用第1项之规定给予税收优惠是适当的。事实上,将诸如合伙企业等实体作为税法上的公司去对待,符合第3条第1款第3项关于公司之定义。只要该主体在某种程度上是缔约国一方居民,且持续365天直接持有支付股息公司至少25%的资本并且满足由缔约国一方公司向缔约国另一方居民公司支付股息的条件,即可享受第2款第1项所规定的税收优惠待遇。第二,对收取股息的公司增加了必须在股息分配之前的相对较长的一段时间内至少拥有25%的资本之规定,即收取股息的公司应当在股息分配之前持续365天持有支付股息公司25%以上的资本。增加受益所有人持股时间限制主要是为了防止条款被滥用,比如某持股在25%以下的公司为了利用上述税收优惠待遇,在股息支付前的短时间内增加其在分配股息公司中的持股份额,或者为了减税而安排符合要求的持股份额以得到税收减免,此种情况下对其进行税收减免不符合宗旨及目的,也会损害来源国的税收利益,故增加持股时间限制以防止人为操纵。当缔约国一方居民公司向在缔约国另一方税法上视为透明实体的合伙企业支付股息时,股息的一部分会被缔约国另一方视为该国居民的收入,收入会被当作向该国居民支付的股息处理。在这种情况下,为了适用第2款第1项,在认定是否直接持有支付股息公司至少25%的资本时,应当将该合伙人在财政透明实体或者安排中持有的比例与其他方式持有的其他资本比例相加,在认定是否满足直接持有365天的规定时,有必要既考虑其在透明实体中的财政透明实体中持有相关权益的期限,又考虑该实体持有支付股息公司的期限,如果上述任何一个期间都不满足365天的要求,则不能适用第1项之规定,应该对相关部分股息适用第2项之规定。

It is noteworthy that, compared with the previous version, the taxation rules on dividends in subparagraph a) of Paragraph 2 of Article 10 was amended in 2017. First, the expectation that beneficial owner should be a company rather than a partnership was deleted in recognition of the fact that if a partnership is treated as a company for tax purpose by the contracting state in which it is established, it is appropriate for the other state to grant the benefits of subparagraph a) to that partnership. Indeed, an entity or arrangement (e.g. a partnership) that is treated as a company for

---

① 2017年OECD范本修订之前,对股息的征税规则如下:"一、缔约国一方居民公司支付给缔约国另一方居民的股息,可以在该缔约国一方征税。二、然而这些股息也可以在支付股息的公司是其居民的缔约国,按照该缔约国法律征税。但是如果股息受益所有人是缔约国另一方的居民,则所征税款:(1)如果受益所有人是直接持有支付股息公司至少25%资本的公司(不是合伙企业),不应超过股息总额的5%;(2)其他情况下,不应超过股息总额的15%。"

tax purposes qualifies as a company under the definition of in subparagraph C of Paragraph 1 of Article 3 and, to that extent that it is a resident of a contracting state, is therefore entitled to the benefits of subparagraph a) of Paragraph 2 with respect to dividends paid by a company resident of the other state, as long as it holds directly at least 25 per cent of the capital of that company. Second, a limitation has been added that companies receiving dividends must hold at least 25% of their capital for a relatively long period (throughout 365 days) before the dividend is paid in case of the abuse of this provision. For example, where a company with a holding of less than 25 per cent has, shortly before the dividends become payable, increased its holding primarily for the purpose of securing the benefits of the provision mentioned above, or otherwise, where the qualifying holding was arranged primarily in order to obtain the reduction or exemption. Not only are such abuses inconsistent with the object and purpose of the provision, but also do great harm to the benefits of tax of source state. Therefore, the time limit of stock holding is added to prevent manipulation. When a company resident of State A pays a dividend to a partnership that State B treats as a transparent entity, the part of that dividend that State B treats as the income of a partner resident of State B, will, for the purposes of Paragraph 2 of the convention between States A and B, be treated as a dividend paid to a resident of State B. Also, for the purposes of the application of subparagraph a) of Paragraph 2 in such a case, a member that is a company should be considered to hold directly, in proportion to its interest in the fiscally transparent entity or arrangement, the part of the capital of the company paying the dividend that is held through that entity or arrangement and, in order to determine whether the member holds directly at least 25 per cent of the capital of the company paying the dividends, that part of the capital will be added to other parts of that capital that the member may otherwise hold directly. In that case, for the purposes of the application of the requirement that at least 25 per cent of the capital of the company paying the dividends be held throughout a 365 day period, it will be necessary to take account of both the period during which the member held the relevant interest in the fiscally transparent entity or arrangement and the period during which the part of the capital of the company paying the dividend was held through that entity or arrangement. If either period does not satisfy the 365 day requirement, subparagraph a) will not apply and subparagraph b) will therefore apply to the relevant part of the dividend.

此外，还应当注意关于"资本"的认定。该款所用的"资本"一词，指的是与股息（即分配给股东的利润）征税相关的资本。因此，作为一般原则，"资本"一词应当按照其在公司法中的含义范围进行理解。公司法意义上的资本是指大多数情况下以资本的形式反映在公司资产负债表上的所有股票的票面价值。因为股票种类更多地与股东权利的性质相关，而不能影响股东对资本的所有权，对于股票的种类（普通股、优先股、多重表决权股、无表决权股、无记名股、记名股等）以及其他因素，特别是企业提留的储备金，均不在考虑范围之内。当一项贷款或者其他形式的出资，严格按照公司法不能被视为"资本"时，但基于国内法或惯例（资本弱化或者将贷款视为股本），因此获得的收入适用第10条之规定处理时，此时贷款或者其他形式的出资的价值也会被视为本项规定的"资本"范围。对于不具有公司法意义上资本的实体而言，第1项所称"资本"是指在分配利润时应当给予考虑的对该实体所有投入总额。实际上，在双边谈判中，缔约国双方可以不采纳第2款第1项给出的"资本"标准，可以使用"表决权"标准。

Moreover, attentions should be paid to the term "capital" used here. In subparagraph a) of Paragraph 2, "capital" is used in relation to the taxation treatment of dividends, i.e. distributions of profits to shareholders. Therefore, as a general rule, capital should be understood in the scope of company law. As understood in company law, capital should be indicated in terms of par value of all shares which in the majority of cases will be shown as capital in company's balance sheet. No account need be taken of differences due to the different classes of shares issued (ordinary shares, preference shares, plural shares, non-voting shares, bearer shares, registered shares, etc.) and other elements, especially the reserves, as such differences relate more to the nature of the shareholder's right than to the extent of his or her ownership of the capital. When a loan or other contribution to the company does not, strictly speaking, come as capital under company law but when on basis of internal law or practice (thin capitalization, or assimilation of a loan to share capital), the income derived in respect thereof is treated as dividend under Article 10, the value of such loan or contribution is also to be taken as "capital" within the meaning of subparagraph a). In the case of bodies which do not have capital within the meaning of company law, for the purpose of subparagraph a) is to be taken as meaning of the total of all contributions to the body which are taken into account for the purpose of distribution profits. In bilateral negotiations, contracting states may depart from the criterion of "capital" used in subparagraph a) of Paragraph 2, and use criterion of "voting power" instead.

（二）股息的定义和范围
Definition and Scope of Dividends

鉴于经合发组织成员国之间的公司法和税法一般差异较大，不可能对"股息"作出充分详尽的定义。因此只能通过列举那些在经合发组织大多数成员国国内法中都能找到，且在任何情况下都会给予同等方式处理的例子，从中概括出一个关于"股息"的一般定义。本条所称股息是指从股份、"享受"股份或者"享受"权利、矿业股份、发起人股份或者非债权关系而分享利润的其他权利中获得的收入，以及按照分配利润的公司是其居民的国家法律，视为股份所得而同样征税的其他公司权利取得的所得。① 此外，还应当注意到，合伙企业的利润分配不应属于股息，除非合伙企业在其实际管理场所所在地国家的税收地位与股份有限公司实质上相似，否则合伙企业的利润分配应当作为合伙企业的经营所得征税。②

In view of great dissimilarities in the field of company law and tax law among the OECD member countries, it is impossible to define "dividends" fully and exhaustively. Consequently, the definition is generalized from the examples which are to be found in the majority of member

---

① 参见OECD范本第10条第3款。
② 参见OECD范本第10条第3款注释第27段。

countries' laws and which, in any case, are treated coequally. The term "dividends" as used in this Article means income from shares, "jouissance" shares or "jouissance" rights, mining shares, founders' shares or other rights, not being debt-claims, participating in profits, as well as income from other corporate rights which is subjected to the same taxation treatment as income from shares by the laws of the state of which the company making the distribution is a resident. Also, we should know that distributions of profits by partnerships are not dividends within the meaning of the definition, unless the partnerships are subject, in the state where their place of effective management is situated, to a fiscal treatment substantially similar to that applied to that companies limited by shares, otherwise, the distribution of profits of partnership should be treated as business income.

在认定股息时，需要考虑以下几个问题：首先，股息主要是就公司的利润分配而言的，而此处所称"公司"，则需要符合第3条第1款第2项之条件，即其实体在税法上应被视为法人。[①]其次，股息的定义同样适用于公司发行的具有利润分享权但不具有债权请求权的证券，相应地，参与利润分配的债权以及可转换债券的利息不包括在内；再次，第10条之规定不仅解决股息征税问题，而且适用于贷款人实际分担公司经营风险情况下，即支付结算汇报主要取决于公司经营是否成功时，相关贷款利息征税问题。也就是说，OECD范本并不禁止借款人所在国根据资本弱化的国内法将利息作为股息处理。贷款人是否分担公司经营风险需要综合个案情况加以具体认定，认定时可以参照下列情况：第一，贷款大幅超过其他投资形式（或者被用于弥补重要的资本损失），并与可变现资产严重不匹配；第二，债权人可以分享公司的任何利润；第三，贷款的偿还优先于其他债权人的债权或者股息支付；第四，利息支付水平取决于公司利润水平；第五，签订的贷款合同没有对偿还日期作出明确规定。

Several problems should be put into consideration when identify dividends. In the first instance, the notion of dividends basically concerns distributions by company with the meaning of subparagraph b) of Paragraph 1 of Article 3, that is the entity is treated as a body corporate for tax purposes. In the second place, the definition assimilates to share all securities issued by companies which carry a right to participate in the companies' profits without being debt-claims, that's to say, debt-claims participating in profits and interest on convertible debentures do not come into the category of dividend. Last, Article 10 deals not only with dividends as such but also with interest on loans insofar as the lender effectively shares the risks run by the company, i.e. when repayment depends largely on the success of otherwise of the enterprise's business. Article 10 and Article 11 do not therefore prevent the treatment of this type of interest as dividends under the national rules on thin capitalization applied in the borrower's country. The question whether the contributor of the loan shares the risks run by the enterprise must be determined in each individual case in the light of all the circumstances, the following content could be put into consideration. First, the loan very heavily outweighs any other contribution to the enterprise's capital (or was taken out to replace a substantial proportion of capital which has been lost) and is substantially unmatched by redeemable assets. Second, the creditor will share

---

① 参见OECD范本第3条第1款第2项。

in any profits of the company. Third, repayment of the loan is subordinated to claims of other creditors or to the payment of dividends. Fourth, the level or payment of interest would depend on the profits of the company; Fifth, the loan contract contains no fixed provisions for repayment by a definite date.

股息支付范围不仅包括每年股东大会决定的利润分配,也包括其他货币或者具有货币价值的收益分配,比如红利股、红利、清算利润或者股权回购以及变相分配的利润。只要支付公司居住国将该项收益作为股息征税,即可适用第10条之规定。至于所分配的利润是来自当年利润还是来自历年结存利润,在所不问。通常情况下,公司减少股东权益的分配,比如通过任何形式构成返还出资的付款,都不被视为股息。作为一般原则,持有公司股份的收益权只属于股东自身,若将收益分配给公司法上不具有股东身份的人,则该收益不能被认定为股息,但是存在例外情况:如果此人与公司之间的法律关系类似于在公司中持有股份(隐蔽持股)而且此人与股东关系极为密切,比如接收人是股东的亲戚或者与拥有股份的公司同属于一家集团的公司,则支付给接收人的收益仍被视为股息。当股东与利益接收人不属于同一个国家的居民,且来源国已经缔结协定,或者来源国仅与其中一国缔结协定而未与另一方缔结协定,此时便会产生适用哪个协定的争议。这种矛盾会影响其他收入的类型,此类冲突只能通过相互协商程序加以解决。①

Payments regarded as dividends may include not only distributions of profits decided by annual general meetings of shareholders, but also other benefits in money or money's worth, such as bonus shares, bonuses, profits on a liquidation or redemption of shares and disguised distributions of profits. The Article 10 will be applied so long as the state of which the paying company is a resident regards such benefits as dividends. It is immaterial whether any such benefits are paid out of current profits made by the company or are derived, for example, from reserves, i.e. profits of previous financial years. Normally, distributions by a company which have the effect of reducing the membership rights, for instance, payments constituting a reimbursement of capital in any form whatever, are not regarded as dividends. As a general rule, the benefits to which a holding in a company confers entitlement are available solely to the shareholders themselves. However, certain of such benefits are made available to persons who are not shareholders within the meaning of company law, that is, they may constitute dividends if the legal relations between such persons and the company are assimilated to a holding in a company (concealed holding) and the persons receiving such benefits are closely connected with a shareholder, for example, where the recipient is a relative or is a company belonging to the same group as the company owning the shares. When the shareholder and the person receiving such benefits are residents of two different states with which or one of them the state of source has concluded conventions, differences of views may arise as to which of these conventions is applicable. This, however, is a conflict which may affect other types of income, and the solution to it can be found only through an arrangement under the mutual agreement procedure.

---

① OECD范本第10条注释第28—30段。

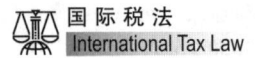

（三）禁止对股息境外征税以及对未分配利润征税
Taxation of Dividends Abroad and Taxation of Undistributed Profits are Prohibited

关于股息的征税规则仅适用于缔约国一方居民公司向缔约国另一方居民支付股息的情形。但是，一些国家不仅对本国境内居民公司支付的股息进行征税，而且对非居民公司源于本国境内取得的利润进行征税。虽然依照第7条，国家对非居民公司源于本国境内的收益有征税的权力，但是在支付股息的情况下，这些公司的股东都不应该被征税，除非公司股东是该国居民，因而自然地服从于国家税收主权。因此，第10条第5款规定：缔约国一方居民公司从缔约国另一方取得利润或者所得，该缔约国另一方不得对该公司支付的股息征收任何税收（但支付给该缔约国另一方居民的股息或者据以支付股息的股份与设在缔约国另一方的常设机构有实际联系的除外），即使支付的股息或未分配的利润全部或者部分发生于该缔约国另一方的利润或者所得，也不得对该公司未分配的利润征收任何税收。第5款将股息境外征税排除在外，即缔约国不得以用于分配的利润来自其境内为由（比如通过其境内的常设机构实现）对非居民公司分配的股息征税。因为在税收协定中，关于股息来源地认定采用以居民公司支付为准的原则，即股息来源地为分配股息的公司居住地，而非股息利润的实际来源地。当公司利益来源国对支付给本国居民股东或境内常设机构的股息征税时，则不存在境外征税问题。①此外，第5款进一步规定了不得对非居民公司的未分配利润征收任何特别税种，不能将该款理解为限制纳税人居民国依据其受控外国公司立法或者具有类似效果的规则对纳税人的国外未分配利润进行征税，事实上，第5款是对来源地国征税的限制，并不会对居民国依照此类立法或者具有相同效力的规则所进行的征税产生影响。但是此类立法或者规则可能会引起第23条关于消除双重征税方法的适用复杂化。

The Article deals only with dividends paid by a company which is a resident of a contracting state to a resident of the other state. Certain states, however, tax not only dividends paid by companies resident therein but even distributions by non-resident companies of profits arising within their territory. Each state, of course, is entitled to tax profits arising in its territory which are made by non-resident companies, to the extent provided in the Convention (in particular in Article 7). The shareholders of such companies should not be taxed as well at any rate, unless they are residents of the state and so naturally subject to its fiscal sovereignty. Therefore, the paragraph stipulates where a company which is a resident of a contracting state derives profits or income from the other contracting State, that other state may not impose any tax on the dividends paid by the company, except insofar as such dividends are paid to a resident of that other state or insofar as the holding in respect of which the dividends are paid is effectively connected with a permanent establishment situated in that other state, nor subject the company's undistributed profits to a tax on the company's undistributed profits, even if the dividends paid or the undistributed profits consist wholly or partly of profits or income arising in such

---

① OECD范本第10条注释第33—35段。

other state. Paragraph 5 rules out the extra-territorial taxation of dividends, i.e. the practice by which states tax dividends distributed by a non-resident company solely because the corporate profits from which the distributions are made originated in their territory. Because in the tax convention, the criterion for tax liability is the fact of payment of the dividends, and not the origin of the cooperate profits allotted for distribution. There is no question of extra-territorial taxation when the source of the corporate profits taxes the dividends because they are paid to a shareholder who is a resident of that state or to a permanent establishment situated in that state. Paragraph 5 further provides that non-resident companies are not to be subjected to special taxes on undistributed profits. It is noteworthy that Paragraph 5 cannot be interpreted as preventing the state of residence of a taxpayer from taxing that taxpayer, pursuant to its controlled foreign company legislation or other rules with similar effect, on profits which have not been distributed by a foreign company. Moreover, it should be noted that the paragraph is confined to taxation at source and, thus, has no bearing on the taxation at residence under such legislation or rules. However, the application of such legislation or rules may complicate the application of Article 23.

二、利息
Interest

（一）对利息的征税规则
The Taxation Rules of Interest

OECD范本第11条对利息征税规则作出规定："一、发生于缔约国一方并支付给缔约国另一方居民的利息，可以在该缔约国另一方征税。二、然而这些利息也可以在发生该利息的缔约国，按照该国法律征税。但是，如果利息的受益所有人是缔约国另一方的居民，则所征税款不应超过利息总额的10%。缔约国双方主管当局应通过相互协商，确定实施该限制税率的方式。" UN范本第11条第1款也确定了税收分享原则，但是第2款中未明确规定支付利息的公司的所在国一方对利息的预提税比例，而是规定限制税率由缔约国双方通过谈判具体确定。

Article 11 of OECD Model Tax Convention stipulates the rule of taxation on interest: "Interest arising in a contracting state and paid to a resident of the other contracting state may be taxed in that other state. However, interest arising in a contracting state may also be taxed in that state according to the laws of that state, but if the beneficial owner of the interest is a resident of the other contracting state, the tax so charged shall not exceed 10 per cent of the gross amount of the interest. The competent authorities of the contracting states shall by mutual agreement settle the mode of application of this limitation." Paragraph 1 of Article 11 of UN Model Tax Convention also lays down the principle of tax sharing, but Paragraph 2 does not expressly prescribe the withholding tax rate of interest in the country where the company pays the interest. Instead, it provides that the limited tax rate shall be specifically determined by the contracting states through negotiations.

OECD范本第11条第2款保留了来源国对利息的征税权,同时设定税率上限以限制来源地国征税权,考虑到来源国有权对本国境内通过借入资金投资产生的利润或者所得进行征税,不超过10%的税率被认为是合理的。缔约国双方可以通过双边谈判确定更低的税率或者双边协商确定受益人是其居民国的缔约国对一些具体的利息种类甚至全部利息享有独占征税权。上述可以由受益人是其居民的缔约国独占征税的利息种类主要包括:支付给一国、其所属行政区和中央银行的利息;由一国或者其所属行政区支付的利息;根据出口融资计划支付的利息;支付给金融机构的利息;赊销利息;支付给某些免税实体的利息(如退休基金)等。第2款没有规定程序问题,各国可以适用国内法规定的程序进行征税,也没有明确来源国的税收减免是否附条件,这一问题可以通过双边协商加以解决。

Paragraph 2 reserves a right to tax interest for the state in which the interest arises, but it limits the exercise of that right by determining a ceiling for the tax, which may not exceed 10 per cent. This rate may be considered a reasonable maximum bearing in mind that the state of source is already entitled to tax profits or income produced on its territory by investments financed out of borrowed capital. The contracting states may agree in bilateral negotiations upon a lower tax or on exclusive taxation in the state of the beneficiary's residence with respect to all interest payments or, as explained below, as regards some specific categories of interest. The categories of interest mentioned above consist of interests paid to a state, its political subdivisions and to central bank, interest paid by a state or its political subdivisions, interest paid pursuant to export financing programmes, interest paid to financial institutions, interest on sales on credit and interest paid to some tax-exempt entities (e.g. pension funds). Procedural questions are not dealt with in this Article, each state should apply the procedure provided in its own law. Also, it does not specify whether or not the relief in the state of source should be conditional upon the interest being subject to tax in the state of residence, this question shall be settled by bilateral negotiations.

在特定情况下,第11条第2款采用的允许对利息进行源泉课税的方法,可能形成对国际贸易的阻碍或者因为其他原因而被认为是不适当的。比如,当利息受益人对据以获得利息的业务提供的借款是向他人所借时,利息受益人以利息形式获得的利润可能会远远小于名义上收到的利息,如果所收到的利息等于或者小于其所支付的利息,此次投资利润为零甚至还要承担亏损。这种问题,居民国是无法解决的,因为受益人所在国是以其从交易中获得的净利润征税的,所以该国征收很少的税甚至征不到税。产生该问题的原因在于来源国按照利息的毛收入额计算征税,并不考虑产生该利息的成本。为了避免此类情况,实践中债权人倾向于将来源国对利息的课税负担转移给债务人,从而增加债务人负担的利率,债务人也随之增加了与应纳来源国税额相对应的财务负担。

In certain cases, the approach adopted in Paragraph 2, which is to allow source taxation on payments of interest, can constitute an obstacle to international trade or may be considered inappropriate for other reasons. For instance, when the beneficiary of the interest has borrowed in order to finance the operation which earns the interest, the profit realized by way of interest will be much smaller than the nominal amount of interest received; if the interest paid is equal to or exceeds the interest received, there will be either no profit at all or even a loss. The problem, in that case, cannot be solved by the state of residence, since little or no tax will be levied in that state where the beneficiary is taxed on the net profit derived from the transaction. That problem arises because the tax in the state of source is typically levied on the gross amount of the interest regardless of expenses incurred in order to earn such interest. In order to avoid that problem, creditors will, in practice, tend to shift to the debtor the burden of the tax levied by the state of source on the interest and therefore increase the rate of interest charged to the debtor, whose financial burden is then increased by an amount corresponding to the tax payable to the state of source.

（二）利息的定义和范围
The Definition and Scope of Interest

本条所称"利息"是指从各种债权中取得的所得,不论其有无抵押担保或者是否有权分享债务人的利润;特别是指从政府证券取得的所得、从债券或者信用债券取得的所得,包括附属于这些证券、债券或者信用债券的溢价和奖金。因延期支付的罚款,一般不应视为本条所规定的利息。[①] "各种债权"主要包括现金存款、货币形态的有价证券以及政府证券、债券和信用证券,后三种债券因其重要性和其所呈现的特殊性而被提及。通常情况下,参与利润分配的债券的利息不应视为股息,可转换债券在没有转换为股份之前,其利息也不被认为是股息。但是,如果该项债券贷款实际分担了债务人公司的风险,则证券贷款的利息应当被视为股息。在推定资本弱化的情况下,有时很难区分股息和利息,为了避免任何第10条和第11条所得种类可能产生重合的问题,应当注意第11条所称的"利息"不包括第10条规定的按照"股息"处理的所得项目。第11条第3款前半部分所述的"利息"通常不包括一些非传统的缺乏基础性债务交易的金融工具的支付,比如利率掉期,但是如果根据"实质优于形式""权利滥用原则"以及其他类似的原则认为贷款存在,那么仍可以适用上述利息的定义。第3款后半部分将因延期支付的利息罚款排除在"利息"定义之外,但是缔约国可以忽略这条规定在双边税收协定中将因延期支付的罚款作为利息处理。年金也不应当被认定为利息,一方面,第18条提到考虑到过去就业情况而发给的年金,遵守有关养老金的规定。另一方面,虽然分期购买年金具备资本购买和资本返还的利息因素,但分期付款的法定孳息以日为单位增加,许多国家很难区别其中代表资本回报的要素与代表资本收入的要素,因而不能将收入成分与来自动产的收入放在同一种类征税。税法往往规定特别条款将年金分为薪金、工资以及养老金,并对其分别征税。应当注意的是,第11条第3款所述的关于"利息"的定义原则上是穷尽的,出于以下几点考虑,文本没有附带提出国内法上关于这一问题的参考具有一定的可取性:首先,本条关于"利息"的定义实际上已经包含各国国内法上视为利息的所有类型的所得。其次,从法律层面去看,该定义能够确保协定不会因国内法将来的变化而缺乏稳定性,更加具有保障性。最后,符合协定应当尽可能避免援引国内法之要求,然而,在缔约国双方在双边协定中扩大利息范围,虽然定义上没有涉及,但按照任何

---

① 参见OECD范本第11条第3款,UN范本第11条第3款。

一方的国内法将所得视为利息征税时，可以援引国内法。① 此外，第11条第6款还规定了如果支付利息的人与受益所有人或者两者与其他人之间存在特殊关系，有关债权的利息支付超过了在没有这层特殊关系情况下支付人所能同意的数额时，利息应仅仅包括正常情况下债权人所能获得的利息数额，超过该数额的部分不能被当作税收协定中规定的"利息"处理，而应当按照缔约国的国内法征税，但应当考虑协定其他条款的规定。上述特殊关系通常包括不同于因法律关系而支付利息的任何共同利益关系，如关联企业关系、血缘和婚姻关系。

  The term "interest" as used in this Article means income from debt-claims of every kind, whether or not secured by mortgage and whether or not carrying a right to participate in the debtor's profits, and in particular, income from government securities and income from bonds or debentures, including premiums and prizes attaching to such securities, bonds or debentures. Penalty charges for late payment shall not be regarded as interest for the purpose of this Article. The term "debt-claims of every kind" obviously embraces cash deposits and security in the form of money, as well as government securities, and bonds and debentures, although the three latter are specially mentioned because of their importance and of certain peculiarities that they may present. Normally, Interest on participating bonds should not be considered as a dividend, and neither should interest on convertible bonds until such time as the bonds are actually converted into shares. However, the interest on such bonds should be considered as a dividend if the loan effectively shares the risks run by the debtor company. In situations of presumed thin capitalization, it is sometimes difficult to distinguish between dividends and interest and in order to avoid any possibility of overlap between the categories of income dealt with in Article 10 and Article 11 respectively, it should be noted that the term "interest" as used in Article 11 does not include items of income which are dealt with under Article 10. The definition of interest in the first sentence of Paragraph 3 does not normally apply to payments made under certain kinds of nontraditional financial instruments where there is no underlying debt (for example, interest rate swaps). However, the definition will apply to the extent that a loan is considered to exist under a "substance over form" rule, an "abuse of rights" principle, or any similar doctrine. The second sentence of Paragraph 3 excludes from the definition of interest penalty charges for late payment but contracting states are free to omit this sentence and treat penalty charges as interest in their bilateral conventions. The annuities ought not to be assimilated to interest. On the one hand, annuities granted in consideration of past employment are referred to in Article 18 and are subject to the rules governing pensions. On the other hand, although it is true that instalments of purchased annuities include an interest element on the purchase capital as well as return of capital, such instalments thus constituting "fruits civils" which accrue from day to day, it would be difficult for many countries to make a distinction between the element representing income from capital and the element representing a return of capital in order merely to tax the income element under the same category as income from

---

① 参见OECD范本第11条注释第18—23段。

movable capital. Taxation laws often contain special provisions classifying annuities in the category of salaries, wages and pensions, and taxing them accordingly. It's noteworthy that the definition of interest in the Paragraph 3 of Article 11 is, in principle, exhaustive. It has seemed preferable not to include a subsidiary reference to domestic laws in the text, which is justified by the following considerations. First, the definition covers practically all kinds of income which are regarded as interest in the various domestic laws. Second, the formula employed offers greater security from the legal point of view and ensures that conventions would be unaffected by future changes in any country's domestic laws. Last, in the Model Convention references to domestic laws should as far as possible be avoided. However, in a bilateral convention two contracting states may widen the formula employed so as to include in it any income which is taxed as interest under either of their domestic laws but which is not covered by the definition and in these circumstances may find it preferable to make reference to their domestic laws. Also, the Paragraph 6 of Article 11 stipulates that the amount of interest, having regard to the debt-claim for which it is paid, exceeds the amount of which would have been agreed upon by the payer and the beneficial owner in the absence of such relationship, by reason of a special relationship between the payer and the beneficial owner or between both of them and some other person, the provisions of this Article shall apply only to the last-mentioned amount. In such case, the excess part of the payments shall remain taxable according to the laws of each contracting state, due regard being had to the other provisions of this convention. The concept of special relationship also covers relationships by blood or marriage and, in general, any community of interest as distinct from the legal relationship giving rise to the payment of the interest.

(三) 利息来源地认定
Identification of Source of Interest

第11条第5款规定：当利息支付人是缔约国一方居民时，应当认定该利息发生于该缔约国。然而，无论利息支付人是否为缔约国一方居民，在缔约国一方设有常设机构或固定基地，支付该利息的债务与该常设机构或固定基地有联系，并由其负担利息，上述利息应当认为发生于该常设机构所在缔约国。第5款确立了利息来源国是利息支付人为其居民的国家的原则，同时也规定了一个例外情形，即该项贷款与利息支付人在缔约国另一方拥有的常设机构有明显的经济联系。利息支付人应常设机构的需要而签订贷款合同，且支付利息由该常设机构承担，不管该机构的所有人为哪国居民，即使其居住在第三国，也应认为利息的来源地应当是常设机构所在的缔约国。当贷款利息与常设机构缺乏经济联系时，常设机构所在缔约国不能被认为是利息的来源国，即便是在与常设机构的重要性相称的应税配额范围内，它也无权对这种利息征税。此外，只有在贷款和常设机构之间的经济联系足够明确的情况下，才能作为第5款前半部分规定的例外情况。在此规定下，可以具体区分出以下情况：第一，常设机构的管理部门应常设机构的具体要求签订贷款合同，将借入款项作为该机构的债务并由其直接向债权人偿付。第二，企业总部为设立于其他国家的常设机构单独使用的贷款订立贷款合同并支付利息，所付利息最终由常设机构承担。

第三,贷款合同由企业总部签订,但所贷款项由设立在不同国家境内的常设机构使用。上述三种情形下,前两种均符合第5款规定的常设机构例外原则,常设机构所在缔约国可被视为利息发生地。但是第三种情形不属于第5款规定的例外情形,从字面意思上来看,该规定排除了同一笔贷款有多个来源地的可能性。同时,这种情况会增加管理上的复杂性,并使债权人无法事前计算出该利息所要承担的税收。当然,缔约国双方可以根据自己的意愿将第5款适用的范围限制在第一种情形或者扩展至第三种情形。实践中还存在利息支付人和受益人均为缔约国居民,但是贷款是应利息支付人在第三国境内设立的常设机构的要求借入,并由该常设机构负担利息的情形,第11条第5款并没有对这种排除情形提出解决方法。因此按照本款的现有规定,只能将第5款规定的第一句适用于此类情形,即以利息支付人的缔约居民国为利息来源国,而不是使用贷款并实际支付利息的常设机构所在的第三国。因此利息将在利息支付人为其居民的缔约国和受益人为其居民的缔约国双方征税。但是,虽然按照本条规定,可以避免对该笔利息进行双重征税,但是不能避免支付人与受益人居民国和第三国之间因对其境内产生常设机构所负担的贷款利息征税而产生的双重征税。①

The Paragraph 5 of Article 11 stipulates that when the payer of interest is a resident of a contracting state, the interest shall be deemed to have occurred in that contracting state. However, regardless of whether the payer of interest is a resident of a contracting state, in the contracting state one party has a permanent establishment or a fixed base, and the debt to pay the interest is related to the permanent establishment or the fixed base, and the interest shall be borne by it. The above-mentioned interest shall be deemed to have occurred in the contracting state where the permanent establishment is located. Paragraph 5 establishes the source of interest. The principle that the country is a country where the interest payer is a resident also provides for an exception, that is, the loan has an obvious economic connection with a permanent establishment owned by the interest payer in the other party of the contracting state. The interest payer shall sign a loan contract according to the needs of a permanent establishment, and the payment of interest shall be borne by the permanent establishment. No matter which country the owner of the establishment is a resident of, even if he or she lives in a third country, the source of interest should be considered as a permanent establishment state party in which it is located. In the absence of an economic link between the loan on which the interest arises and the permanent establishment, the state where the latter is situated cannot on that account be regarded as the state where the interest arises; it is not entitled to tax such interest, not even within the limits of a "taxable quota" proportional to the importance of the permanent establishment. Moreover, any departure from the rule fixed in the first sentence of Paragraph 5 is justified only where the economic link between the loan and the permanent establishment is sufficiently clear-cut. In this connection, a number of possible cases may be distinguished. First, the management of the permanent establishment has contracted a loan which it uses for the specific requirements of the permanent establishment; it shows it among

---

① 参见OECD范本第11条第5款,第11条注释第26—28段。

its liabilities and pays the interest thereon directly to the creditor. Second, the head office of the enterprise has contracted a loan the proceeds of which are used solely for the purposes of a permanent establishment situated in another country. The interest is serviced by the head office but is ultimately borne by the permanent establishment. Third, the loan is contracted by the head office of the enterprise and its proceeds are used for several permanent establishments situated in different countries. In the first two cases, the conditions laid down in the second sentence of Paragraph 5 are fulfilled, and the state where the permanent establishment is situated is to be regarded as the state where the interest arises. The third case, however, falls outside the provisions of Paragraph 5, the text of which precludes the attribution of more than one source to the same loan. Such a solution, moreover, would give rise to considerable administrative complications and make it impossible for lenders to calculate in advance the taxation that interest would attract. It is, however, opening to two contracting states to restrict the application of the final provision in Paragraph 5 to the first case or to extend it to the third case.

三、特许权使用费
Royalties

（一）特许权使用费征税规则
Rules for Taxation of Royalties

如前所述，对于特许权使用费的征税协调问题，两大范本采用了不同的征税原则。OECD范本第12条确立了对特许权使用费的独占征税原则，规定发生于缔约国一方并由缔约国另一方居民受益所有的特许权使用费应仅在该缔约国另一方征税。UN范本第12条则确立了税收分享原则，规定发生在缔约国一方并支付给缔约国另一方居民的特许权使用费，可以在另一国征税。然而，这些特许权使用费也可以在其发生的缔约国，按照该国法律征税。但是如果收款人是特许权使用费的受益所有人，则所征税款不得超过特许权使用费总额的____%（百分数通过双边谈判确定）。

As mentioned above, OECD Model Tax Convention and UN Model Tax Convention apply different tax principles to the issue of tax harmonization on royalties. Article 12 of OECD Model Tax Convention lays down the principle of exclusive taxation of royalties in the state of the beneficial owner's residence. The principle stipulates that royalties arising in a contracting state and beneficially owned by a resident of the other contracting state shall be taxable only in that other state. While the Article 12 of UN Model Tax Convention lays down the principle of tax sharing. The principle stipulates that royalties arising in a contracting state and beneficial owned by a resident of the other state may be taxed in that other state. However, royalties arising in a contracting state may also be taxed in that state according to the laws of that state, but if the recipient is the beneficiary owner, the tax so charged shall not exceed ____% (percentage is determined through bilateral negotiations).

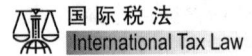

(二) 特许权使用费的定义
Definition of Royalties

本条所称特许权使用费通常是指因使用或者授权使用构成各种形式的文学与艺术的权利或者财产，工业、商业和科学经验的文本和情报资料中确定的知识产权要素而支付的款项。对于上述概念的理解要注意以下几个方面：第一，上述概念中提及的权利或财产不论是否已经登记或者被要求在公共注册部门登记，均构成特许权使用费的对象；第二，支付款项必须因"使用或者有权使用"上述权利而产生，并非基于转移上述权利的完全所有权而产生。如果是为了取得上述权利的完全所有权而支付的报酬，原则上应当认定为营业所得或者营业利润，而非特许权使用费；第三，概念中因使用权利而支付的款项，既包括有权使用相关权利而支付的费用，也包括因欺诈性复制或侵权使用相关权利而被责令支付的赔偿款。①

The royalties used in this Article generally refer to the payments for the use of, or the entitlement to use the rights and the property constituting the different forms of literary and artistic property, the elements of intellectual property specified in the text and information concerning industrial, commercial, or scientific experience. The understanding of the concept mentioned above should pay attention to the following aspects. First, whether the right or property mentioned in the concept have been registered or required to be registered in a public register could be the objects of royalties. Second, the payments must derive from the "use or the right to use" the relevant elements of property instead of the transferring of the full ownership of an element of the property referred to in the definition. If the consideration was paid to alienate the full ownership of the right or property mentioned above, in principle, the payment should be recognized as business income or business profit rather than royalties. Third, the payments deriving from the use of the right and property cover both payments made under a license and compensation which a person would be obliged to pay for fraudulently copying or infringing the right.

(三) 特许权使用费的认定
Identification of Royalties

关于特许权使用费的认定，需要从特许权使用费的概念入手。如前所述，特许权使用费通常是指因使用或者授权使用构成各种形式的文学与艺术的权利或者财产，工业、商业和科学经验的文本和情报资料中确定的知识产权要素而支付的款项。在对因使用有关工业、商业或科学经验中情报而产生的特许权使用费进行分类时，第2款指"专有技术"这一概念。专有技术是指不为公众所知悉能够在应用过程中为权利人带来经济利益的工业、商业以及科学信息。从概念中我们可以看出构成特许权使用费的报酬应当是为了获取专有技术的使用权，因此，尽管实践中交易错综复杂，有关款项的实质支付目的是认定是否构成特许权使用费的关键标准。

---

① 参见OECD范本第12条注释第8段、第8.2段。

The identification of royalties needs to start with the concept of royalties. As mentioned above, the royalties generally refer to the payments for the use of, or the entitlement to use the rights and the property constituting the different forms of literary and artistic property, the elements of intellectual property specified in the text and information concerning industrial, commercial, or scientific experience. In classifying as royalties, payments received as consideration for information concerning industrial, commercial or scientific experience, Paragraph 2 is referring to the concept of "know-how". It generally corresponds to undivulged information of an industrial, commercial or scientific nature arising from previous experience, which has practical application in the operation of an enterprise and from the disclosure of which an economic benefit can be derived. We can find that the payment for the purpose to use or right to use "know how" constitutes the royalties within the meaning of Paragraph 2. Even though the transactions are complex in practice, the essential consideration of payments is the key point of the determination of royalties.

首先，多数设备租赁协议中因不涉及专有技术使用权转让，所支付的报酬不能认定为特许权使用费。1977年税收协定范本对特许权使用费的表述为"为了使用或者有权使用工业、商业以及科学设备"，考虑到工业、商业以及科学设备租赁收入的性质，财政事务委员会决定将租赁收入排除在特许权使用费范围之外，不适用第12条之规定，纳入第5条、第7条规定的营业利润范畴。比如，多数情况下，卫星运营商与广播公司或者远程通信企业之间签订的"转发器租赁协议"中，卫星运营商允许其客户使用卫星并在较大的地理区域内传输信号，承租人支付的报酬通常不能认定为特许权使用费。因为在此类协议中承租人支付的报酬仅仅为了利用卫星传输能力，而不涉及使用设备中包含的情报中的知识产权要素，因此不符合第2款之规定，相关报酬不能被认定为特许权使用费，而应当认定为第7条所规定的营业利润予以征税。但是在少数情况下，卫星运营商将设备租赁给承租人，承租人或可以按照自己的意愿操作设备，或利用其数据传输能力向第三方提供服务，此种情况下，卫星运营者向卫星所有者提供的报酬便可认定为工业、商业以及科学设备租赁。同样，在远程通信网络运营商的"漫游协议"和广播公司"频谱执照"中，承租人向出租人支付的报酬也不能认定为特许权使用费，因为在此协议中，并没有进行专有技术转让，不属于第2款所规定的专有技术，因此相关报酬不能被认定为特许权使用费。

First of all, most equipment leasing agreements do not involve the transfer of "know-how", so the payments of the agreement cannot be regarded as royalties. In 1977 Model Convention, the definition of royalties included payments "for the use of, or the right to use, industrial, commercial or scientific equipment", but given the nature of income from the leasing of industrial, commercial or scientific equipment, the Committee on Fiscal Affairs decided to exclude income from such leasing from the definition of royalties and, consequently, to remove it from the application of Article 12 in order to make sure that it would fall under the rules for the taxation of business profits, as defined in the Article 5 and Article 7. For example, in many cases, satellite operators and broadcasting and telecommunication enterprises frequently enter into "transponder leasing" agreements under which the satellite operator allows the customer to utilize the capacity of a satellite transponder to transmit over large geographical areas. Payments made by customers under typical "transponder leasing" agreements are made for the use of the transponder transmitting capacity instead of using any elements of intellectual property, and will not constitute royalties under the definition of Paragraph 2 and the payments should be treated as the business profit under the definition in Article 5 and Article 7. However, in less frequent cases, the owner of satellite leases it to another party so that the latter may operate it and either use it or for its own purpose or offer its data transmission capacity to third parties. In such cases, the payment made by the satellite operator to the satellite owner could well be considered as a payment for the leasing of industrial, commercial or scientific equipment. Similarly, payments made by lessee to leaser in "roaming agreement" and "spectrum license" will not constitute royalties under the definition of Paragraph 2 because there is no information transfer.

其次，相关款项的实质支付目的是否为获得专有技术的使用权在区分传授某种专有技术而收取的特许权使用费与提供某种专业技术服务而获得的劳动报酬中也发挥着重要作用。OECD范本的注释中提出区分上述两种合同的参考标准：提供专有技术的合同涉及的是特许权使用费中所述的已经存在或者是开发或者创造后提供的情报资料，并且合同中有关于情报资料的保密规定；在提供服务的合同中，服务提供方在提供服务的过程中可能也会使用到特殊知识、技能和专门技术，但是并不将其转让给另外一方；在涉及提供专有技术的合同中，提供方除了提供相关情报或者专有技术，通常不参与受让方的生产经营活动，而在服务合同中，提供方基于履行合同义务的目的，需要亲自完成为另一方服务的工作。总的来说，在传授专有技术合同中，受让人支付报酬的实质目的是获得相关情报、经验或者专有技术的使用权并依照自己的意愿加以使用，而在提供某种专业技术服务的合同中，支付报酬是为了使合同另一方利用其职业技能亲自开展工作。两种合同的支付目的截然不同，对区分两种报酬的性质提供了重要的突破口。OECD范本的注释还具体列举一些不应当认定为特许权使用费的支付情形，包括售后服务报酬、单纯的技术协助服务报酬等。商业实践中，经常存在既包含提供专有技术又包含提供技术服务的混合合同，比如特许经营合同。在特许经营合同中，特许经营授权者将其经营知识和经验传授给特许经营者，同时还向特许经营者提供经济支持以及商品供应等多种技术协助。原则上，此类混合合同的处理需要将合同内容分解为提供专有技术的条款与提供技术服务的条款，然后对各部分涉及的费用分别按照特许权使用费与营业利润适用相应的税收待遇。但是如果混合合同中，某一部分构成了合同的最主要的目的，另一部分仅是辅助性的或者大部分不重要的，一般可对报酬的总额按照主要部分应当适用的税收规则进行征税。[①]

Secondly, whether the actual purpose of payment is to obtain the right to use proprietary technology also plays an important role in distinguishing between the royalty for imparting a certain proprietary technology and the labor remuneration for providing a certain professional technical service. The following relevant criteria of the OECD Model Tax Convention are put

---

① 参见OECD范本第12条的注释第11—11.6段。

forward for the purpose of making that distinction. First, contracts for the supply of know-how concern information of the kind described in Paragraph 11 that already exists or concern the supply of that type of information after its development or creation and include specific provisions concerning the confidentiality of that information. Second, in the case of contracts for the provision of services, the supplier undertakes to perform services which may require the use, by that supplier, of special knowledge, skill and expertise but not the transfer of such special knowledge, skill or expertise to the other party. Third, in most cases involving the supply of know-how, there would generally be very little more which needs to be done by the supplier under the contract other than to supply existing information or reproduce existing material, but in a contract for the performance of services would, in the majority of cases, involve a very much greater level of expenditure by the supplier in order to perform his or her contractual obligations. In short, in the know-how contract, the payments made by transferee is to obtain the use right of unrevealed special knowledge and experience from the transferor so that the transferee can use it on his or her own purpose. But in the contract for the provision of services, transferor undertakes to use the customary skills of his or her calling to execute work himself or herself for the transferee. The essential considerations for the payments are totally different which provides a breakthrough to distinguish two types of contract. The OECD Model Tax Convention enumerate examples of payments which should therefore not be considered to be received as consideration for the provision of know-how, but rather, for the provision of services, including payments obtained as consideration for after-sales service, payments for pure technical assistance and so on. In business practice, contracts are encountered which cover both know-how and the provision of technical assistance, for example franchising, where the franchisor imparts his or her knowledge and experience to the franchisee and, in addition, provides him or her with varied technical assistance, which, in certain cases, is backed up with financial assistance and the supply of goods. The appropriate course to take with a mixed contract is, in principle, to break down, on the basis of the information contained in the contract or by means of a reasonable apportionment, the whole amount of the stipulated consideration according to the various parts of what is being provided under the contract, and then to apply to each part of it so determined the taxation treatment proper thereto. If, however, one part of what is being provided constitutes by far the principal purpose of the contract and the other parts stipulated therein are only of an ancillary and largely unimportant character, then the treatment applicable to the principal part should generally be applied to the whole amount of the consideration.

伴随着计算机技术的迅速发展与跨境计算机技术交易的不断增多,计算机软件的报酬是否属于特许权使用费一直是实践中的一个重大难题,我们仍然可以借助实质支付目的这一标准进行区分。OECD范本的注释中指出:"计算机软件交易报酬的认定与传输方式与支付方式等因素无关,计算机软件转让交易中所收取的报酬的性质,取决于在有关程序使用或者开发的具体安排下受让方取得的权利性质。"如果支付报酬是为了通过某种方式取得使用该软件的权利(没有这种授权将构成侵权),为了获取版权中部分权利而支付的款项构成特许权使用费。如果获得的与版权相关的权利仅限于使用者能够对程序进行操作所必需的权利,无论这种权利是由法律授予还是通过与版权所有人签订特许权使用协议授予的,将程序复制到计算机硬盘或者随机存取到储存器上或者为了存档而进行拷贝,都是利用该程序的必要步骤。因此,当这些与复制行为有关的权利只是为了使受让方能够对程序进行有效操作时,此类交易支付的费用不应当认定为特许权使用费,而应当认定为第7条所规定的营业收入。如果在混合合同中,既包括提供服务的条款,又包括提供软件使用权的条款,则应当按照第12条的注释第11.6段提出的原则进行处理。上述关于软件报酬的规则同样适用于其他种类的数字产品的交易,比如影像、声音或者文本等,在认定上述交易中产生的支付款项是否构成特许权使用费时,主要是辨别有关款项的实质支付目的。①

Whether the payments received as consideration for computer software may be classified as royalties poses difficult problems. But it is a matter of considerable importance in view of the rapid development of computer technology in recent years, and the extent of transfers of such technology across national borders. However, we can still tell it by the essential consideration of payments. Commentary on Article 12 of OECD Model Tax Convention points out that: "The character of payments received in transactions involving the transfer of computer software depends on the nature of the right that the transferee acquires under the particular arrangements regarding the use and exploitation of the program rather than the method of transferring and the form of payments." Payments made for the acquisition of partial rights in the copyright (without the transferor fully alienating the copyright rights), will represent a royalty where the consideration is for granting of rights to use the program in a manner that would, without such license, constitute an infringement of copyright. In some types of transactions, the rights acquired in relation to the copyright are limited to those necessary to enable the user to operate the program. Regardless of whether this right is granted under law or under a license agreement with the copyright holder, copying the program onto the computer's hard drive or random access memory or making an archival copy is an essential step in utilizing the program. Therefore, the payments for rights in relation to these acts of copying, where they do no more than enable the effective operation of the program by the user, should be regarded as commercial income in accordance with Article 7 instead of royalties. If software payments are made under mixed contract, which includes concession of right to use software combined with the provision of services, the payments in such contract should be treated under the principle that put forward in Paragraph 11.6. The principles expressed above as regards software payments are also applicable as regards transactions concerning other types of digital products such as images, sounds or text. In deciding whether or not payments arising in these transactions constitute royalties, the main question to be addressed is the identification of that for which the payment is essentially made.

---

① 参见OECD 范本第13.1段,第14段,第14.1段,第16段,第17.1段。

第三节 相关案例
Section 3　Related Cases

（一）美利坚合众国泛美卫星国际系统责任有限公司诉北京市国家税务局对外分局第二税务所代扣代缴预提所得税决定案

Pan Am Satellite International System Liability Co., Ltd. of the United States of America v. the Second Tax Bureau of the External Branch of the State Taxation Bureau of Beijing over Decision on withholding and paying withholding income tax

（一）案情介绍
Introduction to the Case

1996年4月3日，泛美卫星国际系统责任有限公司（以下简称泛美卫星公司）与中央电视台签订协议，该协议有效期至2006年6月30日。1997年10月19日，双方对协议的部分条款进行了修改并签订修正案。根据协议及修正案约定，泛美卫星公司向中央电视台提供全时的固定期限的、不可再转让（除优先单独决定权外）的压缩数字视频服务。服务范围包括：太平洋地区（环太平洋服务）、非洲地区（非洲服务）、印度洋地区（南亚／中东服务）、拉美地区（美洲服务）。协议第1条第1款A项约定，泛美卫星公司提供地面设备，以提供下行、美国传输、美洲、非洲服务，除了支付各服务费，中央电视台同意支付设备费。第1条第2款约定，泛美卫星公司只用于传送中央电视台的电视信号，中央电视台可以自己使用，也可以允许中国省级以上的广播电视台使用中央电视台未使用的部分，经泛美卫星公司提前许可，中央电视台允许非中国法人的广播电视台使用其未使用的部分，传送电视信号。第1条第6款约定：对每个服务的空中载波参数的监督将由泛美卫星公司"载波监督系统"进行，该系统由泛美卫星公司工程和技术运行中心的职员进行全天候运行。第3条第1款、第3条第2款约定：中央电视台支付季度服务费和设备费，中央电视台在协议签订之后30日内向泛美卫星公司支付订金，此订金用于支付服务期限的头3个月和最后1个月的服务费和设备费；为确保中央电视台向泛美卫星公司支付服务费和设备费，中央电视台将于1996年5月3日向泛美卫星公司支付相当于1 961 496美元的保证金，保证金将在本协议最后服务费到期时使用，如果中央电视台未能按期支付，泛美卫星公司将不通知中央电视台立即从保证金上提取现金，在这种情况下，中央电视台以后的付款在补齐从保证金账户上支取的数额后，用于支付其余的服务费。

On 3 April 1996, Inter-American Satellite International Systems Liability Ltd.(hereinafter referred to as Pan American Satellite Company) and CCTV signed the agreement, which was valid until 30 June 2006. On 19 October 1997, the parties amended some of the terms of the agreement and signed the amendment. Under the agreement and the amendment, Pan Am Satellite provides CCTV with a full-time, fixed-term, non-transferable (with the exception of a separate priority) compressed digital video services. The services cover the Pacific (Pacific Rim Service), Africa (African Service), Indian Ocean (South Asia/Middle East Service) and Latin America (Americas). According to section 1.1 A agreement: Pan Am Satellite supplies ground equipment, to provide downlink, US transmission, America, Africa, in addition to paying the fees, CCTV agreed to pay for the equipment. According to section 1.2, Pan Am Satellite is only used to transmit CCTV television signals, CCTV can use it for itself, Chinese radio and television stations above the provincial level may also be allowed to use parts not used by CCTV. With the prior permission of Pan Am Satellite, CCTV allows non-Chinese corporate broadcasters to use their unused parts, transmit TV signals. According to Section 1.6, the monitoring of the air carrier parameters for each service will be carried out by the Inter-American Satellite Company Carrier Surveillance System. The system is operated on a round-the-clock basis by staff of the Pan Am Satellite Engineering and Technology Operations Centre. According to Section 3.1 it 3.2, it is agreed that CCTV shall pay quarterly service fees and equipment fees, and that CCTV shall pay a deposit to Pan Am Satellite Company within 30 days after the signing of the agreement, which shall be used to the service fees and equipment fees for the first three months and the last one month of the service period. In order to ensure payment by CCTV of services and equipment to Pan Am Satellite Company, CCTV will pay Pan Am Satellite Company a deposit equivalent to US $1,961,496 on 3 May 1996, which will be used when the final service fee of this Agreement expires. If CCTV fails to pay on time, Pan Am Satellite Company will not notify CCTV to withdraw cash from the deposit immediately. In this case, the subsequent payment by CCTV will be used to pay the remaining service fee after the amount withdrawn from the deposit account is filled.

协议签订后,中央电视台按约定向泛美卫星公司支付了订金和保证金,此后定期向泛美卫星公司支付季度服务费和设备费。2000年6月30日,北京市国家税务局对外分局第二税务所(以下简称对外分局二所)向中央电视台发出京国税外分税二[2002]第319号《关于对中央电视台与泛美卫星公司签署〈数字压缩电视全时卫星传送服务协议〉所支付的费用代扣代缴预提所得税的通知》(以下简称319号《通知》)。该《通知》要求,中央电视台履行代扣代缴的义务,并认定泛美卫星公司于1999年3月25日交纳的1 546 631美元是应由中央电视台依法代扣代缴的预提所得税。泛美卫星公司不服,向北京市国家税务局对外分局(以下简称对外分局)提出复议,对外分局于同年11月17日作出维持319号《通知》的决定。2000年11月29日,原告以北京国税第二税务所为被告,央视为第三人诉至北京市第一中级人民法院。

After the signing of the agreement, CCTV paid the Pan Am Satellite Company a deposit and a security deposit as agreed. Since then, quarterly service and equipment fees have been paid regularly to Pan Am Satellite. On 30 June 2000, Beijing State Taxation Bureau Foreign Branch Second Tax Office (hereinafter referred to as the Foreign Branch Bureau II) issued to CCTV the Notice No. 319 of the [2002] on the Deduction of the Advance Income Tax for

第九章 跨国投资所得征税的协调
CHAPTER IX Tax Harmonization on Cross-border Investment Income

expenses paid by CCTV and Pan Am Satellite Company (Digital Compressed Television Full-time Satellite Transmission Service Agreement)(hereinafter referred to as Circular 319). The "Notice" required that CCTV fulfill the obligation of withholding and paying, and determined that the US $1,546,631 paid by Pan Am Satellite on March 25, 1999 was the withholding income tax that should be withheld and paid by CCTV in accordance with the law. Pan Am Satellite Company refused to accept it and filed a reconsideration with the Foreign Branch of the Beijing Municipal State Administration of Taxation (hereinafter referred to as the Foreign Branch). The Foreign Branch made a decision to maintain the No. 319 Notice on November 17 of the same year. On 29 November, 2000, the plaintiff took the Beijing National Taxation Office No. 2 as the defendant, and the central government regarded it as a third party to Beijing, which was the No. 1 Intermediate People's Court.

原告诉称：(1) 对于"协议"性质的认定，应以合同法为依据。租赁合同的主要法律特征是租赁物的交付，即有体物占有、使用权的转移。"协议"约定由原告通过操作使用其位于外层空间的卫星及美国的地面设施，为第三人提供传输服务。在该过程中，未发生任何设施的占有和使用权的转移，不符合租赁合同的特征。故原告的收入不属于租金。(2)《中美税收协定》第11条中"使用或有权使用工业设备"的使用者应是积极的实际使用。整个信号传输过程中，全部设施完全由原告独立操作使用，第三人无权且未实际使用原告的任何设施，原告的收入不是特许权使用费。(3) 原告的收入是靠长年不断的工作取得的积极收入，应属于营业利润，且其在中国未设立常设机构，故不应在中国纳税。(4) 201号"通知"和566号"批复"违反法律和国际税收协定的规定，应当不予适用。(5) 被告在计算应税收入时，将订金和保证金计算在内是错误的。故被告的具体行政行为认定事实错误，适用法律不当，请求法院依法予以撤销并责令被告返还不当征收的税款。

The plaintiff stated: (1) The nature of the agreement should be based on contract law. The main legal feature of the lease contract is the delivery of the lease item, that is, the transfer of possession and right of use. The agreement provides for the plaintiff to provide transport services to third parties by operating its satellite in outer space and United States ground facilities. In this process, there is no transfer of possession and use of any facilities, which does not conform to the characteristics of the lease contract. Therefore, the plaintiff's income does not belong to the rent. (2) The user who "uses or has the right to use industrial equipment" in Article 11 of the Sino-US Tax Agreement shall be actively used in practice. In the whole process of signal transmission, all the facilities are operated independently by the plaintiff, the third party has no right and does not actually use any of the plaintiff's facilities, and the plaintiff's income is not royalties. (3) The plaintiff's income is a positive income derived from perennial work and should be operating profit, and it does not have a permanent establishment in China, so it should not be taxed in China. (4) No. 201 "Notice" and No. 566 "Reply" violate the provisions of the law and international tax agreement and should not be applied. (5) It was a mistake for the defendant to include the deposit and margin in the calculation of taxable income. Therefore, the defendant's specific administrative act is wrong in ascertaining the facts and improper in applying the law, so he requests the court to cancel it and order the defendant to return the tax improperly collected.

被告辩称：(1)《中美税收协定》中特许权使用包括对有形财产和无形资产的使用。使用当然并非仅限于对实物的实际操作，操作只是使用的一种方式，"使用"的正确理解应当是利用某客体的使用功能达到预期的目的；(2) 根据"协议"的约定，第三人利用原告所拥有的卫星设备进行电视信号的转发，即有权使用原告的卫星转发器，其向原告支付的季度服务费和设备费，属于《中美税收协定》中特许权使用费；(3) 原告卫星中专门转发器的全部或部分由第三人专有使用，符合我国税法关于将财产租给中国境内租用者的规定，也符合租赁合同中关于转移财产使用权的特征，故原告的收入属于租金；(4) 根据"协议"约定，订金和安全保证金的性质是原告的收入，因原告所缴纳的是预提所得税，根据我国税法规定，应当将其计算在应纳税额中。因此，319号"通知"认定事实清楚，适用法律正确，执法程序合法，请求法院予以维持。

The defendant argued that: (1) The use of concessions in the Sino-US Tax Agreement included the use of tangible and intangible assets. (2) According to the agreement, a third party uses the satellite equipment owned by the plaintiff for the transmission of television signals, i.e. the right to use the plaintiff's satellite transponder, and the quarterly service and equipment fees paid to the plaintiff are royalties under the Sino-US Tax Agreement. (3) All or part of the special transponder in the plaintiff's satellite is used exclusively by a third party, in accordance with the provisions of our tax law concerning the lease of property to renters in China, as well as the characteristics of the lease contract concerning the transfer of the right to use property, so the plaintiff's income belongs to the rent. (4) According to the agreement, the nature of the deposit and security deposit is the plaintiff's income, as the plaintiff pays withholding income tax, which should be calculated in the taxable amount according to the provisions of our tax law. Therefore, Notice 319 found that the facts were clear, the applicable law was correct, and the law enforcement procedure was lawful, and requested the court to uphold it.

第三人认为：原告提起诉讼所依据的事实符合实际情况，但其没有资格对原告所得的性质进行认定，请法院公正裁断。

The third party holds that the facts on which the plaintiff filed the lawsuit are in accordance with the actual situation, but they are not qualified to determine the nature of the plaintiff's income, and ask the court to adjudicate fairly.

2001年10月11日，一审法院审理后判决，被告作出319号"通知"，认定事实清楚，程序合法，适用法律并无不当，法院予以维持。原告要求撤销319号"通知"并责令被告返还不当征收税款的诉讼请求法院不予支持。原告泛美卫星公司不服一审判决提起上诉，2002年12月26日北京市高院作出终审判决，驳回上诉，维持原判。

On 11 October 2001, the court of first instance, after hearing the judgment, the defendant made 319 "Notice", found that the facts were clear, the procedure was lawful, and the applicable law was not improper, and the court upheld it. The plaintiff's claim to revoke Notice 319 and order the defendant to return improper tax collection is not supported by the Court. The plaintiff Pan Am Satellite Company appealed against the first instance judgment, and on December 26,

2002, the Beijing Municipal High Court issued a final judgment, rejected the appeal and upheld the original judgment.

（二）案件分析
Case Analysis

结合本案中原告被告双方的观点来看，案件争议焦点是：《卫星传输服务协议》以及协议中相关收入的定性问题，即《卫星传输服务协议》应当认定为租赁合同还是服务合同？依照协议内容产生的收入应当认定为特许权使用费还是营业收入？第一，《卫星传输服务协议》具有典型的租赁合同特征。租赁合同的构成要件包括：（1）转移占有和使用权，（2）使用人支付相应对价，（3）双方约定维修费用承担，（4）约定期满后返还原物。从协议的内容来看，泛美卫星公司负责发射、运行、检修、干预卫星并转让特定卫星频道的使用权，央视在约定期限内专有使用特定卫星发射器与特定带宽并支付对价。显然，协议内容符合租赁合同后三个要件。此时央视是否占有使用卫星特定转发器与特定带宽成为协议是否构成租赁合同的关键点。根据"协议"约定，在正常情况下，卫星中指定的转发器带宽只能用于传输第三人的电视信号，即这些指定带宽的使用权为第三人专有。带宽是由卫星系统提供的，第三人有权使用带宽应视为有权使用卫星系统。此外，泛美卫星公司以聘请技术人员对卫星进行运营为理由而主张的卫星传输协议属于服务协议缺乏说服力。协议的标的为特定卫星频道的使用权而非技术人员的运营维修服务，卫星传输信号需要通过人员对地面设备的操作来完成，人员的操作服务是为了保障卫星系统的正常运行，实现传输信号的使用功能。虽然双方签订的协议内容包括由原告通过技术人员操作其各地面配套设施来提供服务，但这种服务是从属于第三人有权使用原告卫星系统的，仅占辅助地位，不足以影响传输服务协议的性质，因此卫星传输协议属于租赁合同。另外，协议中相关收入应当认定为特许权使用费而非营业利润。原告主张相关收入来源于其发射卫星并雇佣技术人员运营设备，且央视没有实际使用卫星，系从事积极的运营活动，是积极性收入而非消极性收入，因此构成营业利润而非特许权使用费。本案中，央视支付对价的本质目的是使用特定卫星频道进行信号传输，因此泛美收入取得是基于央视对特定频道的使用而产生，具有被动性特征。《中美税收协定》第11条并未明确有权使用工业、商业、科学设备应限定为实际占有操作有体物，故原告认为第三人未实际操作使用其卫星设备，不能构成使用或有权使用工业设备，原告的收入是由于提供服务而取得的积极收入，应属于营业利润等诉讼理由没有法律依据。综上，援引《中美税收协定》中有关特许权使用费的规定对原告提供的服务性质进行定性，相关所得为特许权使用费，又因"卫星中专门转发器的全部或者部分由第三人专有使用"符合我国税法将财产租给中国境内租用者的规定，也符合租赁合同中关于转移财产使用权的特征，故原告的收入属于租金。

According to the viewpoint of the plaintiff and defendant in this case, the dispute focus of the case is "Satellite Transmission Service Agreement" and the qualitative problem of the related income in the agreement, that is, should "Satellite Transmission Service Agreement" be regarded as a lease contract or a service contract? and should revenue generated in accordance with the content of the agreement be recognized as royalties or operating income? First, the Satellite Transmission Service Agreement has typical lease contract characteristics. The constituent elements of the lease contract include (1) transfer of possession and right of use, (2) payment of corresponding consideration by the user, (3) commitment of maintenance expenses by both parties, and(4) return of the original property after the expiration of the agreement. From the content of the agreement, Pan Am Satellite Company is responsible for launching, running, overhauling, interfering with satellites and transferring the right to use specific satellite channels. CCTV exclusively uses specific satellite launchers and specific bandwidth and pays consideration within the agreed time limit. Obviously, the contents of the agreement meet the three requirements of the lease contract. At this time, whether CCTV occupies and uses satellite specific transponders and specific bandwidth becomes the key point of whether the protocol constitutes a lease contract. According to the "protocol", under normal circumstances, the designated transponder bandwidth in the satellite can only be used to transmit third-party television signals, that is, the right to use these specified bandwidth is exclusive to third-party users. The bandwidth is provided by the satellite system, and the third party's right to use the bandwidth shall be regarded as the right to use the satellite system. In addition, the satellite transmission protocol advocated by Pan Am Satellite Company on the grounds of hiring technicians to operate the satellite is a service protocol that is unconvincing. The object of the protocol is the right to use a specific satellite channel rather than the operation and maintenance service of the technical personnel. The satellite transmission signal needs to be completed through the operation of the ground equipment by the personnel. The operation service of the personnel is to ensure the normal operation of the satellite system. Although the agreement between the two parties includes the provision of services by the plaintiff through the operation of its ground supporting facilities by technical personnel, such services are subordinate to the right of the third party to use the plaintiff's satellite system and occupy only an auxiliary position. Inaddition, the relevant income in the agreement shall be recognized as royalties rather than operating profits. The plaintiff claimed that the related income came from its satellite launch and hired technicians to operate the equipment, and CCTV did not actually use the satellite, which was engaged in active operating activities, positive income rather than negative income. As a result, operating profits are not royalties. In this case, the essential purpose of CCTV to pay consideration is to use a specific satellite channel for signal transmission, so Pan American revenue acquisition is based on CCTV's use of a specific channel and has passive characteristics. Article 11 of the Sino-US Tax Agreement does not specify that the right to use industrial, commercial and scientific equipment shall be limited to the actual possession of operational objects, so the plaintiff considers that the third party's failure to actually use its satellite equipment can not constitute the use or right to use industrial equipment, that the plaintiff's income is a positive income derived from the provision of services, and that there is no legal basis for litigation reasons such as operating profits. In summary, the nature of the services provided by the plaintiff is characterized by the use of royalties under the Sino-US Tax Agreement, and the proceeds are concessions.

二、美国硅谷公司特许权使用费和利息纳税案
Case of Royalties and Interest Taxes for Silicon Valley Company

(一)案情介绍
Introduction to the case

硅谷公司是依照美国纽约州法律注册设立的、总部位于纽约市的一家专营药品开发和生产业务的企业。2008年5月,硅谷公司与中国上海医药集团公司在上海依照中国法律合资成立以药品制造和销售为主营业务的中外合资硅沪公司,公司注册资金为1 000万元人民币,硅谷公司出资600万元人民币,持有硅沪公司60%股权,上海医药集团出资400万元人民币,持有40%股权。2009年11月,双方签订了有关授权使用硅谷公司开发的某种新型药品的专利技术和授权硅沪公司在中国独家经销硅谷公司生产的消炎药的协议。根据协议规定,硅谷公司授权硅沪公司使用其专利技术的5年期间内,硅沪公司每年按其销售该种药品的年销售额的10%支付硅谷公司专利技术使用费。

Silicon Valley Corporation is a New York City-based pharmaceutical development and manufacturing company registered under the laws of New York. In May 2008, silicon Valley Corporation and Shanghai Pharmaceutical Corporation of China established a Sino-foreign joint venture in Shanghai in accordance with the laws of China, and the registered capital was 10 million yuan, to which Silicon Valley contributed 6 million yuan, holding a 60% stake in Sihu, and Shanghai Pharmaceutical Group contributed 4 million yuan, holding a 40% stake. In november 2009, the two sides signed agreements to authorize the use of patent technology for a new drug developed by Silicon Valley and to authorize the exclusive distribution of anti-inflammatory drugs produced by Silicon Shanghai in China. According to the agreement, within five years of Silicon Valley's licensing of its patented technology, Silicon Shanghai pays Silicon Valley royalties annually for its patented technology at 10% of its annual sales.

(1)2010年年底,硅沪公司根据协议内容和年度新型药品的销售总额的10%计算支付硅谷公司应收取的1 000万元专利使用费时,上海市国税局通知要求硅沪公司在向硅谷公司支付相关费用时按照10%的税率代为扣缴100万元企业所得税和相应的营业税及附加。硅谷公司知悉后,遂通过驻北京办事处与上海国税局交涉,认为研究开发和转让药品生产技术是硅谷公司的主营业务内容,其与硅沪公司依照协议所取得专利权使用费收入,属于硅谷公司在正常营业范围内的收入,依照《中美税收协定》,中方不应征收企业所得税。试分析硅谷公司的主张是否具有法律依据?

(1) At the end of 2010, when Sihu paid 10 million yuan royalties due to Silicon Valley companies on the basis of the terms of the agreement and 10 per cent of the total annual sales of new drugs, the Shanghai Municipal Bureau of Internal Revenue notified the company that it was required to withhold 1 million yuan corporate income tax and corresponding business tax and additions at a rate of 10 per cent when paying related fees to Silicon Valley companies. After being informed, the company negotiated with the Shanghai Internal Revenue Bureau through its

Beijing office, arguing that research, development and transfer of drug production technology was the main business content of Silicon Valley Company, and that its patent fee income obtained under the agreement with Silicon Shanghai Company belonged to the income of Silicon Valley Company within the normal business scope. According to the Sino-US Tax Agreement, China should not levy enterprise income tax. Does Silicon Valley's claim have a legal basis?

（2）根据协议中硅谷公司与硅沪公司有关授权硅沪公司在中国独家经营经销消炎药的条款规定，硅沪公司应按年度向硅谷公司支付硅谷公司提供给硅沪公司的消炎药销售货款，并按照每年度该药品销售总额提取15%的经销费后将余款支付给硅谷公司。已知该新型消炎药2008年在中国境内销售额为1 000万元，硅沪公司作为经销商从中提取经销费用150万元，上海市国税局认为硅谷公司通过硅沪公司代理经销在中国境内取得的消炎药品销售收入1 000万元应在中国履行缴纳企业所得税。由于硅谷公司本身未向上海市税务机关提供硅谷公司生产销售消炎药的成本、费用资料，上海市国税局决定采用核定利润率方式征税，依照国内同类药品制售行业的20%利润率核定其应税所得额为200万元，并责成硅沪公司按照25%的税率计算其应纳税额代扣企业所得税50万元。试分析上海市国税局的征税行为是否正确。

(2) In accordance with the terms of the agreement between Silicon Valley and Sihu to authorize Sihu to exclusively distribute anti-inflammatory drugs in China, Silicon Shanghai should pay annual sales of anti-inflammatory drugs from Silicon Valley to Silicon Shanghai, and according to the annual total sales of the drug 15% of the distribution fee will be paid to Silicon Valley companies. The new anti-inflammatory drug is known to have sales of 10 million in China in 2008, Silicon Shanghai Company as a distributor to extract distribution costs of 1.5 million, the Shanghai State Taxation Bureau believed that Silicon Valley companies should pay corporate income tax in China for 10 million sales of anti-inflammatory drugs obtained in China through the agency distribution of Silicon Shanghai. Since Silicon Valley companies themselves did not provide the Shanghai tax authorities with information on the costs and costs of producing and selling anti-inflammatory drugs, the Shanghai Municipal Bureau of Internal Revenue decided to use the approved profit margin to tax, according to the domestic similar drug production and sale industry 20% profit margin approved its taxable income amount is 2 million, and ordered Sihu company according to 25% tax rate to calculate its tax payable withholding enterprise income tax 500,000. Try to analyze whether the tax collection behavior of Shanghai Internal Revenue Bureau is correct.

（3）为解决上述新型药品生产资金问题，经硅谷公司担保，硅沪公司于2009年与美国花旗银行纽约总部签订总额为600万美元年利率为10%期限为5年的贷款协议。为执行上述贷款合同，美国花旗银行委托上海分行向硅沪公司发放贷款并协助监督硅沪公司将上述贷款用于药品研发及销售，以确保硅沪公司届时有能力履行其与硅谷公司之间协议的专利使用费以及贷款合同规定的向花旗银行总部还本付息的义务。依照贷款合同内容，硅沪公司在2010年12月应支付花旗银行纽约总部上述贷款利息60万美元，上海市国税局按照《中美税收协定》要求硅沪公司在支付上述利息时应当代为扣缴10%的预提所得税。上海市国税局对美国花旗银行上述利息所得的课税行为是否具有法律依据？

(3) In order to solve the problem of financing the production of these new drugs, Silicon Shanghai signed a bandwidth agreement with Citibank New York headquarters in 2009, with a total annual interest rate of $6 million and a 10-year term of five years, under the guarantee of Silicon Valley. In order to implement the loan contract, Citibank commissioned the Shanghai Branch to issue loans to Sihu and to assist in supervising the use of the loans for drug development and sales to ensure that Sihu would be able to meet its agreement with Silicon Valley royalty and loan contract obligations to Citibank headquarters. In accordance with the terms of the loan contract, Sihu should pay Citibank's New York headquarters $600,000 in interest on the loan in December 2010, and the Shanghai IRS required Sihu to withhold 10% of its withholding income tax on its behalf when paying the interest. Is there a legal basis for the Shanghai Internal Revenue Service to tax the above interest earned by Citibank?

（二）案件分析
Case Analysis

（1）本案中，硅沪公司向硅谷公司支付费用是为了使用其药品专利，应当认定为特许权使用费。依照《中美税收协定》第11条的规定，发生于缔约国一方而支付给缔约国另一方居民的特许权使用费，可以在该缔约国另一方征税。然而，这些特许权使用费也可以在其发生的缔约国按照该缔约国的法律征税。但是如果收款人是特许权使用费的受益所有人，则所征税款不应超过特许权使用费总额的10%。所以上海市国税局要求硅沪公司在向硅谷公司支付专利使用费时按照10%的预提税率代为扣缴税款是符合《中美税收协定》之规定的。因此硅谷公司的关于相关费用是营业收入的异议是没有合法依据的。

(1) In this case, Sihu paid the Silicon Valley Company for the use of its drug patents and the payment should be recognized as royalties. In accordance with Article 11 of the Sino-US Tax Agreement, royalties paid to residents of the other contracting party arising from one of the contracting parties may be taxed in the other contracting party. However, these royalties may also be taxed in the state party in which they occur, in accordance with the laws of that state party. However, if the payee is the beneficial owner of the royalty, the tax levied shall not exceed 10% of the total royalty. So the Shanghai Internal Revenue Service requires Silicon Shanghai to withhold taxes at a 10% withholding rate when paying royalties to Silicon Valley companies. It is compliance with the Sino-US Tax Agreement. So there is no legal basis for the Silicon Valley Company's objection that the related expenses are operating income.

（2）依据《中美税收协定》，缔约国一方企业的利润应仅在该缔约国征税，但该企业通过设在缔约国另一方常设机构在缔约国另一方营业的除外，其利润以属于该常设机构的利润为限可以在缔约国另一方进行征税。此外，在确定常设机构利润时，应允许扣除营业发生的各项费用，但不包括特许权使用费和利息等类似款项。依据我国《企业所得税法》，非居民企业在中国境内设立机构、场所的，应就其所设机构、场所的来源于中国境内的所得，以及发生在中国境外，但与所设机构、场所有实际联系的所得缴纳企业所得税。对非居民企业取得的该法规定的所得应缴纳的所得税，实行源泉扣缴，以支付人为扣缴义务人。企业不能提供与关联方之间业务往来资料的，未能如实反映业务往来情况的，税务机关有权依法核定其应纳税所得额。本案中,硅谷公司通过硅沪公司进行药品销售,符合上述纳税条件,应当履行缴纳企业所得税义务。又因硅谷公司未向上海市税务机关登记手续和申报材料,经销商硅沪公司也无法提供上述材料,上海市国税局依照我国税法规定采用核定利润率方式征税,符合《中美税收协定》和《企业所得税法》之规定,因此上海市国税局的征税行为是正确的。

(2) Under the Sino-US Tax Agreement, the profits of an enterprise of a contracting state shall be taxed in that contracting state only, except where the enterprise operates in the other contracting state through a permanent establishment located in the other contracting state, whose profits may be taxed in the other contracting state only to the extent that it is a profit belonging to that permanent establishment. In addition, in determining the profits of the permanent establishment, deductions should be allowed for operating expenses, excluding similar amounts such as royalties and interest. In accordance with the Enterprise Income Tax Law of China, a non-resident enterprise that establishes an institution or place within the territory of China shall pay the enterprise income tax on the income derived from the establishment of the institution or place, as well as the income derived from the establishment of the institution or place outside the territory of China, but having actual connection with the establishment of the institution or place. The income tax payable by non-resident enterprises under this law shall be withheld from the source, and the payer shall be the withholding agent. If an enterprise fails to provide information on business transactions with related parties and fails to truthfully reflect the business transactions, the tax authorities shall have the right to approve their taxable income according to law. In this case, Silicon Valley Company through Silicon Shanghai Company for drug sales, meet the above tax conditions, should fulfill the obligation to pay corporate income tax. Because Silicon Valley Company did not register and declare materials with the Shanghai tax authorities, and the dealer Sihu Company was unable to provide the above materials, the Shanghai Internal Revenue Bureau taxed the approved profit margin in accordance with the provisions of our tax law. In accordance with the Sino-US Tax Agreement and the Enterprise Income Tax Law, the tax collection behavior of Shanghai Internal Revenue Bureau is correct.

(3)上海市国税局对美国花旗银行利息所得征税是有法律依据的。根据《中美税收协定》之规定,发生于缔约国一方而支付给缔约国另一方居民的利息,可以在该缔约国一方征税。然而这些利息也可以在该利息发生的缔约国,按照缔约国的法律征税。但是如果收款人是该利息的受益所有人,则所征税款不应超过利息总额的10%。本案中利息所得发生地为我国,受益所有人花旗银行为美国居民企业,符合上述规定之条件,因此上海市国税局有权对花旗银行上述利息所得按照规定征税。[①]

(3) There is a legal basis for the Shanghai Internal Revenue Service to tax interest income from Citibank. Under the Sino-US Tax Agreement, interest paid to a resident of the other contracting state in respect of one of the contracting states may be taxed on that Contracting State. However, such interest may also be taxed in the state party in which the interest occurred, in accordance with the law of the state party. However, if the payee is the beneficial owner of the

---

① 龙英锋主编:《国际税法案例教程》,立信会计出版社2011年版,第88—92页。

interest, the tax levied shall not exceed 10% of the total interest. In this case, the interest income occurred in China, and the beneficial owner of Citibank was a resident enterprise in the United States, which met the above requirements, so the Shanghai Internal Revenue Bureau had the right to tax the interest income of Citibank in accordance with the regulations.

学习思考题 / Questions for Study

1. 简述税收分享原则的适用前提以及例外情形。
   Please briefly explain the application prerequisites and exceptional circumstances of principle of tax sharing.
2. OECD范本对股息、利息以及特许权使用费是如何征税的?
   How are dividends, interest and royalties taxed in OECD Model?
3. 简述股息和利息的范围。
   Please briefly explain the scope of dividends and interest.
4. 如何认定股息和利息的来源地?
   How to identify the source of dividends and interest?
5. 如何区分提供专有技术合同与提供专有技术服务合同?
   How to distinguish between contracts for the supply of know-how and contracts for the provision of services?

第十章 CHAPTER X

跨国不动产所得、财产收益、财产价值征税的协调
Tax Harmonization on Cross-border Income from Immovable Property, Capital Gains and Property Value

对包括不动产在内的财产及财产要素所课的税收可有不同的形式,如专门针对财产转让所得的课税、对财产交易的课税、对财产持有的课税等。本章聚焦不动产所得、财产转让收益和财产价值相关征税规则在国际层面的协调。这些协调主要分为两个层面:一是国内所得税法的相关规定,二是税收协定中的内容。在探讨国内法和税收协定的规则之前,首先应明确的是"不动产所得""财产收益"和"财产价值"这三个概念。

The taxation of property and property elements including immovable property can take different forms, such as taxation of the income from property transfer, taxation of the property transactions, taxation of the possession of property, etc. This chapter focuses on the international coordination of tax rules related to the income from immovable property, the income from property transfer and the property value. The coordination is mainly divided into two levels, one is relevant provisions of the domestic income tax law, and the other is the content of the tax treaties. Before discussing the rules of domestic laws and tax treaties, the three concepts of "income from immovable property", "capital gains" and "property value" should be clarified first.

"不动产所得"是税收协定中的概念,在中国国内法中并未出现,也没有明确定义。在中国所签署的税收协定中,不动产所得指使用、出租不动产所获的收益,不包括不动产转让的所得。[①] 与之对应的是国内法中的不动产的"租赁所得"。

"Income from immovable property" is a concept derived from tax treaties, which does not appear in Chinese domestic law and is not clearly defined. In the tax treaties signed by China, income from immovable property refers to the income derived from the direct use or letting of immovable property, excluding the income from the transfer of immovable property.[②] The corresponding concept is "rental income" of immovable property in domestic law.

---

① 参见国家税务总局《〈中华人民共和国政府和新加坡共和国政府关于对所得避免双重征税和防止偷漏税的协定〉及议定书条文解释》(国税发[2010]75号),第6条。

② See the State Administration of Taxation "'The Agreement between the Government of the People's Republic of China and the Government of the Republic of Singapore on Avoidance of Double Taxation and Prevention of Fiscal Evasion with Respect to Taxes on Income' and the Interpretation of the Provisions of the Protocol" (No. 75 [2010] of the State Administration of Taxation), Article 6.

第十章 跨国不动产所得、财产收益、财产价值征税的协调
CHAPTER X Tax Harmonization on Cross-border Income from Immovable Property, Capital Gains and Property Value

财产收益,即财产转让所得,指纳税人因转让各种具有资本性质的财产的所有权而取得的收入。①《中华人民共和国企业所得税法》中,财产收益被称为"转让财产收入",指企业转让固定资产、生物资产、无形资产、股权、债权等财产取得的收入。②《中华人民共和国个人所得税法》中,财产收益被称为"财产转让所得",指个人转让有价证券、股权、合伙企业中的财产份额、不动产、机器设备、车船以及其他财产取得的所得。③国家税务总局将税收协定中的"财产收益"解释为"因财产所有权发生转移而取得的所得"。④无论是国内法还是税收协定,不动产转让取得的收入都涵盖在财产收益的范围内。

"Capital gains", the income from property transfer, refers to the income obtained by the taxpayer from the transfer of ownership of various capital properties. In the Enterprise Income Tax Law, "Capital gains", known as "property transfer income", refers to the income obtained by enterprises from transferring fixed assets, biological assets, intangible assets, equity, debts and other properties. In the Individual Income Tax Law, capital gains, known as "income from the transfer of property", refers to the income obtained by individuals from the transfer of securities, stock rights, property shares in partnerships, immovable property, machinery and equipment, vehicles and ships, and other properties. The State Administration of Taxation interprets "capital gains" in tax treaties as "the income derived from the transfer of property ownership." Regardless of the domestic law or tax treaties, the income from the transfer of immovable property is covered by the scope of capital gains.

财产价值,通常指蕴含在财产中的潜在收益,尚未通过转售实现。这是财产价值与财产收益、不动产所得等已实现收益的最大差异。从理论角度出发,财产价值和财产收益并不是泾渭分明的。例如,根据纯资产增加说的所得理论,无论财产本身的价值是否通过转售得以实现,都属于所得的一部分。⑤但实践中,各国原则上均将未实现的财产价值排除在所得税的征税范围之外。其主要原因是,对财产价值课征所得税不仅将使征税范围过广,产生过度课税之虞,还在征管层面难以执行,难以准确对财产估值。⑥因此,对财产价值课税并非通过所得税,而是通过财产税实现。财产税指对纳税人在某一日期拥有的动产或不动产从价征收的税种。⑦在国际税收实务中,财产税是对所得税的补充,其目的在于把握财产所具有的潜在收益能力。⑧

"Property value", which has not been realized through resale, usually refers to the potential income contained in the property. This is the biggest difference between property value and realized income such as capital gains and income from immovable property. From a theoretical

---

① 参见廖益新主编:《国际税法学》,高等教育出版社2008年版,第190页。
② 参见《中华人民共和国企业所得税法》第6条,《中华人民共和国企业所得税法实施条例》第17条。
③ 参见《中华人民共和国个人所得税法》第2条,《中华人民共和国个人所得税法实施条例》第6条。
④ 国家税务总局:《税收协定条款解读之十——财产收益》,http://www.chinatax.gov.cn/n810219/n810744/n1671176/n1705734/c1707078/content.html。
⑤ 参见柯格钟:《论所得税法上的所得概念》,载《台湾大学法学论丛》2008年第37卷3期,第129—188页。
⑥ 参见陈清秀:《量能课税与实质课税原则(上)》,载《月旦法学杂志》2010年第183期,第76页。
⑦ 参见《元照英美法词典》。
⑧ 参见陈清秀:《国际税法上财产课税之探讨》,载《税务旬刊》2017年第2832期,第7—14页。

point of view, property value and capital gains are not clearly distinct. For example, according to the comprehensive income theory, regardless of whether the value of the property itself is realized through resale, it is part of the income. In practice, in principle, all countries exclude unrealized property value from the scope of income tax. The main reason is that imposing income tax on property value will not only make the scope of taxation too wide and cause excessive taxation, but also make it difficult to exercise the collection and to value the property accurately. Therefore, the taxation of property value is not realized through income tax, but through property tax. Property tax refers to an ad valorem tax levied on movable or immovable property owned by a taxpayer on a certain date. In international taxation practice, property tax is a supplement to income tax, and its purpose is to grasp the potential profitability of property.

第一节 跨国不动产所得征税的协调
Section 1　Tax Harmonization on Cross-border Income from Immovable Property

跨国不动产所得征税的协调中包含了国内法对非居民不动产租赁所得的课税规则和税收协定中不动产所得的管辖权划分规则。

The coordination of tax rules on cross-border income from immovable property includes the tax rules relating to non-residents' rental income from immovable property in domestic law and the jurisdictional division rules for income from immovable property in tax treaties.

一、国内法对非居民不动产租赁所得的课税规则
Tax Rules for Non-residents' Rental Income from Immovable Property in Domestic Law

针对非居民的不动产租赁所得课税的国内法规则，明确了中国单方面如何划分跨国不动产租赁所得的管辖权范围。对于非居民企业和非居民个人，国内法遵从不动产所在地课税的一般规则。

The domestic rules on the taxation of non-residents' rental income from immovable property clarify how China unilaterally allocates the jurisdiction of cross-border rental income from immovable property. For non-resident enterprises and non-resident individuals, domestic law follows the general rules which attribute the taxing right to the place where immovable property is located.

（一）对非居民企业不动产租金所得的课税规则
Tax Rules for Non-resident Enterprises' Rental Income from Immovable Property

中国向非居民企业的所得主张管辖权具体分为两种情形：其一，非居民企业在中国境

第十章 跨国不动产所得、财产收益、财产价值征税的协调
CHAPTER X　Tax Harmonization on Cross-border Income from Immovable Property, Capital Gains and Property Value

内设立机构、场所的,应当就其所设机构、场所取得的来源于中国境内的所得,以及发生在中国境外但与其所设机构、场所有实际联系的所得,缴纳企业所得税;其二,非居民企业在中国境内未设立机构、场所的,或者虽设立机构、场所但取得的所得与其所设机构、场所没有实际联系的,应当就其来源于中国境内的所得缴纳企业所得税。① 两种情形在税率、缴税方式上皆有所区分。第一种情形中,非居民企业同居民企业一样申报企业所得税,适用25%的税率;第二种情形中,非居民企业的所得实行源泉扣缴,并适用20%的税率。② 源泉扣缴的含义是,非居民企业未在境内设立机构、场所,或取得的收入与境内所设机构场所无实际联系,非居民企业的支付人应履行扣缴义务。③ 一方面,税务机关难以监管未在境内设有机构场、所的非居民企业的境内所得,另一方面,境内机构、场所若与该所得之间缺乏实际联系,可能无法提供准确的纳税信息。因此,源泉扣缴不仅便于境内税务机关掌控税源,提升境内税务机关征管效率,还有利于减轻非居民企业遵从成本。

　　Chinese jurisdiction over non-resident enterprises' income is specifically divided into two situations. Firstly, if a non-resident enterprise establishes an institution or premises in China, it shall pay enterprise income tax on the income derived from or accruing by its institution or premises in China and on the income derived from or accruing outside China with which the established institution or premises has a de facto relationship. Secondly, for a non-resident enterprise having no institution or premises inside China, or for a non-resident enterprise whose incomes have no de facto relationship with its institution or premises inside China, it shall pay enterprise income tax on the incomes derived from or accruing in China. The two situations are distinguished in tax rate and tax payment method. In the first case, non-resident enterprises report enterprise income tax at the same rate as resident enterprises, while a 25% tax rate applies. In the second case, non-resident enterprises' income is subject to withholding at source, while a 20% tax rate applies. The meaning of withholding at source is that non-resident enterprises have not established an institution or premises in China, or the income obtained has no de facto relationship with the institution or premises established in China, and the payer of the non-resident enterprise shall act as withholding agent. On the one hand, it is difficult for tax authorities to supervise the domestic income of non-resident enterprises that do not have an institution or premises in China. On the other hand, if there is no de facto relationship between premises and the income, they may not be able to provide accurate tax information. Therefore, withholding at source not only facilitates the control of tax source by domestic tax authorities and improves the efficiency of domestic tax authorities' collection and management, but also helps to reduce compliance costs for non-resident enterprises.

　　非居民企业的所得是否需要缴纳中国企业所得税,主要取决于非居民企业是否在境内设有机构、场所,其取得的所得是否与该机构、场所有实际联系,其所得来源于境内还是境外这三个因素。非居民企业设立的机构、场所指在中国境内从事生产经营活动的机构、场所,

---

① 参见《中华人民共和国企业所得税法》第3条。
② 参见《中华人民共和国企业所得税法》第3条、第4条、第37条。
③ 参见《中华人民共和国企业所得税法》第3条、第37条。

包括管理机构、营业机构、办事机构、工厂等物理存在,也包括非居民企业委托从事生产经营活动的营业代理人。① 所谓与场所、机构有实际联系,是指该场所和机构有据以取得所得的股权、债券,以及拥有、管理、控制据以取得所得的财产等。② 无论非居民企业在境内是否设有机构、场所,或者是否取得与机构、场所有实际联系的所得,只要来自境内的所得都需要缴纳企业所得税。相比于前两个因素,判断所得是否来源于境内的标准更加细致而多元。

Whether a non-resident enterprise's income is subject to Chinese enterprise income tax depends mainly on whether the non-resident enterprise has an institution or premises in China, whether the income obtained is de facto related to the institution or premises, and whether the income is from domestic or overseas. Institutions or premises established by non-resident enterprises shall refer to the institutions or premises that are engaged in production and business activities within the territory of China, including management institutions, operational institutions, offices, factories and other physical presence, and also include business agents entrusted by non-resident enterprises to carry out production and business activities. The so-called de facto relationship with an institution or premises refers to the connection whereby the institution or premises acquires its equity or credit, and owns, manages or controls its property, etc. Regardless of whether a non-resident enterprise has an institution or premises in China, or whether it obtains income de facto related to the premises, as long as the income derives from the territory, it is subject to enterprise income tax. Compared with the first two factors, the criteria for judging whether the income derives from within the territory is more detailed and diverse.

非居民企业不动产租赁所得采用所得来源地管辖权规则,以不动产所在地为所得来源地。根据《中华人民共和国企业所得税法实施条例》,不动产租金所得来源于境内或境外,取决于负担、支付所得的企业或个人的所在地或住所地。③ 国家税务总局在有关非居民企业所得税的文件中补充,非居民企业出租位于中国境内的房屋、建筑物等不动产,对未在境内设立机构、场所进行日常管理的,由境内承租人履行代扣代缴义务。两项规定虽然看似采用不同的课税标准,但内在逻辑却存在统一,即默认负担、支付所得的企业或个人就是承租人,其所在地或住所地是不动产所在国。因此,国内法针对非居民企业获得的不动产租赁所得,符合不动产所在地课税的基本原则。然而,负担、支付所得的企业或个人和实际承租人分别位于境外和境内的情况在实践中确实存在。例如,境外总公司为境内办事处租用境内不动产支付租金及相关费用。此时,不动产位于境内,而租金所得可能无法被认定为来源于境内。如果国内法不在立法中明确承租人和支付租金的主体之间的关系,则中国可能面临非居民企业不动产租赁所得流失的风险。另外,对于判断取得不动产租金所得的非居民企业是否在境内设有机构,存在一项特殊规则。如果该企业委派人员在中国境内或委托境内单位或个人对位于境内的不动产进行日常管理,则该企业将被视为在中国境内设立机构、场所,需就来源于境内的所得和与机构、场所有实际联系的境外所得自行申报纳税。④

---

① 参见《中华人民共和国企业所得税法实施条例》第5条。
② 参见《中华人民共和国企业所得税法实施条例》第8条。
③ 参见《中华人民共和国企业所得税法实施条例》第7条。
④ 参见《关于非居民企业所得税管理若干问题的公告》(国家税务总局公告2011年第24号)。

第十章 跨国不动产所得、财产收益、财产价值征税的协调
CHAPTER X Tax Harmonization on Cross-border Income from Immovable Property, Capital Gains and Property Value

For non-resident enterprises' rental income from immovable property, the source jurisdiction rules shall be adopted, and the place of the immovable property shall be the source of income. According to the Regulation on the Implementation of the Enterprise Income Tax Law, whether the rental income from immovable property derives from China or overseas, depending on the location of the enterprise (the domicile of the individual) bearing and paying the income. The State Administration of Taxation has added in the relevant documents concerning non-resident enterprises' income tax that if a non-resident enterprise rents out immovable property such as houses and buildings in China and doesn't establish any institution or premises to conduct daily management buildings, the domestic lessee shall perform the withholding obligation to pay. Although the two regulations seem to adopt different taxation standards, the internal logic is unified, which tacitly admit that the enterprise or individual who bears and pays the rent is the lessee, and its location or domicile is the country where the immovable property is located. Therefore, the domestic law for non-resident enterprises' rental income from immovable property is in line with the basic principle of taxation of immovable property. However, it does exist in practice that the enterprise or individual that bears and pays the income and the actual lessee are located in overseas and China respectively. For example, an overseas head office pays rent and related expenses for renting domestic immovable property for its domestic offices. At this time, the immovable property is located in the territory, and the rental income may not be recognized as deriving from the territory. If the domestic law does not clarify the relationship between the lessee and the entity who pays the rent, China may face the risk of the loss of rental income from the immovable property obtained by non-resident enterprises. In addition, there is a special rule for determining whether a non-resident enterprise that obtains rental income from immovable property has an institution or premises in China. If the enterprise appoints personnel in China or entrusts a domestic unit or individual to conduct daily management of immovable property located in China, the enterprise will be deemed to have established an institution or premises in China, and should report its income derived from China and the overseas income de factor related to its institution and premises.

（二）对非居民个人不动产租赁所得的课税规则
Tax Rules for Non-resident Individuals' Rental Income from Immovable Property

非居民个人不动产所得的课税原则遵从所得来源地原则，由不动产所在地主张税收管辖权。非居民个人从中国境内取得的所得，应在中国缴纳个人所得税。① 就不动产租赁而言，出租不动产给承租人在中国境内使用的所得，属于来源于境内的所得，无论支付地点是否在中国境内。② 承租人在中国境内使用的不动产必然也位于中国境内。因此，非居民个人和非居民企业租赁不动产的所得，考虑到不动产所在地与纳税人取得的所得存在密切经济联系，皆由不动产所在地主张税收管辖权。

---

① 参见《中华人民共和国个人所得税法》第1条。
② 参见《中华人民共和国个人所得税法实施条例》第3条。

The taxation principle of non-resident individuals' income from immovable property follows the source principle, and the tax jurisdiction is allocated to the location of the immovable property. Non-resident individuals shall pay individual income tax in China for income obtained from China. In terms of the lease of immovable property, the income obtained from renting out immovable property to lessees for use in China, notwithstanding the payment is made in China or not, shall be considered income derived from China. The immovable property used by the lessee in China must also be located in China. Therefore, considering the close economic relationship between the location of the immovable property and the income obtained by the taxpayer, the rental income from immovable property of non-resident individuals and non-resident enterprises, should be taxed by the country where the immovable property is located.

（二）税收协定中跨国不动产所得的协调
Coordination of Tax on Cross-border Income from Immovable Property in Tax Treaties

不动产所得的协调规则在不同税收协定中基本一致。因此，本部分将以《中华人民共和国政府和新加坡共和国政府关于对所得避免双重征税和防止偷漏税的协定》（以下简称《中国-新加坡协定》）[①]为例加以阐释。

The coordination rules of income from immovable property are basically consistent in different tax treaties. Therefore, this part will take "the Agreement between the Government of the People's Republic of China and the Government of the Republic of Singapore for the Avoidance of Double Taxation and the Prevention of Fiscal Evasion with Respect to Taxes on Income" (hereinafter referred to as "the Agreement between China and Singapore") as an example.

（一）"不动产"和"不动产所得"的定义
Definition of "Immovable property" and "Incomes from Immovable Property"

"不动产"的概念对于跨国不动产所得的所得税协调至关重要，也频繁出现在税收协定的不同条款中。中国所签署的税收协定吸收了《OECD关于对所得和财产避免双重征税的协定范本》（下文简称"OECD税收协定范本"）第6条对不动产的阐释。依照《中国-新加坡协定》第6条第2款的规定，"不动产"一语应当具有财产所在地的缔约国的法律所规定的含义。该用语在任何情况下应包括附属于不动产的财产，农业和林业所使用的牲畜和设备，有关地产的一般法律规定所适用的权利，不动产的用益权以及由于开采或有权开采矿藏、水源和其他自然资源取得的不固定或者固定收入的权利。船舶、船只和飞机不应视为不动产。该条款首先明确了双边协定中不动产的含义应以财产所在地缔约国法律为准。此规定一方面考虑到"不动产"这一用语是缔约国各方国内财产法中的重要概念，采用缔约国一方国内法比另行确定一个概念更易于双方协调，[②]另一方面也兼顾了不动产所在地国家与不动产之

---

① 本章引用不同协定时都将简化成"中国-X国协定"这一表述。
② 参见廖益新主编：《国际税法学》，高等教育出版社2008年版，第197页。

第十章 跨国不动产所得、财产收益、财产价值征税的协调
CHAPTER X Tax Harmonization on Cross-border Income from Immovable Property, Capital Gains and Property Value

间具有密切的经济联系。为了进一步缩小缔约国双方对于不动产的规定,OECD税收协定范本第6条第2款进一步限定了不动产的内涵。

The concept of "immovable property" is very important to the income tax coordination of cross-border incomes from immovable property, and often appears in different provisions of tax treaties. The tax treaties signed by China absorb the interpretation of Article 6 of "The Model Convention of the Organization for Economic Cooperation and Development for the Avoidance of Double Taxation on Incomes and Property" (hereinafter referred to as "the OECD Model Tax Convention"). According to Article 6, Paragraph 2, of the Agreement between China and Singapore, the term "immovable property" shall have the meaning prescribed by the law of the contracting state in which the property is located. The term shall in any case include property attached to immovable property, livestock and equipment used in agriculture and forestry, rights applicable to general legal provisions relating to real estate, usufruct of immovable property and right to variable or fixed income derived from the exploitation or right to exploit mineral deposits, water resources and other natural resources. Ships, vessels and aircraft shall not be considered as immovable property. The article first makes clear that the meaning of immovable property in bilateral agreements should be subject to the law of the contracting state where the property is located. This provision, on the one hand, considers that the term "immovable property" is an important concept in the domestic property law of each contracting state, and it is easier for both parties to coordinate by adopting the domestic law of one contracting state than by adopting a new concept. On the other hand, it also takes into account the close economic relationship between the immovable property and the state where the immovable property is located. In order to further narrow the differences between the provisions on immovable property between the contracting states, Article 6 (2) of the OECD Model Tax Convention further limits the connotation of immovable property.

反观中国国内法,《中华人民共和国企业所得税法》和《中华人民共和国个人所得税法》均未对不动产加以阐释。增值税法律规范中的"不动产"是指不能移动或者移动后会引起性质、形状改变的财产,包括建筑物、构筑物等。①《中华人民共和国担保法》中的不动产是指"土地以及房屋、林木等地上定着物,与增值税法律规范中的不动产含义相类似"。但这些定义在覆盖范围上都不及OECD税收协定范本第6条广泛。因此,国家税务总局专门明确了中国税收协定中"不动产"的定义,"包括各种营业用或非营业用房屋等建筑物和土地使用权,以及附属于不动产的财产"。②该定义在国内法的基础上作出一定扩充。对于第6条规定的其他内容,中国承认其应包含在"不动产"概念之中。③

In contrast, Chinese domestic law, both the Enterprise Income Tax Law and the Personal Income Tax Law do not interpret the immovable property. In the legal norms of value-added tax,

---

① 参见《财政部、国家税务总局关于全面推开营业税改征增值税试点的通知》,销售服务、无形资产、不动产注释。
② 《国家税务总局关于税收协定中财产收益条款有关问题的公告》(国家税务总局公告2012年第59号),第1条。
③ 参见国家税务总局关于印发《〈中华人民共和国政府和新加坡共和国政府关于对所得避免双重征税和防止偷漏税的协定〉及议定书条文解释》的通知,第6条第(二)款。

"immovable property" means the properties which are immovable or the natures or shapes of which will change after being moved, including buildings and structures, etc. The fixed property described in the Guarantee Law before repeal refers to lands and fixed objects on the ground such as buildings and forest woods, which is similar to the immovable property in the value-added tax regulations. However, the scope of these definitions is not as wide as Article 6 of the OECD Model Tax Convention. Therefore, the State Administration of Taxation has specifically defined the concept of "immovable property" in Chinese tax treaties, "including various operating or non-operating housing and other buildings and land use rights, as well as accessories attached to the immovable properties". The definition is expanded compared to domestic law. As for other contents of Article 6, China recognizes that they should be included in the concept of "immovable property".

"不动产所得"在税收协定中有其独特含义。"不动产所得"并非国内法中的概念,仅在税收协定中出现。中国将税收协定中的"不动产所得"定义为"在不动产所有权不转移的情况下,使用不动产所获得的收益,包括直接使用、出租或者以任何其他形式使用该不动产取得的所得"。转让不动产取得的所得、来源于房地产抵押的利息收入等不符合上述定义的所得,则被排除在"不动产所得"的范围之外。[①]

"Income from immovable property" has its unique meaning in tax treaties. "Income from immovable property" is not a concept in domestic law, and only appears in tax treaties. China defines "income from immovable property" in tax treaties as "the gains derived from the use of immovable property provided that the ownership of the immovable property is not alienated, including income derived from the direct use, lease, or use in any other form of the immovable property". Income from the transfer of immovable property, interest income from real estate mortgage and other income that does not correspond to the above definition are excluded from the scope of "income from immovable property".

(二)不动产所得的所得税管辖权划分规则
Rules for Allocating Jurisdiction of Immovable Property Income Tax

在中国与不同国家签署的税收协定中,不动产所在地享有优先对不动产所得征税的权利。依照《中国-新加坡协定》第6条,缔约国一方居民从位于缔约国另一方的不动产取得的所得(包括农业或林业所得),可以在该缔约国另一方征税。该条款仅适用于缔约国一方居民从位于缔约国另一方的不动产取得所得的情形,不适用于其从居民国境内或从位于第三国的不动产取得的所得。[②] 这与中国国内法中不动产租赁所得的划分原则一致。当然,该条款并未排除居民国的征税权。居民国对境外不动产所得征税时,应采用消除双重征税的方法,确保该所得不被重复征税。

---

① 参见国家税务总局关于印发《〈中华人民共和国政府和新加坡共和国政府关于对所得避免双重征税和防止偷漏税的协定〉及议定书条文解释》的通知,第6条。
② OECD, Commentaries on the Articles of the Model Tax Convention, 2010, p. 128.

第十章 跨国不动产所得、财产收益、财产价值征税的协调
CHAPTER X Tax Harmonization on Cross-border Income from Immovable Property, Capital Gains and Property Value

In the tax treaties signed between China and different countries, the location of immovable property has the priority to tax the income from immovable property. According to Article 6 of the Agreement between China and Singapore, income derived by a resident of a contracting state from immovable property (including income from agriculture or forestry) situated in the other contracting state may be taxed in that other State. The article deals only with income which a resident of a contracting state derives from immovable property situated in the other contracting state. It does not, therefore, apply to income from immovable property situated in the contracting state of which the recipient is a resident or situated in a third state. This is consistent with the allocation principle of rental income from immovable property in Chinese domestic law. Of course, the article does not exclude the right of the resident state to tax. When the resident country taxes the cross-border incomes from immovable property, it should adopt the method of eliminating double taxation to ensure that the income is not subject to double taxation.

至于不动产转让所得,间接转让价值来源于不动产的收益性资产的所得,皆在双边协定第13条财产收益条款中约定,并不适用"不动产所得"的协调规则。

As for the income from the transfer of immovable property, and the income from the indirect transfer of equity investment assets of immovable property, are stipulated in the property income clause of Article 13 of tax treaties and do not apply to the coordination rules of "income from immovable property".

第二节 跨国财产收益征税的协调
Section 2 Tax Harmonization on Cross-border Income from Capital Gains

无论所取得的是不动产所得,还是财产收益,非居民是否需要缴纳中国所得税取决于所得是否来源于境内和所得是否与境内机构、场所有实际联系。对于不同类型的所得,非居民是否设立境内机构、场所的认定标准,所得与境内机构、场所是否有实际联系的认定标准,大体一致。发生变化的是所得来源于境内的标准。

Regardless of the income obtained is immovable property income or other property income, whether non-residents need to pay Chinese income tax depends on whether the income is derived from China and whether the income is de facto related to its domestic institutions and premises. Regarding different types of income, the standards for determining whether non-residents have established domestic institutions and premises, and whether the income is de facto related to domestic institutions and premises are generally the same. What has changed is the standard of judging whether the income is derived from China.

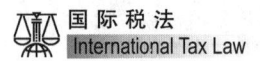

一、国内法对非居民财产收益的课税规则
Tax Rules for Non-residents' Capital Gains in Domestic Law

(一)非居民企业财产所得的课税规则
Tax Rules for Non-resident Enterprises' Capital Gains

转让财产所得来源地的判断标准根据财产类型而变化。不动产转让所得和动产转让所得来源于境内的标准相对明确;权益性投资财产转让所得来源于境内的标准,因涉及反避税规则、税收优惠而更加多元。

The criteria for judging the source of income from the transfer of property varies according to the type of property. The standard of the income from immovable property transfer and movable property transfer coming from China is relatively clear. The standard of income from the transfer of equity investment assets derived from China, is more diversified because of the anti-tax avoidance rules and tax incentives.

1. 非居民企业转让不动产所得来源于境内的判断标准

Judgment Criteria for the Source of Non-resident Enterprises' Income from Transfer of Immovable Property

不动产转让所得是否来源于境内,取决于不动产所在地。① 这与中国国内法判断不动产租金所得是否来源于境内的标准基本一致。涉及不动产的各类所得在各国国内法和全球范围内的税收协定中统一程度较高,大多遵从由不动产所在地独占管辖权或者优先课税的规则。该规则充分考虑到不动产与不动产所在地的联系,兼顾了税收公平和税收效率。在公平方面,不动产不仅蕴含着巨大的经济价值,还具有创造收入的能力。这些经济价值和未来收入一定程度上是由不动产的地理位置带来的,反映了"地域租金"。由不动产所在地对地域租金征税可更好地体现受益原则。在效率方面,不动产所在地不存在信息不对称的问题,可更好地把握不动产的全部价值。②

Whether the income from the transfer of immovable property derives from China depends on the location of the immovable property. This is basically the same as Chinese domestic law to determine whether the rental income from immovable property derives from the country. Various types of income related to immovable property are highly unified in the domestic laws of various countries and global tax treaties, and most of them follow the rules of exclusive jurisdiction or prior taxation by the location of the real property. This rule fully takes into account the connection between immovable property and its location, and takes into account both tax fairness and tax efficiency. In terms of fairness, immovable property not only involves huge economic value, but also contains the ability to create income. These economic values and future income are brought to a certain extent by the geographical location of the real property, reflecting "the location specific

---

① 参见《企业所得税法实施条例》第7条。
② See IMF, OECD, UN & WBG, The Platform for Collaboration on Tax, The Taxation of Offshore Indirect Transfers—A Toolkit, 2018, pp. 17–23.

rents" (LSRs). Taxation of LSRs by the location of the immovable property can better reflect the principle of benefit. In terms of efficiency, there is no information asymmetry in the location of immovable property, and the full value of immovable property can be better grasped.

2. 非居民企业转让动产所得来源于境内的判断标准

Judgment Criteria for the Source of Non-resident Enterprises' Income from Transfer of Movable Property

动产转让所得按照转让动产的企业或者机构、场所所在地判定其是否来源于境内。① 非居民企业动产转让所得的课税采用的是让与人所在地标准。非居民企业如果在境内未设有机构、场所,则无需就动产转让缴纳中国企业所得税;非居民企业如果在境内设有机构、场所并转让动产给其他单位或个人,需要就动产转让所得缴纳企业所得税。

The income from the transfer of movable property shall be determined according to the place where the enterprise, institution or premises transferring the property is located. The jurisdiction of income from the transfer of movable property of non-resident enterprises is allocated to the location of the transferor. If a non-resident enterprise does not have an institution or premises in China, it does not need to pay Chinese enterprise income tax on the transfer of movable property. If a non-resident enterprise has an institution or premises in China and transfers movable property to other units or individuals, it needs to pay the enterprise income tax.

3. 非居民企业转让权益性投资资产所得来源于境内的判断标准

Judgment Criteria for the Source of Non-resident Enterprises' Income from Transfer of Equity Investment Assets

一般情况下,权益性投资资产转让所得依照被投资企业所在地来确定。② 根据一般规则,如果非居民企业转让境外企业的权益性投资资产时,由于被投资企业位于境外,该非居民企业无需在中国缴纳企业所得税。只要被转让的资产是中国居民企业的股权、债权等权益性投资资产,该所得为来源于中国境内的所得,应缴纳企业所得税。③ 值得一提的是,企业重组中财产转让虽然可适用特殊性税务处理,但并未调整所得税管辖权的划分。国家为了鼓励企业兼并重组、优化产业结构,降低企业负担,允许满足特定条件的非居民企业在跨境重组中向非居民企业转让股权所得适用特殊性税务处理。④ 即便如此,中国并未让渡企业所得税管辖权,只是允许非居民企业递延纳税。⑤

Generally, the income from the transfer of equity investment assets is determined according to the location of the invested enterprise. According to the general rules, if a non-resident enterprise transfers the equity investment assets of an overseas enterprise, the non-resident enterprise does not need to pay enterprise income tax in China because the invested enterprise is

---

① 参见《企业所得税法实施条例》第7条。
② 同上。
③ 参见《非居民企业源泉扣缴指引》。
④ 参见关于《国家税务总局关于企业重组业务企业所得税征收管理若干问题的公告》的解读,http://www.chinatax.gov.cn/n810341/n810760/c1712219/content.html。
⑤ 参见《财政部、国家税务总局关于企业重组业务企业所得税处理若干问题的通知》(财税[2009]59号);参见《国家税务总局关于非居民企业股权转让适用特殊性税务处理有关问题的公告》(2015)。

located abroad. As long as the assets to be transferred are equity investment assets such as equity and creditor's rights of Chinese resident enterprises, the income is derived from China and shall be subject to enterprise income tax. It is worth mentioning that although special tax treatments are applicable to property transfer in corporate restructuring, the division of income tax jurisdiction is not adjusted. In order to encourage enterprise mergers and reorganizations, optimize the industrial structure, and reduce the burden on enterprises, the state allows non-resident enterprises that meet specific conditions to apply special tax treatment to the transfer of equity to non-resident enterprises in cross-border reorganization. Even so, China did not give up corporate income tax jurisdiction, but allowed non-resident enterprises to defer tax payment.

对于非居民企业不具合理商业目的地间接转让中国应税财产的权益性投资资产取得的所得，中国调整了判断所得来源地的标准，一定程度上扩大了其所得来源地管辖权。非居民企业通过转让持有中国应税财产的境外企业的权益性资产，产生与直接转让中国应税财产相近的结果的行为，属于间接转让。如果税务机关认定非居民企业间接转让中国应税财产的行为不具有合理商业目的，该间接转让将被确认为直接转让境内财产，需缴纳中国企业所得税。中国应税财产包括中国境内不动产、中国居民企业的权益性投资资产等应当在中国缴纳企业所得税的财产。该规定是为了避免非居民企业通过间接转让境外企业的权益性资产达到逃避国内企业所得税的目的，其直接依据是《企业所得税法》中的反避税条款。① 对于如何判定是否具有合理商业目的，国家税务总局也制定了详细的标准，综合考虑了境外企业与中国应税财产之间的关联程度。② 间接转让的相关规则虽然以防范非居民企业规避企业所得税为目的，但客观上扩大了来源于境内的所得范围。

Regarding the income obtained from the indirect transfer of equity investment assets of Chinese taxable assets by non-resident companies without a reasonable commercial purpose, China has adjusted the criteria for determining the source of income, and to a certain extent expanded the source jurisdiction. The transfer of equity investment assets of overseas companies holding Chinese taxable assets by non-resident enterprises, whose results are similar to that of direct transfer of Chinese taxable assets, is an indirect transfer. If the tax authority determines that the indirect transfer of Chinese taxable property by a non-resident enterprise does not have a reasonable commercial purpose, the indirect transfer will be confirmed as a direct transfer of domestic property and is subject to Chinese enterprise income tax. Chinese taxable property includes immovable property in China, equity investment assets of Chinese resident enterprises, and other property that should be subject to enterprise income tax in China. This provision is to prevent non-resident enterprises from evading domestic enterprise income tax through indirect transfer of equity assets of overseas companies. The direct legal basis is the anti-avoidance clause in the Enterprise Income Tax Law. With regard to how to determine whether it has a reasonable commercial purpose, the State Administration of Taxation has also formulated detailed standards, taking into account the degree of connection between foreign companies and Chinese taxable

---

① 参见《关于非居民企业间接转让财产企业所得税若干问题的公告》（国家税务总局公告2015年第7号）。
② 同上。

第十章 跨国不动产所得、财产收益、财产价值征税的协调
CHAPTER X Tax Harmonization on Cross-border Income from Immovable Property, Capital Gains and Property Value

assets. Although the relevant rules of indirect transfer aim to prevent non-resident enterprises from evading enterprise income tax, they objectively expand the scope of source jurisdiction.

(二) 非居民个人财产转让所得的课税规则
Tax Rules for Non-resident Individuals' Capital Gains

与非居民企业财产收益适用的规则类似,非居民个人财产转让所得来源的判定标准也根据财产种类变化。

Similar to the rules applicable to the property income of non-resident enterprises, the criteria for determining the source of non-resident individuals' income from alienation of personal property also change according to the type of property.

1. 非居民个人转让不动产所得来源于境内的判断标准

Judgment Criteria for the Source of Non-resident Individuals' Property Income from Alienation of Immovable Property

判断非居民个人不动产转让所得是否来源于境内取决于不动产所在地。① 出于征管实务和政策方面的考虑,非居民个人转让自用达5年以上,并且是唯一的家庭生活用房取得的所得,暂免征收个人所得税。②

Whether the income from the alienation of immovable property comes from China depends on the location of the immovable property. In considerations of collection and management practices and policies, non-resident individuals are temporarily exempted from individual income tax for the income gained from the transfer of house which has been used by oneself for over five years and which is one's only residential house.

2. 非居民个人转让动产所得来源于境内的判断标准

Judgment Criteria for the Source of Non-resident Individuals' Property Income from Alienation of Movable Property

判断动产转让所得是否来源于境内取决于动产转让交易发生地,即动产是否在境内转让。③

Whether the income from the conveyance of movable property comes from China depends on the place where the movable property transfer transaction occurs, that is, whether the movable property is transferred inside China.

3. 非居民个人转让权益性资产所得来源于境内的判断标准

Judgment Criteria for the Source of Non-resident Individuals' Income from the Alienation of Equity Investment Assets

对于权益性资产的转让所得,判断是否来源于境内取决于被投资企业所在地。④ 换

---

① 参见《中华人民共和国个人所得税法实施条例》第3条;另参见《财政部 税务总局关于境外所得有关个人所得税政策的公告》(财政部 税务总局公告2020年第3号)。
② 参见《财政部、国家税务总局关于个人所得税若干政策问题的通知》(财税字[1994]020号)。
③ 参见《中华人民共和国个人所得税法实施条例》第3条;另参见《财政部 税务总局关于境外所得有关个人所得税政策的公告》(财政部 税务总局公告2020年第3号)。
④ 同上。

言之，如果被投资企业或组织位于境外，通常情况下，个人转让企业或其他组织权益性资产所得无需在中国缴纳个人所得税。但是，当权益性资产被转让前三年的任一时间，企业或其他组织的资产价值50%以上来自境内不动产时，该所得为来源于中国境内的所得。①与非居民企业间接转让的规则不同的是，非居民个人间接转让规则并未明确是出于反避税目的，且仅限于境外企业持有境内不动产的情形。结合2018年《中华人民共和国个人所得税法》对一般反避税规则的引入，非居民个人间接转让的新规不排除具有反避税的效果。

For the alienation of equity investment assets, the fact whether it derives from China depends on the location of the invested enterprise. In other words, if the invested enterprise or organization is located outside China, generally, individuals are not required to pay individual income tax in China for the alienation of equity investment assets of the enterprise or other organizations. However, where, at any time within the three years (36 consecutive calendar months) before the transfer of the equity investment assets of an enterprise or organization outside China, more than 50% of the fair value of the assets of the invested enterprise or organization is directly or indirectly derived from the immovable property inside China, the income obtained shall be deemed as the income derived from China. Different from the rules for indirect transfers by non-resident enterprises, the rules for indirect transfers by non-resident individuals are not specifically identified for anti-avoidance purposes, and are limited to situations where foreign companies hold immovable property inside China. In conjunction with the introduction of general anti-avoidance rules in the Personal Income Tax Law in 2018, the new regulations on indirect transfers by non-resident individuals do not rule out anti-avoidance effects.

（二）税收协定对跨国财产收益的协调
Coordination of International Capital Gains in Tax Treaties

税收协定中的"财产收益"是指"因财产所有权发生转移而取得的所得"，②包括不动产转让所得，常设机构营业财产转让所得和固定基地取得的收益，转让国际运输船舶或飞机等动产的收益，转让法人资本中股份或其他权利取得的收益，转让其他财产取得的收益。中国与不同国家签署的税收协定中"财产收益"条款的差异较为明显。该差异主要体现在价值源于不动产的股份或其他权利转让收益和法人资本中股份或其他权利转让收益的相关规则，即第13条第4款、第5款。本部分将以较为典型的《中国-新加坡协定》为例，阐释不同类型财产收益的管辖权划分规则及其与其他协定的主要区别。

"Capital gains" in tax agreements refers to "income derived from the alienation of property ownership", including gains from the alienation of immovable property, gains from the alienation

---

① 参见《财政部 税务总局关于境外所得有关个人所得税政策的公告》（财政部 税务总局公告2020年第3号）。
② 国家税务总局，《税收协定条款解读之十——财产收益》，http://www.chinatax.gov.cn/n810219/n810744/n1671176/n1705734/c1707078/content.html。

第十章 跨国不动产所得、财产收益、财产价值征税的协调
CHAPTER X Tax Harmonization on Cross-border Income from Immovable Property, Capital Gains and Property Value

of the business property of a permanent establishment and fixed base, gains from the alienation of movable property such as ships or aircrafts operated in international traffic, gains from the alienation of shares or other rights of a legal person, and gains from the alienation of other properties. The contents in the "capital gains" clauses in tax agreement signed between China and different countries are relatively various. This difference is mainly reflected in the relevant rules, namely Article 13 (4) and (5), for the proceeds from the alienation of shares or other rights which derive value from immovable property and the proceeds from the alienation of shares or other rights of a legal person. This part will take the Agreement between China and Singapore as a typical example to explain the jurisdictional division rules of different types of capital gains and the main differences from other agreements.

（一）不动产转让所得和价值源于不动产的权益性资产转让所得的协调
Rules for the Coordination of Income from the Alienation of Immovable Property and of Income from the Alienation of Equity Investment Assets Deriving Their Value from an Immovable Property

不动产转让所得和不动产所得的课税规则相同，皆由不动产所在地优先课税。《中国-新加坡协定》第13条第1款规定，缔约国一方居民转让第6条所述位于缔约国另一方的不动产取得的收益，可以在该缔约国另一方征税。收益人的居民国也可以对不动产征税，但需要采取避免双重征税的措施。不同税收协定中，该条款无明显差异。

The rules for income from the alienation of the immovable property and income from immovable property are the same, meaning that the location of the immovable property is granted priority to exercise its taxing right. Article 13 Paragraph 1 of the Agreement between China and Singapore stipulates that gains derived by a resident of a contracting state from the alienation of immovable property referred to in Article 6 and situated in the other contracting state may be taxed in that other state. The residence country of the beneficiary can also tax immovable property, but measures to avoid double taxation are required. There is no significant difference in this clause in different tax agreements.

价值源于不动产的权益性资产转让所得由不动产所在地优先课税。依照《中国-新加坡协定》第13条第4款，缔约国一方居民转让股份取得的收益，如果股份价值的50%以上直接或间接由位于缔约国另一方的不动产构成，可以在缔约国另一方征税。单审视"财产收益"一条，第4款中价值源于不动产的权益性资产转让是对第1款不动产转让规则的补充，与不动产相关的财产收益皆由不动产所在地主张管辖权。而对比税收协定和国内法可见，该条款确定的课税规则与中国国内法中个人/企业间接转让不动产的权益性资产的规则十分类似。国内法这部分内容一定程度上是对税收协定内容的转化和吸收，在加强中国所得税反避税制度构建的同时，更好地与国际税收政策相协调。

The location of the immovable property is granted priority to exercise its taxing right on income from the alienation of equity investment assets deriving their value from an immovable property. According to Article 13 Paragraph 4 of the Agreement between China and Singapore, gains derived by a resident of a contracting state from the alienation of shares deriving more than 50 per cent of their value directly or indirectly from immovable property situated in the other contracting state may be taxed in that other state. In term of the article of "Capital Gains", the alienation of equity investment assets deriving their value from an immovable property in Paragraph 4 is a supplement to the rules of alienation of immovable property in Paragraph 1. The tax jurisdiction of capital gains related to immovable property is allocated to the place where the immovable property is located. Comparing with tax agreements and domestic laws, it can be seen that the rules determined by this clause are very similar to the rules of indirect transfer of equity investment assets deriving their value from the immovable property by individuals/enterprises in Chinese domestic laws. This part of the domestic law is to a certain extent the transformation and absorption of the content of tax treaties, establishes Chinese income tax anti-avoidance system, and better coordinates with international tax policies.

两者不同之处在于，税收协定将间接转让权益性资产的管辖权划分给不动产所在地，并不完全出于反避税的考虑，更是综合了公平和效率原则的选择。这种对公平和效率的追求，与各国国内法将不动产租赁所得和不动产转让所得划分给不动产所在地时追求的价值是一致的，综合考虑了不动产所在地对不动产价值的贡献和对不动产价值课税的优势。[①]该条款在中国与不同国家签署的双边协定中存在明显差异。其差异一方面体现在管辖权划分规则方面，例如部分税收协定（《中国—捷克协定》《中国-叙利亚协定》）并未吸收该条款，导致这类所得将适用财产收益的兜底条款，由转让者为其居民的缔约国征税；另一方面还体现在所得来源地管辖权的行使条件上，例如，《中国—新加坡协定》明确规定，只有当新加坡居民转让的股份价值的50%以上由中国不动产构成时，新加坡居民取得的收益才可由中国征税，而《中国—沙特阿拉伯协定》则未明确规定中国不动产占沙特阿拉伯居民转让财产的价值比例。

The difference between the domestic law and tax treaties is that the reasons why the tax treaties allocate the jurisdiction of the indirect transfer of equity investment assets to the location of the immovable property are not entirely in the considerations of anti-avoidance, but a choice based on the principles of fairness and efficiency. The pursuit of fairness and efficiency is consistent with the value pursued when the rental income from immovable property and the income from the transfer of immovable property are allocated to the location of immovable property by domestic laws. It takes into account the contribution of the location of immovable property to the value of immovable property and its conveniences of taxation on the value of immovable property. This clause is obviously different in the bilateral agreements signed between China and different countries. On one hand, the difference is reflected in the rules for the division of jurisdiction, for example, some tax agreements (the Agreement between China and Czechoslovakia and the Agreement between China and Syria) did not absorb this clause, resulting in that such income would be subject to the miscellaneous provision of capital gains

---

① See IMF, OECD, UN & WBG, The Platform for Collaboration on Tax, The Taxation of Offshore Indirect Transfers — A Toolkit, 2018, pp. 17–23.

第十章 跨国不动产所得、财产收益、财产价值征税的协调
CHAPTER X Tax Harmonization on Cross-border Income from Immovable Property, Capital Gains and Property Value

and taxed by the contracting state in which the transferor was a resident. On the other hand, it is also reflected in the conditions for exercising the source jurisdiction, for example, the Agreement between China and Singapore clearly states that only when more than 50 per cent of the value of the shares transferred by Singapore residents consist of Chinese immovable property, can China impose tax on income received by Singapore residents; the Agreement between China and the Saudi Arabia does not specify the proportion of Chinese immovable property in the value of property transferred by Saudi residents.

管辖权划分规则上的差异,主要取决于中国相对于缔约国另一方是资本输入还是资本输出。如果中国主要输出资本,则更注重维护居民国的税收利益,不倾向采用该条款;如果中国输入资本,则更注重维护来源国的税收利益,更有意愿采用该条款,且尽量扩大该条款的适用范围。所得税来源地管辖权的行使条件与各税收协定范本的更新情况有关。2001年《联合国关于发达国家与发展中国家间避免双重征税的协定范本》(下文简称"UN协定范本")第13条第4款要求公司财产应主要由不动产组成,随后补充"主要"的内涵是指50%以上的价值来源于不动产。① 而2017年的UN协定范本便采用了与OECD协定范本相同的形式,直接明确了转让的权益价值中50%以上来自不动产这一标准。②

The difference in jurisdiction division rules mainly depends on whether China is capital input or capital output relative to the other party of the contracting states. If China is in a position of capital output, it will pay more attention to safeguarding the tax interests of the residence country and is not inclined to adopt this clause. If China is in a position of capital input, it will pay more attention to safeguarding the tax interests of the source country, and is more willing to adopt this clause, and try to expand the scope of application of this clause. The conditions for the exercise of the source jurisdiction are related to the update of the model tax agreements. Article 13 Paragraph 4 of the 2001 "United Nations Model Double Taxation Convention between Developed and Developing Countries" (hereinafter referred to as the "UN Model Tax Convention") requires that company property should be mainly composed of immovable property, and then added "the connotation of 'main' means that more than 50 percent of the value comes from immovable property". However, the 2017 UN Model Tax Convention adopts the same form as the OECD Model Tax Convention, which directly clarifies the standard that more than 50 per cent of the value of the transferred equity comes from immovable property.

(二)常设机构和固定基地转让及相关财产转让所得的协调
Rules for the Coordination of Income from the Alienation of Permanent Establishment and Fixed Base and of Income from the Alienation of Related Property

常设机构和固定基地转让及相关财产转让所得,由常设机构(固定基地)所在地优先课

---

① See U.N. Model Income and Capital Tax Convention 2011.
② See U.N. Model Income and Capital Tax Convention 2017; OECD Model Tax Convention on Income and on Capital 2017.

税。依照《中国-新加坡协定》第13条第2款的规定,转让缔约国一方企业在缔约国另一方的常设机构营业财产部分的动产,或者缔约国一方居民在缔约国另一方从事独立个人劳务的固定基地的动产取得的收益,包括转让常设机构(单独或者随同整个企业)或者固定基地取得的收益,可以在该缔约国另一方征税。此处的动产指不包括在第一款"不动产"中的所有财产。该条款与协定第7条"营业所得"联系密切,都承认常设机构所在地的优先课税权,维护的是所得来源地管辖权。根据第7条第1款的规定,新加坡企业在中国境内构成常设机构,中国对该常设机构取得的利润拥有征税权。"归属于常设机构的利润"不仅包括该常设机构取得的来源于中国境内的利润,还包括其在中国境内外取得的与该常设机构有实际联系的各类所得,包括股息、利息、租金和特许权使用费等所得。[①]转让常设机构和固定基地,转让常设机构和固定基地营业财产,并未被排除在这一范围之外,适用来源地管辖权规则。因此,第7条第1款和第13条第2款的内容相吻合。该条款在不同税收协定中差异并不明显,不存在管辖权划分规则方面的差异。《中国-捷克斯洛伐克协定》中并未涵盖缔约国一方居民在缔约国另一方从事独立个人劳务的固定基地的动产转让收益。这使该条款不能适用于协调收益的个人所得税管辖权冲突。

The location of permanent establishment (fixed base) is granted priority to exercise its taxing right on income from the alienation of permanent establishment and fixed base and of income from the alienation of related property. In accordance with Article 13 Paragraph 2 of the Agreement between China and Singapore, gains from the alienation of movable property forming part of the business property of a permanent establishment which an enterprise of a contracting state has in the other contracting state or of movable property pertaining to a fixed base available to a resident of a contracting state in the other contracting state for the purpose of performing independent personal services, including such gains from the alienation of such a permanent establishment (alone or with the whole enterprise)or of such fixed base, may be taxed in that other state. Movable property here refers to all property that is not included in the first paragraph "immovable property". This clause is closely related to Article 7 "Business Profits" of the agreement. Both recognize the priority taxing right of the location of the permanent establishment and maintain the source jurisdiction. In accordance with the provisions of Article 7, Paragraph 1, where an enterprise of Singapore has a permanent establishment in China, China shall have the right to tax the profits derived by such permanent establishment. The phrase "attributable to the permanent establishment" as mentioned herein shall include not only the profits derived from China by such permanent establishment, but also various other types of income derived in and out of China which are effectively connected with such permanent establishment, including dividends, interest, rents, royalties and other income. The alienation of permanent establishments and fixed bases, and the alienation of business properties of permanent establishments and fixed bases are not excluded from this scope, and apply the source principle. Therefore, the content of Article 7 Paragraph 1 and Article 13 Paragraph 2 are consistent. This clause is not significantly various in different tax agreements,

---

① 参见国税发[2010]75号文第7条。

第十章 跨国不动产所得、财产收益、财产价值征税的协调
CHAPTER X Tax Harmonization on Cross-border Income from Immovable Property, Capital Gains and Property Value

and there is no difference in jurisdictional division rules. The Agreement between China and Czechoslovakia does not cover the gains from the alienation of movable property pertaining to a fixed base available to a resident of a contracting state in the other contracting state for the purpose of performing independent personal services. This makes this clause not applicable to the conflict of individual income tax jurisdiction.

（三）船舶或飞机及其运营相关动产的转让收益的协调
Rules for the Coordination of Income from the Transfer of Movable Property Related to the Ship or Aircraft and its Operation

转让船舶或飞机及其运营相关动产所得由转让者为其居民的缔约国独享税收管辖权。《中国-新加坡协定》第13条第3款规定，缔约国一方居民转让从事国际运输的船舶或飞机，或者转让属于经营上述船舶、飞机的动产取得的收益，应仅在该缔约国征税。该条款与税收协定第8条第1款的规则一致，后者规定了企业为其居民的国家对该企业取得的船舶或飞机经营国际运输业务的利润享有排他性税收管辖权。通常情况下，船舶飞机国际运输业务的利润归属，决定了船舶飞机转让收益的归属。居民国独占管辖权的合理性在于，从事国际运输的企业的所得来源地并不止一处，来源地管辖权很容易导致重复征税。但税收协定实践中，除了居民国外，企业的实际管理所在国也可能独占运输利润的所得税管辖权。

The income from the transfer of the ship or aircraft and movable property related to its operation shall be exclusively taxed in the contracting state in which the assignor is a resident. As provided in Paragraph 3 of Article 13 of the Agreement between China and Singapore, gains derived by a resident of a contracting state from the alienation of ships or aircrafts operated in international traffic, or movable property pertaining to the operation of such ships or aircrafts, shall be taxable only in that state. This provision is consistent with the rules of Article 8, Paragraph 1, of the tax treaty, which provides that profits derived by an enterprise of a contracting state from the operation of ships or aircrafts in international traffic shall be taxable only in that state. Generally, the jurisdiction of profit of shipping and aircraft international transport business determines the jurisdiction of profit of shipping and aircraft transfer. The rationality of the exclusive jurisdiction of the residence country lies in that the enterprises engaged in international transportation normally have more than one source of income, and the adoption of source jurisdiction easily cause double taxation. But in the practice of tax treaties, in addition to residence country, the country where the enterprise is actually administered may also have exclusive jurisdiction over the income tax on transportation profits.

至于管辖权是否应当在居民国和实际管理所在国之间划分，如何划分，各国并未达成一致意见。中国签署的税收协定也反映出两种规则并存的现状。大部分税收协定约定居民国独占管辖权，小部分税收协定是以总机构或实际管理机构所在国独占国际运输所得的管辖权。并存的现状延续到船舶飞机及其运营动产转让收益的管辖权划分规则中。例如，《中国-捷克协定》采用企业实际管理机构所在地标准。无论采用哪种标准，同一税收协定中，船舶或飞机国际运输收益和转让船舶飞机及相关动产的所得适用统一的管辖权划分规则。

There is no agreement as to whether and how jurisdiction should be divided between the state of residence and the state in which it is administered. Chinese tax treaties also reflect the coexistence of two kinds of rules. Most tax treaties provide for the exclusive jurisdiction of the residence country, while a few tax treaties provide for the exclusive jurisdiction of the state in which the head office or the actual governing body is located for the proceeds of international transport. The status quo of coexistence continues into the rules for the division of jurisdiction over the proceeds from the transfer of movable property such as ships, aircrafts and their operations. For example, the Agreement between China and Czechoslovakia adopts the criteria for the location of the actual management body of the enterprise. Regardless of the criteria used, the same tax agreement applies the uniform rules of jurisdiction division of income from the international carriage of ships or aircrafts and income from the transfer of ships, aircrafts and related movables.

（四）法人资本的权益性资产转让所得的协调
Rules for the Coordination of the Income from the Transfer of Equity Assets of the Capital of a Legal Person

转让非居民公司的股份等权利取得的收益允许所得来源国课税。根据《中国-新加坡协定》第13条第5款，除第4款另有规定外，缔约国一方居民转让其在缔约国另一方居民公司或其他法人资本中的股份、参股或其他权利取得的收益，如果该收益人在转让行为前的12个月内，曾经直接或间接参与该公司或其他法人至少25%的资本，可以在该缔约国另一方征税。该段落中的转让与第4款的"间接转让"不同，而是一种"直接转让"，因为缔约国一方居民转让的是其直接持有的股份等权益。① 该条款强调的是所得来源地的征税权。这对于发展中国家而言更为重要，仅在更注重保护发展中国家税收权益的UN协定范本中出现。同时，该条款对所得来源地管辖权作出了一些限制，要求收益人在转让发生前12个月内实质参与被转让企业的资本，即收益人"曾经直接或间接参与该公司或其他法人至少20%的资本"。所谓直接或间接参与该公司或其他法人至少20%的资本，是指缔约国一方居民直接参与缔约国另一方居民公司的资本，或通过具有10%以上直接资本关系的单层或多层公司或其他实体间接参与缔约国另一方居民公司的资本，或是与缔约国一方居民有显著利益关系的关联集团内其他成员成就前两项条件之一。②

The proceeds from the transfer of rights such as shares in a non-resident company are taxable in the country of origin. According to the Paragraph 5 of Article 13 of the Agreement between China and Singapore, subject to Paragraph 4, gains derived by a resident of a contracting state from the alienation of shares, participation, or other rights in the capital of a company or other legal person which is a resident of the other contracting state may be taxed in that

---

① See United Nations Model, Double Taxation Convention between Developed and Developing Countries, 2017, pp. 374–376.
② 参见《国家税务总局关于税收协定中财产收益条款有关问题的公告》（国家税务总局公告2012年第59号），第4条。

第十章 跨国不动产所得、财产收益、财产价值征税的协调
CHAPTER X Tax Harmonization on Cross-border Income from Immovable Property, Capital Gains and Property Value

other contracting state if the recipient of the gains, at any time during the twelve-month period preceding, such alienation had a participation, directly or indirectly, of at least 25 per cent in the capital of that company or other legal person. The transfer in that paragraph is different from the "indirect transfer" in Paragraph 4, but a "direct transfer", because a resident of a contracting state transfers interests such as shares held directly by him or her. This clause emphasizes the source principle. This is even more important for developing countries and can only be seen in UN Model Tax Convention, which focuses more on protecting the tax rights of developing countries. At the same time, this clause imposes some restrictions on the source jurisdiction, requiring the beneficiary to substantially participate in the capital of the transferred enterprise within 12 months before the transfer takes place, that is, the beneficiary "has directly or indirectly participated in at least 20% of the capital of the company or other legal persons". The so-called directly or indirectly participating in the company or other legal person at least 20% of the capital, means that a resident of a contracting state directly participates in the capital of a company which is a resident of the other contracting state, or by more than 10% of the direct relation of single layer or multi-layer company or other entity that indirectly participating in the capital of a company which is a resident of the other contracting state, or other members of an associated company having a significant interest in a resident of a contracting state meet one of the first two conditionsabove.

与不动产的权益性资产转让收益类似,我国税收协定中,其他权益性资产转让条款的差异也体现在管辖权划分规则和所得来源地行使管辖权的条件两个方面。《中国-叙利亚协定》和《中国-阿塞拜疆协定》未采纳该条款,致使这类所得适用兜底条款,由转让者为其居民的缔约国征税。《中国-沙特阿拉伯协定》中未要求转让发生前12个月内这一限制;《中国-捷克斯洛伐克协定》只言明所得来源国的征税权,没有规定任何条件。

Similar to the income from the transfer of equity assets of immovable property, the differences of other equity assets transfer clauses in Chinese tax treaties are also reflected in the jurisdiction division rules and the conditions for the source of income to exercise jurisdiction. This provision is not adopted in the Agreement between China and Syria and the Agreement between China and Azerbaijan, resulting in the application of a miscellaneous provision for such income to be taxed by the residence country of transferor. The Agreement between China and Saudi Arabia does not require this restriction in the 12 months prior to the date of transfer. the Agreement between China and Czechoslovakia specifies only the right to levy taxes in the country of origin and does not provide for any conditions.

(五)其他财产收益所适用的兜底条款
Miscellaneous Provision Applicable to Other Capital Gains

其他财产收益所适用的兜底条款倾向于由居民国独占管辖权。《中国-新加坡协定》第13条第6款,缔约国一方居民转让本条以上各款所述财产以外的其他财产取得的收益,应仅在转让者为其居民的缔约国征税。通过比较中国与部分发达国家签署的旧协定和新协定发现,大部分协定中,原本由所得来源国优先享有的征税权被转移到居民国。同时,中国与大

多数发展中国家的协定也将其他财产所取得的收益,交由居民国征税。中国的居民国立场逐渐凸显。①

The miscellaneous provision applicable to other capital gains generally admit the exclusive jurisdiction of the residence country. According to Article 13, Paragraph 6, of the Agreement between China and Singapore, gains from the alienation of any property other than that referred to in the receding paragraphs of this Article shall be taxable only in the contracting state of which the alienator is a resident. By comparing the old agreements and the new agreements between China and some developed countries, it is found that in most of the agreements, the taxing right was transferred from the source country to the resident country. At the same time, Chinese agreements with most developing countries also allocate the taxing right of proceeds from other property to the resident country. The position of China being a residence country has gradually become clear.

第三节 跨国财产价值征税的协调
Section 3　Tax Harmonization on Cross-border Property Value

无论是财产收益,还是不动产相关所得,中国所得税的征税对象只限于已经实现的所得,不包括蕴含在财产中的价值。财产税对财产蕴含的价值、财产尚未实现的潜在收益课税。正如前文所言,财产税的课税主要补充所得税课税之不足。因此,财产税的课税权通常会被分配给对相应的财产收益享有课税权的国家。OECD协定范本和UN协定范本中仅有一条是对财产税的协调,即两个范本的第22条"财产"(capital)。而在中国与107个国家(地区)签署的"避免双重征税协定"中,仅有与22个国家签署的税收协定③吸收了该条款。虽然中国与部分国家或地区的税收协定吸收了财产条款,但这些协定的税种范围中只列举了中国企业所得税和个人所得税。以房产税、契税为代表的中国财产税目前并未参与税收协定的税收协调。税收协定第2条"税种范围"明确了缔约双方可协调的税种:对全部所得、全部财产或某项所得、某项财产征收的税收,包括对来自转让动产或不动产的收益征收的税

---

① 参见任宛立、熊伟:《全球化视野下中国税收条约政策的调适》,载《国际税收》2017年第6期,第25—31页。
② See OECD, Commentaries on the Article of the Model Tax Convention, Commentary on Article 22 concerning the Taxation of Capital, p. 303.
③ 22个税收协定分别是:《中国-德国协定》《中国-挪威协定》《中国-南斯拉夫协定》《中国-沙特阿拉伯协定》《中国-保加利亚协定》《中国-科威特协定》《中国-塞浦路斯协定》《中国-奥地利协定》《中国-卢森堡协定》《中国-白俄罗斯协定》《中国-以色列协定》《中国-乌克兰协定》《中国-亚美尼亚协定》《中国-立陶宛协定》《中国-拉脱维亚协定》《中国-马其顿协定》《中国-委内瑞拉协定》《中国-阿尔巴尼亚协定》《中国-格鲁吉亚协定》《中国-阿及利亚协定》《中国-塔吉克斯坦协定》《中国-阿根廷协定》。

第十章 跨国不动产所得、财产收益、财产价值征税的协调
CHAPTER X Tax Harmonization on Cross-border Income from Immovable Property, Capital Gains and Property Value

收以及对资本增值征收的税收,应视为对所得和财产征收的税收。依照这一定义,以房产为征税对象的房产税、以城镇土地为征税对象的城镇土地使用税、以产权发生转移变动的不动产为征税对象的契税、车船税、车辆购置税、船舶吨税都属于这一范畴。然而,中国的税收协定,无论签署时间早晚,都未将这些财产税纳入第2条第3款"本协定特别适用的现行税种"范围中。本节以《中国-立陶宛协定》为例,阐释税收协定中不同类型财产相应财产税的管辖权归属。

Whether capital gains or income from immovable property, income tax in China is levied only on income already realized and does not include the value contained in the property. A property tax is a tax on the value of the property and the potential income of the property that has not yet been realized. As mentioned above, property tax is mainly used to cover up the deficiency of income tax. As a result, the right to tax property taxes is usually allocated to the state that has the taxing right of the corresponding capital gains. The only article concerning the harmonization of property tax in the OECD Model Tax Convention and UN Model Tax Convention is the Article 22, "capital". In the tax treaties signed by China with 107 countries, only 22 have incorporated this provision. Although Chinese tax treaties with some countries or regions incorporate property clauses, only Chinese corporate and individual income taxes are listed in the "tax covered" in these agreements. Property tax in China, represented by property tax and deed tax, does not participate in the tax coordination in tax treaties. Article 2 "tax covered" has been clear about the categories of taxes which are coordinated by tax treaties: taxes imposed on total income, on total capital, or on elements of income or capital, including taxes on gains from the alienation of movable or immovable property, as well as taxes on capital appreciation, shall be regarded as taxes on income and on capital. According to this definition, the property tax, the urban land use tax, and the deed tax, vehicle and ship tax, vehicle purchase tax and ship tonnage tax should have belonged to this category. However, Chinese tax treaties, no matter when they were signed, do not include these property taxes in the scope of Article 2, Paragraph 3, "existing taxes to which this Agreement applies in particular". This section takes the Agreement between China and Lithuania as an example to explain the jurisdiction of property tax on different types of property in the tax agreement.

(一)不动产财产税在不动产所在地优先征税
Property Taxes on Immovable Property shall be Levied in Priority at the Location of Immovable Property

对不动产所课征的财产税通常由不动产所在地优先课税。《中国-立陶宛协定》第24条第1款,第6条所指不动产为代表的财产,为缔约国一方居民所有并坐落在缔约国另一方,可以在该缔约国另一方征税。不动产财产税管辖权归属和该协定第6条不动产所得及第13条第1款不动产转让收益的所得税管辖权归属是一致的,皆由不动产所在地优先课税。居民国采取相应的消除双重征税措施。

Property taxes on immovable property are usually levied in priority on the location of the immovable property. According to Article 24, Paragraph 1 of the Agreement between China and Lithuania, capital represented by immovable property referred to in Article 6, owned by a resident of a contracting state and situated in the other contracting state, may be taxed in that other contracting state. The jurisdiction of property tax on immovable property is the same as that of income tax on immovable property income in Article 6 of the agreement and income tax on immovable property transfer income in Article 13, Paragraph 1 of the agreement, which shall in priority be taxed at the location of immovable property. The residence country shall adopt corresponding measures to eliminate double taxation.

（二）常设机构/固定基地的营业财产由常设机构/固定基地所在地优先征税
Business Property of a Permanent Establishment/fixed Base shall be Taxed at the Place Where the Permanent Establishment/fixed Base is Located

对于构成常设机构和固定基地营业财产的动产，其财产税应优先由常设机构和固定基地所在地课征。依照《中国-立陶宛协定》第24条第2款，缔约国一方企业设在缔约国另一方常设机构构成营业财产部分的动产，或者缔约国一方居民设在缔约国另一方从事独立个人劳务的固定基地所附属的以动产为代表的财产，可以在该缔约国另一方征税。这与该协定第13条第2款常设机构营业动产收益的管辖权划分规则一致，皆由机构或基地所在地优先主张。

For the movable property constituting the business property of permanent establishment and fixed base, the property tax shall be levied in the place of permanent establishment and fixed base in priority. According to the Article 24, Paragraph 2 of the Agreement between China and Lithuania, capital represented by movable property forming part of the business property of a permanent establishment which an enterprise of a contracting state has in the other contracting state or by movable property pertaining to a fixed base available to a resident of a contracting state in the other contracting state for the purpose of performing independent personal services, may be taxed in that other state. This is consistent with the rules for division of jurisdiction of movable property proceeds from the alienation of business property of permanent establishments in Paragraph 2 of Article 13 of the Agreement, which grant the prior jurisdiction to the location of the establishment.

财产构成常设机构动产需要满足的条件的是，该财产的经济所有权归属于常设机构。所谓经济所有权归属于常设机构（固定基地），是指常设机构（固定基地）可获得动产相关收益和承担动产一切损失。常设机构（固定基地）与动产建立紧密的经济联系。动产如果只在会计层面计入常设机构的收支账目，并不能被视为其经济所有权归属于常设机构。[①]

The condition to be satisfied when property constitutes business property of a permanent establishment is that the economic ownership of the property belongs to the permanent establishment. The so-called economic ownership belonging to the permanent organization (fixed base), means that the permanent organization (fixed base) can obtain any profit related to the movable property and bear all losses of movable property. Permanent establishments

---

① See OECD, Commentaries on the Article of the Model Tax Convention (2010), Commentary on Article 22 concerning the Taxation of Capital (2010), Paragraph 3.1.

(fixed bases) establish close economic links with movable property. Movable property cannot be regarded as the economic ownership of a permanent establishment if it is vecorded for accounting purposes, on a balance sheet prepared for the permanent establishment.

（三）船舶飞机及其动产由居民国独占财产税管辖权
Resident State has Exclusive Property Tax Jurisdiction over Ships, Aircrafts and Their Movable Property

从事国际运输的船舶、飞机及其动产由企业居民国独占管辖权。根据《中国-立陶宛协定》第24条第3款的规定，缔约国一方企业从事国际运输的船舶、飞机以及附属于经营上述船舶、飞机的动产为代表的财产，应仅在该缔约国一方征税。这与该协定第13条第3款船舶飞机及其动产转让所得的管辖权归属一致。当然，居民管辖权并非唯一的选择。正如中国税收协定中有关船舶、飞机转让所得相关规则，船舶、飞机及其动产的财产税也可能由企业的实际管理地或总机构所在地独占管辖权。例如，根据《中国-马其顿协定》第23条的规定，船舶、飞机的财产税由企业总机构所在国独占管辖权，与其动产转让所得的归属一致。

The resident state has exclusive jurisdiction over ships, aircrafts and their movable property which is operated in international traffic. According to Article 24(3) of the Agreement between China and Lithuania, capital represented by ships and aircrafts operated in international traffic by an enterprise of a contracting state and by movable property pertaining to the operation of such ships and aircrafts, shall be taxable only in that contracting state. It is consistent with the jurisdiction over the gains derived from the alienation of ships, aircrafts and their movable property in Article 13(3) of the Agreement between China and Lithuania. Of course, resident jurisdiction is not the only option. Just like the relevant rules on income from the transfer of ships and aircraft, in Chinese tax treaties, the country where the enterprise is actually managed or where the head office is located may also have exclusive jurisdiction over property taxes on ships, aircrafts and their movable property. For example, according to Article 23 of the Agreement between China and Macedonia, the property tax on ships and aircrafts shall be under the exclusive jurisdiction of the country where the head office of the enterprise is located, which is consistent with the ownership of the income from the transfer of movable property.

（四）兜底条款承认居民国管辖权
Recognition of Tax Jurisdiction of the Resident Country by the Miscellaneous Provisions

兜底条款中，居民国独占其他财产的财产税管辖权。依照《中国-立陶宛协定》第24条第4款，缔约国一方居民的其他所有财产项目，应仅在该缔约国一方征税。

In the miscellaneous provision, the residence country has exclusive property tax jurisdiction over other property. In accordance with Article 24, Paragraph 4 of the Agreement between China and Lithuania, all other elements of capital of a resident of a contracting state shall be taxable only in that contracting state.

总而言之，同一税收协定中，财产税管辖权和财产收益所得税管辖权的归属通常是统一

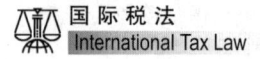

的。针对不同类型财产的条款和兜底条款皆反映了这一点。尤其是不动产、常设机构财产、船舶飞机等财产,即便出现在税收协定不同条款中代表了不同类型的所得,也表现出一以贯之的课税理念。这充分遵循了财产税作为所得税补充的课税规则和税收协定前后内容的协调性。

All in all, property tax jurisdiction and property income tax jurisdiction usually belong to the same subject in the same tax treaty. The clauses for different types of property and the miscellaneous provisions all reflect this. In particular, some property like immovable property, permanent establishment property, ships and aircrafts show a consistent taxing principle, even if they represent different types of income when they appear in different clauses of the same tax treaty. This fully complies with the taxation rules of property tax as a supplement to income tax and the principle that the contents in the same tax treaty should be coordinated.

第四节　相 关 案 例
Section 4　Related Cases

本节选取了两个对跨国财产收益划分管辖权的典型案例。第一个是立足于国内法探讨中国对非居民个人/企业间接转让境内不动产股权的收益如何课税;第二个是立足于税收协定探讨当非居民企业利用境外导管公司滥用税收协定时,中国税收协定和国内法如何应对。

In this section, two typical cases of jurisdiction over transnational property proceeds are selected. The first is based on domestic law to explore how China taxes the proceeds of indirect transfer of domestic real estate equity by non-resident individuals / enterprises. The second is based on tax agreements to explore how China's tax agreements and domestic laws deal with the abuse of tax agreements by non-resident enterprises using overseas conduit companies.

一、非居民间接转让股权案
Non-resident indirect transfer of equity

（一）案情简介
Introduction to the Case

2014年8月加拿大籍华人L、H公司(注册于英属维尔京群岛)、中国居民李某、王某四方共同签署《Z公司整体股权转让协议》,将共同持有的Z公司(注册于开曼群岛)100%的股权转让给注册于开曼群岛的M公司。加籍华人L、H公司、李某和王某在Z公司中所占股权分布为58%、30%、10%和2%。该项交易最终转让价格为4.1亿元人民币。Z公司唯一的子公司是其100%控股的境内企业F公司。F公司拥有的北京市海淀区一座写字楼A大厦,价值约为4亿~5亿元人民币,是该转让交易的核心资产。合同中近90%的篇幅都是关于F公

第十章 跨国不动产所得、财产收益、财产价值征税的协调
CHAPTER X Tax Harmonization on Cross-border Income from Immovable Property, Capital Gains and Property Value

司和A大厦相关事项的约定。股权转让交易的总金额为4.1亿元,全部为A大厦的价值。

In August 2014, the Canadian Chinese L, H Company (registered in the British Virgin Islands), Chinese residents Li and Wang jointly signed the "Z Company Overall Equity Transfer Agreement", to transfer 100% of jointly held Z company (registered in the Cayman Islands) to M company registered in the Cayman Islands. Chinese Canadian L, H Company, Li and Wang in the Z company share in the distribution of 58%, 30%, 10% and 2%. The final transfer price of the transaction is 410 million yuan. Z company's only subsidiary is its 100% holding domestic enterprise F company. F company owns an office A building in Haidian district, Beijing. About 400～500 million yuan is the core asset of the transfer transaction. Nearly 90% of the contract is about the related matters of F company and A building. The total amount of the equity transfer transaction is 410 million yuan, all for the value of A building.

(二)税务机关调查结果、结论与措施
Findings, Conclusions and Measures of the Tax Authorities

此次股权转让交易中被转让的Z公司是一家空壳公司,股权转让交易的实质是通过转让避税地空壳公司股权达到间接转让我国境内实体公司F公司,进而转让A大厦的目的。通过间接转让,非居民个人L和非居民企业H试图规避我国个人所得税和企业所得税。《企业所得税法实施条例》第120条以及国税函〔2009〕698号文第6条规定:"境外投资方(实际控制方)通过滥用组织形式等安排间接转让中国居民企业股权,且不具有合理的商业目的,规避企业所得税纳税义务的,主管税务机关呈报税务总局审核后可以按照经济实质对该股权转让交易重新定性,否定被用作税收安排的境外控股公司的存在。"税务机关因此要求境外注册的H公司需补交税款1 214万元。对于非居民L,由于《中华人民共和国个人所得税法》缺乏反避税条款且国税函〔2009〕698号文无法适用于非居民个人,税务机关以国税函〔2011〕14号《关于非居民个人股权转让相关政策的批复》为依据,要求非居民个人L补交税款。最终,非居民个人L补缴个人所得税款4 651万元,非居民企业H补缴1 215万元企业所得税。①

The Z company transferred in this equity transfer transaction is a shell company, equity transfer transaction is the indirect transfer of the real company i.e. the F company in our country through the transfer of equity of shell companies in tax havens, and then transfer the purpose of A building. Through indirect transfers, non-resident individual L and non-resident enterprise H try to avoid our country individual income tax and enterprise income tax. Article 120 of the Regulations on the Implementation of the Enterprise Income Tax Law and Article 6 of the State Tax Letter (2009) No. 698 provide that: "Foreign investment houses (the actual controlling party) indirectly transfer the shares of Chinese resident enterprises through such as the abuse of organizational forms, without a legitimate commercial purpose, circumventing corporate income tax obligations, the competent tax authority may re-characterize the equity transfer transaction according to the economic essence after the examination by the competent tax authority, deny the existence of an offshore holding company used as a tax arrangement." As a result, tax authorities

---

① 参见田艳春、宋春辉:《海淀地税局追征境外企业股权交易税款》,载《中国税务报》2015年9月22日。

require overseas registered H company to pay 12.14 million yuan in tax. For non-resident L, due to the lack of anti-avoidance provisions in the Personal Income Tax Act and the fact that the National Tax Letter (2009)698 can not be applied to non-resident individuals, the tax authorities based on the State Tax Letter (2011)14, required L to pay the tax. Eventually, non-resident individual L pays 46.51 million yuan in personal income tax, non-resident enterprise H pay 12.15 million yuan enterprise income tax.

（三）案件评述
Case Analysis

本案中，四个股东将共同持有的境外Z公司转让给另一境外企业。无论该所得是否被认定来源于境内，李某和王某作为居民纳税人，需要就该所得缴纳中国个人所得税。本案的焦点是非居民企业H和非居民个人L转让股权所得是否需要在中国缴纳所得税。

In this case, the four shareholders transferred the jointly held overseas Z company to another overseas enterprise. Whether or not the income is recognized as derived from the territory, Li and Wang as resident taxpayers need to pay Chinese personal income tax on the income. The focus of this case is whether the income from equity transfer between the non-resident enterprise H and non-resident individual L needs to pay income tax in China.

在非居民企业间接转让股权所得在境内缴纳所得税的关键前提是，该交易是否不具有合理商业目的。无论是本案中税务机关的执法依据——《国家税务总局关于加强非居民企业股权转让所得企业所得税管理的通知》[国税函（2009）698号文]（下文简称"第698号文"），还是随后取代第698号文的《关于非居民企业间接转让财产企业所得税若干问题的公告》（国家税务总局公告2015年第7号），税务机关对股权转让交易重新定性的前提是，该交易不具有合理的商业目的。有关本案的介绍并未对税务机关认定Z公司是一家空壳公司并滥用组织形式、不具有合理商业目的的过程加以详述。但可以确定的是，境内不动产A大厦是该股权交易的核心资产，几乎占据了交易的全部价值的事实，在税务机关的判断中发挥了关键性的作用。如何认定间接转让交易是否具有合理商业目的，不仅《中华人民共和国企业所得税法实施条例》和国家税务总局公告2015年第7号作出了规定，①而且在司法实践中也发展出一些标准。在儿童投资主基金间接转让境内企业一案中，国家税务总局提出判断交易不具有合理商业目的的三个原因，分别是：（1）境外被转让公司在避税地或低税率地区注册，不从事制造、经销、管理等实质性经营活动；（2）股权转让价主要取决于境内工程项目；（3）股权受让方对外披露收购的实际标的为境内持有项目的公司。这三个原因无论是在初审还是最终的再审判决书中都得到了法院的支持。② 从儿童投资主基金间接转让境内企业

---

① 《中华人民共和国企业所得税法实施条例》第120条规定，《中华人民共和国企业所得税法》第47条所称不具有合理商业目的，是指以减少、免除或者推迟缴纳税款为主要目的。《国家税务总局关于非居民企业间接转让财产企业所得税若干问题的公告》（国家税务总局公告2015年第7号）第3条规定了判断合理商业目的的相关因素，包括境外企业股权主要价值的来源，境外企业资产的投资构成，企业架构的经济实质，股东、业务、组织架构的存续时间，交易的税负等。

② 参见《儿童投资主基金与杭州市西湖区国家税务局行政征收一审行政判决书》，《儿童投资主基金与杭州市西湖区国家税务局再审行政裁定书》。

第十章 跨国不动产所得、财产收益、财产价值征税的协调
CHAPTER X Tax Harmonization on Cross-border Income from Immovable Property, Capital Gains and Property Value

一案和本案可见,不具有合理商业目的这一判断与境外被转让公司是否有实质性经营活动、境外企业的投资构成、股权转让价格构成、交易税负的明显降低等因素都有十分密切的联系。

The key premise of income tax on indirect transfer of equity in non-resident enterprises is whether the transaction has no reasonable commercial purpose. Whether the law enforcement basis of the tax authorities in this case — the notice of the State Administration of Taxation on strengthening the administration of enterprise income tax on the income from equity transfer of non-resident enterprises[State tax letter (2009)698](hereinafter referred to as "Notice 698"), or the subsequent Proclamation on Certain Issues of Income Tax for Indirect Transfer of Property by Non-Resident Enterprises, which replaced Notice 698(State Administration of Taxation Proclamation No. 7 of 2015), if the tax authorities recharacterize the equity transfer transaction, the transaction has no reasonable commercial purposes. A description of the case does not detail the process by which the tax authorities found that Z company was a shell company and abused its organizational form for unreasonable commercial purposes. But one thing is for sure, the fact that the domestic real estate building A is the core asset of the equity transaction, which occupies almost the entire value of the transaction, plays a key role in the judgment of the tax authority. How to determine whether indirect transfer transactions have a reasonable commercial purpose, not only the Regulations on the Implementation of the Enterprise Income Tax Law and the Proclamation of the State Administration of Taxation No.7 of 2015 make relevant provisions, but also the judicial precedent develops some standards. For instance, in the case of Children's Investment Master Fund v. Xihu Distric of State Taxation Bureau, the State Administration of Taxation put forward three reasons for judging that the transaction does not have a reasonable commercial purpose. First, the overseas transferred company is registered in a tax haven or a low tax rate area and does not engage in substantive business activities such as manufacturing, distribution and management. Second, the transfer price of equity mainly depends on the domestic project. Third, the transferee discloses that the actual subject of the acquisition is the company holding the project in China. These three reasons are supported by the court, both in the first instance and in the final retrial decision. It can be seen from the case of indirect transfer of domestic enterprises by the main fund for children's investment and the case that there is no reasonable commercial purpose.

本案中非居民个人间接转让股权适用反避税规则的障碍是缺乏法律依据的。税务机关处理此案时,《中华人民共和国个人所得税法》尚未引入一般反避税条款,国家税务总局公告2015年第7号也无法适用于非居民个人间接转让股权。税务机关最终以国税函〔2011〕14号《关于非居民个人股权转让相关政策的批复》为依据,要求非居民个人L缴纳中国个人所得税,这从合法性角度看也值得商榷。《关于非居民个人股权转让相关政策的批复》适用的情形是香港居民个人通过转让香港企业股权实现对境内物流企业的转让,与本案的案情十分类似,其最终结论也是要求相关居民个人缴纳境内个人所得税。①但是,该批复是国家税务总局对深圳市地方税务局的回函,针对的是香港居民个人这一个案,在法律效力上并不具有普适性,难以成为税务机关处理其他案件的执法依据。

---

① 参见卢勋等:《历时半年深圳地税局跨境追缴1 368万元税款》,载《中国税务报》2011年6月8日版。

In this case, the obstacle to the application of anti-avoidance rules is the lack of legal basis. When the tax authorities deal with this case, the personal income tax law has not yet introduced a general anti-tax avoidance clause, and the State Administration of Taxation Proclamation No. 7 of 2015 can not be applied to indirect transfer of equity by non-resident individuals. Finally, the tax authorities, on the basis of the State tax letter (2011)14, "the approval of the relevant policies on the transfer of individual shares of non-residents", require non-resident individual L pay Chinese personal income tax, which is also debatable from the perspective of legality. The application of the Approval of the Policy on the Transfer of Non-resident Individuals is that the transfer of shares of Hong Kong enterprises by Hong Kong residents to domestic logistics enterprises is very similar to the case, and the final conclusion is that the relevant residents are required to pay personal income tax on their territory. However, the reply is a letter from the State Administration of Taxation to the Shenzhen Local Taxation Bureau. The case against Hong Kong residents is not universal in legal effect and is difficult to become the law enforcement basis for tax authorities to deal with other cases.

显然，2018年《个人所得税法》的一般反避税条款的引入大大缓解这一阻碍。此外，国家税务总局《关于境外所得有关个人所得税政策的公告》(财政部 税务总局公告2020年第3号)规定了非居民个人间接转让权益性资产的情形。该规定仅限于境外被转让企业的资产公允价值50%以上来源于境内不动产的情形，并不包括境外企业持有境内其他类似资产。随着个人所得税反避税规定的逐步完善，本案呈现的缺乏法律依据的问题将逐渐得到解决。

Obviously, the introduction of general anti-tax avoidance provisions in the Personal Income Tax Act 2018 greatly alleviates this obstacle. In addition, the State Administration of Taxation "on foreign income related to personal income tax policy notice" (Ministry of Finance, Administration of Taxation Proclamation No. 3 of 2020) provides for indirect transfer of equity assets by non-resident individuals. This provision is limited to the case where more than 50% of the fair value of the assets of the overseas transferred enterprise comes from the domestic immovable property, and does not include the holding of other similar assets in the territory by the overseas enterprise. With the gradual improvement of individual income tax anti-avoidance regulations, the lack of legal basis in this case will be gradually solved.

（二）"导管公司"滥用《中国-毛里求斯税收协定》第13条财产收益案
Misuse of Article 13 of the China-Mauritius Tax Agreement

（一）案情简介
Introduction to the Case

天津某制造公司是一家中外合资企业。该公司的两个外国股东分别注册于百慕大群岛和毛里求斯共和国。两者签署了一份《股权出售与购买协议》。该协议约定，注册于百慕大群岛的股东购买注册于毛里求斯共和国股东持有的天津公司的股权。根据《中国-毛里求斯协定》第13条第5款的规定，转让第1款至第4款所述财产以外的其他财产取得的收益，应仅在转让者为其居民的缔约国征税。因此，该财产转让收益应仅在转让者为其居民的缔

第十章 跨国不动产所得、财产收益、财产价值征税的协调
CHAPTER X Tax Harmonization on Cross-border Income from Immovable Property, Capital Gains and Property Value

约国毛里求斯共和国征税。

A manufacturing company in Tianjin is a Sino-foreign joint venture. Two foreign shareholders of the company are registered in Bermuda and the Republic of Mauritius. The two signed a share sale and purchase agreement. The agreement provides for shareholders registered in Bermuda to purchase shares in Tianjin Company, which are registered in the Republic of Mauritius. In accordance with Article 13, Paragraph 5, of the China-Mauritius Agreement, proceeds from the transfer of property other than those referred to in Paragraphs 1 to 4 shall be taxed only in the contracting state in which the assignor is a resident. Accordingly, the proceeds from the transfer of the property shall be taxed only in the Republic of Mauritius, the state party in which the assignor is a resident.

（二）税务机关调查结果、结论和措施
Findings, Conclusions and Measures of the Tax Authorities

毛里求斯居民企业成立以来与美国总部关联交易频繁，且其材料、设备采购以及产品销售大部分由美国总部安排并通过美国总部进行。毛里求斯居民公司与美国总部签署了《技术支持和许可协议》，按照所销售产品的销售额的一定比例向美国总部支付特许权使用费。最终，税务机关基于中外合资企业成立之初提交的《合资经营企业合同》中"毛里求斯控股公司是由美国某公司独资，依照毛里求斯共和国法律设立的公司"一条，认定此项财产转让收益的最终受益人是美国公司。税务机关得出结论，该交易不得适用《中国-毛里求斯税收协定》享受协定待遇，而是根据实质交易原则适用《中国-美国协定》。依照《中国-美国协定》第12条第5款，转让第4款所述以外的其他股票取得的收益，该项股票又相当于参与缔约国一方居民公司的股权的25%，可以在该缔约国征税。中国应享有该交易的税收管辖权。随后，美国公司同意补缴税款，由受让股份的一方在支付时代扣代缴。①

Since its inception, Mauritian resident enterprises have had frequent affiliated transactions with United States headquarters, and most of their materials, equipment purchases and product sales have been arranged by and through United States headquarters. MPC has signed a Technical Support and Licensing Agreement with the United States headquarters to pay royalties to the United States headquarters in proportion to the sales of the products sold. Finally, the tax authorities, based on the joint venture contract submitted at the beginning of the establishment of a Sino-foreign joint venture, "the Mauritius holding company is a company wholly owned by a United States company, established in accordance with the laws of the Republic of Mauritius", determine that the ultimate beneficiary of the proceeds of the transfer of this property is a United States company. The tax authorities concluded that the transaction was not subject to the China-Mauritius Tax Agreement but was subject to the China-United States Tax Agreement on the basis of the substantive transaction principle. In accordance with Article 12, Paragraph 5, of the China-United States Agreement, the proceeds from the transfer of shares other than those referred to

---

① 参见《税收贡献每年增加过百亿，中国反避税调查力度逐年加大》，载《法制日报》2014年7月18日，http://www.chinatax.gov.cn/chinatax/n810219/n810780/c1160392/content.html；参见孙文胜、古立杰、冯培进、苗睿：《天津塘沽国税成功突破"管道公司"避税围栏》，新浪博客，http://blog.sina.com.cn/s/blog_493cd61c0100ht21.html。

in Paragraph 4, which in turn amounts to 25 per cent of the equity of a resident company of a participating contracting state, may be taxed in that state. China should have tax jurisdiction over the transaction. Subsequently, the United States company agreed to make up the tax and to withhold the shares from the transferee at the time of payment.

（三）案件评述
Case Analysis

本案的焦点是交易表现出的法律形式是否反映其经济实质。如果不是，税务机关应当依照什么依据采取相应措施。

The focus of this case is whether the legal form of the transaction reflects its economic essence. If not, on what basis should the tax authorities take the appropriate measures.

税务机关否认了股权交易的法律形式，对其经济实质课税。从案情介绍中可见，税务机关的调查结果基本还原了两个非居民企业之间股权转让交易的全貌。如果整个交易的法律形式得到承认，该交易应适用《中国-毛里求斯协定》第13条第5款的规定，享受税收协定待遇。我国作为所得来源地，将放弃一部分税收管辖权，对该交易免税。但税收协定待遇只是按照税收协定可以减轻或者免除按照国内税收法律规定应履行的纳税义务，是缔约国为了避免双重征税自愿限制本国的税收管辖权。通常情况下，所得来源地国会将征税权让渡给居民国行使，但前提是纳税人必须是对方的税收居民。如果第三国居民通过设立在缔约国另一方的导管公司，从而获得缔约国一方给予的税收协定优惠，形成税收套利行为，则这属于滥用税收协定的情况。[1] 对此，税务机关可因交易不符合税收协定的目的，刻意损害所得来源国的税收利益，还原交易的经济实质，认定美国公司为毛里求斯企业的实际控制人和最终受益人，该交易视同美国公司转让天津公司的股权并取得收益。基于这一判断，税务机关适用《中国-美国协定》第12条的规定，对该交易主张税收管辖权。

Tax authorities deny the legal form of equity transactions and tax their economic substance. It can be seen from the introduction of the case that the investigation results of the tax authorities basically restore the whole picture of the equity transfer transaction between the two non-resident enterprises. If the legal form of the transaction as a whole is recognized, the transaction shall be governed by Article 13, Paragraph 5, of the China-Mauritius Agreement and shall be treated as a tax agreement. As a source of income, China will waive part of its tax jurisdiction and exempt the transaction from taxing. However, tax agreement treatment can only reduce or exempt tax obligations under domestic tax law according to tax agreement, which is the voluntary restriction of domestic tax jurisdiction by states parties in order to avoid double taxation. Usually, the congress of the place of origin transfers the tax right to the resident state, provided that the taxpayer is the other party's tax resident. If a third country resident forms a tax arbitrage by establishing a conduit company in the other contracting state, thereby obtaining a tax agreement preference granted by one of the contracting states, this is an abuse of the tax agreement. In this regard, because the transaction is not in accordance with the purpose of the tax agreement, the tax

---

[1] 参见叶姗：《一般反避税条款适用之关键问题分析》，载《法学》2013年第9期，第98页。

第十章　跨国不动产所得、财产收益、财产价值征税的协调
CHAPTER X　Tax Harmonization on Cross-border Income from Immovable Property, Capital Gains and Property Value

authorities may deliberately damage the tax interests of the source country of income, restore the economic essence of the transaction, and determine that the United States company is the actual controller and ultimate beneficiary of the Mauritian enterprise. Based on this judgement, the tax authorities apply Article XII of the China-United States Agreement and claim tax jurisdiction over the transaction.

　　税务机关依照国内法有关一般反避税的规定,否认股权转让交易的法律形式,不履行中毛协定的协定义务,这是否有违国际法？这个问题其实涉及国内法一般反避税规则和税收协定的法律效力问题。本案基本案情并未明确指出税务机关否认该股权交易法律形式、寻求其经济实质的法律依据。《中国-毛里求斯协定》因签署于1994年,并未纳入利益限制条款和主要目的条款规范纳税人择协避税的行为。在税收协定层面,税务机关的行为并没有直接依据。从税务机关介入该案件的时间2010年前后推断,当时该案可援引的国内法规范分别是《企业所得税法》第47条,《关于如何理解和认定税收协定中"受益所有人"的通知》(国税函号〔2009〕601号)(下文简称"601号"),和《国家税务总局关于印发〈特别纳税调整实施办法(试行)〉的通知》(国税发〔2009〕2号)。本案中,税务机关认定毛里求斯企业是以逃避或减少税收,转移或累计利润等的目的而设立,是不从事实质性经营活动的导管公司,不属于可享受税收协定待遇的"受益所有人"。对于美国企业利用导管公司滥用税收协定的行为,税务机关依照国内法启动一般反避税调查,按照经济实质对企业的避税安排重新定性,取消企业从避税安排中获得的税收利益,否认该导管公司的存在。①问题是,在税收协定没有对择协避税行为进行约定的情况下,税务机关能否根据国内法一般反避税规定,否认交易的法律形式,不履行协定义务？虽然中国对税收协定采纳的是法律体系一元论的观点,也在《税收征管法》第91条承认了税收协定优先于国内税法适用,②但这并不当然推断出条约高于国内法,也无法得出在具体问题上条约和国内法之间的关系。国内法的一般反避税条款与税收协定之间的不协调,必须立足于税收协定的目的而加以解决。依照《OECD税收协定范本注释》,税收协定具有防止协定滥用和反避税功能。只要税收协定没有明确限制缔约国双方反避税法律的适用,税收协定便不应被解释为排除国内反避税法律。③如此一来,国内税法中一般反避税法律便与税收协定融合。本案中税务机关的行为也具有税收协定目的的支撑和国内法的依据。除此之外,随着税收协定内容的丰富和国内法的发展,存在其他方式来加强国内法反避税条款和税收协定的协调。第一种是直接在税收协定中约定国内法一般反避税规则优先适用。例如,依照《中国-荷兰协定》第23条的规定,该协定不应妨碍缔约国双方行使其关于防止逃税和避税(不论是否称为逃税和避税)的国内法律及措施的权利,但以不导致与协定冲突的税收为限。第二种在税收协定中约定主要目的条款和限制利益条款,为税收协定打击择协避税行为提供直接依据。

　　In accordance with the provisions of domestic law on general anti-tax avoidance, the tax authorities deny the legal form of equity transfer transations and fail to perform their obligations

---

① 参见《特别纳税调整实施办法(试行)》(国税发〔2009〕2号),第92、94条。
② 《中华人民共和国税收征收管理法》第91条规定:中华人民共和国同外国缔结的有关税收的条约、协定同本法有不同规定的,依照条约、协定的规定办理。
③ 参见熊伟:《税收协定与〈中国企业所得税法〉——基于功能、内容与效力的比较》,载《法学评论》2009年第5期,第35—44页。

in the China Mauritius agreement. Is this contrary to intenational law? This issue actually relates to the legal effect of domestic law's general anti-tax avoidance rules and tax agreements. The basic facts of this case does not clearly state the legal basis for the tax authorities to deny the legal form of the equity transaction and seek its economic substance. The China-Mauritius Agreement was signed in 1994, which does not include interest restriction clause and main purpose clause to regulate taxpayer's behavior of tax avoidance. In tax agreement level, there is no direct basis for the actions of tax authorities. From the time the tax authorities intervened in the case around 2010, at that time, the domestic legal norms that could be invoked in the case were Article 47 of the Enterprise Income Tax Act, Circular on the Understanding and Identification of "Beneficiary Owners" in Tax Agreements (Tax Letter No. [2009].601)(hereinafter referred to as "601"), and the Circular of the State Administration of Taxation on the Issuance of Measures for the Implementation of Special Tax Adjustment (Trial Implementation)(No. 2 of the State Tax [2009]). In this case, the tax authorities have determined that Mauritian enterprises seek to evade or reduce taxes, for purposes such as transfer or accumulation of profits. They are catheter companies that do not engage in substantive business activities, and thus they not belong to the "beneficial owner" who can enjoy the treatment of tax agreement. For US companies who abuse tax agreements, the tax authorities initiate general anti-tax avoidance investigations in accordance with domestic law, recharacterize the corporate tax avoidance arrangements according to the nature of the economy, eliminate tax benefits from tax avoidance arrangements and deny the existence of the catheter company. The problem is that in the absence of relevant provisions on treaty-shopping in the agreement can the tax authorities, in accordance with the general anti-avoidance provisions of the domestic law, deny the legal form of the transaction and refuse to comply with agreement obligations? Although China adopts a monist view of the legal system for tax agreements and recognizes in Article 91 of the Tax Administration Law that tax agreements take precedence over domestic tax laws, this does not of course infer that treaties are superior to domestic laws or that the relationship between treaties and domestic laws can not be drawn on specific issues. The incompatibility between the general anti-tax avoidance provisions of domestic law and tax agreements must be addressed on the basis of the purpose of tax agreements. According to the Notes of the Model OECD Tax Agreement, tax agreements have the function of preventing abuse of agreements and combating tax avoidance. As long as the tax agreement does not explicitly limit the application of anti-tax avoidance laws between the parties, the tax agreement should not be interpreted as excluding domestic anti-tax avoidance laws. In this way, the general anti-tax avoidance law in domestic tax law is integrated with tax agreements. In this case, the behavior of the tax authorities also has the support of the purpose of the tax agreement and the basis of domestic law. In addition, with the enrichment of tax agreements and the development of domestic law, there are other ways to strengthen the coordination of anti-avoidance clauses in domestic laws and tax treaties. The first is to directly stipulate in the tax treaties that general anti-avoidance rules of domestic laws take precedence. For example, in accordance with Article 23 of the China-Netherlands Agreement, nothing in this Agreement shall

CHAPTER X Tax Harmonization on Cross-border Income from Immovable Property, Capital Gains and Property Value

prejudice the right of each contracting state to apply its domestic laws and measures concerning the prevention of tax evasion and avoidance, whether or not described as such, insofar as they do not give rise to taxation contrary to this Agreement. The second is to stipulate the main purpose clauses and benefit-limiting clauses in tax treaties, which provide a direct legal basis for tax treaties to combat treaty-shopping.

学习思考题
Questions for Study

1. 跨国不动产所得、财产所得以及财产价值的定义是什么?
   What are the definitions of transnational real estate income, property income and property value?
2. 国际税法对于跨国不动产所得征税协调规则是什么?
   What are the coordination rules for the taxation of transnational real estate income in International Tax Laws?
3. 国际税法对于跨国财产所得征税协调的规则是什么?
   What are the coordination rules for the taxation of transnational property income in International Tax Laws?
4. 国际税法对于跨国财产价值的征税协调规则是什么?
   What are the coordination rules for the taxation of transnational property value in International Tax Laws?

第十一章 CHAPTER XI

消除国际双重征税的方法
Ways to Eliminate International Double Taxation

在经济全球化时代,对于各国税务机关来说,政策和操作层面都发生了特殊问题。在政策层面,各国需要依据能够在其税收管辖权范围内合理分配的所得和费用来协调其对利润征税的合法权利,目的是避免同一所得被一个以上的税收管辖区域征税,因为此种双重或者多重征税会对商品和服务交易以及资本的流通产生阻碍。伴随着各国对外经贸的发展,如何在维护国家税收利益的基础上避免国际双重征税,平衡经济效率和税收公平、促进对外经济发展,世界各国采取了多种消除或者减缓国际双重征税的方法。

In the era of economic globalization, specific problems arise at both policy and practical levels in tax administrations. At the policy level, countries need to reconcile their legitimate right to tax the profits of a taxpayer based upon income and expenses that can reasonably be considered to arise within their territory with the need to avoid the taxation of the same item of income by more than one tax jurisdiction. Such double or multiple taxation can create an impediment to cross-border transactions in goods and services and the movement of capital. With the development of foreign trade, countries around the world have adopted various methods to relieve or eliminate international double taxation on the basis of national tax interests so as to avoid international double taxation, balance economic efficiency and tax equity, and promote foreign economic development.

第一节 概 述
Section 1 Overview

一、国际双重征税的概念、危害性及主要措施
Concept, Harmfulness and Main Measures of International Double Taxation

(一) 国际双重征税的概念
Concept of International Double Taxation

区别于经济性双重征税,所谓法律性国际双重征税,是指两个以上国家或者地区,依据

自身的税收管辖权,对同一纳税人或者同一征税对象均进行征税。法律性国际双重征税源自国家税收管辖权之间的冲突,主要有以下三种表现形式:居民税收管辖权与来源地税收管辖权之间的冲突;两个国家的居民税收管辖权之间的冲突;两个国家的来源地税收管辖权之间的冲突。目前,普遍接受的法律性双重征税的概念,是经济合作与发展组织于1963年在《关于对所得和财产避免双重征税协定范本草案的报告》中所给出的:法律性双重征税,是指两个或者两个以上的国家,对同一纳税人,就同一征税对象在同一时期内课征相同或者类似的税收。如无特别说明,下文均指法律性国际双重征税。

The so called international double taxation, refers to two or more countries tax the same taxpayer or the same tax object simultaneously according to their tax jurisdictions. International double taxation originates from the conflicts between national tax jurisdiction, which is mainly manifested in the following three forms: the conflict between resident tax jurisdiction and source tax jurisdictions; the conflict between resident jurisdictions in two countries; the conflict between source jurisdictions in two countries. At present, the generally accepted concept of juridical double taxation is given by the OECD in its Report on A Draft Model Agreement on Avoidance of Double Taxation on Income and capital in 1963. Juridical double taxation refers to two or more countries levied the same taxpayerr for his or her same object of taxation in the same period of time.

(二)国际双重征税的危害性
Harmfulness of International Double Taxation

国际双重征税问题的存在,不仅对有关纳税人不利,而且对国际间的资本流动和技术交流也不利。因为国际双重征税使从事跨国投资和其他各种经济活动的纳税人相对于单纯从事国内投资和其他各种经济活动的纳税人,承担了沉重的双重税收义务负担。从税法角度,也违背了税收公平这个基本的税法原则。

The existence of international double taxation is detrimental not only to the taxpayers concerned but also to international capital flows and technological exchanges. Because of international double taxation, taxpayers engaged in transnational investment and other economic activities bear a heavy burden of double taxation obligations compared with those simply engaged in domestic investment and other economic activities. From the angle of tax law, it also violates the basic principle of tax fairness.

(三)主要单边措施
Main Unilateral Measures

国际双重征税的危害性受到国际社会的广泛重视,越来越多的国家采取单边措施予以消除或者减轻。一般来说,单方面避免重复征税的基本方法有免税法和抵免法。需要注意的是,虽然是单边方法,但根据对等原则,一般也会在国际税收条约中得到体现。

The harmfulness of international double taxation has been widely paid attention by the international community, and more and more countries have taken unilateral measures to eliminate or mitigate it. Generally speaking, the basic methods include tax exemption and tax credit method. It should be mentioned that, although it is a unilateral approach, according to the reciprocity principle, it is generally reflected in international tax treaties.

1. 免税法

Exemption Method

免税法即"别国单征，本国放弃"，是指居住国一方对本国居民来源于来源国的已经在来源国纳税的跨国所得，在一定条件下放弃税收管辖权。实行居民管辖权的国家对本国居民的境外所得免予征税，完全放弃征税权，而仅对其来源于国内的所得征税。此法可以有效避免和消除国际重复征税，一般适用于营业利润和个人劳务所得，有的还包括财产。此法多适用于居住国为单一实行地域管辖权的国家。免税法的指导原则是承认收入来源地税收管辖权的独占地位，对居住在本国的跨国纳税人来自外国并已由外国政府征税的那部分所得，完全放弃行使居民税收管辖权，免予课征国内所得税。

Namely, "one country levy, the other country give up". It means that under certain conditions, the host country waives its tax jurisdiction over the transnational income from which its residents has been taxed in source jurisdiction. A state exercising resident jurisdiction shall exempt its residents income derived from abroad totally, and only taxing their income derived from domestic. This method may avoid and eliminate international double taxation effectively. It is generally applicable to business profits and personal service income, and some of them also include property. This method mostly apply to countries exercising single tax jurisdiction. The guiding principle of the tax exemption method is to recognize the exclusive status of the source tax jurisdiction, and to give up resident tax jurisdiction completely for the income of the transnational taxpayer living in the country whose foreign income has been taxed by the foreign government.

2. 抵免法

Credit Method

抵免法即"别国先征，本国补征"，有全额抵免与限额抵免两种。全额抵免是指居住国允许纳税人已经缴纳的来源国税额，可以全部用来冲抵，其居住国的纳税额没有限额的限制。限额抵免是指纳税人可以从居住国应纳税额中冲抵的已缴来源国税额，不得超过纳税人的境外来源所得按照居住国税法规定的税率算出的应纳税额。

The credit method is that "other countries collect tax first, their our country collect tax later", which have two kinds, i.e. full credit and limited credit. Full credit method means that resident country allows its taxpayer's tax paid in source countries being offsetting totally and there are no tax limitations in resident country. While the term "limited credit" refers to the tax paid in source country may offset from tax payable in resident country, the tax payable shall not exceed the tax payable overseas income calculated in accordance with the tax rate stipulated in the resident country's tax law.

因此，抵免法的基本精神是承认收入来源地税收管辖权的优先地位，但并不放弃行使居民税收管辖权。这种方法的最大优点是在来源地管辖权优先的基础上，兼顾了居民税收管辖权，既避免了双重征税，又维护了国家的税收权益。我国也主要采用抵免法，这也是世界上大多数国家为了避免双重征税而选用的方法。

Therefore, the basic spirit of credit method is to recognize the source jurisdiction's priority while not abandon the resident tax jurisdiction.The great advantage of tax credit method is that it based on the source tax jurisdiction priority while having taken into account residential jurisdiction, which may both avoid double taxation and protect states' tax interests. China adopted the tax credit method, just like most countries around the world.

第二节 免 税 法
Section 2　Exemption Methods

所谓免税法,又叫免税制,是指一国政府对本国居民源自国外的所得与位于国外的财产,放弃居民税收管辖权,只按收入来源地税收管辖权征税的方法。免税法一般由国内税法规定,但也常列入国际税收协定。

The so called tax exemption, refers to one government renounce its residents' tax jurisdiction in its citizens income from abroad and property located abroad, and only tax according to resource jurisdiction. Tax exemption method is generally regulated in domestic law, while it is often inclnded in international tax treaties.

按照免税法,居民国只对其居民本国来源的所得征税,对其部分或者全部境外来源的所得,免于征收本国税收。免税法下,居民国放弃了其对境外来源所得的征税权,结果就是该所得仅仅由来源国征税。由于只有一国,即来源国对该所得征税,理论上可以完全消除居民国和来源国之间的国际双重征税。

Under the exemption method, the country of residence taxes its residents on their domestic source income and exempts taxes on some or all of their foreign source income. In effect, the country of residence gives up its right to tax foreign source income, which consequently is taxable exclusively by the source country. In theory, the exemption method completely eliminates residence-source international double taxation because only one jurisdiction, the source country, imposes tax on income.

但是在现实中,居民国也不是对其居民所有的境外来源所得都免税。按免税的彻底与否,可分为两个类型:一类国家对国外所得完全免税,实行彻底的免税法,从而,完全避免了国际双重征税。另一类国家的免税法则不彻底,只对本国居民的境外营业所得和劳务所得免税,对投资所得则不免税,因而,不能完全解决国际双重征税的问题。

However, not all foreign incomes are exempted by resident country in reality. According to whether it is complete or not, tax exemption method may be devided into two typies: one is called complete tax exemption which exempt all incomes deriving from abroad free from tax so as to avoid international double taxation completely; the other is called incomplete tax exemption which only exempt its domestic residents' overseas business income and services income free from tax, while investment income abroad is not tax-free. So this type may not resolve double taxation problems.

在居住国实行累进税率制度的情况下,采用免税法解决双重征税有全额免税法和累进免税法两种不同的计算方法。所谓全额免税法,是指居住国对居民纳税人来源于居住国境内的所得计算征税时,其适用税率的确定,完全以境内这部分应税所得为准,不考虑居民国纳税人来源于境外的免于征税的所得数额的方法。其计算公式为:

居住国的应征所得税额=来源于居住国境内的所得额×居住国所得税税率。

In the case of host country's progressive tax rate system, there are two different calculation methods to solve double taxation by using the tax exemption method: the full tax exemption method and the progressive tax exemption method. The so-called full tax exemption method refers to such a circumstance: when the resident country calculating and leving taxes on its resident taxpayers' income from domestic, its applicable tax rate are totally on the basis of the taxable income within the resident county, and without considering the amount of the income exempted from abroad. Its calculation formula is as follows:

Tax payable in the host country = income originating in the host country × tax rate in the host country

所谓累进免税法,则是指居住国虽然对居民纳税人来源于境外的所得免于征税,但是在对居民纳税人来源于境内的所得确定应适用的累进税率时,要将免于征税的境外所得额考虑在内的方法。其结果是,对居民纳税人来源于境内的所得确定适用的税率,比在采用全额免税法条件下适用的税率要高,居住国采用这种方法对居民纳税人计算征收的所得税额,也比适用全额免税法计征的税额更多。

The so-called progressive tax exemption method means that although the resident country exempts its resident taxpayer's foreign source income's taxation when he determines the progressive tax rate applicable to resident taxpayers' domestic sources' income, the amount of foreign income exempted from taxation should be taken into account.

作为一种消除国际双重征税的措施,免税法最大的优点在于能够彻底消除国际双重征税。因为无论是采取全额免税法还是累进免税法,居住国对居民纳税人来源于境外的所得都放弃了征税权,从而有效避免了国际双重征税的发生。并且来源地国的税率水平不影响居民国放弃的税收,无论来源地国税率与居民国相较而言孰高孰低,居民国放弃的税收都一样。

As an international double taxation eliminating measure, the biggest advantage of tax exemption method is that it can completely eliminate international double taxation. Because whether full tax exemption or progressive exemption is applied, the resident country gives up its tax jurisdiction in its resident taxpayers' foreign income which effectively avoids the occurrence of international double taxation. In addition, the tax rate of source country does not affect the resident country's tax forgone, and the resident country's forgone is the same regardless of the source country's tax rate.

但是免税法的缺陷也广为诟病，主要表现在这种方法是建立在居住国放弃其对居民的境外所得的征税权基础之上的，未能在消除国际双重征税问题上均衡兼顾到居住国、来源地国和跨国纳税人三方的利益，使居住国的权益受到一定的影响，不容易得到居住国的支持。因此，该方法的应用不够广泛。

However, the exemption method is also being criticized widely, and the main reason is that this method is based on the residence country's giving up its overseas income tax jurisdiction, which fails to balance the residence country and source country as well as cross-border tax payers' interests of the three parties when it eliminate international double taxation. So it is not easy to get support from the residence country. Therefore, this method is not widely used.

我国《企业所得税法实施条例》第91条规定了关于免税法的适用条款：

下列所得可以免征企业所得税：

（1）外国政府向中国政府提供贷款取得的利息所得；

（2）国际金融组织向中国政府和居民企业提供优惠贷款取得的利息所得；

（3）经国务院批准的其他所得。

Article 91 of Implementation Regulations for the Enterprise Income Tax Law of the People's Republic of China has regulated the tax exemption applicable terms:

The following income may be exempted from Enterprise Income Tax:

(1) interest income derived by foreign governments from provision of loan to the Chinese government;

(2) interest income derived by international financial institutions from provision of preferential loan to the Chinese government and resident enterprises; and

(3) any other income approved by the State Council.

第三节　抵　免　法
Section 3　Credit Methods

一、抵免法概述
Overview of Credit Method

所谓抵免法，又称外国税收抵免，是各国单方面解决国际双重征税的方法之一，为世界上大多数国家所采用。实行抵免法的国家都承认收入来源地税收管辖权优先的原则，同时，不放弃本国的税收管辖权。根据抵免法，居民纳税人就境外来源所得缴纳的境外税收，一般会减少该所得应缴纳的本国税收，减少的数额就是境外税收的数额。该制度的设计目的，旨在消除国际双重征税，鼓励海外投资，同时应兼顾本国税收利益。

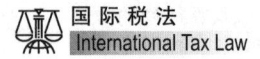

The so-called credit method, also called foreign tax credit, is one of double taxation resolving methods unilaterally by countries and is adopted by most countries in the world. Countries adopted the credit method are all acknowledging source country's jurisdiction first principle, and not abandon their tax jurisdiction meanwhile. Under the credit method, foreign taxes paid by a resident taxpayer on foreign source income will reduce domestic taxes payable on that income by the amount of the foreign taxes generally. The system is designed to eliminate international double taxation to encourage overseas investment, while taking into account domestic tax benefits.

抵免法又可以具体划分为直接抵免和间接抵免两种,我国也是如此。其中,直接抵免是指企业直接作为纳税人就其境外所得在境外缴纳的所得税额在我国应纳税额中抵免。间接抵免是指境外企业就分配股息前的利润缴纳的外国所得税额中由我国居民企业间接负担的部分在我国应纳税额中抵免。

Credit method may be divided into direct credit and indirect credit. It is the same in China. Direct credit means that the overseas income tax paid by an enterprise may be deducted from its tax payable in China directly. Indirect credit means that the foreign income tax by overseas enterprises before the distribution of dividends may be deducted from its tax payable in China by the part directly borne by Chinese resident enterprise.

直接抵免法与间接抵免法的区别在于,前者用于解决法律性国际双重征税,后者用于解决经济性国际双重征税。

The difference between direct and indirect credit method is that the former is used to solve the legal international double taxation problems, while the latter is used to solve the economic international double taxation problems.

 抵免限额

Credit Limitation

抵免限额是抵免法中的一个重要概念,缘起于实行抵免法的国家将境外税收抵免局限于针对外国来源所得的本国税收数额。

Limitation on credit is an important concept in credit method and is arising from countries that use the credit method to limit the credit for foreign taxes to the amount of domestic tax on the foreign source income.

我国境外税收抵免也实行限额抵免政策。抵免限额是指企业来源于境外的所得,依照我国《企业所得税法》等的相关规定计算的应纳税额。

In terms of overseas tax credit, China also implements the credit limitation policy. Credit limitation refers to the tax payable of an enterprise's income derived from overseas accounted according to the relevant provisions of China's Enterprise Income Tax Law, ect.

抵免限额可简单按该境外应纳税所得额直接乘以本国税率得出。这里,境外应纳税所得额是决定境外税收抵免限额的决定性因素。而境外应纳税所得额,是指居民企业来源于境外的所得以及在境内设立机构、场所的非居民企业在境外取得的与境内机构场所有实际

联系的所得,按《企业所得税法》及其实施条例等的相关规定计算的应纳税所得额。具体规定如下:

Credit limitation may be obtained by simply multiplying the taxable income from abroad directly by the domestic tax rate. Here, the overseas taxable income is the decisive factor in determining the tax credit limitation. While the "overseas taxable income" refers to the income derived by resident enterprises from overseas and income derived by non-resident enterprises with establishment or sites in China that have actual connections with domestic establishments or sites, which the taxable income calculated in accordance with the relevant provisions in China Enterprise Income Tax Law and Implementation Regulations for the Enterprise Income Tax Law of the People's Republic of China. The specific provisions are as follows:

《企业所得税法实施条例》第76条规定,《企业所得税法》第22条规定的应纳税额的计算公式为:

应纳税额＝应纳税所得额 × 适用税率−减免税额−抵免税额

As regulated in the Article 76 of Implementation Regulations for the Enterprise Income Tax Law of the People's Republic of China, the formula for computation of tax amount payable stipulated in Article 22 of the Enterprise Income Tax Law shall be:

Tax amount payable = taxable amount of income × applicable tax rate − tax relief − tax credit

公式中的减免税额和抵免税额,是指依照《企业所得税法》和国务院的税收优惠规定减征、免征和抵免的应纳税额。

The tax relief and tax credit in the formula shall mean the tax amount payable after reduction, exemption and relief pursuant to tax incentives stipulated in the Enterprise Income Tax Law and by the State Council.

《企业所得税法实施条例》第77条规定:企业所得税法第23条所称已在境外缴纳的所得税税额,是指企业来源于中国境外的所得依照中国境外税收法律以及相关规定应当缴纳并已经实际缴纳的企业所得税性质的税款。

As regulated in the Article 77 of Implementation Regulations for the Enterprise Income Tax Law of the People's Republic of China, income tax amount paid overseas referred to in Article 23 of the Enterprise Income Tax Law mean that an enterprise shall pay and has paid the Enterprise Income Tax for income sourced outside China payable pursuant to overseas tax laws and the relevant provisions.

《企业所得税法实施条例》第78条规定:《企业所得税法》第23条所称抵免限额,是指企业来源于中国境外的所得,依照《企业所得税法》和本条例的规定计算的应纳税额。除国务院财政、税务主管部门另有规定外,该抵免限额应当分国(地区)不分项计算,计算公式如下:

抵免限额＝中国境内、境外所得依照《企业所得税法》和本条例的规定计算的应纳税总额 × 来源于某国(地区)的应纳税所得额 ÷ 中国境内、境外应纳税所得总额

As regulated in the Article 78 of Implementation Regulations for the Enterprise Income Tax Law of the People's Republic of China, tax set-off limit referred to in Article 23 of the Corporate Income Tax Law shall mean the tax amount payable on income of an enterprise sourced outside China computed pursuant to the provisions of the Enterprise Income Tax Law and these Regulations. Unless otherwise stipulated by the finance and tax departments of the State Council, such tax set-off limit shall be computed by country (region) and not by tax items. The formula shall be as follows:

tax set-off limit = total taxable amount of income for income sourced in China and overseas computed pursuant to the provisions of the Enterprise Income Tax Law and these Regulations × taxable amount of income sourced in a particular country (region) ÷ the total taxable amount of income sourced in China and overseas

《企业所得税法实施条例》第79条规定:《企业所得税法》第23条所称5个年度,是指从企业取得的来源于中国境外的所得,已经在中国境外缴纳的企业所得税性质的税额超过抵免限额的当年的次年起连续5个纳税年度。

As regulated in the Article 79 of Implementation Regulations for the Enterprise Income Tax Law of the People's Republic of China, the five-year period referred to in Article 23 of the Enterprise Income Tax Law shall mean that five tax years have elapsed since the year following the year in which the Enterprise Income Tax paid by an enterprise overseas for income sourced overseas exceeded the tax set-off limit.

《企业所得税法实施条例》第80条规定:《企业所得税法》第24条所称直接控制,是指居民企业直接持有外国企业20%以上股份。《企业所得税法》第24条所称间接控制,是指居民企业以间接持股方式持有外国企业20%以上股份,具体认定办法由国务院财政、税务主管部门另行制定。

As regulated in the Article 80 of Implementation Regulations for the Enterprise Income Tax Law of the People's Republic of China, direct control referred to in Article 24 of the Enterprise Income Tax Law shall mean that a resident enterprise holds 20% or more of the foreign enterprise by direct shareholding. Indirect control referred to in Article 24 of the Enterprise Income Tax Law shall mean that a resident enterprise holds 20% or more of the shares of a foreign enterprise through indirect shareholding. The specific identifying measures shall be separately formulated by the finance and tax departments of the State Council.

《企业所得税法实施条例》第81条规定:按《企业所得税法》第23、第24条的规定抵免企业所得税税额时,应当提供中国境外税务机关出具的税款所属年度的有关纳税凭证。

As regulated in the Article 81 of Implementation Regulations for the Corporate Income Tax Law of the People's Republic of China, when an enterprise sets off corporate income tax pursuant to the provisions of Article 23 and Article 24 of the Enterprise Income Tax Law, it shall provide the relevant tax payment proof issued by the overseas tax authorities for the tax year in respect of the tax amount.

第四节 直接抵免法
Section 4　Direct Credit Method

直接抵免法是出现最早的抵免法,抵免对象限于同一个经济实体,以解决法律意义上的国际双重征税。间接抵免法针对的是经济意义上的重复征税问题。所谓直接抵免法,就是居住国对同一个居民纳税人在来源地国缴纳的税额,如同一居民个人就其境外来源的工资薪金所得在来源地国已缴纳的所得税额,或同一个法人企业的境外分支机构在所在地国缴纳的所得税额,允许用来直接抵免该居民个人或企业的总机构所应汇总缴纳居住国的相应税额的方法。

Direct credit is the earliest credit method, its credit object is limited to one economic entity for resolving international taxation in legal sense, while the indirect credit method is targeting double taxation in economic sense. The so-called direct credit, means the resident country treat the same resident taxpayer's tax paid in source country as the same resident individual's wage and salary taxes paid in source country, or as the same legal person' overseas branch tax paid, allowing for direct credit his or her head office's collective tax payment.

直接抵免法是一种适用于同一经济实体内部的税收抵免法,主要适用于位于居住国的总公司与位于非居住国的分公司之间的税收抵免关系,也适用于跨国自然人与其居住国政府之间的税收抵免关系。一般来说,直接抵免法采用限额抵免规则,允许的抵免额不能超过纳税人的来源国所得按居住国适用税率计算的数额,即直接抵免法允许抵免额一般取纳税人在来源国已纳的所得税额与抵免限额相比较中的较少的数额。

The direct credit method is a tax credit method that applies within the same economic entity, and mainly applies to the tax credit relationship between the head office and its non-residents' branches, and it also applies in the relationship between transnational persons and his or her resident country. In general, the direct credit method adopts limited credit rules, which only allow the credit amount not exceed the taxpayer's source country income calculated according to his or her resident country's applicable tax rate. That is to say, the direct credit method allows the less amount between the taxpayer's income paid in the source country and the credit limitations.

按照我国税法规定,直接抵免是指企业直接作为纳税人就其境外所得在境外缴纳的所得税额在我国应纳税额中抵免。直接抵免主要适用于企业就来源于境外的营业利润所得在境外所缴纳的企业所得税,以及就来源于或发生于境外的股息、红利等权益性投资所得、利息、租金、特许权使用费、财产转让等所得在境外被源泉扣缴的预提所得税。

According to China's tax law, direct credit method means that the income paid by an enterprise directly as a taxpayer's overseas income may be deducted from China's tax payable. The direct credit is mainly applicable to enterprise's company income tax paid for its operating profits overseas, or withholding income tax deducted by foreign source for its equity investment income, interests, rents, royalties, property transfer and other income.

第五节 间接抵免法
Section 5　Indirect Credit Method

间接抵免法，是指当居民公司从其外国关联公司收取股息时，针对由外国关联公司缴纳的境外所得税，而给予居民公司的抵免的方法。允许作为抵免的数额，为由外国关联公司就从支付股息的所得而缴纳的相关境外收入。在通常情况下，境外税收抵免只允许针对居民纳税人直接缴纳的境外所得税。实行间接抵免是股息收入国解决国际双重征税的一项重要措施。

The indirect credit is a credit granted to a resident corporation for the foreign income taxes paid by a foreign affiliate of the resident corporation when it receives a dividend distribution from its foreign affiliate. The amount allowable as a credit is the amount of the underlying foreign tax paid by the foreign affiliate on the income out of which the dividend is paid. The indirect credit is an important measure implemented by dividend income countries to solve international double taxation.

间接抵免只发生在母公司和子公司分设在两国时。由于子公司系独立法人，其在所在国缴纳的税款与母公司并无关联，母公司所在国亦不必给予直接抵免。但是，子公司的资本毕竟是来自母公司的投资，其利润毕竟是母公司的投资收益，在子公司向其所在国纳税后，母公司又须按所收到的股息向自己的所在国纳税，造成税负重叠。有时候母公司所在国会对子公司在其所在国缴纳的公司所得税给予抵免，从而避免国际重叠征税，这种抵免在国际税法上被称作间接抵免。

Indirect credit only occurs when the parent company and its subsidiaries are located in two countries. Since the subsidiary is an independent legal person, the tax paid in its host country has nothing to do with its parent company, and the parent company's country need not to give it direct credit. However, subsidiary's capital is invested by its parent company, and its profit is its parent company's investment interest. After the subsidiary paid taxes in its home country, its parent company has to pay tax to its own home country according to the dividends it received, which may resulting in tax overlap.

间接抵免也存在抵免限额问题。一般国家在直接抵免中关于抵免限额的规定也适用于间接抵免。因此，在实行间接抵免时，也必须确定抵免限额。根据我国税法，间接抵免的适用范围为居民企业直接持有或者间接持有20%以上股份的外国企业。

There are also credit limitation issues in indirect credit methods. Direct credit limitation stipulated by major countries are also applicable to indirect credit. So indirect credit limitation must also be determined when the indirect credit methods are applied. According to China's tax law, the indirect tax credit is applicable to foreign enterprises that are directly or indirectly owned by resident enterprises with more than 20% shares.

第六节 税收饶让制度
Section 6　Tax Sparing Mechanism

税收饶让制度具有影响公司投资决策和改进出境投资竞争力之功能。因此，税收饶让制度经常是双边税收协定中的重要条款之一，主要存在于发达国家与发展中国家之间的税收协定中。

Tax sparing mechanism functions on influencing corporations' investment decision and improving their competitiveness in outbound investment. So tax sparing mechanism is always important provision in double tax treaties, and this provision is primarily a feature of tax treaties between developed and developing countries.

所谓税收饶让，即允许抵免因外国税收优惠或者免税期而未支付的外国税款。税收饶让主要是通过税收饶让抵免实现的。所谓税收饶让抵免，是指居民国对根据来源国通常的税收法规本应缴纳，但是出于某种原因没有实际缴纳的境外税收所给予的抵免。没有缴纳税收的通常原因是，来源国为在该国投资或者开展经营活动的外国投资者规定了免税期或者其他税收激励。如果没有税收饶让，来源国为吸引外国投资而给予的税收激励的实际受益者就是投资者为其居民的国家，而不是外国投资者。其结果，就是来源国税收的减少转而成为居民国税收的增加。①

The so-called tax sparing refers to the allowing of a credit for the amount of foreign taxes that were not paid because of a tax incentive or tax holiday in the foreign country. A tax sparing credit is a credit granted by the residence country for foreign taxes that, for some reason, were not actually paid to the source country but that would have paid under the source country's normal tax rules. The usual reason for the tax not being paid is that the source country has provided a tax holiday or other tax incentive for foreign investors to invest or conduct business in the country. In the abssence of tax spring, the actual beneficiary of a tax incentive provided by a source country to attract foreign investment might be the country in which the investor is resident rather than the foreign investor. This result occurs whenever the reduction in source country tax is replaced by an increase in residence country revenue.②

税收饶让制度的基本运行模式是由资本输出国（居民国）对投资东道国（来源国）所减免的税收予以认可，视同居民国纳税人已经在来源国缴纳过这些被减免的税收，并允许纳税

---
① ［美］布莱恩·J.阿诺德著:《国际税收基础》,《国际税收基础》翻译组译,中国税务出版社2020年版,第164页。
② 同上。

人计算其在居民国应纳税额时抵免这些被饶让的来源国税额。

The basic operation model of tax sparing system is that, the capital exporting (resident country) country acknowledges tax reliefs granted by the host country (source country) and see the tax relief as if it has been truly paid in the source country, meanwhile allows the taxpayer credit these spared taxes in the source country when he or she calculating his or her payable tax amount.

税收饶让制度一方面使居民国纳税人可以保留在来源国被减免的税收，降低了其全球税负；另一方面使来源国的税收优惠能够让居民国纳税人直接受益，以增强来源国对纳税人的吸引力，引导纳税人的投资决策。税收饶让制度实施的前提是，居民国对其纳税居民的全球收入征税，并且使用境外税收抵免法避免双重征税，这是目前世界上大部分国家都在使用的税制。我国从20世纪80年代开始谈签税收协定，第一个包含税收饶让条款的协定是中日税收协定。

On one hand, the tax sparing system may enable the resident taxpayer to keep the tax relieved by source country so to reduce his or her global tax burden. On the other hand, source country's tax preference may directly benefit the resident taxpayer so as to make his or her tax system more attractive and induce taxpyaers' investment decision. The premise of tax sparing implementation is that the resident country implements global jurisdiction and uses tax credit method to avoid double taxation, which is the current tax system used by most countries in the world. In China, we began to negotiate and sign tax treaties in 1980s, among them, the first tax sparing provision is contained in tax treaty between China and Japan.

 学习思考题
Questions for Study

1. 免税法消除国际双重征税的优点和缺点是什么？
   What are the advantages and disadvantages of the tax exemption to eliminate international double taxation?
2. 抵免法消除国际双重征税的优点和缺点是什么？
   What are the advantages and disadvantages of credit method to eliminate international double taxation?
3. 我国企业所得税法采取的"分国不分项"限额抵免法的内容是什么？
   What is the content of "country specific instead of item specific" limit credit method adopted in China's Law of Corporation Income Tax?
4. 什么是饶让抵免？它的法律意义是什么？
   What is the sparing credit? What is its legal significance?

第十二章 CHAPTER XII

国际逃避税及其法律规制
International Tax Evasion and Avoidance as Well as Their Legal Regulations

与国际双重征税相反的一个重要国际税法现象,则是国际逃避税。国际逃避税及其法律规制,是国际税法的第二大重任。

Contrary to international double taxation, there is an important international tax phenomenon which is called international tax evasion and tax avoidance. International tax evasion and tax avoidance and its legal regulation are the second important task in international tax law.

第一节 国际逃税和避税概述
Section 1 Overview of International Tax Evasion and Tax Avoidance

国际交易为国际逃避税提供大量的机会。在法律上,避税和逃税是两种截然不同的行为,面临的法律规制措施也是不一样的。因此,必须将避税与逃税加以区分。然而两者之间彼此边界模糊,有时候很难作出明确界定。长期以来,逃避税行为始终是困扰世界各国税务机关的一道难题。尤其是国际逃避税行为,不仅侵蚀了国家税源,还破坏纳税人间的平等,并且使得法律变得不确定、不清晰进而引发一系列税收遵从问题。

International transactions provide many opportunities for the avoidance of tax. In law, tax avoidance and tax evasion are two distinct behaviors and are confronted different legal regulations. So, we must distinguish one from the other. However, it is difficult to distinguish the two of them because of their indistinct boundary. For a long time, tax evasion and avoidance has been a difficult problem for tax authorities all over the world. Among theses difficulties, international tax evasion and avoidance, which not only corrodes national tax bases but also destroys the equality among taxpayers, makes laws become uncertain and unclear, thus causing a series of tax compliance problems.

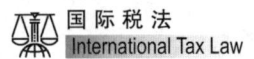

一 国际逃税的法律分析
Legal Analysis of International Tax Evasion

一般认为,逃税是非法的,通常涉及故意隐瞒收入或者欺诈行为。在国际法层面,国际逃税是指发生在国际范围内的逃税行为,即跨国纳税人利用国际税收合作的漏洞,采取种种非法手段,少纳或不纳有关国家税法或税收协定所规定的应纳税款。

It is generally believed that tax evasion is illegal and usually involves international nondisclosure of income or fraud. In international law, international tax evasion refers to tax evasion within the international scope. That is to say, transnational taxpayers take advantage of loopholes in international tax cooperation and take all kinds of illegal means to pay less or no taxes stipulated in relevant national tax law or tax treaties.

关于逃税的定义,各国法律的规定不完全一致。根据《简明牛津英语词典》,"逃税是指故意地不全部交纳法律规定应交的税,是一种犯罪行为"。逃税产生的原因比较复杂,但核心其实就是对利润的追求。为谋取高额利润,在收入确定的情况下,纳税人尽可能地采取能够使其税后利润最大化的各种手段。而在国际市场上,由于各国税收制度不同,包括税收管辖权的不同、税收征管方式和税收优惠措施的差异以及税收管制过程中的缺陷和漏洞,为纳税人提供了国际逃税的机会。

The definition of tax evasion varies in different national laws. According to *The Concise Oxford English Dictionary*, "tax evasion refers to pay in less taxes required by law deliberately, which is an offence". Reasons for tax evasion are complicated, but the core is the pursuit of profits. Under condition of income determination, taxpayers take all kinds of means to maximize their after-tax profits as much as possible. In the international arena, due to the differences of in different countries' tax systems, including different tax jurisdictions, different tax administration and different tax incentives as well as defects and loopholes in tax administration process, taxpayers are provided with opportunities of tax evasion.

二 国际避税的法律分析①
Legal Analysis of International Tax Avoidance

避税较难准确加以定义,通常是指纳税人实施的交易或者安排,目的在于以合法的方式,最大限度地减少应纳税额。避税行为危害严重,不仅侵蚀了国家税源,还破坏纳税人之间的平等,浪费大量社会资源。但是,由于避税行为表面的合法性,反避税并不容易,长期以来,避税行为始终是困扰世界各国税务机关的一道难题。

Tax avoidance is difficult to define precisely, but generally means transactions or arrangements entered into by a taxpayer in order to minimize the amount of tax payable in a lawful manner. Tax avoidance is very harmful for it not only corrodes nations' tax sources but also destroys the equality among taxpayers and wastes a lot of social resources. However, it is

---

① 本部分的内容重点参考了翁武耀:《避税概念的法律分析》,载《中外法学》2015年第3期。

not easy to fight against tax avoidance because of its superficial legality. For a long time, tax avoidance has always been a difficult problem for tax authorities around the world.

避税作为一项重要的税法问题,涉及税法多方面的基础理论。对避税的正确认识关系到对税法的正确认识,一国对避税问题的处理反映一国税收法治的水平。时下,避税现象在规模上已经达到了一个惊人的程度。在类型上,不仅包括传统的所得税等直接税避税,还包括随着时间的推移越来越受到纳税人和税务机关注的增值税等间接税避税。世界各国都已认识到避税严重侵蚀了国家的税收利益,因为形式多样的避税能够陷国库于空虚之深渊。

As an important tax law issue, tax avoidance involves many basic theories. A correct understanding of tax avoidance is related to a correct understanding of tax law. One country's treatment of tax avoidance may reflect its tax law level. Nowadays, Tax avoidance has reached an alarming degree in scale. In its terms, it not only includes traditional direct tax avoidance such as income tax, but also includes indirect tax avoidance such as value-added tax which is paid more and more attention by taxpayers and tax authorities over time. Countries around the world have come to realize its tax base erosion harm for all kinds of tax avoidance may plunge the exchequer into the empty abyss.

不同于逃税这种被明确定性为非法的行为,避税在性质上很难界定为非法还是合法,需要耗费税务机关大量的征管资源。毫无疑问,避税一直以来都是各国需要应对的问题,同时也是一个非常棘手的问题。棘手主要是由于对避税的认定缺乏清晰的标准,反避税措施的实施容易矫枉过正而侵害到纳税人的合法权益,尤其是当引入的一般反避税规则对避税本身缺乏完整、正确界定的时候。

Unlike tax evasion, which is clearly defined as illegal, however, tax avoidance is difficult to be defined as illegal or legal in nature, which needs to consume tax authorities' large amount of tax administration resources. It is no doubt that tax avoidance has always been a very difficult issue for all tax authorities around countries, and all countries have to deal with the problem. The difficulty is mainly due to the lack of clear standards for the identification of tax avoidance, and anti-tax avoidance measures are prone to overcorrect and infringe on the legitimate rights and interest of taxpayers, especially when the general anti-tax avoidance rules are not complete and correctly defined for tax avoidance itself.

虽然避税的概念还不能上升为一个法律范畴,但作为一种特殊现象,避税已经成为现代税法中一个具有独立研究意义的重要内容。可以说,对避税现象的认识,将反映对税法的基本认识和体现对税法基本理论的掌握程度,而对避税现象的处理,某种程度上也将反映一国的税收法治水平。

Although the concept of tax avoidance can't be elevated into a legal category, as a special phenomenon, it has become an important content in modern tax law which is of independent research significance. It can be said that the understanding of tax avoidance phenomenon may reflect the basic understanding of tax law and the mastery of the basic theory of tax law, and to some extent, the treatment of tax avoidance may also reflect the level of a country's tax law.

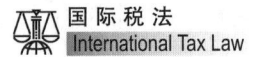

第二节 国际逃税
Section 2　International Tax Evasion

逃税通常存在于这样的情形：纳税人隐匿全部或部分已经发生的应征税行为，比如隐匿或者销毁会计账簿或凭证、使用虚假的会计账簿或凭证等。

Tax evasion usually rests in such a situation that a tax payer hides all or part of the tax behaviors which have already occurred, such as hiding accounting books or destroying of vouchers, using false accounting books or voucher.

有时纳税人直接在会计账簿中计入更少的收益或更多的支出，而不使用虚假的会计凭证、不开具发票、收据或涉税账单等，并伴随欺诈申报、不诚信申报或遗漏申报。结果就是纳税人没有缴纳或缴纳了比应当缴纳的更少的税。

Sometimes, taxpayer reckon less earnings or more spending in accounting books directly, rather than using false accounting vouchers , invoices, receipts, or tax bills, etc., with fraud declaration, dishonesty or omission declaration. The result is that taxpayers have not pay or pay less tax then he should pay.

在国际法层面，国际逃税通常采用的非法手段有：将高税负国收入转移到低税负国；将应税收入转换成免税收入；将较大的应税收入转换成较少的应税收入。目前在国际税法领域，除了跨国公司的国际逃税之外，高净值个人的国际逃税也受到关注。高净值个人的逃税，主要是在域外金融机构的帮助下实现的。离岸金融机构对富人的隐私进行了过度的保护，不追究富人钱财来源是否合法且有银行保密法的支持，使富人逃税的机会大幅度提高。

In terms of international law, international tax evasion usually adopts the following illegal ways such as transfer income from high-tax countries to low tax countries, convert taxable income into tax-free income, convert larger taxable income into less taxable income and so on. In international tax law area, in addition to multinational corporations' tax evasion, there are also high net worth individual's international tax evasion which has attracted more and more attention. HNWIs' tax evasion is mainly realized under the help of overseas financial institutions. Offshore financial institutions have supplied excessive protection in the riches' privacy by not investigating whether their money is legal or not, and backed by bank secrecy law, which increased the richers' tax avoiding chances greatly.

第三节 国际避税的主要方式和各国的法律管制
Section 3 Main Ways to Tax Evasion and its Regulations

一、国际避税的主要方式
Main Ways of International Tax Avoidance

通过国际交易进行避税的方式众多,难以一一列举,但是以下示例说明了产生避税行为的各种可能性。第一,纳税人将其居民身份从一国迁移至征税较低或者不征税的另一国。第二,纳税人将其来源于本国的所得转移至设立在避税地的受控外国实体,比如信托或者公司。第三,纳税人在避税地设立子公司,由其取得来源于境外的所得,或者由其收取设立于其他国家的子公司的利息。第四,在存在可以利用的税收协定的情形下,纳税人可以通过在外国设立的子公司,转移股息、利息、特许权使用费和其他款项,以减少这些款项的预提税数额。在上述手段下,目前主要形成了套用税收协定、资本弱化、成本分摊协议、受控外国公司等避税方式。

There are various ways of international tax avoidance through international transactions to itemize. The following examples, however, illustrate the range of possibilities: First, a taxpayer shift his or her residence from one country to another that levies lower or no taxes. Second, a taxpayer divert domestic source income to a controlled foreign entity, such as a trust or a corporation, established in a tax haven. Third, a taxpayer establish a haven subsidiary to earn foreign source income or to receive dividends from subsidiaries in other foreign countries. Forth, if advantageous treaties exist, a taxpayer route dividends, interests, royalties, and other amounts through subsidiaries established in foreign countries in order to reduce the amount of withholding tax on such amounts.

By the above ways, there has been several measures of tax avoidance, including treaty shopping, thin capitalization, controlled foreign corporation, and cost contribution agreements.

(一)套用税收协定
Treaty Shopping

套用税收协定的根源在于税收条约中规定的税收优惠或者抵免政策。一方面,为了促进国家之间投资和贸易的发展,国家之间往往签订以相互提供税收优惠为目的的税收条约条款;另一方面,在国际税收实践中,由于各主权国家的税收政策之间存在着差异,导致纳税人在进行跨国投资和贸易时经常遭受双重征税问题。为了避免双重征税,各国均采取了不同的措施,除了我们在第11章谈到的免税法、抵免法等基本方法之外,还通过签订税收条约的方式予以消除。

The origin of treaty shopping is the tax preference or credit policies regulated in tax treaties. On one hand, in order to promote the development of investment and trade between countries, countries often sign tax treaties with the purpose of providing tax preferences to each other. On the other hand, in international tax practices, due to the differences in tax policies among sovereign states, taxpayers often suffer from double taxation in transnational investment and trade. In order to avoid double taxation, various countries in the world have taken many different measures. Besides the tax exemption method, tax credit method and other basic methods mentioned in chapter XI, double taxation may also be eliminated by signing tax treaties.

长期以来,无论是以提供税收优惠为目的的税收条约,还是以避免双重征税为目的的税收条约,多以双边形式出现。按照互惠原则,只有协定缔约国的居民纳税人才能享受这些税收协定规定的税收优惠或者抵免政策,非缔约国居民不能享受这些政策。于是,一些非缔约国居民采取各种手段,通过在协定缔约国境内设立非实际经营的公司或者其他法律实体,从而取得其原本不能享受到的税收条约优惠,即所谓的套用税收协定。尽管纳税人从事税收条约套利的主要目的是获得本不应得到的税收条约利益,很多时候,大多数的税收条约套利也是为了获得对股利、利息和特许权使用费的低预提税税率。

For a long time, both tax treaties with the purpose of providing tax incentives and and tax treaties with the purpose of avoiding double taxation, almost are bilateral. According to the reciprocity principle, only residents and nationals of a contracting state are entitled to benefit from a tax treaty, while non residents and nationals are not entitled to the treaty benefits. Tax payers who are not residents or nationals of a contracting state have frequently sought to obtain the benefits of a tax treaty by organizing a corporation or other legal entity in one of the contracting states to serve as a conduit for income earned in the other contracting state. This practice is commonly referred to as treaty shopping. Although a taxpayer may engage in treaty shopping to obtain any treaty benefits not otherwise available, most treaty shopping involves attempts by taxpayers to obtain reduced withholding rates on dividends, interest, and royalties.

(二) 资本弱化
Thin Capitalization

所谓资本弱化,是指企业有意通过加大借贷款(债权性筹资)比重而减少股份资本(权益性筹资)比例的方式增加税前扣除,以降低企业税负的一种行为。

What is called thin capitalization refers to a way in which a corporation deliberately enlarges its debt proportion (debenture financing) while reduces its equity capital (capital financing) proportion so as to increase its tax deductibles and decrease its tax burden.

企业资本由权益资本和债务资本构成。权益资本是所有者投入的资本,包括投入的资本金、资本公积金、盈余公积金和未分配利润等。从企业的筹资决策上来讲,一个母公司可以通过以下三种方式为其分支机构筹资,使用负债、股权和留存收益。其中,债务筹资的税务优势在于,利息可以在税前扣除,降低了投资者的成本;而股权筹资成本则不能税前扣除。财务意义上的资本弱化是企业为了实现其利益最大化,在资本结构的安排中会不自觉地选择高举债、低投资,这是企业资本运营的一种客观结果,也是一般意义上的资本弱化。作为税法调整的对象,资本弱化是一种人为方式,通过带息债务,而非股东持股,唯一目的或主要目的是获得税收方面的好处。

Enterprise capital consists of equity capital and debt capital. Equity capital is capital invested by the owner, including invested capital, capital reserve, surplus reserve, undistributed profits and so on. From the perspective of financing decision, one parent corporation may raise funds for its branch in the following three ways: liability, equity and retained earnings. Financially, in order to maximize their interests, companies will choose high debt and low investment in the arrangement of capital structure unconsciously, which is an object result of the capital operation by enterprises. This is so-called thin capitalization in general sense. As an object of tax adjustment, thin capitalization is an artificial way, through interest-bearing debt rather than shareholder, with sole or primary purpose of obtaining tax benefits.

(三)成本分摊协议
Cost Contribution Arrangement

成本分摊协议在英文中有两种说法,一种是 Cost Contribution Arrangements(CCAs),可以译为成本贡献协议;另一种为 Cost Sharing Arrangements(CSAs),译为成本分摊协议。美国税法对 CSA 的定义是"缔约方之间达成的、在协议下可以合理预期的无形资产开发的未来利益分享份额相应的比例,分摊一项或者多项无形资产开发成本的协议"。OECD 转让定价指南对其作出的定义是:成本分摊协议是企业间达成的一种合同性协议,联合开发、生产或者获得无形资产、有形资产或者服务,目的是让此类无形资产、有形资产或者服务为参与协议的每个个体提供未来预期收益。①

There are two wording of cost contribution arrangement in English, the one is Cost Contribution Arrangements(CCAs), the other is Cost Sharing Arrangements(CSAs). In the US tax code, "a cost sharing arrangement is an arrangement by which controlled participants share the costs and risks of developing cost shared intangibles in proportion to their reasonably anticipated benefits ('RAB') shares". In the OECD Transfer Pricing Guidelines, CCA is a contractual arrangement among business enterprises to share the contributions and risks involved in the joint development, production or the obtaining of intangibles, tangible assets or services with the understanding that such intangibles, tangible assets or services are expected to create benefits for the individual business of each of the participants.

按照美国税法和 OECD 的定义,CSA 与 CCA 是有区别的,两者的主要区别在于 CCA 的范围更加广泛,它是一种框架性协议;而 CSA 被明确定为协议正文。CCA 的定义表明包括风险的分摊,而 CSA 则没有明确风险问题,在定义中没有提到任何风险的字眼。在实践中,CCA 和 CSA 之间也是有区别的,区别在于 CCA 涵盖开发、生产或获得资产、服务或权利,而 CSA 用于无形资产的开发或研究。

According to the US tax law and OECD' definition, there exists difference between CSA

---

① OECD, "OECD Transfer Pricing Guidelines for Multinational Enterprises and Tax Administrations", 2017. Par. 8.3.

and CCA. The main difference is that the CCA's scope is wider than that of CSA, and the CCA is a framework agreement, while the CSA is clearly defined as the body of the agreement. The definition of CCA indicates that it includes the allocation of risks, while CSA does not specify the issue of risks and doesn't mention any word of risks in its definition. In practice, there are also differences between the two. The difference is that CCA covers the development, production, acquisition of assets, services, or rights, while CSA is only used for the development or research of intangible assets.

CSA更加符合成本分摊协议的内涵，因为成本分摊协议主要涉及的是无形资产的联合研发问题。无形资产研发的基本特点是费用高、风险大、周期长。除了这些特点之外，无形资产往往是由实力雄厚的企业集团研发的，而企业集团内部有众多企业，每个企业具有不同的分工与特点，有不同的竞争优势。企业集团内部某一个企业往往不能，或者不愿意独立进行某项无形资产的研发活动。为了降低、分散风险，节约成本，提高无形资产研发成功的概率，作为现代财务工具的成本分摊协议应运而生。

CSA is more in line with the connotation of cost sharing agreement, for cost sharing agreement mainly involves joint research and development of intangible assets. The basic characteristics of the research and development of intangible assets are high cost and high risk as well as long cycle. In addition to the above characteristics, intangible assets are often developed by powerful enterprise groups, and there are many enterprises within the group, each enterprise has different division and priorities as well as competitive strength. One enterprise within the group is often unable or unwilling to carry out the R&D activities of an intangible asset independently. In order to reduce and disperse risks, save costs and improve the possibility of successful R&D of intangible assets, cost sharing agreement as a modern financial tool came into being.

随着经济全球化的发展和无形资产在企业经营中重要性的增强，几乎所有的跨国公司都以削减世界范围内的长期税负为目标，对无形资产进行策略性税务筹划。比如，一个集团公司打算开发有价值的无形资产，并由两个以上集团成员分享利益，可以通过共同承担费用安排，使将来有可能使用无形资产的使用者共同参与开发，这样可以规避转移定价问题，也使所有的无形资产使用者从一开始就都是无形资产的拥有者，而无需在集团成员之间进行资产转让。跨国公司关联企业之间签署的此类协议，往往所涉金额巨大，协议参与方之间的成本分摊和预期收益分配，会对各参与方所在国家的税收利益产生重要影响。跨国公司倾向于将成本分摊无形资产的收益留在低税国从而减少总体税负，这会对所得税税率相对较高的国家产生更大的影响。当前，跨国公司利用成本分摊协议不合理地分摊无形资产开发的成本和风险，进行国际避税的行为越发普遍，此类行为也越来越成为各国政府和国际税法规制的对象。

With the development of economic globalization and the increasing importance of intangible assets in enterprises' operation, almost all transnational corporations have made strategic tax planning for intangible assets so as to reduce the long-term tax burden worldwide. For example, a conglomerate wants to develop valuable intangibles, and two or more of its members will share the intangibles' interests. They may choose to assume a shared expense arrangement so that all of the future users may participate in the development process which may not only circumvent the transfer pricing problems but also make sure all the users of the intangibles are the intangibles' owner from the start, without having to transfer among the group members. Such agreements signed among MNEs' affiliated members often involve huge amount of money and the cost sharing and expected income distribution among the involved parties will have an important impact on the tax benefits of the countries where each participant is located. At present, Multinational companies use CSA to share the costs and risks of intangibles' development unreasonably as a tax avoidance instruments more and more common, and such behaviors are becoming the objects of governments in the world and international tax law.

（四）受控外国公司
Controlled Foreign Corporation

经济全球化和税收竞争条件下，企业需要在国际市场上竞争。为了保持本国企业在国际市场上的竞争力，大部分国家的法律都规定了递延纳税制度，即对居民股东投资于外国企业所实现的投资所得，在被投资外国企业以股息形式分配给股东前，允许暂不计入股东的应税所得中纳税。也就是说，如果设立一个外国公司或者其他法律实体（比如信托），则对外国所得课征的国内税可以被很容易地递延甚至是完全地避免。因为外国的公司或者信托一般被认为是独立的纳税主体，不是控股股东或者受益所有人所在国的居民，不能因为该外国公司或信托赚取了所得就对该控股股东或者受益所有人征税。

Under the background of economic globalization and tax competition, companies need to compete in the international market. In order to maintain the competitiveness of domestic enterprises in the international market, most countries stipulate the tax deferral system, which is designed to allow the resident shareholding foreign investment gains to be temporally not included in their taxable income before the taxable income being distributed to them in the form of dividends. That is to say, domestic tax on foreign source income can easily be deferred or avoided completely by establishing a foreign corporation or other legal entity, such as a trust, to earn the income. Because the foreign corporation or trust is generally considered to be a separate taxable entity and not resident in the country where its controlling shareholders or beneficiaries are residents, those shareholders or beneficiaries are not taxable when the income is earned by the foreign corporations or trust.

递延纳税的预期税收利益可以用现代财务管理学上的现值条款来解释。如果递延持续足够长的时间，就现值而言实际上相当于完全免税，因此，递延纳税制度被跨国公司用作避税的手段之一。全球范围内跨国公司的兴起促使避税港层出不穷，许多公司将利润囤积在设立于避税港或低税地的境外公司，通过利润保留、延迟分配等方式来筹划避税。这些实际由本国居民控制的公司被称为受控外国公司（简称CFC）。

The expected tax benefits of tax deferral system can be explained in terms of the present value clauses in modern financial management. If the deferments lasts long enough, the present value in effect is equivalent to tax exemption. So the tax deferral system is used by multinational companies as a tax avoidance means. The rise of multinational corporations around the world prompts the emergence of tax havens in an endless number of ways. Many companies hoard their profits in overseas companies set up in tax havens or low tax jurisdictions and plan tax avoidance by means of profit retention and deferred distribution and so on. These companies, which are controlled by their own citizens in effect, are called controlled foreign corporations(for short, CFC).

此外,转让定价既是跨国公司的日常经营需求,也被用作税收筹划的方式,我们将会在本章第四节进行专门的介绍,在此不予赘述。

Furthermore, transfer pricing is not only a daily business requirement of international corporations, but also a way of tax planning. We will give a special introduction in Section 4 of this chapter, here we will give no further elaboration.

(二) 各国对避税的法律管制
Anti-tax Avoidance Rules in Various Countries

各国对避税的法律管制各有不同,但是基本上可以分为两类:一类是特别反避税规则,针对特定的反避税类型而开发,主要包括反对税收条约套利的规则、资本弱化规则、受控外国公司制度和成本分摊协议。另一类被称为一般反避税规则,用于处理不属于上述特别反避税规则范畴的情形,但是根据实质重于形式原则,其事实上是为从事避税行为的情形而设置的。

The legal regulations of tax avoidance varies from country to country, but it may be divided into two categories basically. One is special anti-tax avoidance rules, which are developed for specific anti-tax avoidance types, mainly including anti treaty shopping, thin capitalization rules, foreign controlled corporations and cost contribution arrangements. The other one are known as the general anti-tax avoidance rules. They are set up to deal with situations that don't fall within the scope of the above special anti-tax avoidance rules. But according to substantial doctrines, they are actually engaged in tax avoidance activities.

(一) 对税收条约套利的规制
Anti Treaty Shopping Rules

为了防止和消除税收条约套利造成的危害,国际社会开始采取行动来打击税收条约套利,一些国家也依据本国法中的一般反避税规则或者特别反避税规则加以规制。经合发组织和联合国税收协定范本及其注释,也详细规定了在税收条约层面防止税收条约套利的措施。

In order to prevent and eliminate the harm caused by treaty shopping, the international tax community has taken action to curtail treaty shopping, many countries have also adopted anti treaty shopping rules to regulate shopping based on their own general anti tax avoidance rules or special anti tax rules. The OECD and UN Model and their commentaries both have detailed measures to prevent treaty shopping in international tax treaty level.

条约层面的规制措施主要分为一般反对税收条约套利条款和特别反对税收条约套利条款。一般反对税收条约套利条款是普遍适用的、不针对特定对象的反对条约滥用规制措施,具体包括透视法、征税法、渠道法、善意条款和主要目的测试规则等。特别反对税收条约套利措施则是针对特定纳税人或者特定收益类型的反滥用措施,主要包括利益限制条款和收益所有人概念等。

The regulation measures in treaties can be divided into the general anti treaty shopping clauses and the special anti treaty shopping clauses. The general anti treaty shopping clauses are widely applicable which are not targeted at specific objects, including look-through method, tax method, channel method, bona fide clauses and main purpose test rules, etc. The special anti treaty shopping clauses are aimed at specific taxpayer or special income types, which is mainly including limitation-on-benefits and benefit ownership concepts.

BEPS行动六提出了两个重要的反对税收条约滥用的措施,被嵌入了OECD范本,随后被嵌入大量双边税收条约:利益限制条款和主要目的测试条款,两者共同构成防止协定滥用的最低标准。尽管这两个措施在OECD范本中是全新的,但是在很多国家早已在其条约中选择了上述两种措施之一,或者两种措施都选。

BEPS Action 6 proposes two distinct anti abuse measures to be incorporated into the OECD Model Convention and subsequently into the various bilateral tax treaties. A Limitation on Benefits (LoB) clause and Principal Purpose Test (PPT) both shaped as the minimum standard in anti treaty abuse. While both anti-abuse measures are new in the OECD Model Convention, various countries around the world have implemented either LoB or PPT clauses or both into their tax treaties.

利益限制条款的基本做法是否认那些虽然居住在某一缔约国境内,但是事实上是作为第三国居民服务的导管而存在的公司的条约利益。利益限制条款虽然设定了享受税收条约优惠待遇的严格条件,但是也对于从事正常经营活动的居民予以豁免,从而保持其合理性。税收协定主要目的测试条款是指税收协定中的如下表述或者类似表述的条款:虽有本协定其他条款的规定,如果在考虑了所有相关事实与情况后,可以合理地认定就某项所得获取本协定某项优惠是直接或间接产生该优惠的安排或交易的主要目的之一,则不应对该项所得给予该优惠,除非能够证明在此种情形下给予该优惠符合本协定相关规定的宗旨和目的。

The basic policy of the limitation-on-benefits article is to deny treaty benefits to a corporation that is resident in one for the contracting states, but is in effect serving as a conduit for residents of some third country. Although the limitation-on-benefits article sets strict conditions for preferential treatment in treaty benefit quality, it also exempts the residents who are engaged in normal business activities, thus maintaining its rationality. Principal purpose test clause refers to the following terms of expression or similar expression in tax treaties. Despite the other provisions in this treaty, if all of the relevant facts and conditions has been considered, we can reasonably determine to a certain income obtained some discount in the treaty is directly or indirectly from one of the main purpose of the preferential arrangement or transaction, this treaty discount can be denied, unless it can be proved that the reductions in such a case are consistent with the related aim and purpose in this treaty.

(二)资本弱化规制
Thin Capitalization Rules

公司税中对负债的偏爱反映了这样一种事实:公司债务利息是可以从应税利润中扣除的,而股权回报则不能。与这种负债偏好相关的福利成本不能被忽视。更重要的是,过量负债比例提高了欺诈的可能性。世界各国公司所得税法中普遍规定的对负债和股权的不同税收待遇,使资本弱化现象日益突出,迫切需要加以控制。

The debt bias in corporate taxation mirrors the fact that interest payments on corporate debt are deductible from taxable profits, while the return on equity is not. The welfare costs related to this debt bias might not be negligible. More importantly, excessive debt levels increase the probability of default.The different tax treatment between debt and equity makes thin capitalization stronger and should bring under control.

公司股权津贴(ACE)和综合经营所得税(CBIT)作为能够比较彻底解决此类问题的措施,近年来在一些国家得到运用。ACE方式是给股权以负债同样的税收待遇,利息可以在税前扣除;CBIT是在计算应税利润时,使利息不再享受税前扣除的税收待遇。两者的目的都是保持投资的税收中性。从对经济的影响看,ACE改革导致税基变窄、税率提高、资金成本降低;CBIT改革则导致税基变宽、税率降低、资金成本提高。从对投资区位的影响看,在ACE下,法定税率的提高会降低对投资者的投资回报,从而会诱使跨国公司将利润转移到法定税率比较低的国家,但是,由于资金成本下降,相当于提高了公司的投资回报,会产生吸引投资的效果。CBIT下,资金成本上升会引起投资下降。

Allowance for company equity (ACE) and comprehensive business income tax (CBIT), as two measures of solving these problems, have been carried out in some countries. ACE treats equity the same as debt, and interest can be deduced before levying the tax, while under CBIT, interest can not be deduced before computing the business income tax. Both of them are for keeping tax neutrality in investment. Regarding to their economic impact, the reform of ACE has led to the narrowing of tax base, the increase of tax rate and the reduction of capital cost; while CBIT has led to broader tax base, lower tax rate, increasing capital cost. As for their impact to investment, under ACE, the higher tax rate may decrease capital return to investor and making multinational companies shift their profits to lower tax rate countries. However, as capital cost decreasing, the return for investment rise, and this may attract more investment. Under CBIT, capital cost decreasing may cause investment decreasing.

在CBIT方向下,OECD推荐的两种基本方法——独立交易法和固定比率法成为主流。大部分国家采取这两种方法之一或结合这两种方法构建它们的资本弱化税制,由此形成了资本弱化的常见定义:所谓资本弱化规则,是对债务权益比率过高的公司向其非居民股东支付利息的可扣除数额的限制。固定债务/权益比例法的应用以澳大利亚为代表,独立交易法的应用以英国为代表。为保护税收收入,很多国家的立法实施所谓的资本弱化规则。各国资本弱化条款的立法原则、方式和内容存在较大差异。

Follow the direction of CBIT, there are two fundamental ways to regulate thin capitalization in OECD's recommendation: the arm's length method and the fixed ratio method. Most countries adopt one or a combination of these two methods to build their thin capitalization tax system. Thus, the common definition of thin capitalization has been shaped. The so-called thin capitalization rules refer to restrictions on the deductible of interest payments made by corporations with excessive debt-to-equity ratios to their nonresident shareholders. The application of the fixed debt/equity ratio is represented by Australia and the application of the arm's length principle is represented by the United Kingdom. In order to protect tax revenue, more and more countries around the world have also introduced the so-called thin capitalization rules through legislation. There are big differences among countries in capitalization rules' legislation principles, methods and contents.

比如,澳大利亚在应对资本弱化避税方面经验最为丰富,规则最为严厉。澳大利亚税法规定,澳大利亚境内子公司不能将支付给"外国控制方"的超额利息作为费用扣除。具体而言,在某种程度上,如果某个跨国公司在澳大利亚的利息费用超过了规定的水平,则澳大利亚的资本弱化规则永久性地否认利息和其他与负债相关的费用扣除。最大可以允许扣除的利息水平,一般是澳大利亚纳税人经调整后净资产的75%。依据特定的独立交易因素或者世界产权比率,也有可能会提高资本弱化的比率。又如,法国的资本弱化规则适用于任何对关联方的债务利息支付。它包括两个测试:一是独立交易的利率测试,二是依据1.5∶1的产权比率(依据最优惠的利率的结果)进行的二次测试。根据调整后所得的25%或者依据对利息所得限制进行规制。在独立交易原则下否认的利率测试会被永久性地不能税前扣除,而在二次测试下不予税前扣除的利息,则可以无限期地向后结转,但是从次年起每年按照5%的逐渐停止。在美国资本弱化规则下,美国税法典第163节(j)款限制了利息的可扣除性。第163节(j)款主要应用于付款公司在1989年7月10日之后的纳税年度所支付或者积累的利息支付。美国规则被应用于对外国关联方债务的应付利息。固定比率的规定使美国关联集团的产权比率超过了1.5∶1。我国资本弱化税制适用对象应包括企业与关联方之间的融资,在方法选择上采用固定债务/权益比率法。

For example, Australia is the most experienced in anti thin capitalization and has the toughest rules in dealing with thin capitalization. Under Australian tax law, an Australian subsidiary may not deduct its excess interest paid to a "foreign controller" as an expense. To be specific, Australia's thin capitalization rules permanently deny interest and other debt-related deductions to the extent that the debt attributable to the Australian operations of a multinational group exceeds a prescribed level. The maximum allowable level is generally based on 75 percent of the Australian taxpayer's Australian adjusted net assets. There are opportunities to increase the thin capitalization ratio based on certain arm's-length factors or a worldwide debt-to-equity ratio. For instance, France's thin capitalization rules apply to interest payable on debt owing to any related party. The revised rules contain two tests — an arm's-length interest rate test, and a second test based on (depending on which provides the most favourable result) a debt-to-equity ratio of 1.5:1, a limitation based on 25 percent of adjusted earnings or a limitation based on interest income. Interest denied under the arm's-length interest rate test is permanently denied, whereas interest denied under the second test has an indefinitely carry-forward period but is subject to a phaseout of five percent per year from the second subsequent year. Under US thin capitalization rules, section 163(j) of the U.S. Internal Revenue Code ["Code Section 163(j)"] restricts the deductible of interest. Code Section 163(j) generally applies to interest paid or accrued by the payer corporation in its taxable years beginning after July 10, 1989. The US rules apply to interest payable on foreign related party debt. The fixed ratio is regulated as the US Affiliated group's debt-to-equity ratio exceeds 1.5:1. China's thin capitalization rules are applied to financing among enterprises and their related parties, and the fixed debt/equity ratio has been selected.

除了上述常见的以打压负债税收待遇的方式，公司股权津贴制度是一种新型的规制资本弱化的方式，公司股权津贴制度（ACE）是资本弱化税制中最重要的制度之一，其基本理念是通过允许股权资本的机会成本像负债利息一样，从税基中扣除，从而在根源上消除企业由于负债和股权的税收待遇差别而进行资本弱化的动机。但就整体而言，CBIT方向下的资本弱化规则是主流，ACE方向下的资本弱化规则仅仅在少数国家得到实施。

Besides the above methods by depressing the tax treatment of debt financing, there is also a new way to regulate thin capitalization, which is called Allowance on Corporation Equity (ACE). ACE is one of the most important systems in thin capitalization tax law. Its fundamental idea is allowing the shareholder's fund opportunity cost to be deducted from tax base, just the same as the interest expense can, so as to eliminate enterprises' thin capitalization incentives derived from the different tax treatment between debt and equity. But on the whole, the thin capitalization rules under the direction of CBIT are the mainstream while the thin capitalization rules under the direction of ACE are only implemented in a few countries.

（三）受控外国公司制度
Controlled Foreign Corporation Rules

美国由于涉外投资较多，受到递延纳税制度的冲击也最大。特别是到了19世纪60年代，美国经济开始衰退，财政赤字不断增加，美国纳税人利用递延纳税制度避开美国税收的现象最早受到了理论界和实务界的关注。1962年，美国制定受控外国公司规则，如下部分是世界上最早的受控外国公司规则，其他国家纷纷效仿，尽管具体立法存在细微差异。美国受控外国公司规则已经成为其他国家相关立法的模板。比如，在法国，受控外国公司规则首次制定于1980年。法国税收制度是在严格的地域基础上运行的，只有产生于法国的利润才需要纳税。现在受控外国公司规则已经成为包括我国在内的很多国家的反避税法的重要组成部分。

The United States is mostly affected by the deferred tax system due to its large foreign investment. Especially in the 1860s, the American economy began to decline and the fiscal deficit kept increasing. The phenomenon that the American taxpayers avoided the American tax by using the deferred tax system attracted the attention of the theoretical and practical circles. In 1962, the US formulated the CFC rule, known as Division F, which was the first Controlled Foreign Corporation (CFC) rule in the world. After the US enacted the CFC rule, other countries in the world has followed suit. The US CFC rule has become a template for legislation in other countries though there are small differences among them. For example, In France, CFC rules were first enacted in 1980. The French tax regime operates on a strict territorial basis, where only profits generated in the country are subject to tax in France. Now, the CFC rules have become an important part of anti tax avoidance rule system in many countries including China.

从经济学原理上讲，由于纳税人设立受控外国公司的动机在于获得递延纳税利益，消除纳税人在受控外国公司中的税收利益预期，将会消除纳税人利用受控外国公司避税的动机。因此，受控外国公司规则的原理，就是通过取消递延纳税，对符合受控外国公司规则条件的股东在当期课税,使避税地公司无法凭借其独立的法人身份扮演积累所得的角色,从而弥补递延制度带来的立法漏洞。交易法是适用受控外国公司规则的一种具体方法。根据该方法,受控外国企业居民股东,仅仅就受控外国公司的污点所得(消极所得和基地公司所得)负有纳税义务。一般而言,污点所得包括消极投资所得和基地公司所得。

From the pespective of economic principles, because taxpayers' motivation to establish a CFC is to obtain the deferred tax benefits, eliminating taxpayer's expectation of tax deferring benefits will eliminate taxpayer's motivation to use CFC as a tax avoidance tool. So the rationale in CFC rules are taxing the qualified CFC shareholders by canceling deferred tax. By doing so, the companies in haven can't play the accumulated income role by virtue of their independent legal person status, so as to make up the legislative loopholes brought by the tax deferred system. Transactional approach is a specific approach for applying CFC rules under which only the tainted income (passive income and base company income) of CFCs' resident shareholders should pay tax. Generally, tainted income consists of passive investment income and base company income.

(四)成本分摊协议
Cost Contribution Arrangements

成本分摊协议在英文中有两种说法:一种是 Cost Contribution Arrangements(CCAs),可以译为成本贡献协议;另一种为 Cost Sharing Arrangements(CSAs),译为成本分摊协议。前者是 OECD 转让定价指南对成本分摊协议的定义,即"工商企业间所达成的框架性协议,协议分摊开发、生产或获得资产、服务、权利的活动的成本与风险,确定每个参与方从事该活动取得的成果中的利益之性质与范围"。后者则是美国税法对成本分摊协议的定义,即"缔约方之间达成的、在协议下可以合理预期的无形资产开发的未来利益分享份额相应的比例,分摊一项或者多项无形资产开发成本的协议"。《美国成本分摊协议2011年最终规则》对关联企业间以成本分摊方式联合开发无形资产的涉税问题进行了规制,代表了美国在该问题上的最新成果。当前,跨国公司利用成本分摊协议进行税收筹划的行为日益普遍,严重影响了利益相关国的税源控制。美国作为拥有世界上最多跨国公司的国家,它的规则对其他国家税务当局以及跨国纳税人产生了深远影响。

There are two English terms for cost contribution arrangements. One is Cost Contribution Arrangements(CCAs) while the other is Cost Sharing Arrangements(CSAs). CCAs is defined by the OECD Transfer Pricing Guideline as "a framework agreed among enterprises to share the costs and risks of developing, producing, or obtaining assets, services, or rights, and to determine the nature and extent of the interests of each participant in the results of the activity of developing, producing, or obtaining those assets, services, or rights." CSA is defined by the US tax as "a cost sharing arrangement is an arrangement by which controlled participants share the costs and risks of developing cost shared intangibles in proportion to their reasonably anticipated benefits shares." The US Cost Sharing Arrangements 2011 Final Rules and Regulations aim at regulating tax related issues on joint development of intangibles among associated enterprises. This represents the latest development at the issue in US. At present, it is increasingly common for multinational enterprises to take advantage of cost sharing arrangements as tax planning methods and such behaviour has seriously impacted related countries' tax source control. As one of the largest multinational enterprises country, the US Cost Sharing Arrangements 2011 Final Rules and Regulations have been profoundly influenced other countries' tax authorities as well as multinational taxpayers.

如同在本章第四节将会谈到的跨国公司转让定价规则,规制成本分摊协议的基本原则也是独立交易原则,即对成本分摊协议的各参与方贡献,按照独立市场价格予以评估,然后按照成本与收益相匹配原则,将各方投入与预期收益相匹配。对成本分摊协议的法律管制,主要要求协议分摊的成本必须是企业及其关联方在共同开发、受让无形资产,或者共同提供、接受劳务时实际发生的成本数额,而不应在实际成本基础上附加上述共同活动中任何成员公司的属于利润、收益的数据,且这部分成本须与可比情形下没有关联关系的企业在从事上述活动中发生的成本具有可比性。在协议安排期间,CCA 的参与方的成本分摊比例,应与预期获得的资产受益权或劳务服务的分享比例保持一致。

Just as transfer pricing rules in Section 4 of this chapter, the basic principle regulating CCA is also the Arm's Length Principle regulating transfer pricing, that is, the contribution of each party to the CCA is evaluated according to the market force, and then the inputs of each party will be matched with the expected income according to the costs and benefits matching principle. So the main requirement on CCA is that the cost in CCA must be actual cost occurred in companies and their affiliated parties' joint development and transferee of intangible assets, or joint providing or accepting labor services, which should not be additional payment belonging to the data of profit or revenue calculated on the actual cost, and the cost in comparable circumstances should be comparable with independent enterprises. During the period of CCA arrangement, its participants' cost sharing ratio shall consist with the expected future beneficial rights of assets or services.

第四节 转让定价及其法律管制
Section 4　Transfer Pricing and Its Legal Regulations

一、转让定价的概念
Concept of Transfer Pricing

跨国公司产业链日益延伸且日益全球化,有时甚至能够实现"从摇篮到坟墓"的全产业链覆盖。此种情形下,跨国公司集团内部成员之间交易频繁,此种内部交易的定价以及成员之间的利润分配已经成为日常的企业管理行为。即使没有避税动机,也面临定价或者利润分配合理性的挑战。经济全球化背景下,跨国公司通过生产、贸易和金融的跨国经营,从事

第十二章 国际逃避税及其法律规制
CHAPTER XII International Tax Evasion and Avoidance as Well as Their Legal Regulations

"无国界""跨国界"的经济活动,带来了种种国际税法问题,转让定价就是经济全球化及知识经济给国际税法带来的冲击与挑战之一。

The industrial chain of multinational enterprises is increasingly extended and globalized and sometimes may even realize the coverage of the whole industrial chain from cradle to grave. In this case, there are frequent transactions among group members, and the internal transactions' pricing policy and profit distribution among members have become daily business management behaviors. Even if there were no tax avoidance motivation, it is still confronted with the challenge of pricing or profit distribution rationality. Under the current economic globalization background, multinational enterprises are engaging in "stateless" and "cross-border" economic activities which have given rise to a variety of international tax law issues, and transfer pricing is one of most prominent issues among them, which is caused by globalization and intellectual economy.

转让定价是国际税法最为核心的问题,也是最难以规制的问题。转让定价规制的难点在于,跨国公司集团内部成员之间的关系,会给集团成员建立特定条件下不同于独立企业之间的交易定价。当独立企业之间进行交易时,它们之间的商业和财务关系往往是被市场所决定的。当关联企业之间进行交易时,尽管关联企业在交易时也复制市场机制进行定价,但是,它们之间的商业和财务关系可能无法直接被外部市场所影响。一方面,跨国公司进行转让定价行为不一定是出于避税之目的,更是经营战略之所需,我们不能简单地套用反避税规则来规制。另一方面,跨国公司将利润从高税国向低税国转移,实现跨国公司总体税负最小化,转让定价是其基本手段。

Transfer pricing is a core issue in international tax law and the most difficult to regulate. The difficulty to regulate transfer pricing mainly lies in that the relationship among members of an MNE group may permit the group members to establish special conditions in their intra-group relations that differ from those that would have been established between the group members acting as independent enterprises operating in open markets. When independent enterprises transact with each other, the conditions of their commercial and financial relations ordinarily are determined by market forces. When associated enterprises transact with each other, their commercial and financial relations may not be directly affected by external market forces in the samy way, although associated enterprises often seek to replicate the dynamic of market forces in their transactions with each other. On one hand, the transfer pricing behavior of multinationals is not necessarily for the purpose of tax avoidance, but more importantly for business strategies, therefore, we can't simply apply anti-tax-avoidance rules to regulate it. On the other hand, transfer pricing becomes an basic instrument for multinational enterprises to transfer profits from higher tax rate jurisdiction to lower ones to minimize their overall tax burden.

(二) 转让定价的法律管制
Main Regulation on Transfer Pricing

面对越来越多的转让定价问题,转让定价规则的开发,被理论界和实务界共同重视,并形成了体系化的转让定价规则。此类规则限制关联方针对财产或者服务的转让,设定不同于非关联方在类似转让中可能设定的价格的能力。

In confronting with more and more transfer pricing problems, the development of transfer pricing rules has attracted common attention both from theoretical and practical circles, and systematic transfer pricing rules have been formed.Transfer pricing rules are rules that limit the ability of related parties to set prices on transfers of property or services that are different from the prices that would be set in similar transfers involving unrelated parties.

(一)独立交易原则是转让定价规则的基础原则
Arm's Length Principle Is the Foundation Rules of Transfer Pricing

转让定价规则的本质,是基于可比的独立交易,为非独立交易确定合适的价格。用于比较的独立交易,可以是纳税人(即需要对其非独立交易进行定价的一方)与独立交易方之间的交易(即内部可比对象),也可以是非关联独立交易方之间的交易(即外部可比对象)。

The essence of transfer pricing rules is to determine the appropriate price for a non-arm's-length transaction based on a comparable arm's length transaction. The arm's length transaction used for comparison may be a transaction between the taxpayer (the person whose non-arm's-length transactions being priced) and an arm's length person (internal comparable) or between unrelated arm's length persons(external comparable).

独立交易原则是转让定价规则的基本原则,是基于非关联方在类似交易中收取的价格(或在某些情况下取得的利润),对关联方之间交易的转让价格予以确定的方法。所谓的独立交易价格,即针对关联方之间转让商品、服务或者无形资产,依据非关联方之间在类似交易中的价格予以确定的价格。

Arm's length principle is the foundation rule of transfer pricing, which is the establishment of transfer prices in transactions between related parties based on the prices charged (or sometimes the profits derived) in similar transactions between unrelated parties. The so called arm's length price is the price set on a transfer of goods, services, or intangible property between related persons that corresponds to the price that would be set in a similar transfer between unrelated persons.

按照国际惯例,合理的转让价格需要符合独立交易原则。如果纳税人在与关联方的交易中设定的转让价格,与纳税人在非关联方的可比交易中使用的价格相同,则转让价格可以被视为符合独立交易原则。因此,独立交易原则是转让定价规制的基本原则,已经成为国际习惯法。

According to international custom, an appropriate transfer price is one that meets the so-called arm's length principle. This principle is met if a taxpayer sets its transfer prices in its transactions with related persons so that those prices are the same as the prices used in comparable transactions with unrelated persons. Therefore, the arm's length principle is a fundamental principle in transfer pricing regulations and has become an international custom.

（二）独立交易原则下的具体转让定价规制方法
Specific Transfer Pricing Regulation Rules under Arm's Length Principle

到目前为止，在独立交易原则下主要形成了五种基本的转让定价法律管制方法。

Up to now, five basic transfer pricing regulation methods have been formed under the arm's length principle.

1. 可比非受控价格法

Comparable Uncontrolled Price Method

可比非受控价格法参照非关联方之间在类似情况下类似产品的销售，确定独立交易价格。如果存在可比销售交易，则可比非受控价格法就是首选方法。此法广泛应用于对石油、铁矿石、小麦和其他在公开商品市场上出售的商品进行定价。

The comparable uncontrolled price method establishes an arm's length price by reference to sales of similar products made between unrelated persons in similar circumstances. This method is the preferred method if comparable sales exist. It is widely used for pricing oil, iron ore, wheat, and other goods sold on public commodity markets.

2. 再销售价格法

Resale Price Method

再销售价格法即从最终销售给非关联方的售价中，减去适当的利润，以此设定关联方之间销售的独立交易价格。再销售价格法一般适用于再销售者未对商品进行改变外形、性能、结构或者更换商标等实质性增值加工的简单加工或者单纯购销业务。

The resale price method is a way to set the arm's length price for the sale of goods between related parties by subtracting an appropriate markup from the price at which the goods are ultimately sold to unrelated parties. This method is used for simple processing or simple purchase and sale business in which the re-seller has not changed the appearance, performance, structure of the goods or has not changed the trademark and other substantial value-added processing.

再销售价格法的可比性分析，应当特别考察关联交易与非关联交易中企业执行的功能、承担的风险、使用的资产和合同条款的差异，以及影响毛利率的其他因素，具体包括营销、分销、产品保障及服务功能，存货风险，机器、设备的价值及使用年限，无形资产的使用及价值，有价值的营销型无形资产，批发或者零售环节，商业经验，会计处理及管理效率等。

The comparative analysis of the re-sale price method shall examine, in particular, the functions performed by the enterprise in related and non-related transactions, the risks assumed, the assets used and the differences in the terms of the contract, as well as other factors affecting the gross margin, including marketing, distribution, product security and service functions, inventory risk, value and service life of machinery and equipment, use and value of intangible assets, valuable marketing intangible assets, wholesale or retail links, business experience, accounting treatment and management efficiency.

该方法通常适用于涉及购买与转售有形资产的案例中，且转售者不对转售物质进行实质性的改变或者增加实质性的价值。一般而言，包装、再包装、贴标签或者小的装配，不构成实质性的改变。但是如果将无形资产附加于有形资产上，从而增加有形资产价格的，就属于实质性改变，此时再销售价格法不再适用。

This method is generally applicable in cases involving the purchase and resale of tangible assets where the re-seller does not materially alter or add material value to the resale goods. Generally speaking, repackaging, labeling, or simple assembly does not constitute material change scenario. However, if intangible assets are attached to the tangible assets, thereby increasing the tangible assets' price, it is a material change, and the resale price method is no longer applicable.

3. 成本加成法
Cost-Plus Method

成本加成法以关联销售方的制造成本和其他成本作为出发点，确定独立交易价格。销售方的成本乘以适当的利润率，其结果加上销售方的成本，即可确定独立交易价格。利润率的确定，可以参照销售方在与非关联方的交易中，或者可比非关联方在与非关联方的类似交易中所获取的毛利率。成本加成法适用于涉及制造、装配，或者生产向关联方销售的产品的情况。

The cost-plus method uses the manufacturing and other costs of the related seller as the starting point in establishing the arm's length price. The seller's costs are then multiplied by an appropriate profit percentage, and the result is added to the seller's costs to determine the arm's length price. The profit margin can be determined by referring to the gross profit margin obtained by the seller in transactions with non-related parties or comparable to similar transactions between non-related parties and non-related parties. The cost-plus method applies to cases involving the manufacture, assembly, production of products for sale to related parties.

成本加成法的应用缺陷在于，该方法在计算利润时只考虑关联企业生产者的利润，而对关联企业的买方能否获得利润以及获得的利润是否合理则一概不予考虑。这样很容易使利润的计算发生偏差，导致关联企业买方的利润过高或者过低。

The defect of the cost-plus method is that it only considers the associated producer's profits and whether the associated buyer can obtain profits or not. The obtained profits are reasonable nor not will not be considered at all. In this way, it is very easy to make deviation in profit calculation, which may lead to the associated buyer's profit too high or too low.

4. 利润分割法
Profit-Split Method

利润分割法是将跨国公司在全球范围内的利润，按照位于各个国家的成员对利润的贡献比例，分配给各成员的一种方法。当上述三种传统方法都不适用时，通常采用利润分割法。在利润分割法下，在同一业务链开展业务活动的关联方的全球应税收入，根据各关联方对取得该收入所做的贡献，在各关联方之间进行分配。如果关联企业集团有一条以上的产品线，利润分割法可以分别应用于每条产品线。在利润分割法之下，还可以继续划分为可比利润分割法和剩余利润分割法两种更加具体的方法。

Profit split method is a method for the allocation of the worldwide profits of a multinational enterprise among its members in various countries in proportion to their contributions to the earning of the profits. The profit split method typically is employed when none of the three traditional methods can be applied. Under the profit split method, the worldwide taxable income of related parties engaging in a common line of business is allocated among the related parties in proportion to their contributions to earning the income. If a group of affiliated companies has more than one product line, the profit split method might be applied to each product line. Under the profit split method, it can be further divided into two more detailed methods: the comparable profit split method and the residual profit split method.

5. 交易净利润法

Transactional Net Margin Method

交易净利润法是确定关联方交易中转让价格的一种方法。其通常基于从事类似活动的各方取得的利润与某种经济指标(如投资资本或者总收入)的比率。在交易净利润法下,纳税人必须为自己或者关联方(被测试方),针对一系列交易,确定符合独立交易原则的利润区间。如果被测试方这些交易所获得的利润位于该区间内,则其转让价格可以得到税务机关的认可。如果其利润不在该区间之内,则税务机关可能会调整其转让价格,使利润位于该区间内(一般是调整至中位值)。

Transactional net margin method is a method for determining transfer prices in transactions between related parties, typically based on the ratio of profits earned by parties engaged in similar activities to some economic indicator, such as invested capital or gross receipts. Under this method, the taxpayer must establish, either for itself or a related party(the tested party), an arm's length range of profits for a set of transactions. If the tested party's reported profits from those transactions fall within that range, its transfer prices will be accepted by the tax authorities. If its profits fall outside that range, the tax authorities may adjust transfer prices so that the profits fall within the range, typically at the midpoint. The greatest advantage of this method is that the required data is relatively easy to be obtained.

交易净利润法通常也被称为可比利润法,前者是OECD转让定价指南的说法,后者则是美国的说法,实际上两者并无本质区别。可比利润法明确以营业利润作为比较的指标,而营业利润是从毛利润中扣除营业费用所得出的利润,不同的营业费用已经体现出了不同企业之间的功能差异,所以,扣除营业费用也就意味着可以同时排除不同企业间的功能差异,使其营业利润达到相似的程度,这样一来,可比利润法允许独立企业与关联企业之间存在更大的差异,使得该方法的适用范围更加广泛和灵活。

Transactional net margin method is also known as comparable profit method. The former is called by the OECD Transfer Pricing Guideline, while the latter is called by the US transfer pricing rules. There are no essential differences between both of them. The comparable profit method makes it clear that it adopts operating profit as comparative indicator. Because the operating profit is calculated by the gross profit deducted the operating expenses, which may eliminate the functional differences between different enterprises at the same time so as to make the operating profit in similar degree. As a result, the comparable profit method allows a greater difference between independent enterprises and the affiliated enterprises, and makes the application scope of this method more comprehensive and flexible.

简言之,前三种方法以价格比较为基础,后两种方法以利润比较为基础。

In short, the first three methods are based on price comparisons, while the latter two are based on profit comparisons.

(三) 转让定价规则的整体演变
Overall Rule Evolution of Transfer Pricing

目前已经形成了三种转移定价法律调整制度——独立交易法、统一合并公司税基法 (Common Consolidated Corporate Tax Base,简称CCCTB) 和全球公式分摊法。独立交易法是转移定价法律调整的基本制度,OECD、联合国以及代表国际税法另一流派的美国,都主张对转移定价的判断和调整遵循独立交易原则,使其具有了国际习惯法的地位。近年来,受到企业集团内部交易增加、知识产权等无形资产重要性在经营中不断增强的冲击与挑战,独立交易法显现出其适用的局限性和局促,受到很多批评与质疑,但仍然是规制转移定价问题的主要方法。全球公式分摊法被认为是对独立交易法最可能的替代性选择。但是,该方法过于激进,要求的国际合作水平之高,是当前以及短期内,甚至是长期内都难以达到的。欧盟提出的CCCTB则较为温和,是全球公式分摊法在超国家层面上的首次适用。其主要价值在于,成功地解决了独立交易法和全球公式分摊法在现阶段应用的困境,因而成为转移定价法律调整的新思维。全球公式分摊法本是一种国内法,主要在美国的大多数州,加拿大的一些省份以及巴西等少数国家内适用。将其适用于国际税法,则是一种在全球范围内从整体上划分跨国公司利润的方法,但是非跨国公司总部所在国的税收管辖权与税收收入会受到消极影响。该方法有广阔的应用潜力,未来很可能成为国际性转移定价规制的主要方法之一。从发展前景来看,公平交易法、CCCTB和全球公式分摊法这三套规则,各有其合理性与利弊,将来很可能会形成各行其是,在规制转移定价问题上各显身手的局面。

There are three sets of transfer pricing rules, i.e, the arm's length principle, common consolidated corporate tax base rules and global formulary apportionment method. Arm's length principle is the fundamental one. The OECD, UN and the US which represents the other school in international tax law, all advocate that decision and adjustment of transfer pricing being subjected to this principle, thus making it a customary international law rule. In recent years, the arm's length principle has been seriously challenged by great increase of within-MNE group business transaction and of intangibles in manufacturing and marketing. The principle's limitations have been seen and criticized and questioned by many persems. Nevertheless, it is still a main approach in transfer pricing regulation. The global formulary apportionment method might be alternative to the arm's length method. However, it needs very high degree of international cooperation, which can neither be accepted nor be realized by international community in a short period, even in the long run. The EU's CCCTB proposal is more modest and is also the formulary apportionment method's first application at super-national level. Its main value lies in that it can successfully solve the problems that both the arm's length method and global formulary method can't do. Therefore it is a new idea in transfer pricing regulations. The formula apportionment method is a domestic law, mainly being used in most states of the US, some provinces of Canada and some countries such as Brazil. Applying it as the international tax law means that it is a method to divide MNEs' total profit among their enterprises globally. Revenue loss of non-MNEs' headquarter situating countries is inevitable. This approach has great potential and it is very likely to be a main method in international transfer pricing. The arm's length method, CCCTB and global formulary method, each has its rationality and has both good and bad sides. They will play their roles in regulating transfer pricing in the future.

无形资产越来越介入跨国公司生产与经营的各个环节,触动了传统转让定价法律调整制度的基础,诱发了其演变。独立交易法下,传统的三个以价格为基础的规制方法(可比非受控价格法、再销售价格法、成本加价法)的应用基础——价格的可比性,遭到了极大的冲击和挑战。为了克服寻找可比价格的困难,才开发出了以利润比较为基础的方法(即,可比利润法或者说交易净利润法、利润分割法)。随着无形资产在跨国公司价值创造中重要性的凸显,以及无形资产在企业价值创造中的整体性,利润法在规制无形资产转让定价方面也显出乏力与无奈。CCCTB和全球公式分摊法受到重视,主要在于两者是对公司的全球所得作整体处理,把无形资产创造的价值体现在生产、经营的各个环节上,间接地解决了独立交易法下所需要的可比对象寻找、价值评估等难题。

Intangible assets are increasingly involved in all links of the production and operation of multinational corporations, which touches the foundation of the traditional transfer pricing legal adjustment system and induce its evolution. According to the independent transaction method, price comparability, which is the application basis of the three traditional price-based regulation methods (comparable uncontrolled price method, resale price method, cost increase method), has been greatly impacted and challenged. In order to overcome the difficulty of finding comparable prices, a method based on profit comparison has been developed (that is, comparable profit method or transaction net profit method, profit division method). With the importance of intangible assets in the value creation of multinational corporations and the integrity of intangible assets in the value creation of enterprises, profit law also shows fatigue and helplessness in regulating the transfer pricing of intangible assets. CCCTB and global formula allocation method are paid attention to, mainly because they deal with the global income of the company as a whole, embody the value created by intangible assets in all aspects of production and operation, and indirectly solve the problems of finding comparable objects and evaluating the value under the independent trading method.

《OECD转让定价指南》集中在转让定价领域引起的原则性问题上,其财政事务委员会试图持续推进该领域的工作。

OECD Transfer Pricing Guidelines focus on the main issues of principle that arise in the transfer pricing area. Its Committee on Fiscal Affairs intends to continue its work in this area.

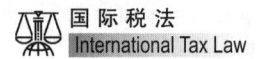

第五节 防止国际逃税与避税的国际税收合作
Section 5　Prevention of International Tax Evasion and Avoidance by International Tax Cooperation

跨国公司在全球经营,各国税务当局的税收管辖权则局限于疆界。随着跨国公司与各国税务当局的博弈能力日益增强,单纯依靠各国国内法措施,很难有效地管制日益严重的国际逃税和避税行为,只有通过国际税收合作,才能有效地制止这种现象。目前已经形成的国际税收合作方式,主要包括税收情报交换、税款征收互助、预约定价安排、联合审计等。

While international corporations operating globally, the tax jurisdiction of national tax authorities is limited to borders. With the increasing gaming capacity between transnational corporations and authorities in different countries, it is difficult to control the increasingly serious international tax evasion and tax avoidance by relying on domestic legal measures. Only through international tax cooperation can this phenomenon be effectively prevented. The main measures of international tax cooperation include information exchange, mutual assistance in tax collection, advance pricing arrangement, joint audit, and so on.

一、税收情报交换
Information Exchange

税收情报交换是指各国税务主管当局之间为了税收征管目的而批次交换情报的过程。为了对跨国经营的纳税人实行合理征税,既避免双重征税,又有效打击国际逃避税,就必须对其跨国经营状况有清楚的了解和把握。一国的税务当局对其居民纳税人在境外经济活动情报的掌握,是防止、纠正国际逃避税的基础。

Information exchange refers to the process in which information exchange is done in batches between competent tax authorities of various countries for tax administration purposes. In order to impose reasonable tax on taxpayers of transnational operation, and avoid double taxation and fight against international tax evasion and avoidance effectively, it is necessary to have a clear understanding and grasp of trans-border taxpayers' transnational operations. One country's tax authorities knowledge of its resident taxpayers' economic activities abroad is the basis for preventing and correcting international tax evasion and avoidance.

纳税人涉税信息的可及性,是税务机关进行税收征管的基础,尤其是对跨境纳税人的相关信息的获得,很多时候决定着税务机关能否进行有效的反避税。但是,一国的税务当局仅靠其自身力量掌握其居民纳税人境外经济活动的情报很难,各国税务当局分别贡献自身力量,与其他国家的税务当局进行税收情报交换合作,是最普遍和最有效的防止国际逃避税的机制之一。

The accessibility of tax-related information is the basis of tax administration, especially the acquisition of cross-border taxpayers' relevant information, which often determines whether tax authorities can carry out effective anti tax avoidance or not. However, it is difficult for one country's tax authorities to grasp the information of its residents tax payers' overseas economic activities information only by themselves. Tax authorities of each country should contribute their own strength to share tax information with tax authorities of other countries. Tax information exchange is one of the most common and effective mechanisms to prevent international tax evasion and tax avoidance.

税收情报交换的法律基础有二:一是在国际双边或多边协定中,一般都订立有有效税收情报交换的条款;二是国家间订立的专项税收情报交换协议。

There are two bases for tax information exchange: one is in international bilateral or multilateral tax treaties, there are generally provisions for effective information exchange; the other is specific tax information exchange agreements concluded between countries.

二、税款征收互助
Mutual Assistance in Tax Collection

光有税收情报交换不能实现各国税务机关依法足额征缴税款的目的。比如,当纳税人在未完全缴纳其应纳税款之前离境,或者纳税人在境内已经没有任何财产可供执行时,该国税务机关根本无法采取任何有效的执行措施。

Tax information exchange alone can't achieve the purpose of tax collection. For example, when a taxpayer has left the country before paying his or her tax payable, or when a taxpayer has no property in the country to enforce, then the country's tax authority can't take any effective enforcement measures at all.

鉴于近年来经济全球化的迅猛发展进一步刺激了纳税人国际逃避税现象的泛滥,加强有关国家税务主管当局之间的税收征收互助,也日益显得必要,2003年修订后的OECD范本增设了缔约国之间进行有关税款征收协助的条款。

In view of the rapid development of economic globalization which further simulates the proliferation of international tax evasion and avoidance, it is increasingly necessary to strengthen the tax collection mutual assistance among relevant national tax authorities. The revised OECD Model Convention in 2003 added the tax collection assistance provisions.

三、预约定价安排
Advance Pricing Arrangement

预约定价安排(APA),是指企业与一个或者多个相关税务机关之间达成的协议。企业就其未来年度关联交易的定价原则和计算方法,向税务机关提出申请,与税务机关按照独立交易原则协商、确认其关联交易的定价事宜。简单来说就是我们常说的税企事前约定，双方在关联交易发生前就通过适当的标准来确定关联交易的价格或者利润率并达成一致。

The advance pricing arrangement (APA) refers to an agreement reached by an enterprise with one or more related tax authorities. The enterprise needs to apply for tax authorities for its future related transactions' pricing issues, and consultant with tax authorities according to the arm's length principle. In short, APA is what we often call the advance agreement between (or among) tax authorities and enterprise, who reach an agreement through appropriate standards to determine the controlled transaction's price or profit margin before the occurrence of controlled transactions.

预约定价安排一般可涵盖各种关联交易类型，如有形资产的购销、转让和使用，无形资产的转让和使用，融通资金，劳务等。一般采取的方式，是以法律法规的形式，纳入特别纳税调整中。当然，具体实施起来，各国仍然有所不同，但大体包括预约定价安排的适用范围、实施程序等内容。预约定价协议也被我国引入，并且在我国得到了蓬勃发展。

The advance pricing arrangement generally covers all kinds of related transactions, such as purchase, sale, transfer and use of tangible assets, transfer and use of intangible assets, financing and services, etc.

对于各国税务当局来说，预约定价协议可以有效降低其反避税成本。对于跨国公司来说，预约定价协议可以使其就关联交易的定价提前取得税务机关的认可，实现对其交易、利润等的稳定预期，从而有效避免税务局后期转让定价调整所带来的经济性双重征税。因此预约定价协议受到跨国公司的青睐，越来越多的跨国公司开始提出预约定价申请。现在，预约定价安排这种税企合作遵从税法的措施，是较为成熟的反避税措施，符合现代民主协商原则，已经被广大国家所采纳。

APA's general way is in the form of law and regulation into the special tax adjustments. For tax authorities of various countries, APA can effectively reduce their anti-tax avoidance burden, while for multinational enterprises, APA can make their controlled price policy being pre-determined by tax authorities which may give them stable expectations on their transaction and profits. Therefore, APA is favored by multinational companies, and more and more multinational companies apply for APA. Now, this tax authorities and enterprises' cooperation to comply with tax law of tax compliance measure is a relatively mature anti-tax measure, which has been adopted by the majority of countries around the world for it conforms to the modern democratic consultation principle.

按照预约定价安排参与主体的范围划分，可以将预约定价安排划分为单边、双边和多边预约定价安排三种类型。单边预约定价安排是一个跨国公司和一个国家的税务机关达成的协议，单边预约定价安排主要适用于涉及的大量交易规模较小的境外交易。单边预约定价安排只能提供给企业关于其在一国境内关联交易的定价方法和计算过程的确定性，但是不能保证有效避免海外税务机关对其实施转让定价审计或者调整，因此，单边预约定价安排不能避免国际双重征税。双边预约定价安排是一个跨国公司与两个国家税务机关达成的协议;我国税务机关对于双边预约定价安排申请,还会考虑案件所涉对方国家(地区)的谈签意愿及其对案件的重视程度。多边预约定价安排,就是一个跨国公司与三个及以上国家税务机关达成预约定价安排协议。多边预约定价安排更加适合于那些具有潜在的大额收入、在外国面临税务调整的高风险或其他为实现有效税务管理而产生的影响因素等复杂的转让定价情形。这些税务机关需要就企业的关联方跨境交易的定价方法和计算方法达成协议。双边或者多边预约定价能够有效避免国际双重征税,提供给纳税人关于转让定价政策的确定性。

An APA may be categorized as unilateral, bilateral or multilateral based on the number of competent authorities involved in the APA. Unilateral APA is an agreement between one multinational company and one country's tax authority and it is mainly applicable to a large number of transactions involving small scale trans-border transactions. A unilateral APA can only provide certainty to the enterprise's pricing methodologies and calculation process with respect to its related party transactions within one country (region), but cannot ensure the effective avoidance of transfer pricing audits or adjustments from the tax authority of the overseas related Parties it transact with. Thus, a unilateral APA cannot prevent international double taxation. Bilateral APA is an agreement among one multinational company and two countries' tax authorities. As for Chinese tax authorities, they will also take into account the negotiation willingness of the other country(region) and the importance they attached to the case when applying for bilateral APA.Multilateral APA is an agreement reached among one multilateral company and three or more countries' tax authorities which is more applicable to those complex transfer pricing situations involving potentially large amounts of revenue, high risk of tax adjustment in foreign countries, or other factors in the implementation of effective tax administrations. These authorities will need to reach an agreement with regard to the pricing methodologies and calculation process used in the cross-border related party transactions of the enterprise in question. Bilateral and multilateral APAs can be used to effectively avoid international double taxation and provide certainty regarding the transfer pricing policies of the enterprise.

预约定价安排的程序即预约定价谈签的程序。各国APA的程序差异不大。我国预约定价安排的谈签和执行经过预备会谈、谈签意向、分析评估、正式申请、协商签署和监控执行6个阶段。

The procedure of APA refers to that of the negotiation and signing of APA stages. There is little difference between different countrys' APA procedures. As for China, APA process involves the following six stages: pre-filing meeting, letter of intent, analysis and evaluation, formal application, negotiation and signing, and implementation and monitoring.

(四) 联合审计

Joint Audit

跨境税收审计合作是国际上反对逃避税合作的重要举措,经历了从境外税务调查和同步税务审计直至联合审计三个发展阶段。其中,前两种方式属于传统上的跨境税收审计合作模式,两者从性质上仍然属于税收情报交换的范畴,并且具体的实施仍然依赖于各国税务当局的单方行为,是比较松散的反对国际逃避税的国际税务合作。

Cross-border tax audit cooperation is an important measure for international anti tax avoidance and evasion, which has gone through three development stages from cross-border tax investigation, simultaneous tax audit to joint audit. Among them, the first two belong to traditional cross-border tax audit cooperation mode, and they still belong to the scope of tax information exchange in nature, and their specific implementation still depends on tax authorities of various countries' unilateral behavior, which are relatively loose international tax cooperation against international tax evasion and avoidance.

联合审计是由税收管理论坛推出的一种国际税收合作新思维。其基本思路是由两个或者多个国家的主管税务当局组成一个审计团队,针对同一跨国公司进行联合税务稽查。联合审计思想的产生虽然来自同步税务稽查的实践,但审计的范围更加广泛,各参与方之间的合作更加紧密。

Joint audit is a new idea in international tax administration cooperation which was proposed by the Tax Administration Forum. Its basic thinking is to organize a joint audit team by two or more competent tax authorities to carry out a joint tax audit which is aiming at one multinational corporation group's tax issues and/or transactions. Although the idea of joint audit comes from the practice of simultaneous tax investigation, its scope is more broader than simultaneous tax investigation and the cooperation among all parties are more closer.

联合审计除了具有反避税和避免双重征税、减少国际税收争端等一般国际税法的价值之外,还对各国税务当局、跨国纳税人和发展中国家等有特殊的价值。当前联合审计发展所面临的挑战主要来自各国相关国内法的限制、纳税人的保密性需求以及发展中国家所面临的特殊挑战等三个方面。但是这些都可以通过交流和合作得到解决。作为资本进出口大国和发展中国家双重身份的中国,既没有同步稽查也没有联合审计的实践经验,我们必须重视联合审计的探究和实践工作,同时从立足中国国情推动联合审计和推进能力建设两方面作出努力。

Besides its general international tax law values such as anti-tax avoidance, prevention of double taxation, international tax disputes reducing etc., joint audit also has special values to the tax authorities around the world, the transnational taxpayers as well as the developing countries. Nowadays the main challenges in the development of joint audit are from the limits in the domestic law and the taxpayers' confidentiality requirements as well as the developing countries' participation. But those difficulties may all be settled by communications and cooperation between participating parties. China has no experience both in simultaneous audit and joint audit. However, as an important capital importing and exporting country, we should pay attention to the research on joint audit, and make efforts in two ways. Firstly, we should promote joint audit based on the national condition in China. Secondly, we should promate the capacity building.

第十二章　国际逃避税及其法律规制
CHAPTER XII International Tax Evasion and Avoidance as Well as Their Legal Regulations

第六节　反避税案例
Section 6　Anti-tax Avoidance Cases

本案例是一个转让定价的案例。①

This is a transfer pricing case.

在对纳税人申报的2017年度关联申报资料进行审核的过程中,淄博市税务局主管税务人员发现某上市公司(母公司)及其关联公司(子公司)在关联交易中将利润留存在低税率地的关联公司,从而造成少缴企业所得税的风险。

In the process of examining the related declaration data declared by taxpayers in 2017, the tax officials in charge of Zibo Taxation Bureau found that a listed company (parent company) and its affiliated company (subsidiary company) have remained their related party transactions' profits in the related company which is located in low tax rate area which increases the risk of corporate income tax underpayment.

一、案例简介
Introduction to the Case

1. 母公司

Parent Company

该公司有员工455余人,注册资本为42 044万元,2010年12月在深交所A股上市。公司产品包括装饰原纸、表层耐磨纸、无纺壁纸原纸三大系列500多个花色品种,产品出口到30多个国家和地区。公司采用直销的销售模式,由终端客户直接向公司下订单,公司直接将货物发给客户并与其结算。该公司2014—2016年度经营收入分别为253 504万元、234 076万元和270 230万元,企业所得税适用税率为25%。

The company has 455 employees, and a registered capital of 420.44 million yuan. It was listed in A shares of Shengzhen Stock Exchange in December 2010. The company's products include decorative base paper, surface wear-resistant paper, non-woven wallpaper base paper three series of more than 500 varieties. The products are exported to more than 30 countries and regions. The company adopts a direct sales model, that is end customers place orders directly to the company, and the company sends the goods directly to the customer and settles with it. The operating income of the company in 2014—2016 was 2.535,4 billion yuan, 2.340,76 billion yuan and 27.023 billion yuan respectively and the applicable tax rate for enterprise income tax is 25%.

---

① 李丽、刘莉、姚书琦著:《一起关联交易转让定价反避税案,补缴税款600多万》,载《国际税收》2019年第1期。

2. 子公司

Subsidiaries

该公司是以生产装饰原纸为主业的特种纸生产企业,有员工1 148余人,注册资本为18 000万元,是国家火炬计划重点高新技术企业,拥有山东省装饰原纸工程技术研究中心、院士工作站和14条国际先进的特种纸生产线。该公司2014—2016年经营收入分别为226 675万元、217 096万元和249 117万元,企业所得税适用税率为15%。

The company is a special paper production enterprise with more than 1,148 employees and a registered capital of 180 million yuan. It is a key high-tech enterprise of the National Torch Program. It has Shandong decorative base paper engineering technology research center, academician workstation and 14 international advanced special paper production lines. The operating income of the company in 2014—2016 was 2.266,75 billion yuan, 2.170,96 billion yuan and 2.491,17 billion yuan respectively, and the applicable tax rate of enterprise income tax is 15%.

3. 母子公司关联交易情况

Associated Transactions of Parent-subsidiary Companies

根据母子公司购销合同约定,交易数量以母公司当月销售数量作为双方的交易数量,交易价格以母公司最终售价扣除1.5%的毛利作为双方的交易价格(表12-1)。

According to the purchase and sale contract of parent and subsidiary company, the transaction quantity is the monthly sales quantity of the parent company as the transaction quantity of both parties, and the transaction price is the final price of the parent company minus 1.5% gross profit as the transaction price of both parties (table 12-1).

表12-1　母子公司2014—2016年关联交易情况　　　　　　　　　　单位:万元

年　度	主要关联方	关联交易类型	关联交易内容	金　额
2014年	子公司	有形资产所有权受让	装饰原纸	226 675
2015年	子公司	有形资产所有权受让	装饰原纸	210 201
2016年	子公司	有形资产所有权受让	装饰原纸	249 031
合　计				685 907

(二) 避税疑点

Suspicion of Tax Avoidance

通过采集企业填报的关联业务往来报告表、财务报表,利用互联网收集可比企业利润水平指标,本书综合绘制盈利能力指标对比表、2012—2016年中国造纸行业毛利润走势图进行疑点分析。

By collecting the related business transaction report form and financial statement, using the Internet to collect the profit level index of comparable enterprises, the comparative table of profitability index and the trend chart of gross profit in China's paper industry in 2012—2016 are comprehensively drawn to analyze the doubtful points.

1. 母子公司利润水平对比

Comparison of Profit Levels of Parent-subsidiary Companies

从表12-2可以看出，子公司息税前营业利润率、营业利润率、毛利率三项指标均高于母公司相关指标，说明子公司的盈利能力远远大于母公司，而母公司与子公司关联销售定价毛利率仅为实际销售价格的1.5%，明显不符合独立交易原则，造成大额利润留在享受高新技术企业优惠的子公司，存在调节利润规避企业所得税的风险。

As can be seen from table 12-2, the operating profit margin before interest and tax, operating profit margin and gross profit margin of the subsidiary company before interest and tax are all higher than those of the parent company, indicating that the profitability of the subsidiary company is far greater than that of the parent company.

表12-2 盈利能力分析指标对比

分析指标	母公司			子公司			A纸业（同行业）			B纸业（同行业）		
	2014年	2015年	2016年	2014年	2015年	2016年	2014年	2015年	2016年	2014年	2015年	2016年
息税前营业利润率	0.016%	0.017%	0.006%	0.14%	0.15%	0.06%	0.05%	0.044%	0.078%	0.12%	0.15%	0.14%
营业利润率	0.008%	0.011%	0.011%	0.132%	0.138%	0.056%	−0.017%	−0.056%	0.03%	0.07%	0.095%	0.1%
毛利率	0.037%	0.035%	0.025%	0.22%	0.22%	0.142%	0.13%	0.118%	0.146%	0.196%	0.23%	0.212%

2. 与可比企业利润水平对比

Comparison with Comparable Enterprise Profit Levels

利用互联网收集山东省同行业A公司、B公司2014—2016年利润率指标与母子公司进行对比后发现，母公司的毛利率远低于A公司、B公司，说明其盈利能力远远低于同行业企业，反映出母公司关联采购、关联销售的定价方面可能存在转让定价不合理的风险。子公司营业利润率指标高于A公司、B公司，说明子公司的盈利能力高于同行业企业。从母子公司与可比企业盈利能力对比来看，母公司盈利能力偏低，不符合经济业务实质，存在利润留存低税率的子公司造成少缴企业所得税的风险。

Using the Internet to collect the profit margin index of Shandong same industry A company and B company in 2014 and 2016, it is found that the gross profit margin of the parent company is much lower than that of A company and B company, which indicates that its profitability is far lower than that of the same industry enterprise. From the comparison between parent and subsidiary companies and comparable enterprises, the profitability of the parent company is on the low side, which does not accord with the essence of economic business, and there is the risk that the subsidiary company with low tax rate of profit retention will pay less enterprise income tax.

3. 与同行业利润水平对比

Comparison with the Profit Level of the Same Industry

从全国造纸行业毛利润走势图（图12-1）的对比分析可以看出，子公司2014、2015年毛利率高出全国造纸行业9%左右，2016年基本持平，总体来看其明显高于全国毛利率水平，存在盈利能力偏高、人为留存大额利润的风险。

From the comparative analysis of the gross profit trend chart of the national paper industry (figure 12-1), it can be seen that the gross profit rate of the subsidiary company in 2014 and 2015 is about 9% higher than that of the national paper industry, and basically flat in 2016. Overall, it is obviously higher than the national gross profit level, and there is the risk of high profitability and artificial retention of large profits.

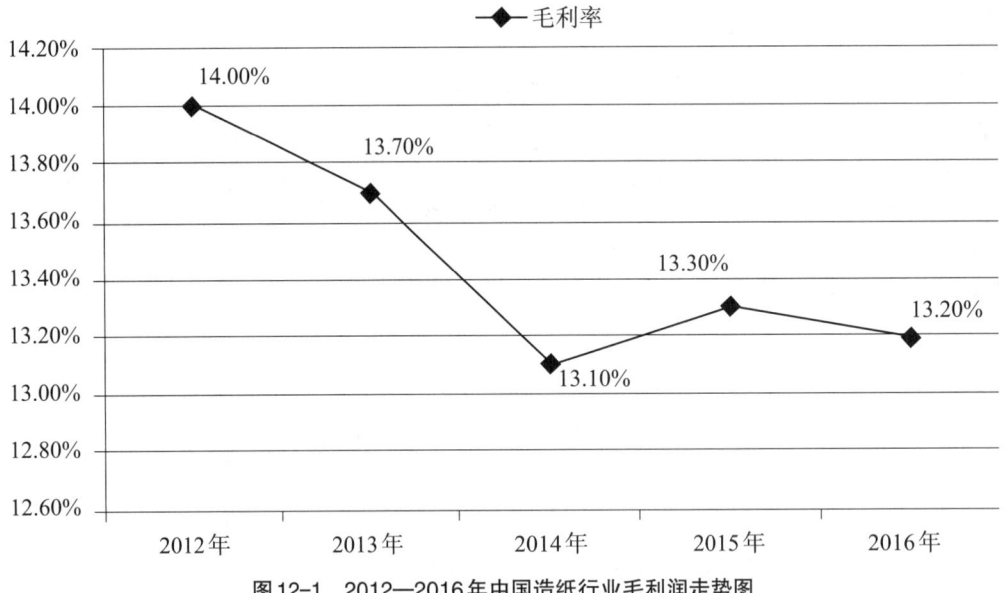

图 12-1　2012—2016年中国造纸行业毛利润走势图

4. 企业功能风险分析对比

Comparison Analysis of Enterprise Functional Risk

根据企业报送的《报告企业信息表》及经主管中心所日常管理，母子公司经营管理与实质控制属于典型的"两个牌子，一套人马"：母公司负担行政、人事和资金等管理和服务职能及风险，同时承担市场推广及销售功能；子公司主要承担全部的生产、研发功能和部分采购功能。结合母子公司利润率指标分析，母子公司在生产经营活动中存在承担的功能风险与利润回报不匹配的风险。

According to the Enterprise Information Form submitted by the enterprise and the daily management of the competent center, the management and substantive control of parent and subsidiary companies belong to the typical "two brands, one set of people". The parent company bears the administrative, personnel and capital management and service functions and risks, as well as marketing and sales functions. The subsidiary mainly bears the whole production, research and development, and procurement functions. Combined with the profit rate index analysis of parent and subsidiary companies, there is a risk that the functional risk and profit return of parent and subsidiary companies do not match in their production and operation activities.

三、工作措施
Working Measures

1. 团队攻关,三级应对
Team Tackling Key Problems and Three-level Response

主管税务机关向上级主管部门汇报并成立了由法规税政科、税源管理科、征管科、稽查局及中心所业务骨干组成的关联申报资料审核小组,在反避税小组的指导下,形成了市、区、中心所三级攻关团队,共同研究探讨确定工作方向。为保证反避税工作顺利开展,关联申报资料审核小组在关键环节和重点问题上及时向省局请示,取得了国家税务总局、省局反避税专家的大力支持和精心的业务指导。

The competent tax authorities reported to the competent departments at higher levels and set up an audit group of relevant declaration materials composed of the administrative departments of laws and regulations, the tax source management department, the collection and management department, the inspection bureau and the business backbone of the center. Under the guidance of the anti-tax avoidance group, a three-level team of the city, district and center was formed to study and determine the direction of work. In order to ensure the smooth development of anti-tax avoidance work, the relevant declaration data audit team promptly asked the provincial bureau for instructions on key links and key issues, and obtained strong support and careful business guidance from the State Administration of Taxation and the provincial bureau anti-tax avoidance experts.

2. 采集资料,验证推断
Collecting Data and Verifying Inference

关联申报资料审核小组要求母子公司提供签订的购销合同、采购计划等资料,同时要求其填写报送《企业功能风险分析表》,深入了解掌握了购销流程、定价原则、运转模式及各自承担的功能等情况,进一步验证了前期的分析判断,为下一步开展谈判工作打下了坚实的基础。

The audit team requested parent-subsidiary companies to provide information on purchase and sale contracts, purchase plans, etc., and requested them to complete and submit the Enterprise Functional Risk Analysis Form, to gain an in-depth understanding of the purchase and sale process, pricing principles, operating modes and their respective functions.

3. 服务引导,提示风险
Providing Guidance, Reminding of Risks

关联申报资料审核小组强化服务意识,以"关联申报说明会"的形式与该公司负责人及财务人员进行了多次座谈,向企业提示存在的纳税风险。

The related declaration data audit team strengthened the service consciousness and held many discussions with the company's responsible person and financial personnel in the form of "related declaration meeting" to prompt the enterprise for the tax risk.

4. 勇于尝试,保障入库

Willing to Try and the collection of Taxes Ensuring

在新上线的"金三"优化版国际税收岗责配置不够健全的前提下,主管所人员会同前台大厅人员大胆尝试,多次对特别纳税调整模块进行测试,从报表填报、基准利率确定、利息加收测算、税款开票等各个环节进行全过程模拟,确保自查补税的顺利入库。

Although the newly launched "Jin San" optimized version of international tax post responsibility allocation is not perfect, the personnel in charge of the institute, together with the front hall personnel, boldly try and test the special tax adjustment module many times, and ensured that the supplementary tax was conected smoothly.

（四）案件处理
Case Processing

1. 企业提出的意见

Comments by Enterprises

（1）对于母公司留存1.5%的毛利作为关联双方的交易价格,是由于母公司只承担管理和销售职能,自身不具备盈利能力,留存1.5%的毛利保证其运营是合理的。

1.5% of the gross profit retained by the parent company as the transaction price of the affiliated parties is due to the fact that the parent company only undertakes management and sales functions and does not have profitability, and the retained 1.5% gross profit ensures that its operation is reasonable.

（2）与同行业的利润水平是没有可比性的,因为每个企业都有其自身的特性,盈利能力往往是由企业自身特性决定的,不能一概而论。

There is no comparability with the profit level of the same industry, because each enterprise has its own characteristics. Profitability is often determined by its own characteristics, and it can not be generalized.

2. 存在的问题

Challenges Faced

一是可比企业的选择难。

First, the choice of comparable enterprises is difficult.

山东省乃至全国范围很难找到生产产品品种、经营规模、运作模式基本相同的企业。

In Shandong Province and even the whole country, it is difficult to find an enterprise with basically the same product variety, business scale and operation mode.

二是企业功能风险分析难。

Second, the analysis of enterprise functional risk is difficult.

关联企业之间的功能往往你中有我、我中有你,很难清晰地划分各自应承担的功能,且功能比例也无明确参数。

The functions of affiliated enterprises are often intertwined, so it is difficult to divide their respective functions clearly, and the proportion of functions has no clear parameters.

三是可参照的典型案例难。

Third, it is difficult to find typical cases for reference.

按照典型案例指引思路,经过筛选,在山东省内未找到可参照的典型案例。

According to the typical case guidelines, through selection, no typical cases can be found in Shandong Province.

3. 案件处理

Case Handling

从母公司填报的《企业功能风险分析表》可以看出,母公司承担行政人事管理服务、市场推广及销售功能,不否认子公司承担的生产、研发功能是经营活动中的重要功能。但母公司留存1.5%的毛利与其承担的功能不匹配,存在将部分利润人为调节到享受税收优惠低税率的子公司的风险。

It can be seen from the Enterprise Function Risk Analysis Form filled out by the parent company that the parent company undertakes the functions of administrative personnel management service, marketing promotion and sales, and does not deny that the production and R & D functions undertaken by the subsidiary company are important functions in business activities. But the parent company retains 1.5% gross profit which does not match its functions. There is a risk of intentionally adjusting some profits to subsidiaries enjoying low tax concessions.

关联申报资料审核小组利用"关联申报说明会"形式上门为企业提供纳税服务,该公司认识到自身存在特别纳税调整风险,同意按照《特别纳税调查调整及相互协商程序管理办法》(国家税务总局公告2017年第6号)的规定自行进行调整补缴税款及利息。经调整,母公司分别调增2014—2016年应纳税所得额1 012万元、852万元和920万元,累计调整应纳税所得额2 784万元,入库企业所得税696万元,加收利息55万元。

The association declaration data audit team uses the "association declaration meeting" to provide tax service to the enterprise, and the company recognizes its risk of special tax adjustments, agrees to adjust and repay tax and interest in accordance with the provisions of the measures for the Administration of Special Tax Investigation Adjustment and Mutual Consultation Procedures (State Administration of Taxation Proclamation No. 6 of 2017). Adjusted, parent companies raised their taxable income by 10.12 million yuan, 8.52 million yuan and 9.2 million yuan from 2014 to 2016 respectively, cumulative adjustment of taxable income of 27.84 million yuan, enterprise income tax 6.96 million yuan, the interest charge is 550,000 yuan.

(五) 案例启示

Case Enlightment

(1) 关联申报是反避税工作的基石。关联申报是税务机关了解和掌握企业关联业务往来的有效手段，税务机关应当就关联交易税收管理开展政策宣传和纳税辅导，提高税收政策落实的确定性，明确告知法律、法规和相关政策对关联申报的规定，使企业清楚自己的权利和应承担的义务，增强企业主动申报意识，努力提高关联申报质量。

(1) Related declaration is the cornerstone of anti-tax avoidance. Affiliated declaration is an effective means for tax authorities to understand and master the related business transactions of enterprises. Tax authorities should carry out policy advocacy and tax guidance on the tax administration of affiliated transactions, improve the certainty of tax policy implementation, clearly inform laws, regulations and related policies of the relevant declaration provisions, make enterprises know clearly their rights and obligations, enhance their awareness of active declaration, and strive to improve the quality of related declaration.

（2）功能风险分析是反避税工作的手段。充分利用企业关联申报的《报告企业信息表》掌握企业职能部门设置、业务运转及关联交易各方履行的功能，借助《企业功能风险分析表》及功能访谈结果，我们可以综合分析企业执行的功能与承担的风险是否相符，从而确定关联各方的功能风险与利润回报是否匹配，加大税务机关在纳税约谈中的筹码，更有利于提高反避税工作质效。

(2) Functional risk analysis is a means of anti-tax avoidance. Making full use of the Report Enterprise Information Table of the enterprise association declaration to master the functions of the establishment of the enterprise's functional departments, the operation of the business and the performance of the parties to the related transactions, and with the help of the Enterprise Function Risk Analysis Form and the results of the functional interviews, we can comprehensively analyze whether the functions performed by the enterprise are consistent with the risks assumed, so as to determine whether the functional risks and profit returns of the related parties match, and to increase the leverage of the tax authorities in tax interviews, which is more conducive to improving the quality and effectiveness of anti-tax avoidance work.

（3）领导重视是反避税工作的保障。淄博市税务局为抓好关联申报和反避税工作，成立了以分管局长为组长，各业务科室及稽查局负责人为副组长，业务骨干为主要成员的关联申报审核小组，为反避税工作提供了组织保障。此外，总局、省局反避税专家的多次业务指导也保障了反避税工作的顺利开展。

(3) The great care by leaders is the guarantee of anti-tax avoidance. In order to do a good job in the related declaration and anti-tax avoidance work, the Zibo Municipal Taxation Bureau has set up a related declaration and audit group with the director in charge as the leader, the responsible person of each business department and the inspection bureau as the deputy leader, and the business backbone as the main members, to provide organizational protection for anti-tax avoidance work. In addition, the General Administration, provincial bureau anti-avoidance experts provided a lot of business guidance which guaranteed the smooth development of anti-avoidance work.

（4）服务意识是反避税工作的关键。关联申报审核小组想纳税人所想，急纳税人所急，帮助纳税人掌握税法，提高纳税申报质量，有效解决纳税人因主观疏忽或对税法理解偏差产生的涉税问题，规避处罚风险，并针对问题提出有效、合理的征管建议，不断深化纳税服务内涵,满足纳税人日益增长的纳税服务需求。

(4) Service awareness is the key to anti-tax avoidance. The affiliated declaration review group help taxpayers master the tax law, improve the quality of tax returns, effectively solve the tax-related problems caused by subjective negligence or deviation in the understanding of the tax law, avoid the risk of punishment, and put forward effective and reasonable suggestions for tax collection and management, deepen the connotation of tax service and meet the increasing demand of tax service.

学习思考题
Questions for Study

1. 什么是国际逃税和国际避税？两者的区别是什么？
   What is international tax evasion and international tax avoidance? What is the difference between the two?
2. 在实践中形成了哪些原则和措施来应对国际避税？
   What principles and measures have been formed in practice to deal with international tax avoidance?
3. 国际逃税的主要方法和相应规制是什么？
   What are the main methods and corresponding regulations of international tax evasion?
4. 国际避税的主要方法和相应规制是什么？
   What are the main methods and corresponding regulations of international tax avoidance?
5. 转移定价的定义和途径有哪些？应对转移定价的原则有哪些以及最近有什么发展？
   What are the definitions and approaches of transfer pricing? What are the principles for dealing with transfer pricing and recent development?
6. 税收信息交换的种类有哪些？分别在何种情形下使用？
   What are the types of tax information exchange? And under what circumstances are they used?
7. 国际税收协助的内容包括哪些？多边税收征管互助公约的内容是什么？
   What are the contents of international tax assistance? What is the content of the Multilateral Convention on Mutual Administrative Assistance in Tax Matters?

第十三章 CHAPTER XIII

国际税务争议的解决
Settlement of International Tax Disputes

第一节 国际税务争议概况
Section 1 Overview of International Tax Disputes

一、国际税务争议的概念
Concept of International Tax Disputes

人类社会形成和发展的过程,就是人们之间的交往由简到繁互动的过程。[①] 有交往就会有争议。从社会学的角度讲,争议是指特定社会主体之间基于权益冲突而产生的对抗行为。争议不仅仅是特定个体之间发生的行为,也是一种社会现象。为了顺利进行交往,人们就必须解决彼此间发生的争议。交往越多,争议也越多,因而争议的解决日益受到重视。通常来说,争议不同,解决争议的方法也不同。

The process of formation and development of human society is the process of communication between people from simplicity to complex interaction. A relationship can be controversial. From the sociological point of view, dispute refers to the antagonistic behavior between specific social subjects based on the conflict of rights and interests. Controversy is not only a behavior between specific individuals, but also a social phenomenon. In order to communicate smoothly, people must solve the disputes between each other. The more communication, the more disputes, so the settlement of disputes is paid more and more attention. Generally speaking, disputes are different and the way to resolve them is different.

国家产生之前,种类繁杂的争议往往局限于一个社群之内。国家产生之后,随着国与国间的频繁交往以及国际社会的形成,由于争议具有跨国界的政治、经济、文化、法律、价值、语言等差异因素,从大的方面说,就产生了国际争议和国内争议之分。国际争议依照不同的标准还可以进一步分为国际法主体之间发生的争议即国际民事争议、国际贸易争议、国际投资争议及国际税务争议等。

Before the emergence of state, the variety of disputes was often confined to a community.

---

① [德]马克思、恩格斯著:《马克思恩格斯选集》(第4卷),人民出版社1995年版,第532页。

第十三章 国际税务争议的解决
CHAPTER XIII Settlement of International Tax Disputes

After the emergence of country, with the frequent exchanges between the countries and the formation of the international community, disputes have cross-border political, economic, cultural, legal, value, language and other factors, and are broadly dirided into international disputes and domestic disputes. International disputes can further be divided into international disputes between subjects of international law, namely, international civil disputes and international trade disputes, international investment disputes and international tax disputes.

关于国际税务争议的定义,目前学界有两种认识。一种认为,国际税务争议仅仅是指有关国家在国际税收利益分配关系中对某项税收利益产生不同主张和要求而产生的争议,即狭义论。按照狭义论,国际税务争议就是国际法律争议,可以通过国际法上的争议解决方法予以解决。另一种认为,国际税务争议不仅是指有关国家在国际税收利益分配关系中对某项税收利益产生不同主张和要求而产生的争议,而且还包括一国政府与跨国纳税人在税收征纳关系中对是否征税、如何征税等问题上产生不同主张和要求而导致的争议,以及国家间在纳税人税收待遇、防止国际逃税和避税、重复征税、避免双重不征税、税收行政互助等问题方面产生的冲突,即广义论。一句话来概括,国际税务争议就是指不同国家之间或一国政府与跨国纳税人之间在国际税收关系中产生的各种争议的总和。[①]很显然,狭义论已不能完全包括经济全球化和贸易自由化这两大世界潮流下,跨国纳税人主要是跨国企业在全球贸易和投资过程中与相关国家税收主管机关之间发生的税收征纳问题。当前,国际性的经济活动非常活跃,人、财(包括无形财产权和技术在内的财产)、资本和服务的国际间转移越来越频繁。在这些国际性经济活动中通常包括两个方面:其一是本国的国民和企业到国外去投资和从事其他经济活动;其二是外国的国民和企业来本国进行投资和从事其他经济活动。而由国际经济活动的快速发展所产生的大量税务争议,无论对国家还是纳税人来说都是至关重要的。税收问题本来是国内法税法解决的问题,但随着税收问题的国际化只靠各国国内法是不足以解决这些税收争议的,逐渐暴露出局限性,如缺乏公正的普遍标准、规则不统一,争议得不到有效救济等,因此也纳入国际法调整和解决的范畴。西方学者也有所谓的狭义论和广义论的划分。狭义论即是指涉及一个以上税收管辖权的争议。而广义论是指所有包括涉外因素的税收争议。[②]本书赞成对国际税务争议概念的广义理解,这也是下文展开论述的基础。

There are two kinds of understanding about the definition of international tax dispute. One view is that international tax disputes only refer to disputes arising from different claims and requirements of a certain tax interest in the distribution of international tax interests. That is a narrow sense. Accordingly, international tax disputes are international legal disputes, which can be solved by means of dispute settlement in international law. The other view is that international tax disputes are not only the disputes arising from the different claims and requirements of a certain tax interest in the distribution of international tax interests, but also include those arising from the different claims between a government and transnational

---

① 廖益新主编:《国际税法学》,高等教育出版社2008年版,第331页。
② LOTFI MAKTOUF, Resolving International Tax Disputes Through Arbitration, Arbitration International, p. 33.

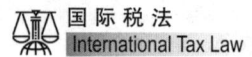

taxpayers on whether or not to tax and how to tax in the tax collection relationship, as well as conflicts between countries on the tax treatment of taxpayers, the prevention of international tax evasion and tax avoidance, double taxation, the avoidance of double non-taxation, and mutual tax administration. That is the broad sense. In a word, it refers to the sum of all kinds of disputes arising in international tax relations between different countries or between a government and transnational taxpayers. Obviously, the narrow theory can not completely cover the tax collection problems between multinational enterprises and relevant national tax authorities in the process of global trade and investment. At present, international economic activity is very active, and international transfers of people, wealth (including intangible property rights and technology), capital and services are becoming more and more frequent. These international economic activities usually include two aspects. One is that their nationals and enterprises go abroad to invest and engage in other economic activities. The other is that foreign nationals and enterprises come in to invest and engage in other economic activities. And a large number of tax disputes arising from the rapid development of international economic activities are crucial to both states and taxpayers. The tax problem is originally solved by domestic tax laws, but with the internationalization of the tax problem, it is not enough to solve these tax disputes by the domestic law of each country, which gradually exposes the limitations, such as the lack of universal standards of justice, the lack of uniformity of rules, the lack of effective remedies for disputes, and therefore, they are also included in the scope of adjustment and settlement of international law. Western scholars also have the so-called narrow theory and the division of broad theory. Narrowly it refers to disputes involving more than one tax jurisdiction. Broadly it refers to all tax disputes including foreign factors. This book supports a broad understanding of the concept of international tax disputes, which is the basis of the discussion below.

 国际税务争议的分类

Classification of International Tax Disputes

依据学界不同的理论标准,国际税务争议的类型主要分为以下三种。

According to different academic standards, the types of international tax disputes are mainly divided into the following three types.

(一)事实争议和法律争议

Factual and Legal Disputes

按照国际税务争议的性质,我们可以将其分为事实争议和法律争议。其中事实争议包括:(1)税收计算;(2)确认税基。而法律争议包括:(1)税收分配;(2)国内税法条文的解释;(3)国际税收条约的解释。争议的定性必然对争议的解决有影响,当事人在争议解决程序中的权利义务也有所差异。

According to the nature of international tax disputes, we can divided them into factual disputes and legal disputes. The factual disputes include: (1) tax calculation; (2) confirmation of the tax base. Legal disputes include: (1) tax distribution; (2) interpretation of the provisions of domestic tax laws; (3) interpretation of international tax treaties. The nature of the dispute surely will have an impact on its settlement, and the rights and obligations of the parties in the dispute settlement procedure are also different.

（二）直接性争议和间接性争议
Direct and Indirect Disputes

按照国际税收争议产生的方式，我们可以将其分为直接性争议和间接性争议。其中直接性国际税收争议指缔约国之间直接因双边或多边税收条约的解释或适用而产生的争议。这类争议属于国际法中的国家争端，与其他种类的国家间争端一样，要么按照条约规定的程序解决，要么根据国际法解决国家间争端的一般规则解决。间接性国际税收争议指缔约国某一纳税人先向缔约国一方主管税务机关提起，再由该缔约国主管税务机关向缔约对方的主管税务机关提起的争议。这类争议是性质较为特殊的一类争议。

According to the way of international tax disputes, we can divide them into direct disputes and indirect disputes. Direct international tax disputes refer to disputes between states parties arising directly from the interpretation or application of bilateral or multilateral tax treaties. Such disputes are state disputes under international law and, like other types of inter-state disputes, are settled either in accordance with the procedures established by the treaty or in accordance with the general rules of international law for the settlement of disputes between states. Indirect international tax dispute refers to a dispute brought by a taxpayer of a contracting state to the competent tax authority of the state and then by the competent tax authority of that state to the competent tax authority of the other contracting state. This kind of dispute is a special kind in nature.

（三）国家间的争议与国家和跨国纳税人之间的争议
Disputes between States and those between State and Transnational Taxpayer

按照国际税收争议的主体不同，我们可以将其分为国家间的争议与国家和跨国纳税人之间的争议。国家间的国际税收争议，产生于主权国家间的国际税收利益分配活动，争议主体的法律地位是平等的。主权国家间往往通过签订国际税收协定的方式来协商它们之间的国际税收利益分配关系。因此，国家间的国际税收争议主要表现为有关国家间就相互签订的税收协定条款的解释、执行、适用范围等问题所产生的争议。如上所述，这类争议的解决比较明确。国家和跨国纳税人之间的国际税收争议，产生于国家和跨国纳税人税收征纳活动中，双方的法律关系类似于国内法上的行政法律关系。其性质较为特殊，将在下文详细分析。当前，跨国企业在数字经济、电子商务蓬勃发展的背景下，以转让定价、滥用国际税收协定等方式导致的税基侵蚀和利润转移活动（base erosion and profit shifting，简称BEPS）日益增加，不仅使征税国和纳税人的争议不断上升，而且也促使全球各大经济体如G20采取一致行动去对付跨国企业的双重不征税问题，这也就是经合发组织2013年出台BEPS行动计划（Action Plan on Base Erosion and Profit Shifting）的直接

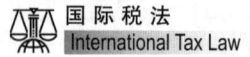

原因。①

According to the main body of international tax dispute, we can divide it into national dispute and transnational taxpayer dispute. The international tax dispute between countries originates from the international tax benefit distribution among sovereign countries, and the legal status of the subjects are equal. The distribution of international tax benefits between sovereign countries is often discussed by signing international tax agreements. Therefore, the international tax disputes between countries are mainly manifested in the disputes arising between the countries on the interpretation, implementation and scope of application of the terms of the tax agreements signed with each other. As noted above, the resolution of such disputes is relatively clear. The international tax dispute between national and transnational taxpayers arises from the tax collection activities of national and transnational taxpayers, and the legal relationship between them is similar to the administrative legal relationship in domestic law. Its nature is relatively special and will be analyzed in detail below. Nowadays, in the context of the booming of digital economy, e-commerce, the increasing activity of tax base erosion and profit transfer (Base Erosion and Profit Shifting, BEPS) caused by transfer pricing, abuse of international tax agreements, etc., not only cause the disputes between tax collectors and taxpayers to rise, but also urge the major economies of the world to take concerted action to deal with the double non-taxation problem of multinational enterprises, which is the direct cause of the action plan (Action Plan on Base Erosion and Profit Shifting) issued by OECD in 2013.

国际税务争议的特点
Characteristics of International Tax Disputes

与国际争端、国际民商事争议和纯国内税收争议相比，大多数国际税务争议中，至少争议一方是代表主权国家的财税主管机关，而且争议具有跨国界的因素，这自然增加了争议解决程序的复杂性和独特性。国际税收争议具有如下特点。

Compared with international disputes, international civil and commercial disputes and purely domestic tax disputes, in most international tax disputes, at least one party to the dispute is the tax authority who represents the sovereign state, and the dispute has cross-border factors, which naturally increase the complexity and uniqueness of the dispute settlement procedure. International tax disputes have the following characteristics.

（一）国际税务争议是一种国际争议
International Tax Dispute is a kind of International Dispute

这里的"国际"，取其广义，即超越一国国境，具有跨国性，从一国的角度看，就是具有涉

---

① See OECD(2013a), Addressing Base Erosion and Profit Shifting, OECD Publishing, Paris.doi:10.1787/9789264192744-en.

外因素。诚如前述,与国际税法学界对国际税务争议定义的广义理解一样,对税收法律关系的涉外或国际性也应作广义理解,即税收法律关系的主体、客体或内容这三个要素中至少有一个与外国相联系,就是涉外或国际税收关系。国际上和我国司法实践亦采这一说法。[①]据此,由这种税收关系引发的争议,即为国际税务争议。国际税务争议的这一特点使其同纯粹的国内税收争议区别开来。

"International" here, in its broad sense, means beyond the territory of a country and transnational in nature. From the point of view of a country, it involves foreign factors. As mentioned above, it is the same with the definition of international tax disputed in the international tax law circles, the internationality of tax legal relations should also be understood in a broad sense, that is, at least one of the three elements of the tax legal relationship is related to foreign countries, that is, foreign or international tax relations. This is also used in international and Chinese judicial practice. Therefore, the dispute caused by this tax relationship is an international tax dispute. This characteristic of international tax disputes distinguishes them from purely domestic tax disputes.

(二)国际税务争议是一种国际性的税收争议
International Tax Dispute is an International Tax Dispute

与其他国际争议比较,例如国际公法上所讲的国际争端,其直接涉及有关国家的政治、军事、外交、领土等关系,其解决一般需要当事国通过外交和司法途径解决。国际民商事争议则是当事人在从事国际民商事活动中所发生的权利义务纠纷,国际民商事争议的内容涉及的是个人的人身关系和财产关系,从实体到程序,当事人依法均享有充分的处分权和自由权。而国际税收争议则是既包括代表征税国的税务主管机关,又包括纳税人的私人主体的国家权力(公权力)和私人权利混合的基于对跨国性的财产和所得征税而产生的一类在性质上较为特殊的争议。

Compared with other international disputes, such as international disputes in public international law, directly involve the political, military, diplomatic and territorial relations of the states concerned, and their settlement generally requires diplomatic and judicial settlement by the states concerned. International civil and commercial disputes are disputes over the rights and obligations of the parties involved in international civil and commercial activities. The contents of international civil and commercial disputes involve personal and property relations of individuals, from entities to procedures. The parties shall enjoy full right of disposition and freedom according to law. The international tax dispute includes not only the tax authorities representing the tax collecting country, but also the state power (public power) and private right of the private subject of the taxpayer.

从性质上说,税收是任何现代国家取得财政收入的一种重要手段和主要途径,税收争议的产生正是因为国家享有税收管辖权。税收管辖权是国家主权在税收领域的体现,是国家主权的重要内容,一国政府行使税收管辖权的依据,就来源于国家的主权。尽管中西方学界

---

① 廖益新主编:《国际税法学》,高等教育出版社2008年版,第333页。

对国家主权的理解存在很大争议,但对作为国际法主要主体的国家在国内享有的完全独立自主的不受外来干预的最高税收权力这一点却是得到普遍承认的。① 一国政府在国内可以依据本国的政治经济状况,按照宪法中确立的"税收法定"的原则来制定税收法律、确立税制和规定纳税人与征税对象等,为国家履行社会管理和提供社会公共产品和公共服务的成本而对其领域内的一切人(除享受豁免权者)和财产以及一切居住在国外的本国人进行征税。具体来说,税收管辖权包括了五方面的内容:(1)由谁征税;(2)对谁征税;(3)对什么征税;(4)征多少税;(5)如何征纳。各国在行使税收管辖权时主要遵守的是属人或者属地管辖权。在属人与属地管辖权下,国家依据纳税人与征税国之间存在的某种人身隶属关系性质的法律事实如居民身份或国籍身份、征税对象与征税国之间存在某种地域上的连接因素如所得来源地或财产所在地主张进行课税。

In nature, taxation is an important means and the main approach for any modern country to obtain fiscal revenue. It is because the state has tax jurisdiction that arouses tax dispute. Tax jurisdiction is the embodiment of national sovereignty in the field of taxation, and is an important part of national sovereignty. The sovereignty of the state is the basis on which a government exercises its tax jurisdiction, Although the Chinese and Western academic understandings of national sovereignty are very controversial, it is generally recognized that the state, which is the main subject of international law, enjoys a completely independent and sovereign right of taxation at the domestic level, free from outside interference. A government can make tax laws, establish tax system and stipulate taxpayer and object according to the principle of "statutory taxation" established in the constitution according to its political and economic situation. All persons (except those who enjoy immunity) and property and all nationals living abroad are taxed by the state to meet the costs of social administration and the provision of social public goods and services. Specifically, tax jurisdiction includes five aspects: (1) who collects taxes; (2) who should be taxed; (3) what is the object of taxation; (4) how much tax is levied; (5) how to collect taxes. In the exercise of tax jurisdiction, states mainly observe personal or territorial jurisdiction. Under personal and territorial jurisdiction, the state claims taxation on the basis of legal facts of the nature of a personal affiliation existing between the taxpayer and the state of taxation, such as resident or national status, the existence of a geographical link between the object of taxation and the state of taxation, such as the place of origin of the income or the place of property.

虽然从国家主权的最高性和权威性角度来看,税收管辖权是一种对一国领土范围内的人和物不受任何约束和限制的权力。但是也应该看到,国际社会是由众多大小不同但主权平等的国家所构成的,从国家主权的独立性来看,各国的税收管辖权都是平等的,这意味着一国政府并不可以随意地扩大其税收管辖权的范围。因为随着跨国商品与服务交易及国际资本和人员流动规模和形式的增加,纳税人的所得与财产也逐渐国际化,出现了两个或两个

---

① Helmut Steinberger, Sovereignty, in R.Bernhardt ed., Encyclopedia of Public International Law, vol.IV, Amsterdam 2000, p. 516.

以上的国家对同一征税对象课税、不同国家税收管辖权发生交叉、重叠的现象,导致国际双重征税等国际税收争议问题的产生。而且一国政府在行使税收管辖权时,绝对地不受任何限制和约束在实践中也是行不通的。①

Although from the point of view of the supremacy and authority of national sovereignty, tax jurisdiction is a kind of power that is not subject to any restriction on people and things within the territory of a country. However, it should also be seen that the international community is composed of many countries of different sizes but sovereign equality. In terms of the independence of national sovereignty, the tax jurisdiction of each country is equal, which means that a government can not arbitrarily expand its tax jurisdiction. Because of the increase of the scale and form of transnational goods and services transactions and international capital and human mobility, the income and property of taxpayers are gradually internationalized, and two or more countries tax the same tax object, and the different national tax jurisdictions cross and overlap, which leads to international tax disputes such as international double taxation. Moreover, it is not feasible in practice for a government to exercise its tax jurisdiction without any restrictions or constraints.

(三)国际税务争议既有平权型争议也有隶属(管辖)型争议
Affirmative and Subordinate Disputes in International Tax Disputes

如前所述,国家间的国际税收争议,产生于主权国家间的国际税收利益分配活动,争议主体的法律地位是平等的。主权国家间往往通过签订国际税收协定的方式来协商它们之间的国际税收利益分配关系。可见,在国际税收协定的限制下,主权国家自愿让渡了一定范围的税收管辖权。国际税收协定的规则主要是征税权(税收管辖权)划分规则。国际税收协定不能为缔约国双方的公民或居民创设权利,除非税收协定的规定按国内立法方式被制定为法律,个人因缺乏国际法地位不得直接依协定主张权利,但根据税收协定中的规定例如相互协商程序(MAP),纳税人享有争议解决的程序权利。缔约主体是国家,权利义务主体也是国家,但税收协定最直接的受益者是跨国纳税人,不是缔约国双方的税务部门,因此,税收协定主要适用于跨国纳税人,作用于缔约国税务机关和纳税人。

As mentioned earlier, international tax disputes between countries arise from the distribution of international tax interests among sovereign countries, and the legal status of the subject of the dispute is equal. Sovereign countries often negotiate the distribution of international tax benefits between them by signing international tax agreements. It can be seen that under the restriction of international tax agreement, sovereign countries voluntarily transfer a certain range of tax jurisdiction. The rules of international tax agreement are mainly the rules of tax right (tax jurisdiction) division. An international tax agreement can not create rights for citizens or residents of both parties, unless the provisions of the tax agreement are

---

① 关于国家主权的特征和我国对国家主权相对性的认识,详见杨泽伟著:《主权论——国际法上的主权问题及其发展趋势研究》,北京大学出版社2006年版,第7—8页,第34—50页。

enacted into law in the form of domestic legislation, and individuals can not claim rights directly under the agreement because of a lack of international law status, but taxpayers have procedural rights to dispute settlement under the provisions of the tax agreement, such as the mutual consultation procedure (MAP), which provides for the procedure. The contracting subject is state, the subject of rights and obligations is also state, but the most direct beneficiary of the tax agreement is the transnational taxpayer, not the tax department of both parties. Therefore, tax agreement mainly applies to transnational taxpayers and acts on the tax authorities and taxpayers of the contracting parties.

如果是国家和跨国纳税人之间的国际税收争议,产生于国家和跨国纳税人税收征纳活动中,则双方的法律关系类似于国内法上的行政法律关系,其性质较为特殊。首先,一方是主权国家,是国际法上的主体;另一方是跨国纳税人,是国内法上的主体。这就使得该类争议很难用传统的争议解决办法来解决,且极易因相关国家行使外交保护权而演变为国家间的争端,使其政治化和复杂化,更难予以解决。其次,这类争议产生的原因也较特殊和复杂。从国际税收的实践看,其产生的缘由可主要归纳为:(1)法律原因,如债务人公司所在国家把利息作为股息看待的情况下,征税国解决资本弱化的国内法适用产生的争议及同样情况下依据税收协定中关联企业规定适用产生的争议。按照税收协定中商业利润相关规定适用常设机构利润归属而产生的争议等。(2)事实原因,即因征税国税务主管机关缺乏认定跨国纳税人实际情况的相关信息而产生的争议,如确定跨国纳税人的居民身份;是否存在常设机构及雇员提供临时服务的性质等。

If an international tax dispute between a state and transnational taxpayers arises from the tax collection activities of the state and transnational taxpayers, the legal relationship is similar to the administrative legal relationship in domestic law. Its nature is relatively special. First of all, one side is a sovereign state as a subject in international law, the other is a transnational taxpayer as a subject in domestic law. This makes it difficult to settle such disputes by traditional dispute resolution, and it is easy to evolve into disputes between states because of the exercise of the right of diplomatic protection by the relevant states, which makes them more politicized and complicated, and more difficult to resolve. Second, the causes of such disputes are also special and complex. From the practice of international taxation, the reasons can be summarized as follows: (1) Legal reasons, such as the case where interest is regarded as a dividend in the country where the debtor's company is located, disputes will arise from the application of domestic law of capital weakening in the tax-paying country and, in the same case, the same are disputes arising from the application of the provisions of the associated enterprise in the tax agreement; disputes arising from the application of the permanent establishment's profit attribution in accordance with the relevant provisions of the commercial profit in the tax agreement. (2) Factual reasons, i.e. disputes arising from the lack of relevant information by the tax authorities of the state of taxation to determine the actual situation of transnational taxpayers, such as the identification of residents of transnational taxpayers, the existence of permanent establishments and the nature of temporary services provided by employees, etc.

第二节 国际税务争议解决的原则和方法
Section 2　Principles and Methods for the Settlement of International Tax Disputes

 国际税务争议解决的原则

Principles for the Settlement of International Tax Disputes

随着经济全球化和贸易自由化的深入发展,跨国人员、技术、服务、所得和资本的流动日益频繁。不同国家基于不同的税收管辖权规则(如有的国家采用属地征税,而有的国家采用属人征税,还有的国家两者兼用),对跨国征税对象和纳税人行使征税权时,会不可避免地产生税收分配的冲突。日益增多的国际税收争议迫切需要快速、高效的争议解决手段。解决冲突的原则和规定(条约)应运而生。这些原则是我们在解决国际税务争议过程中应遵守的指导思想。它们衍生于国际税法的基本原则,保障着公平合理的国际税收新秩序的建立,国际税务争议的各方当事人都应遵守这些解决国际税务争议的基本准则。

With the deepening development of economic globalization and trade liberalization, the flow of transnational people, technology, services, income and capital is becoming more and more frequent. Different countries are based on different rules of tax jurisdiction, such as some countries using territorial taxation, some countries adopting personal taxation, others adopting both, and exercising tax rights against transnational tax objects and taxpayers. The conflict of tax distribution inevitably arises. The growing number of international tax disputes urgently requires rapid and efficient dispute resolution. The principles and provisions of conflict resolution (treaties) are thus applied. These principles are the guiding ideology we should abide by in the settlement of international tax disputes. They derive from the basic principles of international tax law and guarantee the establishment of a fair and reasonable new international tax order. All parties involved in international tax disputes should abide by these basic principles.

(一)维护国家税收主权和税收管辖权原则
Safeguarding the State's Tax Sovereignty and the Principle of Tax Jurisdiction

国家主权平等原则是国际法的基本原则。税收管辖权是国家主权在税收领域的体现,是国家管辖权的一项重要组成部分。国际税务争议的产生是以税收管辖权的存在为前提的,国家享有税收管辖权是其参与国际税收关系的基础,无论是国家与跨国纳税人之间因跨国税收征纳活动而产生的税收争议还是国家之间因国际税收利益分配而产生的税务

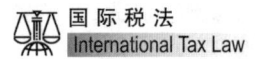

争议，都离不开国家的税收管辖权。因此，国家税收管辖权是各国在国际税务争议中加以维护的根本权益，只有尊重并维护各个国家的税收管辖权，才能合理有效地解决国际税务争议。

The principle of sovereign equality of states is the basic principle of international law. Tax jurisdiction is the embodiment of national sovereignty in the field of taxation and an important part of national jurisdiction. The emergence of international tax disputes is based on the existence of tax jurisdiction, and the national tax jurisdiction is the basis for its participation in international tax relations. Whether it is the tax dispute between the state and the transnational taxpayer due to the transnational tax collection activities or the tax dispute between the state due to the distribution of international tax benefits, it can not be separated from the national tax jurisdiction. Therefore, national tax jurisdiction is the fundamental right and interest of countries to safeguard in international tax disputes. Only by respecting and safeguarding the tax jurisdiction of each country can international tax disputes be reasonably and effectively resolved.

（二）保护纳税人合法权益原则
Principle of Protecting the Lawful Rights and Interests of Taxpayers

纳税人合法权益，指的是国家保障或许可纳税人作为或不作为以及要求税务机关作为或不作为的权利。纳税人合法权益得以实现一般包括三个方面的内容：第一，纳税人依法享有作为或不作为的权利；第二，纳税人依法享有要求税务机关作为或不作为的权利；第三，纳税人依法享有获得各种法律救济的权利，比如提起行政复议、行政诉讼、申请缔约国依国际税收协定发起相互协商程序等。依照我国税法，纳税人除享有上述权利外，还享有要求税务机关保密的权利以及依法享受各种税收优惠待遇的权利。

The legitimate rights and interests of taxpayers refer to the right of the state to protect or permit taxpayers to act or not and to require tax authorities to act or not. The realization of the legitimate rights and interests of taxpayers generally includes three aspects: first, the taxpayer has the right to act or not to act according to law; second, the taxpayer has the right to ask the tax authorities to act or not to act according to law; third, the taxpayer has the right to obtain various legal remedies according to law, such as administrative reconsideration, administrative action, application for the state party to initiate mutual consultation procedures in accordance with international tax agreements, etc. According to the tax law of our country, in addition to the above rights, taxpayers also enjoy the right to require the tax authorities to keep secret and to enjoy all kinds of preferential tax treatment according to law.

20世纪70年代以来，以信息技术革命为基础的科技发展导致市场全球化，直接触发为国际市场的协调建立机制和规范的需求，形成对主权国家进行资源再分配权力的限制。就税收来说，除了全球化的开放性、主动性与国家税收主权的封闭性、被动性之间的矛盾与冲突外，始于第二次世界大战后的现代人权运动深深影响了纳税人权利及其保护的观念。纳税人权利成为讨论的主题是在1975年以后开始的。经合发组织（OECD）1990年发布了关于纳税人权利和义务的一份重要报告，报告中特别强调了纳税人在税收征收和税收执行程序中的权利。2003年经合发组织发布了关于纳税人权利和义务的实务指导说明,在该说明中列举了纳税人的基本权利有:知情权、获得帮助权、听证权、上诉权、法定数额纳税权、确定权、隐私权、保密权。[①]无论是国内法意义上的税务争议,还是国际法意义上的税务争议,其实质就是国家税收主权和纳税人私权发生冲突的表象。对这两种权利关系的不同认识将直接决定国家采取何种税收争议解决方法,观察国家在解决税务争议的规则和做法也直接反映了这个主权国家如何看待纳税人权利和对待纳税人的态度。保护纳税人合法权益是解决国际税务争议要达到的重要目标,同时,只有对纳税人依法享有的各种法律救济权利予以承认和保护,才能促使国际税务争议的顺利解决。

Since the 1970s, the development of science and technology based on the information technology revolution has led to the globalization of the market, which directly triggered the need to establish mechanisms and norms for the coordination of the international market, and formed a restriction on the power of resource redistribution of sovereign countries. As far as taxation is concerned, in addition to the contradiction and conflict between the openness of globalization, initiative and the closeness and passivity of state tax sovereignty, the modern human rights movement after World War II deeply influenced the concept of taxpayer rights and their protection. Taxpayer rights became the subject of discussion after 1975. An important report on the rights and obligations of taxpayers was issued by the OECD in 1990, with particular emphasis on the rights of taxpayers in tax collection and tax enforcement procedures. In 2003, the OECD issued a practical guidance note on the rights and obligations of taxpayers, in which the basic rights of taxpayers are listed: the right to know, the right to help, the right to hear, the right to appeal, the right to pay taxes on legal amounts, the right to determine, the right to privacy, the right to keep secret. Whether it is tax dispute in the sense of domestic law or tax dispute in the sense of international law, its essence is the appearance of conflict between state tax sovereignty and taxpayer's private right. The different understanding of the relationship between the two rights will directly determine the tax dispute settlement method adopted by the state, and the rules and practices of observing the state in resolving the tax dispute also directly reflect how the sovereign country views the rights of taxpayers and the attitude towards taxpayers. Protecting the legitimate rights and interests of taxpayers is an important goal to be achieved in the settlement of international tax disputes. At the same time, only by recognizing and protecting the various legal relief rights enjoyed by taxpayers according to law can the international tax disputes be resolved smoothly.

(三)避免双重征税或双重不征税原则
Principle of Avoidance of Double Taxation or Double Non-taxation

征税权是国家主权的核心之一,各国在设计和制定国内税收规则时,可能并未充分考虑其他国家税收规则的效力。因此各国在按照本国税收规则行使征税权的时候,这些不同的国内法规则在同一时间适用于同一个纳税人的同一笔跨境交易所产生的收入或所得时,

---

① Practice Note on Taxpayer's Rights and Obligations, OECD August 2003.

相互之间就产生了冲突和摩擦。如果是积极的冲突，即各个国家都要按照本国的税法对纳税人征税就产生了双重甚至多重征税的问题。反之消极的冲突，就会对纳税人产生双重甚至多重的不征税。双重征税或双重不征税都违反了国际税法的单一征税原则（the single tax principle）。至少从20世纪20年代国际联盟开始，各国普遍认为国际双重征税是对跨境贸易和投资的阻碍，会损害经济的可持续发展。直到2008年西方国家爆发金融危机之前，国际社会税收规则协调和合作的主要目标在于消除和预防对纳税人跨境交易产生利润的双重征税。

The right to tax is one of the core of national sovereignty, and countries may not fully consider the effectiveness of other countries' tax rules in designing and formulating domestic tax rules. Therefore, when countries exercise their tax rights in accordance with their own tax rules, these different domestic law rules are applicable to the income or income generated by the same cross-border exchange of the same taxpayer at the same time, there is conflict and friction between each other. If there is a positive conflict, the problem of double or even multiple taxation arises when countries tax taxpayers in accordance with their own tax laws. On the contrary, negative conflicts will produce double or even multiple non-taxation of taxpayers. Double taxation or double non-taxation violates the single taxation principle of international tax law (the single tax principle). At least since the 1920s, the League of Nations has widely believed that international double taxation is an obstacle to cross-border trade and investment, which will damage the sustainable development of the economy. Until the financial crisis in the West in 2008, the main goal of international tax harmonization and cooperation was to eliminate and prevent double taxation of taxpayers' profits from cross-border transactions.

但从2008年以来，随着整个西方发达国家国内经济的下行，有些国家出现财政赤字甚至破产，国家税收收入拮据，而与此同时，随着全球数字经济的兴起，那些富可敌国的跨国企业却凭借极具侵略性的税收筹划财源滚滚。八国集团首先在各自国内加强对跨国纳税人的税收监管，然后开始反思现行的以消除国际双重征税的国际税收协定体系。他们的共识是无论是经合发组织的标准还是双边的税收协定模式都无法解决对跨国企业双重不征税的问题。因此从八国集团到二十国集团在这些发达国家的推动及"金砖国家"的共同参与下，二十国集团的财政部长们请求经合发组织以一种协调和全面的方式制定行动计划来应对跨国企业以转让定价、滥用国际税收协定等方式导致的税基侵蚀和利润转移活动。①BEPS的行动计划共包括15项具体行动，每项行动都有具体的时限要求。BEPS的实施将对现行的国际税收协定体系产生重要的影响，尽管BEPS对发展中国家并不能自动适用，但它作为国际税法的第一个软法渊源，针对跨国企业税收套利所确立的标准将对各国自由行使税收主权构成限制。

But since 2008, as the domestic economy of the whole western developed countries has fallen, some countries have even gone bankrupt, and the national tax revenue is tight. At the same time, with the rise of the global digital economy, the multinational enterprises become

---

① OECD(2013a), Addressing Base Erosion and Profit Shifting, OECD Publishing, Paris.doi: 10.1787/9789264192744-en.

so fabulously rich and make a lot of money with aggressive tax planning. The Group of Eight strengthened tax regulation of transnational taxpayers in their respective countries, and then began to reflect on the current system of international tax agreements to eliminate international double non-taxation. Their consensus is that neither the OECD standard nor the bilateral tax agreement model can solve the problem of double non-taxation of multinational enterprises. Therefore, promoted by these developed countries of the Group of Twenty (G20) and with the participation of the BRICs countries, G20 finance ministers have requested OECD to develop action plans in a coordinated and comprehensive manner to address the base erosion and profit transfer activities (Base Erosion and Profit Shifting, BEPS) caused by transnational corporations through transfer pricing and abuse of international tax agreements. A total of 15 specific actions were included in the BEPS action plan, each operation has a specific time frame. BEPS implementation will have an important impact on the current system of international tax agreements, although BEPS is not automatically applicable to developing countries, but as the first soft law source of international tax law, its standards for tax arbitrage of multinational enterprises will limit the free exercise of tax sovereignty.

二、国际税务争议解决的方法
International Tax Dispute Resolution Methodology

从主权国家行使税收管辖权的角度，有关解决国际税务争议的方法主要分为两种。一是国内法程序。从世界范围来看，各国一般都规定，纳税人与税务机关之间发生的税收争议，可以通过行政性救济程序、国内诉讼程序来解决。一般认为，国内法程序是属于各国国内法，准确地说是国内行政程序法研究的对象。因此后文仅介绍一些典型国家的国内法程序，如大陆法系的代表——德国的纳税人权利保护制度及申诉程序、英美法系的代表——美国的纳税人权利保护制度及妥协提议。

From the point of view of sovereign state exercising tax jurisdiction, there are two main methods to solve international tax disputes. One is domestic law procedures. From a worldwide perspective, countries generally stipulate that tax disputes between taxpayers and tax authorities can be resolved through administrative relief procedures and domestic proceedings. The domestic law procedure is generally considered to belong to the domestic law of each country and to be the object of the study of the domestic administrative procedure law. So the following is only a description of the domestic law procedure of some typical countries, the representative of the Mainland law system — German's taxpayer rights protection system and complaint procedure, the representative of the common law system — US taxpayer rights protection system and compromise proposal (an offer in compromise).

二是国际法程序。本部分将分析传统的解决方法——相互协商程序及其延伸仲裁解决程序、预约定价协议。在这些争议解决方法中，相互协商程序作为绝大多数税收协定中的标准条款，在解决国际税收争议和适用、解释税收协定方面发挥了极为重要的作用。通过缔约国税务主管机关的直接交流，而不是通过复杂的外交渠道，相互协商程序在缔约国之间建立了一种灵活的沟通方式。当然随着时间的推移，现实税收争议的日趋增多和日益复杂，相互协商程序在运作中也出现了一系列无法解决的困难。这导致对相互协商程序的批评，如结果的不确定性和耗时，以及进行改善的建议。但相互协商程序的灵活性确实解决了不少法院可能要耗费数年才能解决的国际税务争议问题。

Second, international law procedures. This part will analyze the traditional solution, the mutual negotiation procedure and its extension arbitration settlement procedure, the reservation pricing agreement. Among these dispute settlement methods, the mutual negotiation procedure plays an extremely important role in the settlement of international tax disputes and the application and interpretation of tax agreements as a standard provision in most tax treaties. Through direct communication by the state party's tax authorities, rather than through complex diplomatic channels, mutual consultation procedures create a flexible way of communication between states parties. Of course, with the passage of time, the actual tax disputes are increasing and becoming more and more complex, and the mutual consultation process also has a series of insurmountable difficulties in its operation. This has led to criticism of the mutual consultation process, such as uncertainty and time-consuming results, and suggestions for improvement. But the flexibility of the mutual-consultation process does solve many of the international tax disputes that the court may take years to resolve.

第三节　国际税务争议解决的国内法程序
Section 3　Domestic Law Procedures for the Settlement of International Tax Disputes

一、国际税务争议解决的国内一般方法
General Domestic Approaches to the Settlement of International Tax Disputes

（一）纳税人与本国税务机关协商解决
Taxpayer shall Settle the Matter through Consultation with the Local Tax Authorities

一旦纳税人与本国税务机关发生税收争议，双方解决争议的第一步就是相互协商。对大多数国家的税务机关来说，通过协商解决的优点是明显的，税务官员坚持以讨论、谈判的方式解决，避免耗时且昂贵的国内诉讼程序。例如，美国税务局可以允许纳税人延期缴纳所欠税款或同意纳税人在一定时间内以分期付款的方式缴纳所欠税款。而且国内税务局有

权发出和接受妥协提议,根据提议,纳税人同意缴纳一定比例的所欠税款,以换取免除其他责任。国内税务局基于这些情况可以同意妥协提议:(1)对该税是否得到正确评估存疑;(2)对纳税人是否能足额缴纳税款存疑;(3)有效税收管理提升,即纳税人出现经济困难或其他特殊情形,使国内税务局有正当理由接受其少缴税款。广大发展中国家的税务机关,出于与那些外国纳税人(往往是实力雄厚的跨国公司)保持良好关系的目的,诉讼解决也通常作为解决争议的最后选项。协商解决不成,还可以通过税务机关内部的上诉程序进行复查以避免出现专横的决定。如果内部复查仍无法解决这个问题,就只能启动诉讼程序了。

In the event of a tax dispute between the taxpayer and the local tax authorities, the first step in resolving the dispute is to negotiate with each other. For the tax authorities of most countries, the advantages of a negotiated settlement are obvious, and tax officials insist on a negotiated settlement to avoid time-consuming and expensive domestic proceedings. For example, the United States Inland Revenue Department may allow taxpayers to defer payment of outstanding taxes or agree to pay outstanding taxes in instalments within a certain period of time. And the Inland Revenue Department has the right to issue and accept compromise proposals (an offer in compromise) according to which taxpayers agree to pay a certain proportion of the tax owed in exchange for exemption from other liability. On the basis of these circumstances, the Inland Revenue Department may agree to compromise proposals: (1) doubts as to whether the tax has been correctly assessed; (2) doubts as to whether the taxpayer can pay the tax in full; (3) the promotion of effective tax administration, that is, the taxpayer's financial difficulties or other special circumstances give the Inland Revenue Department a reasonable reason to accept his or her underpayment. For the purpose of maintaining a good relationship with foreign taxpayers (often powerful multinational companies), the tax authorities in developing countries usually take litigation settlement as the last option to settle disputes. A negotiated settlement can also be reviewed through appeal procedures within the tax authorities to avoid arbitrary decisions. If an internal review fails to resolve the issue, proceedings will have to be initiated.

(二)纳税人向上一级行政机关提起行政复议
The Taxpayer Brings an Administrative Reconsideration to the Higher Administrative Organ

行政复议是指行政相对人认为行政主体的具体行政行为侵犯其合法权益时,根据行政相对人的申请,由上一级国家行政机关或者法律法规规定的其他机关依照法定程序对被申请的具体行政行为进行合法性、适当性审查并作出决定的一种行政行为。①

Administrative reconsideration refers to an administrative act in which the administrative counterpart considers that the specific administrative act of the administrative subject infringes upon his or her legitimate rights and interests, according to the application of the administrative counterpart, the state administrative organ at the next higher level or other organ prescribed by laws and regulations shall, in accordance with legal procedures, examine and decide on the

---

① 姜明安主编:《行政法与行政诉讼法》,北京大学出版社、高等教育出版社2007年版,第415页。

legality and appropriateness of the specific administrative act applied for.

在我国,税收领域的行政复议即税收行政复议,是指纳税人、扣缴义务人、纳税担保人等税务行政相对人在认为税务行政主体及其工作人员作出的税务具体行政行为侵犯了其合法权益时,依法向上一级税务机关或者本级人民政府提出复查该具体行政行为的申请,由复议机关对税务具体行政行为的合法性和适当性进行审查并作出裁决的制度。①

In our country, administrative reconsideration in the field of taxation, i.e. administrative reconsideration of taxation, refers to a system in which the administrative counterpart of taxation, such as taxpayers, withholding agents and tax payment guarantors, considers that the specific administrative act of taxation made by the subject of tax administration and its staff has infringed upon their legitimate rights and interests, applies to the tax authorities at the next higher level or to the people's governments at the corresponding level for review of the specific administrative act according to law, and the reconsideration organ shall examine and decide on the legality and appropriateness of the specific administrative act of taxation.

税务行政复议是行政复议制度的组成部分,其制度本身涉及复议范围、复议管辖、复议的当事人、复议申请与受理、复议证据、复议决定等方面的内容。

Tax administrative reconsideration is an integral part of the administrative reconsideration system, which itself involves the scope of reconsideration, the jurisdiction of reconsideration, the parties to reconsideration, the application and acceptance of reconsideration, the evidence of reconsideration, the decision of reconsideration, and so on.

我国有专门的《中华人民共和国行政复议法》(以下简称《行政复议法》),国家税务总局根据《行政复议法》《中华人民共和国税收征收管理法》和《中华人民共和国行政复议法实施条例》的规定,于2010年2月10日发布了修订后的《税务行政复议规则》,自同年4月1日起施行;2004年2月24日国家税务总局以"国税发〔2004〕8号文"发布的《税务行政复议规则(暂行)》同时废止。

China has a special Administrative Review Law of the People's Republic of China (hereinafter referred to as the Administrative Review Law). In accordance with the provisions of the Administrative Review Law, the Law of the People's Republic of China on the Administration of Tax Collection and the Regulations of the People's Republic of China on the Implementation of the Administrative Review Law, the revised Rules on Administrative Review of Tax Matters were issued on 10 February 2010, effective from 1 April of the same year. The Rules for Administrative Review of Tax Administration (Provisional) promulgated by the State Administration of Taxation on 24 February 2004 in document No. 8 of the State Tax Administration shall be repealed at the same time.

根据《税务行政复议规则》第14条的规定,行政复议机关受理的税务行政复议范围包括:税务机关作出的征税行为;税务机关作出的行政许可、行政审批行为;税务机关的发票管理行为;税务机关的不依法确认纳税担保行为;税务机关作出的税收保全措施、税收强制执行措施;税务机关作出的税收行政处罚行为;税务机关不依法履行职责的行为;税务机

---

① 陈少英编著:《税法学教程》,北京大学出版社2011年版,第457页。

关的资格认定行为；税务机关的政府信息公开工作中的具体行政行为；税务机关的纳税信用等级评定行为；税务机关的通知出入境管理机关阻止出境行为；税务机关的其他具体行政行为。①

According to Article 14 of the Rules for Tax Administrative Review, the scope of tax administrative review accepted by the administrative review authorities includes: tax collection acts made by the tax authorities; administrative licensing and examination and approval acts made by the tax authorities; invoice administration acts of the tax authorities; tax guarantee acts of the tax authorities not confirmed in accordance with the law; tax preservation measures, tax enforcement measures taken by the tax authorities; tax administrative punishment acts made by the tax authorities; tax authorities' failure to perform their duties in accordance with the law; tax authorities' qualification determination acts; specific administrative acts of the tax authorities in the public work of government information; the tax authority's tax credit rating; the tax authority's notice to the entry and exit administration authority to prevent the exit; other specific administrative acts of the tax authority.

复议机关审查申请行政复议的具体行政行为是否合法与适当，作出行政复议决定。(1) 具体行政行为认定事实清楚，证据确凿，适用依据正确，程序合法，内容适当的，决定维持。(2) 被申请人不履行法定职责的，决定其在一定期限内履行。(3) 具体行政行为有下列情形之一的，决定撤销、变更或者确认该具体行政行为违法；决定撤销或者确认该具体行政行为违法的，可以责令被申请人在一定期限内重新作出具体行政行为：主要事实不清、证据不足的；适用依据错误的；违反法定程序的；超越或者滥用职权的；具体行政行为明显不当的。(4) 被申请人不按照《税务行政复议规则》第62条的规定提出书面答复，提交当初作出具体行政行为的证据、依据和其他有关材料的，视为该具体行政行为没有证据、依据，决定撤销该具体行政行为。对于行政复议决定，如果纳税人仍然不服的，此时可依法提起行政诉讼。②

The administrative reconsideration organ shall examine whether the specific administrative act applying for administrative reconsideration is lawful and appropriate, and make an administrative reconsideration decision. (1) If the specific administrative act finds that the facts are clear, the evidence is conclusive, the application basis is correct, the procedure is lawful and the content is appropriate, it shall decide to maintain it. (2) If the respondent fails to perform its statutory duties, it shall decide to perform within a certain period of time. (3) If the specific administrative act has one of the following circumstances, it shall decide to revoke, alter or confirm that the specific administrative act is illegal; if a decision is made

---

① 详见《税务行政复议规则》第14条，http://www.gov.cn/flfg/2010-03/01/content_1544560.htm。
② 详见《税务行政复议规则》第75、76条，http://www.gov.cn/flfg/2010-03/01/content_1544560.htm。另《税务行政复议规则》第62条规定，行政复议机构应当自受理行政复议申请之日起7日内，将行政复议申请书副本或者行政复议申请笔录复印件发送被申请人。被申请人应当自收到申请书副本或者申请笔录复印件之日起10日内提出书面答复，并提交当初作出具体行政行为的证据、依据和其他有关材料。对国家税务总局的具体行政行为不服申请行政复议的案件，由原承办具体行政行为的相关机构向行政复议机构提出书面答复，并提交当初作出具体行政行为的证据、依据和其他有关材料。

to revoke or confirm the violation of the specific administrative act, the respondent may be ordered to make a specific administrative act again within a certain period of time: if the main facts are unclear and the evidence is insufficient; if the application basis is wrong; if the legal procedure is violated; if the authority is exceeded or abused; if the specific administrative act is manifestly improper; (4) if the respondent fails to provide a written reply in accordance with the provisions of Article 62 of the Rules for the Administrative Review of Taxation and submit evidence, basis and other relevant materials for the specific administrative act, the specific administrative act shall be deemed to have no evidence or basis and decided to revoke the specific administrative act. For administrative reconsideration decisions, if taxpayers are still dissatisfied, administrative proceedings may be filed according to law.

在美国,如果税务机关完成对纳税人的税务审计后,美国国内税务署(简称IRS)就会向纳税人发出"30天信"(a 30-day letter)。"30天信"中将解释税务审计部门对纳税人税收返还所作出的改变。如果纳税人对税务审计部门的决定不服,则有权向IRS上诉部(IRS Appeals)提出复审。纳税人必须在收到"30天信"的30天内,向IRS上诉部提出书面的复审请求。在该书面请求中,纳税人要提出对税务审计部门决定的异议和支持自己主张的事实及法律依据。①

Within the United States, if the tax authorities complete the tax audit of taxpayers, the United States Internal Revenue Service (IRS) sends a 30-day-letter to taxpayers. The 30-day-letter will explain the tax audit department's changes to taxpayer tax returns. The taxpayer has the right to submit a review to the IRS Appeals Department (IRS Appeals) if he or she disagrees with the decision of the tax audit department. A taxpayer must submit a written request for review to the IRS Appeals Department within 30 days of receipt of the 30-day-letter. In this written request, the taxpayer shall raise the objection to the decision of the tax audit department and the facts and legal basis to support his or her claim.

在德国,对一个税务机关在任一案件中作出的任何终局的、穷尽程序的行政行为都可以提出行政审查,这种书面的救济称为申诉。申诉由受行政决定负担的任何人或人们从该决定生效之日起1个月内提出。申诉程序是免费的。收到申诉后,作出行政决定的税务督查可以自己改正。若其拒绝改正,则该申诉将移交给同一税务办公室内的一个独立审查部门,然后由该部门来决定救济。申诉的最终决定作出之前,纳税人有权要求对案件进行口头讨论。同理,税务机关也有权要求纳税人在合理时间内进一步提供资料和证据。救济的决定对于案件无论是事实上还是法律上都是一项全面、全新的决定。因此,申诉决定并不限于但应特别注意纳税人已提出的异议点。依照规定,提出申诉并不会中止前项决定的执行,然而依照特别程序也可以中止前项决定的执行。该特别程序并不严格只能由纳税人提出,当然实务中基本都是由纳税人提出的。税务机关一旦收到中止的请求,如果对前项决定的合法性存疑,或该决定的执行将对纳税人造成不合

---

① Lawrence M.Hill, Chapter 16 United States, Anuschka Bakker and Marc M.Levey, Transfer Pricing and Dispute Resolution, (IBFD 2011), p. 660.

理且特别的负担,则必须中止前项决定的执行。纳税人在提出中止请求的同时也必须提供担保。如果纳税人已解缴税款或前项决定已经执行,则中止的请求自动变为偿还请求。[①]

In Germany, any final and exhaustive administrative act made by a tax authority in any case may be subject to administrative review, and such a written relief is called complaint. The complaint is filed by any person or person who is liable for the administrative decision within one month from the date on which the decision becomes effective. The complaint procedure is free of charge. After receiving the complaint, the tax inspector who makes the administrative decision can correct it himself or herself. If he or she refuses to correct, the complaint will be transferred to an independent review department within the same tax office, which will then decide on relief. Before the final decision of the complaint is made, the taxpayer has the right to request oral discussion of the case. Similarly, tax authorities have the right to require taxpayers to provide further information and evidence within a reasonable time. The decision of relief is a comprehensive and completely new decision for the case, both in fact and in law. The decision to appeal is therefore not limited to, but should pay particular attention to, the points of disagreement raised by the taxpayer. According to the regulations, filing a complaint does not suspend the implementation of the preceding decision. However, the implementation of the preceding decision may also be suspended under special procedures. The special procedure is not strict only by taxpayers, of course, in practice is basically by taxpayers. Once the tax authority receives a request for suspension, if there is a doubt about the legality of the preceding decision, or if the implementation of the decision will impose an unreasonable and special burden on the taxpayer, the execution of the preceding decision must be suspended. The taxpayer must also provide security when making a request for suspension. If the taxpayer has paid the tax or the previous decision has been implemented, the suspended request automatically becomes a reimbursement request.

(三)纳税人向本国法院提起行政诉讼
Taxpayers Bring Administrative Proceedings to Their Own Courts

诉讼程序是一种耗时、昂贵、公开的国内解决程序。本国纳税人也只有在用尽其他解决方式后才寻求通过诉讼解决。外国纳税人更是担心本国法院法官会倾向于保护本国的税收利益而不是外国纳税人的合法权益。尽管这种担心事实上可能是多余的,但诉讼程序的纯国内色彩、普遍存在的弊端确实动摇了外国纳税人用它来解决国际税务争议的信心。由于各国国内司法体制的不同,国际税务争议既可能由普通法院的法官裁决,也可能由特别法院的法官裁决。例如,在法国,由行政法院来解决国际税务争议,行政法院的裁决最后可以上诉到国务院。在美国,美国国内税务署上诉部(IRS Appeals)收到纳税人书面复审请求后将

---

① Ekkehart Reimer, National Report on Taxpayer Protection in Germany, Protection of Taxpayer's Rights — European, International and Domestic Tax Law Perspective, Edited by Włodzimierz Nykiel and Małgorzata Sęk, Wolters Kluwer Polska Sp.z o.o., 2009, p. 210.

复查纳税人的请求，如果上诉部不予支持纳税人的请求就会向纳税人发出"90天信"（a 90-day letter）。"90天信"是由美国国内税务署发给纳税人补缴税款的通知单。纳税人若不同意国内税务署的纳税决定，可以选择向税务法院、联邦索赔法院和地区法院起诉。纳税人必须在发出补税通知单的90天内向税务法院起诉，如果纳税人不在美国境内则必须在寄出补税通知单的150天内向税务法院起诉。① 纳税人选择向税务法院起诉不需要先缴纳税款也不需要提起退税索赔。对税务法院裁决不服，还可以向联邦巡回上诉法院起诉，及至最后上诉到联邦最高法院。

Litigation is a time-consuming, expensive and open domestic settlement procedure. Domestic taxpayers also seek to settle through litigation only after exhausting other means of settlement. For foreign taxpayers, it is more worried that local court judges will tend to protect their tax interests than the legitimate rights and interests of foreign taxpayers. Although this concern may in fact be superfluous, the purely domestic color of the proceedings and the prevailing drawbacks do shake the confidence of foreign taxpayers to use it to resolve international tax disputes. Because of the differences in national judicial systems, international tax disputes may be decided by judges of ordinary courts or by judges of special courts. In France, for example, international tax disputes are settled by the Administrative Court, whose decision can eventually be appealed to the State Department. Within the United States, the Appeals Department of the United States Internal Revenue Service (IRS Appeals) will review the taxpayer's request upon receipt of the taxpayer's written review request, and if the Appeals Department does not support the taxpayer's request, it will send a 90-day letter to the taxpayer (a 90-day letter). The 90-day letter is a notice issued by the U.S. Internal Revenue Service to taxpayers to make up their taxes. Taxpayers who do not agree to the tax decisions of the domestic tax authorities may choose to sue in tax courts, federal claims courts and district courts. Taxpayers must sue the tax court within 90 days of issuing the tax supplement notice, and if the taxpayer is not in the United States, they must sue the tax court within 150 days of sending the tax supplement notice. Taxpayers choose to sue the tax court without paying taxes or filing tax claims. The decision of the tax court can also be appealed to the Federal Circuit Court of Appeal, and finally to the Federal Supreme Court.

如果纳税人想要向联邦地区法院或索赔法院起诉，则必须先缴纳税款然后才能提起退税索赔之诉。退税索赔之诉必须在纳税人缴纳税款之日起2年内提起。② 如果纳税人对这两个法院之中任何一个法院的裁决不服，还可以向联邦巡回上诉法院起诉，乃至最后上诉到联邦最高法院。

If the taxpayer wants to sue the Federal District Court or the Claims Court, the tax must be paid before the tax refund claim can be filed. Tax refund claims must be filed within 2 years from the date of payment of tax by the taxpayer. If the taxpayer disagrees with the decision of either of the two courts, he or she may also file a complaint with the Federal Circuit Court of Appeal and,

---

① The US Internal Revenue Code of 1986 (the Code) Sec.6213(a).
② Code Sec.6511(a).

finally, appeal to the Federal Supreme Court.

在德国，如果行政申诉不成功，纳税人可以向州税务法院起诉要求撤销或变更税务机关的决定。这种案件通常仅由一个专业法官来听讼。只有对非常复杂的案件，才会由3个专业法官和2个非专业法官（通常都是经验丰富的企业家）组成5人合议庭。一些州也采用1个专业法官和2个非专业法官组成3人合议庭。专业法官经常是从州的税务机关或州的财政局选任。他们都是受过专门税务训练的熟练的律师。作为法官，他们在人身、专业和经济地位方面享有完全的独立性。一位50岁的法官一年的总收入大约是71 500欧元，而同样在州的其他法院法官的收入是65 000欧元。纳税人作为原告向税务法院起诉后，将免费被指派一名律师或税务顾问作为其代理人，这样的协助或代理不是强制的。法院受理后，有义务去调查案件的事实。当然并没有严格的举证规则。如果纳税人应法院请求未能提供有利于自身事实的合理证据，则法院通常会认定该事实不存在。税务法院的裁决必须针对纳税人的诉请且不得超出该诉请。即使纳税人诉请中有合理之处，如果原决定有明显错误但结果正确，税务法院还是会维持原决定。①

In Germany, if the administrative complaint is unsuccessful, taxpayers can sue the state tax court for rescission or change of the tax authority's decision. Such cases are usually heard only by a professional judge. Only in very complex cases will a panel of five be composed of three professional judges and two lay judges, who are usually experienced entrepreneurs. A three-member panel of professional judges and two lay judges was also used in some cantons. Professional judges are often elected from the state tax authorities, including the state finance bureau. They are all skilled lawyers with special tax training. As judges, they enjoy full independence in their personal, professional and economic status. A 50-year-old judge earns about 71, 500 euros a year, compared with 65, 000 euros for other court judges in the same state. The taxpayer, after suing the tax court as plaintiff, will be appointed a lawyer or tax adviser as agent free of charge, although such assistance or agency is not mandatory. The court is obliged to investigate the facts of the case. Of course, there are no strict rules of proof. If the taxpayer fails to provide reasonable evidence in favour of his or her own facts at the request of the court, the court usually finds that the fact does not exist. The decision of the tax court must be directed against the taxpayer and must not exceed that application. Even if the taxpayer's application is reasonable, if the original decision is obviously wrong but the result is correct, the tax court will maintain the original decision.

如果纳税人对州税务法院的裁决不服，还可以向设在慕尼黑的联邦税务法院提起上诉。向联邦税务法院的上诉只能由律师、税务顾问或注册会计师提起。联邦税务法院一旦受理上诉，就会启动对州税务法院裁决的司法复查。这种司法复查仅限于对州税务法院裁决的法律审查，也就是说联邦税务法院既不会听取证据，也不会重新审查事实。联邦税务法院的5名法官组成合议庭，对州税务法院裁决在实体法或程序上是否违反联邦法进行审查。联邦税务法院的裁决以口头程序作出。如果纳税人胜诉，向联邦税务法院上诉的费用由国家承担；反之，纳税人败诉所有费用由其自己承担。例如，在2007年所有向联邦税务法院上诉的

---

① Code Sec.6511(a). p. 211.

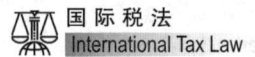

案件中,纳税人的胜诉率只有19.4%。①

If the taxpayer disagrees with the decision of the state tax court, he or she may also appeal to the Federal Tax Court in Munich. Appeals to the Federal Tax Court can only be filed by lawyers, tax advisors or CPAs. Once the Federal Tax Court receives an appeal, it initiates judicial review of the decisions of the State Tax Court. Such judicial review is limited to legal review of decisions of state tax courts, meaning that the federal tax courts neither hear evidence nor re-examine facts. A collegial panel of five judges of the Federal Tax Court examined whether the State Tax Court's decision violated federal law in substantive or procedural terms. The decision of the Federal Tax Court was made orally. If the taxpayer wins the case, the cost of appealing to the Federal Tax Court is borne by the state. Conversely, the taxpayer loses the case and all the expenses are borne by himself or herself. For example, in all cases appealed to the Federal Tax Court in 2007, the rate of success for taxpayers was only 19.4 per cent.

(二) 国际税务争议解决的替代争议解决方法
Alternative Dispute Resolution for International Tax Dispute Settlement

替代性争议解决(ADR)是指由一个公正的人帮助争议当事人解决或缩小他们之间的争议的过程,而不是由法庭或仲裁庭作出裁决。ADR是一种成本效益高、非正式、协商一致、快速解决纠纷的方式。当纳税人不同意税收专员关于税收债务或权利的决定时,就会产生税务纠纷。这些争议主要包括:当事人之间关于税务责任或权利的正式争议,例如提出异议;评估发布前产生的争议,例如纳税人考虑了税务局的立场文件。然而,ADR并不仅仅用于解决实体纠纷,它也可以用来澄清或限制问题,简化程序,消除争议双方关系问题造成的障碍。下面主要介绍澳大利亚税务局适用ADR的实务指南。一般ADR适用于以下情况:税务争议的问题是可以协商的;税务局和纳税人都愿意作出让步;争议能够在现有的解决政策和实践中得到解决;早期解决比司法裁决更可取。

Alternative dispute resolution (ADR) refers to the process by which an impartial person helps the disputing parties to resolve or narrow their disputes, rather than by a court or arbitral tribunal. ADR is a cost-effective, informal, consensual, and rapid resolution of disputes. Tax disputes arise when taxpayers disagree with the tax commissioner's decision on tax debts or rights. It mainly includes: formal disputes between the parties about tax liability or rights, such as raising objections; evaluating disputes arising before publication, such as the taxpayer's consideration of the tax bureau's position paper. However, ADR is not only used to resolve substantive disputes, but can also be used to clarify or limit issues, simplify procedures and remove obstacles caused by issues related to the relationship between the parties to the dispute. We will mainly introduce the Australian Taxation Bureau applicable ADR practice guide below. General ADR applies where the issue of tax disputes is negotiable, both the tax authorities and taxpayers are willing to make concessions,

---

① Bundesfinanzhof, Jahresbericht 2007, http://www.bundesfinanzhof.de//www/jb/jb2007/jb2007.pdf, p. 3.

disputes can be resolved in existing settlement policies and practices, and early resolution is preferable to judicial decisions.

实务中，ADR可能适用于以下情况：能够达成更快或更便宜的解决方案，尤其是当诉讼成本与可能的利益不成比例时；需要缩小或澄清有争议的事实和问题时；为了尽量减少与举证困难相关的风险时；为了促进一定/提前支付税款。一般来说，澳大利亚税务局使用的ADR有三类。

ADR in practice may apply where faster or cheaper solutions can be achieved, especially when the costs of litigation are disproportionate to the potential benefits; when controversial facts and issues need to be narrowed or clarified; in order to minimize the risks associated with evidentiary difficulties; and in order to facilitate certain/early payment of taxes. There are generally three types of ADR used by the Australian Revenue Service.

（1）内部调解。内部调解是由税务局提供的一项免费调解的服务，由一名训练有素的、独立的税务局调解人协助参与者协商争议。内部调解人帮助各方确定有争议的问题，制定备选方案，考虑备选方案，并尝试达成协议。内部调解员不会证实事实，支持任何一方，提供建议，作出决定或决定谁是"对的或错的"。他（她）只是引导双方完成整个过程，并帮助他们确保有明确的沟通渠道，并正确接收信息。

(1) Internal mediation. Internal mediation is a free mediation service provided by the Inland Revenue Department, with a trained, independent Inland Revenue Department mediator assisting participants in negotiating disputes. The internal mediator helps the parties identify contentious issues, develop options, consider options, and attempt to reach agreement. The internal mediator will not confirm the facts, support either party, provide advice, make a decision or decide who is "right or wrong". He (she) just guides both sides to complete the whole process and helps them ensure that there are clear channels of communication and receive information correctly.

如果纳税人要申请内部调解，则需要填写内部调解申请表。在提出内部调解请求后，调解会安排在双方方便的最早日期。调解过程通常不会超过1天。内部调解最好是面对面进行，但如有必要，可通过电话或视频连接进行。调解前，调解人联系纳税人和澳大利亚税务局的办案官员，由调解人概述流程并回答纳税人的问题，通知调解的日期、时间和地点。在调解当天调解人将概述会议流程，强调会议的共同期望和目标，要求纳税人和澳大利亚税务局的办案官在调解开始时提供对争议的看法，协助双方确定争议问题和解决方案，协助纳税人和税务局办案官评估方案并尝试达成解决方案。调解各方要诚信参与，尊重其他参与者，公开透明，愿意谈判。应授权参与者讨论和解决争议。

If taxpayers want to apply for internal mediation, they need to fill out the internal mediation application form. After making an internal mediation request, it will be arranged at the earliest convenient date for both parties. The mediation process usually does not exceed one day. Internal mediation is best done face to face, but if necessary, by telephone or video link. Before mediation, the mediator contacts the taxpayer and the case officer of the Australian Revenue Authority, and the mediator outlines the process and answers the taxpayer's questions, notifying the date, time and place of the mediation. On the day of mediation, the facilitator will outline the process of the meeting, emphasize the common expectations and objectives of the meeting, require taxpayers and the case officer of the Australian Revenue Authority to provide a view of the dispute at the beginning of the mediation, assist both parties in identifying the dispute issues and solutions, assist taxpayers and IRS case officers in evaluating the plan and trying to reach a solution. Mediation parties should participate in good faith, respect other participants, open and transparent, willing to negotiate. Participants should be authorized to discuss and resolve disputes.

调解人的作用是管理参与者之间的讨论，以期解决争议，或至少在解决问题方面取得进展。调解人将接受过调解过程的培训，具有技能和经验，在法律范围内诚信行事，支持流程的完整性和公平性，尝试在合理的时间内完成流程，保持公正，避免任何实际或感知的利益冲突，对案件的最终结果不享有利益，不得在调解过程中接受任何礼物、贿赂或奖励（无论是货币形式还是非货币形式），但调解人作为ATO雇员的当前报酬除外。调解人不得强迫任何参与者同意其不愿意接受的过程、条件或结果中的步骤。未经所有参与者同意，无论是否以ATO员工的身份，调解人之前或将来不得参与案件，应立即向参与者披露可能或可能被视为影响其独立性的任何信息。并且只有在所有参与者同意的情况下，他们才能继续在该过程中充当调解人，遵守保密要求。如果参与者提出合理要求，则应停止行动并退出流程。如果参与者认为程序的继续可能损害或损害一个或多个参与方，或一个或多个参与方不真诚行事，则暂停或终止该程序。

The role of mediators is to manage discussions among participants with a view to resolving disputes or at least making progress in resolving problems. A mediator will have received training, skills and experience in the mediation process, act in good faith within the law, support the integrity and fairness of the process, attempt to complete the process within a reasonable time, maintain justice, avoid any actual or perceived conflict of interest, have no interest in the final outcome of the case, and shall not accept any gift, bribe or reward (whether in monetary or non-monetary form) in the mediation process, except for the current remuneration of the mediator as an ATO employee. Mediators shall not force any participant agree to the steps in the process, conditions or outcome that they are unwilling to accept. Without the consent of all participants, whether as ATO employees or not, mediators shall not to participate in the case before or in the future, and disclose immediately to the participants any information that may or may be considered to affect their independence. Moreover, they continue to act as conciliators in the process only with the consent of all participants, subject to confidentiality requirements. If the participant makes a reasonable request, mediators shall stop acting and exits the process. If the participant believes that the continuation of the process may impair or impairs one or more participants, or if one or more participants do not act in good faith, the program is suspended or terminated.

如果双方同意，调解人可协助记录调解结果。如果没有达成解决方案，审计或异议将根据常规流程确定，或者，就其他选项（包括纳税人的审查或上诉权利）与纳税人讨论。

If the parties agree, the conciliator may assist in recording the results of the mediation. If no solution is reached, the audit or objection will be determined according to the regular process, or other options (including the taxpayer's right to review or appeal) will be discussed with the taxpayer.

(2) 在大型、复杂的税务争议中,澳大利亚税务局可聘请外部从业人员适用ADR。

(2) In large and complex tax disputes, the Australian Revenue Service may employ external practitioners to apply ADR.

(3) 由法院或仲裁庭在裁决案件中适用ADR。

(3) Application of ADR by A Court or Arbitral Tribunal

调解、和解和早期中立评估是解决税务纠纷中最常用的方法。调解是参与者在ADR从业者的协助下进行谈判。ADR从业者帮助双方确定有争议的问题,制定备选方案,考虑替代方案,并尝试达成协议的一种方法。调解员通常不提供咨询意见,除非当事方要求进行咨询/评估性调解或调解。调解通常是自愿的,但可以由法院或仲裁庭下令。如果调解是自愿的,当事人通常分摊相关费用。和解也是一种方法,参与者在ADR从业者的协助下进行谈判,ADR从业者帮助双方确定争议问题,制定备选方案,考虑替代方案,并尝试达成协议。和解人通常在争端领域具有资格。与调解程序不同,和解人可以就解决争端的可能选择向当事方提供专家咨询意见,并积极鼓励参与方达成协议。行政上诉法庭经常在税务纠纷中使用和解。中立评估(也称为早期中立评估)是指争议的参与者向ADR从业者陈述其主张,ADR从业者就解决争议的适当方式提出建议。在税务纠纷中,ADR从业人员通常在税法方面有丰富的经验,并在争议进入诉讼程序时就法院或仲裁庭可能作出的决定提供建议。是否接受评估者的建议以及如何使用这些信息,取决于各方。中立评估可以在争议的任何阶段进行,但通常在法律程序开始之前进行最为有用。

Mediation, reconciliation and early neutral assessment are the most commonly used methods to resolve tax disputes. Mediation is a way for participants to negotiate with the assistance of ADR practitioners to help both parties identify controversial issues, develop options, consider alternatives, and try to reach an agreement. Mediators usually do not provide advice unless the parties request an advisory/assessed mediation or mediation. Mediation is usually voluntary, but may be ordered by a court or arbitral tribunal. If mediation is voluntary, the parties usually share the relevant costs. Reconciliation is also a way in which participants negotiate with the assistance of ADR practitioners, who help both parties identify controversial issues, develop options, consider alternatives, and try to reach an agreement. The conciliator is usually qualified in the field of dispute. Unlike mediation procedures, conciliators can provide expert advice to parties on possible options for the settlement of disputes and actively encourage participants to reach agreement. Administrative Appeals Tribunal (AAT) often uses conciliation in tax disputes. Neutral assessment (also known as early neutral assessment, abbreviated as ENE) means that participants in a dispute present their claims to ADR practitioners and make recommendations on appropriate ways to resolve disputes. ADR practitioners usually have extensive experience in tax law in tax disputes and advise on possible decisions by courts or arbitral tribunals when disputes enter the proceedings. Whether or not to accept the evaluator's recommendations and how to use this information depends on the parties. Neutral assessments can be conducted at any stage of the dispute, but are usually most useful before legal proceedings begin.

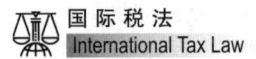

第四节　国际税务争议解决的国际法程序
Section 4　International Legal Procedures for the Settlement of International Tax Disputes

一、相互协商程序
Mutual Agreement Procedure

（一）相互协商程序的概述
Overview of Mutual Agreement Procedure

相互协商程序，在国际税收协定发展的早期也被称为"主管当局协议"或财税机关协议。它是随着税收协定的出现而出现的。奥地利和列支敦士登在1901年的税收协定第8条就首次规定了它的使用，"缔约方的财税机关在必要时应当达成一项协议，并且依据这项协议中防止重复征税的专门条款的规定采取相应措施……"

Mutual Agreement Procedure is also known early in the development of international tax agreements as "competent authority agreements" or fiscal authority agreements. It emerged with the emergence of tax agreements. For the first time, Article 8 of the tax agreement of 1901 between Austria and Liechtenstein provides for its use, "the contracting parties' fiscal authorities shall, if necessary, reach an agreement and take appropriate measures in accordance with the provisions of the special provision of this agreement to prevent double taxation ..."

第一次世界大战后，英国和美国跨国公司的迅猛发展扩大了世界贸易。世界贸易的巨大增长和战后的经济危机导致欧洲很多国家采取重税政策。为了经济的发展和增加国际征税，商人们于1919年在巴黎建立了国际商会。同年同地国际联盟也正式成立。国际联盟于1920年9月24日在布鲁塞尔召开了一次国际财税会议，在会议上国际双重征税被认为是对跨境投资和资本流动的一种阻碍。从1921年9月国际联盟财税委员会委托由四个经济学家组成小组展开关于双重征税的理论研究开始，国际联盟关于双重征税和逃税发布了多份报告。到1922年，主管当局协议被作为一种解决自然人双重国籍、分配商业存在的所得或利润的方法。①

After World War I, the rapid development of British and American multinational corporations expanded world trade. The huge growth of world trade and the postwar economic crisis led many European countries to adopt heavy tax policies. For economic development

---

① Juan Angel Becerra, Interpretation and Application of Tax Treaties in North America, Second Revised Edition. (IBFD 2013), pp. 7-8, 25.

and increased international taxation, businessmen established the International Chamber of Commerce in Paris in 1919. In the same year, the International League of Nations was formally established too. The International Union convened an international finance and taxation conference in Brussels on 24 September 1920, at which international double taxation was considered an obstacle to cross-border investment and capital flows. From September 1921, the International Union Fiscal and Tax Commission commissioned a group of four economists to conduct a theoretical study on double taxation, the International Union issued a number of reports on double taxation and tax evasion. By 1922, the competent authority agreement had been used as a solution to the dual nationality of natural persons and the distribution of proceeds or profits from commercial existence.

目前的相互协商程序是国际联盟财税委员会于1940年和1943年在墨西哥城，以及1946年在伦敦讨论的结果，由此形成了1943年墨西哥城协定范本和1946年伦敦协定范本。这两个范本都对主管当局磋商和主管当局协议作了规定。例如，墨西哥城协定范本第16条和伦敦协定范本第17条规定如下：当一个纳税人有证据证明缔约国一方税务机关的行为已经导致对他的双重征税时，他应当有权利向他的住所地的或他的国籍国的税务机关提出请求。一旦他的请求被接受，他的住所地的或他的国籍国的主管税务机关应当直接和另一缔约国磋商，以达成一项避免双重征税的公正协议。对这两个协定范本的注释也规定：协定范本第16条和协定范本第17条规定的特别程序并非要取代由缔约国税收立法建立的税收上诉程序，而是对它的补充。被双重征税的纳税人不管税收协定的规定，都有权利选择向他的住所地的或他的国籍国的税务机关提出请求。根据双重征税的情况，他应当获得缔约国一方或另一方给予的保护，这对他也是合法合理的。此外，应当指出主管机关磋商不是司法程序，而是所涉税务机关间直接磋商的程序。①

The current mutual agreement procedure was developed during the meetings of the Fiscal Committee of the League of Nations in Mexico City in 1940 and 1943 and in London in 1946, where the Mexico and London Models were framed. Both the Mexico and London Models made reference to competent authority consultations and competent authority agreements. For example, Article 16 of the Model Mexico City Agreement and Article 17 of the Model London Agreement provide that a taxpayer shall have the right to submit a request to the tax authorities of the place of his or her financial domicile or of the country of his or her nationality when there is evidence that the conduct of the tax authorities of one of the contracting states has led to a double taxation of him or her. Once his or her request has been accepted, the competent tax authorities of the place of his or her financial residence or of the state of his or her nationality should consult directly with another state party to reach a just agreement to avoid double taxation. The annotations to the two model agreements also provide that the special procedures provided for in Article 16 of the model agreement and Article 17 of the model agreement are not intended to replace, but to supplement, the tax appeal procedure established by the state party's

---

① Juan Angel Becerra, Interpretation and Application of Tax Treaties in North America, Second Revised Edition. (IBFD 2013), pp. 29-31.

tax legislation. A double-taxed taxpayer, regardless of the provisions of the tax agreement, has the right to choose to submit a request to the tax authorities of his or her financial domicile or of the country of his or her nationality. In the case of double taxation, he or she should be afforded the protection of one or the other of the contracting states, which was also lawful and reasonable for him or her. In addition, it should be noted that consultation by the competent authorities is not a judicial procedure but a procedure for direct consultation between the tax authorities involved.

综上所述，1943年墨西哥城协定范本和1946年伦敦协定范本规定的主管当局磋商程序是现在经合组织税收协定范本第25条相互协商程序的历史渊源。

As a result, the consultation (competent authority consultations) procedures of the competent authorities under the 1943 Mexico City Model Agreement and the 1946 London Model Agreement constitute the historical origin of the mutual consultation procedure now under Article 25 of the OECD Model Tax Agreement.

（二）相互协商程序的基本规则（以OECD税收协定范本第25条第1、第2、第3、第4、第5款为例）

Basic MAP Rules (Using Paragraphs 1, 2, 3, 4 and 5 of Article 25 of the Model OECD Tax Agreement as Examples)

相互协商程序这一术语在国际税收协定用语中是由经合发组织的前身欧洲经济合作组织于1956年首次使用的。用欧洲经济合作组织财政委员会的表述：本报告附件E第25条的目的是在缔约国之间提供一种磋商和协议的程序以及根据该程序的条件和适用来解决相关案件。第25条的前两款规定用来处理与协定不符的征税，除了缔约方国内税法提供的救济方法外。第3款规定了用相互协商程序来解决由协定解释或适用引起的问题以及协定未规定的双重征税的问题。第4款最后规定了由缔约国双方主管税务机关代表组成一个委员会来交换意见。

The term mutual consultation procedure was first used in the terms of international tax agreements by the Organisation for European Economic Co-operation (OEEC), the predecessor of OECD, in 1956. As stated by the Finance Committee of the European Economic Cooperation Organization, Article 25 of Annex E to the present report is intended to provide a procedure for consultation and agreement between states parties and to resolve the relevant cases in accordance with the terms and application of the procedure. The first two paragraphs of Article 25 provide for the treatment of taxes inconsistent with the agreement, in addition to the remedies provided by the domestic tax laws of the contracting parties. Paragraph 3 provides for a process of mutual consultation to resolve issues arising from the interpretation or application of the agreement and the issue of double taxation not provided for in the agreement. Paragraph 4 concludes by providing for a committee of representatives of the competent tax authorities of both parties to exchange views.

2010年OECD税收协定范本第25条的规定实际上与前述第1、第2、第3、第4款是相同的，都规定了原来的相互协商程序。第25条第5款关于仲裁的规定是2008年OECD税收协定范本增加的内容。

Compared to the text of Article 25 of the 2010 Model OECD Tax Agreement, the provisions are in fact identical to those of the preceding Paragraphs 1, 2, 3 and 4, all of which provide for the original mutual consultation procedure. Article 25, Paragraph 5, on arbitration was added to the 2008 Model OECD Tax Agreement.

通常有两种相互协商程序，一种适用于特定纳税人税收协定事项的解决程序，如转让定价的情形或纳税人双重居所冲突的解决；另一种是主管机关就税收协定的解释或适用产生的事项程序。特定纳税人相互协商程序的数量要远远大于通常协定解释程序的数量。根据这两种相互协商程序，由主管机关分别达成两种相互协议。

There are usually two procedures for mutual consultation, one for the settlement of tax agreement matters applicable to specific taxpayers, such as the case of transfer pricing or the settlement of conflicts of dual residence of taxpayers; and the other for matters arising from the interpretation or application of tax agreements by competent authorities. The number of procedures for consultation between specific taxpayers is much greater than the number of procedures for the interpretation of agreements. According to these two procedures for mutual consultation, the competent authorities reach two types of mutual agreement.

第一种是普通相互协议。普通相互协议是由授权主管机关就税收协定具体条款的解释或适用通过协商或谈判达成一致的协议。这种协议对于完善或澄清原来税收协定中缺漏或模糊的规定是非常必要的。另外也会出现，当一个缔约国国内税法发生变化，在不损害税收协定情况下如何就协定中的特定条款的解释或适用由主管机关达成一致协议。这种协议的法律地位在大多数案件中是由缔约国国内宪法或税法界定的。通说认为，它们对法院没有约束力，在协定有效时它们可以被终止。在1988年"Xerox Corp.v.United States"一案中，美国联邦上诉法院裁定：由美英两国主管机关依据美英两国税收协定相互协商程序达成的税收程序既不属于法律也不属于法规，对法院没有法律效力。而且它不能改变税收协定的内容和目的。① 在1992年的另一个案件"Snap-On Tools, Inc.v. United States"中，法院也认为，根据美英两国税收协定相互协商程序达成的一项主管机关协议，有助于法院解释相关法律，但并不能约束法院。②

The first is the common mutual agreement. Ordinary mutual agreement is an agreement by which the competent authority is authorized to reach consensus through consultation or negotiation on the interpretation or application of specific provisions of a tax agreement. This agreement is necessary to perfect or clarify the missing or vague provisions of the original tax agreement. It may also occur that when the domestic tax law of a contracting state changes, it is up to the competent authorities to agree on the interpretation or application of specific provisions of the agreement without prejudice to the tax agreement. The legal status of this agreement is defined in most cases by the domestic constitution or tax laws of the state party. The general view was that they were not binding on the court and could be terminated when the agreement was in force. The United States Federal Court of Appeal ruled in the Xerox Corp.v.United States case in 1988

---

① US:CC, 1988, Xerox Corp.v.United States, 14 Cl.Ct.455(1988).
② US: CC/AC, 1992/1994, Snap-On Tools, Inc.v.United States, 26 Cl.Ct.1045(1992), aff'd, 26 F.3d 137(Fed. Cir.1994), Tax Treaty Case Law IBFD.

that the tax procedure (Revenue Procedure) concluded by the competent authorities of the United States and Britain under the mutual consultation procedure of the United States and Britain under the tax agreement between the two countries is neither a law nor a statute and has no legal effect on the court. And it can not change the content and purpose of tax agreements. In another case, Snap-On Tools, Inc.v.United States, in 1992, the court also found that an agreement of the competent authority reached under the mutual consultation procedure between the United States and Britain in the tax agreement helped the court to interpret the relevant law, but could not bind the court.

第二种是特定案件相互协议。特定案件相互协议是由两个缔约国的主管机关根据两国间税收协定相互协商程序就特定纳税人的特定案件所涉税收协定具体条款的解释或适用达成一致的协议。这种协议在转移定价的情形或解决纳税人双重居所冲突的案件以及特定非歧视的案件中都很常见。这种协议从本质上说是由缔约国双方的主管机关不依照国际公法，而为了一个第三人（纳税人）的特定目的而达成的。达成这项协议的法律基础是2010年经合发组织税收协定范本（以下简称"范本"）第25条相互协商程序的第1、第2款的规定。①如第25条第1款规定，当一个人认为，缔约国一方或者双方的措施，导致或将导致对其不符合该协定规定的征税时，可以不考虑各缔约国国内法律的补救办法，将案情提交本人为其居

---

① Art.25(1)2010 OECD Model("where a person considers that the actions of one or both of the contracting states result or will result for him or her in taxation not in accordance with the provisions of this convention, he or she may, irrespective of the remedies provided by the domestic law of those states, present his or her case to the competent authority of the contracting state of which he or she is a resident, or if his or her case comes under Paragraph 1 of Article 24, to that of the contracting state of which he or she is a national.The case must be presented within three years from the first notification of the action resulting in taxation not in accordance with the provisions of the Convention.")
(2) ("The competent authority shall endeavour, if the objection appears to it to be justified and if it is not itself able to arrive at a satisfactory solution, to resolve the case by mutual agreement with the competent authority of the other contracting state, with a view to the avoidance of taxation which is not in accordance with the Convention. Any agreement reached shall be implemented notwithstanding any time limits in the domestic law of the contracting states.")
(3) The competent authorities of the contracting states shall endeavour to resolve by mutual agreement any difficulties or doubts arising as to the interpretation or application of the Convention. They may also consult together for the elimination of double taxation in cases not provided for in the Convention.
(4) The competent authorities of the contracting states may communicate with each other directly, including through a joint commission consisting of themselves or their representatives, for the purpose of reaching an agreement in the sense of the preceding paragraphs.
(5) Where, a) under paragraph 1, a person has presented a case to the competent authority of a contracting state on the basis that the actions of one or both of the contracting states have resulted for that person in taxation not in accordance with the provisions of this Convention, and b) the competent authorities are unable to reach an agreement to resolve that case pursuant to Paragraph 2 within two years from the presentation of the case to the competent authority of the other contracting State, any unresolved issues arising from the case shall be submitted to arbitration if the person so requests. These unresolved issues shall not, however, be submitted to arbitration if a decision on these issues has already been rendered by a court or administrative tribunal of either state. Unless a person directly affected by the case does not accept the mutual agreement that implements the arbitration decision, that decision shall be binding on both contracting states and shall be implemented notwithstanding any time limits in the domestic laws of these states. The competent authorities of the contracting States shall by mutual agreement settle the mode of application of this paragraph.

民的缔约国主管当局，或者如果其案情属于第24条第1款，可以提交本人为其国民的缔约国主管当局。该项案情必须在不符合该协定规定的征税措施第一次通知之日起3年内提出。根据范本第3条第1款a项的规定，一个人是指一个自然人、一个公司或者是其他人的集合。第3条第一款第b项把公司定义为任何法人或者是在税法上被视为法人的任何组织。第二款规定，上述主管当局如果认为所提意见合理，又不能单方面圆满解决时，应设法同缔约国另一方主管当局相互协商解决，以避免不符合该协定的征税。达成的协议应予执行，而不受各缔约国国内法律的时间限制。根据以上规定，我们可以得出如下三点：第一，相互协商程序并不适用于企业或合伙组织，而是适用于自然人或法人；第二，有权向缔约国主管当局提出案情的必须是某一缔约国的居民纳税人；第三，纳税人向缔约国主管当局提出案情时必须遵守每个缔约国国内的格式要求。此外，因为相互协商程序是一种完全的行政性程序，所以法院并没有权力去发起或强迫税务机关去达成一项协议。还有非常重要的一点，并不是所有纳税人的居民国都许可相互协商程序和诉讼程序的同时进行。例如，加拿大就规定纳税人在继续上诉程序的同时不可以寻求与外国主管当局进行协商。如果在上诉裁决作出后纳税人因为双重征税或与税收协定不符的征税再次提出相互协商程序，加拿大主管当局将向外国主管当局提交上诉裁决作出的细节和理由。而且加拿大国内法院的裁决是不可以被改变的，这也就是说，加拿大主管当局没有任何协商的余地。如上所述，纳税人向缔约国主管当局提出案情前应当要非常了解税收协定中相互协商程序的规定以及缔约国国内的格式要求。在北美，特定案件相互协商程序一直是一种有效的达成共识的机制，在大多数情况下都能对转移定价分配的案件起到充分消除国际双重征税的作用。这一机制在双边转移定价协议的磋商中也发挥了作用，首先由纳税人和其居民国主管机关达成协议；然后由该居民国主管机关和另一缔约国主管机关协商达成双边协议。

The second is a specific case mutual agreement. A specific case mutual agreement is an agreement reached by the competent authorities of the two states parties on the interpretation or application of the specific provisions of the tax agreement in a particular case of a particular taxpayer, in accordance with the mutual consultation procedure of the tax agreement between the two states parties. These agreements are common in cases of transfer pricing or settlement of taxpayer double residence conflicts, as well as in cases of specific non-discrimination. These agreements are, in essence, concluded by the competent authorities of both parties in a contracting state for the specific purpose of a third person (taxpayer), in accordance with public international law. The legal basis for such an agreement is the provisions of Paragraphs 1 and 2 of the 2010 OECD Model Tax Agreement (hereinafter referred to as Model Tax Agreement. Article 25(1) provides that where a person considers that the actions of one or both of the contracting states result or will result for him or her in taxation not in accordance with the provisions of this Convention, he or she may, irrespective of the remedies provided by the domestic law of those states, present his or her case to the competent authority of the contracting state of which he or she is a resident, or if his or her case comes under Paragraph 1 of Article 24, to that of the contracting state of which he or she is a national. The case must be presented within three years from the first notification of the action resulting in taxation not in accordance with the provisions of the Convention. Article 3(1)(a) of the OECD Model defines a person as an individual, a corporation or any other body of persons. Article 3(1)(b) of the OECD Model defines a company as any body corporate or any entity that is treated as a body corporate for tax purposes. Article 25(2) provides that the competent authority shall endeavour, if the objection appears to it to be justified and if it is not itself able to arrive at a satisfactory solution, to resolve the case by mutual agreement with the competent authority of the other contracting state, with a view to the avoidance of taxation which is not in accordance with the Convention. Any agreement reached shall be implemented notwithstanding any time limits in the domestic law of the contracting states. On the basis of the above, we can draw the following three points. First, the procedure of mutual consultation does not apply to enterprises or partnerships, but to natural or legal persons. Second, the competent authority of a state party must have the right to bring a case before the competent authority of a state party against a resident taxpayer of a state party; and third, the taxpayer must comply with the domestic format requirements of each state party when presenting the case to the competent authority of a state party. Moreover, because the procedure of mutual consultation is a complete administrative procedure, the court does not have the power to initiate or force the tax authorities to reach an agreement. It is also important that not all taxpayers' residents allow mutual consultation and litigation to take place simultaneously. Canada, for example, provides that taxpayers should not seek consultation with the competent foreign authority while continuing the appeal proceedings, and the competent Canadian authority will submit the details and reasons of the appeal decision to the competent foreign authority if, after the appeal decision is made, the taxpayer again submits the mutual consultation procedure because of double taxation or taxation inconsistent with the tax agreement. Moreover, the decisions of the Canadian domestic courts can not be changed, which means that the Canadian authorities have no room for consultation. As noted above, taxpayers should have a good understanding of the provisions of the mutual consultation procedure in the tax agreement and the format requirements in the state party before presenting their case to the competent authorities of the state party. In North America, the case-specific mutual consultation process has been an effective consensus-building mechanism, which in most cases can fully eliminate international double taxation in cases of transfer pricing distribution. This mechanism also plays a role in the negotiation of bilateral transfer pricing agreements, beginning with an agreement between the taxpayer and the competent authority of the country of residence, and then between the competent authority of that country and the competent authority of another state party.

2010年OECD税收协定范本第25条共有5款。第1款规定了相互协商程序的发起。第2款规定了主管当局的义务。第1款给予了纳税人向其居住国提出申诉的权利，第2款则规定了一国税务机关如何将纳税人与税务机关的争议转化为两国税务机关之间的争议。居住国有义务考虑纳税人的申请异议是否合理以及能否单方面解决。在缔约国一方提出进行谈判时，另一方有义务进行谈判，但仅有义务尽力谈判，没有义务一定要达成结果。因此，第1款和第2款适用于间接的国际税务争议。第3款规定当局通过相互协商程序解决什么问题。第3款适用于缔约国税务机关在解释或适用税收协定时的争议的处理，因此其适用于直接国际税务争议。该款要求税务机关,如果可能的话,通过相互协商程序来解决解释和适用协定中的困难。这些困难主要涉及或可能涉及某类纳税人的一般性问题。因此,缔约国主管当局没有义务启动此类争议的相互协商程序。另外,第3款还具有填补条约空白的作用,即用于解决税收协定未规定的双重征税问题。第4款规定了当局沟通的方式。第5款规定对未决事项,纳税人可以要求仲裁。具体方式包括:纳税人发起、主管税务机关采取相互协商、咨询、直接沟通(包括成立联合委员会)、调解、专家程序(仅适用纯事实争议方式)。

Article 25 of the 2010 Model OECD Tax Agreement contains five paragraphs. MAP initiation is provided for in Paragraph 1. Paragraph 2 sets out the obligations of the competent authorities. Paragraph 1 gives the taxpayer the right to lodge a complaint with the state of residence, Paragraph 2 sets out how a country's tax authorities translate disputes between taxpayers and tax authorities into disputes between the two countries' tax authorities. The state of residence is obliged to consider whether the taxpayer's application objection is reasonable and whether it can be settled unilaterally. When a party offers to negotiate, the other party is obliged to negotiate, but it's only an obligation to negotiate, but there is no obligation to reach results. Therefore, Paragraphs 1 and 2 apply to indirect international tax disputes. Paragraph 3 provides for the MAP of the authorities to resolve any problems. Paragraph 3 applies to the handling of disputes between the tax authorities of a contracting state in the interpretation or application of tax agreements. Therefore, it is applicable to direct international tax disputes. It requires tax authorities, if possible, difficulties in the interpretation and application of agreements are resolved through mutual consultation procedures. These difficulties relate mainly to or may involve general issues of a particular type of taxpayer. Therefore, the competent authorities of the state party are not obliged to initiate a mutual consultation procedure for such disputes. Besides, Paragraph 3 also serves to fill the treaty gap, that is, to solve the problem of double taxation not stipulated in the tax agreement. Paragraph 4 sets out the manner in which the authorities communicate. Paragraph 5 provides for outstanding matters, taxpayers may request arbitration. Specific methods include taxpayer initiation, mutual consultation by the competent tax authorities, consultation, direct communication (including the establishment of joint committees), mediation, expert procedures (only in the form of purely factual disputes).

(三)互相协商程序的特点
MAP's Characteristics

(1)相互协商程序是通过税收协定缔约国双方的税务主管机关解决纳税人税收争议的机制。相互协商程序是由代表缔约国的税务主管机关之间进行的国际程序。该程序虽然属于解决国际争端的外交手段,但不是通过外交部门,而是由两国税务主管机关谈判进行,并可自由决定协商的具体程序和规则,并可设立联合委员会。

(1) Mutual consultation procedure is a mechanism to resolve taxpayer tax disputes through the tax authorities of both parties to the tax agreement. The mutual consultation procedure is

an international procedure between the tax authorities representing the state party. While this procedure is a diplomatic instrument for the settlement of international disputes, it is negotiated not through the diplomatic service, but by the tax authorities of the two countries and is free to decide on specific procedures and rules for consultation and may establish joint committees.

（2）相互协商程序是一种给予纳税人的类似外交保护的特殊程序。纳税人居住国税务机关受理了纳税人的申请后，并不一定要启动相互协商程序。如果税务机关认为申诉合理，其问题主要由于纳税人居住国采取的税收措施所致，就可单方面解决。在这种情况下，就没有必要通过相互协商程序解决问题。

(2) The procedure of mutual consultation is a special procedure that gives taxpayers similar diplomatic protection to the procedure. After accepting the taxpayer's application, the tax authorities of the country where the taxpayer lives do not have to initiate mutual consultation procedures. If the tax authorities consider that the complaint is reasonable, the problem can be solved unilaterally, mainly due to the tax measures taken by the taxpayer's country of residence. In such cases, there is no need to resolve the issue through a process of mutual consultation.

但是，如果居住国税务机关不能单方面令人满意地解决纳税人的税务问题，认为纳税人申诉的税收问题全部或部分是由于缔约国对方税务主管机关采取措施所致，其就有义务启动相互协商程序了。不过，如果纳税人居住国在此情况下仍不启动相互协商程序，对纳税人来说，由于不是国际法主体，也不能在国际层面上就税务当局不启动相互协商程序提出申诉，这需要看其居住国的国内法是否有相应规定。比如，纳税人是否可向法院就税务机关不启动相互协商程序的决定提出司法审查。

However, if the tax authorities of the state of residence are unable to solve the tax problems of the taxpayer unilaterally and satisfactorily, they are obliged to initiate a mutual consultation procedure if they consider that the tax problems complained by the taxpayer are due in whole or in part to the measures taken by the tax authorities of the other state party. However, if the state of residence of the taxpayer does not initiate a mutual consultation procedure in such a case, for taxpayers, since they are not subjects of international law and can not appeal at the international level against the failure of the tax authorities to initiate a mutual consultation procedure, this depends on whether the domestic law of the state of residence has a corresponding provision. For example, whether a taxpayer can submit a judicial review to a court of the tax authorities' decision not to initiate a mutual consultation procedure.

从税务主管机关没有义务必须启动相互协商程序这点来看，该程序与国际法中的外交保护具有类似之处，都是一国保护本国居民或国民利益的制度，而且国家在该程序中占据主动，是否启动不在于当事人。不过，相互协商程序又不同于一般意义的外交保护，因为相互协商程序的启动不以用尽当地救济为前提，即使纳税人不寻求国内法的救济，也不排斥纳税人寻求国内法的救济。

From the point of view that the tax authorities are not obliged to initiate a procedure of mutual consultation, the procedure has similarities with diplomatic protection in international law, i.e. it is a system for a state to protect the interests of its own residents or nationals, and the state takes the initiative in the procedure, and whether or not to initiate it does not lie with the parties. However, the procedure of mutual consultation is different from that of diplomatic protection in the general sense, since the procedure of mutual consultation is not initiated on the premise of exhaustion of local remedies, even if the taxpayer does not seek relief from domestic law, it does not exclude the taxpayer from seeking relief from domestic law.

不过，实践中可能出现这样的情况，相互协商已经启动，税务机关已经达成了协议，但由于纳税人也将案件提交了缔约国国内法院审理，法院尚未作出终审判决，此时税务机关没有理由拒绝纳税人的要求，即允许其在法院作出判决前，延缓接受执行相互协商程序结果所提出的解决办法。这就存在着法院判决与协商协议相冲突的可能，而有的国家国内法禁止缔约国税务机关作出与该国法院判决不同的行政决定。为避免这种冲突，防止相互协商程序执行中的困难及对该程序的滥用，实践中税务机关在启动相互协商程序时，一般要求纳税人撤回向国内法院的诉讼。简言之，执行相互协商程序决议通常必须具备下列条件：纳税人接受该相互协商决议，且纳税人撤销了其已经在相互协商决议中解决问题的法律诉讼。

However, this may be the case in practice, where mutual consultations have been initiated and the tax authorities have reached an agreement, but since the taxpayer has also referred the case to the domestic courts of the contracting state, the court has not yet rendered a final judgment, at which time the tax authorities have no reason to reject the taxpayer's request to defer the settlement proposed as a result of the mutual consultation procedure before the court makes its decision. There was the possibility that court decisions would conflict with the agreement on consultation, while domestic law in some countries prohibited the tax authorities of a state party from making administrative decisions different from those of its courts. In order to avoid such conflicts and prevent difficulties in the implementation of the mutual consultation procedure and the abuse of the procedure, tax authorities in practice generally require taxpayers to withdraw their actions to domestic courts when initiating the mutual consultation procedure. In short, the implementation of a mutual consultation procedure resolution usually requires the following conditions: the taxpayer accepts the mutual consultation resolution and the taxpayer withdraws the legal action that it has already resolved in the mutual consultation resolution.

（3）纳税人不是相互协商程序的主体。国际税收协定为缔约国创设权利与义务，纳税人并不是该协定的主体，只是可根据税收条约享受税收协定给予的利益。因此，国家间通过相互协商程序解决其税收争议时，纳税人也不是相互协商程序的当事人。

(3) Taxpayers are not the subject of mutual consultation procedures. The international tax agreement creates rights and obligations for the parties, and the taxpayer is not the subject of the agreement, but can enjoy the benefits of the tax agreement under the tax treaty. Therefore, when states settle their tax disputes through mutual consultation procedures, taxpayers are not parties to mutual consultation procedures.

纳税人能否参加相互协商程序，能否在税务当局面前陈述观点，完全取决于缔约国税务机关的同意。当然，缔约国国内法中有规定是另一个问题。在一些OECD国家，纳税人在主管当局作出正式结论前应被通知磋商结果。

The ability of taxpayers to participate in the mutual consultation process and to present their views before the tax authorities depends entirely on the consent of the tax authorities of the state party. Of course, the existence of provisions in the domestic law of states parties is another issue. In some OECD countries, taxpayers should be informed of the outcome of the consultations before the competent authorities reach a formal conclusion.

相互协商程序不仅是税收协定缔约国解决它们之间税收争议的一种方法,而且也是缔约国税收机关保护它们的居民纳税人的手段。然而这种对纳税人的法律保护手段还有一些不足之处。

The mutual consultation procedure is not only a way for the states parties to the tax agreement to resolve their tax disputes, but also a means for the tax authorities of the states parties to protect their resident taxpayers. However, there are still some shortcomings in this legal protection of taxpayers.

首先,纳税人必须根据缔约国国内法的规定发起相互协商程序。税收协定本身并不能给缔约国国内个人创设权利和义务。税收协定也没有赋予纳税人可以直接发起争端解决主体的地位。尽管纳税人居民国主管税务机关为了纳税人的利益有义务启动相互协商程序,它也认为纳税人提出异议的征税行为是由另一缔约国全部或部分的措施造成的。但是若该居民国主管税务机关自己不能或不情愿解决另一缔约国违反税收协定的征税,纳税人在国际法层面也无法强制该居民国实施这一义务。

First, taxpayers must initiate a mutual consultation procedure in accordance with the provisions of the domestic law of the state party. Tax agreements themselves do not create rights and obligations for individuals in the state party. There is also no tax agreement that gives taxpayers the status of direct dispute settlement subjects. Although the competent tax authorities of the resident state have an obligation to initiate a process of mutual consultation in the interest of the taxpayer, it also considers that the taxpayer's objection to the taxation is caused by measures taken in whole or in part by the other contracting state. The taxpayer can not impose this obligation on the resident state at the level of international law if the competent tax authorities of the resident state themselves are unable or unwilling to resolve the taxation of a breach of a tax agreement by another contracting state.

其次,即使启动了相互协商程序,居民国主管税务机关也没有必须要达成解决方法的义务。纳税人可以向主管税务机关要求发起相互协商程序,但最后能否避免与协定不符的征税是不确定的。关于这一点,经济合作组织财政事务委员会自己也认为,无法保证达成解决问题的结果是相互协商程序的基本缺陷。[①]

Secondly, even if a mutual consultation procedure was initiated, the competent tax authorities of the resident state had no obligation to reach a solution. Taxpayers can ask the competent tax authorities to initiate a mutual consultation process, but it is uncertain whether taxes that are inconsistent with the agreement can be avoided in the end. In this regard, the Finance Committee of the Economic Cooperation Organization itself believes that the failure to ensure a solution to the problem is a fundamental flaw in the mutual consultation process.

最后,相互协商程序仅在缔约国主管机关之间进行。纳税人并不是该程序的当事人,

---

① Art.25(37) 2010 OECD Commentary.

除非缔约国国内法另有规定,其既没有查阅案件资料的权利,也没有当面陈述自己意见的权利。税务当局希望仅给予纳税人本人或通过他的代表提交书面或口头陈述的权利。因此,在实践中绝大多数相互协商的案件是由相关主管机关的高层官员通过个人联络解决的。经合发组织范本注释中提出的纳税人的参与权几乎不具有可行性。总之,正如有学者所说:"相互协商程序并不是一种令人满意的争议解决方法,因为是由缔约国的税务行政当局来解决,所以从本质上它是一种政治程序而不是一种司法程序。还应当增加其他如国际仲裁或诉讼的司法性的争议解决方法。"①所以,实践中一些国家在双边的税收协定中规定,一旦相互协商程序未能解决税收争议就可寻求通过仲裁的方式来解决。

Finally, the procedure for mutual consultation takes place only between the competent authorities of states parties. The taxpayer is not a party to the procedure, unless the domestic law of the state party provides otherwise that it has neither access to the information of the case nor the right to present its opinion in person. The tax authorities wish to grant the taxpayer the right to submit written or oral statements only in person or through his or her representative. Thus, in practice, the vast majority of cases of mutual consultation are resolved by senior officials of the relevant authorities through personal contact. The right of taxpayers to participate, as set out in the OECD Model Notes, is hardly feasible. In conclusion, as some scholars have said, "The procedure of mutual consultation is not a satisfactory dispute settlement, because it is settled by the tax administration of the state party, so it is essentially a political procedure rather than a judicial procedure. Other judicial dispute resolution methods, such as international arbitration or litigation, should also be added." Therefore, in practice, some countries have stipulated in bilateral tax agreements that once the mutual consultation process fails to resolve tax disputes, they can seek to resolve them by arbitration.

(四) 我国相互协商程序的规定
Provisions of Our Mutual Agreement Procedure

国家税务总局于2013年9月24日制定了《税收协定相互协商程序实施办法》(以下简称《实施办法》),以国家税务总局公告2013年第56号予以发布,自2013年11月1日起施行。《实施办法》共6章,41条。下面就结合《实施办法》的规定来分析我国的相互协商程序。

On 24 September 2013, the State Administration of Taxation in China formulated the Measures for the Implementation of the Procedures for Mutual Consultation of Tax Agreements (hereinafter referred to as the Implementation Measures). It was promulgated by the State Administration of Taxation Proclamation No. 56 of 2013 and came into force on November 1, 2013. The Implementation Measures consist of 6 chapters and 41 articles. The following is an analysis of the country's mutual consultation process in the light of the provisions of the Implementation Measures.

第一,《实施办法》规定了相互协商程序的定义。相互协商程序,是指我国主管当局根

---

① Mario Züger, Arbitration under Tax Treaties; Improving Legal Protection in International Tax Law, Doctoral Series, vol.5 (IBFD 2001), pp. 13-15.

据税收协定有关条款规定,与缔约对方主管当局之间通过协商共同处理涉及税收协定解释和适用问题的过程。这里的缔约对方是指与中国签订税收协定,且该税收协定已经生效执行的国家或地区。① 据此,我国相互协商程序的协商主体限于与我国已经缔结税收协定国家的税收主管当局,纳税人是不能主动参加协商程序的。②

First, the Implementation Measures provide a definition of MAP. Mutual agreement procedure (MAP) refers to the process in which the competent authorities of our country deal with the interpretation and application of tax agreements through consultation with the competent authorities of the other contracting party in accordance with the relevant provisions of tax agreements. In this case, the contracting party refers to the signing of a tax agreement with China, which has entered into force in a country or region. Accordingly, the subject of consultation in our MAP is limited to the tax authorities of the countries that have concluded tax agreements with China, and taxpayers can not take part in the consultation procedure on their own initiative.

第二,《实施办法》规定了相互协商程序的目标。相互协商程序的主要目的在于确保税收协定正确和有效适用,切实避免双重征税,消除缔约双方对税收协定的解释或适用产生的分歧。③ 其确保通过相互协商程序解决税收争议的统一、规范和高效。

Second, the Implementation Measures set out the objectives of the MAP. The main purpose of the mutual consultation procedure is to ensure the correct and effective application of tax agreements, to effectively avoid double taxation and to eliminate differences between the parties in the interpretation or application of tax agreements. Ensure consistency, standardization and efficiency in resolving tax disputes through mutual consultation procedures.

第三,《实施办法》规定了相互协商程序的适用范围。相互协商的事项限于税收协定适用范围内的事项,但超出税收协定适用范围,且会造成双重征税后果或对缔约一方或双方利益产生重大影响的事项,经我国主管当局和缔约对方主管当局同意,也可以进行相互协商,但关于特别纳税调整的相互协商程序实施除外。

Third, the Measures of Implementation provide the scope of application of the MAP. The matter of mutual consultation is limited to matters within the scope of application of tax agreements, but beyond the scope of application of tax agreements, and may also be subject to mutual consultation with the consent of the competent authorities of China and the competent authorities of the other contracting party, except for the implementation of the mutual consultation procedure on special tax adjustments.

第四,《实施办法》规定了我国负责相互协商程序的主管当局。我国负责相互协商工作的主管当局为国家税务总局(以下简称税务总局);处理相互协商程序事务的税务总局授权代表为税务总局国际税务司司长或副司长,以及税务总局指定的其他人员。省、自治区、直辖市和计划单列市国家税务局或地方税务局(以下简称省税务机关)及以下各级税务机关

---

① 《实施办法》第2、6条。
② 见附录二,在《启动税收协定相互协商程序申请表》中对纳税人有这样的要求:"我了解并同意,相互协商过程仅在缔约双方主管当局授权代表间进行,我仅在缔约双方主管当局授权代表邀请时才可以参与。"
③ 《实施办法》第2.2条。

负责协助税务总局处理相互协商程序涉及的本辖区内事务。

Fourth, the Implementation Measures provide for the competent authorities responsible for MAP in China. The competent authority responsible for mutual consultation in our country is the State Administration of Taxation (hereinafter referred to as the State Administration of Taxation); the authorized representative of the State Administration of Taxation dealing with the procedure of mutual consultation is the Director or Deputy Director of the International Taxation Department of the State Administration of Taxation, as well as other personnel designated by the State Administration of Taxation. The State Taxation Bureau or Local Taxation Bureau of provinces, autonomous regions, municipalities directly under the Central Government and municipalities separately listed in the plan (hereinafter referred to as the provincial tax authorities) and the tax authorities at the following levels shall be responsible for assisting the State Administration of Taxation in handling the affairs within their respective jurisdictions involved in the mutual consultation procedures.

第五,《实施办法》规定了我国纳税人[①]提出申请相互协商程序的条件。

Fifth, the Implementation Measures set out the conditions for the MAP of the application of taxpayers in China.

(1) 申请形式的要求。如果中国居民(国民)认为,缔约对方所采取的措施,已经或将会导致不符合税收协定所规定的征税行为,可以向省税务机关提出申请,请求税务总局与缔约对方主管当局通过相互协商程序解决有关问题。[②]

(1) The requirements of the form of application. If Chinese residents (nationals) believe that the measures taken by the contracting party have or will lead to a tax act that is not in accordance with the provisions of the tax agreement, they may apply to the provincial tax authorities to request the General Administration of Taxation and the competent authorities of the other party to solve the relevant problems through mutual consultation procedures.

申请人应在有关税收协定规定的期限内,以书面形式(需提供纸质版和电子版)向省税务机关提出启动相互协商程序的申请。[③]申请表的内容一般包括:申请人基本情况,申请案件的事实和争议,附件清单和纳税人声明。其中案件的事实应包括:案件涉及的国家(地区)、相关经济活动的内容、纳税年度、所得(收入)类型、税种、税额、缔约对方税务机关第一次发出征税通知的时间和内容。还特别说明,如有可能,申请人可将了解到的在缔约对方发生的相关、类似或相同案件的判例作为附件的一部分报省税务机关。[④]

The applicant shall, within the time limit stipulated in the relevant tax agreement, submit an application in writing (in paper and electronic versions) to the provincial tax authorities for

---

[①] 包括中国居民和中国国民。其中,中国居民,是指按照《中华人民共和国个人所得税法》和《中华人民共和国企业所得税法》,就来源于中国境内境外的所得在中国负有纳税义务的个人、法人或其他组织。中国国民,是指具有中国国籍的个人,以及依照中国法律成立的法人或其他组织。见《实施办法》第8条。与美国的规定相比,我国规定的人的范围要窄。

[②] 《实施办法》第7条。

[③] 《实施办法》第11条。

[④] 见附录二,填表说明。

the initiation of mutual consultation procedures. The contents of the application form generally include: the applicant's basic information, the facts and disputes of the application case, the attached list and the taxpayer's statement. The facts of the case shall include: the country (region) involved in the case, the content of the relevant economic activities, the tax year, the type of income (income), the type of taxes, tax amount, the time and content of the first tax notice issued by the tax authority of the other party. In particular, it is stated that, if possible, the applicant may report to the provincial tax authorities, as part of the annex, the relevant, similar or identical cases that have occurred in the other party.

申请人向省税务机关提起相互协商程序申请的,填报或提交的资料应采用中文文本。相关资料原件为外文文本且税务机关根据有关规定要求翻译成中文文本的,申请人应按照税务机关的要求翻译成中文文本。① 各级税务机关应对缔约对方主管当局与相关纳税人、扣缴义务人、代理人等在相互协商程序中提供的资料保密。②

If the applicant applies to the provincial tax authorities for mutual consultation, the information submitted shall be in Chinese. If the original of the relevant materials is a foreign language text and the tax authorities require translation into Chinese according to the relevant regulations, the applicant shall translate it into Chinese in accordance with the requirements of the tax authorities. Tax authorities at all levels shall keep confidential the information provided by the competent authorities of the other contracting party and relevant taxpayers, withholding agents and agents in the process of mutual consultation.

(2)申请实质的要求。中国居民有下列情形之一的,可以申请启动相互协商程序:③

① 对居民身份的认定存有异议,特别是相关税收协定规定双重居民身份情况下需要通过相互协商程序进行最终确认的;

② 对常设机构的判定,或者常设机构的利润归属和费用扣除存有异议的;

③ 对各项所得或财产的征免税或适用税率存有异议的;

④ 违反税收协定非歧视待遇(无差别待遇)条款的规定,可能或已经形成税收歧视的;

⑤ 对税收协定其他条款的理解和适用出现争议而不能自行解决的;

⑥ 其他可能或已经形成不同税收管辖权之间重复征税的。

此外中国国民认为缔约对方违背了税收协定非歧视待遇(无差别待遇)条款的规定,对其可能或已经形成税收歧视时,也可以申请启动相互协商程序。

(2) The substantive requirements of the application. If a Chinese resident has one of the following circumstances, he or she may apply for the initiation of a mutual consultation procedure:

(i) there are objections to the determination of resident status, in particular where the relevant tax agreements provide for the final confirmation of dual resident status through mutual consultation procedures;

---

① 《实施办法》第38条。
② 《实施办法》第5条。
③ 《实施办法》第9条。

(ii) where there are objections to the determination of the permanent establishment, or to the attribution of profits and deduction of expenses of the permanent establishment;

(iii) where there is any objection to the tax exemption or applicable tax rate for all proceeds or property;

(iv) in violation of the provisions of the non-discriminatory treatment (non-discriminatory treatment) provisions of tax agreements, tax discrimination may or has occurred;

(v) the interpretation and application of other provisions of the tax agreement is disputed and can not be settled on its own;

(vi) other taxes that may or have formed between different tax jurisdictions.

In addition, Chinese nationals believe that the contracting party has violated the provisions of the non-discriminatory treatment (non-discriminatory treatment) clause of the tax agreement, and may apply for the initiation of mutual consultation procedures when tax discrimination may or has been formed.

第六,《实施办法》规定了税务机关受理相互协商程序的条件。申请人按规定提出的相互协商申请符合以下全部条件的,税务机关应当受理:①

① 申请人为按照该办法第9条或第10条规定可以提起相互协商请求的中国居民或中国国民;

② 提出申请的时间没有超过税收协定规定的时限;

③ 申请协商的事项为缔约对方已经或有可能发生的违反税收协定规定的行为;

④ 申请人提供的事实和证据能够证实或者不能合理排除缔约对方的行为存在违反税收协定规定的嫌疑;

⑤ 申请相互协商的事项不存在该办法第19条规定的情形。

对于不符合上款规定全部条件的申请,税务机关认为涉及严重双重征税或损害我国税收权益、有必要进行相互协商的,也可以决定受理。② 可以看出,通过列举和概括的规定,税务机关在是否受理申请上享有较大的自由裁量权,也有很大的灵活性。这既可能是好事但也可能是坏事,在操作层面有很多细节要考虑。

The Measures for Implementation set out the conditions for tax authorities to accept MAP. If the applicant's application for mutual consultation according to the regulations meets all the following conditions, the tax authorities shall accept:

(i) the applicant is a Chinese resident or a Chinese national who may file a request for mutual consultation in accordance with the provisions of Article 9 or Article 10 of these measures;

(ii) the time limit for filing an application does not exceed the time limit stipulated in the tax agreement;

(iii) the application for consultation is a breach of the provisions of the tax agreement that has occurred or is likely to occur by the contracting party;

---

① 《实施办法》第14.1条。
② 《实施办法》第14.2条。

(iv) the facts and evidence provided by the applicant can prove or can not reasonably exclude the suspicion that the conduct of the contracting party is contrary to the provisions of the tax agreement;

(v) there are no circumstances under Article 19 of the Measures for the application for mutual consultation.

For applications that do not meet all the conditions stipulated in the preceding paragraph, the tax authorities may also decide to accept applications that involve serious double taxation or damage to the tax rights and interests of China and are necessary for mutual consultation. It can be seen that through enumeration and generalization, tax authorities have greater discretion and flexibility in accepting applications. This can be both good and bad, and there are many details to consider at the operational level.

第七,《实施办法》规定了税务机关受理相互协商程序后的内部处理程序。受理申请的省税务机关应在15个工作日内,将申请上报税务总局,并将情况告知申请人,同时通知省以下主管税务机关。因申请人提交的信息不全等原因导致申请不具备启动相互协商程序条件的,省税务机关可以要求申请人补充材料。申请人补充材料后仍不具备启动相互协商程序条件的,省税务机关可以拒绝受理,并以书面形式告知申请人。申请人对省税务机关拒绝受理的决定不服的,可在收到书面告知之日起15个工作日内向省税务机关或税务总局提出(需提供纸质版和电子版)异议申请。省税务机关收到异议后,应在5个工作日内将申请人的材料,连同省税务机关的意见和依据上报税务总局。①

The Measures for Implementation provide for internal procedures for tax authorities after accepting MAP. The provincial tax authorities that accept the application shall, within 15 working days, report the application to the State Administration of Taxation, inform the applicant of the situation, and notify the competent tax authorities below the province at the same time. If the application does not meet the conditions for initiating mutual consultation procedures due to incomplete information submitted by the applicant, the provincial tax authority may request the applicant to supplement the materials. If the applicant does not have the conditions to initiate mutual consultation procedures after the supplementary materials, the provincial tax authorities may refuse to accept them and inform the applicant in writing. If the applicant is not satisfied with the decision of the provincial tax authority to refuse to accept it, he or she may, within 15 working days from the date of receipt of the written notification, submit an application for objection to the provincial tax authority or the State Administration of Taxation (both paper and electronic) to be provided. After receiving the objection, the provincial tax authorities shall, within five working days, report the applicant's materials, together with the opinions and basis of the provincial tax authorities, to the State Administration of Taxation.

税务总局收到省税务机关上报的申请后,应在20个工作日内按下列情况分别处理:②

① 申请具备启动相互协商程序条件的,决定启动相互协商程序,并将情况告知受理申

---

① 《实施办法》第15、16条。
② 《实施办法》第17条。

请的省税务机关,省税务机关应告知申请人;

② 申请已超过税收协定规定的期限,或申请人的申请明显缺乏事实法律依据,或出现其他不具备相互协商条件情形的,不予启动相互协商程序,并以书面形式告知受理申请的省税务机关,省税务机关应告知申请人;

③ 因申请人提交的信息不全等原因导致申请不具备启动相互协商程序条件的,通过受理申请的省税务机关要求申请人补充材料或说明情况。申请人补充材料或说明情况后,再按前两项规定处理。

税务总局启动相互协商程序后,可通过受理申请的省税务机关要求申请人进一步补充材料或说明情况,申请人应在规定的时间内提交,并确保材料的真实与全面。对于紧急案件,税务总局可以直接与申请人联系。①

After receiving the application submitted by the provincial tax authorities, the State Administration of Taxation shall, within 20 working days, deal with the following cases separately:

(i) if the application has the conditions for initiating the mutual consultation procedure, it shall decide to initiate the mutual consultation procedure and inform the provincial tax authorities that accept the application, and the provincial tax authorities shall inform the applicant;

(ii) If the application has exceeded the time limit stipulated in the tax agreement, or the applicant's application is obviously lack of factual legal basis, or there are other circumstances that do not meet the conditions for mutual negotiation, the mutual negotiation procedure shall not be started, and the provincial tax authority accepting the application shall be informed in written form, and the provincial tax authority shall inform the applicant;

(iii) if the application does not meet the conditions for initiating the mutual consultation procedure due to incomplete information submitted by the applicant, the provincial tax authorities accepting the application shall require the applicant to supplement the materials or explain the situation. After the applicant adds the material or explains the situation, then according to the first two provisions processing.

After the State Administration of Taxation has initiated the procedure of mutual consultation, it may request the applicant to further supplement the materials or explain the situation through the provincial tax authorities accepting the application. The applicant shall submit the materials within the prescribed time and ensure the authenticity and comprehensiveness of the materials. For urgent cases, the State Administration of Taxation can contact the applicant directly.

税务总局可以在发生下列情形之一的情况下,决定终止相互协商程序,并以书面形式告知省税务机关。省税务机关应告知申请人:②

① 申请人故意隐瞒重要事实,或在提交的资料中弄虚作假的;

② 申请人拒绝提供税务机关要求的、与案件有关的必要资料的;

③ 因各种原因,申请人与税务机关均无法取得必要的证据,导致相关事实或申请人立

---

① 《实施办法》第18条。
② 《实施办法》第19条。

场无法被证明,相互协商程序无法继续进行的;

④ 缔约对方主管当局单方拒绝或终止相互协商程序的;

⑤ 其他导致相互协商程序无法进行,或相互协商程序无法达到预期目标的。

同样,在两国主管当局达成一致意见之前,申请人也可以以书面方式撤回相互协商申请。一旦申请人撤回申请或者拒绝接受缔约双方主管当局达成一致的相互协商结果,税务机关将不再受理基于同一事实和理由的申请。①

The State Administration of Taxation may, in one of the following circumstances, decide to terminate the procedure of mutual consultation and report to the provincial tax authorities in writing. The provincial tax authorities shall inform the applicant:

(i) the applicant intentionally conceals important facts or defrauds information submitted;

(ii) if the applicant refuses to provide the necessary information requested by the tax authorities relating to the case;

(iii) if, for various reasons, neither the applicant nor the tax authorities can obtain the necessary evidence, resulting in the fact that the relevant facts or the applicant's position can not be proved, and the mutual consultation procedure can not continue;

(iv) unilateral refusal or termination of the mutual consultation procedure by the competent authority of the other contracting party;

(v) others that result in the failure of the mutual consultation process or the failure of the mutual consultation process to achieve the desired objectives.

Similarly, before the competent authorities of the two countries agree, the applicant may withdraw the application for mutual consultation in writing. Once the applicant withdraws the application or refuses to accept the result of mutual consultation reached by the competent authorities of both parties, the tax authorities will no longer accept the application on the same facts and grounds.

第八,《实施办法》规定了缔约对方主管当局相互协商请求的程序要求。其在受案范围上与我国纳税人的要求是相同的。②税务总局在拒绝缔约对方主管当局启动相互协商程序的请求,或者要求缔约对方主管当局补充材料的规定方面,也非常灵活,有很大的自由裁量权。③税务总局在收到缔约对方启动相互协商程序的函后,查清事实,决定是否同意启动相互协商程序,并书面回复对方。④如果我国相关税务机关的处理决定尚未作出,税务总局应将对方提起相互协商程序的情况告知相关税务机关。但相互协商程序不影响相关税务机关对有关案件的调查与处理,相互协商程序进行期间,也不停止税务机关已生效决定的执行,当然税务总局认为需要停止调查和处理的除外。⑤税务总局决定启动相互协商程序后,如有必要,则可以要求相关省税务机关予以协助在规定期限内完成核查。如果涉及需要对方补充材料或就某一事项作出进一步说明,税务总局同意向缔约对方主管当局提出补充要求的,

---

① 《实施办法》第20条。
② 《实施办法》第22条。
③ 《实施办法》第23条。
④ 《实施办法》第24条。
⑤ 《实施办法》第25、26条。

等待对方回复的时间不计入核查时间。① 这些规定借鉴了发达国家相互协商程序的相关程序,是合理和先进的。

Eighth, the Measures of Implementation set out the procedural requirements for requests for mutual consultation between the competent authorities of the contracting parties. In the scope of the case, it is the same as the taxpayer requirements in China. The Directorate of Taxation also has considerable flexibility and discretion in rejecting requests from the competent authorities of the other contracting party to initiate a mutual consultation process or in requiring the competent authorities of the other contracting party to supplement their information. After receiving the letter from the other party to initiate the mutual consultation procedure, the State Administration of Taxation ascertained the facts, decided whether to agree to initiate the mutual consultation procedure, and replied to the other party in writing. If the decision of the relevant tax authorities in China has not been made, the State Administration of Taxation shall inform the relevant tax authorities of the circumstances in which the other party initiated a mutual consultation procedure. However, the mutual consultation procedure does not affect the investigation and handling of the relevant cases by the relevant tax authorities, and during the period of the mutual consultation procedure, it does not stop the implementation of the effective decisions of the tax authorities, except, of course, where the General Administration of Taxation considers it necessary to stop the investigation and handling. After the State Administration of Taxation decides to initiate the procedure of mutual consultation, if necessary, it may request the relevant provincial tax authorities to assist in the completion of the verification within the prescribed time limit. Where there is a need for additional information or for further clarification of a matter, where the State Administration of Taxation agrees to make a supplementary request to the competent authority of the other party, the time to wait for the other party's reply is not included in the verification time. These provisions are reasonable and advanced, drawing on the relevant procedures of the mutual consultation procedure of developing countries.

第九,《实施办法》还规定了税务总局可以主动向缔约对方主管当局提出相互协商请求的条件。比如: ① 发现过去相互协商达成一致的案件或事项存在错误,或有新情况需要变更处理的; ② 对税收协定中某一问题的解释及相关适用程序需要达成一致意见的; ③ 税务总局认为有必要与缔约对方主管当局对其他税收协定适用问题进行相互协商的。② 如前,根据国外学者在学理上对相互协商程序的分类,税务总局的主动请求属于普通相互协议,而前面由纳税人启动的请求则属于特定案件的相互协议。

The Measures of Implementation also set out the conditions under which the General Administration of Taxation may, on its own initiative, submit a request for mutual consultation to the competent authorities of the other contracting party. For example: (i) where errors have been found in cases or matters that have been agreed upon by mutual agreement in the past, or where new circumstances need to be changed; (ii) where agreement is needed on the interpretation

---

① 《实施办法》第28、29、30条。
② 《实施办法》第32条。

of an issue in a tax agreement and the relevant application procedures; (iii) where the General Administration of Taxation deems it necessary to consult with the competent authorities of the other contracting party on the application of other tax agreements. Previously, according to the classification of MAP by foreign scholars, the active request of the General Administration of Taxation belongs to the ordinary mutual agreement (a general mutual agreement), while the previous request initiated by the taxpayer belongs to the mutual agreement (a particular taxpayer mutual agreement).

第十,《实施办法》最后规定了双方税收主管当局经过相互协商达成协议时,对协议的执行。执行如下:① 双方就协定的某一条文解释或某一事项的理解达成共识的,税务总局应将结果以公告形式发布;② 双方就具体案件的处理达成共识,需要涉案税务机关执行的,税务总局应将结果以书面形式通知相关税务机关。相关税务机关应在收到通知之日起3个月内执行完毕,并将情况报告税务总局。

Tenth, the Implementation Measures finally provide for the implementation of the agreement when the tax authorities of both parties reach an agreement through mutual consultation. The implementation is as follows: (i) if the two parties reach a consensus on the interpretation of a provision of the agreement or on the understanding of a matter, the State Administration of Taxation shall publish the results in the form of a public announcement; (ii) if the two parties reach a consensus on the handling of specific cases and need to be executed by the tax authorities involved, the State Administration of Taxation shall notify the relevant tax authorities in writing of the results. The relevant tax authorities shall complete the execution within three months from the date of receipt of the notice and report the situation to the General Administration of Taxation.

根据上述《国家税务总局关于发布〈税收协定相互协商程序实施办法〉的公告》(国家税务总局公告2013年第56号),我国"走出去"企业在境外遇到涉及其重大利益的税收争议事项都可以启动相互协商程序。然而,实践中真正愿意启动该程序的企业并不多。据一定范围内的"走出去"企业问卷调查结果,绝大多数"走出去"企业都会遇到税收争议,但是选择愿意告知主管税务机关并呈报国家税务总局解决的只占调查企业的11%,而实践中提起相互协商程序的比例相当低。究其原因主要是企业对相互协商程序不了解、对协商结果的信心不足。

According to the above notice of the State Administration of Taxation on issuing the measures for the implementation of the procedure for mutual consultation of tax agreements (No. 56 of 2013 of the State Administration of Taxation), Chinese "going out" enterprises may initiate mutual consultation procedures when they encounter tax disputes involving their major interests abroad. However, in practice, there are not many enterprises that are truly willing to start the process. According to a certain range of "going out" enterprise questionnaire results, the vast majority of "going out" enterprises will encounter tax disputes, but the choice to inform the competent tax authorities and report to the State Administration of Taxation only accounts for 11% of the surveyed enterprises. In practice, the proportion of mutual agreement procedures is quite low. The main reason is that enterprises do not understand the mutual agreement process

二、仲裁
Arbitration

(一)税务仲裁概述
Overview of Tax Arbitration

仲裁解决国际税务争议的设想早在20世纪20年代就由国际联盟任命的专家提出,其在主管当局未能就某一税收协定达成一致解释时适用。① 例如,由国际联盟财政委员会起草的多边税收协定报告从第17条到21条包含了详细的仲裁条款。② 然而,这些建议并未引起各成员国的注意。后来在英国和爱尔兰1926年的所得税协定以及1934年捷克斯洛伐克和罗马尼亚的遗产税协定中包含了仲裁条款。③ 但这些国家是否适用仲裁解决过税收争议不得而知。直到20世纪60年代,由投资保护公约建立的仲裁机构才开始解决一些争议激烈的税收争议。④ 经合发组织在1984年的转移定价报告中详细讨论了仲裁程序的使用。⑤ 此后,经合发组织的一些成员国开始在双边税收协定中系统地引入了仲裁条款。1985年西德和瑞典起草的税收协定草案第44条中,规定了创新性的仲裁解决国际税收争议的方法,被学者称为是在国际税收争议解决领域革命性的一步。⑥

The idea of arbitration for the settlement of international tax disputes was advanced in the 1920s by experts appointed by the League of Nations, applicable as the competent authority in the absence of an agreed interpretation of a tax agreement. For example, multilateral tax agreement reports prepared by the Finance Committee of the League of Nations contain detailed arbitration clauses from Articles 17 to 21. However, those recommendations had not attracted the attention of member states. The arbitration clause was later included in the British and Irish income tax agreements of 1926 and the estate tax agreements of Czechoslovakia and Romania of 1934. But it is not clear whether these countries have applied arbitration to settle tax disputes. Until the 1960s, the arbitration body established by the Investment Protection Convention began to resolve some controversial tax disputes. The use of arbitration procedures was discussed in detail in the OECD Transfer Pricing Report 1984. Thereafter, some OECD member countries have begun to systematically introduce arbitration clauses in bilateral tax agreements. In Article 44 of the draft tax agreement prepared by West Germany and Sweden in 1985, innovative

---

① Lindencrona, How To Resolve International Tax Disputes? New Approaches to an Old Problem, Intertax 1990, 266.
② Documents of the League of Nations C.415.M.171.1931.II.A〔F./Fiscal/73〕4236.
③ Hinnekens, The European Tax Arbitration Convention and Its Legal Framework, British Tax Review 1996, 141.
④ Guttentag/Misback, Resolving Tax Treaty Issues: A Novel Solution, Bulletin for International Fiscal Documentation 1986, p. 354.
⑤ OECD Report Transfer Pricing, Corresponding Adjustments and the Mutual Agreement Procedure(1982), para 41.
⑥ Guttentag, Misbach, Resolving Tax Treaty Issues: A Novel Solution, 40 Bulletin for Int'l Fiscal Documentation, 350(1986).

arbitration methods for resolving international tax disputes are provided, known by scholars as a revolutionary step in the field of international tax dispute resolution.

根据国际财政文献局的统计,有200多个双边税收协定中规定了仲裁条款。如美国在与加拿大、法国、德国、爱尔兰、意大利、哈萨克斯坦、墨西哥和瑞士等国家的双边税收协定中规定了仲裁条款。加拿大在与智利、厄瓜多尔、法国、德国、冰岛、哈萨克斯坦、秘鲁和南非的双边税收协定谈判中也要规定仲裁条款。特别是荷兰,其除了已经与十多个国家签订了包含有仲裁条款的税收协定外,在所有新的税收协定中都包含了仲裁解决的规定。从国际税收争议解决的理论和实践看,通过仲裁解决目前主要可以分为两种:一种就是通过在双边税收协定中规定仲裁条款来实施的选择性仲裁(optional arbitration);另一种是以欧共体仲裁公约(准确的名称是欧共体转移定价公约)为里程碑的强制性仲裁(compulsory arbitration)。[①]本节主要讨论选择性仲裁,强制性仲裁将在下文中结合欧共体转移定价公约作专门论述。

According to the International Bureau of Fiscal Documentation, more than 200 bilateral tax agreements have stipulated arbitration provisions. For example, the United States provides arbitration clauses in bilateral tax agreements with Canada, France, Germany, Ireland, Italy, Kazakhstan, Mexico and Switzerland. Canada also provides for arbitration clauses in bilateral tax agreements negotiations with Chile, Ecuador, France, Germany, Iceland, Kazakhstan, Peru and South Africa. In particular, the Netherlands, in addition to having concluded tax agreements with more than a dozen countries containing arbitration clauses, included arbitration settlement provisions in all new tax agreements. Judging from the theory and practice of international tax dispute settlement, arbitration settlement can be divided into two main types: one is selective arbitration (optional arbitration) by providing arbitration clauses in bilateral tax agreements; the other is mandatory arbitration (compulsory arbitration) with the European Community Arbitration Convention (the exact name is the European Community Transfer Pricing Convention) as a milestone (EC Transfer Pricing Convention). This section mainly discusses selective arbitration, mandatory arbitration will be discussed below in conjunction with the EC Transfer Pricing Convention.

选择性仲裁,如前所说,是国家间在签订的避免双重征税协定中,解决协定适用或解释出现的问题,而在相互协商程序失败后给予当事各方通过仲裁来解决它们之间争议的一种方法。不同国家的法制不同,各国间签订的税收协定中对适用仲裁的规定也有很多细节性的不同。

Selective arbitration, as has been said previously, is a method of settling disputes between the parties through arbitration in agreements concluded between states to avoid double taxation as a solution to problems arising from the application or interpretation of the agreement and after the failure of the mutual consultation process. Different countries have different legal systems, and there are many details of the application of arbitration in tax agreements between countries.

---

① Mario Züger, Arbitration under Tax Treaties; Improving Legal Protection in International Tax Law, Doctoral Series, vol.5(IBFD 2001), p. 17, 65.

以现实中税收协定包含的仲裁条款模式来划分,选择性仲裁大致可以分为三种模式。

According to the arbitration clause mode contained in the tax agreement in reality, selective arbitration can be roughly divided into three modes.

第一种模式是1992年美国和墨西哥的双边税收协定中的仲裁条款(第26条第5款),其标准条文表述为:如果缔约国主管当局不能依据本条前款的相互协商程序来解决就本协定的解释或适用产生的任何困难和疑义,在缔约国双方主管当局和纳税人都同意的条件下,如果纳税人以书面形式同意接受仲裁庭裁决的约束,则此案可提交仲裁解决。仲裁庭就个案的裁决对缔约国双方应当具有个案的约束力。缔约国间应通过外交渠道的换文来建立仲裁程序规则。本款规定在缔约国通过外交换文达成同意后生效。①1992年以后国家间签订的大多数双边税收协定,都以第一种模式规定了仲裁解决的条款。仔细研读该条款,我们可以简单归纳它的特征:首先,发起仲裁的条件之一是,缔约国主管当局和纳税人或相关的纳税人们都同意选择仲裁作为解决他们之间税收争议的方法;其次,受将来仲裁裁决约束的纳税人必须以书面的方式表明其接受裁决的意愿;再次,仲裁庭针对缔约国和纳税人某个案件争议作出的裁决,对缔约国双方都具有制约效力,但该效力仅止于个案,而不能成为之后案件的先例。当然,如果以后的案件涉及的是相同的纳税人(们)、相同的税收争议,主要事实也相同,这些裁决还是会予以考虑。②最后,至于仲裁程序如何进行,要由缔约国通过外交渠道来沟通解决。

The first model is the arbitration clause in the United States-Mexico bilateral tax agreement of 1992(Art. 26, Para. 5), the standard provision of which states that if the competent authorities of a contracting state are unable to resolve any difficulties and doubts arising from the interpretation or application of this Agreement in accordance with the procedure of mutual consultation in the preceding paragraph of this article, the case may be referred to arbitration for settlement, subject to the agreement of the competent authorities of both contracting states and the taxpayer, if the taxpayer agrees in writing to be bound by the arbitral tribunal's award. Arbitral tribunal decisions on individual cases shall be binding on both parties. Rules of procedure for arbitration should be established between states parties through exchange of letters through diplomatic channels. The provisions of this paragraph shall enter into force upon the agreement of the states parties through an exchange of diplomatic communications. Most

---

① Article 26(5) Double Taxation Convention Mexico-USA, 18 September 1992("If any difficulty or doubt arising as to the interpretation or application of this Convention cannot be resolved by the competent authorities pursuant to the previous paragraphs of this Article, the case may, if both competent authorities and the taxpayer(s) agree, be submitted for arbitration, provided that the taxpayer agrees in writing to be bound by the decision of the arbitration board.The decision of the arbitration board in a particular case shall be binding on both states with respect to that case.The procedures shall be established between the states by notes to be exchanged through diplomatic channels.The provisions of this paragraph shall have effect after the states have so agreed through the exchange of diplomatic notes.")

② Article 18.(b) (v) of Exchange of Notes on the US treaties with Mexico: "While the decision of the arbitration board shall not have precedential effect, it is expected that such decisions ordinarily will be taken into account in subsequent competent authority cases involving the same taxpayer(s), the same issue(s), and substantially similar facts, and may also be taken into account in other cases where appropriate."

bilateral tax agreements concluded between states after 1992 provided for arbitration settlement clauses in the first model. A closer look at this provision would allow us to summarize its features briefly: first, one of the conditions for initiating arbitration, where the competent authorities of the contracting state and the taxpayer or the relevant taxpayer agree to choose arbitration as a means of settling tax disputes between them; second, where the taxpayer bound by a future arbitral award must indicate in writing his or her will to accept the award; and, again, where the arbitral tribunal's award in respect of a dispute between the contracting state and the taxpayer in a particular case has binding effect on both contracting states, it is only in the individual case and can not be a precedent in subsequent cases. Of course, these decisions will be taken into account if future cases involve the same taxpayers, the same tax disputes and the same main facts. Finally, as to how the arbitral proceedings were to be conducted, it was for the states parties to communicate through diplomatic channels.

第二种模式是1994年拉脱维亚与荷兰双边税收协定中的仲裁条款(第27条第5款),其标准条文表述为:如果缔约国主管当局不能依据该条前款的相互协商程序在争议产生之日起两年内解决任何就本协定的解释或适用产生的困难和疑议,则应任一缔约国请求,该争议可提交仲裁解决,但这仅在用尽与条第1—4款的程序后以及获得另一缔约国主管当局同意,并且纳税人或相关纳税人们以书面形式同意接受仲裁庭裁决的约束。仲裁庭就个案的裁决对缔约国双方和纳税人应当具有个案的约束力。[1]

The second model is the arbitration clause in the 1994 bilateral tax agreement between Latvia and Netherlands (Art. 27, Para. 5), the standard provision of which reads as follows: if the competent authorities of a contracting state are unable to resolve any difficulties or doubts arising from the interpretation or application of this Agreement within two years from the date of the dispute arising under the procedure of mutual consultation of the preceding paragraph of this article, at the request of any contracting state, the dispute may be submitted to arbitration for settlement only after the procedure of paragraphs 1–4 of this article has been exhausted and with the consent of the competent authorities of the other contracting state, and the taxpayer or the relevant taxpayer agrees in writing to be bound by the arbitral tribunal's award. The arbitral tribunal's decision on a case shall be binding on both parties and taxpayers.

第三种模式是2008年经合发组织税收协定范本第25条第5款的规定。在采用仲裁方式解决双边国际税收争议实践的推动下,经合发组织对其范本也作了增加。在OECD税收

---

[1] Article 27(5) Double Taxation Convention Latvia-Netherlands, 14 March 1994 ("If any difficulty or doubt arising as to the interpretation or application of the Convention cannot be resolved by the competent authorities of the contracting states in a mutual agreement procedure pursuant to the previous paragraphs of this Article within a period of two years after the question was raised, the case may, at the request of either contracting states, be submitted for arbitration, but only after fully exhausting the procedures available under paragraphs 1 to 4 of this Article and provided the competent authority of the other contracting state agrees and the taxpayer or taxpayers involved agree in writing to be bound by the decision of the arbitration board.The decision of the arbitration board in a particular case shall be binding on both contracting states and the taxpayer or taxpayers involved with respect to that case.")

协定范本2008年第25条相互协商程序中加了第5款,其条文表述为:根据本条第1款,当一个人基于缔约国一方或双方的行动已经导致对其不符合本协定规定的征税时,他把案情提交缔约国一方的主管当局后,缔约国双方主管当局如果不能通过本条第2款的相互协商程序在把案情提交给缔约国另一方主管当局之日起2年内解决,则应该由纳税人请求,该案的任何未决争议可提交仲裁解决。然而如果这些争议已由任一缔约国的法院或行政法庭作出裁决,则这些争议不可提交仲裁。除非受本案直接影响的纳税人不接受执行仲裁裁决的相互协商,否则该仲裁裁决对缔约国双方都有约束力,都应予执行,而且不受缔约国国内法律的任何时间限制。缔约国双方主管当局应当通过相互协商来解决本款适用的方法。

The third model is provided for in Article 25, Paragraph 5, of the 2008 OECD Model Tax Agreement. The OECD Model has also been added to the practice of using arbitration to resolve bilateral international tax disputes. Paragraph 5 has been added to the mutual consultation procedure under Article 25 of the 2008 OECD Model Tax Agreement, which states that, in accordance with paragraph 1 of this article, when a person, on the basis of the actions of one or both parties, has led to the taxation of a non-conformity with the provisions of this Agreement, submits the case to the competent authority of one of the parties, and if the competent authority of both parties can not resolve the case within two years from the date of submitting the case to the competent authority of the other party through the mutual consultation procedure under paragraph 2 of this article, any outstanding dispute in the case may be submitted to arbitration for settlement at the request of the taxpayer. However, such disputes may not be submitted to arbitration if they have already been decided by a court or administrative tribunal of any contracting state. Unless the taxpayer directly affected by the case does not accept mutual consultation on the enforcement of the arbitral award, the arbitral award shall be binding on both parties and shall not be subject to any time limit under the domestic law of the state party. The competent authorities of both states parties shall resolve the method of application of this paragraph through mutual consultation.

上述三种模式无论条文表述如何,作为选择性仲裁仍然有很多共同的地方。明显的不足在于:税收协定本身并未规定纳税人参与仲裁程序的可能性;仲裁程序的发起要由缔约国主管税务当局都同意,而主管当局并不一定要发起仲裁程序;与相互协商程序相比,选择性仲裁并没有实质进步。总之,选择性仲裁在对纳税人的法律保护方面几乎没有改善。

These three models, regardless of the formulation of the provisions, still have much in common as selective arbitration. The obvious shortcomings are that the tax agreement itself does not provide for the possibility of taxpayers participating in the arbitration proceedings; that the initiation of the arbitration proceedings is subject to the consent of the competent tax authorities of the contracting states, which do not necessarily initiate the arbitration proceedings; and that there is no substantial progress in selective arbitration compared to the mutual consultation procedure. In short, selective arbitration has hardly improved in terms of legal protection for taxpayers.

（二）税务仲裁程序的理论分析
Theoretical Analysis of Tax Arbitration Proceedings

1. 税务争议适裁性分析
Analysis of Admissibility of Tax Disputes

赞成通过仲裁解决商事、财税争议的主要理由如下：第一，与诉讼相比，仲裁是一种快速高效的争议解决手段。诉讼往往以其复杂和耗时而为人诟病。第二，与诉讼相比，仲裁更为经济。第三，与诉讼相比，仲裁并不需要向公众公开。对机密的保证，特别是在敏感的工业、商业和投资领域，争议的细节只有双方当事人和仲裁员了解，成为提请仲裁解决的强烈动因。第四，与法院的法官相比，仲裁员可能更为独立且中立。在商事争议，特别是国际投资争议方面，国内法院法官往往被迫去保护本国利益，而作出损害外国投资者利益的裁决。外国投资者，特别是一些跨国公司倾向于夸大这些事实，在那些不发达国家，法院完全被行政机构所操控而且这些国家的法律制度是如此落后、未知和不确定，所以外国投资者的合法利益是不可能得到法院公正保护的。所有这些因素综合起来，使仲裁成为解决国际商事和国际投资争议的方式之一。大量仲裁规则的产生、国际条约的出现（特别是1958年纽约公约的签订）以及诸如国际商会（ICC）、解决投资争端国际中心（ICSID）和美国仲裁协会（AAA）等仲裁机构的建立，都使得仲裁成为解决国际贸易、投资争议的普遍方式之一。其后仲裁条款在双边税收协定和投资条约法中出现。例如，1986年法国与阿尔及利亚的投资条约中就规定了仲裁解决税收争议的方法。

The main reasons in favour of resolving commercial and fiscal disputes through arbitration are as follows. First, arbitration is a fast and efficient means of dispute resolution compared with litigation. Litigation is often criticized for its complexity and time-consuming. Second, arbitration is more economical than litigation. Third, arbitration does not need to be made public compared with litigation. Guarantees of confidentiality, especially in sensitive industrial, commercial and investment fields, the details of the dispute are known only to the parties and arbitrators, and are a strong motivation for bringing them to arbitration. Fourth, arbitrators may be more independent and neutral than court judges. In commercial disputes, especially international investment disputes, domestic court judges are forced to protect their domestic interests and make decisions that harm the interests of foreign investors. Foreign investors, especially some transnational corporations, tend to exaggerate these facts. In those underdeveloped countries, the courts are completely manipulated by administrative bodies and the legal systems of these countries are so backward, unknown and uncertain that the legitimate interests of foreign investors can not be fairly protected by the courts. All these factors combine to make arbitration one of the ways to resolve international commercial and international investment disputes. The emergence of a large number of arbitration rules, the emergence of international treaties (in particular the signing of the 1958 New York Convention) and the establishment of arbitration institutions such as the International Chamber of Commerce (ICC), the International Centre for the Settlement of Investment Disputes (ICSID) and the American Arbitration Association (AAA) have made arbitration one of the universal means of resolving international trade and investment disputes.

Arbitration clauses then emerged in bilateral tax agreements and investment treaty law. For example, the French and Algerian investment treaties of 1986 provided for arbitration in the settlement of tax disputes.

尽管仲裁在解决国际商事争议方面的效用和比较优势获得大家一致认可,但仲裁解决国际税务争议的案件却并不多见。究其原因,作为当事人一方的主权国家很不情愿把自己手中的部分或全部征税权交给仲裁庭,而且事先同意将受仲裁裁决的制约。

Although the utility and comparative advantage of arbitration in the settlement of international commercial disputes have been unanimously recognized, arbitration in the settlement of international tax disputes is rare. The reason is that the sovereign state, as one of the parties, is reluctant to hand over part or all of its tax rights to the arbitral tribunal, and prior consent will be subject to the arbitral award.

2. 税务仲裁程序的特点

Characteristics of Tax Arbitration Procedures

(1) 解决国际税收争议的仲裁不同于国际商事仲裁。国际商事仲裁解决的是私人主体之间的民商事争议,而税收国际仲裁解决的是国家之间的争议,而且这种税收争议具有公法的性质。因此,相关国家的商事仲裁法律不能适用于税收国际仲裁。税收国际仲裁适用的法律应当是相关的国际税收协定,涉及税收协定解释时还适用《维也纳条约法公约》,有时也需适用国内法。美国和墨西哥税收协定的议定书换文中规定,仲裁裁决应当基于税收协定,适当考虑缔约国国内法和国际法原则。

(1) Arbitration for the settlement of international tax disputes is different from international commercial arbitration. International commercial arbitration resolves civil and commercial disputes between private subjects, while tax international arbitration resolves disputes between countries, and this tax dispute has the nature of public law. Therefore, the commercial arbitration law of the relevant countries can not be applied to tax international arbitration. The law applicable to international tax arbitration should be the relevant international tax agreement, which also applies the Vienna Convention on the Law of Treaties to the interpretation of tax agreements and sometimes domestic law. The exchange of protocols to the United States-Mexico Tax Agreements provided that arbitral awards should be based on tax agreements, giving due consideration to the domestic law of states parties and the principles of international law.

(2) 仲裁是解决争议的最后手段。税收协定的仲裁条款一般规定只有经相互协商程序不能解决的税收争议才能提交仲裁,因此仲裁是最后使用的手段。这意味着仲裁并不是争端当事方可以选择的争议解决方式。这不同于国际商事仲裁。国际商事仲裁的当事人可以选择仲裁,也可选择调解、诉讼等方式,而且一旦选择了仲裁就排除了司法管辖。

(2) Arbitration as a last resort for the settlement of disputes. The arbitration clause of a tax agreement generally provides that only a tax dispute that can not be settled through mutual negotiation can be submitted to arbitration, so arbitration is used as a last resort. This means that arbitration is not a dispute settlement option for the parties to the dispute. This is different from international commercial arbitration. The parties to international commercial arbitration can choose arbitration, mediation, litigation and so on, and once they choose arbitration, they

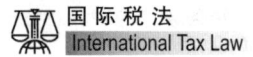

exclude jurisdiction.

（3）仲裁解决的争议范围。国家间的税收争议包括间接和直接两类。上述美国、荷兰的两个仲裁条款均规定适用于税收协定的解释和适用中产生的争议，这实际上指向直接的国际税收争议。不过，美国和墨西哥的税收协定中仲裁条款要求仲裁的启动取得纳税人的同意和事先受仲裁决定约束的声明，意味着主管当局只能将通过相互协商程序不能解决的涉及纳税人的案件提交仲裁。爱沙尼亚与荷兰的税收协定中的仲裁条款没有要求纳税人的同意启动仲裁，但要求纳税人事先同意受仲裁决定的约束，这意味着只有涉及纳税人的案件才能提交仲裁。不过，加拿大与智利的税收协定中的仲裁条款，并没有要求纳税人的同意提起仲裁，也没有要求纳税人事先书面同意受仲裁决定约束，这意味着直接和间接税务争议都可仲裁。另外，美国的一些税收协定中明确将"税收政策和国内法"排除出仲裁范围。

(3) Scope of dispute to be settled by arbitration. Tax disputes between countries include indirect and direct categories. Both of the above-mentioned arbitration clauses in the United States and Netherlands provide for disputes arising from the interpretation and application of tax agreements, which in fact point to direct international tax disputes. However, the arbitration clause in the tax agreements between the United States and Mexico, which requires that the commencement of arbitration be subject to the consent of the taxpayer and the prior declaration of the arbitration decision, means that the competent authority can only refer to arbitration cases involving taxpayers that can not be resolved through mutual consultation procedures. The arbitration clause in the tax agreement between Estonia and Netherlands does not require the consent of the taxpayer to initiate arbitration, but requires the prior consent of the taxpayer to be bound by the arbitration decision, which means that only cases involving taxpayers can be submitted to arbitration. However, the arbitration clause in the tax agreement between Canada and Chile does not require the consent of the taxpayer to initiate arbitration, nor does it require the taxpayer to be bound by the arbitration decision in writing in advance, which means that both direct and indirect tax disputes can be arbitrated. In addition, some United States tax agreements explicitly exclude "tax policy and domestic law" from arbitration.

（4）仲裁的自愿性和强制性。大多数仲裁条款要求缔约国双方主管当局的同意才能启动仲裁，这意味着仲裁是自愿性的。仲裁条款只是确立了可提交仲裁的机制，但是否提起仍然需要个案的当局是否同意，也不能保证任何相互协商程序下的任何问题都可能提交仲裁解决。当然，也有的仲裁条款将仲裁设定为强制性的。德国与奥地利的税收协定规定，税收协定解释和适用中的争议，在纳税人的请求下，可提交欧洲法院仲裁。欧盟的仲裁公约第7条规定，转让定价争议不能通过相互协商解决时必须提交仲裁。有的学者认为仲裁是否设定为强制性的，也与仲裁的争议事项有关。有的主张涉及税收协定适用的事实争议比税收协定解释的争议更适合于仲裁：因为仲裁员是某些领域的专家，比税务主管当局更有经验处理税收协定适用的事实纠纷，其裁决也不会影响缔约国财政主权。这也是欧盟仲裁公约提供转让定价调整争议的强制性仲裁的原因。

(4) Voluntary and mandatory. Most arbitration clauses require the consent of the competent authorities of both parties to initiate arbitration, which means that arbitration is voluntary. The arbitration clause merely established a mechanism for referral to arbitration, but the consent

of the authorities who still required the case to be initiated did not guarantee that any issue under any mutual consultation procedure could be referred to arbitration. Of course, there are arbitration clauses that make arbitration mandatory. The tax agreement between Germany and Austria provides that disputes in the interpretation and application of the tax agreement may be submitted to the European Court of Justice for arbitration at the request of the taxpayer. Article 7 of the European Union Arbitration Convention stipulates that transfer pricing disputes must be submitted to arbitration if they can not be settled through mutual negotiation. Some scholars believe that whether arbitration is mandatory or not is also related to the dispute of arbitration. Some argued that factual disputes involving the application of tax agreements were more appropriate for arbitration than those relating to the interpretation of tax agreements: since arbitrators were experts in certain fields and had more experience than tax authorities in dealing with factual disputes applicable to tax agreements, their decisions would not affect the financial sovereignty of states parties. This is also the reason why the EU Arbitration Convention provides mandatory arbitration for transfer pricing adjustment disputes.

（5）纳税人的地位。纳税人也不是仲裁程序的主体，尽管有的税收协定规定需要纳税人的同意才能启动仲裁。对于遭受双重征税的纳税人来讲，同意仲裁的可能性比阻止的可能性大。不过，即使纳税人同意仲裁，也需要缔约国主管机关的同意才能最终启动仲裁。仲裁条款一般要求纳税人事先同意受仲裁决定的约束，这样做的目的与相互协商程序中的理由是一致的。

(5) Taxpayer status. Taxpayers are not the subject of arbitration proceedings, although some tax agreements require the consent of the taxpayer to initiate arbitration. For taxpayers subject to double taxation, consent to arbitration is more likely than prevention. However, even if the taxpayer agrees to arbitration, the consent of the competent authority of the contracting state is required for the eventual commencement of arbitration. The arbitration clause generally requires the prior consent of the taxpayer to be bound by the arbitration decision, the purpose of which is consistent with the reasons in the mutual consultation procedure.

（6）仲裁裁决的效力。尽管仲裁条款规定仲裁裁决对缔约国有约束力，但裁决能否在缔约国执行仍取决于国内法。由于纳税人不是仲裁的主体，仲裁裁决也不指向纳税人，因此纳税人也不能在国际层面上申请执行仲裁裁决。如果仲裁裁决要求税务机关重新进行税收核定，而这又与国内法中的司法判决不一致，就要看国内法中是否允许税务机关和法院重新进行税收核定。

(6) The validity of the arbitral award. Although the arbitration clause provides that an arbitral award is binding on a contracting state, the enforcement of an award in a contracting state remains subject to domestic law. Since the taxpayer is not the subject of arbitration and the arbitral award does not point to the taxpayer, the taxpayer can not apply for enforcement of the arbitral award at the international level. If the arbitral award requires the tax authority to re-examine the tax approval, which is inconsistent with the judicial decision in the domestic law, it depends on whether the domestic law allows the tax authority and the court to re-examine the tax approval.

在荷兰，法院不能适用与国际条约或政府间国际组织的决定不符的国内法。这需要该决定指向荷兰政府及其居民纳税人，为纳税人创设明确的权利和义务，并予以公开。不过，税务仲裁庭是否是国际组织值得探讨。如果把仲裁裁决认定为是对荷兰有约束力的税收协定的解释，就可能被执行。

In Netherlands, courts can not apply domestic laws that are inconsistent with international treaties or decisions of intergovernmental international organizations. This requires that the decision be directed to the Dutch government and its resident taxpayers, and that clear rights and obligations be created and made public for taxpayers. However, whether the tax tribunal was an international organization was worth exploring. Interpretation of an arbitral award as a tax agreement binding on Netherlands may be enforced.

此外，仲裁裁决不具有先例的作用，缔约国没有义务根据个案的仲裁裁决解释和适用其他类似案件。这是由于仲裁不公开进行，裁决一般也不公开，公众无法获知；作出裁决所依据的法律个案可能不同；每个案件的仲裁程序也可能不同。

Moreover, the arbitral award had no precedent-setting effect and the state party was not obliged to interpret and apply other similar cases on the basis of the arbitral award in each case. This is due to the fact that the arbitration is held in private and the award is generally not made public and is not known to the public, the legal cases on which the award is based may also be different, and the arbitral proceedings in each case may be different.

（三）税务仲裁程序的缺陷
Defects in Tax Arbitration Proceedings

仲裁程序虽然是相互协商程序的扩大，目的是增强相互协商程序的有效性，但也存在着一些缺陷。

Although the arbitration procedure is an extension of the mutual consultation procedure, the purpose is to enhance the effectiveness of the mutual consultation procedure, but there are some flaws.

（1）仲裁程序不能独立于相互协商程序的适用问题。无论是OECD税收协定范本的注释，还是相关税收协定的规定，都把仲裁程序作为相互协商程序的组成部分，其不能单独适用。这意味着即使税收协定中规定了强制性的仲裁解决方法，缔约国也可以通过在相互协商程序中排除特定事项的做法来规避仲裁解决方法的适用。[①]在实践中纳税人被税务机关审计之后，自己并不能启动仲裁程序，必须先启动相互协商程序，然后等2年，即使缔约国主管当局没有达成协议。让纳税人耗费时间成本可能就会影响纳税人把仲裁作为解决争议的一种令人满意的选择。对税收主管当局来说，仲裁解决方法依附于相互协商程序可以节省很多人力、物力和组织成本。但从设立仲裁解决的本源看，就是要激励税收主管当局打破相互协商程序拖拉、积案甚多的僵局。事实上从很多税收协定中加入仲裁解决的方法确实达到了这一目的。问题是为什么仲裁解决就不能成为一种独立的争议解决方法而仅仅是一种

---

① 详见美国和法国于1994年8月31日签订的税收协定第26条第2款的规定，美国和德国于1989年8月29日签订的税收协定第25条第2款的规定。

第十三章 国际税务争议的解决
CHAPTER XIII Settlement of International Tax Disputes

激励呢？对纳税人来说，如果在相互协商程序和直接仲裁解决之间选择的话，仲裁解决的迅捷优势无疑是非常明显的。

(1) Arbitration proceedings can not be independent of the use of mutual consultation proceedings. The arbitration procedure can not be used separately as an integral part of the MAP, either under the notes of the model OECD tax agreement or under the relevant tax agreement. Even if mandatory arbitration solutions were provided for in tax agreements, states parties could circumvent the application of arbitration solutions by excluding specific matters in MAP. After being audited by the tax authorities, taxpayers in practice can not initiate arbitration proceedings themselves and must start MAP then wait for two years, even if the competent authorities of the state party have not reached an agreement. The cost of taxpayers' time may discourage taxpayers from using arbitration as a satisfactory alternative to dispute resolution. For tax authorities, arbitration solutions attached to MAP can save a lot of human, material and organizational costs. But from the point of view of the establishment of arbitration settlement, it is necessary to encourage tax authorities to break the deadlock of MAP procrastination and many cases. In fact, the inclusion of arbitration settlements from many tax agreements did do that. The question is, why can't arbitration be a stand-alone dispute resolution rather than an incentive? For taxpayers, if they make a choice between MAP and direct arbitration settlement, the quick advantage of arbitration settlement is undoubtedly very obvious.

（2）仲裁条款不具有操作性。税收协定中的仲裁条款并不完善，体现为仲裁条款没有约定下列事项：仲裁员的任命和仲裁庭的组成、作出仲裁的期限、仲裁适用的法律和仲裁程序等。这样的条款不具有可操作性。即使缔约国主管当局同意仲裁，如果在仲裁员任命和仲裁程序上不能达成一致，仲裁实际上也无法进行。比如，对于缔约国一方可启动仲裁的仲裁条款，如果仍需要双方同意才能任命仲裁员，则一国可通过拒绝任命仲裁员而逃避仲裁条款中本已经事先给予的仲裁同意。

(2) Arbitration clause is not operable. The arbitration clause in the tax agreement is not perfect, which is reflected in the fact that the arbitration clause does not stipulate the following matters: the appointment of arbitrators and the composition of the arbitration tribunal, the time limit for arbitration, the law applicable to arbitration and the arbitration procedure. Such clauses are not operational. Even if the competent authorities of a contracting state agreed to arbitration, arbitration could not actually take place if agreement could not be reached on the appointment of arbitrators and on the arbitral proceedings. For example, in the case of an arbitration clause in which a contracting state may initiate arbitration, if the consent of both parties is still required for the appointment of an arbitrator, a state may evade the prior consent to arbitration in the arbitration clause by refusing to appoint the arbitrator.

（3）纳税人在仲裁程序中参与度的问题。这是与相互协商程序同样存在的问题。依据目前的仲裁程序，纳税人不能参加仲裁程序。即使纳税人被允许提交自己的意见，也不能参加或参与到仲裁裁决的决定过程。如此一来，即便是解决程序与纳税人有重大利害关系，纳税人也无法为自己进行辩护或对裁决结果产生影响。特别是当纳税人有权拒绝仲裁裁决时，纳税人参与仲裁程序能防止已经投入的时间和金钱的浪费。另外，纳税人对案件事实和争议最为了解，如果纳税人不能直接向仲裁庭提交这些材料而是必须通过税收主管当局去提交，这不仅会影响仲裁程序的效率，更有可能会因信息传递过程中的失误导致对纳税人不利的后果。

(3) The participation of taxpayers in arbitration proceedings. This is the same problem as the mutual consultation process. According to the current arbitration procedure, taxpayers can not participate in the arbitration procedure. Even if the taxpayer is allowed to submit his or her own opinion, he or she can not participate in the decision process of the arbitral award. Thus, the taxpayer has a significant interest in the settlement process, but the taxpayer can not defend himself or herself or influence the outcome of the ruling. Especially when the taxpayer has the right to reject the arbitration award, the taxpayer's participation in the arbitration procedure can prevent the waste of time and money already invested. In addition, taxpayers are most aware of the facts and disputes of the case. If taxpayers can not submit these materials directly to the arbitral tribunal, they must submit them through the tax authority. This will not only affect the efficiency of the arbitration process, but also lead to adverse consequences for taxpayers due to errors in the transmission of information.

综上所述，仲裁作为解决税务争议的手段，不是相互协商程序的上诉程序，具有优于相互协商程序之处，但也存在着一些缺陷。

To sum up, arbitration, as a means of resolving tax disputes, is not an appeal procedure of mutual negotiation procedure, and has advantages over mutual negotiation procedure. But there are also some defects in arbitration.

（四）欧盟《欧洲仲裁公约》的相关规定
Relevant Provisions of the European Arbitration Convention

1990年《欧洲仲裁公约》（以下简称《公约》）是第一个规定强制仲裁程序的国际税收条约。根据《公约》规定，如果主管当局通过相互协商未能在2年内就跨国公司利润调整消除双重征税，则它必须启动强制仲裁程序。只有在下列情况下才不需要启动强制仲裁：已构成税收犯罪；国内规定仲裁程序仅作为法律诉讼的一种可能选择，并且纳税人选择了国内诉讼；纳税人没有把案件提交给仲裁庭。顾及缔约国的主权，《公约》并未规定仲裁裁决的约束效力，而是正式把关于消除双重征税的决定权留给主管当局，同时给予他们6个月的时间去找到双方都能接受的解决办法。然而如果主管当局不能在6个月内找到各方一致同意的解决办法，一旦裁决作出，则该裁决对当事方就具有约束效力。《公约》给予受利润调整的纳税人广泛地参与仲裁程序的权利。仲裁裁决依据相关国内法规定来执行。《公约》生效以来，只有一起在法国和意大利税务主管机关之间就转移定价发生的争议进入强制仲裁裁决程序，[①]这也说明了《公约》的目标是确保在所有缔约国内统一适用转移定价的原则以及由相关税务主管机关通过相互协商消除它们适用的任何困难以得到实现。这也是《公约》期待的效果，即调动相互协商程序中的税务主管当局相互妥协，以避免发起强制仲裁程序。

---

① Joseph, Ghislain T J, Transfer pricing: The EC arbitratio convention as a dispute resolution mechanism, *The International Tax Journal*; Spring 2002; 28, 2; Accounting & Tax, p. 37.

第十三章 国际税务争议的解决
CHAPTER XIII Settlement of International Tax Disputes

在许多案件中税务主管当局就在启动强制仲裁程序的最后一刻解决了转移定价的争议。《公约》因此能够保证利润不会被重复征税,因为转移定价调整的存在。然而,《公约》也受制于它有限的适用范围,它仅适用于欧盟内部跨国关联企业利润调整而产生的争议,因为转让定价争端在实践中的重要性,所以解决此类争端对欧盟委员会就显得特别紧迫,这也就是欧盟委员会为什么仅针对此类争端来制定行动守则的原因。此外,《公约》有效期很短,它于1999年12月31日到期,对《公约》自动延期5年的修改议定书到目前还没有得到所有成员国的批准。而这一程序是复杂且耗时的,事实上缔约国并未授权欧盟法院解释《公约》或欧洲委员会监督和审查《公约》。尽管如此,《公约》在多边的基础上为欧盟各成员国的税务主管当局解决转移定价争议建立了一套普遍的税法原则和程序。而最重要的是,《公约》真正创新的地方是它建立的争议解决机制。强制仲裁确保了每一个由相互协商程序产生的案件得到解决,或者是由主管当局来解决,抑或是由仲裁庭来解决。一方面,纳税人(关联企业)不仅有非常充足的时间(3年)向税务主管当局提起案件;另一方面,对税务主管当局和咨询委员会作出决定或提出建议规定了严格的时间限制(3年内)。与经合发组织税收协定范本规定的双边税收协定中的争议解决过程相比,这是一个巨大的提速。因此,强制仲裁程序有效地保护了纳税人,加强了纳税人在税收协定中的地位。基于此,欧盟的《欧洲仲裁公约》是极具参考价值的,它构建了一套有效消除国际双重征税的多边仲裁解决程序,无论是在转移定价调整方面还是其他税收方面。而这是通过传统在双边税收协定中规定仲裁条款来实施的选择性仲裁来解决争议所做不到的。

The 1990 Arbitration Convention was the first international tax treaty to provide for compulsory arbitration proceedings, under which a competent authority must initiate compulsory arbitration proceedings if, through mutual consultation, it fails to eliminate double taxation on profit adjustments of transnational corporations within two years. It was only in those cases that compulsory arbitration did not need to be initiated: it had already constituted a tax offence; domestic arbitration proceedings had been provided only as a possible option for legal proceedings and the taxpayer had opted for domestic proceedings; the taxpayer had not referred the case to the arbitral tribunal. Taking into account the sovereignty of states parties, the Convention did not provide for the binding effect of arbitral awards, but formally left the right to decide on the elimination of double taxation to the competent authorities, giving them six months to find a mutually acceptable solution. However, if the competent authorities are unable to find a consensual solution within six months, once the award is rendered, the award is binding on the parties. The Convention gives taxpayers subject to profit adjustment the right to participate extensively in arbitral proceedings. The arbitral award shall be executed in accordance with the provisions of the relevant domestic law. Since the entry into force of the Convention, only one dispute concerning transfer pricing between the competent tax authorities of France and Italy has entered the compulsory arbitral award procedure, which also illustrates the objective of the Convention: to ensure the uniform application of the principle of transfer pricing in all contracting states and to have the relevant tax authorities remove, through mutual consultation, any difficulties that they apply. This is also the desired effect of the Convention, which is to mobilize the tax authorities in the mutual consultation process to compromise with each other in order to avoid initiating compulsory arbitration proceedings. In many cases, the tax authorities resolved the transfer pricing dispute at the last minute of the commencement of compulsory arbitration proceedings. The Convention thus ensures that profits are not subject to double taxation because of transfer pricing adjustments. However, the Convention is also subject to its limited scope of application, and it applies only to disputes arising from the adjustment of profits of transnational affiliated enterprises within the European Union, since the importance of transfer pricing disputes in practice makes the settlement of such disputes particularly urgent for the European Commission, which is why the European Commission has developed a code of action for such disputes only. In addition, the Convention had a very short period of validity and had expired on 31 December 1999, and the Protocol to amend the Convention for an automatic five-year extension had not yet been ratified by all member states. This procedure is complex and time-consuming, and in fact the state party does not authorize the European Court of Justice to interpret the Convention or the Council of Europe to monitor and review it. Nevertheless, the Convention establishes, on a multilateral basis, a universal set of tax principles and procedures for the tax authorities of EU member states to resolve transfer pricing disputes. Most importantly, the dispute resolution mechanism it had established was the one that had truly innovated the Convention. Compulsory arbitration ensures that each case arising from a mutual consultation process is resolved either by the competent authority or by the arbitral tribunal. On one hand, taxpayers (affiliated enterprises) not only have very sufficient time (3 years) to bring cases to the tax authorities, but on the other hand, strict time limits are set for tax authorities and advisory committees to make decisions or make recommendations (3 years). This is a significant acceleration compared to the dispute resolution process in bilateral tax agreements under the OECD Model Tax Agreement. Therefore, the compulsory arbitration procedure effectively protects the taxpayer and strengthens the taxpayer's position in the tax agreement. Based on this, the European Arbitration Convention of the European Union is of great reference value. It constructs a set of multilateral arbitration settlement procedures which can effectively eliminate international double taxation, whether in terms of transfer pricing adjustment or other taxes. And this is not possible through selective arbitration, which is traditionally provided for in bilateral tax agreements.

（五）税务仲裁解决程序的比较及最新发展
Comparison of Settlement Procedures for Tax Arbitration and Recent Developments

通过仲裁解决国际税收争议的最新发展是由美国引领的。尽管美国2006版的所得税协定范本没有规定强制仲裁的条款，但在实践中强制仲裁程序深受美国政府和纳税人团体的青睐。美国计划与7个国家的所得税协定中包含强制仲裁程序，到2013年美国已经与加拿大、比利时、法国和德国4个国家的双边税收协定中规定了强制性的仲裁条款。据美国财政部的官员介绍，在参议院待批的是与瑞士的双边协定，已经与日本、西班牙签订的双边税收协定中都规定了强制性的、有约束力的仲裁条款。而且，在将来新修订的所得税协定范本中都将规定强制仲裁的条款。[①]

The latest development in the settlement of international tax disputes through arbitration is led by the United States. Although the 2006 US model income tax agreement does not provide for mandatory arbitration, in practice, mandatory arbitration procedures are favored by the US government and taxpayer groups. The United States plans to include mandatory arbitration procedures in income tax agreements with seven countries, and by 2013 the United States has established mandatory arbitration clauses in bilateral tax agreements with four countries, Canada, Belgium, France and Germany. According to US Treasury officials, the Senate is awaiting approval of bilateral agreements with Switzerland, and bilateral tax agreements with Japan and Spain already contain mandatory binding arbitration provisions. Moreover, provisions for compulsory arbitration would be included in the new revised model income tax agreement.

第五节　相关案例
Section 5　Related Cases

一、泛美公司所得税争议案
Pan Am Income Tax Controversy

本案是美利坚合众国泛美卫星国际系统责任有限公司诉北京市国家税务局对外分局第二税务所代扣代缴预提所得税争议案。

In this case, Pan Am Satellite International System Liability Co., Ltd. of the United States of America sues the Second Tax Office of the Foreign Branch of the Beijing Tax Bureau on the withholding of income tax.

（一）案情介绍
Introduction to the Case

1996年4月3日,泛美卫星国际系统责任有限公司（以下简称"泛美公司"）与中国中央电视台（以下简称"央视"）签订了《数字压缩电视全时卫星传送服务协议》。双方约定,泛美卫星公司向央视提供压缩数字视频服务,提供27 MHz带宽和相关的功率所组成的转发器,包括地面设备；央视向泛美卫星公司支付季度服务费和设备费。

A Digital Compressed Television Full-time Satellite Transmission Service Agreement was

---

① United States: Treasury Official Says Mandatory Arbitration Expected in Update to US Model Tax Treaty, 2013 Tax Management, 966 (Vol. 21, No. 19).

signed on 3 April 1996 between Pan Am Satellite International Systems (Pan Am) and China Central Television (CCTV). The two parties agreed that Pan Am Satellite would provide CCTV with compressed digital video services and a transponder consisting of 27 MHz bandwidth and associated power, including ground equipment. CCTV pays quarterly service and equipment fees to Pan Am Satellite Company.

1999年1月,北京市国税局在税务检查中认为,央视在支付上述款项时应当履行代扣代缴所得税义务,故作出了要求央视于1999年1月28日前申报缴纳相应税款的行政通知。泛美公司得知后,于1999年3月26日缴纳了外国企业所得税,并于1999年5月22日向国税局对外分局申请行政复议。8月23日对外分局作出复议决定,维持行政行为。泛美卫星公司遂对国税局提起行政诉讼。审理中,国税局对外分局于2000年6月26日撤销了此通知,泛美公司遂撤诉。

In January 1999, Beijing Tax Bureau held that CCTV should fulfill the obligation of withholding income tax when making the above payment, so it made an administrative notice requiring CCTV to declare and pay corresponding tax before 28 January, 1999. Pan American paid the foreign corporate income tax on 26 March, 1999, and applied for administrative reconsideration to the foreign branch of the National Tax Bureau on 22 May, 1999. On 23 August, the foreign branch of the National Tax Bureau made a reconsideration decision and maintained the original administrative action. Pan American satellite then filed an administrative lawsuit against the Beijing Tax bureau. During the trial, the foreign branch of the National Tax Bureau cancelled the reconsideration decision on June 26, 2000, and Pan American company withdrew the lawsuit.

2000年6月30日,北京市国税局对外分局第二税务所作出了第319号《关于对中央电视台与泛美卫星公司签署〈数字压缩电视全时卫星传送服务协议〉所支付费用代扣代缴预提所得税的通知》,认定央视与泛美公司签订的电视卫星传送协议所支付的费用,属于《中美税收协定》第11条、《外商投资企业和外国企业所得税法》第19条、国家税务总局《关于外国企业出租卫星通信线路所取得的收入征税问题的通知》及国家税务总局《关于泛美卫星公司从中央电视台取得卫星通信线路租金征收所得税问题的批复》确定的预提所得税征税范围。因此,税务机关要求央视履行代扣代缴的义务并将该决定内容告知泛美公司。

On 30 June 2000, the Second Tax Office of the External Branch of the Beijing Municipal Bureau of Internal Revenue issued Notice No. 319 on the withholding of income tax on the fees paid for the full-time satellite transmission service agreement signed between CCTV and Pan American Satellite Company, and determined that the expenses paid for the television satellite transmission agreement signed between CCTV and Pan American Company, belongs to the scope of withholding income tax determined in Article 11 of the Sino-US Tax Agreement, Article 19 of the Law on Income Tax of Enterprises with Foreign Investment and Foreign Enterprises, the Notice of the State Administration of Taxation on the Tax Collection of Income from the Rental of Satellite Communication Lines by Foreign Enterprises and the Approval of the State Administration of Taxation on the Collection of Income Tax from the Rent Collection of Satellite Communication Lines by Pan American Satellite Company from CCTV. Therefore, the tax authorities require CCTV to fulfill its withholding obligations and inform Pan Am of the contents of the decision.

泛美卫星公司对此不服,向北京市国家税务局对外分局申请行政复议。该局经复议维持了第319号通知。泛美卫星公司仍不服,故又将北京市国家税务局对外分局第二税务所作为被告、将央视作为第三人诉至北京市第一中级人民法院。

Pan Am Satellite Company disagrees with this, and apply for administrative reconsideration to the Foreign Branch of Beijing State Taxation Bureau. The Board upheld Circular 319 on reconsideration. Pan Am Satellite Company was still not convinced, so it brought the Second Tax Office of the Foreign Branch of Beijing Municipal State Taxation Bureau as the defendant and CCTV as the third party to the Beijing First Intermediate People's Court.

北京市第一中级人民法院经审理,于2001年12月20日判决维持了被告第二税务所的第319号通知,驳回了泛美公司的其他诉讼请求。

On 20 December 2001, the First Intermediate People's Court of Beijing upheld the defendant's Notice No. 319 of the Second Tax Office, rejecting other Pan Am claims.

一审判决后,泛美卫星公司不服,向北京市高级人民法院提出上诉,要求判决撤销一审判决,并依法予以改判。

After the first instance judgment, Pan Am Satellite Company appealed to the Beijing Higher People's Court, demanding that the judgment be annulled and revised according to law.

北京市高级人民法院二审认为,原审判决认定事实清楚,适用法律正确,审判程序合法,故依法驳回泛美公司的上诉请求,维持一审判决。

The second instance of the Beijing Higher People's Court held that the original judgment found that the facts were clear, the applicable law was correct, and the trial procedure was lawful, so it rejected the appeal request of Pan American Company according to law and upheld the judgment of first instance.

(二) 法理分析
Legal Analysis

1. 知识点提示
Knowledge Points

本案是我国首起卫星业务涉外税收争议案,它反映了我国与涉外纳税人之间税务争议解决的国内法程序。解决国家和涉外纳税人之间的国际税务争议的国内法程序主要有行政复议和行政诉讼制度。

This case is the first foreign tax dispute case of satellite business in China, which reflects the domestic law procedure of tax dispute settlement between China and foreign taxpayers. The domestic legal procedures for resolving international tax disputes between the state and foreign taxpayers mainly include administrative reconsideration and administrative litigation system.

2. 行政复议
Administrative Review

行政复议是指国家行政机关在行使其行政管理职权时,与作为被管理对象的相对方发生争议,根据行政相对方的申请,由上一级国家行政机关或者法律法规规定的其他机关依法对引起争议的具体行政行为进行复查并作出决定的一种活动。

Administrative reconsideration refers to an activity in which in the exercise of its administrative functions and powers, and as the object of management of the opposite party disputes, according to the application of the administrative counterpart, an activity in which the state administrative organ at the next higher level or other organs prescribed by laws and regulations review and decide on the specific administrative act in dispute according to law.

在我国,税务领域的行政复议即税收行政复议是指纳税人、扣缴义务人、纳税担保人等税务当事人或者其他行政相对人认为税务机关及其工作人员作出的税务具体行政行为侵犯其合法权益,依法向上一级税务机关或者本级人民政府提出复查该具体行政行为的申请,由复议机关对税务具体行政行为的合法性和适当性进行审查并作出裁决的制度。

In China, administrative reconsideration in the field of taxation, i.e. administrative reconsideration of taxation, refers to a system in which taxpayers, withholding agents, tax pay guarantors and other tax parties or other administrative counterparts believe that specific administrative acts of taxation made by tax authorities and their staff members infringe upon their legitimate rights and interests, and apply to the tax authorities at the next higher level or to the people's governments at the corresponding levels for review of such specific administrative acts in accordance with the law, and they shall examine and decide on the legality and appropriateness of specific administrative acts of taxation.

税务行政复议是行政复议制度的组成部分,其制度本身涉及复议范围、复议管辖、复议申请与受理、复议决定等方面的内容。

Tax administrative reconsideration is an integral part of the administrative reconsideration system, which involves the scope of reconsideration, the jurisdiction of reconsideration, the application and acceptance of reconsideration, and the decision of reconsideration.

我国有专门的《中华人民共和国行政复议法》(以下简称《行政复议法》)。国家税务总局根据《行政复议法》和其他法律法规的规定,于1999年9月23日发表了修订后的《税务行政复议规则(试行)》,自同年10月1日起施行。1993年11月6日国家税务总局以"国税发〔1993〕119号文"发布的《税务行政复议规则》同时废止。

China has a special Administrative Review Law of the People's Republic of China (hereinafter referred to as the Administrative Review Law). In accordance with the Administrative Review Law and other laws and regulations, the revised Rules on Administrative Review of Taxation (Trial Implementation) were published on 23 September 1999, effective from 1 October of the same year. The Tax Administrative Review Rules issued by the State Administration of Taxation on 6 November,1993, with Taxation〔1993〕No. 119, were repealed at the same time.

根据《税务行政复议规则(试行)》第7条,涉及所得税领域的税务行政复议范围包括:税务机关作出的征税行为;税务机关作出的责令纳税人提供纳税担保行为;税务机关作出的税收保全行为;税务机关未及时解除税收保全措施,使纳税人等合法权益遭受损失的行为;税务机关作出的税收强制执行措施;税务机关作出的税收行政处罚行为;税务机关不予依法办理或答复的行为等。

According to Article 7 of the Rules for Tax Administrative Review (Trial Implementation), the scope of tax administrative review in the area of income tax includes: tax collection acts made by tax authorities; tax security acts ordered by tax authorities to provide tax payment; tax preservation acts made by tax authorities; tax authorities' failure to lift tax protection measures in time to cause losses to taxpayers and other legitimate rights and interests; tax enforcement measures made by tax authorities; tax administrative penalties imposed by tax authorities; and acts not handled or answered by tax authorities according to law.

复议机关审查申请行政复议的具体行政行为是否合法与适当,作出行政复议决定:(1)具体行政行为认定事实清楚,证据确凿,适用依据正确,程序合法,内容适当的,决定维持;(2)被申请人不履行法定职责的,决定其在一定期限内履行;(3)具体行政行为有下列情形之一的,决定撤销、变更或者确认该具体行政行为违法,决定撤销或者确认该具体行政行为违法的,可以责令被申请人在一定期限内重新作出具体行政行为:事实不清、证据不足的;适用依据错误的;违反法定程序的;超越或者滥用职权的;具体行政行为明显不当的;(4)被申请人不按照《税务行政复议规则(试行)》第26条的规定提出书面答复,提交当初作出具体行政行为的证据、依据和其他有关材料的,视为该具体行政行为没有证据、依据,决定撤销该具体行政行为。

The administrative reconsideration organ shall examine whether the specific administrative act applying for administrative reconsideration is lawful and appropriate, and make an administrative reconsideration decision: (1) if the specific administrative act finds that the facts are clear, the evidence is conclusive, the application basis is correct, the procedure is lawful and the content is appropriate, it shall decide to maintain it; (2) if the respondent fails to perform its statutory duties, it shall decide to perform within a certain period of time; (3) if the specific administrative act has one of the following circumstances, it shall decide to revoke, alter or confirm that the specific administrative act is illegal; if a decision is made to revoke or confirm the violation of the specific administrative act, the respondent may be ordered to re-do the specific administrative act within a certain period of time: if the facts are unclear and the evidence is insufficient; if the application basis is wrong; if the legal procedure is violated; if the authority is exceeded or abused; if the specific administrative act is manifestly improper; (4) if the respondent fails to provide a written reply in accordance with the provisions of Article 26 of the Rules for the Administrative Review of Tax Administration (Trial Implementation) and submits the evidence, basis and other relevant materials for the specific administrative act, it shall be deemed that the specific administrative act has no evidence or basis and decides to revoke the specific administrative act.

对于行政复议结果,如果纳税人仍然不服的,则可依法提起行政诉讼。

For the result of administrative reconsideration, if the taxpayer is still dissatisfied, administrative proceedings may be brought according to law.

3. 行政诉讼

Administrative Litigation

税务行政诉讼是行政诉讼和司法审查制度的组成部分。在我国,税务行政诉讼是指公民、法人和其他组织认为税务机关及其工作人员作出的税务具体行政行为违法或者不当,侵害了其合法权益,依法向人民法院提起行政诉讼,由人民法院对税务具体行政行为的合法性、适当性进行审查并作出判决的司法制度。

国际税法
International Tax Law

Tax administrative litigation is an integral part of administrative litigation and judicial review system. In China, tax administrative litigation refers to the judicial system in which citizens, legal persons and other organizations believe that specific tax administrative acts made by tax authorities and their staff members are illegal or improper, infringe upon their legitimate rights and interests, file administrative proceedings in a people's court according to law, and the people's court examines and decides on the legality and appropriateness of specific tax administrative acts.

行政复议和行政诉讼都是解决税务争议的法律途径,但两者的法律性质不同:税务行政复议仍然是在行政领域内解决争议,行政复议决定仍然是一种行政行为;行政诉讼是司法机关对行政机关行政行为的司法审查,是司法行为。

Administrative reconsideration and administrative litigation are both legal ways to resolve tax disputes, but their legal nature is different. Tax administrative reconsideration is still to resolve disputes in the administrative field, and administrative reconsideration decision is still an administrative act. Administrative litigation is the judicial examination of administrative acts by judicial organs and judicial acts.

在行政复议和行政诉讼的关系上,一般有两种做法:(1)行政复议是行政诉讼的必经程序,即当事人提起行政诉讼之前必须先提起行政复议;(2)当事人可以选择直接提起行政诉讼,而不需经过行政复议程序。

In the relationship between administrative reconsideration and administrative litigation, there are generally two ways. First, administrative reconsideration is the necessary procedure of administrative litigation, that is, the parties must bring administrative reconsideration before filing administrative litigation. Second, the parties may choose to file administrative litigation directly without administrative reconsideration.

《中华人民共和国税收征收管理法》第88条规定:纳税人、扣缴义务人、纳税担保人同税务机关在纳税上发生争议时,必须先依照税务机关的纳税决定缴纳或者解缴税款及滞纳金或者提供相应的担保,然后可以依法申请行政复议;对行政复议决定不服的,可以依法向人民法院起诉。当事人对税务机关的处罚决定、强制执行措施或者税收保全措施不服的,可以依法申请行政复议,也可依法向人民法院起诉。

Article 88 of the Law of the People's Republic of China on Tax Collection and Administration stipulates that in the event of a dispute between a taxpayer, a withholding agent, a tax payer and a tax-paying guarantor and a tax-paying organ, they must first pay or remit the tax and late fees or provide corresponding guarantees in accordance with the tax-paying decision of the tax-paying organ, and may then apply for administrative reconsideration in accordance with the law. If they are not satisfied with the administrative reconsideration decision, they may bring a suit in a people's court in accordance with the law. If the parties are not satisfied with the decision of punishment, enforcement measures or tax preservation measures of the tax authorities, they may apply for administrative reconsideration according to law or bring a suit in a people's court according to law.

我国没有专门的行政法院或税务法院,有关税务行政诉讼由人民法院依照其管辖权受理,法院内部设立行政审判庭专门负责审理行政案件。税务行政诉讼适用《中华人民共和国行政诉讼法》和有关法律、法规的规定。

There is no special administrative court or tax court in China. The relevant tax administrative litigation is accepted by the people's court in accordance with its jurisdiction, and the administrative trial court is set up within the court to handle the administrative case. The Administrative Procedure Law of the People's Republic of China and the relevant laws and regulations shall apply to tax administrative litigation.

税务行政复议和行政诉讼是处理税务机关和涉外纳税人之间税务争议的主要方式。此外,有的国家还使用仲裁解决税务争议。比如,美国税法规定,当税务争议发生后,当事人可以通过仲裁程序解决任何事实争议。

Tax administrative reconsideration and administrative litigation are the main ways to deal with tax disputes between tax authorities and foreign taxpayers. In addition, some countries use arbitration to settle tax disputes. For example, the United States tax law provides that when a tax dispute arises, the parties may settle any factual dispute through arbitral proceedings.

(三)案件分析
Case Analysis

本案从程序法的角度看,泛美公司作为涉外纳税人取得了来自中国的收入,且就该收入是否应向中国税务机关缴纳所得税,与征税机关,即北京市国家税务局对外分局第二税务所发生了争议。泛美公司在缴纳了外国企业所得税后,按照我国行政复议法的规定,向第二税务所的上一级税务机关,即北京市国家税务局对外分局提起了行政复议。北京市国家税务局对外分局经复议,维持了第二税务所有权征税的行政行为。

In this case, from the point of view of procedural law, Pan American Company, as a foreign taxpayer, has obtained income from China and has a dispute with the Second Tax Bureau of the Beijing State Taxation Bureau. over whether the income should be paid to the Chinese tax authorities. The Foreign Branch of Beijing State Taxation Bureau has maintained the administrative act of taxing the Second Tax Office after reconsideration.

泛美卫星公司对复议决定不服,故又将北京市国家税务局对外分局第二税务所作为被告、将央视作为第三人诉至北京市第一中级法院,启动了行政诉讼的一审程序。

Pan Am Satellite Company is not satisfied with the reconsideration decision. So the Second Tax Office of the Foreign Branch of the Beijing Taxation Bureau is taken as the defendant, CCTV as the third party to the First Intermediate Court of Beijing, and the first instance procedure of administrative proceedings has been initiated.

北京市第一中级法院经审理,判决维持了被告第二税务所的第319号通知,驳回了泛美公司的诉讼请求。泛美公司一审败诉。

After trial, the Beijing No. 1 Intermediate Court upheld the defendant's No. 319 Notice of the Second Tax Office and rejected Pan Am's claims. Pan Am lost first instance.

一审判决后,泛美卫星公司不服,向北京市高级人民法院提出上诉,要求判决撤销一审判决,并依法予以改判,启动了行政诉讼的二审程序。

After the first instance judgment, Pan American Satellite Company appealed to the Beijing Higher People's Court, asked the judgment to rescind the first instance judgment, revised the sentence according to law, and started the second instance procedure of the administrative lawsuit.

北京市高级人民法院二审认为,原审判决认定事实清楚,适用法律正确,审判程序合法,故依法驳回泛美公司的上诉请求,维持一审判决。泛美公司二审败诉。

The second instance of the Beijing Higher People's Court held that the original judgment found that the facts were clear, the applicable law was correct, and the trial procedure was lawful, so it rejected the appeal request of Pan American Company according to law and upheld the judgment of first instance. The Pan American Company lost the second trial.

至此,泛美公司用尽了我国解决与涉外纳税人税务争议的所有国内法程序。若泛美公司仍然不服,还有解决此争议的其他救济程序吗?答案是肯定的。泛美公司可寻求解决国际税务争议的国际法程序主要为双边税收协定中的相互协商程序。

At this point, Pan Am has exhausted all domestic legal procedures in China for resolving tax disputes with foreign taxpayers. If Pan Am still not convinced, are there any other remedies to resolve the dispute? The answer is yes. The international law procedure that Pan Am may seek to resolve international tax disputes is primarily a mutual consultation procedure in bilateral tax agreements.

国际税收协定中都有相互协商程序的规定,基本采用经合发组织范本或联合国范本的模式。中美两国于1984年4月30日签署关于对所得避免双重征税和防止偷漏税的协定(以下简称"中美税收协定"),该协定1986年11月21日生效,从1987年1月1日起执行。

International tax agreements contain provisions for mutual consultation procedures, the model of OECD or United Nations model is basically adopted. On 30 April 1984, China and the United States signed an agreement on the avoidance of double taxation of income and the prevention of tax evasion (hereinafter referred to as the Sino-US Tax Agreement). The Agreement entered into force on 21 November 1986, and it was implemented since 1 January 1987.

中美税收协定中有关相互协商程序的内容规定在第24条,共4款:

The content of the Sino-US tax agreement on mutual consultation procedures is stipulated in Article 24, which consists of four paragraphs.

(1)当一个人认为,缔约国一方或者双方的措施,导致或将导致对其不符合本协定规定的征税时,可以不考虑各缔约国国内法律的补救办法,将案情提交本人为其居民的缔约国主管当局,或者如果其案情属于第二十三条第一款,可以提交本人为其国民的缔约国主管当局。该项案情必须在不符合本协定规定的征税措施第一次通知之日起,3年内提出。

(1) When a person considers that the measures taken by one or both of the contracting states have led to or will result in a tax on him or her that is not in conformity with the provisions of this Agreement, he or she may refer the case to the competent authorities of the contracting state in which he or she is a resident, without taking into account the remedies available to him or her under the domestic law of each contracting state, or to the competent authorities of the

contracting state in which he or she is a national. The case must be filed within three years from the date of the first notification of the tax measures not in accordance with this Agreement.

（2）上述主管当局如果认为所提意见合理，又不能单方面圆满解决，应设法同缔约国另一方主管当局相互协商解决，以避免不符合本协定的征税。达成的协议应予执行，而不受各缔约国国内法律的时间限制。

(2) If the said competent authority considers that the observations made are reasonable and can not be satisfactorily resolved unilaterally, it shall seek to settle them in consultation with the competent authority of the other contracting state in order to avoid taxation that is inconsistent with this Agreement. Agreements reached should be implemented without time limits under the domestic law of each state party.

（3）缔约国双方主管当局应通过协议设法解决在解释或实施本协定时发生的困难或疑义，也可以对本协定未作规定的消除双重征税问题进行协商。

(3) The competent authorities of both parties shall, by agreement, seek to resolve difficulties or doubts arising in the interpretation or implementation of this Agreement, or may consult on the elimination of double taxation not provided for in this Agreement.

（4）缔约国双方主管当局为达成第二款和第三款的协议，可以相互直接联系。为有助于达成协议，双方主管当局可以进行会谈，口头交换意见。

(4) The competent authorities of both parties may communicate directly with each other in order to reach an agreement on Paragraphs 2 and 3. In order to facilitate agreement, the competent authorities of both parties may hold talks and exchange views orally.

从上述条文可以看出：

As can be seen from the above provisions:

第（1）款给予了纳税人向其居住国提出申诉的权利，第（2）款则规定了一国税务机关如何将纳税人与税务机关的争议转化为两国税务机关之间的争议。居住国有义务考虑纳税人的申请异议是否合理以及能否单方面解决。在缔约国一方提出进行谈判时，另一方有义务进行谈判，但仅有义务尽力谈判，却没有义务一定要达成结果。因此，第（1）款和第（2）款适用于间接的国际税务争议。第（3）款适用于缔约国税务机关在解释或适用税收协定时的争议的处理，因此适用于直接国际税务争议。该款要求税务机关，如果可能的话，通过相互协商程序解决解释和适用协定中的困难。这些困难主要涉及或可能涉及某类纳税人的一般性问题。因此，缔约国主管当局没有义务启动此类争议的相互协商程序。另外，第（3）款还具有填补条约空白的作用，即用于解决税收协定未规定的双重征税问题。

Paragraph (1) gives taxpayers the right to appeal to their country of residence, while Paragraph (2) sets out how a country's tax authorities translate a dispute between taxpayers and tax authorities into a dispute between the tax authorities of the two countries. The state of residence is obliged to consider whether the taxpayer's application objection is reasonable and whether it can be settled unilaterally. When one party offers to negotiate, the other party is obliged to negotiate, only to try to negotiate, but not necessarily to reach a result. Paragraphs (1) and (1) therefore apply to indirect international tax disputes. Paragraph (3) applies to the handling of disputes by the tax authorities of a contracting state in the interpretation or application of tax agreements, and therefore to direct international tax disputes. The paragraph requires tax authorities, if possible, to resolve difficulties in the interpretation and application of agreements through mutual consultation procedures. These difficulties relate mainly to or may involve general issues of a particular type of taxpayer. The competent authorities of states parties are therefore not obliged to initiate a mutual consultation procedure for such disputes. In addition, Paragraph 3 had the function of filling the treaty gap by addressing the issue of double taxation not provided for in tax agreements.

税收协定的主要功能之一是消除双重征税。不过,适用相互协商程序的条件并不要求一定产生了双重征税,只要产生了与税收协定不符的征税即可。事实上,税务机关没有导致双重征税的征税措施可能会不符合税收协定,而导致双重征税的行为并不一定就与税收协定不符。

One of the main functions of tax agreements is to eliminate double taxation. However, the conditions for the application of the procedure of mutual consultation do not require that double taxation must arise. As long as the taxation is not in conformity with the tax agreement, the procedure of mutual consultation is applicable. In fact, the absence of tax measures by tax authorities that lead to double taxation may be inconsistent with tax agreements, and acts that lead to double taxation may not necessarily be inconsistent with tax agreements.

(二) 冰岛政府与瑞士公司 Alusuisse 公司税务争议案
The Iceland/Alusuisse Arbitration Case

1986年3月29日冰岛政府与瑞士公司Alusuisse税务争议案,是仲裁解决国际税务争议的第一案。

A tax dispute between the government of Iceland and a Swiss company Alusuisse in 29 March 1986 was the first case in which international tax disputes were settled by arbitration.

(一) 案情介绍
Overview of the Case

案件的事实: 1986年3月29日,冰岛政府与瑞士公司Alusuisse签订了一份关于建设和运营加工铝工厂及附属设施的主协议,铝厂属于瑞士公司Alusuisse持有绝大多数股份的冰岛铝业公司所有。主协议相关的文件还包括瑞士公司Alusuisse和冰岛铝业公司之间的技术协助合同。依据主协议的规定,冰岛铝业公司将每年按其净利润向冰岛政府缴纳统一的税收。主协议中也规定了通货贬值规则、分配方法和转移定价等事项。随后冰岛铝业公司在向冰岛政府缴税的数额上发生了争议,特别是在储备金结构的分配方法和技术协助合同条款的解释以及确定原材料的价格方面都有争议,而这些争议都对计算冰岛铝业公司的净利润产生重要影响。

The facts of the case are as follows. On 29 March 1986, the government of Iceland and the Swiss company Alusuisse signed a master agreement on the construction and operation of processing aluminum plants and ancillary facilities owned by the Swiss company Alusuisse Icelandic Aluminium, which holds an overwhelming majority of its shares. Documents relating to the main agreement also include technical assistance contracts between Swiss company Alusuisse and Icelandic Aluminium. According to the main agreement, Alcoa will pay a unified tax to the Icelandic government on its net profit every year. The main agreement also provides for currency depreciation rules, distribution methods and transfer pricing. Subsequently, there were disputes over the amount of tax paid to the Icelandic government by Alcoa, particularly with regard to the allocation of the reserve structure and the interpretation of the terms of the technical assistance contract and the determination of the price of raw materials, which had an important impact on the calculation of the net profit of Alcoa Iceland.

争议解决过程：双方协商未果后，依据主协议的规定把争议提交给解决投资争端国际中心，通过仲裁来解决。在向解决投资争端国际中心提起仲裁后不久，双方又签订了临时协议决定通过专家仲裁来解决它们的争议。双方改由专家仲裁的原因是希望能够以友好和快速的方式解决它们之间的争议。仲裁庭由三名税务专家组成。双方各自指定一名专家担任仲裁员，第三名即仲裁庭的主席既不能是瑞士公民也不能是冰岛公民，由已指定的两名专家协议指定产生。作为仲裁庭的补充，由冰岛的税务专家组成了一个独立的专家组。这个独立的专家组将解决如下事项：

Dispute settlement process are as follows. After the negotiation between the two parties fails, the dispute shall be submitted to the International Center for the Settlement of Investment Disputes for arbitration in accordance with the provisions of the main agreement. Shortly after the arbitration was initiated at ICSID, the parties signed an interim agreement to resolve their dispute through expert arbitration (an ad hoc arbitration). The agreement was signed. The reason the parties had moved to expert arbitration was the desire to resolve their disputes in a friendly and expeditious manner. The tribunal consists of three tax experts. Each party appoints an expert as arbitrator, and the third, the chairman of the arbitral tribunal, can neither be a Swiss citizen nor an Icelandic citizen, and is appointed by agreement between the two experts appointed. As a complement to the arbitral tribunal, an independent expert group was formed by tax experts from Iceland. This independent expert group will address the following questions:

第一，冰岛铝业公司为了缴税而产生的货币汇兑损失问题；
第二，冰岛铝业公司使用的防污设备的贬值问题；
第三，依据主协议利润分配产生的一项特别储备金的问题；
第四，依据主协议冰岛政府估算罚款的权利问题。

First, the issue of currency exchange losses incurred by Alcoa Iceland for tax purposes;

Second, the devaluation of anti-fouling equipment used by Alcoa Iceland;

Third, the issue of a special reserve arising from the distribution of profits under the main agreement;

Fourth, according to the main agreement, the Icelandic government estimates the right to fine.

冰岛铝业公司和冰岛政府在双方签订的临时协议中授予仲裁庭和独立专家组很大的自由权。例如，临时协议中规定：仲裁庭和独立专家组都有自裁管辖权，应当按照普遍适用的民事诉讼的基本原则来决定自己的裁决程序。专家组应当就他们的观点陈述理由。如果专家组的意见不一致，则以多数意见为准。另外临时协议中规定的时间限制也表明了仲

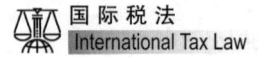

裁解决的快速和高效。如组成专家组的时间是4周,专家组作出裁决的时间是从成立后6个月内。在两个专家组分别作出他们的裁决提交给当事人后的2周内,冰岛铝业公司和冰岛政府将再组成第三个专家组。这第三个专家组分别由冰岛政府的国家审计长、冰岛铝业公司的法定审计员以及一个独立的注册会计师组成,专家组的主席由独立的注册会计师担任。第三个专家组的职责是重新计算冰岛铝业公司以前年度的纳税责任。重新计算的结果必须在3个月内提交。而这一结果对双方当事人都有效力而且是终局裁决。至于仲裁的费用,每个当事人各自承担自己选定的专家的费用,每个专家组主席的费用由双方当事人平均分担。本案的仲裁程序是保密的。裁决作出后得到了成功履行。

The Icelandic Aluminium Corporation and the government of Iceland, in an interim agreement between the two parties, granted the arbitral tribunal and the independent panel a great deal of freedom. The interim agreement, for example, provides that both the arbitral tribunal and the independent expert group have jurisdiction to adjudicate and that their own adjudication procedures should be determined in accordance with the basic principles of universally applicable civil action. The group of experts should present reasons for their views. In the event of disagreement, the majority opinion shall prevail. In addition, the time limit stipulated in the interim agreement also shows the speed and efficiency of arbitration settlement. If the time for the formation of the group of experts is four weeks, the group's decision will take place within six months of its establishment. Within two weeks of their respective decisions being submitted to the parties, the Icelandic Aluminium Corporation and the Icelandic government will form a third panel. The third group of experts is composed of the State Auditor-General of the Government of Iceland (the State Auditor), the statutory auditor of Alcoa Iceland and an independent CPA, chaired by an independent CPA. The role of the third panel was to recalculate the tax liability of Alcoa Iceland for previous years. The results of the recalculation must be submitted within three months. This result is valid for both parties and final. As for the costs of arbitration, each party bears the costs of the experts of its own choosing, and the costs of the chair of each expert group are shared equally between the parties. The arbitration proceedings in this case are confidential. The decision was successfully carried out.

(二)法理分析
Legal Analysis

从上述案件可以看出,仲裁程序进行得非常有效,而且最后的裁决也得到了成功的履行。基于税务争议的专业性,由税务专家来裁决是其取得成功的重要保证。当然,国际税收争议由于涉及管辖权问题、经济主权等,一个国家和非本国公民或非居民纳税人在所有案件中都通过仲裁解决税收争议可能并不是恰当的。

As can be seen from the above cases, the arbitration proceedings were very effective and the final award was successfully performed. Based on the professionalism of tax disputes, tax experts are an important guarantee of their success. Of course, international tax disputes may not be appropriate for a state and non-national or non-resident taxpayers to settle tax disputes by arbitration in all cases because of jurisdiction issues, economic sovereignty, etc.

仲裁程序给纳税人提供了一个通过仲裁来解决相互协商程序无法解决的税收争议的机会。如前所述,仲裁发起的条件是由纳税人发起。但在有些国家因为国内法、国内政策或行政管理方面的考量,仲裁程序是不可以解决税收争议的或者只能解决一些特定的争议,例如仅涉及事实争议的案件。此外纳税人要求仲裁的事项如果已经在国内进行诉讼,则纳税人不能在任何缔约国提起仲裁。依据OECD税收协定范本注释76、77的规定,我们可以得出仲裁与国内救济的关系如下:

The arbitration procedure provides an opportunity for taxpayers to solve the tax disputes that can not be solved by MAP. As mentioned earlier, the conditions for arbitration to be initiated are by taxpayers. However, in some countries, because of domestic law, domestic policy or administrative considerations, arbitration proceedings can not resolve tax disputes or can only resolve specific disputes, such as cases involving only factual disputes. In addition, the taxpayer can not initiate arbitration in any state party if the matter for arbitration has already been litigated domestically. According to Notes 76 and 77 of the Model OECD Tax Agreement, we can conclude that the relationship between arbitration and domestic remedies is as follows.

(1)纳税人不能同时寻求仲裁程序和国内法律救济。若国内救济适用,则主管机关一般要么要求纳税人暂停国内救济程序,或如果纳税人不同意暂停,则推迟仲裁程序,直到纳税人用尽了国内法律救济程序。

(1) Taxpayers can not seek both arbitration procedures and domestic legal remedies. If domestic remedies are applicable, the competent authority will normally either require the taxpayer to suspend the domestic remedies procedure or, if the taxpayer does not agree to the suspension, postpone the arbitration procedure until the taxpayer has exhausted the domestic remedies procedure.

(2)若相互协商程序在先适用,并且主管机关之间已达成了协议,则纳税人和其他直接受本案影响的当事人就有机会拒绝相互达成的协议,同时寻求已被中止的国内救济程序。另一方面,如果上述当事人愿意适用达成的协议,他们必须宣布放弃就协议所设事项进行的国内救济。

(2) The taxpayer and other parties directly affected by the case have the opportunity to reject the mutual agreement if the MAP applies first and the competent authority has reached a mutual agreement. At the same time, the domestic relief procedure that has been suspended is sought. On the other hand, if the above-mentioned parties are willing to apply the agreement reached, they will have to renounce domestic remedies in respect of matters established by the agreement.

(3)若纳税人先寻求国内救济方法,并且在缔约国内已用尽该救济,则纳税人只能寻求相互协商程序,为了获得在另一缔约国对于双重征税的救济。但事实上,如果就某一案件已由缔约国一方国内作出法律裁决,大多数国家认为,通过相互协商程序推翻该裁决是不可能的,因此也将限制随后为尽力获得另一缔约国救济的相互协商程序的适用。相同的一般原则在相互协商程序案件中也可适用,且该相互协商程序涉及一项或多项提起仲裁的事项。如果事先已知某一缔约国在执行仲裁裁决受限,则把该事项提起仲裁,是无任何帮助的。这种情况当然不适用于某一缔约国在相互协商程序中能背离该国法院的一项裁决的情形。这样的话，仲裁程序即可适用。当然如果纳税人未用尽国内救济程序（或未寻求国内救济）的情况下，国内救济程序将被中止以等待仲裁程序的结果。实践证明纳税人很少会拒绝仲裁程序而转向寻求国内救济程序。①

(3) If the taxpayer first seeks domestic remedies and has exhausted such remedies in the contracting state, the taxpayer can only seek MAP, in order to obtain relief for double taxation in the other contracting state. However, in fact, if a legal decision had been made in one of the states parties in a particular case, most states considered it impossible to overturn it by MAP. Consequently, the application of subsequent MAP to seek relief from another state party to the extent possible would also be limited. The same general principles may also apply in MAP cases, and the MAP procedure involves one or more matters for which arbitration is initiated. It would be of no assistance to bring the matter to arbitration if it was known in advance that a contracting state was limited in the execution of the arbitral award. Certainly this does not apply to a state party which, in MAP proceedings, can depart from a decision of its courts. In that case, the arbitral proceedings would be applicable. Of course, if the taxpayer fails to exhaust domestic remedies (or does not seek domestic remedies), domestic remedies will be suspended pending the outcome of the arbitration proceedings. Taxpayers rarely turn to domestic remedies by refusing arbitration proceedings.

学习思考题 / Questions for Study

1. 国际税收争议的分类和特点是什么？
   What are the classification and characteristics of international tax dispute?
2. 国内法解决国际税收争议的途径有哪些？其各自的特点是什么？
   How to resolve international tax disputes in domestic law? And what are their characteristics?
3. 相互协商程序解决国际税收争议的缺点或不足是什么？
   What are the disadvantages or shortcomings of the mutual consultation procedure in resolving international tax disputes?
4. 完善相互协商程序的途径是什么？
   How to improve the procedure of mutual consultation?

---

① 2010 OECD Model Convention, Commentary on Art. 25, Para. 76 and 77.

参考文献
Reference

[1] 刘隆亨.国际税法[M].2版.北京:法律出版社,2007.

[2] 刘剑文.国际税法学[M].2版.北京:北京大学出版社,2004.

[3] 崔晓静.国际税收行政合作的新发展及其法律问题研究[M].北京:中国社会科学出版社,2014.

[4] 汤贡亮.2012年中国税收发展报告:中国国际税收发展战略研究[M].北京:中国税务出版社,2013.

[5] 张泽平.国际税法[M].北京:北京大学出版社,2014.

[6] 付志宇,张帆,陈龙.国际税法[M].北京:清华大学出版社,2015.

[7] 廖益新.国际税法学[M].北京:高等教育出版社,2008.

[8] 廖益新.国际税法学[M].北京:北京大学出版社,2001.

[9] 王丽华.常设机构利润归属问题研究[M].上海:东华大学出版社,2011.

[10] 国家税务总局国际税务司.税收协定执行案例集[M].北京:中国税务出版社,2019.

[11] 迈克尔·朗.避免双重征税协定法导论[M].2版.朱炎生,译.北京:法律出版社,2017.

[12] 雷霆.国际税收实务与协定适用指南:原理、实务与疑难问题[M].北京:法律出版社,2018.

[13] 张泽平.国际税法[M].北京:北京大学出版社,2016.

[14] 龙英锋.国际税法案例教程[M].上海:立信会计出版社,2011.

[15] 姜明安.行政法与行政诉讼法[M].北京:北京大学出版社;高等教育出版社,2007.

[16] 陈少英.税法学教程[M].北京:北京大学出版社,2011.

[17] 赵鹏."一带一路"合作中的国际税收争议解决机制研究[M].上海:立信会计出版社,2020.

[18] 马克思,恩格斯.马克思恩格斯选集:第4卷[M].北京:人民出版社,1995.

[19] 布莱恩·J.阿诺德.国际税收基础[M].《国际税收基础》翻译组,译.北京:中国

税务出版社,2020.

[20] 叶莉娜.常设机构利润归属:独立交易法VS公式分摊法[J].税收经济研究,2012(3).

[21] 刘奇超,郑莹,曹明星.CCCTB机制阐发:公式分配法欧美比较与中国引申[J].国际税收,2016(7).

[22] 延峰,冯炜,崔煜晨.数字经济对国际税收的影响及典型案例分析[J].国际税收,2015(3).

[23] 柯格钟.论所得税法上的所得概念[J].台湾大学法学论丛,2008(3).

[24] 陈清秀.量能课税与实质课税原则(上)[J].月旦法学杂志,2010(183).

[25] 任宛立,熊伟.全球化视野下中国税收条约政策的调适[J].国际税收,2017(6).

[26] 叶姗.一般反避税条款适用之关键问题分析[J].法学,2013(9).

[27] 熊伟.税收协定与《中国企业所得税法》:基于功能、内容与效力的比较[J].法学评论,2009(5).

[28] 王禹娇,李丽,刘莉,等.某造纸上市公司转让定价反避税案例分析[J].国际税收,2018(10).